Criminal Justice and Law Enforcement Books

of

WEST PUBLISHING COMPANY

St. Paul, Minnesota 55102

CONSTITUTIONAL LAW

MADDEX'S CASES AND COMMENTS ON CONSTITUTIONAL LAW

James L. Maddex
Professor of Criminal Justice, Georgia State University

The book is designed as a classroom text and covers the following subjects by chapter: Introduction to the Study of Constitutional Law; The Development of Due Process and Individual Protection; The Right to Counsel; Unreasonable Searches and Seizures; Compulsory Self-Incrimination; Additional Pre-Trial Issues; Fair Trial; Cruel and Unusual Punishment; Double Jeopardy; Constitutional Rights in the Correctional Setting; Constitutional Limitations upon Defining Criminal Conduct; The First Amendment; Equal Protection of the Laws; Constitutional Limitations upon Juvenile Courts; Peripheral Rights. Appendices and Index included.

816 pages-1974

CORRECTIONS

KERPER AND KERPER'S LEGAL RIGHTS OF THE CONVICTED

Mrs. Hazel B. Kerper
Professor of Sociology and Criminal Law, Sam Houston State University

Ms. Janeen Kerper
Attorney, San Francisco, Calif.

The book is designed as a classroom text and covers the following subjects by chapter: Conviction and Its Consequences—I; Conviction and Its Consequences—II; Adjudication of Delinquency and Its Consequences; Sentencing—I; Sentencing—II; Direct Attack Upon the Validity of a Conviction—Appeals;

CORRECTIONS—Continued

Collateral Attack Upon the Validity of a Conviction—Post-Conviction; Procedures; Legal Rights of Probationers; The Legal Rights of Prisoners—An Overview; State Remedies for Enforcement of Prisoners' Rights; Federal Remedies for Enforcement of Prisoners' Rights; Particular Rights of Prisoners—I; Particular Rights of Prisoners—II; Legal Rights of Parolees; Minimizing the Effects of a Conviction.

677 pages-1974

KILLINGER AND CROMWELL'S SELECTED READINGS ON CORRECTIONS IN THE COMMUNITY

George G. Killinger
Director of the Institute of Contemporary Corrections, Sam Houston State University

Paul F. Cromwell
Professor of Sociology, San Antonio College

The book can be used as a classroom text or collateral reading source and covers the following subjects by chapter: Diversion From the Criminal Justice System; Special Community Programs; Probation; Parole. Appendix included.

Paperback, 579 pages-1974

KILLINGER AND CROMWELL'S READINGS ON PENOLOGY—THE EVOLUTION OF CORRECTIONS IN AMERICA

George G. Killinger
Director of the Institute of Contemporary Corrections, Sam Houston State University

Paul F. Cromwell, Jr.
Professor of Sociology, San Antonio College

The book can be used as a classroom text or collateral reading source and covers the following subjects by chapter: Philosophical Foundations of Punishment; Historical Developments in American Penology; Corrections in Contemporary America; New Frontiers in Corrections.

Paperback, 426 pages-1973

MODEL RULES AND REGULATIONS ON PRISONERS' RIGHTS AND RESPONSIBILITIES

The book is designed for collateral use and contains proposed rules and regulations in the following areas: Rules and Commentary on Prisoners' Rights; Rules and Commentary on Classification and Reclassification; Rules and Commentary on Institutional Standards; Rules and Commentary on Inmate Offenses; Rules and Commentary on Disciplinary Procedures; Rules and Commentary on Transfers; Rules and Commentary on Grievance Procedures.

Paperback, 212 pages-1973

CORRECTIONS—Continued

RUBIN'S LAW OF CRIMINAL CORRECTION, 2nd EDITION (STUDENT EDITION)

Sol Rubin

Counsel Emeritus, Council on Crime and Delinquency

The book may be used as a classroom text or for collateral reference and covers the following subjects by chapter: Historical Development of the Law of Criminal Correction; The Guilty Plea and Related Sentence Considerations; The Presentence Investigation and the Hearing on the Sentence; Imposing Sentence—Commitments; Suspended Sentence and Discharge; Probation; Fine and Restitution; Imprisonment; Capital Punishment, Sterilization and Castration, Corporal Punishment; Cruel, Unusual and Excessive Punishments; The Repeated or Multiple Offender; Youthful Offenders; The Misdemeanant and Lesser Offender; The Mentally Ill Defendant; Parole; Pardon and Other Forms of Clemency; Civil Rights, Their Loss and Restoration; Punishment and Treatment; A Field of Law; Criminal Correction. Index included.

Paperback, 873 pages-1973

CRIMINAL JUSTICE SYSTEM

KERPER'S INTRODUCTION TO THE CRIMINAL JUSTICE SYSTEM

Hazel B. Kerper

Professor of Sociology and Criminal Law, Sam Houston State University

The book is designed as a classroom text and covers the following subjects: The Nature of Crime and Criminal Responsibility; The Criminal Justice Process—Basic Concepts of Criminal Law, The Criminal Courts, Investigation and Accusation, Adjudication and Conviction, Sentencing and Correction, The Juvenile Court Process, Habeas Corpus and Extradition; The Professionals in the Criminal Justice System—The Police, The Judicial Officers, The Correctional Officer, Related Professionals (Psychiatrists, Social Workers). Tables and Index included.

558 pages-1972

CRIMINAL LAW

DIX AND SHARLOT'S CASES AND MATERIALS ON BASIC CRIMINAL LAW

George E. Dix

Professor of Law, University of Texas

M. Michael Sharlot

Professor of Law, University of Texas

The book is designed as a classroom text and covers the following subjects by chapter: Introduction; The Criminalization Decision; Principles of Criminal Liability; The Inchoate Crimes; Specific Offenses: Crimes Against Property; Specific Offenses: Crimes Against the Person; Defenses Not Directly Related to the Basic Requirements for Liability. Table of Cases and Index included.

649 pages-1974

CRIMINAL LAW—Continued

FERGUSON'S READINGS ON CONCEPTS OF CRIMINAL LAW

Robert W. Ferguson
Administration of Justice Dept. Director, Saddleback College

The book can be used as a classroom text or collateral reading source and covers the following subjects by chapter: Legal Research and Methodology; Philosophical and Historical Development; The Nature of Criminal Law; Classification and Application of Crimes; Elements of Crime; Capacity to Commit Crime.

CRIMINAL PROCEDURE

KAMISAR, LaFAVE AND ISRAEL'S CASES, COMMENTS AND QUESTIONS ON BASIC CRIMINAL PROCEDURE, 4th EDITION

Yale Kamisar
Professor of Law, University of Michigan

Wayne R. LaFave
Professor of Law, University of Illinois

Jerold H. Israel
Professor of Law, University of Michigan

The book is reprinted from Kamisar, LaFave and Israel's Cases, Comments and Questions on Modern Criminal Procedure, 4th edition and is designed as a classroom text covering the following subjects by chapter: A General View of the Criminal Justice System; The Nature and Scope of the Fourteenth Amendment Due Process—The Applicability of the Bill of Rights to the States; The Right to Counsel, Transcripts and Other Aids—Poverty, Equality and the Adversary System; Some General Reflections on the Police, the Courts and the Criminal Process; Arrest, Search and Seizure; Wiretapping, Electronic Eavesdropping, the Use of Secret Agents to Obtain Incriminating Statements, and the Fourth Amendment; Police "Encouragement" and the Defense of Entrapment; Police Interrogation and Confessions; Lineups, Showups and Other Pre-Trial Identification Procedures; The Retroactive Effect of a Holding of Unconstitutionality; The Scope of the Exclusionary Rules; The Administration of the Exclusionary Rules. Table of Cases included. New supplement annually.

Paperback, 790 pages-1974
Annual Supplement

ISRAEL AND LaFAVE'S CRIMINAL PROCEDURE IN A NUTSHELL

Jerold H. Israel
Professor of Law, University of Michigan

Wayne R. LaFave
Professor of Law, University of Illinois

The book can be used as a classroom text or collateral reading source and covers the following subjects by chapter: The Constitutionalization of Crim-

CRIMINAL PROCEDURE—Continued

inal Procedure; Arrest, Search and Seizure; Wiretapping, Electronic Eavesdropping, and the Use of Secret Agents; Police Interrogation and Confessions; Lineups and Other Pre-Trial Identification Procedures: Application of the Exclusionary Rule; Right to Counsel; Raising Constitutional Claims. Table of Cases and Index included.

Paperback, 423 pages-1971

EVIDENCE

KLEIN'S LAW OF EVIDENCE FOR POLICE

Irving J. Klein

Professor of Law and Police Science, John Jay College of Criminal Justice, The City University of New York

The book is designed as a classroom text containing text and cases and covers the following subjects by chapter: Introduction; Examination of Witnesses and Trial Procedures; Opinion Evidence; The Best Evidence Rule; Hearsay; Hearsay—Admission Exception; Hearsay—Res Gestae Exceptions; Hearsay—Dying Declaration Exception; Hearsay—Business Records Exception; Privileged Communications; Declarations against Interest; Self-Serving Declarations; Public Documents; Presumptions; Judicial Notice; Illegally Obtained Evidence. Teacher's manual available.

416 pages-1973

ROTHSTEIN'S EVIDENCE IN A NUTSHELL

Paul F. Rothstein

Professor of Law, Georgetown Law Center

The book can be used as a classroom text or collateral reading source and covers the following subjects by chapter: Basic Principles of Evidence; Burdens of Proof and Presumptions; Hearsay; Exceptions to the Hearsay Rule; Admissions and Confessions; Impeachment of Witnesses; Some Selected Evidentiary Privileges. Table of Cases and Index included.

Paperback, 406 pages-1970

INTRODUCTION TO LAW ENFORCEMENT

SCHWARTZ AND GOLDSTEIN'S LAW ENFORCEMENT HANDBOOK FOR POLICE

Louis B. Schwartz
Professor of Law, University of Pennsylvania

Stephen R. Goldstein
Professor of Law, University of Pennsylvania

The book is designed as a classroom text and covers the following subjects by chapter: The Policeman's Role in Criminal Justice; The Police Career;

INTRODUCTION TO LAW ENFORCEMENT—Continued

Criminology for Policemen; Patrol, Frisk and Arrest; Search and Seizure; Vice and Organized Crime; Preserving Order and Keeping the Peace; Traffic; Juvenile Delinquency; Demonstrations, Picketing and Riots. Index included.

Paperback, 333 pages-1970

INVESTIGATION

UVILLER'S THE PROCESSES OF CRIMINAL JUSTICE–INVESTIGATION

H. Richard Uviller

Professor of Law, Columbia University

The book is designed as a classroom text and covers the following subjects by chapter: The Police; Enforcing the Fourth Amendment: The "Exclusionary Rule"; Gathering Tangible Objects; Acquiring the Evidence of Witnesses; Surveillance of the Suspect as Sources of Evidence; Examination of the Suspect in Custody; Developing Evidence From the Defendant After Accusation.

Paperback, 744 pages-1974

JUVENILE JUSTICE

FAUST AND BRANTINGHAM'S JUVENILE JUSTICE PHILOSOPHY: READINGS, CASES AND COMMENTS

Frederic L. Faust

Professor of Criminology, Florida State Univerity

Paul J. Brantingham

Professor of Criminology, Florida State University

The book is designed as a classroom text or collateral reading source and covers the following subjects by part: The Origin of the Juvenile Court—19th Century Philosophies—Introduction Reading; The Origin of the Juvenile Court—Precipitating Conditions—Introduction Reading; The Era of the "Socialized" Juvenile Court—1899 to 1967—Introduction Reading; The Constitutionalists' Argument—Introduction Reading; The Constitutionalist Revision of Juvenile Court Philosophy and Procedure—1967 to Present—Introduction Reading; Models of Juvenile Justice.

Paperback, 600 pages-1974

FOX'S LAW OF JUVENILE COURTS IN A NUTSHELL

Sanford J. Fox

Professor of Law, Boston College

The book can be used as a supplemental classroom text or collateral reading source and contains the following subjects by part: Introduction to Juvenile Courts; Jurisdiction; The Roles of Law Enforcement Agents; The Judicial Process; Fact-Finding Hearings; Dispositions; Waiver; Appeals; Philosophy of the Juvenile Court. Table of Cases and Index included.

Paperback, 286 pages-1971

POLICE-COMMUNITY RELATIONS

CROMWELL AND KEEFER'S READINGS ON POLICE-COMMUNITY RELATIONS

Paul F. Cromwell, Jr.
Professor of Sociology, San Antonio College

George Keefer
Former F.B.I. Agent

The book can be used as a classroom text or collateral reading source and covers the following subjects by chapter: The Police Role and Function; Psycho-Social Aspects of Community Relations; The Police and Minority Groups; Special Considerations in Police Community Relations.

Paperback, 368 pages-1973

VICE CONTROL

FERGUSON'S THE NATURE OF VICE CONTROL IN THE ADMINISTRATION OF JUSTICE

Robert W. Ferguson
Administration of Justice Dept. Director, Saddleback College

The book is designed as a classroom text and covers the following subjects by chapter: Organizing the Enforcement Unit; Enforcement Techniques; Prostitution; Homosexuality; Pornography; Gambling; Bookmaking; Loanshark Operations; Control of Alcoholic Beverage Abuses; Organized Crime. Table of Cases and Index included.

UELMAN AND HADDOX' CASES, TEXT AND MATERIALS ON DRUG ABUSE LAW

Gerald F. Uelman
Professor of Law, Loyola University, Los Angeles

Victor G. Haddox
Professor of Criminology, California State University at Long Beach and Clinical Professor of Psychiatry, Institute of Psychiatry, Law and Behavorial Sciences, University of Southern California School of Medicine

The book is designed as a classroom text and covers the following subjects by chapter: Introduction: Drugs of Abuse; Legal Classification of Drugs; Criminal Offenses; Constitutional Limits on the Criminal Sanction; Enforcing the Criminal Sanction; Sentencing the Drug Offender; Alternative for Treatment.

564 pages-1974

*

CORRECTIONS IN THE COMMUNITY:
Alternatives to Imprisonment
Selected Readings

by

GEORGE G. KILLINGER
Director, The Institute of Contemporary Corrections
and Behavioral Science, Sam Houston State University,
Huntsville, Texas

and

PAUL F. CROMWELL, JR.
Assistant Professor of Criminology
San Antonio College, San Antonio, Texas

ST. PAUL, MINN.
WEST PUBLISHING CO.
1974

Killinger & Cromwell–Corr. in Comm.CrJS

1st Reprint—1974

DEDICATION

To the "Dean of American Corrections"
Austin H. MacCormick

*

III

PREFACE

This book was designed to fill what heretofore has been a significant gap in the literature. Developed as a text or supplement to other texts in Probation and Parole, it incorporates the newly emerging phenomenon of Diversion and Community Based Corrections, therefore offering the reader, whether student or practitioner, a comprehensive view of corrections outside the prison.

In recent years in the United States an increasing emphasis has been placed upon the development of community oriented correctional programs. For the most part correctional institutions have been located outside metropolitan areas, with the inmates isolated from the community and from normal community activities. Increased knowledge in corrections has pointed to the need for closer ties between offenders and their families and community.

It appears, furthermore, that imprisonment as a method of correction has assumed too great a role in dealing with the offender. Increasing utilization of probation and parole illustrate the major trend away from institutional confinement. Within the past decade additional programs and methods have been developed, either as alternatives or supplements to confinement in correctional institutions.

Diversion is increasingly being suggested as a viable alternative to traditional processing of offenders through the criminal justice system. Diversion refers to formally organized efforts to utilize alternatives to initial or continued induction into the justice system. It implies halting or suspending formal criminal or juvenile justice proceedings against a person who has violated a statute in favor of processing through a non-criminal disposition or means.[1]

This volume reviews the history and practice of Diversion and presents two major papers, each a comprehensive and exhaustive study of the process. Robert M. Carter explores the origins of diversion and identifies the major operational and philosophical problems associated with the movement while the report of the National Advisory Commission on Criminal Justice Standards and Goals identifies various programs of Diversion currently in use and suggests further means by which Diversion may be

---

1. National Advisory Commission on Criminal Justice Standards and Goals, *Task Force Report on Corrections*, (Washington, D.C., 1973), p. 73.

V

utilized. *Standards Relating to Diversion* are included from the Report of the National Advisory Commission.

Community Treatment Programs

Community treatment programs, other than probation and parole, for offenders are still in an early stage of development. Programs now in use or suggested include: Half-way Houses, Work or Study Release, Furloughs and Probation Hostels. The concept is summarized by the Task Force on Corrections of the President's Crime Commission (1967):

> The general underlying premise for the new directions in corrections is that crime and delinquency are symptoms of failure and disorganization of the community as well as the individual offender. In particular, these failures are seen as depriving offenders of contact with institutions (of society) that are basically responsible for assuring the development of law abiding conduct . . .

> The task of corrections, therefore, includes building or rebuilding solid ties between the offender and the community, integrating or re-integrating the offender into community life—restoring family ties, obtaining employment and education, securing in a larger sense a place for the offender in the routine functioning of society—. This requires not only efforts directed toward changing the individual offender, which has been almost the exclusive focus of rehabilitation, but also mobilization and change of the community and its institutions.

Efforts are being made by a number of states and the Federal Government to develop ways to reestablish offenders into the community through community treatment programs. This volume undertakes to analyze this trend in American corrections. Significantly, extensive use is made of the newly published *Report of the National Advisory Commission on Criminal Justice Standards and Goals and the American Bar Association's Project on Standards for Criminal Justice*. The contributors include some of the leading authorities in criminal justice; correctional administrators, members of the judiciary, the bar and the academic community. Suggested *Standards and Goals Relating to Community Programs* supplement the narrative accounts.

Probation

The basic idea underlying a sentence to probation is very simple. Sentencing is in large part concerned with avoiding future crimes by helping the defendant learn to live productively in the community against which he has offended. Probation proceeds on the theory that the best way to pursue this goal is to orient the criminal sanction toward the community setting in those cases where it is compatible with the other objectives of sentencing.[2] The emergence of probation during the last half of the 19th Century marked a definite advance in the disposition and treatment of the offender. Over the years the concept has been expanded far beyond that envisioned by its founders.

In this chapter the origins and evolution of probation services are traced. Problems of supervision, the Pre-sentence Report, counseling and probation revocation are considered. Standards are presented as established by the American Bar Association and the National Advisory Commission on Criminal Justice Standards and Goals.

Parole

Almost every offender who enters a correctional institution is eventually released. The only relevant questions are: When? Under what conditions? Parole is the predominant mode of release for prison inmates today, and it is likely to become even more so.[3] Parole resembles probation in a number of aspects. In both, information about an offender is gathered and presented to a decision making authority with the power to release him to community supervision under specific conditions. If he violates those conditions, the offender may be placed in, or returned to, a correctional institution. Parole, however, differs from probation in a significant way. Parole implies that the offender has been incarcerated in a correctional institution before he is released, while probation usually is granted by a Court in lieu of any kind of confinement.[4]

This chapter will review the origins of parole and analyze methods of parole supervision, procedures, and the use of parole in association with other community programs. *Standards Relating to Parole* are presented as a supplement to the narrative.

A major purpose of this book is to provide for college students a collection of original material from professionals in the field of corrections. In comparison with a book written by one author,

---

2. The American Bar Association, Project on Minimum Standards for Criminal Justice, *Probation*, (1970), p. 1.
3. *National Advisory Commission on Criminal Justice Standards and Goals*, supra, at p. 389.
4. Supra, at p. 390.

PREFACE

a compendium has the advantage of placing before the reader exactly what an author had to say on his subject and provides a wider range of knowledge than can be gained by a single author in a lifetime.

The editors wish to thank the authors and publishers who kindly consented to the reprinting of their work in this book.

GEORGE G. KILLINGER
PAUL F. CROMWELL JR.

Huntsville, Texas
April, 1974

SUMMARY OF CONTENTS

TABLE OF CONTENTS

TABLE OF CONTENTS

TABLE OF CONTENTS

†

CORRECTIONS
IN THE
COMMUNITY

Chapter 1

DIVERSION FROM THE CRIMINAL JUSTICE SYSTEM

THE DIVERSION OF OFFENDERS*

Diversion is increasingly being suggested as a viable alternative to traditional processing of offenders through the criminal justice system. This article is in two parts. The first segment attributes the current emphasis on diversion to three factors: (1) increasing recognition of deficiencies in the nonsystem of justice, (2) rediscovery of the ancient truth that the community itself significantly impacts upon behavior, and (3) growing demands of the citizenry to be active participants in the affairs of government. The second section identifies major unresolved problem areas in the diversion process, such as the absence of guidelines for diversion fiscal complexities, political and social issues, inadequate and uneven community resources, lack of assessment or evaluation of diversion programs, and the need for redefining traditional roles.

I.   ORIGINS OF DIVERSION

Although there is considerable discussion and writing by academicians, administrators, and researchers about the system of

---

* Robert M. Carter, "The Diversion of Offenders", *Federal Probation*, December, 1972.   Reprinted with permission.

criminal and/or juvenile justice, the United States does not have a single system of justice. Each level of government, indeed each jurisdiction, has its own unique system. These many "systems"— all established to enforce the standards of conduct believed necessary for the protection of individuals and the preservation of the community—are a collectivity of some 40 thousand law enforcement agencies and a multiplicity of courts, prosecution and defense agencies, probation and parole departments, correctional institutions and related community-based organizations. It is clear that our approach to criminal and juvenile justice sacrifices much in the way of efficiency and effectiveness in order to preserve local autonomy and to protect the individual.

The many systems of justice in existence in the United States in the early 1970's are not the same as those which emerged following the American Revolution. Indeed this 200-year evolution has not been uniform or consistent; some of the innovations and changes in our systems have been generated by judicial decisions and legislative decrees; others have evolved more by chance than by design. Trial by jury and the principle of bail, for example, are relatively old and date back to our European heritage in general and the English Common Law in particular. Probation and parole began in the 19th century and the juvenile court is a 20th century innovation.

Coupled with the numerous criminal and juvenile justice arrangements in the United States and their uneven development is the separation of functions within the systems. There are similar components in all systems ranging from apprehension through prosecution and adjudication to correction. Although in fact interwoven and interdependent one with the other, these components typically function independently and autonomously. This separateness of functions, which on one hand prevents the possibility of a "police state," on the other leads to some extraordinary complex problems. Not the least of these is that the systems of justice are not integrated, coordinated, and effective entities, but rather are fragmented nonsystems with agencies tied together by the processing of an increasing number of adult and juvenile offenders. These nonsystems are marked by an unequal quality of justice, inadequate fiscal, manpower and training resources, shortages in equipment and facilities, lack of relevant research and evaluation to provide some measure of effectiveness and, until recently, a general indifference and apathy on the part of the public which the systems were designed to serve.

Society Itself Contributes to Criminal Behavior

Society deals with crime in a manner which reflects its beliefs about the nature and cause of crime. Many centuries ago, for example, when crime was believed to be the product of the possession of the mind and body by an evil spirit, the primitive response was simple: drive the devil out of the body by whatever means were available for such purposes. The American tradition as relates to the etiology of crime has focused, until recently, upon the individual as a free agent—able to choose between good and evil and aware of the differences between right and wrong. Our "treatment" of crime accordingly reflected the simplistic notion that criminality was housed solely within the psyche and soma of the offender. Regardless of whether the prevalent philosophy was revenge, retaliation, retribution or rehabilitation, the individual was seen as being of primary importance.

We have long assumed that the criminal or delinquent either willfully disregards legitimate authority by his illegal acts or suffers from some personal defect or shortcoming. There is much to learn, however, about the mysteries by which a society generates abnormal responses within its own circles. But this has become increasingly apparent: Society itself contributes significantly to such behavior. Indeed, it is the self-same social structure expressing its force and influence in an ambivalent manner which helps create on one hand the conforming individual—the person respectful of the social and legal codes—and on the other the deviant and lawbreaker who are disrespectful of the law. We have only recently become aware that crime and delinquency are symptoms of failures and disorganization of the community as well as of individual offenders. In particular, these failures may be seen as depriving offenders of contact with those social institutions which are basically responsible for assuring the development of law-abiding conduct.

Note, for example, that it has become increasingly common to discuss the "decline in respect for law and order." In every quarter, and with increasing intensity, we hear that the citizenry, for reasons as yet unclear, is not only failing to honor specific laws, but also displays a mounting disregard for the "rule of law" itself as an essential aspect of the democratic way of life. But even as this concern is echoed, it is not clear that we are all agreed as to what is meant by "decline in respect for law and order" or precisely to whom or to what we are referring. It may be that a large amount of what we observe and label as "disrespect for law" in a wide range and diversity of communities is in fact a normal reaction of normal persons to an abnormal condition or situation.

As knowledge expands to recognize the role of society in the creation of deviance, justice systems themselves will be modified. The implementation of knowledge, of course, always lags behind the development of knowledge.

Mass Disaffection by Large Segment of Population

Concurrent with the recognition that (1) the justice system is but a nonsystem and (2) the community itself has an enormous impact upon the crime problem, there has been—particularly within the past decade—the emergence of mass disaffection of a large segment of our population. This disaffection with the American system is often described in terms which suggest that citizens are not involved in decision-making and are acted upon by the government rather than impacting upon government. The disaffection has been manifested in many communities and in various ways.

We have, for example, been witness to mass civil disorder unparalleled in recent times. We have seen our young people in revolt against the war in Vietnam, the grape industry, selective service, marihuana laws, prison administration, presidential and congressional candidates, Supreme Court nominees, and Dow Chemical. We have observed rebellion against the establishment ranging from burning ghettos and campuses everywhere to looters in the North, freedom riders in the South, and maniacal bombers from East to West. Young and old, black and white, rich and poor have withstood tear gas and mace, billy clubs and bullets, insults and assaults, jail and prison in order to lie down in front of troop trains, sit-in at university administration buildings, love-in in public parks, wade-in at nonintegrated beaches and lie-in within legislative buildings. The establishment has been challenged on such issues as the legal-oriented entities of the draft, the rights of Blacks to use the same rest-rooms and drinking fountains as whites, the death penalty, and free speech. Young people have challenged socially oriented norms with "mod" dress and hair styles, language, rock music, and psychedelic forms, colors, and patterns. We have seen the emergence of the hippy and yippy, the youthful drug culture, black, yellow, red, and brown power advocates, and organizations such as the Panthers, Women's Lib, the Third World Liberation Front, and the Peace and Freedom Party.

But this disaffection or unrest is not restricted to youth alone. Increasingly, adults are rebelling against the system. One need look no further than the recent slowdowns, work stoppages, and strikes of such tradition-oriented groups as police and fire officials, military personnel, social workers, school teachers, and indeed even prison inmates. Adult participation in protest has generally been more moderate than that of youth; some have been through membership in political organizations of a left wing orientation; others have joined conservative right wing organizations such as the Birch Society or Minutemen. Millions of Americans protested against the political establishment by voting for a third or fourth party or not voting at all in the last Presidential election.

Movement Toward Diversion

These three phenomena—recognition that the community impacts significantly upon behavior, the uncertainty as to the effectiveness or quality of justice in the nonsystem of justice, and the growing desire of the citizenry for active relevant and meaningful participation in every area of governmental affairs and community life—are moving the responses to the challenge of crime in a new direction. This direction is typically referred to as "diversion" and relates specifically to movement away from the justice system. It is most likely a prelude to "absorption" . . . a process in which communities engage a wide variety of deviant behavior without referral to or only minimum interaction with the traditional establishment agencies.

Diversion is justice-system oriented and focuses upon the development of specific alternatives for the justice system processing of offenders. The diversion model and its application has been generated from a belief that the control of crime and delinquency would be improved by handling criminals and delinquents outside the traditional system. Diversion is also predicated upon the reported effects of the "labeling" process and the impact of the "self-fulfilling prophecy." Whether diversion, at long range, is more effective than the established justice system and whether the "labeling" and "self-fulfilling" phenomena are operationally significant is unclear. These uncertainties do not dictate against diversion models, but rather should serve to restrain unbounded enthusiasm based upon belief and emotion rather than fact.

Absorption may be defined generally as the attempts of parents, peers, police, schools, and neighborhoods to address social problems—including those of crime and delinquency—by minimizing referral to or entry into one or more of the official governmental agencies designated to handle those manifesting deviant behavior. If there has already been a referral, absorption involves the removal of the transgressor from the official processes by offering solutions, techniques or methods of dealing with him outside of the usual agency channels. Absorption is not restricted to the criminal offender or delinquent. It is, for example, equally applicable to deviants within the educational process. Absorption is adaptive behavior within the community in which alternative strategies are developed for coping with social problems. These involve the extensive use of community and personal resources.

II. DIVERSION: SOME PRACTI-CAL/OPERATIONAL ISSUES

There are issues about diversion—involving both philosophy and practice—which demand in depth examination. Failure to address these completely interwoven issues is likely to result in diversion efforts which are every bit as fragmented and disjointed as those justice system practices which, in some measure, led to the diversion movement. Rather clearly, there is a need to explore operational aspects of diversion, examine the community, its role and resources and determine the latent and manifest impact of diversion on the justice system. These requirements are in fact, mandates for assessment and evaluation. There is an explicit need to: (1) Determine the guidelines and standards which define those eligible or ineligible for diversion, those agencies which are appropriate to receive those who are diverted, and programmatic activities of the agencies which receive diverted cases; (2) identify or develop, and mobilize, resources in a community, determine techniques for increasing community "tolerance" levels, enhance the delivery system for these resources and, make more equitable the availability of resources to diverse types of communities; (3) determine the impact of diversion practices on the justice systems over-all as well as their component parts and examine the need for possible administrative, organizational and legal changes; (4) prepare a complete methodology for evaluating the effectiveness of diversion, keeping in mind that being "progressive" is not synonymous with being "successful."

The need for diversion guidelines is critical. Without some minimum standards for practice and procedure and general concensus or agreement on philosophy, there is a distinct possibility that diversion may become the source of continuing and substantial inequities. Basic questions—such as who is (or is not) to be diverted, by whom, on what basis, and to what programmatic activities—should be answered by some shared understandings. Without such common understandings, the justice system— through increased use of nonsystematic diversion—may become more confused, autonomous, and fragmented.

Some minimum standards are needed, for example, to guide the *selection of individuals* for diversion. Diversion practices may be exclusionary and identify types of offenders who are deemed ineligible, such as those with a history of violence or felony offenders. Or practice may be permissive and allow that all offenders who will benefit from nonjustice system treatment are to be considered eligible, regardless of other considerations. Diversion may be restricted to adjudicated offenders, or it may include nonadjudicated offenders. If the former, diversion is from the system after entry; if the latter, diversion is an alternative to entry into the system. Both raise substantial legal issues.

Determinations as to time frames are required, i. e., the optimum time for diversion, the length of time or duration of diversion, and so on. Guidelines are also needed as to actions to be taken if the person diverted fails to comply with the actual or implied conditions of diversion or if it appears that the diversion plan is inappropriate.

Meaningful standards are necessary, for the *selection of agencies* to receive those who are diverted. Diversion need not necessarily be made to private agencies; it may be appropriate for there to be diversion to those public agencies which normally have been either minimally or not at all concerned with the offender population. And it may be appropriate for diversion to be to individuals rather than agencies. The selection of agencies requires community inventories which in turn may indicate the need for new private and/or public agencies or combinations/consortiums/conglomerates of established agencies which address needs of offenders.

Of equal significance is the complex and politically sensitive problem of sifting through a wide variety of potential diversion agencies including those with "unusual" or nontraditional characteristics such as those with an ex-offender or ex-addict staff. Underlying many of these guidelines are fiscal considerations— including possible requirements for subsidies to agencies which handle those who are diverted. A delicate issue arises from public support of private agencies in terms of performance objectives and standards, constraints and expectations. The subsidy issue is made even more complex as the need arises to determine which public agency at what level of government pays the subsidies to these new partners in the justice system.

There is, of course, a requirement to examine the *programmatic activities* of the agencies which receive diverted offenders. While an inventory of these various programs and some estimate of their effectiveness are essential to rational diversion practice, a basic question emerges as to whether offenders should be diverted if appropriate (or at least similar) programs exist within the justice system. And if such programs already exist in the justice system, the advantages, if any, which accrue by transfer of these programs and clientele to community-based, nonjustice system organizations must be established.

The movement of programs and offenders to nonjustice system organizations will require new roles for justice and nonjustice system personnel. As an example, the probation or parole officer realistically might be required to become a catalyst and seek to activate a community and its caretakers to absorb the offender as a member of that community. This would require a complete knowledge of community resources and diagnosis of clientele needs. There would be an emphasis on reducing the alienation of the offender from his community by impairing the continued maintenance of a criminal identity and encouraging a community identity. The officer would no longer find employment for the offender, but instead direct him into the normal channels of job seeking in the community. Residential, marital, medical, financial or other problems would be addressed by assisting the offender engage those community resources which deal with these problem areas. This new role, then, might be one of insuring a process of community, not correctional absorption. Again illustrating interrelationships of these issues, note that the "new role" phenomenon itself raises questions about training for and acceptance of the role and methods or techniques of implementation.

Imbalance in Community Resources a Problem

Other issues arise as one examines the role and resources of the community. Not at all insignificant is the complex issue of imbalance among communities to accept cases which are diverted and to provide necessary services and resources. Some communities have distinct economic advantages over others—and it is clear that diversion has an economic, as well as a motivation base. Middle- and upper-class communities and their citizens, socially and economically secure, often have internal financial resources available to mobilize a wide range of agencies of diversion or specialized services ranging from psychiatric care through private schools. The differences in resource levels need scrutiny, for it would be socially disastrous to deny diversion to those who are economically disadvantaged; diversion cannot be restricted to the affluent. Without action to balance resource requirements with the capacity of delivering services, the poor and the disadvantaged will continue to flow into and through the justice agencies.

A parallel community-based problem occurs where there is a low community tolerance for diversion. How is community tolerance to be increased? A simple demonstration of need may be insufficient. Numerous examples of low or non-tolerance may be cited ranging from open through latent resistance and hostility directed against self-help groups and agency halfway houses. And besides the very difficult "how," there is the related question of "who" is responsible for dealing with community fears and anxieties. Is every justice agency seeking to divert offenders responsible for its own resource development or is some overall plan among cooperating justice agencies more rational?   And again, as one question leads to another, if a plan is necessary, who designs and implements it, and how are activities financed and monitored?

Diversion Will Result in Significant Changes

Although changes in justice systems are inevitable consequences of an increased use of diversion, there is a distinct probability that the changes will be both unplanned and unsystematic. These changes may range from administrative and organizational restructuring and modification in procedure and policy on one hand through major changes in the populations which are serviced by the justice systems on the other.

As justice agencies become partners with communities, there may be requirements in all agencies for organizational change to include new bureaus or divisions of "community service." This would require new personnel or reassignment of personnel, development and acceptance of new roles such as those of diagnostician and/or catalyst, innovative training, perhaps additional funding and different kinds of facilities, and new understandings within the agencies and communities themselves. Permanent linkages with community organizations may be required. Traditional pyramid, hierarchical organizational models may have to be flattened. New information systems will be required, and continuing involvement or monitoring of diverted cases may be desirable.

The large scale diversion of offenders—either from or after entry into the justice system—may have other consequences for the justice agencies. If, for example, substantial numbers of offenders are diverted by local law enforcement to community-based agencies, there will be, in all likelihood, reduced inputs to prosecution, adjudication and correctional agencies. Lessened inputs will alleviate some of the backlog in the judicial system and reduce caseload pressure in probation and parole and size of institutional population. While these occurrences are desirable, at some point in time the bureaucratic instinct for survival may be threatened. Reactions protective of the establishment may set in. Of greater significance, however, is that increased diversion may leave the justice system with a unique clientele of hardened, recalcitrant, difficult offenders who seem unlikely to "make it" in the community. These offenders may have complex problems requiring long-range treatment and they may represent a major threat to and be rejected by their communities. In addition to creating major management problems, these offenders will require new and different programs, facilities and staff for treatment. In short, extensive diversion may not only "threaten" the justice establishment, it may change the justice system population and alter the system itself.

Planning and Evaluation Necessary

There are yet other important aspects of diversion which require attention—planning and evaluation. A lack of mid-range and strategic planning and systematic evaluation has long been a major defect in justice operations from law enforcement through corrections. The movement toward diversion of offenders mandates that planning and evaluation not be "tacked on" to operational processes, but rather be built-in, continually updated, constantly reviewed. The questions about planning and evaluation are familiar—criteria must be established, funds must be made available, personnel, software and hardware must be obtained, methodologies developed, responsibilities delineated.   Without such planning and evaluation, it appears certain that diversion practices will produce more confusion and chaos than clarity and consistency.

Conclusion

This article has explored the origins of diversion and identified some of the major operational and philosophical problems associated with the movement. Diversion is seen as an outgrowth of a fragmented justice system which has been neither just nor efficient, the increasing demands of our citizenry to be participants in the affairs of government including the justice system, and recognition that the community is an appropriate base for many justice operations. But even as there is increasing momentum toward diversion, there is a pressing need for guidelines, standards and shared understandings, examination of the role and resources of the community, study of the long range impact of diversion on the justice system and society, and planning and evaluation.

Diversion is both a challenge and an opportunity. As a potentially major mechanism of the justice system, diversion requires considered attention. Although changes in our justice systems are indicated, rapid movement to untested and ill-defined alternatives is inappropriate.

DIVERSION FROM THE CRIMINAL
JUSTICE PROCESS*

Diversion has been used informally and unoffically at all stages of the criminal justice process since its inception, but without being clearly identified and labelled. Desire to accommodate varying individuals and circumstances and to minimize the use of co-

-----

* National Advisory Commission on
Criminal Justice Standards and
Goals, *Report on Corrections*, 1973.

ercion resulted in many deviations from a formal justice system model that hypothesized arrest, conviction, and punishment without exception. When such deviations have been acknowledged at all, they have been called "discretion," "screening," or "minimizing penetration."

As used in this chapter, the term "diversion" refers to formally acknowledged and organized efforts to utilize alternatives to initial or continued processing into the justice system. To qualify as diversion, such efforts must be undertaken prior to adjudication and after a legally proscribed action has occurred.

In terms of process, diversion implies halting or suspending formal criminal or juvenile justice proceedings against a person who has violated a statute, in favor of processing through a noncriminal disposition or means.

Diversion is differentiated from prevention in that the latter refers to efforts to avoid or prevent behavior in violation of statute, while diversion concerns efforts after a legally proscribed action has occurred. For example, programs of character building for youths represent prevention efforts.

Diversion is also differentiated from the concept of "minimizing penetration" in that the latter refers to efforts to utilize less drastic means or alternatives at any point throughout official criminal or juvenile justice processing, while diversion attempts to avoid or halt official processing altogether. Probation in lieu of institutionalization represents an example of minimizing penetration.

There are a few gray areas within this definition which require clarification. For example, programs aimed at increasing the use of bail or release on recognizance instead of pretrial detention are sometimes called diversion on the grounds that research has shown that those detained prior to trial are more likely to be convicted than those released. However, since pretrial release programs utilize a less drastic means of continuing with official processing rather than stopping official processing altogether, such activities fall within the scope of minimizing penetration.

Similarly, activities such as plea bargaining and charge reductions have sometimes been referred to as diversion. Again, however, such efforts are not directed at halting all official processing and thus should not be characterized as diversion.

Some confusion may arise in discussions of diversion due to efforts to remove certain categories of behavior from the purview of the criminal law or the delinquency jurisdiction of the courts. For example, where drunkenness is a criminal offense, programs that provide alternatives to criminal processing for a drunkenness offender would qualify as diversion. In places where drunkenness has been decriminalized, however, treatment programs for drunkenness in the community would not technically be diversion programs under the definition given in this chapter since criminal processing would not be an option. Similarly, this report recommends that juveniles who have not committed acts that would be criminal if committed by adults should not be subject to the delinquency jurisdiction of the courts. Until that recommendation is implemented, however, programs that avoid formal court processing for truants, "minors in need of supervision," etc., fit the definition of diversion.

Unless otherwise specified, discussion of "victimless crimes" or juvenile status offenses in this chapter will assume that such categories of behavior are legally proscribed and that justice system processing may result if alternatives are not made available.

One last definitional note is needed. Throughout this report on corrections, the term "criminal justice system" is used in the generic sense to include the juvenile justice system even though it does not technically involve a criminal process. Given the fact that diversion programs are usually directed toward *either* adults in the criminal justice system *or* juveniles in the juvenile justice system, the two will frequently be differentiated throughout this chapter.

THE ARGUMENT FOR DIVERSION

The significance of diversion is evidenced primarily by the role it plays in keeping the criminal justice system in operation. For various reasons, people refuse to report offenses; police refuse to make arrests; prosecutors refuse to prosecute; and courts refuse to convict. Yet if all law violations were processed officially as the arrest-conviction-imprisonment model calls for, the system obviously would collapse from its voluminous caseloads and from community opposition. Cost of resources needed to handle violations officially would be prohibitive financially and socially.

To illustrate, consider some national data for the year 1971. In that year, approximately 5,995,000 major felonies—murder, aggravated assault, rape, robbery, burglary, grand larceny, and auto theft—were reported to the police. These reports resulted in 1,707,600 arrests, with juvenile courts assuming jurisdiction over about 628,000 cases. Among the remaining cases, 82 percent were processed in criminal court. Sixty percent of the cases processed resulted in conviction as originally charged, and 11 percent for a lesser charge.[1]

On the basis of these figures it can be estimated that nearly 30 percent of all reported offenses result in arrest, and almost one-third of all arrests in criminal convictions. Not included among criminal convictions are cases handled by juvenile courts. The figures also fail to account for multiple reports against single offenders, and they are compromised by the notoriously inadequate records kept by most agencies. Nevertheless, they convey some impression concerning the extent to which the arrest-conviction-imprisonment model is circumvented in practice.

Preadjudication dispositions (diversion) occur in both the juvenile and adult justice system and for many of the same reasons. First, even with the best legislative formulations, definitions of legally proscribed conduct are likely to be ambiguous. The decision to divert out of the justice system is affected by many factors including the nature of the offense, the circumstances of its commission, the attitude of the victim, and the character and social status of the accused. The use of discretion is encouraged by the stigma associated with official processing. The stigma may seriously limit the social and economic opportunities of the accused or impose upon him deviant roles leading to further antisocial acts. Finally, the volume of cases processed is so large as to require some screening of less serious offenders in order to allow law enforcement, courts, and corrections to concentrate on the more serious cases.

INADEQUACY OF THE CURRENT SYSTEM

Essentially, the argument generally put forth for diversion is a negative argument against the existing system. The assumption is that the present justice system is so bad that any alternative for diverting most offenders out of it, is better than any that will move the offender farther into it. In the current literature and knowledge in the field, there is evidence to support this assumption. But as the justice system becomes more rational, as

1. Federal Bureau of Investigation, *Crime in the United States: Uniform Crime Reports, 1971* (Washington: Government Printing Office, 1971), pp. 35, 61, 115. Referred to hereinafter as *UCR*, with appropriate date.

called for by this Commission, a method or process is needed by which equitable and logical choices are made to exclude individuals who truly do not need the services and resources of the justice system agencies, even though they may need forms of help from outside the justice system. Thus far, no classification schema or system has successfully addressed this issue.

Although many of the diversion programs of the past are based on humanitarian interests, experience has demonstrated that humanitarian intentions alone do not guarantee either more humane treatment or more successful programs. The juvenile court and its procedures were developed to divert children and youth from the criminal justice system. Yet, it has been found that the court itself often infringes on the rights of the child and involves a problem of stigma equal to those associated with a child being handled through criminal procedures or processes.

California juvenile court practices offer an excellent example of the injustice experienced by many children and youth coming into the justice system for behavior that would not be an offense if engaged in by adults. Recent figures show that arrests for major offenses equivalent to adult felony offenses accounted for only 17 percent of all juvenile arrests. Arrests for offenses generally comparable at the adult level with misdemeanors accounted for 20 percent. The remaining 63 percent was made up of arrests of youths who were "in need of supervision." [2] In many of the cases the juveniles referred to as being in need of supervision were treated in exactly the same way as, or worse than, those referred for felony and misdemeanor offenses.

A study of the fates of serious delinquents (youths adjudicated on the equivalent of serious criminal charges) and youths in need of supervision (juveniles charged with acts that would not be criminal if committed by adults) in 19 major cities revealed the following results: [3]

1.   Youths in need of supervision are more likely to be detained in detention facilities than serious delinquents (54 percent vs. 31 percent);

2. California Department of Justice, *Crime and Delinquency in California, 1970* (Sacramento: 1971), pp. 71–110.

3. Statement by Allen F. Breed at the Critical Decision Maker Conference sponsored by the U. S. Youth Development and Delinquency Prevention Administration, Los Angeles, May 24, 1972.

2. Once detained, youths in need of supervision are twice as likely as serious delinquents to be detained for more than 30 days (51 percent vs. 25 percent);

3. Youths in need of supervision are more likely to receive harsher dispositions in juvenile court and to be sent to confinement placement than serious delinquents (25 percent vs. 23 percent), with the average length of stay being much longer for the nondelinquent group.

Such findings raise serious questions about the way the resources of the juvenile justice system are being utilized. If evidence could convince us that current criminal and juvenile justice and correctional practices were effective in altering socially disapproved behavior, it is possible that we would continue to support such treatment of troublesome persons. However, the best of current evidence points strongly in the opposite direction.

More than three-fourths of the felonies processed in criminal courts are committed by repeaters. Recidivism rates ordinarily are highest among offenders discharged from prison at the expiration of their sentences, lower among parolees, and lowest among probationers.[4] It therefore seems clear that prisons are failing to achieve their correctional objectives. In spite of the vocal support given rehabilitation and reintegration of the offender into community life, the fact remains that many prisoners, adult and juvenile, live under conditions more debilitating than rehabilitating—conditions that encourage patterns of immorality, dependency, manipulation, irresponsibility, and destructiveness.

In recognition of this, much effort has recently been directed toward improvement of institutional programs. Among the programs developed in the last few decades are psychiatric therapy, group counseling, casework, role playing, and academic and vocational training. Prisoners, if sufficiently motivated, can gain proficiency in an occupation. But they may be unable to find related employment when released. Or they may not have learned how to get along with other people or how to perform the various nonoccupational tasks necessary for success in the community.

4. See National Council on Crime and Delinquency, *Policies and Background Information* (Hackensack, N. J.: NCCD, 1972), p. 14; and California Assembly, Committee on Criminal Procedure, *Deterrent Effects of Criminal Sanctions* (Sacramento: 1968).

Programs may alleviate some pains of imprisonment and foster better institutional adjustment. Life in the free community, however, is an entirely different matter. Prison virtues such as dependency, subordination, and compliance are not always rewarded in the world outside. Thus a good prisoner does not necessarily make a good parolee or a good citizen.

The result is that prisoners who receive special "treatment" in the institution apparently have about the same recidivism rates as those who do not.[5] Even where treatment is institutionally successful, its effects seem to dissipate once the offender returns to the community. An illustration is the Fricot Ranch Project in California, which initially produced a drastic reduction in recidivism rates for offenders who received intensive treatment. A year after release the group that received treatment had a recidivism rate of 37 percent, compared with 52 percent for a matched control group.[6] Five years after release, however, the recidivism rates were 88 and 90 percent, respectively.

Neither do long sentences, with or without "treatment," necessarily protect society better than short ones. In fact, if offense type, previous record, and similar variables are held constant, the probability of recidivism increases with the length of the sentence.[7] And the greater the number of times an offender is confined, the greater the risk of failure.

If, on the whole, the effects of incarceration are harmful, the prison, instead of deterring crime, may deter the offender's successful community performance. Diversionary methods, accordingly, work better than incarceration. Diverted offenders do not have to contend with the prison's criminogenic environment.

5. See, for example, Walter Bailey, "Correctional Outcome: An Evaluation of One Hundred Reports," *Journal of Criminal Law, Criminology, and Police Science*, 57 (1966), 153–160; Gene Kassebaum et al., *Prison Treatment and Its Outcome* (Wiley, 1970); James Robison and Gerald Smith, "The Effectiveness of Correctional Programs," *Crime and Delinquency*, 17 (1971), 67–80.

6. Carl F. Jesness, "Comparative Effectiveness of Two Institutional Programs for Delinquents," unpublished paper, 1972.

7. See, for example, Carol Crowther, "Crimes, Penalties, and Legislatures," *Annals of the American Academy of Political and Social Science*, 381 (1969), 147–158; Paul Mueller, *Advanced Releases to Parole* (Sacramento: California Department of Corrections, 1965); Dorothy Jaman and Robert Dickover, *A Study of Parole Outcome as a Function of Time Served* (Sacramento: California Department of Corrections, 1969).

Their lives are disrupted less seriously. Contacts with the community are not severed. Stigmatization is less severe. It seems that the earlier diversion occurs in the criminal or juvenile justice system, the greater its relative advantages.

THE DILEMMA OF THE TREATMENT MODEL

Even with such growing evidence of the counter-productive effects of incarceration and other forms of correctional treatment, there has been substantial reluctance to adopt alternate methods of dealing with criminal and quasi-criminal behavior. One reason for this reluctance centers around a deeply rooted adherence to a treatment model as the answer to problems of crime and delinquency.

Many efforts to correct the deficiencies of the justice system are seriously limited by the medical model adopted for the correctional system. Tremendous pressures are put on staff and resources to offer "treatment" to those persons who are made subjects of the justice system. As a result of the assumption that all persons who find themselves within the correctional and justice system are necessarily in need of help or "treatment," many persons argue that there cannot be a diversionary program without in fact offering some kind of alternative service or help.

Perhaps the classic example of this dilemma is in relation to children with delinquent tendencies. At the moment there is considerable doubt in the field of juvenile justice as to whether these children should be subjected to "help." Yet, there is a consistent unwillingness to legislatively remove these children and youth from the system until such time as there is some other treatment to provide help. Apparently doing something, no matter how bad, is perceived as being better than doing nothing, even though evidence does not support this position.

Legislative or administrative action that excluded these children and youth from the "help" of the justice system would force development of whatever private or community alternatives were needed. Both indecision and ambivalence enable the field to avoid facing the issue of legislatively excluding from the juvenile justice system juveniles and youths who have not committed acts that would be criminal if committed by adults—a decision that would reduce workloads and offer greater opportunity for constructive work with delinquents remaining within the system.

Our society reflects a phenomenon that sociologist Erving Goffman [8] has identified as "ritual maintenance," which he describes as a universal feeling that when some sort of antisocial or disapproved act occurs something must happen. What happens need not necessarily be punitive, nor must it necessarily be therapeutic. The point is that there are alternatives to both punishment and treatment and a wide range between these two extremes if a willingness exists to consider them. The alternatives run a gamut from reprimand, release, fines, and informal supervision to forms of custody and restriction on freedom. Some imply treatment, but many do not. Most imply a willingness to consider noncriminal program dispositions—forms of help that are often best offered by non-justice system agencies, groups and individuals.

Society must act in some visible way against behavior that is defined as illegal. Action is a necessity; treatment is not—not necessarily.

To the extent that the foregoing has validity, the strategy and argument for diversion presents itself; namely, every effort should be made to keep juveniles and adults out of the justice system. Secondly, every effort should be made to minimize a juvenile's or an adult offender's penetration into the correctional system. This does not suggest that the agents of the system simply take advantage of ambiguities within the existing system. It does suggest that planned programs be developed as alternatives to needless processing into the justice system. To this end, every available alternative must be explored at each decision point; i. e., police contact, arrest, intake, detention, jail, court wardship, conviction, commitment, probation, parole, and, ultimately, even revocation. At each critical step, efforts should be made to exhaust and select the less rejecting, less stigmatizing recourses before taking the next expulsive step. This becomes particularly important during that short time between arrest and adjudication within which diversion for appropriate cases can be planned.

A POSITIVE ARGUMENT FOR DIVERSION

The positive argument for diversion is that it gives society the opportunity to consider the possibility of reallocating existing

---

8.   Erving Goffman, *Asylums* (Doubleday, 1961).

resources to programs that promise greater success in bringing about correctional reform and social restoration of offenders. Given the choice between expanding the capacities of police, courts, and institutions to the point where they could accommodate the present and projected rates of criminal activity and the opportunity to establish diversion programs with public funds, the economics of the matter clearly favor a social policy decision for diversion. For example, the Project Crossroads diversion program in the District of Columbia had a per capita program cost of approximately $6.00 per day. The per capita cost of institutionalization in D.C. correctional facilities was averaging close to $17.00 a day at the time. Furthermore, the recidivism rate among Crossroads participants was 22 percent, as opposed to 46 percent among a control group which did not receive project services.[9]

Diversion is an opportunity. It is not a solution.[10] If it is seen exclusively as a solution, diversion programs, like their correctional predecessors, will fail. To develop a system that utilizes diversion in a planned and constructive fashion, there must be a radical overhaul in the nature and character of some of today's most cherished social institutions. Commitment to diversion is a commitment to the principle of change.

Probably the most significant contribution to the field of criminal justice today would be development of a schema that systematically, and on a selected basis, effectively screens subjects out of the criminal justice system in terms of their real danger to society rather than the prejudices of individual members of the criminal justice system. As we now operate, diversion is advocated in the funding standards of the Law Enforcement Assistance Administration, the Youth Development and Delinquency Prevention Administration, and the American Correctional Association without uniform methods, theories, or procedures being given to describe specifically at what points diversion should occur, who should be diverted, under what conditions, to what programs, and for what purposes. National standards to guide the continuing development of diversion programs are essential.

9. American Correctional Association, *Juvenile Diversion: A Perspective* (College Park, Md.: ACA, 1972), pp. 1–2.

10. Allen F. Breed, "Diversion: Program, Rationalization, or Excuse?" address to the National Institute on Crime and Delinquency, Portland, Or., June 19, 1972.

IMPLEMENTATION OF DIVERSION

For communities interested in maximizing the planned use of diversion, it is necessary to identify the points at which diversion may occur and the individuals or groups primarily responsible for it at each of these points. There are three main points at which diversion may occur: prior to police contact, prior to official police processing, and prior to official court processing. Analysis of each of these potential points of diversion yields three basic models in terms of responsibility for diversion: community-based diversion programs, police-based diversion programs, and court-based diversion programs. While each of these models usually involves more than one agency or group, programs will be grouped according to who initiates and is primarily responsible for their operation.

COMMUNITY-BASED DIVERSION PROGRAMS

For a variety of reasons, many illegal acts that come to the attention of citizens are not reported to the police. A national victimization survey was conducted on a sample of 10,000 households from July 1965 through June 1966.[11] These studies attempt to estimate the number of unreported offenses by asking persons if they or members of their families were victimized by crime during the preceding year. Some of the results are given in Table 3.1, with comparable statistics from the Federal Bureau of Investigation.

Two facts stand out in the comparison. The relative frequencies of specific serious crimes uncovered by the victimization survey are fairly similar to those obtained by the FBI from police agencies. Offenses are ranked in an identical order. However, the survey found a much greater number of offenses than were reported by the police—2,116.6 offenses per 100,000 population as compared with 974.7 offenses.

There can be little doubt that a large number of law violators go free because people fail to report offenses.

One of the main reasons for failure to report offenses, according to the survey, is that many people believe the authorities are unwilling or unable to do much about crimes that have occurred.

---

11. Philip H. Ennis, *Criminal Victimization in the United States* (Washington: Government Printing Office, 1967), p. 8.

Table 3.1   Comparison of Victimization Reports and Police
Data on the Amount of Crime.

| | Rate per 100,000 Population | |
Offense	Victimization Survey	FBI Reports
Homicide	(Too few cases)	5.1
Forcible Rape	42.5	11.6
Robbery	94.0	61.4
Assault	218.3	106.6
Burglary, Grand Larceny, Auto Theft	1,761.8	790.0

Source: Philip H. Ennis, *Criminal Victimization in the United
States,* (Washington: Government Printing Office, 1967), p. 8.

[A8882]

Such attitudes are especially prevalent in disadvantaged areas
where the crime rates are highest.

On the other hand, it is becoming increasingly clear that numerous responsible individuals and groups do not report some illegal incidents to the police because they think the matters can
be handled better outside the criminal justice system.   While
some of this reaction may be characterized simply as toleration
or lack of concern, much of it is quite to the contrary.   That is,
community agencies and residents around the country are seeking planned alternatives to official criminal justice processing
that they hope will have better results.   Such citizens and agencies are taking action of varying degrees of formality to increase
the community's capability to respond to unwanted behaviors.

School Diversion Programs

One of the oldest community-based diversion models centers
around the school.   Since the school as a social institution is responsible for young people a large portion of the day and is highly
concerned with their socialization, and since many behaviors that
are categorized as delinquent are school-related (truancy, incorrigibility, vandalism), most schools maintain procedures for dealing with the majority of their behavior problems without re-
course to legal authorities.

For example, 40 percent of the offenses committed by Los Angeles school children and coming to the attention of the authorities in 1968–1969—involving cases of drug violations, assault

against school personnel, damage to school property, etc.—were processed without referral to the police.[12] Schools utilize counseling, disciplinary action, family conferences, special classes or special schools, referral to community social service agencies, and a whole range of other techniques before finally resorting to police help. While most schools probably do not think of themselves as operating diversion programs, they are doing just that when they deal with illegal behavior unofficially.

There are, in addition, other agencies or groups that are organizing diversion efforts as at least one of their stated objectives.

Comprehensive Youth Service Delivery System

An example of a major prevention-diversion effort is to be found in projects currently being funded by the Youth Development and Delinquency Prevention Administration of the U. S. Department of Health, Education, and Welfare. Called Comprehensive Youth Service Delivery Systems, pilot projects are being established in Florida, Oklahoma, and California to develop a network of youth services which will create the ties between service institutions and the recipients of the service. They have as their objective a 2- to 3-percent diversion rate per year from the juvenile justice system as measured by reduced arrests and filings before the juvenile court.

The program specifically incorporates these basic ingredients: 1) diversion of youth from the juvenile justice system within a given target area by 2 to 3 percent per year; 2) development of an integrative, jointly funded youth service system containing programs and services that enhance both prevention and diversion activities; 3) involvement of youth themselves in the planning, development, and execution of the programs and service delivery systems.

As designed, the programs are intended to eliminate the need to label children as delinquent before rendering service. Units of State and local government traditionally have been constrained in their delinquency prevention and diversion efforts because they had no jurisdiction to intervene with a juvenile or his family until the youth committed one or a series of delinquent acts.

12. Edwin M. Lemert, *Instead of Court: Diversion in Juvenile Justice* (Rockville, Md.: National Institute of Mental Health, Center for Studies of Crime, and Delinquency, 1971).

The basic idea of this project is to provide a broad range of services, preventive, rehabilitative, health, tutorial, etc., to *all* youths, delinquent and nondelinquent, in a narrowly restricted target area containing large percentages of children and families at risk without regard to traditional eligibility requirements.

It is the aim of such projects to coordinate all service programs to youth in the target area—Federal, State, county, city, private —and determine from model experimentation which agencies should eventually operate these services—private or public sector, local or State government, etc. The underlying hypothesis of the program is that crime and delinquency are due not so much to a lack of resources as to a failure on the part of the system to adequately focus on the needs of youth at appropriate times and places in ways that make existing services effective. The projects propose to provide new resources to the police and courts, on a 24-hour, 7-day-a-week basis, that will enable these agencies to divert children and youth.

Community Responsibility Programs

Community responsibility programs are increasing throughout the United States. Frequently located in predominantly low-income minority communities (particularly in California, Illinois, New York, and Puerto Rico), these projects are designed to assist youth involved in delinquent activities. The main focus of the programs is community involvement and community responsibility for their own children and youth. A panel of community members, both youth and adult, act as judges listening to cases of youthful offenders who have been referred by various agencies, most frequently by law enforcement agencies. Minors who have committed violations of the law appear before the citizen panel which determines the minor's responsibility. If it is determined that an alleged act did in fact occur which in some way injured the community, the youth may be required to carry out some useful community work under supervision. He is also asked to undergo a program of counseling with volunteers, paraprofessionals, or even established agency personnel on an informal basis.

Programs of this nature, greatly expanded through funding by the Office of Economic Opportunity, the Law Enforcement Assistance Administration, and the Department of Health, Education, and Welfare, are increasingly gaining citizen support and public agency respect. In addition to evidencing an ability to deal with youthful offenders outside of the justice system, the community responsibility and concern for delinquent activities within the community also has a tendency to reduce the total volume of crime and delinquency within that area. It is hypothesized that some of the success of such programs is due to the fact that juveniles respond better to members of their own community than to personnel of the justice system, who are seen as part of the establishment. Many adult drug treatment programs have similar qualities and procedures.

The Youth Service Bureau

Of all of the recommendations made by the President's Crime Commission in 1967, none was regarded with more hope for diverting children and youth from the juvenile justice system than the Youth Service Bureau. Yet, in 1972, a national study was able to identify only 150 bureaus spread throughout the United States and supported by only $25,000,000 of Federal funds.[13] The Youth Service Bureau does not appear to be the Nation's most popularly supported diversion effort.

The Youth Service Bureau was intended to be a community agency to provide those necessary services to youth that would permit law enforcement and the courts to divert youthful offenders from the justice system. It was intended to involve the entire community, its agencies and resources in effective programs of crime prevention, diversion, rehabilitation, care, and control.

Today, the future of Youth Service Bureaus appears to be financially uncertain, and those bureaus that are surviving tend to be related to established agencies. Those related to the police, probation, or the courts are expanding and show the greatest evidence of being able to offer acceptable alternatives to justice system processing. Some may be incorporated with comprehensive youth service delivery systems.

The national study reports that on the basis of a national 500-case sample, a majority (87 percent) of the youth who were provided services were between the ages of 12 and 18. Approximately 79 percent were of school age, and the predominant source of referral was self, friends, or family. Schools referred approx-

13. Sherwood Norman, *The Youth Service Bureau* (Paramus, N. J.: National Council on Crime and Delinquency, 1972). See also William Underwood, *A National Study of Youth Services Bureaus* (Washington: U. S. Youth Development and Delinquency Prevention Administration, in process).

imately 21 percent and police only 13 percent. Problems at home, incorrigibility, runaways, not getting along, and school problems accounted for 28 percent of the referrals.

Preliminary data indicate that Youth Service Bureaus are providing an alternative service for children in need of supervision. Whether or not they have been able to establish a new agency to serve children and youth effectively on a continuing basis is a question that only time will answer.

POLICE-BASED DIVERSION MODELS

Police-based diversion programs may be administered internally or through use of referral relationships with other community agencies. Neither arrangement, however, has met with much use in the past. On a national basis, less than 2 percent of arrested juveniles are referred to other community agencies by police departments,[14] and probably even fewer are served through police-run diversion programs.

The reasons for past police reluctance to engage in formal diversion efforts are numerous and understandable. Perhaps the most common reason relates to community and police perceptions of the police role. Where the role of police is defined mainly in terms of rigorous detection and apprehension of all violations of law, rather than such responsibilities tempered by roles in prevention, fairness, community interests, individual circumstances, and the like, it is not surprising that diversionary efforts are not made highly visible. Sometimes, a choice not to process an offender officially even appears to be contrary to the law. Thus for example, the Wisconsin statutes provide that a police officer "shall arrest . . . every person found . . . in a state of intoxication or engaged in any disturbance of the peace or violating any law of the state or ordinance . . . " Some places, such as the District of Columbia, make it a criminal offense for a police officer to fail to make an arrest.

These impediments to a police role in diversion are compounded by such real problems as: the conflicting demands on police manpower and resources posed by law enforcement and diversion objectives; the lack of police officers with training in the behavioral

14. *UCR, 1971*, p. 112 (includes all offenses except traffic and neglect cases).

sciences; and the general absence of cooperative relationships between police departments and community groups.

To state that police involvement in formalized diversion programs has been minimal is not to minimize the very considerable impact of police discretion not to arrest.

Studies show that informal procedures aimed at avoiding arrest are especially prevalent in rural areas, small cities with a large upperclass population,[15] and large metropolitan communities where the police force has not been highly professionalized.[16] Similar results are obtained in other studies. In addition, some juvenile courts are excluding certain types of cases, especially those involving dependency, runaways, ungovernable conduct, and other kinds of family problems. These cases are often aggravated by official court intervention and probably can be resolved more effectively by social service agencies or counseling clinics. A program of this kind has recently been instituted in King County (Seattle) Washington to avoid the use of official sanctions unless they are necessary for community protection or offender control.

The same objective applies to adult offenders. Even where guilt probably could be established by a trial, official sanctions are often avoided to preserve the offender's community ties, keep neighborhood peace, protect a wage earner's job, maintain family unity, or provide treatment without marring the lawbreaker's record by a criminal conviction. Again, the primary responsibility for initiating informal procedures, instead of official sanctions, is delegated to the police.

For example, the police commonly use alternatives to arrest, such as reprimanding a suspected offender, referring him to his family or other agencies, requiring that he make restitution to the victim or that he seek some kind of treatment. There are many situations in which arrest is clearly inappropriate. This is normally true when the police are trying to resolve conflicts between husbands and wives, landlords and tenants, businessmen and customers, or management and labor. It is often the case when the police are questioning people, collecting information, engaging in surveillance, asking for assistance, or attempting to remove persons from the scene of a crime or an accident. In these

15. Nathan Goldman, *The Differential Selection of Juvenile Offenders* (New York: National Council on Crime and Delinquency, 1963).

16. James Q. Wilson, "The Police and the Delinquent in Two Cities," in Stanton Wheeler, ed., *Controlling Delinquents* (Wiley, 1968).

circumstances, the police are called upon to play the roles of counselor, technical expert, or referral agent. The more effective they are in those roles, the less often they need to rely on arrest, force, and other legal sanctions.

When an offense is reported, the police need to decide if it warrants investigation. Likewise, it must be determined if the offender should be arrested, if he should be taken into custody, and if he should be detained. Before any court action can occur, the nature of the official charges must be decided. On each of these issues the police have access to a variety of alternatives.

Many police officers have doubts about the effectiveness of prosecution and are reluctant to make an arrest unless they believe it necessary. Judgments concerning the necessity of an arrest are influenced by numerous subjective factors. Probably one of the most important is the attitude or demeanor of the suspected offender. If the suspect is contrite, cooperative, and compliant, the likelihood of an arrest is lessened. But if he displays a bold, brusque, and belligerent attitude, the probability of action is greatly increased.[17] Other factors affecting discretionary decisions are the roles played by the victim, the complainant, and any witnesses; the community's attitudes and interests; the perceived severity of the offense; and the policies of courts and other agencies.[18]

Recently there has been an increase in the number of police agencies acknowledging the crucial role of individual police discretion and some have begun to develop policies to guide and structure its use. A number of those agencies have arrived at the point of adopting formal diversion programs.

Family Crisis Intervention Projects

There are indications that the police, by identifying conflict situations at an early stage of development, can prevent the escala-

17. See Irving Piliavin and Scott Briar, "Police Encounters with Juveniles," *American Journal of Sociology*, 70 (1964), 206–214; Lyle Shannon, "Referral in a Middle-Sized City," *British Journal of Criminology*, 3 (1963), 24–26; Robert Terry, "Discrimination in the Handling of Juvenile Offenders by Social Control Agencies," *Journal of Research in Crime and Delinquency*, 3 (1967), 218–230; and Wayne La Fave, *Arrest: The Decision to Take a Suspect into Custody* (Little, Brown, 1965).

18. Donald Black, "Production of Crime Rates," *American Sociological Review*, 35 (1970), 733–748; Donald Black and Albert Reiss, "Police Control of Juveniles," *American Sociological Review*, 35 (1970), 63–77.

tion of violence. A conspicuous example is the Family Crisis Intervention Project in New York City.[19] Officers from a high-risk precinct are trained to work in teams to intervene in family disturbance calls attempting to resolve the conflict on the scene. If unsuccessful, they refer the antagonists to a community agency. The New York program has been successful in many other cities including Oakland, Denver, and Chicago.

In the New York experience, not one homicide occurred in 926 families handled by intervention teams. Nor was a single officer injured, even though the teams were exposed to an unusually large number of dangerous incidents. Families having had experience with the teams referred other families to the project, and many troubled individuals sought out team members for advice. It is believed that police-community relations were improved as a result and that a number of incidents were averted that otherwise might have led to arrests.

The 601 Diversion Project

The County of Santa Clara, California, proposed a project for funding to the State planning agency that would divert 77 percent of those children arrested and previously referred to the probation department.[20] Referred to as the 601 Diversion Project, 12 law enforcement agencies in the county receive a reward commensurate with the degree of reduction in referrals of children "in need of supervision" to alternative community-based programs. The funds received by the law enforcement agencies are used to purchase services for the children referred from other private and public agencies or resources. The probation department administers the program, and all 12 law enforcement agencies voluntarily participate in its design and implementation.

The program identifies a kind of police behavior—diversion of children in need of supervision from the juvenile justice system—and rewards those engaging in the approved behavior. Further, the proposal identifies levels for performance; i. e., 77 percent reduction from past practice of law enforcement agencies. The

19. Morton Bard, *Training Police as Specialists in Family Crisis Intervention* (Washington: Government Printing Office, 1970).

20. "Predelinquent Diversion Project," proposal submitted by Santa Clara County Juvenile Probation Department, 1972, and funded by the California Council on Criminal Justice, Sacramento. The name of the project derives from Sec. 601 of the State Welfare and Institutions Code, which deals with juveniles with delinquent tendencies.

program specifies objectives, outlines activities, and requires evaluation for reimbursement. It proposes a planned diversion to identified programs. It is highly visible as well as measurable.

A Police Youth Service Bureau

The first Youth Service Bureau to be affiliated with the local police department was started in July of 1971 in Pleasant Hill, California. Like other Youth Service Bureaus, the Pleasant Hill bureau is designed to divert young offenders and potential delinquents from the regular channels of juvenile corrections. In place of the traditional methods of dealing with teenage lawbreakers, the youth service bureau offers a variety of counseling programs, including family and school visits by the bureau's staff. In addition to offering counseling, tutoring, job assistance or other professional help, the bureau has initiated a wide variety of delinquency-preventive programs, including special classes for girls exhibiting delinquent tendencies, classes in drug education, a speakers bureau, and police-youth rap sessions.

The program is staffed by two civilian aids and three policemen. The initial emphasis is to curb truancy and the number of runaway teenagers. Guidelines for the police department have been drafted which provide for the referral of all runaways to the bureau. A youth may be sent to juvenile hall only when he presents a danger to himself and others.

In its first year of operation, 49 percent of the arrests by the Pleasant Hill police—about 294—were of juveniles. Of these, 80 percent were handled within the police department. The other 20 percent of the youths were sent to juvenile hall or cited to probation.

The Pleasant Hill Youth Services Bureau is being funded jointly by the Federal Government and the city. Sixty percent of the bureau's $89,000 annual budget comes from a Federal grant administered by the California Council on Criminal Justice. The remaining 40 percent has been allocated to the bureau by the Pleasant Hill city council.[21]

21. "Police Department Opens Youth Bureau," *Contra Costa Times*, Nov. 11, 1971.

Richmond, California Police Diversion Program

Another example of a police-based diversion program is occurring in Richmond, California. The Richmond Police Department's Juvenile Diversion Program, funded on a pilot basis by LEAA and subsequently aided by the California Youth Authority, is testing the feasibility of the police providing direct helping and counseling services to youth involved in predelinquent and certain delinquent activities.[22] Program elements include crisis intervention, behavior management training for parents, counseling, tutorial services, and employment assistance. These services traditionally have been provided by other agencies such as probation staffs, the school department, or paroling authorities. The intent is to provide direct services and eliminate the wasted hours, days, and weeks of time that sometimes expire before offenders referred for service actually receive service.

The basic thrust of this project is that the police are on the cutting edge of the entire juvenile justice system and are in this sense the primary gatekeepers to that system. With adequate resources and properly trained staff, the police feel they are in the position to provide 24-hour services of a helping nature to youthful offenders who are at risk of coming into the formal juvenile justice system if care and service are not immediately provided.

Los Angeles County Diversion Program

Early in 1970, the Los Angeles County Delinquency and Crime Commission recommended that the Los Angeles County Department of Community Services and the Los Angeles County Sheriff's Department enter into discussions relative to the establishment of a county-wide delinquency prevention program. After careful examination of numerous prevention strategies, it was determined that a juvenile diversion program would provide the most effective and mutually beneficial prevention effort directly applicable to the highly diversified areas and the $1\frac{3}{4}$ million people served directly by the 14 sheriff's stations in Los Angeles County.[23]

The decision was made to focus on juveniles as the target population for the Los Angeles County Sheriff's Department diversion

22. Information supplied by the California Youth Authority.

23. Information supplied by the Los Angeles County Sheriff's Department.

program. An important first step in planning the program was analysis of the current juvenile disposition data for the department. This analysis revealed that the department traditionally "counseled and released" the least serious 55 percent of all juvenile arrests. About 25 percent were released to the custody of their parents and a non-detained petition filed with the probation department requesting a juvenile court hearing. The remaining 20 percent of the cases represented the most serious of the offenders. Because they were viewed as a hazard to themselves or the community, these offenders were referred to juvenile hall for detention via detained petition requests.

By more detailed analysis of the characteristics of the juveniles comprising each of the above three groups, it appeared that a significant portion of the youth in the mid-range of seriousness appeared to be in a "high-risk" situation in regard to developing delinquent lifestyles. Although many of the juveniles in this area would not be termed delinquent, records indicated that they were the most likely of all those in the non-delinquent category to have further contacts with law enforcement and thus create the "cycle of failure" which ultimately leads to a delinquent and criminal lifestyle.

On the basis of this information and in an effort to break the "cycle of failure," it was decided to select a target of 10 percent of youths in this category to be diverted to community-based organizations trained specifically to provide personal, non-stigmatizing supportive guidance.

An important aspect of the program was the decision to make complete referrals as opposed to merely "forwarding problems." That is, the department assumed responsibility for gaining extensive knowledge of community resources, making evaluations of them, communicating directly with agency personnel to familiarize them with problems at hand, preparing the juvenile to accept the agency, and following up after referral to see that contact actually was carried out. The decision was also made to deal with agencies offering direct services and those with aggressive outreach and follow-up services, rather than umbrella agencies engaging in referral.

COURT-BASED DIVERSION MODELS

The opportunity to divert does not cease even after an arrest has been made.[24] Many arrested offenders are diverted at a later stage in the judicial process. Whether or not these various discretions constitute diversion is another question. In some cases, the district attorney, the court, the public defender, and others have specific programs aimed at diverting people out of the criminal justice system. They have a specific target population and specific programs to which offenders can be diverted. To the extent that these activities are formally designed to divert a defined offender population, they are diversion programs, as the term is used in this chapter.

Diversionary methods have been used most extensively for persons accused of white-collar offenses, shoplifting, family disturbances, misdemeanors of all kinds, and first offenses. They are employed at all stages of the judicial process. In many cases diversionary decisions have such low visibility that it is difficult to describe them and nearly impossible to assess their value. However, some of the decisions reflect more or less standardized policies, and they are indicative of general trends in informal procedure.

Minor offenses have long been characterized by a low incidence of official sanctions. This is especially true of what have been called crimes without victims and class crimes. Victimless crimes include liquor and drug violations, gambling, numbers rackets, prostitution, homosexuality, and so on. Class crimes involve offenses categorized as vagrancy, drunkenness, disorderly conduct, and suspicious behavior.

These offenses are notoriously resistant to law enforcement tactics. Unless they seriously disturb the public conceptions of order and decency, they are not likely to arouse official reaction. Indeed, the authorities sometimes may try to regulate these activities to minimize their public visibility. In spite of sporadic

---

24. See Martin Gold, *Delinquent Behavior in an American City* (Brooks-Cole, 1970); Eugene Doleschal, Hidden Crime, *Crime and Delinquency Literature*, No. 2 (New York: National Council on Crime and Delinquency, 1970); Roger Hood and Richard Sparks, *Key Issues in Criminology* (McGraw-Hill, 1970); Clarence Schrag, *Crime and Justice: American Style* (Rockville, Md.: National Institute of Mental Health, Center for Studies of Crime and Delinquency, 1971).

and half-hearted enforcement, however, the offenses mentioned were responsible for 45 percent of the 8.6 million arrests that occurred in 1971 in the United States.[25]

Civil Commitment

Criminal justice concepts are being revised because of the increasing tendency of courts and the public to hold authorities responsible for the consequences of their decisions. This is perhaps best evidenced in the rapid expansion of civil commitment and other procedures based on a medical model that holds that some types of deviance, instead of indicating criminal intent, are symptoms of illness.

Civil commitment can be described as a procedure, theoretically noncriminal and employed without stigmatization, for diverting selected types of deviants from the criminal justice system. Such diversions can occur either before or after trial. The offenders—juveniles, drug abusers, sex offenders, and the mentally ill or retarded, for example—are hospitalized for treatment instead of being imprisoned. Community protection is promised by removal of the "sick" person and by therapies aimed at restoration of health or normalcy before the patient is returned to free society.

Yet there are some doubts about the wisdom of civil commitments. Such commitments are ordinarily viewed by the patient as involuntary, and his rights may be violated even though no criminal charges are made against him. Moreover, there is much concern that the treatment given may not be any different or any more effective than that received in many correctional facilities. Although these charges present some problems, the Commission endorses the use of civil commitment under certain conditions. A discussion of this concept may be found in the Commission's Report on Police and in the chapter dealing with drug abuse in its Report on Community Crime Prevention.

Pretrial Intervention Programs

Many pretrial programs aimed at reducing criminalization have been developed. Their main process is screening cases appearing on the first arraignment calendar to select those that are good prospects for diversion. The screening is done by interview with some corroborative investigation. Interviews are conducted by different personnel in different programs—probation officers,

25. *UCR, 1971,* p. 115.

public defenders, prosecuting attorneys, court staff, law students, ex-offenders, VISTA volunteers, or special project employees.

Court-based diversion programs are administered either directly by the court or by public or private agencies working in cooperation with the court.   For example, Project Crossroads, to be described shortly, began as an independently administered diversion resource that accepted referrals from juvenile court intake and judges.   In 1971, when the project's grant was terminated, its staff and program were incorporated in the local court system.

The purpose of the growing number of pretrial diversion programs is to provide the court and individuals involved with a chance to minimize the exercise of coercive power and still have the opportunity to try to treat the behavior problem that was the basis for concern.   They also fill the usual service gap between apprehension and trial.   These projects have built-in safety mechanisms (i. e., they are based on conditional diversion) to increase the likelihood that state interests are not jeopardized.

Pretrial intervention projects basically operate in two ways. In a number of the projects, no formal charges are lodged.   Instead, after an individual has been arrested, he is screened on a number of criteria to determine whether he is eligible for participation in a formal diversion program.   Such screening criteria vary, depending on the scope and range of the particular project. For example, a project may be willing to accept only juvenile first offenders or offenders who have not committed offenses in certain categories.   If an individual meets the particular criteria, the project staff explains the program to the individual.   If he is interested in participating, the staff will ask the court to defer formal charging.   If the individual successfully completes the program, which usually involves regular participation in certain activities and acceptance of assistance, the staff will ask the prosecutor to dispense entirely with the case.   For those individuals who do not wish to participate or who indicate a desire to participate but then withdraw or are terminated unfavorably, charging will proceed as otherwise would have occurred.

In the other model, formal charges are lodged but individuals are screened for eligibility in a particular intervention project. If they and the court agree, further criminal proceedings are suspended pending the outcome of the individual's participation.   In these programs, successful completion of the program results in a request that charges be dropped. Unsuccessful participation results in regular proceedings on the charges.

The attractive feature of both approaches is that further opportunities to avoid criminalization are introduced without the prosecutor and the court having to terminate their interest and authority in the matter. The individual is able to avoid criminal prosecution and at the same time avail himself of whatever services he may need. In this sense, the programs are planned interventions, not simply the result of chance fluctuations in the broad range of discretions represented in the justice system.

The added services require more staff and better facilities, of course, but they promise greatly increasing use of pretrial intervention beyond the present level, which is approximately 10 percent of the cases on the arraignment calendar, according to the reports from several cities. Such intervention requires skill and patience on the part of staff, since many clients are alienated, suspicious, unable to present themselves effectively, and initially resistant to any kind of social agreement that involves making a commitment on their part.

DEPARTMENT OF LABOR PRETRIAL INTERVENTION PROJECTS

Under the Manpower Development and Training Act, the Manpower Administration of the Department of Labor has funded some of the most notable pretrial intervention projects. These projects aim at giving first offenders a chance through their performance in special diversion programs, to get into a lifestyle of worthwhile employment and stability with the help of manpower services and training.

Pretrial intervention projects have been funded for an average of 18 months with the hope that local sources will pick up the funding once Federal funding stops. This was the case in the first two, Project Crossroads in Washington, D. C., and the Manhattan Court Employment Project in New York City, which were experimental and demonstration projects. Sponsorship for pretrial projects can include cities and counties as well as private nonprofit corporations.

Project staffs include both paid workers and community volunteers with responsibilities in one of the following areas: screening of potential participants, counseling, employment services, and education. Nonprofessional staff members with backgrounds similar to those of the offenders are used in what have been traditionally professional occupational roles.

Program counselors screen all defendants prior to each day's arraignment. If an eligible defendant wants to participate in the program, the counselor, with the approval of the prosecuting attorney, makes a recommendation to the judge in arraignment court for a continuance of the case to permit the defendant to participate in the project (usually for 90 days). The enrollment criteria vary. Different projects have considered such factors as sex, age, residence, employment status, present charge, pretrial release status, and previous record. Accused offenders have been accepted while facing such various charges as petty larceny, attempted auto theft, receipt of stolen property, use of false pretenses, forgery, solicitation for prostitution, attempted burglary, simple assault, unlawful entry, and destruction of property.

At the end of the prescribed period of the continuance, the participant's counselor may recommend one of the following three actions to the court:

• Dismissal of pending charges based on satisfactory project participation and demonstrated self-improvement.

• Extension of the continuance to allow the program staff more time to work with the person (usually for an additional 30 to 90 days).

• Return of the defendant to normal court processing, without prejudice, because of unsatisfactory performance in the program.

Of 753 young first offenders enrolled in one of the first projects, charges were dropped for 468 who completed the program successfully, while 285 offenders were returned to face prosecution because of unsatisfactory performance. The recidivism rate (using a 15-month period following arrest as the base) was 14 percent lower for project participants than for a control group of first offenders.[26]

Recently pretrial pilot projects have been funded by the Manpower Administration in Baltimore, Boston, Cleveland, Minneapolis, San Antonio, and the San Francisco Bay Area. A similar project has been funded in Newark, N. J., by the Law Enforcement Assistance Administration.

26. *Manpower Programs for Offenders* (Washington: Manpower Administration, U. S. Department of Labor, 1972), p. 12.

New Haven Pretrial Diversion Program

An interesting example of a spin-off from the pilot projects funded by the Manpower Administration is the establishment of the New Haven Pretrial Diversion Program in the Sixth Circuit Court in New Haven.[27] The program was developed by the New Haven Pretrial Services Council, a body established to bring together representatives of the criminal justice system and other interested agencies to focus on the problems of pretrial criminal justice.

Formation of the Council in 1971 marked the first effort in New Haven to develop a formal mechanism for coordinating activities of local criminal justice agencies. The decision was made to focus upon the pretrial stage of the criminal process in order to enable the Council to concentrate upon a critical problem area.

The New Haven criminal justice community responded favorably to the idea of establishing a local Pretrial Services Council. The agencies which designated local representatives included:

> New Haven Department of Police Services
> Department of Corrections
> Department of Adult Probation
> Sixth Circuit Court Prosecutor's Office
> Sixth Circuit Court Public Defender's Office
> New Haven County State's Attorney's Office
> New Haven County Public Defender's Office
> New Haven Legal Assistance Association
> Judicial Department; Circuit Court Clerk's Office
> Connecticut Bail Commission
> New Haven County Bar Association
> Yale Law School

A full-time professional staff was hired to assist the Council in program planning and implementation under the close supervision of Council members. Federal assistance under the provisions of the Omnibus Crime Control and Safe Streets Act was secured to enable the project to get underway.

The Pretrial Services Council is designed to serve a double function for the New Haven criminal justice system. First, the Council improves the ability of New Haven criminal justice agen-

27. Information from Pretrial Diversion Program, Sixth Circuit Court, New Haven.

cies to both coordinate and cooperate in upgrading the pretrial criminal process. Second, the Council through its staff can institute and operate pilot projects which require interagency coordination.

The New Haven Pretrial Diversion Project is the first program developed by the Pretrial Services Council. It is modelled after successful diversion programs which have been operating in New York City and Washington, D. C., for over four years. The program is designed to channel eligible defendants into a specifically developed set of services focusing upon employment and counseling.

The ultimate goals of the program are to assist in reducing congestion in the Circuit Court System; avoid unnecessary prosecution, trial, and the development of conviction records; and lower the recidivism rate in the defendant population.

SPECIAL PROBLEM AREAS

The preceding sections of this chapter have dealt with diversion programs or models in terms of the groups or agencies having primary responsibility for them (police, courts, or community). To develop a clear picture of the ways in which diversion programs may operate, it should be useful to focus on selected special problem areas to illustrate the variety of programs that are being implemented in response to those problems. The following section focuses on programs that provide alternatives to criminal or delinquency processing for drunkenness, drug abuse, and mental illness.

PUBLIC DRUNKENNESS

Public drunkenness accounts for more than 2 million arrests each year.[28] The fact that most persons arrested for drunkenness are homeless and indigent chronic offenders [29] suggests that drunkenness and related offenses should be treated through social service rather than law enforcement agencies. But a shortage of money in the social services leaves the problem to the police, courts, and jails. The policies of local police departments

28. Robert T. Nimmer, *Two Million Unnecessary Arrests* (Chicago: American Bar Foundation, 1971), p. 1.

29. Gerald Stern, "Public Drunkenness: Crime or Health Problem?" *Annals of the American Academy of Political and Social Science*, 374 (1967), 148.

determine the number of arrests, the criteria for arrest, and the manner of handling a drunkenness offender.

To reduce the number of drunkenness arrests, the President's Commission on Law Enforcement and Administration of Justice in 1967 recommended the creation of community detoxification centers operated under the auspices of local police departments.[30] The proposed centers were to provide medical and social services for the rehabilitation of drunkenness offenders and reduce the involvement of the criminal justice system in the solution of social ills.

Experimental programs in three cities—St. Louis, Washington, D. C., and New York—present models for the diversion of public inebriates.

Detoxification Centers
St. Louis and the District of Columbia

St. Louis opened the first police-sponsored detoxification center in 1966 for the diversion of drunkenness offenders.[31] The project was funded by the Office of Law Enforcement Assistance (now the Law Enforcement Assistance Administration) to provide medical and rehabilitative services for a projected 1600 cases. In 1967 the State of Missouri took over funding for the present facility in the St. Louis State Hospital.

Persons arrested on a drunkenness charge in St. Louis now have a choice between treatment at the center and criminal prosecution. For those who choose to undergo treatment, criminal charges are suspended pending completion of the 7-day program. At the center, patients are given food and medical care, with optional counseling and referral services.

The District of Columbia received Federal funds for a similar detoxification program shortly after the creation of the St. Louis center. In Washington, a 1- to 3-day program is available to "walk-ins" and is mandatory for intoxicated persons picked up by the police.

30. President's Commission on Law Enforcement and Administration of Justice, *The Challenge of Crime in a Free Society* (Washington: Government Printing Office, 1967), pp. 236–237.

31. Data on St. Louis and Washington centers from Nimmer, *Two Million Unnecessary Arrests*, and Helen Erskine, *Alcoholism and the Criminal Justice System: Challenge and Response* (Washington: Law Enforcement Assistance Administration, 1972).

After spending a day at the center, where medical attention and food are provided, some patients are released. Others stay for 3 days, and those patients in more serious condition are referred to a subacute treatment unit of an alcoholism treatment hospital. The goal of the program is not to cure alcoholics but to divert nuisance cases from jail and court and, at the same time, to offer short-term care for recuperating inebriates. Before the detoxification centers opened, public inebriates in the District of Columbia generally spent 30 days in jail. Critics of the centers feel that a 30-day sentence at least gave an offender the opportunity to "dry out" and a place to sleep. Now the large turnover and volume of cases make rehabilitation difficult, if not impossible.

St. Louis claims that its graduates have shown some improvement in health and drinking habits, but the short treatment period in both cities precludes complete withdrawal from alcohol. St. Louis spends $40.00 per patient day for 7 days as compared to the District's $20.00 per patient day for a maximum of 3 days. The St. Louis center has been much more expensive to operate than the previous arrest system; the District has reduced costs by over 40 percent.

The courts and jails have benefited from the detoxification programs, now that all public drunkenness offenders in D. C. and those who prefer treatment to arrest in St. Louis are routed through the centers. No police time is saved, however, as police are still responsible for keeping inebriates off the streets. Police dissatisfaction with the new procedure causes many inebriates to be ignored.

In addition to the lack of police support, both programs suffer from a lack of money. Overcrowding is a chronic problem in both centers, in effect reducing them to corrals for herds of unfortunates. A minimum of services is provided and individual programming is nonexistent.

Manhattan Bowery Project

The Manhattan Bowery Project in New York City is a detoxification center operated by the Vera Institute of Justice in cooperation with public agencies. Created in 1967 and receiving money from Federal, State, and local sources, the program is now supported by the New York State Department of Mental Hygiene and the New York City Community Mental Health Board.

Its stated purpose is to provide both emergency and long-term medical and rehabilitative services to homeless alcoholics in the Bowery.[32]

A rescue team consisting of a recovered alcoholic and a plain-clothes police officer patrols the area offering transportation to the center to persons severely intoxicated or in need of medical aid. Agency and self-referrals are admitted, but 75 percent of the patients are recruited on the street. All cases are voluntary.

The program consists of 3 days of intensive care and treatment followed by a day or two in the aftercare unit. There is an emergency health clinic on the premises which serves anyone in need, intoxicated or not. The aftercare unit offers counseling and referral services and transportation to other agencies upon release.

About 67 percent of the inebriates approached on the street accept aid, and, upon release, over half of the patients accept referrals. The cost of treatment is about $38.00 per patient day, and the staff claims credit for overwhelming reduction in drunkenness arrests in the Bowery.

Conclusions

The response to the voluntary aspect of the Bowery and District of Columbia programs demonstrates the willingness of many problem drinkers to accept treatment, if only for free room and board. Opening the D. C. center to walk-ins has resulted in a patient population that is 50 percent self-referred.[33]

With the virtual decriminalization of public drunkenness in St. Louis and Washington, the next logical step is to remove it completely from the realm of the criminal justice process, entrusting care and cure to social service agencies that can better address long-range projects for housing and employment. Prison does not rehabilitate drunkenness offenders and neither does forced, short-term treatment. To rehabilitate problem drinkers, an alternate lifestyle must be offered, and the problem drinker must bring him with a desire to change his habits.

32. Criminal Justice Coordinating Council of New York City and Vera Institute of Justice, *The Manhattan Bowery Project* (New York: CJC, 1969).

33. Nimmer, *Two Million Unnecessary Arrests*, p. 20.

Until the distribution of public monies makes feasible a transfer of responsibility, drunkenness offenses will continue to drain law enforcement resources. Diversion of such cases into therapy may, in the long run, prove to be the most practical means of dealing with this problem.

DRUG ABUSE

Narcotics offenses have become more and more prevalent in recent years, burdening the criminal justice system with cases that might better be treated medically. Drug offenders today come from middle-class suburban as well as urban core areas and thus create public interest in preventive and rehabilitative programs. Diversion into therapeutic programs offers drug offenders an alternative to criminal prosecution. It completely avoids legislative and judicial entanglements, imprisonment, and the controversy over legalization of the possession of some drugs, especially marijuana. Dealing with the social and medical aspects of drug abuse is a positive approach with potential benefits both for society and for the individual.

In establishing a plan for diversion, several questions must be resolved: when diversion is appropriate; whether treatment should be voluntary or imposed; whether there should be a specified length of treatment; and whether it should be available to anyone, including non-offenders. For the success of any diversion scheme for narcotics offenders, eligibility requirements must be clearly defined. The population to be served must be a cohesive group with similar problems and treatment goals. The nature of the pending charge is also crucial: hard-core addicts should be treated separately from first offenders charged with possession. The goal of any diversion plan is to reorient the offender in society and to spare the criminal justice system the time and expense of prosecuting cases that are medical, rather than criminal, in nature.

Illinois Drug Abuse Program

The Illinois Dangerous Drug Abuse Act in 1967 provided a diversionary procedure for narcotics offenders, especially heroin addicts, and in 1968, the Illinois Drug Abuse Program (IDAP) was established. Financed entirely by the State Department of Mental Health, the program provides for group therapy, methadone maintenance, and medical and social services in halfway houses and therapeutic communities. After 1968, Federal funds made available through the Narcotic Addict Rehabilitation Act were channeled to the program through the National Institute of Mental Health (NIMH). IDAP's budget increased from $185,-000 in 1968 to $2.4 million in 1971, with the State gradually assuming more financial responsibility. By 1972, the budget increased to $4.5 million, with NIMH funds acounting for only 14 percent.[34]

IDAP has been expanded to treat users of amphetamines, barbiturates, and hallucinogenic drugs so that by July, 1971, about 2,000 individuals had received treatment in over 20 clinics. In 1972, IDAP had resources and facilities to handle 3,000 patients. Twenty-five percent of the patient population are referred from criminal court.

The structure and function of every agency involved are defined by State law. The court determines eligibility for offenders according to statutory requirements. Not eligible are offenders charged with violent crimes, drug-related criminal conspiracy, sale of specified drugs or sale of drugs to young persons, or possession of more than a certain quantity of specified drugs. Two or more previous convictions for violent crimes or a pending felony charge disqualify a person from treatment, as do two previous enrollments in a drug program within any consecutive 2-year period.[35]

An IDAP intake representative screens arrestees for drug use. Potential candidates are interviewed and given a medical examination to detect signs of addiction and to determine the likelihood of rehabilitation. The Illinois law (Ill.Rev.Stat. ch. 91½, 120.3–4, Smith-Hurd Supp., 1972) incorporates the Federal definition of addiction: "habitual use . . . so as to endanger the public morals, health, safety, or welfare" and "loss of self-control with reference to . . . addiction."

IDAP reserves the right to refuse any candidate, a safeguard against overcrowding its facilities. If IDAP approves a referral,

34. Except as otherwise noted, information on IDAP is from American Psychiatric Association and National Association for Mental Health, *The Treatment of Drug Abuse: Programs, Problems, Prospects* (Washington: Joint Information Service, 1972), pp. 127–152.

35. Wayne Kerstetter, "Diversion of Narcotics Offenders Three Formats," unpublished paper prepared for the Law Enforcement Assistance Administration, 1971, p. 8.

the court makes a final ruling, either continuing the case for the duration of treatment or granting convicted persons probation, with drug treatment a condition.

To treat offenders who are technically ineligible for treatment, IDAP has contractual agreements with government and private agencies. One such organization is Gateway Houses Foundation, a private nonprofit corporation operating three therapeutic communities for first offenders charged with possession of marijuana and other drugs. IDAP operates two multimodality residential centers, one in downtown Chicago and one outside the city. These centers serve narcotic drug users, non-narcotic drug users, those who have been detoxified by methadone, methadone-maintained patients, and those now abstaining from drugs. Some of the staff are rehabilitated addicts.

The maximum referral period is 2 years for pre-adjudication cases. Under the statute, treatment can be successfully completed at any time during that period. If an offender leaves the program or if IDAP dismisses him, pending criminal charges are brought to court. If a person faithfully participates in the program for 2 years but cannot be certified cured by staff, the court exercises discretion in dropping the charges or resuming prosecution. The maximum term of treatment for persons assigned to the program as probationers is 5 years or the length of probation, whichever is less.

The program's minimum goal is to turn out law-abiding citizens. Its maximum goal is to enable its patients to lead productive, drug-free lives. Its multimodality approach serves the patients' diverse needs, and its flexibility allows for modifications.

Cook County State's Attorney's Program

The Cook County State's Attorney's Program for the Prevention of Drug Abuse depends on judicial and prosecutorial discretion rather than statute. The State's Attorney's office works with the director of the program to divert from prosecution first offenders charged with possession of small amounts of marijuana, stimulants, depressants, and hallucinogens. The Illinois Cannabis Control Act offers guidelines to determine whether the quantity of a drug in an offender's possession is for personal use or for sale.

Eligible offenders must waive the right to a speedy trial, and the court continues the case for the program's 2 or 3 months' duration.   Participants attend five weekly group therapy sessions and submit urine samples for up to 3 months.   Arrest, absence from group therapy, or traces of opiates, amphetamines, or barbiturates in the urine are cause for removal from treatment and either a resumption of prosecution or enrollment in a more intensive program, such as IDAP or Gateway House.

The State's Attorney moves to nolle prosequi charges against persons who successfully complete treatment and refrain from further arrest.   Failure in the program does not influence the court in cases where prosecution is resumed.   The State's Attorney's Office plans to expand the process of diverting users of "soft" drugs from prosecution.   Approximately 80 percent of the cases have been successful, lending credence to the argument for diversion of drug offenders.[36]

Daytop Village

In 1963 Daytop Village began a treatment program for convicted drug addicts on probation in the Second Judicial District of New York.   Originally financed by a $390,000 research grant through the National Institute of Mental Health, Daytop Village is now a private nonprofit foundation receiving funds from the New York State Narcotic Addiction Control Commission.   It operates three residential communities in the New York City area with a combined capacity for 550 patients.   The average annual intake for the years 1969 through 1971 was 500 addicts; the annual dropout rate was 50 percent.[37]

The program is no longer restricted to probationers.   There are no set eligibility requirements, but persons involved in violent crimes or the sale of narcotics or dangerous drugs are automatically excluded.   Reduction of these charges, however, is common practice to allow for admission to the program.   Judicial and prosecutorial discretion determine referrals after recommendation from the Daytop court liaison officer.   There is no statutory provision for diversion, but about 25 to 33 percent of the patients are referred from court as probationers and parolees. Almost 75 percent of the patients have been arrested for drug offenses, and 50 percent convicted of that crime.

The preadjudication diversion procedure is informal.   The court liaison officer meets with individual candidates to evalu-

36. Kerstetter, "Diversion of Nar-   37. APA–NAMH, *The Treatment of*
    cotics Offenders," p. 25.   *Drug Abuse*, pp. 83–103, 242–244.

ate their eligibility and willingness to be treated. If the person is approved for admission to the program, his case is adjourned for 2 months. Adjournment must be renewed every 2 months, and renewal is based on his progress at Daytop. After 6 to 8 months of compliance with program requirements, his case is dropped.

Daytop's program includes daily meetings at the Village, chores, seminars, classes, and encounter groups led by a staff of former addicts. Younger participants (under 20 years) and marijuana users report to storefront day-care centers for daily therapy. These storefronts have a dual purpose: to reorient offenders into their everyday environment without drugs and to force community awareness of the drug problem and Daytop's program. Although the number of cases diverted through Daytop has been small—100 cases in 1969—it serves as a hopeful alternative to criminal processing of drug offenders.

All Daytop programs depend on a preliminary interview with each candidate to determine his willingness to accept treatment, and all reserve the right to refuse a referral. For preconviction referrals, charges are dismissed at a hearing after the completion of drug treatment.

Narcotics Treatment Administration

The District of Columbia's Narcotics Treatment Administration (NTA) differs from the models described above in its primary goal: to treat all the addicts in the community, regardless of their previous offenses and program failures. The only prerequisite for enrollment is a desire to break the drug habit, and failure in treatment does not result in expulsion.

NTA's long-term objective is to enable every participant to live a life free of illegal drug use and arrest and to function as a contributing member of society. Beginning with one clinic serving 100 patients, the program has expanded its services to treat 3,500 addicts in 12 centers and four private contract facilities.[38] With the exception of the most affluent residential area, heroin use is spread throughout the city. Because heroin addiction is known to be related to criminality, NTA treatment centers are

38. Comptroller General of the U. S., *Narcotic Addiction Treatment and Rehabilitation Programs in Washington, D. C.*, Report to Subcommittee No. 4, House Committee on the Judiciary, 92 Cong., 2 Sess., 1972.

strategically located in areas with high crime rates.[39]   A few are outside the core area where heroin use is not yet rampant.

A budget of $7 million in 1972 supported units for methadone maintenance, methadone detoxification, urine surveillance only, and total abstinence.   There is no waiting list for voluntary patients.   They are sent immediately to a holding facility and begin methadone maintenance until the appropriate treatment modality is determined.   Each week about 175 heroin users volunteer for treatment.[40]

Each day NTA representatives screen all defendants entering Superior Court to identify heroin users.   The court approves the administration of narcotics tests, and eligible offenders are released to NTA's Criminal Justice Intake Service on bail.   Thorough examinations are performed, and a counselor refers each patient to the treatment facility nearest his home that can best serve his needs.   NTA operates separate units for those not yet 18 years old.

Six bureaus at NTA provide medical, management, youth, research, information, and special services.   The Special Services Bureau supervises and coordinates counseling, criminal justice referrals, and patient referrals to other programs and agencies. Legal advice is available through Legal Services to Addicts, a special project of NTA and the Washington Lawyer's Committee for Civil Rights under Law.[41]   A central computerized data bank compiles information from all facilities for program evaluation including patients' arrest records, employment status, urinalysis reports, and length of treatment.

From May, 1970, to November, 1971, NTA studied the progress of 450 adult and 150 youth patients, selected at random.[42]   Most of the adult patients were enrolled in methadone maintenance; most of the youths were in a methadone detoxification program.

39.   Barry S. Brown, Robert L. DuPont, and Nicholas J. Kozel, "Heroin Addiction in the City of Washington," unpublished paper for Narcotics Treatment Administration, Washington, 1971.

40.   Robert L. DuPont, "Trying to Reach All the Heroin Addicts in a Community," unpublished paper, Narcotics Treatment Administration, Washington, 1971, pp. 2, 5.

41.   Comprehensive Plan for Law Enforcement and Criminal Justice in the District of Columbia (Washington: Office of Criminal Justice Planning, D. C. Government, 1971), p. 197.

42.   Comptroller General, Narcotic Addiction Treatment, pp. 22–24.

After 18 months, 46 percent of the adults were still in treatment; 19 percent were meeting all program goals of abstinence from illegal drug use, no arrests, and employment or training. Twenty-seven percent of those still in treatment failed to meet one or more treatment goals, usually employment. Twenty-eight percent of the sample had been arrested within the study period.

In the youth sample, 18 percent remained in the program for 18 months, with only 1 percent satisfying all treatment goals. Twelve percent of those in treatment failed to meet one or more program goals. Ninety-two percent were arrested within the study period. No follow-up data concerning dropouts are available.

Results of the study seem discouraging, but in a city with an estimated 20,000 addicts, success will not be immediate. NTA has extended its original city-wide treatment deadline of 3 years to 5 years and blames its failures on inadequate planning and management. Since 1971, efforts have been made to broaden and restructure existing services, with expansion of referral services and recruitment of a highly professional staff as priorities.

Public endorsement is essential if NTA is to reach the entire addict population. Because of the cooperation and interaction of law enforcement and social service agencies with NTA, duplication of efforts has been avoided and criminal prosecution of addicts reduced.

Conclusions

Drug treatment programs have been springing up around the Nation to deal wtih the growing problem of drug abuse. One result of the widespread interest has been a duplication of services between State and local, public and private agencies. Coordination and cooperation among social service and law enforcement agencies can greatly reduce waste and confusion and improve the potential capabilities of treatment programs.

The President set an example in 1971 by creating a White House Special Action Office for Drug Abuse Prevention responsible for the overall planning, policy, and budget of all Federal drug programs. Although the multiplicity of approaches to treatment is extensive, a variety of modes is necessary to reach the large numbers of addicts, because no "cure" for addiction exists. With multimodality treatment, a patient failing in one type of treatment may succeed in another.[43]

Criminal prosecution does not rehabilitate the drug user; in fact, his knowledge of drug use may be increased after a prison term.[44] Diversion into treatment programs may not break the habit of every addict or prevent his return to drug-related crime, but it does offer an alternative for those who may desire rehabilitation.

MENTAL ILLNESS

Cases involving mental illness are an appropriate field for diversion, but few statutes or consistent local policies exist to facilitate its development. A shortage of money in social services, red tape involved in commitment procedures, and general ignorance regarding mental disorders combine to place emergencies in the hands of the police. A doctor's certificate is required for commitment to a mental hospital, and in most States even emergency admissions require either a doctor's certificate or a court order or both. To expedite commitment, some social service agencies recommend filing a disorderly conduct complaint against a person in need of care, leaving the responsibility for psychiatric examination to the court. Obviously, this solution is unfair to the individual and a burden on the criminal justice system.[45]

Insane and mentally incompetent offenders can be excused from criminal prosecution, but they are processed through jail and court before an official diagnosis is made. Diversion of such persons from the criminal justice system at the outset, eliminating the record of arrest, would be more humane and expedient.

Police Emergency Programs

State laws provide for emergency detention, authorizing a police officer to take into custody and transport to a mental health

43. Roger E. Meyer, *Guide to Drug Rehabilitation: A Public Health Approach* (Beacon Press, 1972), p. 37.

44. John P. Bellassai and Phyllis N. Segal, "Note, Addict Diversion: An Alternative Approach for the Criminal Justice System," *Georgetown Law Journal*, reprinted in *TASC: Treatment Alternatives to* *Street Crime* (Washington: Special Action Office for Drug Abuse Prevention, 1972), pp. 18–61.

45. Arthur R. Matthews, Jr. "Observations on Police Policy and Procedures for Emergency Detention of the Mentally Ill," unpublished paper prepared for the Law Enforcement Assistance Administration, 1972, p. 18.

center for short-term detention anyone he considers to be mentally incompetent and an immediate danger to himself or to other persons. Admissions procedures at most receiving centers, however, preclude expediency. A signed petition is usually required, and police officers, whose legal authority ends at the center, refuse to sign.

The Los Angeles Police Department, in cooperation with the county hospital, has assigned a detail of seven officers to expedite cases of mental illness.[46] All such cases are screened by the hospital detail for disposition: release, arrest, or admission to the hospital for 72 hours of emergency detention. Detail officers do not receive special training, but they are made familiar with admissions procedures and the guidelines for determining a need for hospitalization. California law provides for emergency detention, and the Los Angeles Police Department has taken the responsibility of acting as petitioner for admission when no family member or friend of the offender is available. The final decision for admission is left to the admitting physician, so that the petition is a mere formality.

New York and San Francisco have reception facilities in large hospitals to accept emergency cases brought by the police. An admissions staff perform psychiatric examinations, and police officers file an application or petition for admission.[47] Because the judgment of the hospital staff is the basis for admission, a policeman's signature is only a formality. He is not held responsible for the admission, and the court and health officers are eliminated from the process.

Most hospitals, however, do not have sufficient staff for round-the-clock admissions and, as a result, in many jurisdictions police officers spend hours waiting for a psychiatrist to examine an offender. In States where laws do not provide for speedy admission to mental hospitals, cooperation between the police and receiving centers is necessary to reduce police involvement. For example, the Wheaton, Ill., police department, in cooperation with the Graduate School of Social Work of the University of Illinois, operates a crisis intervention program offering services 24 hours a day to youths referred by the police.[48]

46. Matthews, "Observations on Police Policy," p. 26.

47. Matthews, "Observations on Police Policy," pp. 23–24.

48. *Models for Delinquency Diversion* (Athens, Ga.: Institute of Government, University of Georgia, 1971).

To deal effectively with the problem of mental illness, public health services must be funded and staffed with professionals to treat those persons who cannot afford private care and those who have neglected a mental disturbance until it has reached a dangerous stage. The police deal with cases of mental illness daily because people have nowhere else to go or are unaware of existing social service organizations. The public must be made aware of available services so that the mentally ill may receive treatment before crises arise.

Community Mental Health Centers

Because of their location in inner-city neighborhoods where few residents are familiar with mental health services and even fewer can afford private care, community centers are ideal facilities for the diversion of the mentally ill. The National Institute of Mental Health has recently sponsored community health centers in urban areas and plans the opening of 2,000 centers by 1980, some with satellites in storefronts, some with day-care programs, all with an informal atmosphere. Services will be free or priced according to a patient's ability to pay; funds will be contributed by State and Federal governments; existing agencies will cooperate with private organizations and public agencies on local, State, and Federal levels. An example is the St. Joseph Hospital Mid-Houston Community Health Center which has satellites offering screening and intake services for welfare, vocational rehabilitation, and employment counseling.[49]

Public relations is an important element in the community center project; the center must be known and accepted by the neighborhood residents in order to accomplish its therapeutic and educational goals. At some centers, local leaders—teachers, clergymen, probation officers—are a liaison to the community. Many centers recruit foreign-speaking and ethnic personnel to create better relations and communication with the public. Rehabilitative programs for reentry into society as well as vocational training and counseling are part of the treatment for the mentally ill. Job placements and on-the-job training are secured for patients, with a goal of reducing the future rate of hospitalization and arrest. The spread of available services in community

49. National Institute of Mental Health, Office of Program Planning and Evaluation, *The Mental Health of Urban America* (Chevy Chase, Md.: NIMH, 1969), p. 76.

health centers should reduce the number of police contacts with the mentally ill. In addition it will offer to police officers a receiving facility for unstable offenders without complicated and lengthy admissions procedures.

NIMH has heavily funded local public facilities and encouraged the development of comprehensive programs to serve the poor. Public awareness and support depend on local agencies. Hospitals that receive emergency cases brought by police officers must cooperate by eliminating the red tape in admissions. Public health and law enforcement officials must press to erase legal barriers to fast service for the needy. The public must learn that programs for the mentally ill exist, eliminating the need for police intervention.

Whatever arrangements are made to coordinate police and social service efforts, provisions must insure a clear and simple procedure for police to follow without the fear of liability. Vague regulations and unnecessary restrictions must be eliminated for the success of a diversion program.

STRATEGIES FOR CHANGE

Every day correctional agencies, legislators, the judiciary, and law enforcement have the option to modify procedures in the interest of doing a better correctional or justice job. Frequently, the modifications require no additional funding since they represent changes in policy, procedure, or law, which often have more to do with changing behavior and attitudes toward it than individual treatment per se.

POLITICAL-LEGAL STRATEGIES

Probably one of the most potent strategies available for proponents of diversion programs is the political-legal approach. If in fact there are individuals within the justice system who need not be there, then one of the most obvious solutions is to change the law regarding the behavior that brings these individuals into the justice system. The State of Connecticut offers a specific example with its recent statutory enactment that permits law enforcement agents to deliver an intoxicated person (alcohol or drugs) to a treatment facility rather than a custodial facility. Unfortunately, however, the legislative mandate was not supported with resources for treatment centers or massive educational programs or administrative direction to insure that the law was followed. An excellent theoretical model for diversion was subverted since the idea could not be translated into a "real" program. The concept, however, is very important. In writing statutes regarding legally proscribed acts, for example, the legislature should provide that the police *may* make an arrest, rather than that they *shall* do so.

Decriminalization also could be applied to class crimes such as vagrancy and disorderly conduct. Definitions of these offenses are lacking in clarity, and the laws are applied in a capricious manner for purposes having little to do with the protection of society. The same thing is true of many juvenile offenses listed under ambiguous categories such as "ungovernable," "runaway," or "curfew violation."   Indeed, it seems probable that indiscretions of these kinds could be handled better without official court intervention by counseling and social and mental health agencies. The stigma of an official court hearing should probably be reserved for violations that are defined without regard to age, that is, for acts that would be crimes if committed by adults. It is unlikely that the rights of juveniles assured by decisions such as *Gault* can be meaningful if the definitions of offense categories are unconstitutionally vague.

LEGISLATIVE AUTHORIZATION OF DIVERSION PROGRAMS

Another important way that legislatures can enhance and extend diversion is by authorization or creation of diversion programs. Formal legislative authorization of diversion programs introduces safeguards unlikely in informal diversion techniques. By increasing the visibility of diversion and specifying broad criteria of eligibility and procedure, protection against discriminatory or random application of discretion is introduced. In addition, formal programs are much more amenable to research and evaluation. Finally, legislatures can not only authorize diversion programs but also provide funding for staff and facilities to operate them.

A good example is a bill introduced in the 92d Congress to provide opportunities for diversion of Federal defendants. The legislation would have authorized automatic diversion of Federal first offenders who meet certain criteria, and funding for diversion programs within the administrative framework of Federal district courts. Although the bill did not come to the floor in 1972, it is expected that similar legislation will be introduced in 1973.

ADMINISTRATIVE-POLICY STRATEGIES

Every organization and agency engages in activity that is governed by administrative practice and policy. Law is not the limiting constraint; tradition and practice are. Many of the new programs of law enforcement consciously violate traditional practice. An administrative decision is made to change the way regular business is transacted. Procedures are changed, not law. Take for instance the chief of police in a large metropolitan area who, in written orders, instructed his field force to ignore persons selling flowers at the public freeway entrances, a misdemeanor in the State. By administrative order a diversion program of "no action" was operationalized. Take for example another police chief who established a policy that juvenile behavior that would constitute misdemeanors for adults would be referred to the local Youth Service Agency. He made no exceptions; on the contrary, he demanded a lengthy written explanation by officers violating his new departmental policy.

A colleague in an adjoining city went even further. He declared the same policy and set a limit on the distance offenders could be transported to custody. Interested in improving the "street time" for his force, this chief set a five-mile limit on the distance officers could travel to deliver prisoners to custody, unless they presented a serious threat to property, other persons, or self. He, too, required written explanations for exceptions.

Probation department intake units frequently employ crisis intervention teams, volunteers, and advocates as substitutes for detention and petitions. All of these practices reflect administrative decision, policy, and program. They are new administrative ways of taking care of old justice system practices.

An interesting example of an administrative strategy, funded by the Youth Development and Delinquency Prevention Administration of the Department of Health, Education, and Welfare, is operating in St. Louis, Missouri. The juvenile court, in cooperation with the Research Analysis Corporation, has developed a program patterned after the European program of house arrest. Called the "House Detention" program, children who would otherwise be held in detention are offered help and control at home and school by paraprofessionals pending some dispositional decision before the juvenile court. Whether or not the court acts is determined by the juveniles' behavior while in house detention.

The project makes extensive use of paraprofessionals and sets qualifications for employees. It seeks to find individuals within the community who have the same cultural and socioeconomic backgrounds as the youth being supervised. Hired on a full-time basis, the paraprofessionals are paid salaries equal to those received by regular employees working in the detention center. Although they have no offices (hence, no regularly scheduled office hours), they are required to provide services to their clients when needed. Caseloads of five children and/or families permit the paraprofessionals to be almost another member of the child's family. The limited caseload permits the worker to become involved in real problem-solving activities with the client, his family, the school, law enforcement agencies, and others. Practical in approach, the paraprofessional's efforts are directed at the immediate resolution of the practical problems that may have led to the child's arrest.[50]

RAMIFICATIONS OF DIVERSION

It is obvious that diversion is both a new idea and a very old practice. It is also obvious that prevention, diversion, screening, and minimizing penetration are closely related concepts that become easily confused by those attempting to deal with alternatives to criminal justice processing. Each, however, is predicated on the assumption that the existing system is often destructive and that it is better to direct many offenders to programs that are less stigmatizing, less restricting, less punitive, than it is to escalate them through the justice system. Unfortunately, however, diversion may be used as an excuse for not addressing the very real problems associated with the development of effective preventive, correctional, differential care, custody, and treatment programs. Many programs that are labeled diversion did not originate as formal efforts to divert people from the criminal justice process but came about through ambiguities in the law or the discretionary practices of individual agents of the justice system. Real programs of diversion specify objectives, identify a target group, outline means and activities for

50. Information from Youth Development and Delinquency Prevention Administration, U. S. Department of Health, Education, and Welfare.

achieving the goals, implement programs, and produce evidence of a plan to at least attempt to evaluate whether or not the means employed are successful in achieving the goals desired.

Because of the variety of diversionary methods, it is essential that the community obtain reliable information concerning their effectiveness in crime control. Information is needed regarding diversion's impact on the justice system, the role diversion plays in crime prevention, and the relative rates of success on cases diverted from the system at different stages as compared with cases subjected to varying degrees of criminalization. Such information is not now available, nor will it be available until records are kept on diversion as well as on cases processed officially.

When two or more control methods appear to be about equally effective, researchers need to decide between them. Research involves experimental design and random assignment of cases to alternative treatment or control methods, and it requires most of all that judgments of authorities be assessed in terms of their empirical consequences, not their intended effects.

In the absence of research and experimentation, the assessment of correctional policies is largely a matter of guesswork. But the evidence that does exist suggests that diversion may warrant consideration as the preferred method of control for a far greater number of offenders. Moreover, it appears that diversion plays a significant role in crime prevention and in maintaining the justice system so that it is not swamped by its own activity.

Diversion provides society with the opportunity to begin the reordering of the justice system, by redistributing resources to achieve justice and correctional goals—to develop truly effective prevention, justice, control, and social restoration programs.

Perhaps the single greatest contribution that diversion can make during the next decade is to make society more conscious and sensitive to the deficiencies of the justice system, and hence to force radical changes within the system so that appropriate offenders are successfully diverted from the system while others are provided with programs within the system that offer social restoration instead of criminal contamination.

STANDARDS FOR USE OF DIVERSION*

USE OF DIVERSION

Each local jurisdiction, in cooperation with related State agencies, should develop and implement by 1975 formally organized programs of diversion that can be applied in the criminal justice process from the time an illegal act occurs to adjudication.

1.   The planning process and the identification of diversion services to be provided should follow generally and be associated with "total system planning" as outlined in Standard 9.1.

> a. With planning data available, the responsible authorities at each step in the criminal justice process where diversion may occur should develop priorities, lines of responsibility, courses of procedure, and other policies to serve as guidelines to its use.

> b. Mechanisms for review and evaluation of policies and practices should be established.

> c. Criminal justice agencies should seek the cooperation and resources of other community agencies to which persons can be diverted for services relating to their problems and needs.

2.   Each diversion program should operate under a set of written guidelines that insure periodic review of policies and decisions.   The guidelines should specify:

> a. The objectives of the program and the types of cases to which it is to apply.

> b. The means to be used to evaluate the outcome of diversion decisions.

> c. A requirement that the official making the diversion decision state in writing the basis for his determination denying or approving diversion in the case of each offender.

> d. A requirement that the agency operating diversion programs maintain a current and complete listing of

* The National Advisory Commission
on Criminal Justice Standards and
Goals, *Report on Corrections*, 1973.

various resource dispositions available to diversion decisionmakers.

3. The factors to be used in determining whether an offender, following arrest but prior to adjudication, should be selected for diversion to a noncriminal program, should include the following:

a. Prosecution toward conviction may cause undue harm to the defendant or exacerbate the social problems that led to his criminal acts.

b. Services to meet the offender's needs and problems are unavailable within the criminal justice system or may be provided more effectively outside the system.

c. The arrest has already served as a desired deterrent.

d. The needs and interests of the victim and society are served better by diversion than by official processing.

e. The offender does not present a substantial danger to others.

f. The offender voluntarily accepts the offered alternative to further justice system processing.

g. The facts of the case sufficiently establish that the defendant committed the alleged act.

COMMENTARY

Alternatives to criminalization should be developed for use from the time an illegal act occurs to adjudication. These procedures should be preferred over traditional punitive measures for those offenders who do not present a serious threat to others.

Diversion programs should be a part of the same planning process that is performed for the rest of the criminal justice process, and particularly corrections. The methodology is outlined in Standard 9.1, Total System Planning. Planning for diversion should include the procedures to be used and the points at which diversion may occur. As with other correctional programs, systematic review and evaluation of policies and procedures should be provided for. The community should be represented in the planning process, and the community resources that may be used in the program identified and enlisted.

A number of factors justify noncriminal treatment, counseling, or restitution programs. The existing system has failed to achieve reformation in any large number of cases; it is discriminatory in nature; and it is costly in relation to outcomes. Personal values, costs, and humanitarian interests also contribute to the arguments for diversion.

Most of the diversion processes operating today are informal and are not mandated by statute. On the contrary, they are the result of ambiguities in existing legislation as well as the broad administrative discretion of officials administering criminal justice. The discretionary decisions are influenced by a variety of factors, but of most importance is the scarcity of system resources. Diversion often occurs because of the pragmatic and pressing realization that there are not enough resources to handle the potential, if not actual, caseload.

It is impossible to specify all of the factors which might be desirable in determining whether or not diversion is a correct alternative. In general, however, there seem to be guiding principles which help determine the desirability of diversion to formal justice system processing. They relate to existing programs, visibility, stated goals, methods for measuring success, and finally, the willingness of specific communities to participate in the development of rational, community-based alternatives to justice system processing.

If diversion programs are to perform as they are intended, then the decisions of those referring to these programs must be subject to review and evaluation. In a similar vein, decision-makers cannot make referrals outside their system unless they have necessary information about alternative programs and the authority to make decisions referring cases out of the system. Guidelines outline the information necessary to meet the requirements of both of these conditions.

The first step in establishing accountability is to disclose the basis of decisions. Too often the rationale for discretionary decisions is undisclosed and unstated. Simply requiring written statements for each decision forces the process to become more open while it also permits administrative or judicial review. Review can be through the courts, the legislature, or whatever source seems most appropriate in seeing that goals have been achieved and standards complied with.

Chapter 2

SPECIAL COMMUNITY PROGRAMS

SPECIAL COMMUNITY PROGRAMS: ALTERNATIVES TO INSTITUTIONALIZATION*

In recent years a number of experimental community programs have been set up in various parts of the country, differing substantially in content and structure but all offering greater supervision and guidance than the traditional probation and parole programs. The new programs take many forms, ranging from the more familiar foster homes and group homes to halfway houses, "guided group interaction" programs, and intensive community treatment. As such, they offer a set of alternatives between regular probation supervision and incarceration, providing more guidance than probation services commonly offer without the various disruptive effects of total confinement. They also greatly enrich the alternatives available in parole supervision. The advent of these programs in the postwar decades and their recent growth in numbers and prominence are perhaps the most promising developments in corrections today.

These programs are by and large less costly, often far less costly, than incarceration in an institution. Evaluation has indicated that they are usually at least as effective in reducing recidivism and in some cases significantly more so. They therefore represent an important means for coping with the mounting volume of offenders that will be pouring into corrections in the next decade. Although population forecasts indicate that the number of adult criminals who will be incarcerated in the next 10 years will increase only slightly, the projections for juveniles on the basis of present trends are alarming. As noted in chapter 4, it is estimated that by 1975 the number of juveniles who would be confined would increase by 70 percent; whereas in 1965, there were about 44,000 juveniles in State and Federal correctional in-

* From *Task Force Report: Corrections*. The President's Commission on Law Enforcement and Administration of Justice (Washington, D. C.: U. S. Government Printing Office, 1967), pp. 38–44. [Footnotes omitted.]

61

stitutions, by 1975 this number would reach about 74,000. Such an increase would place a burden on the correctional system that increased community programming could go far to alleviate.

Among the special community programs at least five types are important enough to warrant special discussion: guided group interaction programs; foster homes and group homes; prerelease guidance centers; intensive treatment programs; and reception center parole. These programs are reviewed here as examples of approaches that are capable of, and deserve, widespread application in a variety of modifications.

GUIDED GROUP INTERACTION PROGRAMS

Underlying one of the newer programs for treating the young delinquent in the community is the premise that juvenile delinquency is commonly a group experience and that therefore efforts to change delinquent behavior should focus primarily on a group like that within which the individual operates. A number of group counseling methods have been employed but the method called guided group interaction has been used most extensively in those programs which involved a research component.

The general strategy of guided group interaction calls for involving the offenders in frequent, prolonged, and intensive discussions of the behavior of individuals in the group and the motivations underlying it. Concentrating on participants' current experiences and problems, the approach attempts to develop a group "culture" that encourages those involved to assume responsibility for helping and controlling each other. The theory is that the offender-participants will be more responsive to the influence of their fellow offenders, their peers, than to the admonitions of staff, and less likely to succeed in hoodwinking and manipulating each other.

As the culture develops and the group begins to act responsibly, the group leader, a staff member, seeks to encourage a broader sharing of power between the offenders and the staff. At first, group decisions will be limited to routine matters, such as the schedule of the day, but over time they may extend to disciplinary measures against a group member or even to decisions concerning readiness for release from the program.

Highfields

The Highfields project in New Jersey was the pioneer effort in guided group interaction.   Initiated in 1950, it has been duplicated in communities and also in institutions and used with both juveniles and adults.   Highfields limits its population to 20 boys aged 16 and 17, who are assigned directly to it from the juvenile court.   Boys with former commitments to correctional schools are not accepted, nor are deeply disturbed or mentally retarded youths.   The goal is to effect rehabilitation within 3 to 4 months, about half the average period of incarceration in the State training school.

The youths are housed in the old Lindbergh mansion.   They work during the day at a mental institution immediately adjacent to their residence.   In the evening they participate in the group counseling sessions.   On Saturdays, they clean up the residence.   Saturday afternoon is free, and Sunday is reserved for receiving visitors and going to religious services.   Formal rules are few.

Early efforts to evaluate the effects of the project on recidivism, as compared with those of the State reformatory, are still the subject of academic dispute.   However, it is clear that Highfields was at least as effective as the reformatory, perhaps more effective, and that it accomplished its results in a much shorter period of time at greatly reduced monthly costs.

Pinehills and Other Developments

Important variations on the Highfields project developed at Essexfields, also in New Jersey, and at Pinehills in Provo, Utah. As at Highfields, program content at Essexfields and Pinehills centered around gainful employment in the community, school, and daily group meetings.   The most significant difference was that, in the Essexfields and Pinehills experiments, the offenders continued to live at home.

The regimen at both Essexfields and Pinehills was rigorous. At Pinehills, for example, all boys were employed by the city. They put in a full day's work on the city streets, on the golf course, in the cemetery, wherever they were needed.   They were paid 50 cents an hour.   During the late afternoon, after the day's work was finished, all boys returned to the program headquarters where they met in daily group sessions.   About 7 p. m. they were free to return home.   They were also free on Sundays.

In the daily group sessions all group members, not just adult staff, were responsible for defining problems and finding solutions to them. By making the program operations to some extent the work of all involved, both offenders and staff, it was possible to make a better estimate of just how much responsibility for his own life a given offender could take.

The fact that these guided group interaction programs are located in the community means that the problems with which the group struggles are those that confront them daily in contacts with their families, friends, teachers, and employers. This is one great strength of a community program over an institutional program. The artificiality of institutional life is avoided, and concentration can be placed upon the issues with which every offender eventually has to deal.

The Pinehills experiment was one of the first to set up an experimental design by which to assess the effectiveness of the project. Offenders assigned to the program were compared with two control groups: One group which was placed on probation, and another which was committed to a training school. The initial design was such that all three groups could be drawn randomly from a common population of persistent offenders living in the same county. Although there was some difficulty in exactly maintaining the research design, the data appear significant. The results, as measured in terms of recidivism, are shown in table 1.

TABLE 1

Effectiveness of Three Programs for Juvenile
Delinquents, Utah, 1964, as Measured
by Percentages of Releasees Not Arrested
Within 6 Months of Release

Program	Percentage of releasees not arrested within 6 months	
	All boys assigned to program	All boys completing program
Pinehills (experimental)	73	84
Probation (controls)	73	77
State school (controls)	42	42

Other variations of guided group interaction projects have been developed in the Parkland project in Louisville, Ky., in the GUIDE (Girls Unit for Intensive Daytime Education) program in Richmond, Calif., and in another girls' program in San Mateo, Calif. All three of these projects entail the daily gathering of the group in a center for participation in a combination of educational activities, craft projects, center development and beautification, and group and individual counseling. The Parkland project took its name from its location in two portable classrooms on the grounds of the Parkland Junior High School. In addition to morning classes in the school, the program entails afternoon work in and about the Louisville Zoo and terminates with group counseling sessions and dinner.

Contributions of Guided Group Programs

These projects, like Highfields, represent an authentic departure from traditional community programs for delinquents. The Highfields type of program is unique in that the group process itself shapes the culture and social system of the total program. The key element seems to be the amount of decision-making authority permitted the group, which has considerably more authority to decide than in traditional group therapy programs. J. Robert Weber, who made a study of promising programs for delinquents, said of the Highfields type of program:

> If one asks a youth in most conventional institutions, "How do you get out?" one invariably hears some version of, "Be good. Do what you are told. Behave yourself." If one asks a youth in a group treatment program, "How do you get out?" one hears, "I have to help myself with my problems," or "When my group thinks I have been helped." This implies a basic difference in the social system of the organization, including staff roles and functions.

In the large institution, Weber concluded, the youth perceives getting out in terms of the problem of meeting the institutional need for conformity. In the group treatment program the youth sees getting out in terms of his solution to his own problems, or how that is perceived by other youths in the group.

FOSTER HOMES AND GROUP HOMES

Foster-home placement has long been one of the most commonly used alternatives to institutionalization for juvenile probationers. The National Survey of Corrections reported that 42 percent of the 233 probation departments surveyed utilized this resource. A sizeable proportion of juvenile aftercare programs also make foster placements a routine part of their work.

The utilization of foster homes or group homes in lieu of institutional confinement has several obvious advantages, provided the offender does not require the controls of an institution. Such placements keep the offender in the community where he must eventually work out his future. They carry less stigma and less sense of criminal identity, and they are far less expensive than incarceration.

Weber reported in 1966:

> Discussions with State administrators would seem to indicate that foster care is in an eclipse. Reception center staffs report disillusionment with foster care for delinquents. Yet a look at actual placement practices of the State agencies and local courts indicates an unabated use of foster care.

The opinions encountered by Weber may be a reflection of the long and controversial history of foster-home placement for delinquents. The decision to sever family ties, even temporarily, is a hard one to make for the youth who might otherwise be placed on probation at home. And more difficult juveniles who might be sent to institutions are often beyond the capacity of the usual foster home to manage. It is obvious, however, that many delinquent youngsters come from badly deteriorated family situations and that such conditions are significant, perhaps critical, factors in generating delinquent behavior. When the delinquency-inducing impact of a slum neighborhood is added to a destructive family setting, placement of the delinquent away from home becomes increasingly necessary.

A number of States have begun to develop group homes as a variant to traditional foster-home care for youths who need a somewhat more institutional setting or cannot adjust to family life. The Youth Commission of Minnesota, for example, reported using seven group homes under arrangements with the home operator or with an intermediate agency. A nominal retaining fee was paid for each bed licensed; and, when a youth actually was placed in the home, the rate of pay was increased.

The Wisconsin Division of Corrections in 1966 was operating an even more ambitious program. Thirty-three homes for boys or girls were in use under a payment plan similar to that employed in Minnesota. With four to eight adolescents in each home, the total population handled was equivalent to that of at least one institution, but operating costs were one-third to one-fourth less.

In both States the adolescents placed in group homes were those who had been received on court commitment as candidates for institutional placement. In Wisconsin, approximately one-fourth of the group had been released from institutions for placement in a foster home. Other jurisdictions are experimenting with the group-home technique. Michigan, for example, reported a plan to use larger homes operated by State employees for parolees from their institutions.

There is some doubt about the wisdom of committing offenders to State agencies for placement in foster homes or group homes, when this function could as readily be performed by the courts through associated probation and welfare services. It is far less expensive for a local court to commit a youth to the State, even though that commitment entails some additional stigmatization, than to undertake the development and operation of local resources of the same kind. This problem derives from the fragmented administrative structure of American corrections, and could be overcome by a carefully planned program of subsidies from State to local governments. Such a plan was developed in California in 1965. Under its terms subsidies are given to those county probation departments which are successful in reducing commitments to State institutions by the development of improved community-based programs.

HALFWAY PROGRAMS: THE PRERELEASE
GUIDANCE CENTER

In corrections as in related fields, the "halfway house" is an increasingly familiar program. Initially, such programs were conceived for offenders "halfway out" of institutions, as a means of easing the stresses involved in transition from rigid control to freedom in the community. The prerelease guidance centers of the Federal Bureau of Prisons are the best known halfway out programs in the United States. Recently the halfway house has come to be viewed as a potential alternative to institutionalization, and thus a program for those "half-way in" between probation and institutional control.

Federal Prerelease Guidance Centers

The first prerelease guidance centers of the Federal Bureau of Prisons were opened in 1961 in New York, Chicago, and Los Angeles, and others were established subsequently in Detroit, Washington, and Kansas City. Each center accommodates about 20 Federal prisoners who are transferred to it several months before their expected parole date. Thus they complete their terms in the community but under careful control.

Some of the centers are located in what were large, single-family houses; some occupy a small section or scattered rooms in a YMCA hotel; and one is located in a building once operated as a small home for needy boys. All are in neighborhoods with mixed land usage, racial integration, and nearby transportation.

Offenders transferred to these centers wear civilian clothes. They generally move from prison to the centers by public transportation without escort. For a day or two they are restricted to the building, although they may receive visitors there. In the YMCA's they eat in a public cafeteria in the building and use the public recreation areas, taking out YMCA memberships. Following a day or two of orientation and counseling, they go out to look for jobs. After they are on a job, they are gradually given more extensive leaves for recreational purposes and for visits with their families. As their parole date approaches, some may even be permitted to move out of the center, although they are still required to return to the center for conferences several times a week.

These centers are staffed in large part by persons rotated from regular institution staff who are highly oriented to counseling. One full-time employee is an employment counseling specialist. Several others, such as college students in the behavioral sciences, are employed on a part-time basis and provide the only staff coverage during the late night hours and part of the weekend. In addition to individual counseling, there are several group sessions a week. Federal probation officers, who will supervise the offenders when they go on parole, participate in the center's counseling activities. By the time a resident is ready to begin his parole, almost all of his individual counseling has been assumed by his parole supervision officer.

A major function of these temporary release programs has been to augment the information available to correctional staff. This information includes both diagnostic data on the individuals temporarily released and information on the assets and deficiencies of correctional programs and personnel. In addition, they provide optimum circumstances for counseling, since the counseling can deal with immediate realities as they are encountered, rather than with the abstract and hypothetical visions of the past and the future or the purely institutional problems to which counseling in institutions is largely restricted.

Inmate misbehavior while on work release or in prerelease guidance centers is not a rare thing, particularly for youthful offenders. Although a majority adjust quite satisfactorily, some get drunk, some get involved in fights and auto accidents when out with old or new friends, and some are late in returning to the center. An appreciable number of the youth have difficulty in holding jobs, some fail to go to work or to school when they are supposed to be there, a few abscond, and a few get involved in further crime. The important point is that they would be doing these things in any case, and probably more extensively, if they had been released more completely on their own through parole or discharge. Under the latter circumstances, however, correctional staff would know of the releasee's difficulties, if at all, not nearly so promptly as is possible with temporary release measures.

When an individual returns from a temporary release to home, work, or school, his experience can be discussed with him by staff, to try to assess his probable adjustment and to note incipient problems. Many difficulties can be anticipated in this way. The inmate's anxieties can be relieved by discussion, and discussion may also help him develop realistic plans for coping with prospective problems. When persistent or serious misbehavior occurs, sanctions are available to staff, ranging from restriction of further leaves or temporary incarceration to renewed institutionalization, with a recommendation to the parole board that the date of parole be deferred.

A number of offenders on work release, live in prerelease guidance centers. Some of them attend school part- or full-time, in addition to or instead of working; this sometimes is called "study release." It is particularly appropriate for juvenile and youthful offenders and is highly developed at several State establishments resembling the Federal prerelease guidance centers.

State Prerelease Centers

The Kentucky Department of Corrections, under a grant from the Office of Economic Opportunity, has a series of vocational training courses in its State reformatory which are identical with courses established at several centers in the State under the Department of Labor. Prerelease guidance centers were established near these centers in three cities, so that reformatory inmates could continue their institution courses in the community, where as trainees they receive a small stipend, in addition to highly developed job placement services.

The Federal Bureau of Prisons assisted in establishing these centers and sends Federal inmates from these cities to the centers. Conversely, State correctional agencies share in the operation of the Federal prerelease guidance centers in Detroit and Kansas City, assigning some State inmates there, and the District of Columbia Department of Corrections plays a major role in the operation of the center in Washington. This State-Federal collaboration could well serve as a model for many types of correctional undertaking.

INTENSIVE COMMUNITY TREATMENT

Perhaps the best known of the country's efforts at controlled experimentation in the correctional field is the California Youth Authority's Community Treatment Project, now in its sixth year. Operating within a rigorous evaluative design, it offers an excellent illustration of the profitable partnership which can develop when carefully devised program innovations are combined with sound research.

The subjects of the project consist of boys and girls committed to the Youth Authority from two adjacent counties, Sacramento and San Joaquin. While under study in a reception center, each new group is subjected to a screening process which excludes some 25 percent of the boys and 5 to 10 percent of the girls because of the serious nature of their offenses, the presence of mental abnormality, or strenuous community objections to their direct release. The remaining youngsters are then either assigned randomly to the community project—in which case they form part of the experimental group—or are channeled routinely into an institution and eventually paroled.

An interview by a member of the research staff provides the basis for classification of the offender subgroups. This categorization is made in terms of the maturity of the youths, as reflected in his relationships with others, in the manner in which he perceives the world, and in the way he goes about gaining satisfaction of his needs. A variety of standardized tests seeks to measure the extent of his identification with delinquent values as well as his general personality characteristics.

The program provided for the experimental group offers singly or in combination most of the techniques of treatment and control which are in use in corrections today: individual counseling, group counseling, group therapy, family therapy, involvement in various other group activities, and school tutoring services by a certificated teacher with long experience in working with delinquents. The goal is to develop a treatment plan which is tailored to the needs of each type of offender. The resulting plan is then implemented at a level of high intensity, made possible by the availability of carefully selected and experienced staff on a ratio of 1 staff member for each 12 youths.

A program center serves as the hub of activity; it houses the staff and provides a recreation area, classrooms, and a music-room. A limited outdoor sports activities area also is available. In the later afternoon and some evenings, the center resembles a small settlement house operation as the wards come in after school for counseling, tutoring, and recreational activity.

An unusual and controversial feature of the experiment is the frequent use of short-term detention at the agency's reception center to assure compliance with program requirements and to "set limits" on the behavior of the participants. The detention may vary from a few hours to a few days.

Results have been measured in several ways. A repetition of the psychological test battery seeks to determine what movement has occurred in the socialization of the individual offender. The responses of the various categories of youth have revealed greater success with some than with others, and may eventually provide a more reliable indicator of who should be institutionalized. Finally, the "failure rate," as measured by the proportion who are later institutionalized because they have committed additional offenses, is carefully compared with similar information on members of the control group who have been institutionalized and then returned to the community under regular parole supervision.

The latest report of the project activity available to the Commission revealed that checks of parolees, at the end of 15 months of parole exposure, showed that 28 percent of the experimental group had been subject to revocation of parole, as compared to 52 percent of the control group which was afforded regular institution and parole handling.

After several years of pilot work, the California Youth Authority decided in 1964 to extend the community treatment format to the Watts area of Los Angeles and to a neighborhood in west Oakland. Both are high-delinquency areas; both are heavily Negro in population. Essentially duplications of the original experiment, the two new program units do not have a research component. Instead of random assignment of the subject, the youths committed from a given area are screened by project staff for direct release from the reception center.

In the absence of a control group, the success of the program has been measured by comparing the failure rate of the youth assigned to it with equivalent statewide rates for youths of the same middle to older adolescent age range. At the end of 15 months of parole exposure, 39 percent of project wards had been subject to parole revocation as compared to a statewide revocation rate of 48 percent for youths of the same age bracket.

The Los Angeles and Oakland adaptations of the original demonstration were initiated, in part, to alleviate acute population pressures in the institutions. With caseloads of 15 youths per officer, the $150 per month cost per boy is three to four times as much as that of regular parole. But it is less than half the average monthly cost of institutionalizing an offender. These experiments are now handling a group that is larger than the capacity of one of the new institutions that the Youth Authority is building. Thus they obviate the investment of $6 to $8 million.

RECEPTION CENTER PAROLE AND SHORT–TERM TREATMENT PROGRAMS

Diagnostic parole is a program whereby all commitments from the juvenile court are referred to a reception center where they can be screened for eligibility for parole, either immediately or after a short period of treatment. This program has reached significant proportions in an increasing number of States.

While most State systems have long had some informal arrangements for returning a few cases to the community at an early date, more organized procedures developed almost simultaneously in New York, Washington, Kentucky, and California in the early 1960's. These programs were conceived in part as a response to acute population pressures in overcrowded institutions. The seemingly successful results have led to a substantial increase in the volume of cases diverted from the training school to short, intensive treatment programs followed by parole in the community.

In New York the screening is undertaken by special aftercare staff while the youngsters are in New York City's Youth House awaiting delivery to the State school system. The youths selected to return to the community are those who are thought to be amendable to conventional casework procedures. Those selected are placed in an intensive casework program. The apparent success of the original unit in New York City has led to an expansion of the program and to the practice of returning still other youngsters to the community after the intake studies carried on in the State schools.

Washington, another State with a central reception center for juvenile offenders, is also screening those committed. A significant percentage of cases are assigned to immediate placement in foster homes or other community-based programs, including four halfway houses.

The California Youth Authority apparently is making the greatest use of the reception center release procedure. Currently some 20 percent of the boys and 35 percent of the girls processed are being released to regular parole or to foster-home placement at the termination of reception period. This is typically a month long, but in some instances release may be postponed for another 30 to 90 days.

The California Youth Authority's Marshall Program represents an interesting variation in the practices discussed above. The program was initiated 3 years ago as a device for easing population pressures in the institutions. It provides for the selection of cases by the clinical staff and the project director for a 3-month intensive treatment program at the reception center at Norwalk.

Based on "therapeutic community" concepts, the project involves the youths in a half-day work program in institution operation and maintenance, some specialized education classes, and daily group counseling. Active participation is rewarded by progressively longer and more frequent home furloughs. Parents provide the transportation, and furloughs are scheduled so that parents can participate in group counseling activities as they return their sons to the center. Parental involvement is seen as a significant program component.

While the performance of the project graduates has not been subjected to comparison with a control group, agency research staff have sought to match the subjects with youths possessed of the same characteristics who have been processed through the regular institution programs. With 15 months of parole exposure time, 44 percent of the Marshall youths, as against 47 percent of the matched group, were subject to parole revocation. Moreover, the relatively short program period of 3 months, as compared against the average stay of 8 to 9 months in the State schools, means a significant saving of public funds.

The success of reception center parole has been encouraging. Other States will undoubtedly develop reception centers that features sophisticated screening techniques and intensive treatment for those offenders who are deemed most susceptible. To date, parole from reception centers has been confined to the juvenile field. However, there is no inherent reason why this approach should not be taken with adults, and hopefully it will be so used in the near future.

PROSPECTS FOR DEVELOPING ALTERNATIVE PROGRAMS

This chapter has described some of the most promising programs in the correctional field. Unfortunately, however, only a few correctional agencies are developing any of them. The great bulk of correctional programs in this country today still consists of either traditional supervision in the community under probation or parole or confinement in institutions.   And further, the newer alternatives to institutionalization are not even known to many correctional personnel.

Comprehensive Programing

Some programs can be developed with effective leadership. The State of New York, for example, has established a particularly comprehensive set of programs as alternatives to incarceration of juveniles.   The Division for Youth was launched initially as an agency for dispersing funds to local jurisdictions for general delinquency-prevention and character-building programs.   In 1962 it initiated an imaginative effort to modify the conventional probation-incarceration sequence.   Operating as an independent entity in State government, it has provided a series of community programs for youthful offenders who might otherwise have been committed to either State training schools or the prison system. Approximately three-fourths of its intake comes through referrals or commitments from the juvenile and criminal courts. The others are referred from other agencies or come in on their own initiative.

The agency has developed three distinct program forms. For the more sophisticated delinquent there are a number of installations that replicate the Highfields model. Work during the day at some State facility is followed by daily group counseling sessions in a nearby residence that houses 20 to 25 older adolescents. Other program elements are minimal and are left largely to the residents' ingenuity.   For the more immature and dependent youngster, a small forestry camp operation provides a combination of work, academic instruction, and group counseling.

Finally, for the youth who is not too committed to delinquency and who possesses some stability and maturity, there are residential centers in the cities of the State.   These take two organizational forms.   The earlier projects were located in houses that would accommodate 20 to 25 youths.   Recently the division has experimented with the use of large apartments in conventional apartment houses.   The pattern calls for a cluster of three units, each housing seven or eight wards and house parents. A program director supervises and divides his time among the three operations.   The organized program is minimal, although the group counseling pattern prevails on a daily basis.   Primarily, jobs or schooling are sought within the communities adjacent to the centers.

The Division for Youth is providing some postrelease supervision, although it would not be described as a strong aspect of this innovative effort. An interesting feature is the employment of graduates of the program in modified staff roles in both the residential and postrelease phases of the operation.

The division's research arm, only recently organized, is attempting some objective evaluation of operational effectiveness. An analysis of the postrelease performance of all youthful graduates after 7½ months of exposure to the community indicated that 13 percent had been convicted of further offenses, and only 8 percent reconfined. While the nature of this operation precludes the establishment of a control group and thus prevents the creation of a yardstick against which performance can be measured, the "failure" rate appears impressively low as compared with performance of typical State school releasees.

Problems to be Confronted

Extensive development of alternatives to institutions requires that several problems be solved, and solved simultaneously. First is the need to make administrators and legislators aware of these programs and thus create conditions favorable for developing them. Demonstration projects which duplicate successful alternatives to institutionalization will have to be set up in various parts of the country. Such a process would require changes in the funding policies of many Federal and private agencies, which usually will support only a new type of program and not a duplication of one already proved successful. Such duplication is essential if correctional personnel and citizens are to become aware of the potentials of alternatives to institutions.

A second major problem is the familiar one of manpower. Most of these programs require skills which many correctional personnel do not have. Several centers should be established at sites of successful programs of all kinds, to train workers in the skills involved. This proposal would have particular application to training personnel for the special community programs described here.

The variety among correctional administrative structures in the country makes it difficult to determine how the new community programs could best be administered. The limited history of the prototypes indicates that the State itself will have to play a major and continuing role in order to coordinate services.

In some jurisdictions, the State may well operate virtually all of the alternative programs; in others, only part of them. For example, it is anticipated that the State will usually operate community programs for parolees. For probationers the situation is different, since a number of counties will continue to operate probation services. Where the State does not operate all community programs, it should at least supply leadership and subsidies in order to promote their development.

Whatever the administrative arrangement, it is essential that all elements of corrections should be involved. Special community programs must be perceived by all parts of the correctional apparatus as legitimate and integral parts of the system. There is a great tendency for each part of the system to push forward with its own existing programs. For example, institutional managers are apt to urge new institutions rather than looking at the possibility of alternative programs. Failure to involve important elements of the correctional community can jeopardize not only the creation of new community programs but the survival of those which prove successful. The Pinehills project in Provo, Utah, described earlier in this chapter as exciting both in its operation and in its research design, does not exist today. This project and other successful ones were not picked up by a correctional agency once the initial grant moneys were exhausted. It is clear that new community programs must be integrated into the main line of corrections if they are to succeed and survive.

It is also essential that representatives of allied service agencies, such as welfare and mental health, be involved in planning for community programs. Correctional foster-home placements, for example, are closely involved with such placements by welfare agencies, and consideration must be given to the needs of both systems. Many of the specialized community programs in corrections will lay demands on the same resources as mental health agencies. It is essential that corrections and the mental health field work out accommodations, so that there is a functional relationship.

Finally, one of the most critical problems in developing new community programs is to secure the involvement and participation of the community itself. Too often, promising programs such as halfway houses have failed simply because the community was not prepared to tolerate them. Thus it is essential that the public be brought into planning early and that correctional managers make intense efforts to insure citizen understanding and support.

HISTORY OF HALFWAY HOUSES
IN THE UNITED STATES*

Halfway houses received their first trial in the United States when New York, Pennsylvania and Massachusetts established such facilities in the early part of the Nineteenth Century.[1]

Although there is evidence of early interest in halfway houses by some governmental bodies (a Massachusetts Commission recommended the establishment of such facilities in 1820),[2] the main thrust for the movement came from religious and private volunteer groups.[3] Both groups were composed of idealistic, hardworking, humane and highly dedicated people who all too frequently lacked the requisite skills to administer an agency or to provide a treatment program.

Their purpose, which they met effectively, was to provide such services as a temporary place of shelter, food, clothing, friendly advice and sometimes, efforts to assist the ex-offender in securing gainful employment. The public offender usually did not have the above-named services at his disposal upon release from an institution.[4] In addition, they helped cushion the impact of release from an institution to open society and, although no hard data is available (a chronic problem in corrections), it does not

* John M. McCartt and Thomas Mangogna, *Guidelines and Standards for Halfway Houses and Community Treatment Centers*, United States Department of Justice, L.E.A.A. Publication, May, 1973.

1. *"Halfway Houses: Community-Centered Corrections and Treatment"*, by Oliver J. Keller and Benedict S. Alper; D. C. Heath & Co., p. 7. Also, *"Crime and Its Corrections"*, by John Conrad, University of California Press, Berkeley, Calif., 1965, p. 275.

2. Keller and Alper, op. cit., p. 7.

3. Ibid., p. 7.

4. *"Administration of Justice in a Changing Society"*, A Report of Developments in the United States —1965-70, prepared for the Fourth United Nations Congress on the Prevention of Crime and Treatment of Offenders, p. 69.

seem unreasonable to assume that they had a beneficial effect on their clients.[5]

The early halfway houses were self-contained and relatively isolated from the correctional staff and facilities providing them with releasees.[6] This is one of several factors which may have led to their eventual failure to survive as a permanent part of the correctional system, if indeed they could have been considered part of the system as it existed at that time. From all available evidence, it is not too much to assume that the early halfway houses were not considered a part of the correctional system and, although this may have been a factor in their failure to flourish, it was (in all probability) a factor which was attractive to the ex-offender who needed assistance.

More than forty years after the Massachusetts Commission made its recommendation, a halfway house for women released from institutions opened in Boston in 1864. It remained in operation for about twenty years.[7]

Amidst public indifference and even hostility, a group of Quakers opened a halfway house in New York City, which has survived to the present as the Isaac T. Hopper House. The House of Industry, established in Philadelphia, Pennsylvania, in 1889, also continues to receive parolees from Pennsylvania prisons.[8]

Despite opposition by the American Prison Association, a temporary shelter for ex-offenders was opened in New York City in the late 1890's. In September of 1896, Maud Booth, along with her husband, co-leader of the Volunteers of America, rented a building in the Washington Heights section of Manhattan. The facility, known as Hope Hall, came under such harassment from the police that Mrs. Booth was forced to appeal directly to Theodore Roosevelt for help.[9]

A second Hope Hall was established in Chicago, Illinois in 1903, and eventually, under the same auspices, halfway houses were established in New Orleans, Louisiana; Columbus, Ohio; Fort

5. "Halfway Houses for Reformatory Releasees", by Robert H. Vasoli and Frank J. Fahey, *Crime and Delinquency*, Vol. 16, No. 3, July, 1970, p. 293.

6. Vasoli and Fahey, op. cit., p. 294.
7. Keller and Alper, op. cit., p. 7.

8. Ibid., p. 7. Also see "Halfway Houses: An Historical Perspective", by Edwin Powers, *American Journal of Corrections*, Vol. XXI, July-August, 1959, p. 35.

9. Keller and Alper, op. cit., p. 7.

Dodge, Iowa; San Francisco, California; Hampton, Florida; and Waco, Texas.[10]

Several of the Hope Halls remained in existence for only a short period of time, while others managed to survive for many years. Eventually, however, they all ceased operations. It seems ironic that as more such facilities were established, Parole authorities argued increasingly against them. The basic objection used was that association with former prisoners was forbidden by parole regulations.[11]

Although there were many instances of halfway houses being established in the early and middle 1800's, it was not until the close of the Nineteenth Century that enough facilities had been established to assist any sizable number of ex-offenders.[12]

The founders of the halfway houses in the 1800's were the true pioneers of community treatment centers, but they often were looked upon with contempt or, at most, tolerance, by most professional correctional workers. They met with public as well as official hostility and/or indifference. Their work, in the main, was with the offender released from a penal institution. They also sowed the seed and laid the groundwork that others, who were to follow decades later, were to reap and build upon.

REVIVAL OF THE HALFWAY HOUSE MOVEMENT IN THE UNITED STATES

It was not until the 1950's that the halfway house movement was revived with the founding of such facilities as St. Leonard's House, Dismas House, and 308 West Residence. Acute awareness of the multitude of problems facing the ex-offender released from a penal institution, as well as a growing dissatisfaction with high recidivism rates, helped to spark the revival of halfway houses in general and also served to commence the beginnings of a national halfway house movement.[13]

There are certain parallels between the halfway houses founded over one hundred years ago and those which came into existence approximately fifteen years ago. Both were started by religiously-oriented or volunteer groups. Both lacked professionally trained personnel and dealt primarily with the ex-offender

10. Keller and Alper, op. cit., p. 7.   12. Ibid., p. 8.

11. Ibid., p. 7.   13. Keller and Alper, op. cit., p. 8.

released from a penal institution. Both lacked "programs" as such, but had as their aim the goal to meet the offender's basic needs for survival and re-entry into the community. Treatment, as such, was not an integral part of either the early halfway houses or those founded little less than two decades ago. Both were meant to be a buffer, a halfway step between the highly structured and regimental setting of the traditional correctional institution, to free and constructive life in the community. Both were relatively isolated from the correctional staff and institution providing them with releasees and both met with resistance from the community as well as from some correctional workers.

One factor present in modern day corrections which was absent over one hundred years ago was a century of dismal failure of the traditional correctional system. This factor, the recognition of it by many in the correctional field, and the renewed advent of halfway houses as a means of assisting offenders released from institutions, all served to create a favorable climate for the "evolutionary development" of the halfway house concept.[14]

As mentioned in the *Introduction*, it was not until 1964, only eight years ago, that some of those involved in the halfway house movement met and formed what is now the International Halfway House Association. Since that time, a host of agencies, private and public, have established community treatment centers to service a wide variety of target populations.

While most halfway houses have and still are serving the general public offender, some are now specializing in the treatment of specific problem areas, such as alcoholism, and here again, private agencies have pioneered and paved the way "as a result of the indifference of professional and governmental agencies".[15]

---

14. For a description of the operation of one of the early prototypes of modern-day halfway houses, see "The Lessons of Norman House", by Merfyn Turner, "*Annals of the American Academy of Political and Social Science*", January, 1969, p. 39.

15. "Task Force Report: Drunkenness", *The President's Commission on Law Enforcement and the Administration of Justice*, U. S. Government Printing Office, 1967, p. 19.

OVERVIEW OF ISSUES RELATING TO HALFWAY HOUSES AND COMMUNITY TREATMENT CENTERS*

A. HALFWAY HOUSES—A HETEROGENOUS CONCEPT

The term *halfway house* or *community treatment center* does not convey a homogeneous meaning. Halfway houses are as varied and different from each other as "closed" institutions such as jails, prisons, training schools and mental hospitals vary among and between themselves.

There is no single definition or description which can possibly be devised at this time which would adequately encompass the wide range of facilities which call themselves or which are called halfway houses or community treatment centers.[1]

Intake criteria, length of stay, treatment goals, target population serviced, services offered, quantity and quality of staffing, physical plant, physical location, and numerous other factors are so diverse that a unified, capsulized definition is virtually impossible.[2]

For example, there are in existence today, halfway houses or community treatment centers for the psychiatric patient, the neglected child, the delinquent child (the latter two are variously called halfway houses, group homes and even group foster homes), the adult public offender—both misdemeanant and felon —for the homeless adult with social or adjustment problems, and for individuals with specialized problems such as drug abuse, alcoholism and mental retardation.

The point is that each type of halfway house or community center mentioned above differs, often widely, from others which logically could be grouped in the same type.

---

* John M. McCartt and Thomas Mangogna, *Guidelines and Standards for Halfway Houses and Community Treatment Centers*, United States Dept. of Justice, L.E.A.A. Publication, May, 1973.

1. *"Halfway Houses: Community-Centered Corrections and Treatment"*, Oliver J. Keller and Benedict S. Alper; D. C. Heath & Co., pp. 11 and 12.

2. Keller and Alper, op. cit., pp. 13 and 14.

One reason halfway houses have developed in this manner was to meet varying needs for different target populations and communities. A second, and more valid reason, is that with no standards or guidelines to follow, halfway houses reflected the personal treatment and other philosophies of their founders or directors.[3] To establish a halfway house ten or even five years ago was a formidable task for anyone, whether the facility was privately or publicly sponsored. Those who assumed the responsibility were usually driving, energetic, creative and individualistic. In an area of practice which was very new to the modern correctional field, and which demanded the kind of qualities listed above, homogeneity could not be expected. Indeed, even at this stage of development, diversity—as wide as it is currently—should be viewed as an asset rather than a liability. Differing ideas, programs, goals, treatment modalities, staffing patterns and techniques need to be implemented; however, there is a desperate need for their evaluation. More will be said of evaluation later.

Suffice it to say now that there has been little of it in the halfway house and community treatment center field, as is true of most other areas of corrections.[4] As diverse as they currently are, halfway houses provide a rich and fertile ground for research in the area of community corrections.[5]

In the short period of time that halfway houses have been a part of the correctional scene, many have evolved rapidly into highly sophisticated programs. The evolution probably has taken place more out of necessity to meet ever-increasing demands for services for varying groups of clientele, and the demonstrated need for those services, as well as a change in our correctional approach.[6]

The halfway house whose average length of stay is thirty days is undoubtedly serving as a "way station" for its clientele, more than anything else. On the other hand, halfway houses whose

3. Keller and Alper, op. cit., p. 123.

4. "The Continuum of Corrections", H. G. Moeller, *Annals of the American Academy of Political and Social Science*, January, 1971, p. 86.

5. For a broad discussion on the topic of correctional research, see *Crime and Delinquency*, Vol. 17, No. 1, January, 1971, in which the entire issue is devoted to the problem.

6. "*Administration of Justice in a Changing Society*", A Report of Developments in the United States —1965–70, prepared for the Fourth United Nations Congress on the Prevention of Crime and Treatment of Offenders, p. 7. Cf. Moeller, op. cit., p. 82.

average length of stay is a year to eighteen months are probably serving groups with specialized problems, such as drug abuse and alcoholism. The first type of house mentioned probably has little or no "program", as such. The second, more often than not, uses various modifications of "therapeutic community" techniques. Most halfway houses, with the exception of those just noted and those serving juveniles, usually have their clients in residence from eighty to one hundred and twenty days.[7]

Some halfway houses and community treatment centers have as few as six to eight residents, while others may have as many as eighty. "A small population is an essential characteristic of the halfway house idea, and is found almost universally." "Most authorities maintain that a population of approximately twenty is close to ideal, permitting informal and close interaction among the residents." [8]

B. The Halfway House in the Criminal Justice System— Where Does it Belong?

It was noted earlier in this report that the early halfway houses were relatively isolated from the correctional staff and facilities providing them with releasees. They were not considered a part of the correctional or criminal justice system.[9] Some halfway houses in existence today are still somewhat isolated from the "system" and indeed, prefer to remain so. Some community-based services, such as the Youth Services Bureau concept, as formulated by the National Council on Crime and Delinquency, insist on remaining not only independent of, but apart from, the juvenile justice system.[10]

7. See Question No. 6 in Appendix F, Section II of the questionnaire sent to halfway houses throughout the United States. It was considered to be "essential" by the majority of respondents that the length of a client's stay should be determined on a case-by-case basis. Therefore, the figures eighty to one hundred and twenty days are not viewed as a recommendation, only as a report of widespread current practice.

8. Keller and Alper, op. cit., p. 12. Cf. U. S. Bureau of Prisons, "Trends in the Administration of Justice and Correctional Programs in the United States", a Report prepared for the Third United Nations Congress on the Prevention of Crime and Treatment of Offenders, U. S. Government Printing Office, Washington, D. C., 1965, p. 34.

9. Vasoli and Fahey, op. cit., p. 293.

10. Sherwood, Norman, "The Youth Services Bureau: A Key to Delinquency Prevention", National Council on Crime & Delinquency, Paramus, New Jersey, 1972, pp. 8, 16 and 17.

Vasoli and Fahey note that in comparison to its forebears, the halfway house of today is more frequently closely coordinated with and even a part of the correctional system.[11] It is common knowledge that the criminal justice system as it exists today, and even components within that system, such as corrections, are too fragmented, and thus lose much of their effectiveness. Increasingly, reference is made not to the "system" but to the "nonsystem". It also has been recognized that there have been histories of barriers between institutional and community programs themselves, such as probation and parole, which are frequently administered by different agencies.[12]

As the Task Force on Corrections notes, "It is clear that new community programs must be integrated into the main line of corrections, if they are to succeed and survive." [13] This would seem to support the contention made earlier in this report that the self-containment and isolation of the early halfway houses was one of several factors leading to their failure to survive.

By grants and contracts awarded to both public and private agencies, governmental funding bodies have fostered the phenomenal growth of halfway houses. As a practical stipulation of most grants and contracts, cooperation with other agencies, especially correctional agencies, is required. Such cooperation is an absolute necessity if halfway house programs are to have any measure of success, much less survive. More will be said of cooperative relationships later, but it is noted here to emphasize the fact that halfway houses, no matter who operates them, must have solid ties with other segments of the criminal justice system, and corrections in particular.

Keller and Alper consider halfway houses organizationally related to corrections.[14] Controversy about where halfway houses "belong" in the organizational structure of the system have arisen among and between public agencies as they have become involved in their establishment and operation.[15] The most reasonable viewpoint offered on this controversy seems to be that, "Despite differing views, it probably matters little whether the management of a center falls under the sponsorship of a public or private

11. Vasoli and Fahey, op. cit., p. 294.

12. "Task Force Report: Corrections", op. cit., p. 6. Cf. Moeller, op. cit., p. 87.

13. "Task Force Report: Corrections", op. cit., p. 44.

14. Keller and Alper, op. cit., p. 15.

15. Moeller, op. cit., p. 87.

agency, or in fact, becomes part of the responsibilities of a probation, parole or correctional institution administrator. Of far greater importance are the quality of the programs offered, the competence and integrity of the center's staff and the working relationships between the center and the correctional agencies that use the resources." [16]

The issue, therefore, does not seem to be which agency, public or private, should operate halfway houses, but:

1. Are halfway houses, public or private, a part of the correctional system?

2. If they are part of the correctional system, what is their function in relationship to that system?

For public agencies, we can be safe in answering the first question in the affirmative. For private agencies, the majority seem to view themselves as part of the correctional system, but this view is by no means unanimous. As a practical matter, those private agencies who wish to remain isolated from the system will find it increasingly difficult, not only to survive as an increasing amount of public funds go to support privately operated programs, but also will find that the services they could offer to the offender will be severely restricted because of their isolation. As the early halfway houses did, they will undoubtedly continue to service only those released from institutions. In isolation, they will be unable to participate in the "more positive and dynamic role for community treatment centers" that is "a hopeful substitute for the large prison".[17] Furthermore, they will be unable to assist the offender by offering many services now being delivered by halfway houses over and above the traditional "transitional facility" concept.

If halfway houses, public or private, are truly to be a part of the criminal justice system and serve their clientele most effectively, then strong relationships must be developed with the other components of the system—both at the administrative and line staff levels. This means the whole spectrum of the justice system: chiefs of police and police officers, prosecutors, defense attorneys (especially public defenders), jails, judges, probation and

16. "The Residential Center: Corrections in the Community", United States Bureau of Prisons, Department of Justice, Washington, D. C.

17. "Administration of Justice in a Changing Society", op. cit., p. 69.

parole authorities (both adult and juvenile), workhouses, houses of detention, prisons and reformatories, training schools and other community treatment center programs in the same geographical area. Here we have spoken only of the relationships which must be developed within the system. Many other community relationships need to be developed also.[18]

At this point, a question should be asked: "Why corrections in the community?" Our communities are conditioned to the "correctional process" taking place elsewhere. Corrections is too frequently equated with prisons. Unfortunately, notions of punishment still underlie much of the community's attitude toward corrections,[19] and the symbol of punishment is prison.

Although most offenders currently incarcerated in our prisons are from large metropolitan areas, the prisons themselves are usually located away from urban areas. The original reasons for establishing these institutions in remote locations were diverse. To a large extent, those reasons are now outdated, i. e., the communities' interest in banishing the offender to a remote locale, the deside of rural legislators to provide public employment for their constituents and the belief that a rural setting was beneficial and salutary for individuals reared in cities, are just a few.[20]

Two factors, of which many unfamiliar with the field of corrections are unaware, however, are that only about one-third of all offenders are in institutions, while two-thirds are already under supervision in the community,[21] and that approximately 95% of all offenders committed to penal institutions are eventually released and returned to the community. Even though two-thirds are in the community under supervision, the treatment afforded them is more illusion than reality.[22]

Crime and delinquency are symptoms of failure and disfunctioning of the community as well as of the individual offender.[23] The community has its share of responsibility to bear for the conditions conducive to crime and as a result must share in the "responsibility to deal with the results of these conditions".[24] With

18. "The Residential Center: Corrections in the Community", op. cit., p. 11.

19. "Task Force Report: Corrections", op. cit., p. 2.

20. Ibid., p. 4.

21. Ibid., p. 1.

22. Ibid., p. 4.

23. "Task Force Report: Corrections", op. cit., p. 7.

24. Keller and Alper, op. cit., p. 108.

the recognition that traditional penal institutions have not adequately performed their rehabilitative functions, community programs such as halfway houses are being developed in order to reduce the flow of individuals into those institutions.[25] While institutional populations have been showing a decrease in many areas of the country, community-based treatment programs are showing a considerable increase.

The best opportunity for successful integration or reintegration of the offender seems to lie in the community itself.[26]

The field of mental health has paved the way for corrections by establishing community-based programs whose aims are to ease the patient's transition back into the community and to prevent their removal from it in the first place, if possible.[27] Adequately trained personnel and other resources which only the community can offer with any degree of quality or quantity are essential for the rehabilitative process. Physicians, dentists, psychiatrists, psychologists, social workers, para-professionals, including indigenous personnel, teachers, vocational counselors, and other personnel, are not to be found in sufficient numbers in places other than metropolitan areas. Resources such as schools, diverse vocational training courses and employment opportunities, mental health centers, recreational opportunities and not least of all, family and friends, are also located in metropolitan areas.

It was noted earlier that we have spoken only of relationships which the halfway house must develop with other components of the criminal justice system, but that many other community resources and relationships must also be developed. To provide a successful and viable program for its clients as well as to achieve its purpose as a community-based program, a halfway house must develop strong relationship with a host of non-correctional or criminal justice agencies, public and private, as well as various citizen and neighborhood groups.

Vocational rehabilitation agencies, including vocational training centers, public and private, medical and mental health facilities, schools, including colleges and universities as well as centers for adult and juvenile basic education, agencies providing family

---

25. Ibid., p. 110.

26. "The Residential Center: Corrections in the Community," op. cit., p. 1.

27. Keller and Alper, op. cit., p. 5.

counseling and recreational facilities, chambers of commerce, labor unions, the news media (radio, television, press), employers, civic and fraternal groups such as the Lions, Rotary Clubs, U. S. Jaycees, citizen groups interested in the criminal justice field such as the Alliance for Shaping a Safer Community, and various neighborhood improvement and association groups, are just a few samples of the type of community agencies, groups and resources with which halfway houses must develop strong relationships.

A key function of corrections today is to help the offenders avail themselves of the variety of services they need in order to take advantage of the opportunity structure which they have previously lacked, or to open doors to services which have been denied them in the past.[28]

Therefore, those who work in corrections must develop the knowledge and skill it requires to see that those services are made available to the offender.[29]   The answer to the question: "Why corrections in the community?" should now be obvious. The next issue we need to address i. the function and place of halfway houses or community treatment centers in relation to the correctional system.

C.   THE FUNCTION AND PLACE OF THE HALFWAY HOUSE IN THE CORRECTIONAL SYSTEM

Traditionally, the early halfway houses, including those founded fifteen to twenty years ago, served the parolee or mandatory releasee from penal institutions almost exclusively. Some halfway houses or community treatment centers, however, have developed rather sophisticated programs, and have broadened not only the scope of services they offer, but also the target populations being serviced. Corrections is moving away increasingly from traditional methods of confinement, and community-based programs are being utilized in numerous ways as the appropriate alternatives. Halfway houses or community treatment centers are being developed rapidly and as the range of alternatives for courts and correctional officials broadens for the treatment of the

28. Moeller, op. cit., p. 84.

29. For a discussion of the availability of community resources in conjunction with correctional agencies, see Mandall, Wallace, "Making Corrections a Community Agency", *Crime & Delinquency*, Vol. 17, July, 1971.

public offender, such alternatives will be increasingly utilized in preference to traditional methods.[30]

As corrections becomes increasingly more community-based, the range of possible alternatives available to our courts and correctional officials will offer a flexibility for the treatment of the offender hitherto unknown to corrections, and will allow for the flow of offenders from one alternative to another, as need dictates.[31]

While the place of halfway houses or community treatment centers has not been decided from an organizational standpoint for either public or private agencies,[32] the present and possible future functions of such facilities have become increasingly clear. As indicated above, many halfway houses are serving a much wider target population and are being utilized for many other purposes than just the parolee or mandatory releasee. Starting with the traditional populations served by halfway houses, we will list the current uses of community-based residential treatment facilities.

1. *Mandatory Releasee and Parolee*

The mandatory releasee or parolee who is in need of a transitional center, and the range of services it offers (see Standards Nos. 10, 11 and 12 under "Program") has always been and still is being served by the community treatment center. The rationale for servicing this population has been to ease their transition back into free society and to buffer the many negative effects of their period of incarceration and isolation from the community.

Until the recent past, parolees were usually received directly upon release from the institution. One innovation, however, recently formalized by Federal law for Federal parolees, is the use of halfway houses for the parolee who is already "on the street", but who is having difficulty in his adjustment and perhaps stands the risk of revocation. Instead of waiting for failure, and sending such an offender back to the institution, the alternative to send him to community treatment centers for more intensive treatment and supervision, while keeping him in the community, is now available. While we are unaware of any state or local

---

30. "Administration of Justice in a Changing Society", op. cit., p. 7.

31. "Task Force Report: Corrections", op. cit., p. 11.

32. Moeller, op. cit., p. 82.

jurisdictions which have such formal provisions written into statute or ordinance, parole officers at those levels are using community treatment centers informally for this purpose already.
Here is one added alternative to the traditional options of parole
or reinstitutionalization.

2.   *The Probationer*

Many halfway houses are increasingly accepting persons placed
on probation. Probationers are referred to a halfway house under two sets of general circumstances: First, the court may consider the individual too much of a risk to simply place him on
probation to be supervised by an already overworked probation
officer, who will be unable to give the needed time and attention
to the prospective probationer. At the same time, the court may
recognize that the individual in question does not need incarceration in the traditional institutional setting. Therefore, the court
may choose to stipulate that, as a condition of probation, the individual agree to participate in a halfway house or community
treatment center program. This stipulation takes place prior to
the time the person is placed on probation. The alternative just
described has been practiced informally by courts and probation
officers at all jurisdictional levels throughout various parts of
the United States for the past few years. Its use has been dependent largely upon the intake policies of a given halfway house
and whether they have been willing to accept such potential probationers.

Second, an individual may have been placed on probation already, but like the parolee described earlier, may be experiencing adjustment problems in the community, and running the risk
of revocation. Rather than revoke an individual in such a situation, the court or probation officer may refer them to a halfway
house. Again, intensity of treatment and supervision is much
greater, but the benefits of remaining in the community are
maintained. The Federal government has also passed legislation
formalizing the procedure for utilizing halfway houses for probationers in the situation just described. This alternative is also
being utilized informally by many state and local courts and probation officers.

3.   *The Pre-releasee*

For several years, Federal law, and more recently, the laws of
several states, have allowed for the release of prisoners to half-

way houses or community treatment centers prior to their actual mandatory release or release on parole. The period of time for which an individual is released under this provision ranges from thirty to one hundred and twenty days, although some jurisdictions allow for pre-release status for up to six months. While the pre-release of such individuals is considered an administrative transfer from one "institution" to another "institution", the pre-releasee receives the benefit of community-based treatment and supervision *prior* in time to the mandatory release or parole. Therefore, when the pre-releasee reaches mandatory release or parole status, he has had the opportunity of working through many of the problems of adjustment, and utilizing the necessary community resources, such as vocational training, employment placement, psychiatric and medical resources, housing, re-establishing family and other community ties, with which the parolee or mandatory releasee newly released to a halfway house is just beginning to cope. Many halfway houses, public and private, are accepting pre-releasees from Federal and state referral sources.

4.   *Study and Diagnostic Services to Offenders*

Depending on their level of sophistication, many halfway houses are now capable of offering study and diagnostic services to courts. Such services are rendered prior to final disposition in court. It was mentioned earlier that the court may consider an individual too great of a risk to place on probation and yet recognizes that the individual does not need incarceration and, therefore, stipulates that they enter a halfway house program as a condition of probation. The court may be able to arrive at this conclusion based on information provided by the pre-sentence report.

Study and diagnostic services, however, is a more formalized method of assisting the court to arrive at a final disposition, especially when the pre-sentence investigation cannot provide enough information about special problematic areas facing the offender. In such instances, the court of jurisdiction may place the offender in a halfway house or community treatment center for "study and observation" for a sixty-to-ninety-day period. During this time, a complete battery of psychiatric or psychological tests are administered, as well as psychiatric or psychological interviews with an accompanying assessment; a complete social history is also developed along with an assessment of the offender's prior record, if any; vocational and/or employment history, assessment and potential, and a record of the individual's progress and behavior while at the halfway house. A prognosis and recommendation is submitted to the court for its consideration for final disposition. Upon completion of study and diagnostic services, the individual may be placed on probation and/or possibly required to remain in the community treatment center, either as a condition of probation with the provisions of the "split sentence" * procedure, or sent to a more traditional correctional institution.

While study and diagnostic services have been utilized with community treatment centers primarily by the Federal justice system, there is much promise that such services will be rendered to offenders at the state and local levels if "correctional center complexes" as described in the *Task Force Report on Corrections* are constructed in metropolitan areas.[33]

5. *The Juvenile—Neglected and Delinquent*

Halfway houses, or group homes, as they are often called, are being utilized increasingly for the child who is neglected or delinquent. The establishment of such group homes has been increasing at an extremely rapid pace. Many times in the past, the neglected child was placed in detention facilities or training schools along with delinquent children, simply because there were no other resources to draw upon. Without any violation of the Juvenile Code, a child could, in effect, be incarcerated. Not enough foster parents are available to care for these children, and as a result, group homes have been established to meet this pressing need.

Group homes for the delinquent child are serving several purposes. First, they give the court of jurisdiction an alternative to incarceration if the child does not respond to the supervision of his probation officer or social worker. This prevents the child from being sent to training schools, which often are ill equipped to meet the child's needs. A child may be in residence in such a home for well over a year. The child's inability to care for himself, secure gainful employment, and be exclusively responsible

---

* That sentence in which the offender is initially committed for a brief period prior to supervision on probation.

33. "Task Force Report: Corrections", op. cit., p. 11.

for his own welfare, often makes a longer length of stay in a group home necessary.

Second, the group home may be used as a short-term facility for the delinquent child while community resources are brought to bear on the root of his problems, such as family difficulties which may be resolved by intensive counseling in a relatively short period of time.

Third, the group home is also used as a "halfway out" facility for children who have been incarcerated and do not have an adequate home plan.

The group home may be used flexibly as one of many alternatives for the delinquent child. Community correctional centers seem to be approaching reality more quickly for the juvenile delinquent than for the adult offender. Relatively small institutions with greater security but also intensive treatment for the hyper-aggressive child are being established in metropolitan areas, in lieu of "training schools" located in rural areas. In addition to regular probation supervision, intensive treatment units are being established for children still living in their own homes. Intensive treatment units may have a ratio of one social worker or counselor for every six to ten children. The establishment of group homes in conjunction with the other alternatives listed above will give courts of jurisdiction tremendous flexibility to move the child from one component of the "system" to another as need or progress dictates. It should be noted that all of the alternatives listed above would be based in the community.

6.   *Use of Halfway Houses for Individuals with Special Difficulties, such as Drug Abuse, Alcoholism and Psychiatric Problems*

Halfway houses or community treatment centers are being utilized for target populations with special difficulties such as drug abuse, alcoholism or psychiatric problems. Due to the nature of the problems being treated, the length of stay in such centers is usually much longer than in those servicing the general offender population, often for as long as eighteen months. Many, perhaps most such centers, utilize one form or another of the therapeutic community technique. Especially in the case of drug abuse and alcoholism, such centers are frequently staffed by individuals who have experienced and successfully worked through the problem. In many such centers, professionally trained personnel who have not experienced the problem being treated, were often excluded from the staffing pattern as a matter of treatment philosophy. However, there is evidence that professionally trained staff are now being accepted more readily as a part of the treatment team. Because of the nature of the difficulties experienced by drug abusers and alcoholics, many of them have passed through our criminal justice system. This has occurred usually as a direct result of their problems.

7. Use of Halfway Houses for Individuals Released on Bail Prior to Final Disposition

We have been speaking of some of the traditional and more recent uses and functions of the halfway house in relation to the correctional system. What are some other innovative uses which may be made of halfway houses? What other functions may it serve in the correctional system?

Bail reform has been spreading rapidly in the United States. Federal and many state and local jurisdictions have enacted bail reform measures. Although innocent until proven guilty, it is known that most individuals accused of crimes are from lower socio-economic groups,[34] and cannot afford ten per cent of the bail set by the court, which is usually required by professional bondsmen. As a result, the poor remain in jail to await final disposition while those more affluent are able to obtain their release.

To remedy the inequity of this situation, "Recognizance Bond" legislation has been and still is being enacted in various parts of the nation. If the individual meets certain criteria, he may be released upon his own signature, promising to reappear in court on the appropriate date. This provision does away with the need for the accused to produce a certain amount of cash or property for his bail.

One of the usual standard requirements is that the individual have roots in the community in which he stands accused, i. e., family, friends, job, etc. Many accused individuals, however, have poor family ties, and poor work histories, which are often the result of educational and cultural deprivation. Not meeting some of the basic criteria, they are excluded from the use of recognizance bond and must await final disposition in jail. The bad effects of this situation have been expounded by governmen-

34. "Task Force Report: Corrections", op. cit., p. 2.

tal commissions, hearings by committees of Congress, and state legislatures, and several publications in professional journals and books.

The halfway house should consider the possibility (and some already have) of providing services to an individual enabling him to become eligible for recognizance bond. At a minimum, this would include providing shelter and supervision prior to final disposition. However, whether the accused is found guilty or not, they are usually in need of a range of services which the halfway house is often in a position to provide, directly or indirectly. Medical, dental, psychological and psychiatric services, individual and group counseling services, vocational evaluation and counseling services, as well as employment placement services, can all be provided to the accused who has not been found guilty, but who is in need of such services. The delays which occur between the time of arrest and final disposition are often lengthy, ranging from six months to a year or more. Even if the process is speeded up, and the time from arrest to final disposition is reduced to two or three months, there is still much that can be accomplished during this period of time.

The next point is obvious: as most halfway houses deliver their range of services between an eighty to one hundred and twenty day period, a question should be asked: Why not intervene on the client's behalf long before final disposition, and why not deliver needed services prior to final disposition?

If the accused are found not guilty, they are in a much better position after the delivery of these services to pursue a more meaningful and constructive life. In one sense, this approach might be considered crime prevention in the true sense of the word. If the accused is found guilty, a range of services has been delivered already which may well affect the outcome of final disposition, e. g., probation rather than incarceration. In this instance, the halfway house would be in a position to offer valuable information to the court even before a pre-sentence investigation commences. The progress (or lack of it) of the individual found guilty could be reviewed with the court of jurisdiction as well as the investigating probation officer.

Additional or continued treatment plans could be formulated prior to the time of sentencing and if the person is to be placed on probation, made a part of the probation treatment plan. Even if the person is to be incarcerated, the services rendered, progress made, and information obtained need not be wasted, but could be shared with institutional treatment staff to help them formulate a plan for treatment with the client while he is incarcerated. Even if incarcerated, the fact that the individual was willing to avail himself of needed services while on recognizance bond could have a positive effect on how quickly he is released back into the community.

Few halfway houses have experimented in this area, but it seems to be a fertile ground for new uses of the halfway house.

8. Use of the Halfway House for Diversion from the Criminal Justice System

Halfway houses or community treatment centers can be utilized in the future to divert individuals from the criminal justice system. The question of diversion has been discussed in criminal justice circles for some time. Some that were formerly arrested and convicted repeatedly for an offense such as public intoxication are now being diverted from the criminal justice system in some jurisdictions.

When it is realized that in 1965, one-third of all the arrests in the United States were for the offense of public drunkenness, the magnitude of the problem of processing these individuals through the criminal justice system can be appreciated. The burden on police departments, courts, prosecutors, probation and parole officers and jails, as well as other penal institutions, is tremendous.[35]

The criminal justice system seems to be ineffective to alter the behavior of the chronic alcoholic and to meet his underlying medical and social problems. The "system" only served to remove the publicly intoxicated individual from public view.[36] *The Task Force Report on Drunkenness* states that, "The commission seriously doubts that drunkenness alone (as distinguished from disorderly conduct) should continue to be treated as a crime." [37]

A general trend seems to be developing in the United States to restrict the scope of the criminal sanction by removing those statutes which tend to regulate the private moral conduct of individuals. Channeling through the criminal justice system those

---

35. "Task Force Report: Drunkenness", op. cit., p. 1.

36. "Task Force Report: Drunkenness", op. cit., p. 3.

37. Ibid., p. 4.

who have committed "victimless crimes" gravely dissipates the resources at the command of that system.

Time, energy, manpower, financial and other resources are diverted from coping with the type of offenses that threaten a community most, and affect the quality of life of its citizens, i. e., various forms of violence and theft.[38]

If alternative mechanisms are established to deal with victimless crimes, not only is the individual diverted from the criminal justice system, and relieved of the burden of the lasting stigma which is the result of the formal adjudication process, but a greater opportunity exists for obtaining the desired results of rehabilitation.[39]

The Board of Trustees of the National Council on Crime and Delinquency has issued a policy statement in support of abolition of victimless crime statutes.[40] There are also a substantial number of individuals at both the juvenile and adult offender levels, who could be diverted from the justice system, well before the point of sentencing, to alternative treatment programs.[41] As far as juveniles are concerned, this is certainly the thrust of the Youth Service Bureau as espoused by the National Council on Crime and Delinquency.

Legislation has been enacted already by the Federal government permitting drug abusers, for instance, to commit themselves voluntarily for treatment. Federal legislation also allows drug abusers who have been apprehended to be committed for treatment with the consent of the United States Attorney. If the individual successfully completes treatment, criminal charges against him are dropped.

In some areas of the United States, it is the policy of local police departments to take those who are publicly intoxicated to detoxification centers for treatment, rather than charging them with such petty offenses as disorderly conduct and vagrancy. If the person arrested consents to treatment, charges are not brought against him.

---

38. "Administration of Justice in a Changing Society", op. cit., p. 10.

39. Ibid., p. 11.

40. "Crimes without Victims—A Policy Statement", Board of Trustees, National Council on Crime and Delinquency, *Crime and Delinquency*, Vol. 17, No. 2, April, 1971.

41. "Task Force Report: Corrections", op. cit., p. 22.

Halfway houses as well as public health facilities can be utilized to divert and treat a substantial number of people such as alcoholics, drug abusers, and petty offenders who are currently being channeled through our criminal justice system. Obviously, not all such persons will want treatment, and in those instances, the mechanisms have been created to protect the individual and the community. With the proper legislation, halfway houses can be the focal point of a whole new direction for the diversion of individuals from the criminal justice system.

To return to an issue raised earlier would now be appropriate: if halfway houses serving the offender (primarily the privately-operated halfway houses) do not consider themselves a part of the correctional system, and if they do not establish cooperative relationships with correctional and other agencies but prefer to remain relatively isolated, they will be limiting the scope of their services and seriously restricting their participation in future innovative programs. We see this as being true for two reasons:

1.   Correctional authorities will be increasingly hesitant to refer individuals to a house or center which does not have some type of cooperative relationship with them, especially as the numbers of such centers grow and the authorities have alternative houses or centers to which they may turn.

2.   Without such cooperative relationships, which in themselves make a house or center a part of the correctional system, in fact if not by law, public funds will be increasingly difficult to obtain, whether by grant or contract with public agencies. Relying solely on private sources of income, the vast majority of private halfway houses would have extreme difficulty not only in offering a wide range of quality services to meet the varying needs of its clientele but also in simply surviving. Those who would suffer most, of course, would be the clientele halfway houses are serving, and the community of which both the client and the halfway house are a part.

HOMEWARD BOUND: AN ALTERNATIVE TO THE INSTITUTIONALIZATION OF ADJUDICATED JUVENILE OFFENDERS*

In 1847 the Lyman School for Boys was established in Westboro, Massachusetts.[1] Thus began, on that day, a new and enlightened era in the handling of juvenile offenders. No longer would a juvenile be incarcerated with adult felons, nor would cruel and unusual punishments be inflicted on the young.

The Training School—An Overview

In subsequent years, more and more states, following Massachusetts' leadership in the field, developed "reform" or "training" schools. Regimentation was foremost. To conform to rules and regulations was to be "rehabilitated." Days leading into weeks, then into months were spent walking in line, two abreast, with hands in trouser pockets,[2] lining up for "headcounts"[3] and sleeping in large impersonal dormitories.

As it was so aptly phrased in the Newman report:

> They are fed and housed and to some extent clothed. They receive a minimum of medical and dental attention. They go to classes, where some who cannot read are taught to read. They learn a few skills—though the farm work, which is probably the best taught and most interesting, is of little use upon release. They have no privacy and virtually no personal possessions. They spend months or years in a situation of almost total conformity and irresponsibility, with no chance to develop independence of thought or self-reliance . . . they do not learn how to handle money—to earn it or even to spend it. They are isolated from their families by a sys-

* Herb C. Willman, Jr., and Ron Y. F. Chun, *Federal Probation*, September, 1973. Reprinted with permission.

1. *Task Force Report: Juvenile Delinquency and Youth Crime.* The President's Commission on Law Enforcement and the Administration of Justice, 1967.

2. This is a common practice in "control" institutions to prevent one boy from touching another.

3. Generally, religiously adhered to, three or four times daily.

tem which permits two parental visits per month. They are isolated from outside friends . . . they never meet or associate with girls. They go out with no resources into a world that is totally strange. It is no wonder that so many graduate to become inmates of our correctional institutions.[4]

Or as depicted by Shaw 40 years earlier:

Haircuts were (and are) short, blue dungarees and shirt are the uniform of the day . . . they have already achieved fame in the world of crime, and proceed to impress that fact upon the other boys. They loiter about the place, congregate in small groups, talking about their achievements and ambitions in their common vocation, crime.[5]

Shaw's description of delinquent boys attempting to impress their peers with talk about "their achievements and ambitions in their common vocation, crime," was written in 1930, and has changed little to this day, although, admittedly, there is now much more talk of "doing dope," or "clouting cars."

From that day in 1847 to the present, literally thousands of children have "done their time" as described by Newman and Shaw. In spite of the fact that training school administrations have hired increased numbers of educators, social workers, counselors, psychologists, and psychiatrists, most have proven well-meaning but their impact equivocal.

We have attempted in our training schools "compensatory education," [6] "individual therapy," [7] "group counseling," [8] and "group therapy," [9] among others. Many of these innovations show

4. Mary B. Newman, *The Newman Committee Investigation Into Conditions in Training Schools in Massachusetts*, 1971, State House Library.

5. Clifford R. Shaw, *The Jack-Roller: A Delinquent Boy's Own Story*, chapter 5, p. 57, 1930.

6. Title I, Elementary and Secondary Education Act: *An Evaluation of Compensatory Educational Programs for Institutionalized Children*, 1971, Department of Health, Education and Welfare.

7. Stuart Adams, "The Pico Project," *The Sociology of Punishment and Correction*, New York, 1962, pp. 213–224, Norman Johnson, et al.

8. Norman Fenton, *An Introduction to Group Counseling in State Correctional Service*, New York: American Correctional Association, 1958.

9. California Department of Corrections, Second Annual Report.

some promise in given situations, however, most have shown little or no lasting differences between control and experimental groups examined. Change criteria have been elusive.

As a result, we are still turning out of our training schools more youngsters going on to further criminal activities and future incarceration in adult prisons, than youngsters who reenter the mainstream of society.

With this record of repeated failure in mind, let us reexamine what we assume to be true about the training school youngster.

> Disproportionately, he is a child of the slums, he is 15 or 16 years old, perhaps one of numerous children, possibly from a broken home; from adults and older children in charge of him, he has had leniency, sternness, affection, perhaps indifference in erratic and unpredictable succession. He may well have dropped out of school, he may well be unemployed and have little to offer an employer. His crimes are much more frequently thefts than crimes of violence.[10]

He is also resentful, impatient, and insecure because of repeated failure; he is searching desperately for masculine identity, and craves excitement, adventure, recognition, and acceptance.

The Outward Bound Schools

In England, during World War II, there was considerable concern about the large numbers of British seamen who would literally give up their lives with little struggle when forced to abandon ship in the cold waters of the North Atlantic—while many older, more experienced sailors, although in poorer physical shape, would survive this same ordeal.

As a result of this concern, Dr. Kurt Hahn was commissioned to establish the first Outward Bound School in Aberdovey, Wales. Hahn was interested in developing more than muscle in young merchant seamen for, in addition to physical conditioning, he stressed the importance of group pride, personal contribution, and trust in yourself and others. This school, as in other Outward Bound Schools to follow, recognized the value of structuring stressful situations to unify groups toward a common goal, as

10. *Task Force Report: Juvenile Delinquency and Youth Crime Understanding and Preventing Delinquency*, p. 43, 1967 (not a verbatim quotation).

well as the value of repeated and hard-won successes in establishing confidence and a more positive self-image.

Hahn's efforts met with such success that some 34 Outward Bound Schools have since been established throughout the world.

Outward Bound and Juvenile Delinquency

The Colorado Outward Bound School which opened in 1962 is located on the snow-crested western slopes of the Rocky Mountains at an altitude of 8,800 feet. The program, which involves mountain walking, backpacking, high altitude camping, solo survival, rappelling and rock climbing, accepted its first adjudicated delinquents, five in all, from the Massachusetts Department of Youth Services in 1964.

The following year, 25 more adjudicated youngsters from Massachusetts completed the Outward Bound Program in Colorado, and in newly opened Outward Bound Schools in Minnesota and Maine. This early success led to the funding of a study to determine whether a program of severe physical challenge can be effective in reducing further delinquency among adolescent boys as shown by a comparison of recidivism rates, control vs. experimental.[11]

The Homeward Bound Program

In September 1960 the Massachusetts Department of Youth Services established the Stephen L. French Youth Forestry Camp, located in Nickerson State Park in East Brewster, Massachusetts.

This camp was designed to run on a work-therapy model for adjudicated delinquent boys, 16 years of age or older, who would provide, during a 6- to 9-month stay, labor for the Department of Natural Resources in building and cleaning campsites, clearing trails, and other park projects.

The 18–20 boys in the camp were housed in a converted hunting lodge located in the 1,777 acre State Park.

As the years passed, and the Department's success with delinquents attending Outward Bound schools grew, pressures both

11. F. J. Kelly and D. J. Baer, *Outward Bound Schools as an Alternative to Institutionalization for Adolescent Delinquent Boys*, Boston, Massachusetts: Fandel Press, 1968. Funded by the Office of Juvenile Delinquency, Childrens Bureau, U. S. Department of Health, Education and Welfare, Grant No. 66013; the Massachusetts Department of Youth Services; and the Committee of the Permanent Charity Fund, Boston.

from within the Forestry Camp and from the Department's administration called for a radical change from the camp's work-therapy model to an adventure training, self-discipline model.

Following a reorganization of the Department of Youth Services and a change in the administration of the Forestry Camp, sufficient money and trained personnel [12] were available to enable the Homeward Bound Program to evolve from a series of pilot programs [13] to a full-time Homeward Bound School, in October 1970.

Using the best elements of the Outward Bound model developed by Kurt Hahn in Aberdovey, Wales, and taking full advantage of the experiences gleaned from association with the Colorado, Minnesota and Maine Outward Bound Schools, the Massachusetts Department of Youth Services initiated a series of pilot programs which evolved into a two-phase program of 6 weeks' duration called Homeward Bound.[14]

Boys are selected for participation in Homeward Bound based on the day they are received from the court. On alternate days during the first 2 weeks of the program boys whose offenses in the community—whether they be stubborn child, use of a motor vehicle, or murder—are "committed or referred" to the Homeward Bound Program on a "space available" basis where they are immediately welcomed by the assistant superintendent and a counselor, at the lodge where they were to live during Phase I.

Prior to coming to Homeward Bound, it is carefully explained to each boy that the program: (1) Is very rugged; (2) has limited openings; (3) is voluntary; (4) once begun must be completed; (5) once completed allows the graduate to be paroled directly home. During the study no boys declined to participate in Homeward Bound.

12. Money was made available from Title I of the Elementary and Secondary Education Act, private donations of $8,000 and the reallocation of existing state appropriations. Twelve of the Department's personnel volunteered to attend Outward Bound schools in Minnesota and Maine for training.

13. A pilot program, called Overlanders, based on the Outward Bound model, was run in a separate cottage on the grounds of the Lyman School for Boys during portions of a 2-year period. At the same time, a similar pilot program was being run at the Forestry Camp. In October 1970, both programs merged into the Homeward Bound Program.

14. During its first full year of operation, Homeward Bound has offered this 6-week program to 300 court-acquainted boys or boys adjudicated as delinquent.

The assistant superintendent and the counselor explain a few basic rules to each new enrollee. There are no locks, no fences, and no secure rooms. Visiting is permitted, mail is not censored, personal clothing may be worn, phone calls may be made and received—all permitted during Phase I but not in Phase II where much of the program takes place on the Appalachian Trail or at sea.

Following this initial orientation, the incoming boys are introduced to several boys working at the camp as assistant brigade leaders, who in turn orient the boys in their fashion (probably more effectively) about the rigors of the program and those few rules enforced by staff.

The physical site for the "Homeplace" for Phase II of Homeward Bound is located a quarter of a mile away from the Lodge, on the shores of crystal clear Cliff Pond. It is here that each brigade lives in its own A-frame while in camp, and it is the home from which at 6:00 a. m., staff and boys begin each day with a 2-mile run and dip—regardless of the weather or season.

After the first few days of Phase I, 32 boys are assembled—divided into brigades of eight each—and begin the early or intermediate phase of Homeward Bound.

Days are devoted to community service projects, short hikes along the National Seashore, some running, minimal calisthenics, and a few choice obstacle courses.[15] There are also hours spent with a counselor helping to develop a realistic plan for release, as each boy is thoroughly involved in working up his own postrelease plan and has time to reflect a bit on who he is and how he got there.

Evenings are not for play; there are classes from Homeward Bound-instructors in ecology, orienteering, survival, search and rescue, overnight expeditions, ropes and knots, and seamanship.

For those who do not pay attention during class—and this is the majority—the first overnight expedition is an eye-opener. Packs are not packed properly, some gear is left behind, not enough of the right kind of food is brought along, and most end up the first overnight cold, wet, and miserable. Thereafter, however, evening classes become more lively and more questions are asked. As the 2-week period in Phase I comes to a close, most

15. There is a certain amount of weeding out; 1 to 2 percent of the boys refuse to participate despite all efforts by staff and peers.

boys move ahead with a mixture of fear and apprehension toward Phase II.

On the first day of Phase II, following the run and dip, all brigades assemble for an orientation concerning the nature of the particular program they will undertake. Each program varies with the time of the year, weather conditions, and the availability of specialized safety equipment. Equipment is then issued and each brigade is allowed a brief period to settle into its A-frame.

From 1700 hours until long after dark, the program director conducts what is known of as a "quiet walk." This is neither quiet, nor a walk; it is instead, a cross-country trot over forest trails, through swamps, across rivers, and nearly impenetrable woodlands. Some 5 or 6 hours after it began in daylight, it ends in darkness, with all participants fully exhausted, thoroughly wet and mud-covered, and well aware of what it means to give more than you thought you had.

Following the quiet walk, each boy is then asked to step forward to sign a pledge, reiterating his desire to continue on and complete the Homeward Bound Program. This is a soul-searching time for each youth, as his commitment is requested at a time when he feels defeated, frustrated, and incapable of meeting Homeward Bound's standards. Seldom does a boy refuse to sign. This may be due in part to peer pressure and marks the first of many personal successes he will experience in the month to follow.

One day then rapidly falls upon another, as each brigade learns the intricacies of survival, circuit training, land and/or sea expeditions, navigation, first aid and firefighting, silviculture, logistics, ecology, search and rescue, ropes and knots, rock climbing and rappelling.

In the beginning, there is an overnight training expedition, bringing together much of what is being learned. Later, a 3-day expedition tests the brigade even further, although it barely prepares them for the 10-day mobile course across the Appalachian Trail, often in four or more feet of snow.

A brigade can only move as fast and accomplish as much as its slowest, most inept member. This leads to increased group interaction and an eventual sharing and reaching out to one another. The 100-foot rappell, while one of the safest of exercises, can bring fear to the hearts of many brigade members, and it is here that one's peers, together with the skill of the brigade instructor and assistant brigade instructor, can make the seemingly impossible come true.

After a series of repeated successes on the high rappell, in rock-climbing, on expeditions and circuit training, comes the solo—a 3-day experience of survival suddenly with no peer pressure and no peers, no instructors to push, no one. It is here that each boy must put together all he has learned. With a few matches, a plastic sheet, a cooking pail and water, he must fend for himself for 3 days and 3 nights, far from the safety of any town or the comforts of home.

Following solo, the remainder of the long expedition seems to be anticlimactic for each boy now knows that he has what it takes. The return to the "homeplace" and the final competition between brigades passes all too quickly, as does the 7-mile run for individual honors.

The final evening is a blending of happy and sad. Even though there are smiles and congratulations when each boy receives his certificate and emblem; and even though the blisters have hardened and the muscles no longer hurt, each remembers all the good times—sitting around the fire in the evening, the first good hot meal after expeditions, and the newly won pride of knowing he did something no one could do for him.

Attempting to capsulize or summarize Homeward Bound is not an easy task. It is certainly a program of severe physical challenge, extreme excitement and perceived danger, followed by periods of relative calm, where participants can absorb and reflect on their accomplishments.

As shown by Kelly and Baer,[16] it is of little value to attempt to point out to an adjudicated delinquent that he is far more capable than he feels himself to be. What is necessary, however, is to devise a set of circumstances whereby the delinquent boy can clearly demonstrate this competence to himself. Only then will opportunities for concrete, impressive accomplishment promote personal growth.

The need to pace oneself, and the requirements of persistence in the morning run and dip, the circuit training, and the 90- to

16. F. J. Kelly and D. J. Baer, "Physical Challenge as a Treatment for Delinquency," *Crime and* *Delinquency,* October 1971, pp. 437–445.

100-mile overland expeditions challenge the delinquent's impulsivity and endurance.

The necessity of safety rules and climbing regulations in rappelling, sea expeditions, and search and rescue operations, causes him to question his previous concept that laws and regulations are to be ignored or treated lightly.

The placing of larger measures of responsibility on him as he holds the safety line of a peer who is rappelling, or assumes leadership of his brigade in stressful situations, forces him to re-evaluate his worth in relationship to his peers.

His dependence on his brigade leader and peers for success, safety and well-being cause him not only to reexamine his attitude towards authority, but also to understand and accept the strength and weaknesses of himself and others.

Lastly, the sobering experience of the solo, causes him to think deeply and long about his accomplishments, and consider what brought him to Homeward Bound, and where and how he is going from here.

Research Results

The Homeward Bound Program as a model, utilizing the lure of adventure and challenge as in Outward Bound, gives strong evidence that a positive rather than a negative orientation can create better correctional results with concomitant public safety.

On a 7- to 14-month follow-up our study demonstrated that 20.8 percent of the Homeward Bound Group recidivated as opposed to 42.7 percent of the control group. This finding remarkably supports the earlier study of Kelly and Baer whose research showed that 20 percent of the experimental group and 42 percent of the comparison group recidivate.[17]

Selection of boys for Homeward Bound versus Lyman School for Boys was based solely on a "space available basis" with 32 boys going directly from the court to Homeward Bound during the first 2 weeks of each 6-week cycle and all other commitments going to Lyman School during the last 4 weeks.

While chi square tests of the background characteristics of the Homeward Bound participants (178 boys) and the Lyman School

17. Kelly and Baer, "Physical Challenge," op. cit., p. 437.

participants (75 boys) showed no significant differences between either group, several interesting factors were observed:

(1) Homeward Bound participants are able to stay out of trouble longer than participants in regular institutional programs. Only 38 percent of those who recidivated following the Homeward Bound program did so within the first 6 months as compared to 72 percent of the institutional or control group.

(2) There was an increased chance of success in Homeward Bound as the chronological age of the participants increased.

(3) The marital status of the parents affected success or failure in the Homeward Bound Program. Participants whose parents were "separated" showed poorer results (22.6 percent failure) than in any other marital status category.

(4) There was a significant difference in "Last school grade attended" and success-failure in the Homeward Bound Program. The higher the school grade attained, the better the chance for success.

(5) Strong tendency noted that persons who committed "assault against persons" and "larceny" are more apt to experience success in the Homeward Bound Program. Contrariwise, persons in "stubborn child" category have a marked tendency toward failure within the program.

Conclusion and Future Implications

In their report on the Outward Bound Study, mentioned earlier in this article, Kelly and Baer state:

> Persistence is a virtue, and giving-up is hard to tolerate. Students feel that what they have to do at Outward Bound is what *should* be done. It becomes very difficult for a boy to "walk away" from a challenge. Students are often kept in the challenging situation for a period of time to encourage their meeting it. There are few "acceptable" reasons for not doing parts of the program, or for leaving the course. Serious physical injury like a broken leg, is one such acceptable reason. Injuries which allow for "malingering," like sprains, are rarely acceptable. Psychological problems, like fear of the mountains, are not easily understood, sometimes ridiculed.

Challenges, particularly when they are felt as dangerous, when one's life is "at stake" take on an irresistible quality. The excitement of the challenge, the sense of adventure, is contagious. Exciting events intensively involve the students in Outward Bound. More dangerout tasks generate more excitement. As on the climb up the rock face, much of the excitement stems from a conflict about whether one should make a certain move or should not. Many students feel they have come to Outward Bound specifically to meet challenges. Challenges are often seen as the highlights of the Outward Bound experience.

The opportunity to really test one's limits is very important. Challenges, particularly those felt as dangerous are often approached as opportunities for defining oneself. For many students, the question "Who am I?" is very pressing. As suggested by many writers, adolescents' sense of identity is in formation. For many, the challenges of Outward Bound provide an opportunity to gain some clarity about "who they are." They look upon Outward Bound as an "initiation rite," a not particularly pleasant but "real" way of finding out who they are, what their limits are. Many students approach Outward Bound as if it were the initiation rite which will effect their transition from boyhood to manhood.

The development of competence and confidence in meeting the Outward Bound tasks becomes important. Competence (mastery) generates a sense of personal worth and a feeling of accomplishment. Students develop pride in their competence, an almost professional feeling about their sailing, climbing or canoeing abilities. There is also a strong desire to be able to deal with danger confidently. It becomes important to be able to face one's fear about a dangerous situation, and still complete the task. Students are not comfortable with the feeling that "I'd never do that again, it was too scarey."

There is a strong desire among students to be seen as "men" not "boys." They do not want to be considered soft or cowardly. Hard work becomes intrinsically rewarding and a source of pride when one wants to avoid appearing soft. After a hard day of hiking or paddling, students feel a meaningful sense of accomplishment. Many of the tales told by students deal with the weight of the pack they carried, or the number of hours they rowed. Students who take short cuts, or have a lazy attitude, rarely occupy positions of influence or respect. Outward Bound is "hard work," not "fun." Rarely does a student enjoy Outward Bound. Rather, it is something he *should* go through. To be considered "chicken" and not to be able to disprove this claim is a supreme insult at Outward Bound.

Peer, staff, and family expectations exert great pressure toward conforming to the Outward Bound culture. As on the climb up the rock face, when everyone is doing it, the individual student finds it hard not to join in. This is particularly so when he realized that the camaraderie which develops is based on a sharing of common experiences. Anyone who did not climb the rock face that day was "left out" in a very important sense. The watch patrol or brigade as a unit also exerts strong pressure on completing tasks and the course. Intergroup competition is based on individuals' performances on tasks, particularly on their completing tasks.

Staff members are persons who have completed tasks similar to or more demanding than the Outward Bound program. Their almost unquestioned expectation is that their students will also complete the Outward Bound course. In fact, part of their reputation as instructors depends on how all their group completes a task or finishes the course.

Parents add a final pressure toward completing the course. It seems that there is an increase in the number of boys who are "sent to Outward Bound in order to become a man." There is also the more usual expectation that when one goes to a school, one finishes the course and gets his diploma, or in this case, certificate.[18]

People-changing organizations vary in mode, direction and extent of change. Too often the change is symbolic—the affixing of a new title or label on an old program. Happily we do not con-

18. Kelly and Baer, op. cit., pp. 116–119.

sider the Homeward Bound program to be a symbolic change in dealing with offenders, but rather a substantively new program. The thrust is to accept the offender, emphasize his worthfulness, build up his self-esteem and confidence and through personal achievement grant him an identity that hopefully will not be prone to extinction or rapid diminution once he leaves the program. Through activity-with-purpose, the debilitating effects of a correctional institution are held minimal.

We agree with Kelly and Baer that many features of the Outward Bound or Homeward Bound Program could, though with much difficulty, be incorporated into a regular training school structure and that this could supplement, if not provide an alternative to, institutionalization.

We feel, however, that for those states who undertake such a program, they will be faced rather quickly with the decision of closing one or more large and generally ineffective training schools. For it is obvious that Massachusetts, which has already closed three large training schools for boys, was aided immeasurably by sending 300 14- to 17-year-old adjudicated delinquents through a 6-week program (Homeward Bound) rather than through a traditional 6- to 9-month training school experience.

PROBATION HOSTELS IN GREAT BRITAIN*

It is now 53 years since probation hostels first found a place in British legislation. Several decades on, it might naturally be expected that they would hold an honoured place within the penal system, would be found to operate upon a soundly constructed conceptual basis tested out empirically as well as in the light of systematic research, and would thus serve as a model upon which those interested in establishing hostels in other countries could base their first experiments.

Such claims as can be made must be on a more modest basis. Hostels are not infrequently described by those in the best position to know, as the "poor relation" of the probation system. It

* Mark Monger, *Federal Probation,*
September, 1967. Reprinted with
permission.

will be suggested later that such conceptual basis as exists is of a very rule-of-thumb kind; little research has been carried out until very recently, and the findings of the Home Office Research unit still await publication. It may be, therefore, that the lessons to be learnt from British experience are limited in scope, and that interest must derive largely from belief in the potential of hostels as an adjunct of a probation system.

Some Problems Confronting the Hostel System

Four reasons for this perhaps surprising situation may be identified.

The first is the general assumption which has operated until very recently that hostels had something to offer only to adolescents, which means that Britain has no experience in the provision of this facility for adult probationers. Historically, it may well be that hostels were thought of as suitable for young people because for many years probation itself was regarded in this way. The legend that probation is for first offenders and young people dies hard, as witness the highly inaccurate description still given in a recent edition of the Concise Oxford Dictionary: "Probation: . . . system of releasing young criminals esp. first offenders on suspended sentence during good behaviour under supervision of person acting as friend and adviser."

Thus in 1924, an official report referred to the hostel provision in Birmingham:

> In nearly every case these boys have had no proper home or the surroundings have been undesirable, and but for the establishment of a hostel would probably have been committed to reform schools at considerable cost to the city. Instead they are living a comparatively normal life, learning steady habits under decent conditions, keeping their individuality—an important matter —saving a little money for the future and no public money is being incurred.

A major opportunity for this limited concept to be enlarged in favour of more imaginative thinking was thrown away by the Morison Committee in 1962. In its second report, specifically dealing with the hostel aspect of the probation system, it was clear that consideration had been given to the possibility of establishing hostels for adult probationers, but with negative conclusions:

> We recognize that there may be some adult probationers, who, although of adult years, are immature and likely to benefit from the support of supervision which approved hostels provide. We are not, however, satisfied on present evidence, that there is a sufficient number of such adults to justify provision being made for them in the approved hostel system.

From this it would seem that the Committee was still influenced by the idea of probation for the young, since the only type of adult they quoted was the "immature," and, as later investigators have suggested, there are many others. Probation, furthermore, is now used for offenders at most stages of criminality, and not merely for those who are either young or immature. In passing, the Morison Committee's conclusion was the more surprising, since the National Association of Probation Officers, in evidence, expressed itself in favour of hostels for adults.

Secondly, the development of the hostel system has been affected by an administrative arrangement commonly found in this country, by which the central government refrains from taking initiative, expecting and encouraging it from local interested individuals and bodies, provides finance only when this is unavoidable, and sees its real contribution as inspectorial, concerned with the establishment and maintenance of adequate standards. This system has many advantages, but it can lead to the acceptance and perpetuation of standards which are only just above questionable level.

The report of 1924 on the Birmingham hostel, quoted above, illustrates some aspects of this point of view, with its favourable references to lack of cost to the city and saving of public money.

In the period between the wars it became increasingly obvious that central government funds were needed; these were first added to local government provisions in 1928. Not until 20 years later, by the Criminal Justice Act of 1948, did the central government make itself responsible for capital expenditure. Since that time, a resident has been maintained partly by the state, partly by the probation committee who sent him, and partly by his own contribution out of earnings.

Thirdly, hostels might today present a more impressive front had provision in Scotland, England, and Wales been uniform. There has, however, been a sharp difference of opinion north and south of the border on the question whether probationers can best be helped by provision which segregates them, or which provides for a hostel community only partly consisting of probationers, the rest being people of similar age for whom residence away from home is necessary for reasons other than delinquency.

Scottish opinion, until very recently, has always held the latter view. In 1946, the Scottish Advisory Council on the Treatment and Rehabilitation of Offenders said that a hostel catering for probationers only would not, they thought, serve the best interests of the probationer; that it was most important that he should, during the whole of his probationary period, feel that he was living so far as possible as an ordinary citizen. They noted that in the voluntary homes and hostels which then catered for probationers considerably less than half the number of residents might be the subject of a probation order, and they considered that this system . . . ought to be continued.[1]

By 1964, however, Scottish opinion had shifted to some extent. The Probation Advisory and Training Council, after considering English experience, concluded that for some probationers, notably those in need of casework help, a "special" hostel—that is, one solely for probationers—would be appropriate, while for others with lesser problems an "ordinary" hostel, that is, one in which probationers and other residents would live together, would be suitable.

This cross-border debate was part of a fourth important factor which has been discussed intermittently through the years, the part which "training" should play in hostel life. As far back as 1927, a Departmental Committee made a basic distinction between young people who needed "character training" and those who did not. Only the latter, they felt, were suitable candidates for a hostel. These, broadly, would be young people with environmental difficulties who needed somewhere to lodge from which they could go out to work under normally free conditions, and who needed only help in finding employment and guidance about leisure-time activities.

1. I am indebted to Mr. Ian Sinclair of the Home Office Research Unit for assistance with the historical aspects of this paper.

In 1948, however, it was clear that ideas about training had altered, and official thinking was that hostels "should have regard to the paramount importance of character training." Each hostel was required to have a scheme of training, directed mainly to ensuring regular attendance at work, industrious application to it, and worthwhile leisure-time activities. By this definition, which included by implication such other matters as punctuality, politeness, cooperation with others, personal cleanliness, and so on, "training" appeared as the kind of provision which would normally be made by a good home, and nothing more.

This was at least coherent in the terms of the time, since probation practice was hardly yet seen as an aspect of social casework. This emerged in the early fifties and, as far as hostels are concerned, has inevitably added complexities for probation officers and hostel wardens. In 1948, both could realistically be seen as engaged in character training, through the aspects outlined above plus the centrally important personal influence of each worker. In the years since 1948, however, it would broadly be true to suggest that most hostel wardens have remained wedded to the 1948 idea of training, while probation officers have moved away from this in the light of developing understanding and teaching of casework. Much of the confusion and uncertainty which is to be seen among those concerned with hostels today, it can be claimed, springs from this divergence.

How Hostels Operate

Turning now to present aspects of the hostel system, it must first be mentioned that residence in a probation hostel takes place as one of the terms of a probation order; the order may last for as long as 3 years but hostel residence is limited to 12 months from the date of the order. The consent of the resident must be obtained, a provision which applies to any measure in connection with probation for those over 14 years of age.

Something of the administrative arrangements has already been outlined. Ownership of hostels is vested in management committees, but financial assistance in purchasing property is given by the central government, subject to provisions which make it impossible for the committee to sell it for private gain, and which, in the event of closure, ensures the return of the monetary outlay to the government. The detailed administration is governed by Rules made under the Act of 1948, which cover such diverse matters as the appointment of the Management Committee and its duties, restrictions on those who may be admitted under a probation order (for example, no severe epileptics or mental defectives), appointment and duties of staff, and general care and welfare of residents, down to such matters as adequate pocket money and daily fresh air! Periodic inspections are carried out by officials from the Probation and After Care, and the Children's Departments of the Home Office.

From the point of view of the resident, these provisions are matters he (or she) will take for granted. The two important figures in his life are the warden and the liaison probation officer. The former is responsible for the running of the hostel; the latter is appointed to exercise supervision under the probation order. The balance of power between the two may vary from place to place and from time to time, depending upon such factors as the relative experience and strength of personality of each.

The regime is an ordered one. It follows its regular weekly pattern for the most part, which is predictable and simple; the boy or girl rises at a certain time, goes out to employment, returns in the evening, and thereafter follows a regular programme of activities which will vary according to the evening of the week. This regularity and predictability is itself a new experience for many residents.

There are about 35 hostels in Britain at the present time, a third of which are for girls. They usually are situated in or near large centres of population, where employment and social services are readily available, and where travelling difficulties and expense are minimal. A hostel will accommodate around 20 residents. Usually buildings are older-type large houses, few if any being purpose-built, though some have added extensions since purchase.

A normal hostel for lads will be staffed by a warden and matron who are usually a married couple. There will be an assistant warden, usually a single man, and perhaps one or two other members of staff. The pay and conditions of service of hostel staff are poor in the extreme. The maximum salary payable to a warden is about £1100 (about $3,080) compared to about £1500 (about $4,200) for a probation officer. Very few wardens are satisfied with their pay, and most feel that a new structure is necessary, related either to salaries of probation officers or of staffs of residential schools for offenders. There is even stronger feeling on the question of the salaries of assistants.[2]

Academic qualifications amongst wardens are few and far between. About half are completely untrained; some have child care or youth leadership qualifications. As there is no recognized training course at present for wardens of hostels as such, it is hardly surprising that a school of thought amongst them exists which doubts the value of training and extols the virtues of experience. Most, however, see the advantages of some kind of qualification. Opinions are divided as to the best kind of training. The possibilities of child care, probation, and even legal training are debated, with, on the women's side, some emphasis upon nursing.

The difficulties encountered by an inadequately paid and probably unqualified warden may clearly be considerable. There is another factor which is equally unhelpful, namely, the position of assistant staff. One of the most frequently heard complaints relates to the lack of satisfactory accommodation for assistants, which means, in effect, that it is usually difficult, if not impossible, to appoint a second married couple. Separate staff accommodation away from the hostel is even rarer, so that a burden which may prove intolerable is thrown upon the warden and matron (assuming they are husband and wife) since they can seldom get way from the establishment and much of their "leisure" time is spent on the premises. Inadequate accommodation for staff also means that the turnover of assistants is rapid, making consistency in outlook and relationship with the residents extremely difficult for the warden to maintain.

Despite these disadvantages, a number of wardens remain in post over long periods, so that the situation must offer to some people adequate incentives. The work certainly cannot be said to lack interest. As with other residential work, there are certain perquisites which make unattractive salaries a little better than they look; accommodation is often more spacious than an ordinary family house would afford; and perhaps there are not so many occupations of comparable responsibility and interest open to those who may be unqualified in any technical sense.

2. This and other information which follows derives from a survey made privately by the writer earlier this year.

How Probationers Are Selected for Hostel Treatment

How are probationers selected for a period of residence? As with most matters connected with hostels, there is no universal answer. A position must first arise in which a court feels that such a period away from home is desirable. This usually presupposes a suggestion to that effect by a probation officer which, in turn, should presuppose an adequate discussion with the probationer in order to explain what it is which is intended, and to ensure in advance that he is in agreement with the proposal. From this point, however, a wide variety of proceedings is possible.

The commonest method is for the probation officer who wishes to send a probationer to get in touch with the warden, establish that a vacancy exists, send details of the probationer to the warden who agrees that if the court concerned desires, he will accept the probationer.

Several aspects of this procedure deserve comment. One is that it would seem that probation officers much more often contact the warden in the first instance, than their opposite number in the person of the liaison probation officer (who will assume supervision in the event of the probationer residing at the hostel). This could be because the warden's name appears in the probation directory, while the liaison probation officer does not in that capacity, but only as one of a number of officers working in the area; except by telephoning the office, he is therefore unidentifiable.

A more curious factor is that by no means all liaison officers are invited by the warden to participate in the selection process. This means, assuming that a period of residence is seen as an aspect of the casework help offered by all concerned to the probationer, that his suitability for this particular kind of help is assessed by the only person in the situation who is not (in all probability) a trained caseworker.

A third surprising factor is that few probationers are interviewed by the warden before acceptance and usually the whole process carries through on the basis of paper—information about the probationer for the warden and information about the hostel for the probationer and probation officer, plus the telephone. Nor are the distances in Britain always so great as to make personal interviewing impossible.

Under the circumstances which normally govern selection, the position of the sending probation officer assumes great importance. For the most part, they are felt by wardens to give a fairly good picture of the prospective resident, but there would seem to be a sizable minority of whom this cannot be said. This could be because the probation officer concerned is not well informed about hostels and what they can offer, or because he is so concerned to get the probationer away that a too favourable picture of him may be painted. This may especially occur where the probation officer sees the hostel as a last-ditch alternative to a more severe form of treatment. The rough-and-ready nature of the whole process is also reflected in the views of wardens, some of whom it would appear, select half-heartedly, aware of their own inadequacy and that of the system under which they work, preferring to take what comes and rely upon their own know-how in welding together a heterogeneous group; aware, also, that good prognosis or bad often is defied by the unpredictability of the reactions of the probationer to this new situation and the new people in his life.

Many wardens and liaison probation officers are aware that selection could be carried out more efficiently. Classification is sometimes suggested, with hostels required to take probationers of a certain type or with a certain kind of problem. More extensive knowledge by courts about hostels would be useful. Here the new compulsory training for British magistrates, most of whom are unpaid laymen, will help in due course. Personal contact with prospective residents is seen by some as important. By liaison officers, it is not surprising to find that greater participation by them in selection is seen as an important part of the total answer.

Haphazard as the selection process undoubtedly is, it is predictable that the objectives in the minds of wardens and liaison officers will be found to vary widely. Since statutory provisions require hostels to take any probationer who is not deemed unsuitable by the Rules, it is at first sight surprising that there is any choice. This comes about from a situation in which there are fewer vacancies than candidates, so that those responsible for selection are able to influence to a greater extent than the statutory position would imply the kind of probationer who is accepted. Broadly, probationers with institutional experience are not popular, nor are those with severe emotional disturbance symptoms; but beyond such wide generalizations it is impossible to distinguish.

Wardens View Their Roles Differently

Selection is also likely to be carried out in terms of the objectives in the mind of the warden, not so much related to the individual candidate as to his own ideas about his establishment, and how he sees his own role. This factor, though largely unrecognized, is undoubtedly important. It would be possible, for instance, for a warden to feel that he and his hostel exist primarily for the purpose of providing the advantages of a good home during a period in which a probationer will be helped through the casework of the liaison probation officer. Or he might feel that the help given would normally be via the probation officer in the home area. It is arguable that in most cases defective relationships and attitudes and standards within the family have contributed to the need for the probationer to live away for a while, and that it therefore would be a considerable waste of time and effort for the probationer, after this period, to be returned to a home which would instantly present him with all the old problems. Or he might see his hostel as a place, and himself as a person, from which and from whom the probationer could receive such help and guidance as would enable him to return to an unmodified home situation, but better equipped to deal with it, and live within it without the need for further antisocial behaviour.

This last alternative could be seen either in very simple terms, whereby basic social training and a period of stable relationships would be felt to provide an adequate measure of help, even if over a very short period of time; or in more sophisticated terms, in which the hostel would be seen as a therapeutic community in which intensive treatment would be carried out as far as the short period allowed.

There is no doubt that in Britain most hostel wardens see their work in terms of the penultimate suggestion above. Some information is given below to indicate the elements in the training which hostels provide, from which it will be clear that the 1948 idea of the benefits of the good home still holds sway; there is limited awareness of the limitations imposed by time, and a considerable degree of optimism as to the effectiveness of the unavoidably superficial means of help provided by untrained personnel over a very short period. What may be a more serious problem is that wardens as a whole place little emphasis upon the value of casework, either as carried out by the liaison probation officer with whom nominally they work in close cooperation, or by the probation officer in the home area who has been responsible for initiating the proceedings which have brought the probationer to the hostel.

An interesting divergence of views and emphasis appears between men and women wardens. The latter would seem to be less sanguine about the effects of the hostel regime itself, and to rely far more upon, and presumably hold a higher opinion of, the casework of their probation officer colleagues. It is also clear that they see work in the home area during the period of residence as of considerable significance.

Training Program at Hostels

The statutory Rules provide that a scheme of training shall be submitted to and approved by the Secretary of State, but no guidance in matters of detail is given. Hostels, in fact, provide much the same kind of training wherever they are situated, and this falls roughly under four headings: Social training in matters such as personal cleanliness, punctuality, courtesy, cooperation with others; work training in the sense of regular attendance at and application to employment; leisure-time training, in which encouragement is given to develop hobbies and play games; and further formal education either to make up for deficiencies in basic education or to pursue an area of interest to a more advanced stage.

Theoretically, it would have been possible for hostels to offer training at two levels: That required by the Rules, and also some additional form of experience. This has occurred in a few hostels, but not in many. Experiments have taken place in group work, for instance, the hostel as a whole or in part being geared to this approach. Incentive schemes also have been tried with the idea of encouraging initiative and effort on the part of the probationer. Variations in the structure of the regime have been explored; normally the hostel group is an ever-changing one, as probationers leave and others take their place, but it is of course possible to gear residence to a set period within which certain objectives will be borne in mind, and at the end of which all the probationers will leave, their places being taken by another group who will have been selected during the period of residence of their predecessors.

Role of the Liaison Probation Officer

Whatever training is organized and carried out within the hostel itself is, of course, only part of the total process through which the probationer passes while he lives in the hostel. The other part, less apparent but no less important, is the casework carried out on an individual basis by the liaison probation officer. His position within the hostel framework is curiously indeterminate but nevertheless significant.

Technically he exists to maintain probation supervision while the probationer resides at the hostel. Perusal of the Rules might suggest that his contact with the hostel is intended only to be tenuous. He is not ex officio a member of the hostel Managing Committee. His rights extend only as far as being notified in cases of absconding or where the Committee intends to terminate a probationer's period of residence, being provided with a private place in which to interview a probationer, and with a written report from the warden on the progress of a resident upon request.

Through the years, liaison probation officers have interpreted their duties in various ways, but mostly in a more positive fashion than the Rules suggest. It is possible that the very intangibility of their function has compelled them to develop their function empirically to a point where the outcome of much unrelated experience could now usefully be drawn together. By and large it seems likely that they have operated in several identifiable ways. Firstly, they have played an often vital role in the life of the hostel as a whole. Some have been members of the Managing Committee. Others have found themselves providing a certain continuity, especially if wardens did not stay for more than a few years. Even where the liaison officers themselves changed based as they were upon the probation service with its relatively clearly defined outlook, continuity could still be provided to some extent. It was also open to them to play a major part in the day-to-day affairs of the hostel, partly as they chose, partly according to the wishes of the warden, and the extent to which he was an acceptable colleague. But where liaison officers interviewed their probationers at the hostel rather than in their offices, and where they cared to drop in for casual contacts, obviously they could assume a central role.

Another and less apparent function has involved interpreting "liaison" as broadly as possible. While a liaison officer might or might not be involved in the selection of residents, according to the wishes of the warden, it was always important that as soon as possible, he liaised with the probation officer in the resident's home area who was responsible for sending him, both with a view to supplementing the information provided by the warden and also, and perhaps more importantly, discovering all he could about the resident's background, problems, and proposed future. Information would, of course, come his way in the shape of paper, but it would be essential to supplement this by as much personal contact with his colleague as possible. On the assumption that it was to this colleague's further supervision that the probationer would return, it would also be essential to ascertain the probationer's feelings towards this officer—which might well be ambivalent or hostile—and deal with these, a more difficult task if seen only through the probationer's eyes.

Home area contacts were also imperative from another point of view, that of keeping abreast with the problems which had contributed to the need for a hostel placement, how they were developing or being dealt with by the home probation officer, and above all, how they were affecting the probationer during his period of residence at the hostel. Finally, they were central because the whole period of hostel residence was so short that almost from the beginning, plans had to be made for the resident's return. These could not realistically be made at short notice, say a few weeks before the end of the residence period.

Most difficult of all to assess is the contribution made by the supervision carried out by the liaison officer. Within a normal probation period of say 2 or 3 years, no probation officer would welcome passing over a probationer to a colleague for the best part of a year and then receiving him back. The continuity of relationship would be broken, a conflict of loyalties could be anticipated; this would also apply to a probation officer required to accept a probationer for a short period and pass him back.

Add to the complexities of this basic situation further ones appertaining to the hostel, where the sending probation officer's motives in suggesting a period away from home have to be explained to and accepted by the probationer, where the group situation has to be encountered and accepted, where there is a duality of supervision from two people, warden and liaison probation officer, whose outlook and attitudes may appear to the probationer widely different, and the task of the liaison officer is seen as an unenviable one.

In reality the position is less complex than might be supposed. Wardens and liaison officers often appear to work well together, even though the partnership may sometimes be an uneasy one. Most liaison officers would appear to see the work of the hostel in much the same terms as the warden. This is not surprising if it is appreciated that some element of self-selection must take place within the general process whereby one or two out of a larger number of probation officers are chosen for this particular work. It is arguable that those who see their work in fairly straightforward terms, and who will not be disturbed by the problems of the short term provided and the need to work closely with somebody who is not a caseworker, are more likely to come forward than others.

Role of the Sending Probation Officer

More problematic is the position of the sending probation officer. Comment was made earlier to the effect that few wardens appear to attribute much importance to one possible role for their hostel, that of providing a place where a probationer can live while the home area probation officer is dealing with the familial problems. There is also a good deal of evidence to suggest that wardens, and to a lesser extent liaison probation officers, have no great opinion of the ability of their colleagues to select the right probationers for hostel treatment, and that this may be suggested with a view to providing a breathing space for home and probation officer in some instances, rather than with any more scientific objective in view. The sources of such feeling are difficult to determine. It could be that wardens, finding themselves saddled with some difficult probationers, conclude that the home probation officer is not likely to carry out effective work with the home. Or it could be that experience has shown that this is sometimes the case, and general conclusions have been drawn from particular instances. Research is needed into the motives and activities of probation officers who send probationers to hostels, short of which, as with so much else in this sphere, uncertainty must continue.

It is, of course, open to an individual probation officer to establish that he has well conceived ideas as to hostel treatment, and a strong desire to make the best use of it for the benefit of a probationer. Some such officers seem to find this easier to establish if they work repeatedly with certain hostels. The elements in good work may comprise the following: Helping the prospective resident and his parents to share in the decision to seek a hostel placement; effective cooperation with the warden and liaison probation officer to ensure that both will in their different ways meet the probationer's particular needs; continuing to work with the home in the probationer's absence with a view to ameliorating the residual problems; keeping in close touch with the hostel end while the probationer is away from home, and as part of this, planning for his return; making use of the period away in his subsequent casework.

Effectiveness of Hostel Treatment

In view of the foregoing, it is perhaps not surprising that no systematic attempt is made on a national basis to assess the effectiveness of hostel treatment. How such assessment could validly be made is not easy to visualise under the present arrangements. Most hostels, though not all, try to satisfy themselves that they are serving a useful purpose. Some follow up their ex-residents by enquiries of the supervising probation officers. Of those who do, some appear to seek evidence of acceptable behaviour in terms of personal relationships, other in terms of non-conflict with the law over a period. The period may vary from a few months to several years. All hostels have in addition certain even less scientific yardsticks which nevertheless may well be meaningful. Note is taken of the number of probation officers who make repeated requests for placements, and of the number of ex-residents who keep in touch.

The applicability of the British experience to other countries must from one point of view appear limited. So much must hinge on the system of probation evolved, what kind and severity of problems it exists to deal with, indeed upon the place within a penal system of probation as a whole. The relevance is also clear of the means adopted to give personal help to delinquents, which itself must be seen as part of whatever approach is accepted by a society towards its needy members as a whole. An important aspect of this will be the availability of social casework and psychotherapeutic services.

Even with these reservations, however, some food for thought may be provided by a system such as the British, which was never conceived as a whole but "just growed." Are hostels to be provided for all age groups? If so, the British system would need considerable modification in some aspects, notably the paternalistic and authoritarian, before it could be applied to adults.

What is the existing legal framework within which a hostel must operate, if seen in the light of British experience? It would, of course, be possible to use hostels, residence in which was voluntary. Is it desirable to segregate delinquents in special hostels? What kind of delinquents is it possible to help via this means, and how long a period is considered necessary if the objectives in mind are to be attained? What are the objectives? These identified, how are hostels staffed? What staff-resident ratio is in mind? With what kind of training are hostel staffs to be equipped, and at what rate are they to be paid? Underlying these last questions, from what group in the community is it desired to draw staff? What relationship is to be established between hostel staff and probation officers? Are they to be one and the same?

British experience may not provide many clear answers but it certainly poses some interesting questions. Perhaps the most important of these relates to potential. The degree of success enjoyed by the British system so far has depended massively upon the sterling personal qualities of those involved, especially wardens. If such qualities could be backed by appropriate training and the use of far greater material and technical resources, there is no reason to doubt that much more might be achieved.

COMMUNITY–BASED CORRECTIONAL PROGRAMS: A SURVEY AND ANALYSIS*

This article focuses on programs designed to facilitate the transition of adult offenders, male and female, from prison back into the community via community-based correctional programs. An attempt was made (1) to trace the rate of growth and development of community-based programs, (2) to identify the sources

* Bertram S. Griggs and Gary R. Mc-Cune, *Federal Probation*, June 1972. Reprinted with permission.

of funding, (3) to ascertain the need, if any, for legislation, (4) to determine the various types of programs, (5) to identify the populations serviced, and (6) to review and comment on problem areas.

The basic method of gathering information was by questionnaire and telephone calls to state correctional agencies and state planning agencies (LEAA). Additional information was secured from the International Association of Halfway Houses and the U.S. Bureau of Prisons. Also, on site visits were made to community-based programs operated by (1) a private agency that contracted for federal prisoners, (2) state programs operated on the grounds of institutions, and (3) state programs operated in the community without the usual prison safeguards.

Limitations of the Study

There are community treatment programs for adults and juveniles, for males and females, for felons and misdemeanants, for parolees, probationers, and offenders committed to these centers as an alternative to incarceration. The variety of populations served made it necessary to narrow the scope of this study to adult felons, male and female, who are programmed in the community *prior* to release or parole.

Initially, the focus was to be confined to a survey and analysis of just those persons residing in community-based facilities. It soon became apparent that the focus would have to be expanded to include those housed in local jails and institutions, because they are being programmed in the community for reasons identical to our original target group and are considered by many as being involved in community-based programs despite their residence.

It appears that sometimes these programs are operated out of jails and state correctional facilities primarily for legal considerations and, more often than not, for budgetary considerations. Obviously, programs in local jails or correctional institutions also allow for participation by a larger number of eligible inmates. It is anticipated that as funds become available there will be a shift from jails and prisons to "genuine" community facilities, *i. e.*, hotels, apartments, large boarding homes, etc.

Background of the Study

It is estimated that by 1975 the average daily population in corrections will be 1.8 million.[1] Approximately 98 percent of that

1. *The Challenge of Crime in A Free Society*, 1967, p. 160.

population will eventually be released. Most of the offenders will return to the same community, even the same homes. Many will be under some kind of supervision. Will society be ready and willing to accept them? Perhaps even more important, will they, by virtue of their institutional experience, be ready to take their place in society?

It is difficult under our present system to prepare a person confined in prison for months, or years, to make the transition from prison back to the community. Fear, lack of information, distrust, and a variety of other forces combine to cause the releasee to approach the experience with trepidation and a sense of helplessness.

The President's Crime Commission focused on one aspect of the problem when it stated: "Institutions tend to isolate offenders from society, both physically and psychologically, cutting them off from schools, jobs, families, and other supportive influences and increasing the probability that the label of criminal will be indelibly impressed upon them. The goal in reintegration is likely to be furthered much more readily by working with the offender in the community than by incarceration." [2]

The Report further states: "with two-thirds of the total corrections caseload under probation or parole supervision, the central question is no longer whether to handle offenders in the community but how to do so safely and successfully." [3]

Over the years there have been sporadic attempts, mostly by religious and other humanitarian groups, to operate small community and prison institution programs for offenders. These pioneering programs, for the most part met only the bare necessities and did not allow for enough active offender participation in organizing, planning, and day-to-day operations. Borrowing from the experiences of these small, private agencies, government agencies have developed a rationale for residential centers, i. e., community treatment programs. The concept was clearly delineated by the Task Force on Corrections of the President's Crime Commission:

> The general underlying premise for the new directions
> in corrections is that crime and delinquency are symp-
> toms of failure and disorganization of the community
> as well as the individual offenders. In particular, these
> failures are seen as depriving offenders of contact with

2. Ibid., p. 165.   3. Ibid.

institutions (of society) that are basically responsible for assuring the development of law-abiding conduct . . .

The task of corrections therefore included building or rebuilding solid ties between the offender and the community, integrating or reintegrating the offender into community life—restoring family ties, obtaining employment and education, securing in a larger sense a place for the offender in the routine functioning of society . . . . This requires not only efforts directed toward changing the individual offender, which has been almost the exclusive focus of rehabilitation, but also mobilization and change of the community and its institutions.

Maximum effort, therefore, will be required of departments of corrections to influence those conditions that will assist the offender to build a solid bridge back to the community. That bridge must enable offenders to participate in work, education, training and other aspects of community life.

Some efforts have been made by a number of states to develop ways to reestablish offenders in the community through the use of community treatment programs. Many such programs focus on offenders after they have been paroled. This approach is more or less traditional, making use of postrelease "halfway houses" operated by state and private agencies.

We are concerned in this article with a more modern trend, i. e., the programming of offenders in the community *prior* to release or parole. Without attempting to evaluate the effectiveness of these programs, we have attempted to determine their extent, rate of growth and the trends that may be developing, and the present status of prerelease community-based correctional programs.

Results of Study

The responses from the state departments of corrections were excellent—46 out of 51, or 90 percent, completed and returned the questionnaire.[4] Of the 46 responses, 28 departments of corrections (59 percent) have community treatment programs, al-

---

4. The 50 states plus the District of Columbia. The Federal Bureau of Prisons is treated separately, see pages 10 and 11.

though as already noted, some of them are operated out of local jails and state institutions.[5]

Presently there are five departments of corrections without programs, but with definite plans to establish programs within the next 2 years.[6] There are 13 departments of corrections without programs and are not presently planning any.[7]

Approximately 4,143 inmates were participating in treatment programs (all categories), ranging from a high of 437 in one state to a low of 10.[8] It is significant that the high of 437 represents less than 2 percent of that state's total prison population.

STATES WITH COMMUNITY TREATMENT PROGRAMS FOR ADULT FELONS, MALE AND FEMALE, PRIOR TO RELEASE ON PAROLE

State	Residents			Source of Referrals				Source of Funding				Type of Facility		
	Capac-ity	M.	F.	State insti-tution	Fed-eral prisons	Courts	Other	State (LEAA)	State (other)	Fed-eral	Pri-vate	Hotel or Apt.	Jail	State (insti-tution)
Total	4,143	27	19	27	5	6	1	13	25	3	4	20	9	16
Calif.	437	X	X	X					X			X	X	X
Colo.	60	X		X				X	X					X
Conn.	112	X		X		X			X	X			X	
Fla.	150	X	X	X	X			X	X			X	X	
Ga.	138	X	X	X				X				X	X	
Hawaii	145	X		X					X			X		X
Ill.	60	X	X	X					X			X		X
Ind.	214	X	X	X				X	X		X	X		X
La.	150	X	X	X				X	X		X	X	X	X
Me.	10		X	X					X			X		
Md.	189	X	X	X				X	X	X		X		
Mass.	72	X	X	X				X	X					X
Mich.	125	X	X	X				X	X			X		X
Minn.	70	X	X	X		X		X	X		X	X	X	
Neb.	25	X		X					X			X		
N.J.	30	X	X	X					X			X		
N.C.	151	X	X	X					X			X		X
Okla.	48	X		X					X			X		
Oreg.	183	X	X	X	X	X		X	X			X	X	X
R.I.	50	X		X					X					X
S.C.	311	X		X	X	X		X	X			X		
Tenn.	50	X	X	X				X	X			X		X
Texas	350	X		X				X	X					X
Vt.	298	X	X	X	X	X			X					X
Va.	105	X	X	X					X				X	X
Wash.	25	X		X					X		X	X		
Wis.	250	X	X	X					X				X	X
D.C.	335	X	X		X	X	X		X			X		

5. See table on page 9.

6. Arizona, Delaware, Missouri, New Hampshire, West Virginia.

7. Alabama, Arkansas, Idaho, Iowa, Kansas, Kentucky, Mississippi, Nevada, New York, North Dakota, Ohio, South Dakota, Wyoming.

8. The average length of participation is approximately 90 days. This means a turnover of four times per year or a potential capacity of 16,572 cases. Should the capacity be increased by 70 percent within 2 years, as anticipated, the annual capacity would be over 28,000 cases.

Nine of the state programs are limited to males and 18 have programs serving both sexes, including several that are coeducational to the extent that both men and women are housed in the same building. One state program serves females only. All of the states reporting programs service their own clients, and four of the 28 states also handled federal inmates.[9]

The major source of funds came from state budgets, but there were other sources—especially LEAA. Thirteen of the 28 states used state funds exclusively, one was financed totally by Federal funds, and the balance were combinations of state, Federal, and private funds.[10]

Types of Facilities

The study revealed that many types and combinations of physical facilities were used by states in operating their community treatment programs.[11] In those states which have a combination of community-based and institutional or jail-based community programs, the work-study release programs usually preceded the state's involvement in community-based operations. However, in regard to strictly community-based programs (operated out of noncorrectional facilities in the community), only 8 states reported having programs of this type without also operating work-study release out of jails and correctional institutions.

In most states which submitted copies of their work release laws, the legislation was similar and usually required that the

9. The authors are aware of programs in some states, operated primarily by private agencies, which serve federal offenders on a contractual basis, but which do not serve state prisoners in the same status. Most of these programs have a combination of federal prisoners who participate prior to release and state offenders who participate while on parole, or on a postrelease basis. Programs of this nature were not included in the survey data but are covered in the section on federal programs.

10. Eight used combinations of state and state LEAA funds; three used combinations of state, state LEAA, and private funds; one each used state and federal

funds (e. g., Model Cities, Department of Labor, HEW), state and private funds, and state, state LEAA, and Federal funds.

11. Eight states used noncorrectional facilities only, such as hotels, YMCA's, apartments, etc. Five used state correctional institutions only. One used county jails only. Two used a combination of state correctional institutions and county jails. Six used a combination of state correctional institutions and noncorrectional facilities. Three used county jails and noncorrectional facilities. And three used a combination of county jails, state correctional institutions, and noncorrectional facilities.

inmate be "returned to a penal or correctional institution at night." In those instances, new legislation would be required to permit participation in community programs where the prisoners are housed in noncorrectional facilities. In those states which have only institution or jail-based work-study release, practically all indicated intentions to expand existing programs in the same facilities, as well as plans to establish new community treatment programs.

Program Emphasis

Without exception, each of the 28 correction departments with community treatment programs featured work release or work furlough. Of these 28, 12 also included "school release"—or study release. Most of these programs included one or more of the following: individual and group counseling, prerelease orientation, family counseling, accelerated release for those participating in the program, community involvement and use of volunteers, and maximum use of all community resources. There are also some special programs in cooperation with public and private agencies that provide assistance to individuals with psychiatric, narcotic, and related health and emotional problems.

We were struck by the similarity rather than the difference in the programs described in the information we received. Many departments believe that allowing inmates serving time in prison to go into the community is a unique and giant step in the right direction. Based on the past history of corrections, it is difficult to argue with that. Five or 10 years from now, hopefully that feeling will have changed significantly to one that sees programming in the community as being "routine" and imprisonment, in the traditional sense, the exception.

Problem Areas

Because community treatment programs for inmates still serving sentences are relatively new, it seemed appropriate to provide an opportunity for respondents to our survey to discuss "problem areas." The most sensitive issue for all of the programs was the reaction of the community. Other comments related to lack of funding and the need for statutory and programmatic changes. Some typical comments are the following:

> We have encountered problems in preparing the community to accept a house with offenders. It is our ex-

perience that a great deal of public relations is necessary before moving into a neighborhood and that if possible the citizens should become part of the policy making of the house.

Correctional centers have both detention and sentenced population. Most problems are related to the inability to segregate the two classes. This requires too high a degree of security for prerelease prisoners. (Our only problem.)

. . . begin actively involving members of the community 1 to 2 years prior to the planned opening of the center . . .

The original legislation is ambiguous and omitted some important items.

Need for a weekend furlough program.

We would anticipate community reaction if we were attempting to establish a house in the community; we have maintained fairly rigid house rules and our experience has been this is preferable to more permissive procedures; we have found a large untreated alcohol problem which surfaces when men are placed in the program and for which a treatment program is needed.

. . . Negative community attitudes to be overcome and the appointment of a blue ribbon committee to study the needs and sites for these problems.

Legislation

Twenty-one of the 28 departments making use of community treatment programs stated that special legislation had been required before they could permit inmates to participate in such programs. Four states indicated that no additional legislation was necessary, and three did not respond to that specific question.

Most of the new laws stated in essence that the directors of corrections may utilize facilities located off the regular institution grounds as community correctional facilities and the director may enter into agreements with city or county jails and transfer inmates to such facilities for purposes of work release or work furlough. A small number of states required only limited modifications of their statutes. In the District of Columbia, Congress had to enact laws authorizing the establishment of community correctional center programs.

The Federal Program

For the purposes of this survey, the community treatment programs operated by the Federal Bureau of Prisons and those programs which serve Federal prisoners on a contract basis are treated separately and summarized in this section. Although the Bureau of Prisons operates work release programs out of most of their institutions, this summary focused only on their community treatment centers and those contract community-based programs where Federal prisoners are sent prior to release. At the present time the Bureau of Prisons operates a total of 14 community treatment centers (CTC) programs. The first CTC was established in Chicago in 1961. The combined capacity of these programs is approximately 350, out of an inmate population of approximately 21,500.[12] A majority of the centers are operated out of hotels or apartment facilities. Over half of them serve both male and female offenders. Although most of these facilities are funded exclusively by the Bureau of Prisons, one is partially funded by both state and the Vocational Rehabilitation Administration and one receives some private funding.

Until recently, the federally operated community treatment centers served prisoners scheduled for release from Federal, and, in some cases, state institutions. However, the passage of Public Law 91–492 in October 1970 now makes it possible for Federal courts to direct a probationer to reside or participate in the program of a CTC as a condition of probation when such facilities are available. Similarly, the U.S. Board of Parole may require a parolee or mandatory releasee to reside or participate in the program of a CTC as a condition of parole or mandatory release.

This "half-way-in" approach to dealing with offenders as an alternative to imprisonment is a major step forward, and one which will necessitate the development of additional facilities. In the Federal program at this time, the actual, as well as projected, populations of the CTC's will consist of approximately 10 percent probationers and parolees and 90 percent inmates scheduled for release.[13] The Bureau of Prisons has plans to expand existing programs by developing more satellite units in the larger metropolitan areas, as well as establishing new centers in areas

12. As of March 31, 1972.

13. From February 1971 to February 1972, 134, or 9.5 percent, of 1500 CTC residents were probationers or parolees.

where they can be justified in terms of referrals from institutions, courts, and the parole board.

The CTC program has undergone substantial expansion, especially during the past 4 years. Possibly even more significant has been the increase in the number of contracts initiated with state, local, and private agencies which provide similar programs to Federal prisoners in areas where the concentration of releasees has been too small to justify a Federal facility. The Bureau currently has contracts with 35 such programs (representing 60 facilities) located in 15 states and the District of Columbia. A significant number of these programs are at least partially funded by private agencies and organizations. A few of them are operated in states such as Massachusetts, where laws now preclude participation of state offenders, except after release or while on parole. One would hope that these programs would serve to demonstrate the value of such a resource to states which are not now using their program for prerelease purposes. The Bureau of Prisons expects to continue expanding its contract programs as more resources become available.

A review of the laws and program policies of those states with community-based programs (including work release) indicates that many were modeled after the Federal program. Although the Bureau of Prisons may not have pioneered in community treatment programs, it has been an important transmitter of this innovation to the state and local systems.

Growth and Trends

The period of greatest growth in community treatment programs was during 1968 and 1969, when six states implemented programs during each of those years.[14] The slower growth in 1970 may be explained by the mild recession the Nation experienced. Also, it appears that there has been a shift in emphasis, as reflected in some recent state plans (LEAA), toward development of community treatment programs as alternatives to any imprisonment. It may well be that the rate of growth in these programs will slow down or level off because of the shift in emphasis to the beginning of the correctional process. It should be pointed out, however, that 21 of the states presently involved in community-based programs have specific plans to expand ex-

---

14. Before 1968, programs had been implemented in two states in 1963, one in 1964, three in 1965, two in 1966, and four in 1967.

isting programs substantially and/or to increase their community-based facilities within the next 2 to 5 years. These increases would account for an additional 64 units or facilities and 2,891 beds or program spaces. This represents an increase of approximately 70 percent over present level. If these plans materialize, the total program capacity would be approximately 7,000.[15] However, considering the total prison population, and the recognized need to increase the efficiency of correctional programs, the number is relatively insignificant.

Where considering the question of introducing community-based treatment programs into correctional systems that are complex and often under critical attack, one must be aware of the many forces operating in the communities that may determine the programs' effectiveness.[16] As we have seen, the most crucial area, based on the experience of those operating such programs, is *community acceptance* of the idea that inmates serving time would not be a serious risk to the community. Even though over 93 percent of the inmates currently confined will eventually be released, the paramount question continues to be how to do so safely and successfully. Community-based treatment programs offer some hope.

Recommendations

Community treatment programs for offenders due to be released from prison are still in a relatively early stage of development. Before any firm conclusions can be drawn regarding their effect on reducing recidivism, or other criteria of success, considerably more research will be required. However, there is no question but that programs of this type do help facilitate the offender's inevitable reentry into the community by: (1) providing some continuity with education and training programs begun in the correctional institutions; (2) assisting the offender in obtaining adequate employment; (3) increasing utilization of community resources; and (4) providing needed support during this difficult initial period of adjustment. On this basis alone, the question is not one of whether a correctional agency should be-

15. See footnote 8.

16. LEAA announced in 1971 a grant of $194,544 for the development of a research plan for evaluating community-based correctional treatment programs and analyzing their cost effectiveness, by the Pacific Northwest Laboratory of the Battelle Memorial Institute, Richland, Washington, *Criminal Justice Newsletter*, Vol. 2, No. 8, April 19, 1971.

come involved in community treatment programs, but rather how and to what extent.

At the conclusion of the survey, it became obvious that there is an evolutionary process in the development of community treatment programs. On a nationwide basis, the stages of this process range from states with "no programs—no plans" to states with a variety of progressive programs. Somewhere in between lie the bulk of states which are operating or have recently initiated work release programs in their correctional and detention facility as well as those states which are operating or planning to establish community-based treatment centers. This evolutionary process could be shortened considerably through a greater exchange of information and experience, as well as more efficient use of funding resources and technical assistance. With this in mind, the following recommendations are offered:

(1) The Federal Bureau of Prisons has considerable experience in both the operation of community-based treatment programs and work-study release which is institution-based. Their expertise and leadership in this area is well established. By virtue of the LEAA Technical Assistance Program, the Bureau of Prisons is able to provide direct assistance, including on site visits, to state correctional agencies. This assistance can include drafting legislation, planning and implementing community treatment programs, and devising methodology for and actually conducting evaluation. It is recommended that the states make use of this excellent resource.

(2) The International Halfway House Association, an affiliate of the American Correctional Association, has as its purpose to "exchange ideas on developing programs and techniques, to provide training programs and organizational assistance to new agencies, and to provide an ongoing program of public information and education. These goals are achieved through issuance of a newsletter, periodic training programs, an annual conference, and other contracts between member agencies." This organization is in an excellent position to serve as a clearinghouse for ideas and information regarding community treatment programs. It is recommended that correctional agencies take advantage of this resource in planning and operating their program.

(3) An increasing number of private agencies and foundations have become involved in operating community-based treatment programs which serve correctional agencies on a contract basis.

Many of these programs are excellent. They offer an alternative to states which are unable to establish their own capabilities in this area for reasons of funding, other priorities, or volume of offenders to be served. It is recommended that states explore the use of privately operated programs and cultivate private agency interest in this area as an alternative or as an adjunct to state-operated programs.

(4) Correctional agencies frequently encounter strong resistance in establishing community residential facilities for offenders. This is especially true of programs for offenders who are still serving sentences. Sometimes this resistance is less when community programs are operated out of local or county jails. However, programs in local jails are not as desirable as those in non-correctional facilities. Since penal and correctional institutions are frequently located in isolated areas, the use of local jails does allow many offenders to be returned to their home community prior to release. It is recommended that states explore the use of local jail facilities as another alternative in establishing community treatment programs.

(5) An additional and important source of funding for correctional programs, including community treatment programs, is the Law Enforcement Assistance Administration (LEAA). From our survey, it would appear that many states have not made use of LEAA funds for prerelease community treatment programs. The reason for this may be the result of other higher correctional priorities. However, it is recommended (1) that LEAA be considered by states in combination with other sources of funding; (2) that LEAA be more active in encouraging the development of plans for community-based programs; and (3) that state planning agencies, in administering LEAA funds, give high priority to community-based programs. In addition, it is recommended that state correctional agencies and state planning agencies (LEAA) develop closer coordination with regard to long-range planning in the area of community treatment programs.

(6) The American Correctional Association in its *Manual of Correctional Standards* has developed a section on standards for community correctional centers. These standards, currently being revised, and upgraded, would serve as an excellent source of information for the operation of community-based programs. It is recommended that states consult this additional source of information.

STANDARDS FOR COMMUNITY–BASED PROGRAMS*

Legislation should be enacted immediately authorizing the chief executive officer of the correctional agency to extend the limits of confinement of a committed offender so the offender can participate in a wide variety of community-based programs. Such legislation should include these provisions:

1.   Authorization for the following programs:

    a.   Foster homes and group homes, primarily for juvenile and youthful offenders.

    b.   Prerelease guidance centers and halfway houses.

    c.   Work-release programs providing that rates of pay and other conditions of employment are similar to those of free employees.

    d.   Community-based vocational training programs, either public or private.

    e.   Participation in academic programs in the community.

    f.   Utilization of community medical, social rehabilitation, vocational rehabilitation, or similar resources.

    g.   Furloughs of short duration to visit relatives and family, contact prospective employers, or for any other reason consistent with the public interest.

2.   Authorization for the development of community-based residential centers either directly or through contract with governmental agencies or private parties, and authorization to assign offenders to such centers while they are participating in community programs.

3.   Authorization to cooperate with and contract for a wide range of community resources.

4.   Specific exemption for participants in community-based work programs from State-use and other laws restricting employment of offenders or sale of "convict-made" goods.

* National Advisory Commission on
Criminal Justice Standards and
Goals, *Report on Corrections*, 1973.

5.   Requirement that the correctional agency promulgate rules and regulations specifying conduct that will result in revocation of community-based privileges and procedures for such revocation.   Such procedures should be governed by the same standards as disciplinary proceedings involving a substantial change in status of the offender.

Commentary

The most dramatic development in corrections in the United States over the last several years is the extension of correctional programing into the community.   Probation and parole have always involved supervision in the community; now institutional programs located in the community provide a gradual diminishment of control leading toward parole and outright release.

Work-release programs that allowed the committed offender to work in the community by day and return to the institution during nonworking hours began in Wisconsin for misdemeanants in 1913 and have spread through many States on the felony level.   Approximately 31 States have some work-release authority.   Federal prisoners were provided work-release opportunities by the Prisoner Rehabilitation Act of 1965.

Offenders participating in employment programs should continue to be protected against economic exploitation.   Most work-release laws require that prisoners receive equal wages and work under employment conditions equal to those of free employees.

The flexibility of community-based programs is limited only by the availability of community resources and the imagination of correctional administrators.   Employment opportunities are only one example.   Legislation should authorize correctional agencies to utilize any community resource with reasonable relation to efforts to reintegrate the offender into the community on release.

Full utilization of community resources may require more from the legislature than authorization.   Present laws which prohibit the sale of "prison-made goods" are, in some States, sufficiently ambiguous as applied to community-based programs as to require clarification.   Some occupations regulated by government may prohibit employment of felons unless pardoned, which would curtail utilization of offenders prior to their outright release.   Although it may be useful to list specific programs in authorizing legislation for clarification, an open-ended provision allowing experimentation should be provided.

Temporary furloughs likewise should be authorized for a wide variety of reasons. Most States have furlough laws allowing incarcerated individuals to attend a funeral of a relative or to visit a sick or dying family member. These programs should be expanded to include family visits, seeking employment and educational placements, and other reasons consistent with the public interest. Since furloughs for family visitation are controversial in some locations, the legislature should specifically authorize such a program.

Contemporary correctional thinking is that offenders will be given gradual responsibility and more freedom until parole or outright release. Thus, each new decrease in control is a test for eventual release. A violation of trust at any one stage of the process inevitably will affect the date when the offender will be paroled. Decisions that revoke community-based privileges thus have a substantial impact on an offender's liberty. Procedural safeguards should be required in revocation of community-based privileges.

PAROLE LEGISLATION

Each State should enact by 1975 legislation (1) authorizing parole for all committed offenders and (2) establishing criteria and procedures for (a) parole eligibility, (b) granting of parole, (c) parole conditions, (d) parole revocation, and (e) length of parole.

In authorizing parole for all committed offenders the legislation should:

1. Not exclude offenders from parole eligibility on account of the particular offense committed.

2. Not exclude offenders from parole eligibility because of number of convictions or past history of parole violations.

3. Authorize parole or aftercare release for adults and juveniles from all correctional institutions.

4. Authorize the parole of an offender at any time unless a minimum sentence is imposed by the court in connection with

an extended term (Standard 5.3), in which event parole may be authorized prior to service of the minimum sentence with the permission of the sentencing court.

In establishing procedures for the granting of parole to both adults and juveniles the legislation should require:

1. Parole decisions by a professional board of parole, independent of the institutional staff. Hearing examiners should be empowered to hear and decide parole cases under policies established by the board.

2. Automatic periodic consideration of parole for each offender.

3. A hearing to determine whether an offender is entitled to parole at which the offender may be represented by counsel and present evidence.

4. Agency assistance to the offender in developing a plan for his parole.

5. A written statement by the board explaining decisions denying parole.

6. Authorization for judicial review of board decisions.

7. Each offender to be released prior to the expiration of his term because of the accumulation of "good time" credits to be released to parole supervision until the expiration of his term.

8. Each offender to be released on parole no later than 90 days prior to the expiration of his maximum term.

In establishing criteria for granting parole the legislation should be patterned after Sec. 305.9 of the Model Penal Code and should:

1. Require parole over continued confinement unless specified conditions exist.

2. Stipulate factors that should be considered by the parole board in arriving at its decision.

3. Direct the parole decision toward factors relating to the individual offender and his chance for successful return to the community.

4. Not require a favorable recommendation by the institutional staff, the court, the police, or the prosecutor before parole may be granted.

In establishing criteria for parole conditions, the legislation should be patterned after Sec. 305.13 of the Model Penal Code and should:

1. Authorize but not require the imposition of specified conditions.

2. Require that any condition imposed in an individual case be reasonably related to the correctional program of the defendant and not unduly restrictive of his liberty or incompatible with his constitutional rights.

3. Direct that conditions be fashioned on the basis of factors relating to the individual offender rather than to the offense committed.

In establishing criteria and procedures for parole revocation, the legislation should provide:

1. A parolee charged with a violation should not be detained unless there is a hearing at which probable cause to believe that the parolee did violate a condition of his parole is shown.

    a. Such a hearing should be held promptly near the locality to which the parolee is paroled.

    b. The hearing should be conducted by an impartial person other than the parole officer.

    c. The parolee should be granted notice of the charges against him, the right to present evidence, the right to confront and cross-examine witnesses against him, and the right to be represented by counsel or to have counsel appointed for him if he is indigent.

2. Parole should not be revoked unless:

    a. There is substantial evidence of a violation of one of the conditions of parole.

    b. The parolee, in advance of a hearing on revocation, is informed of the nature of the violation charged against him and is given the opportunity to examine the State's evidence against him.

    c. The parolee is provided with a hearing on the charge of revocation. Hearing examiners should be empowered to hear and decide parole revocation cases under policies established by the parole board. At the hearing the parolee should be given the opportunity to present evidence on his behalf, to confront and cross-examine witnesses against him, and to be represented by counsel or to have counsel appointed for him if he is indigent.

    d. The board or hearing examiner provides a written statement of findings, the reasons for the decision, and the evidence relied upon.

3.   Time spent under parole supervision until the date of the violation for which parole is revoked should be credited against the sentence imposed by the court.

4.   Judicial review of parole revocation decisions should be available to offenders.

In defining the term for which parole should be granted, the legislation should prohibit the term from extending beyond the maximum prison term imposed on the offender by the sentencing court and should authorize the parole board to discharge the parolee from parole at any time.

Commentary

Historically, parole was the only procedure, short of pardon, to diminish an original sentence to confinement. Parole was one method of controlling excessive sentences. It developed, as did probation, with the rhetoric of leniency rather than as an affirmative tool of corrections.

The widespread adoption of indeterminate sentencing gave boards of parole new functions to serve. The theory was, and still remains, that the judicially imposed sentence was the best estimate of the term of imprisonment necessary to serve the needs of the particular offender or the punitive needs of society. In recognition of the fact that changes in attitude and development might drastically alter the needs of the offender, wide discretion was granted to the parole board to select the most appropriate date for release.

The function of the paroling authority now is undergoing change. With a blurring of the distinctions between institutional confinement and community supervision, many offenders have participated in various community-based programs prior to their release on parole. As the trend toward community-oriented programs continues, the decision to parole, at least under traditional notions of parole, becomes less critical for the offender. As community-based programs ranging from halfway houses to non-supervised work- and education-release programs expand, the role of the parole board will become increasingly one of reviewing institutional decisions that deny certain offenders access to community-based programs. Under present circumstances, the parole board has some direct influence over all confined offenders.

Legislation in many States grants broad discretion to paroling authorities with few statutory criteria to guide them and yet precludes violators convicted of certain offenses from consideration. Likewise, some States, directly or indirectly, prohibit more than one opportunity for parole; i. e., one violation precludes further consideration. Mandatory statutory prohibitions against parole for some offenders are as unwise as mandatory sentencing provisions generally. They can take into account only the offense, never the offender.

With 99 percent of institutionalized offenders returning to the community, the question for legislators and paroling authorities is not whether a person will be released, but when and under what conditions. In practice, the choice is between parole—release with supervision and assistance of the State during the critical stage of reentry into society—or outright release with no such supervision and assistance. Prohibitions against parole of certain offenders tend to be found most often in regard to crimes of violence—committed generally by offenders more in need of parole supervision than offenders committing nonviolent offenses.

In most States, parole eligibility begins when the minimum sentence is served. This report proposes the elimination of all legislatively imposed minimum sentences and the infrequent use of judicial minimums. With the exception of those rare instances where the retributive feelings of the community require a minimum term—the standard proposed for judicial imposition—there is no apparent reason why offenders should not be eligible for parole at any time.

The tradition in most States, either in practice or through legislation, is that either the offender applies for parole or he is recommended for parole by the institutional staff. Neither procedure is consistent with the role parole and the paroling agency should play in the correctional process. Incarceration should be viewed as the last alternative at the time of sentencing and continued incarceration undesirable unless there is no other choice. Thus, confined offenders should be assured that at regular reasonable intervals the paroling authority will consider them for parole.

Studies indicate that the first three months after the release of an institutionalized offender are the most critical in his avoidance of further criminal conduct. When it is clearly understood that toward the end of an offender's term the choice is between outright release without supervision and release on parole, a requirement that every offender spend some time on parole becomes manifest. Several States and the Federal Government now have mandatory conditional release provisions.

Imposition of parole conditions raises the same issues as the imposition of conditions of probation. (See Standard 16.11.) The approach of the Model Penal Code is similar in both instances and should be followed.

Parole revocation has a dramatic effect on the offender; it is similar to his original arrest and detention. His ties to family, friends, and employment are severed. He is again subjected to the emotional strains of accusation and potential sanction. The Supreme Court has recently recognized the impact of parole revocations and has ruled that due process requires certain procedural safeguards. The decision resolved a dispute among many courts as to whether a revocation of parole required any procedural rights. This standard is consistent with that decision.

The Court in Morrissey v. Brewer, 408 U.S. 471 (1972), neither determined that a parolee is entitled to bring his own counsel to the hearing or that the State is obligated to provide counsel for indigents. Other Supreme Court decisions strongly suggest that, when given the opportunity, the Court will rule that the Constitution requires counsel at these hearings. The standard recommends that counsel be provided not only to meet constitutional standards but also to insure sound correctional decisions by protecting the offender from arbitrary or misinformed decisions.

In many States, the time an offender serves on parole is not considered service of sentence. Thus, if an offender is sentenced to a maximum of 5 years and serves 1 year in confinement and 3 on parole before it is revoked, he is still required to serve 4 more years in confinement unless again paroled. In other States, parole time is deemed to be part of the sentence. The latter is the preferable course. With development of community-based programs operated by the institution—participation in which is credited toward the offender's sentence—offenders under very similar circumstances may be treated in disparate ways. Offenders thus may refuse parole. Likewise, parole revocation can have a dramatic effect on lengthening the time that the State exercises control over the offender. Parole, if considered as another option in corrections, should be considered as service of sentence.

An offender should not be subjected to a longer period of State control because he is assigned to a parole program. The Model Penal Code does provide a "parole term" that is above and beyond the maximum term imposed by the court. The major argument for this extension is that the offenders most in need of extended parole supervision are generally those who are not paroled until late in their sentence, whereas the least dangerous and most tractable offender is released early and can serve longer on parole. The "parole term" thus extends the period of State control over those offenders who need it the most.

The answer to this argument is twofold: First, the "parole term" effectively lengthens sentences when most authorities agree American sentences are already too long. Parole revocation within the parole term would result in continued confinement. Thus, an offender actually could be confined for a longer period than his maximum term by agreeing to parole. Second, it has been argued that the Model Penal Code "parole term" will encourage parole authorities to defer release since the length of the term is based on the length of confinement and thus, by holding an offender longer in confinement, the amount of time the parole authority can retain control is lengthened.

Without clear evidence that longer periods of confinement, followed by longer periods of parole supervision, are beneficial, extension of State control beyond the initial maximum term is unwarranted.

———

INMATE INVOLVEMENT IN COMMUNITY PROGRAMS

———

Correctional agencies should begin immediately to develop arrangements and procedures for offenders sentenced to correctional institutions to assume increasing individual responsibility and community contact. A variety of levels of individual choice, supervision, and community contact should be specified in these arrangements, with explicit statements as to how the transitions between levels are to be accomplished. Progress from one level to another should be based on specified behavioral criteria rather than on sentence, time served, or subjective judgments regarding attitudes.

The arrangements and procedures should be incorporated in the classification system to be used at an institution and reflect the following:

1. When an offender is received at a correctional institution, he should meet with the classification unit (committee, team, or the like) to develop a plan for increasing personal responsibility and community contact.

2. At the initial meeting, behavioral objectives should be established, to be accomplished within a specified period. After that time another meeting should be held to make adjustments in the individual's plan which, assuming that the objectives have been met, will provide for transition to a lower level of custody and increasing personal responsibility and community involvement.

3. Similarly, at regular time intervals, each inmate's status should be reviewed, and if no strong reasons exist to the contrary, further favorable adjustments should be made.

4. Allowing for individual differences in time and progress or lack of progress, the inmate should move through a series of levels broadly encompassing movement from (a) initial security involving few outside privileges and minimal contact with community participants in institutional programs to (b) lesser degrees of custody with participation in institutional and community programs involving both citizens and offenders, to (c) partial-release programs under which he would sleep in the institution but have maximum participation in institutional and outside activities involving community residents, to (d) residence in a halfway house or similar noninstitutional residence, to (e) residence in the community at the place of his choice with moderate supervision, and finally to release from correctional supervision.

5. The presumption should be in favor of decreasing levels of supervision and increasing levels of individual responsibility.

6. When an inmate fails to meet behavioral objectives, the team may decide to keep him in the same status for another period or move him back. On the other hand, his behavioral achievements may indicate that he can be moved forward rapidly without having to go through all the successive stages.

7. Throughout the process, the primary emphasis should be on individualization—on behavioral changes based on the individual's interests, abilities, and priorities. Offenders also should be afforded opportunities to give of their talents, time, and efforts to others, including other inmates and community residents.

8. A guiding principle should be the use of positive reinforcement in bringing about behavioral improvements rather than negative reinforcement in the form of punishment.

Commentary

If there is one thing on which the criminal justice world is agreed, it is the difficulty of evaluating "readiness for release." In large part, the difficulty is related to the "either/or" philosophy evident in current practice. Today, some person or group of persons must decide whether an inmate is or is not ready for release. While it is true that mechanisms such as partial release programs, halfway houses, and parole sometimes are used, their use generally is limited to individuals whose release date already has been set.

Given the acknowledged "unnaturalness" of a prison environment, inability to assess release readiness is not surprising. The range for exercise of individual choice and responsibility is limited in today's institutions.

Officials charged with assessing release readiness thus have meager grounds for evaluating an individual's likelihood of responsible behavior in the community. They have tended to be inclined favorably toward offenders who evidence cooperation and a "good attitude." But, given the institutional environment, a "good adjustment" is not necessarily indicative of the behavior to be expected on the outside. The tendency to reward cooperation also may stem more from concern with smooth operations than from belief about its relationship to outside adjustment.

Attempts to assess offenders' attitudes probably are even less successful than assessing behavior. Given the state of knowledge about causation, control of crime, and individual motivations, "evaluative assessments" of psychological states are of questionable usefulness. The tendency has been to rely on an offender's verbalization of contrition, strong desire to change, and agreement with staff values as he perceives them. This is perhaps the ultimate "con game," involving extremely high stakes. If the offender says the right things, he will be released; if not, he will have a period of months to prepare for his next performance. The ritual is made even more distasteful by the "faddism" and inconsistency frequently characteristic of treatment teams and hearing examiners. Thus, an offender may rehearse his part well, only to learn that the script has been changed since his last appearance.

Corrections has failed to utilize fully the theories and experience of other areas of the behavioral sciences—such as child development, education, training, and social work—particularly with reference to behavior modification and positive reinforcement and the importance of the individual's increasing assumption of responsibility and choice as preparation for full independence.

Within a slight range of variation, offenders either are greatly restricted (incarcerated) or have few restrictions (probation and parole) in their opportunity to exercise individual choice. Such a sharp distinction clearly is not in the interests of the individual or the community. Corrections must acknowledge that the only reasonable way to assess an individual's "readiness" for a particular program is to allow him progressively more responsibility and choice under controlled conditions. The either/or approach should be modified greatly.

The offender's goal (release) currently is related chiefly to factors of time, attitude of staff and parole board, sentence, and absence of major disruptive or violent behavior, except for the very indirect and delayed reinforcement of "good time." New motivations for change should be introduced in the form of more immediate rewards.

The Non-Prison: A New Approach to Treating Youthful Offenders provides a good example of recent thought on how to avoid extended periods of incarceration followed by an abrupt transition to community living. The book presents a model for rapid transition of a cohort of offenders and staff through a community correctional center, using a group process in which each individual offender develops a program plan and schedule with the advice and consent of the rest of the group, including both staff and inmates. A series of transitional phases emphasizing progressively more responsibility and choice is used, with continuing but decreasing amounts of supervision, to process a group of offenders through the residential portion in a few months. While this model was designed for youthful offenders meeting certain criteria, the approach has broad applicability.

Implementation of the standards recommended in Chapter 5, Sentencing, would allow incorporation of a series of levels, with varying amounts of supervision and individual responsibility and choice, into all correctional programs, including institutional confinement. In fact, it is at the institutional level that such a change is most strikingly needed.

For example, an individual arriving at a correctional institution would meet with a committee or team to develop an individualized progress plan. The plan would incorporate specific behavioral objectives to be met in a specified period of time, preparatory to transition into a new level with different or additional behavioral objectives.

Such a plan might specify that for a certain period of time, the individual would be assigned medium security status, in which he would follow a regular schedule and participate in an educational and training aptitude and interest program. Depending on the individual's preferences, he also might agree to accept responsibility for part of a certain recreational activity, observing inmate advisory council meetings, or other such activities. It should be stressed that each plan might be different from every other plan, because each should emphasize those activities and responsibilities the individual felt to be important, interesting, or rewarding. A date would be set for the next such team meeting when a new and less controlling plan would be developed, assuming the basic behavioral objectives were not violated.

At the next meeting, the individual would make program choices such as whether to take educational courses, participate in vocational training, join a group therapy session, begin to participate in an arts and crafts program, etc. Again, he would help determine a daily schedule, but this time with more flexibility built in. He would also have the option to begin participating in institutional-community programs in the institution and certain types of such activities in the community.

At the following meeting, assuming no major problems under the existing plan, further changes would be made. The inmate might progress now to attending an adult education course at a nearby high school to which he would be provided transportation. He also might wish to seek a position on the inmate advisory council or to undertake supervision of an evening recreational period involving community and institution residents. In this phase, his allowable participation in cooperative programs would be greater, but he would still be subject to regular supervision.

The next phase might involve full-time attendance at a local school, eligibility for furlough, and continuation of the activities begun in the third phase.

A possible next step would be reassignment to a halfway house or community correctional center, where progression would continue in assuming individual responsibility and choice, until a release to the community with supervision was made, followed by release from all correctional supervision.

The above case is merely illustrative. There would be great variation in the rate and detail of individual plans. In general, however, current rates of progression should be speeded up greatly. There also might be some backward steps when change had been made too quickly and behavior problems resulted. The important point, however, is that a number of transitional phases would be employed instead of the current one or two, greatly separated in time, by which individuals now typically move from confinement status to that of free citizen.

The advantages in terms of protection of community interests are obvious. Many of the random practices of release today would be eliminated, and an offender proved to be responsible would be released. The advantages to the individual involved also would be substantial. It would give him an immediate, realizable goal to work for, and above all, hope and feelings of worthiness as an individual reintegrated into society.

REDISTRIBUTION OF CORRECTIONAL MANPOWER RESOURCES TO COMMUNITY–BASED PROGRAMS

Correctional and other agencies, in implementing the recommendations of Chapters 7 and 11 for reducing the use of major institutions and increasing the use of community resources for correctional purposes, should undertake immediate cooperative studies to determine proper redistribution of manpower from institutional to community-based programs. This plan should include the following:

1. Development of a statewide correctional manpower profile including appropriate data on each worker.

2. Proposals for retraining staff relocated by institutional closures.

3. A process of updating information on program effectiveness and needed role changes for correctional staff working in community-based programs.

4. Methods for formal, official corrections to cooperate effectively with informal and private correctional efforts found increasingly in the community. Both should develop collaboratively rather than competitively.

Commentary

Most correctional resources—dollars, manpower, and attention—have been invested in traditional institutional services outside the mainstream of urban life. As indicated throughout this report, the trend now is away from isolating the offender in large, rural prisons and toward treatment near his home. There are major obstacles to full implementation of this change, however, not the least of which are the tremendous implications for correctional personnel.

As stated earlier, the majority of correctional personnel are now, and have been in the past, employed in institutions. Given the size, physical characteristics, and predominant institutional attitudes toward offenders, most of these staff have been trained and rewarded for a custody and control orientation. In addition, correctional staff have generally had a predominantly rural background and, in many cases, a lifestyle that has been heavily centered around institutional life. Thus, a dual problem is presented in switching to community-based corrections: a change in job function and a change in community of orientation.

Obviously, current staff cannot be dismissed and replaced by new staff. Nor can it be assumed that simply relocating and changing job descriptions will solve the problem. Correctional agencies that have made major shifts from institutional corrections to community corrections have learned this lesson the hard way. When insufficient attention has been given to staffing in effecting these major program changes, problems have resulted. In some cases institutional staff have been notified only days or weeks before the institution in which they had been working was, closed. Naturally, the persons so affected have been angered, and some have become vigorous opponents of such moves. Such opposition may serve to slow or halt further implementation of community corrections. Thus lack of adequate anticipatory planning and retraining for staff may block program change.

Too often advocates of reform have concentrated solely on the political and social change strategies necessary to convince administrators and funders to change their priorities and emphasize community corrections programs. However, by the time agreement is reached on the desirability of moving toward such a change, in one sense it is already too late to begin thinking about the problems that will result from existing staff.

It is of critical importance for correctional administrators to acknowledge the changes in the wind and begin preparing for them immediately. The first step required is to gather an overall picture of current personnel, including data on education, training, and experience. Such a statewide correctional manpower profile can then be used in conjunction with other information as long-range planning is done. Such material can serve as a basis for developing comprehensive plans for retraining staff, both for those already relocated and in anticipation of future manpower requirements.

Much of this training will take the form of introducing correctional personnel to a new role—that of broker, resource manager, change agent, etc.—that will be required in community corrections. If training precedes actual relocation, consideration should be given to using rotating assignments as, for example, moving a group of institutional staff into the community with a cohort of parolees and later returning the staff to another institutional shift. Such a project is now being tried in California. Another possibility would involve utilizing institutional staff in expanded roles, such as carrying the functions of release planning and employment placement assistance from the institution into the community. Thus, personnel may adopt more fluid assignments so that "institutional staff" may have responsibilities that require working in the community on a part-time basis.

Many variations are possible, but it is important that adequate provisions are made for giving those undergoing training an opportunity to utilize and expand their new skills.

Experimenting with new roles for correctional staff can also serve a valuable function in developing effective relationships with private correctional efforts in the community. Administrators should realize that beginning to work with community agencies and representatives should not wait until a complete transition to community corrections is achieved. In order to plan effectively for new manpower needs, it is necessary to work with community agencies to learn what services are presently available, what could be done by community groups, and what the critical roles to be filled by correctional personnel will be.

As new manpower programs and assignments are implemented, evaluation components should be included, at least on a sample basis, that will provide feedback on actual services performed, additional services needed, problems encountered, etc., as a basis for continuing planning and training.

Chapter 3

PROBATION

The basic idea underlying a sentence to probation is very simple. Sentencing is in large part concerned with avoiding future crimes by helping the defendant learn to live productively in the community which he has offended against. Probation proceeds on the theory that the best way to pursue this goal is to orient the criminal sanction toward the community setting in those cases where it is compatible with the other objectives of sentencing. Other things being equal, the odds are that a given defendant will learn how to live successfully in the general community if he is dealt with in that community rather than shipped off to the artificial and atypical environment of an institution of confinement. Banishment from society, in a word, is not the way to integrate someone into society. Yet imprisonment involves just such banishment—albeit for a temporary sojourn in most cases.

This is of course not to say that probation should be used in all cases, or that it will always produce better results. There are many goals of sentencing, some of which in a given case may require the imposition of a sentence to imprisonment even in the face of a conclusion that probation is more likely to assure the public that the particular defendant will not offend again. And there are defendants as to whom forced removal from the environment which may in some part have contributed to their offense may be the best beginning to a constructive and useful life.

By the same token, however, it is to say that probation is a good bit more than the "matter of grace" or "leniency" which characterizes the philosophy of the general public and of many judges and legislatures on the subject. Probation is an affirmative correctional tool, a tool which is used not because it is of maximum benefit to the defendant (though, of course, this is an important side product), but because it is of maximum benefit to the society which is sought to be served by the sentencing of criminals. The automatic response of many in the criminal justice system that imprisonment is the best sentence for crime unless particular reasons exist for "mitigating" the sentence is not a sound starting point in the framing of criminal sanctions. The premise of this report is that quite the opposite ought to be the case—that the automatic response in a sentencing situation ought to be probation, unless particular aggravating factors emerge in the case at hand. At least if such aggravating factors cannot be advanced as the basis for a more repressive sentence, probation offers more hope than a sentence to prison that the defendant will not become part of the depressing cycle which makes the gates of our prisons resemble a revolving door rather than a barrier to crime.

It must of course also be realized that this thesis cannot be practiced in a vacuum. Too often a sentencing judge is faced with the Hobson's choice of a sentence to an overcrowded prison that is almost a guarantee that the defendant will emerge a more dangerous man than when he entered or a sentence to an essentially unsupervised probation that is little more than a release of the defendant without sanction, as well as without incentive to avoid the commission of a new offense. Such a state of affairs represents a failure of the legislative process of the highest order. The criminal justice system has failed in this country for this reason more than any other; not enough attention has been paid to providing adequate correctional choices to those who much operate the system. The thesis of these standards is that an adequate correctional system will place great reliance on appropriately funded and manned probation services. Within such a context, probation can lead to significant improvement in the preventive effects of the criminal law, at much less of a financial burden than the more typical prison sentence. This much has been proven in those jurisdictions where it has had a chance to work. One should not treat lightly an approach to crime control that offers the hope of better results at less cost. This, in a sentence, is the hope of probation.

The American Bar Association Project on Minimum Standards and Goals—*Probation*

THE ORIGINS OF PROBATION: FROM COMMON LAW ROOTS*

Several attempts have been made to trace back the legal origins of probation to medieval and early modern European law. The precedents found in this period of legal history, however, generally relate to the suspension of punishment subject to good behavior rather than to probation as such, that is, a *combination* of the conditional suspension of punishment and the personal supervision of the released offender during a trial period. There can be little doubt that there has not been any continuous process of historical development linking early Continental instances of the use of the conditional suspension of punishment with contemporary probation. Probation as it is known today has been derived from the practical extension of the English common law, and an analysis of the legal origins of probation must therefore be principally concerned with England and America.

In England and in the United States of America probation developed out of various methods for the conditional suspension of punishment. Generally speaking, the court practices in question were inaugurated, or adopted from previously existing practices, as attempts to avoid the mechanical application of the harsh and cruel precepts of a rigorous, repressive criminal law. Among these Anglo-American judicial expedients which have been mentioned as direct precursors of probation, are the so-called benefit of clergy, the judicial reprieve, the release of an offender on his own recognizance, provisional "filing" of a case, and other legal devices for the suspension of either the imposition or the execution of sentence. With a view to a full understanding of the legal origins of probation, it is necessary to review briefly the nature of these practices.

The Benefit of Clergy

The so-called benefit of clergy was a special plea of devious origin by virtue of which certain categories of offenders could, after conviction, but before judgment, claim exemption from, or

---

* Reprinted in part by permission of the United Nations, Department of Social Affairs, *Probation and* *Related Measures*, 1951, pp. 16–26. Footnotes are omitted.

mitigation of, punishment. In practice it was primarily a device to avoid capital punishment. The importance of this plea in the criminal proceedings of the eighteenth and early nineteenth century is beyond any doubt: "according to the common practice in England of working out modern improvements through antiquated forms, this exemption was made the means of modifying the severity of the criminal law." It is, however, extremely doubtful whether this device had any direct influence on the later development of the suspension of sentence or of any other immediate precursor of probation.

The Judicial Reprieve

The judicial reprieve was a temporary suspension by the court of either the imposition or the execution of a sentence. It was used for specific purposes such as to permit a convicted person to apply for a pardon, or under circumstances such as where the judge was not satisfied with the verdict or where the evidence was suspicious. Although this measure involved only a temporary stay of imposition or execution of sentence, it did lead, in some cases, to an abandonment of prosecution. It does not appear, however, that in England this device was ever extended to embrace what is now termed an indefinite suspension of sentence, particularly in cases which presented no peculiar reason, arising out the lack of or limitations on procedure, for withholding execution of sentence. On the other hand, there is, no doubt, more than a modicum of good reason in tracing the later pretensions of American courts to a power of indefinite suspension of sentence back to this early practice of reprieve in the English courts.

The Recognizance

The recognizance is a legal device deeply embedded in English law. It originated as a measure of preventive justice, and as such it consists in obliging those persons, whom there is a probable ground to suspect of future misbehavior, to stipulate with and to give full assurance to the public, that such offense as is apprehended shall not happen. . . . This "assurance to the public" is given by entering into a recognizance or bond (with or without sureties) creating a debt to the State which becomes enforceable, however, only when the specified conditions are not observed. The recognizance is entered into for a specified period of time.

At an early date the use of the principle of the recognizance (or binding-over) was also extended to actual offenders arraigned before the criminal courts. The device came to be used both to ensure the appearance of an offender before the court at a future date when called upon, and as a disposition (or part thereof) in the case of convicted offenders. With the passing of time, the recognizance came to be used almost exclusively with reference to criminal proceedings rather than as a measure of preventive justice. It should be noted, however, that the recognizance, when used in connection with persons arraigned before criminal courts, does not lose its character as a measure of preventive justice but is actually designed to ensure the future lawful behaviour of the offender or, as Blackstone said, "must be understood rather as a caution against the repetition of the offence, than (as) any immediate pain or punishment."

For centuries the courts of England on occasion bound over and released minor offenders on their own recognizance, *with* or *without sureties*. Similarly, instances of this practice can be found in the records of the American colonies. During the first half of the nineteenth century this device was adopted with increasing frequency, particularly in the case of youthful and petty offenders, the imprisonment of whom did not appear to be warranted. The practice seems to have been common in New England (particularly Massachusetts) at the time and was to be found also in other jurisdictions of the United States of America.

The device of binding-over was used extensively and imaginatively by Judge Peter Oxenbridge Thacher during his term of office (1823–1843) in the Municipal Court of Boston, and the practices developed by him were of particular significance in the later development of probation in Massachusetts. The earliest recorded case in this connection is the case of Commonwealth v. Chase (1830). In Judge Thacher's opinion we find in this case a clear statement of the nature of the practice of binding-over as employed by him:

> "The indictment against Jerusha Chase was found at the January term of this court, 1830. She pleaded guilty to the same, and sentence would have been pronounced at that time, but upon the application of her friends, and with the consent of the attorney of the commonwealth, she was permitted, upon her recognizance for her appearance in this court whenever she

should be called for, to go at large. It has sometimes
been practiced in this court, in cases of peculiar interest, and in the hope that the party would avoid the
commission of any offense afterwards, to discharge him
on a recognizance of this description. The effect is,
that no sentence will ever be pronounced against him,
if he shall behave himself well afterwards, and avoid
any further violation of the law. . . ."

In 1836, the State of Massachusetts, as part of a general revision of its statutory law, gave legislative recognition to the
practice of release upon recognizance, *with sureties,* at any stage
of the proceedings, insofar as it applied to petty offenders in
the lower courts. In the report of the commissioners charged
with the revision of the statutory law of the State, the commissioners formulated the theoretical basis of this alteration in the
law relating to the punishment of petty offenders, as follows:

"This alteration consists in the discretionary power
proposed to be given to the courts and magistrates, before whom this class of offenders may be brought, to
discharge them, if they have any friends who will give
satisfactory security for their future good behavior,
for a reasonable time. When such sureties can be obtained, it can hardly fail to operate as powerful check
upon the conduct of the party, who is thus put upon
his good behavior. And if his character and habits are
such that no one will consent to be sponsor for him, it
must forcibly impress on his mind the value of a good
character, while it deprives him of all ground of just
complaint of the severity of the law, or the magistrate."

It is significant to compare this formulation of the theory underlying the use of release on recognizance, with a British formulation of the second half of the nineteenth century. In a book
published in 1877, Edward William Cox, Recorder of Portsmouth,
specifically described the release of offenders on their own
recognizance, with sureties, as a "substitute for punishment,"
and he noted that, while the conduct of the released offenders
was proper, no further action was taken. In particular, he was
strongly motivated by the desire to avoid the demoralizing and
contaminating influence of short terms of imprisonment, especially in the case of first and juvenile offenders. As for the *ra-*

tionale of the use of the recognizances, with sureties, he says, "The suspension only of the judgment, the knowledge that if he (the offender) offends he may yet be punished—the hold which his bail thus has upon him, to a great extent guarantee that if there is in him an inclination to redeem himself he will return to a life of honesty."

Provisional Release on Bail

It has been noted in the preceding paragraphs that the device of releasing an offender on his own recognizance (binding-over) may be used *with,* or, *without, sureties.* Conversely, the device of sureties (or bail) may be employed with or without simultaneously binding over the defendant on his own recognizance. The significance of the device of sureties, when combined with the recognizance, as a precursor of probation, has already been discussed; it remains to be pointed out, however, that both in England and in the United States of America the device of bail as such (that is, when not used in conjunction with the recognizance) has similarly been of major historical significance in the evolution of probation, namely, as a device for the provisional suspension of punishment in relation to rudimentary probation practices.

Binding-Over, Bail and the Origins of Probation

It has been noted above, that the recognizance is essentially a preventive rather than a punitive measure of dealing with actual or potential offenders. In the early nineteenth century the increased use of this device was motivated, no doubt, to a considerable extent by considerations of mercy and in this respect the device was one of the measures employed to reduce the hardships involved in the mechanical application of a rigorous criminal law. The rehabilitative object of the measure—i. e., the prevention of crime by the restoration of the offender as a law-abiding member of society—was, however, always present. Nevertheless, during this era the device came to be applied with an increasing realization of its rehabilitative potentialities, and same to be accompanied by increasingly effective safeguards and aids in the form of the personal supervision of, and assistance to the released offender during the trial period. It should further be noted that the recognizance has always contained the germs of supervision—it involves the conditional suspension of punishment, and some vigilance is required to ascertain whether the conditions concerned are being complied with.

It is clear that the provisional release of offenders in the charge of sureties similarly contained the germs of probationary supervision (irrespective of whether this device was combined with the recognizance or not). In view of their financial interest in the conduct of the provisionally released offender, sureties are bound to try to ensure the good behavior of the offender through personal supervision, assistance or influence. The deliberate use, by the courts, of the salutory influence of sureties on offenders released conditionally, either on their own recognizance or on bail, indeed seems to have been in a very real sense the first, rudimentary stage in the development of probation.

The Provisional "Filing" of Cases

The practice of provisionally "filing" a case seems to have been peculiar to Massachusetts. This device consisted of the suspension of the imposition of sentence when, "after verdict of guilty in a criminal case . . . the Court is satisfied that, by reason of extenuating circumstances, or of the pendency of a question of law in a like case before a higher court, or other sufficient reason, public justice does not require an immediate sentence. . . ." The use of this procedure was subject to the consent of the defendant and of the prosecuting attorney, and the suspension was made subject to such conditions as the court in its discretion might impose. The order that a case be laid on file was not equivalent to a final judgment, but left it within the power of the court to take action on the case at any time, upon motion of either party.

The Suspension of Sentences at Common Law

By way of summary, it may be noted that there existed, during the nineteenth century and earlier, several legal devices which enabled the English and the American courts to suspend either the imposition of sentence (recognizance to keep the peace or to be of good behavior and to appear for judgment when called upon, provisional release on bail, the provisional "filing of a case," and the judicial reprieve) or the execution of sentence (also the judicial reprieve). That these devices existed, and allowed *at least* for the temporary suspension of sentence for *specific purposes,* is beyond any doubt. The question whether the

English and American courts possess, at common law, an inherent power to suspend sentence *indefinitely* is, however, more problematic.

In analyzing the question of an inherent judicial power to suspend sentence *indefinitely,* it is necessary to distinguish clearly between the use of the special devices of the recognizance and bail, on the one hand, and other devices used for the provisional suspension of punishment, on the other hand. Prior to statutory provisions to this effect, the courts both in England and in the United States of America *did,* in fact, engage in the suspension of the imposition of sentence when releasing offenders on their own recognizances, and took no further action with regard to the infliction of punishment if the condition of good behavior was complied with. Similarly, this procedure was followed, prior to statutory authorization, in at least two of the other countries of the British Commonwealth, viz., New England and Canada. Both in England and in certain jurisdictions of the United States of America (notably Massachusetts), the conditional suspension of the imposition of sentence, with the ultimate release of the offender from all punishment in case of good behavior, was practiced (without statutory authorization) also in relation to the provisional release of offenders on bail.

For all practical purposes it may be said that—beyond the relatively circumscribed practice of suspending the imposition of a sentence by means of releasing an offender on a recognizance and/or bail—the English courts *did not* assume the existence of an inherent common law power to suspend sentence indefinitely. In the United States of America, however, a variety of practices developed, with a tendency to extend the suspension of sentence beyond the employment of the recognizance and/or bail. In particular, this involved the suspension of the imposition or of the execution of sentence on the basis of the common law precedent of the judicial reprieve. With the increasing use of the conditional suspension of punishment, with or without some sort of probationary supervision, courts in different jurisdictions adopted contradictory points of view on the question of the existence, at common law, of an inherent judicial power of indefinite suspension of sentence. While some held that the courts had such a power, others rejected this view arguing either that the conditions justifying the recognition of such a power in England did not obtain in the United States, or that the indefinite suspension of sentence by the court constituted an encroachment on the executive prerogative of pardon and reprieve, and thus infringes upon the doctrine of the separation of powers.

The United States Supreme Court finally expressed itself on the issue in question in the so-called *Killits* case. In his opinion in this case, the late Chief Justice White decided that the English common law did not give the Federal courts the power to suspend sentence indefinitely.

> "It is true that, owing to the want of power in common law courts to grant new trials and to the absence of a right to review convictions in a higher court, it is we think, to be conceded: (a) that both suspensions of sentence and suspensions of the enforcement of sentence, temporary in character, were often resorted to on grounds of error or miscarriage of justice which under our system would be corrected either by new trials or by the exercise of the power to review; (b) that not infrequently, where the suspension either of the imposition of a sentence or of its execution was made for the purpose of enabling a pardon to be sought or bestowed, by a failure to further proceed in the criminal cause in the future, although no pardon had been sought or obtained, the punishment fixed by law was escaped. But neither of these conditions serves to convert the mere exercise of a judicial discretion to temporarily suspend for the accomplishment of a purpose contemplated by law into the existence of an arbitrary judicial power to permanently refuse to enforce the law."

With reference to the decision in the *Killits* case, the Attorney General's Survey concludes as follows:

> "For practical purposes it may be said that this decision served to explode the erroneous belief that had grown up in some states. . . . It may be concluded, therefore, that there is no historical warrant in the English common law for the claim that American courts have an inherent power to suspend sentence indefinitely. Where this power has been asserted, it has been based on a misconception of English authorities or recognized because it tempered the criminal law with mercy and had grown as a local practice."

It should be noted that the Court's decision in the *Killits* case did not seek to invalidate the practice of releasing offenders on their own recognizances, but referred to "the fact that common law courts possessed the power by recognizances to secure good behavior, that is, to enforce the law. . . ." This fact did not, however, afford support for "the proposition that those courts possessed the arbitrary discretion to permanently decline to enforce the law."

From the point of view of the development of probation as a distinct method for the treatment of offenders, the extent to which the judicial devices in which it had its historical origins, were, in fact, extra-legal and not warranted by the English common law, is of small significance. The important point is that these devices developed, and could in fact only develop, in a system of common law jurisdiction which is flexible enough to allow for the gradual adjustment of existing practices to new needs and new objectives. In England this process of adjustment was more conservative and it is probable that the courts stayed within their common law powers, in any case, the legality of the devices used for the conditional suspension of punishment, in relation to early pre-statutory probation practices, was never challenged in England, in Canada, or in New Zealand. In the United States of America, the courts overstepped their common law powers, and the resulting diversity and confusion of principles and authorities necessitated the authoritative revision of the legal bases of the practices that have developed. Nevertheless, the definitive explosion of the doctrine of an inherent judicial power to suspend any part of the administration of criminal justice, and when public opinion had already been fully prepared for this new method for the treatment of offenders. Consequently, the final rejection by the Supreme Court of the doctrine of a common law judicial power of indefinite suspension of sentence actually served as a stimulus for the enactment of statutes expressly authorizing the suspension of sentence and probation.

PROBATION*

Extensive use of institutions has been giving way to expanded use of community-based programs during the past decade. This is true not only in corrections, but also in services for the mentally ill, the aging, and dependent and neglected children.

The movement away from institutionalization has occurred not only because institutions are very costly, but also because they have debilitating effects on inmates, who have great difficulty in reintegrating themselves into the community. Therefore, it is essential that alternatives to institutionalization be expanded in use and enhanced in resources. The most promising process by which this can be accomplished in corrections—probation—is now being used more as a disposition. Even greater use can be projected for the future.

Broad use of probation does not increase risk to the community. Any risk increased by allowing offenders to remain in the community will be more than offset by increased safety due to offenders' increased respect for society and their maintenance of favorable community ties. Results of probation are as good, if not better, than those of incarceration.[1] With increased concern about crime, reduction of recidivism, and allocation of limited tax dollars, more attention should be given to probation, as a system and as a sentencing disposition.

Although probation is viewed as the brightest hope for corrections, its full potential cannot be reached unless consideration is given to two major factors. The first is the development of a system for determining which offenders should receive a sentence of probation. The second is the development of a system that enables offenders to receive the support and services they need so that ultimately they can live independently in a socially acceptable way.

Currently, probation has failed to realize either of these. Probation is not adequately structured, financed, staffed, or equipped

---

* National Advisory Commission on Criminal Justice Standards and Goals, *Report on Corrections*, 1973.

1. See National Council on Crime and Delinquency, *Policies and Background Information* (Hackensack, N. J.: NCCD, 1972), pp. 14–15.

with necessary resources. A major shift of money and manpower to community-based corrections is necessary if probation is to be adopted nationally as the preferred disposition, as this Commission recommends. The shift will require strengthening the position of probation in the framework of government, defining goals and objectives for the probation system, and developing an organization that can meet the goals and objectives. In this chapter, consideration will be given to what must be done if probation is to fulfill its potential as a system and as a disposition.

DEFINITIONS

In corrections, the word "probation" is used in four ways. It can refer to a disposition, a status, a system or subsystem, and a process.

Probation as a court disposition was first used as a suspension of sentence. Under probation, a convicted offender's freedom in the community was continued, subject to supervision and certain conditions established by the court. A shift now is occurring, and probation is being used increasingly as a sentence in itself. The American Bar Association Project on Standards for Criminal Justice defines probation as:

> A sentence not involving confinement which imposes conditions and retains authority in the sentencing court to modify the conditions of sentence or to re-sentence the offender if he violates the conditions. Such a sentence should not involve or require suspension of the imposition or execution of any other sentence. .   .   .
>
> A sentence to probation should be treated as a final judgment for purposes of appeal and similar procedural purposes.[2]

Probation as a status reflects the position of an offender sentenced to probation. For the offender, probation status has implications different from the status of either free citizen or confined offender.

Probation is a subsystem of corrections, itself a subsystem of the criminal and juvenile justice system. Unless otherwise specified, "probation" will be used throughout this chapter to refer

2. American Bar Association Project on Standards for Criminal Justice, *Standards Relating to Probation* (New York: Institute of Judicial Administration, 1970), p. 9.

to the probation subsystem. When used in this context, probation refers to the agency or organization that administers the probation process for juveniles and adults.

The probation process refers to the set of functions, activities, and services that characterize the system's transactions with the courts, the offender, and the community. The process includes preparation of reports for the court, supervision of probationers, and obtaining or providing services for them.

The terms written report or "report" will be used to denote both presentence investigation reports and social studies prepared for the courts. The term "presentence investigation report" is used for those dealing with adults and "social study" for those dealing with juveniles.

"Intake" refers to the process of screening cases prior to court appearance, in order to take or recommend a course of action. It involves discretion to resolve a matter informally, to arrange court-based diversion services, or to proceed with a court hearing. It also may include investigative or assessment activities and pre-trial release or detention decisions.

EVOLUTION OF PROBATION

Probation's origins go back to English common law and the efforts to alleviate the severity of criminal sanctions. The earliest probation device appears to have been "benefit of clergy," which was used originally to release clergymen from criminal court on the theory that only church courts had jurisdiction over their personnel. Later, "benefit of the clergy" was extended to include anyone who could read.

Judicial reprieve, another device used in the Middle Ages, was the precedent for the practice of suspension of sentence, which was brought to America from England. Recognizance practice also was developed in England, apparently in the 14th century, involving release with some type of surety or bail to assure good behavior.

John Augustus, a Boston shoemaker, is recognized as the father of probation in this country. As a volunteer, he asked the court to release certain offenders he thought he could assist. Practices he began using in 1841 have stood the test of time: investigation and screening, interviewing, supervision of those released, and services such as employment, relief, and education.

His efforts were so successful that legislation formally establishing probation and providing for paid staff was enacted in Massachusetts in 1878. By 1900, six States had enacted probation legislation; four dealt with adult probation and two related only to children.

Probation as a disposition and a system is essentially a development of the 20th century. The first directory of probation officers in the United States, published in 1907, identified 795 probation officers, mostly serving juvenile courts. Some were volunteers, some welfare workers, some attached to courts, and some employed part-time. By 1937 more than 3,800 persons were identified as probation officers, of whom 80 percent worked full-time and the rest had additional duties such as sheriff, welfare worker, minister, attendance officer, or attorney. In 1947, the directories began to include both probation and parole. In 1970, nearly 25,000 persons were identified as probation and parole personnel, and only 2 percent had other duties such as county welfare worker or sheriff.

As probation use increased, growing interest in its effectiveness developed. One demonstration of its effectiveness was the Saginaw Project conducted in Michigan between 1957 and 1962. The project staffed by trained workers with manageable workloads, had three objectives. First, probation should be used for 70 to 75 percent of convicted offenders. Second, there should be no increased risk to community safety. Third, actual tax dollar savings should be achieved by reduced construction and maintenance of institutions. All objectives were accomplished.[3]

Follow-up studies of probation elsewhere indicated that failure rates of persons on probation were relatively low.[4] Although many of these studies were not conducted under controlled conditions, with definitive information about variables such as service rendered and matched groups of offenders, the gross evidence cannot be discounted.

3. National Probation and Parole Association, Michigan Council, *The Saginaw Probation Demonstration Project* (New York: National Council on Crime and Delinquency, 1963).

4. See Robert L. Smith, *A Quiet Revolution* (Washington: U. S. Department of Health, Education, and Welfare, 1972).

GOVERNMENTAL FRAMEWORK OF PROBATION

The position of probation in the government framework varies among the States. The continuing controversy over the most appropriate placement of probation centers on two main issues: whether it should be a part of the judicial or executive branch of government; and whether it should be administered by State or local government.

In all States, corrections components and subsystems, except probation and some juvenile detention facilities, operate within the executive branch. Probation is found in the executive branch in some States, in the judicial in others, and under mixed arrangements elsewhere.

State governments operate most subsystems of corrections. The exceptions are probation, jails, and some juvenile detention facilities. Juvenile probation usually developed in juvenile courts and thus became a local function. As adult probation services developed, they generally were combined with existing statewide parole services or into a unified corrections department that also included parole and institutions. The exceptions were in major cities that had already created probation organizations for the adult courts and States in which probation responsibilities were divided.

Variations in the way probation has been organized and placed within the government framework have created differences between States as well as within States. Ohio provides an example of the complicated arrangements that have developed. There, juvenile probation is a local function in the judicial branch, but the State aid program is in the executive branch. Adult probation can be either a State or local function. A State agency in the executive branch can provide probation service to local courts, or they may establish their own. Where local probation exists, the control may be shared by both branches in an arrangement under which the county commissioners and judges of the court of common pleas must concur on appointments.

In New York State the State Division of Probation is in the executive branch as are all local probation agencies except those in New York City, which are in the judicial branch.

Such variations appear to have arisen as emphasis was given to one or the other of the two traditional functions of probation officers: to provide presentence reports and other services for the courts; and to supervise and provide services for probationers. These are different tasks with different objectives.

Variations occur within probation itself. There may be one agency for all offenders or separate agencies for juveniles and adults. Adult probation may be divided into one agency for felons and another for misdemeanants.

The question of where probation should be placed in the framework of government becomes more critical as its use expands and staff numbers increase. It is time to take a serious look at where probation could function most effectively, rather than using chance and history to support the status quo.

JUDICIAL VS. EXECUTIVE BRANCH

In the debate over the appropriate governmental branch for the probation system, those who favor the judicial branch give the following rationale.

1. Probation would be more responsive to court direction. Throughout the probation process, the court could provide guidance to probation workers and take corrective action when policies were not followed or proved ineffective.

2. This arrangement would provide the judiciary with an automatic feedback mechanism on effectiveness of dispositions through reports filed by probation staff. Judges, it is urged, may place more trust in reports from their own staff than in those from an outside agency.

3. Courts have a greater awareness of needed resources and may become advocates for their staffs in obtaining better services.

4. Increased use of pretrial diversion may be furthered by placing probation in the judicial branch. Courts have not been inclined to transfer authority and therefore may set more stringent limitations on the discretion of nonjudicial personnel to release or divert than on judicial staff.

The arguments for keeping probation in the judicial branch, which center around the direct relationship between the courts and probation, are not persuasive. Subsystems of the criminal justice system in the executive branch are able to work effectively with the courts.

Those who oppose placement of probation within the judiciary argue that:

1.　Under this arrangement judges frequently become the administrators of probation in their jurisdictions—a role for which they usually are ill-equipped. The current trend toward use of court administrators reflects the belief that judges cannot be expected to have the time, orientation, or training to perform two such distinct roles.

2.　When probation is within the judicial system, the staff is likely to give priority to services for the courts rather than to services to probationers.

3.　Probation staff may be assigned functions that serve legal processes of the court and are unrelated to probation, such as issuing summonses, serving subpenas, and running errands for judges.

4.　Courts, particularly the criminal courts, are adjudicatory and regulatory rather than service-oriented bodies. Therefore, as long as probation remains part of the court setting, it will be subservient to the court and will not develop an identity of its own.

Another class of arguments supports placement of probation in the executive branch of government, rather than merely opposing placement in the judicial branch.

1.　All other subsystems for carrying out court dispositions of offenders are in the executive branch. Closer coordination and functional integration with other corrections personnel could be achieved by a common organizational placement, particularly as community-based corrections programs increase. Furthermore, job mobility would be enhanced if related functions are administratively tied.

2.　The executive branch contains the allied human service agencies including social and rehabilitation services, medical services, employment services, education, and housing. Where probation also is in the executive branch, opportunities are increased for coordination, cooperative endeavors, and comprehensive planning.

3.　Decisions involving resource allocations and establishment of priorities are made by the executive branch. It initiates requests to the legislative bodies, either local or State, for appropriation of funds, and by so doing sets priorities for allocating limited tax dollars. When probation is included in the total corrections system, more rational decisions about the best distribution of resources can be made.

4. Probation administrators are in position to negotiate and present their case more strongly, if they are in the executive branch. When probation is part of the court system the judge, not the probation administrator, is responsible for presenting the budget request and acting as negotiator. The latter is not a role traditionally undertaken by the judiciary.

On balance, the arguments for placement of probation in the executive branch of government are more persuasive. Such placement would facilitate a more rational allocation of probation staff services, increase interaction and administrative coordination with corrections and allied human services, increase access to the budget process and establishment of priorities, and remove the courts from an inappropriate role.

For these reasons, this report calls for inclusion of probation departments within unified State correctional systems. (See Chapter 16, Statutory Framework of Corrections.) Moreover the chapters which deal with intake services (Chapter 8 for juveniles and Chapter 9 for adults) recommend that staff performing services for the courts (as against services to pretrial releasees and probationers) should be under the administrative control of the courts.

This is, in the Commission's view, the proper long-range objective. It would do away with the current duality of roles for probation staff. However, in view of the current variety of local arrangements, it may for the present be appropriate for personnel carrying out services to the courts to be employed by the probation division of a unified State corrections system but detailed to perform court services. It would be essential in such an arrangement that probation staff take direction from the court and the court administration in establishment of policies, procedures, and performance standards for carrying out their tasks and that the probation division be responsive to the needs of the courts. Where such an arrangement appears to be desirable, written agreements setting out and defining the relationship between the court and the corrections system should be developed and agreed to by both.

STATE VS. LOCAL ADMINISTRATION

Few States in which probation is a local function have provided any leadership or supervision for probation agencies. Tremendous variations are likely to exist within a State in terms of number of staff employed in counties of similar size, qualifications of personnel employed, and relative emphasis on services to courts and probationers. County probation agencies often are small and lack resources for staff training and development, research and program planning, and, more basically, services to the probationers.

State Efforts to Set Standards

Attempts to bring about some degree of uniformity have been limited. In a few States where probation is a local function, standards are set by the State in either the judicial or executive branch. For example, in New Jersey the judicial branch is responsible for setting standards for its local probation systems, while in California the responsibility is placed in the executive branch.

The degree to which local probation systems comply with State standards is dependent upon the rewards and sanctions used. As a reward for meeting specified standards, the State may provide either revenue or manpower. Michigan assigns State-paid probation officers to work alongside local probation officers. The more common practice, however, is direct payment by the State to local governments for part of the costs of probation services. New York State reimburses local communities up to 50 percent of the operating costs for probation programs, provided that local communities meet State staffing standards. This subsidy has nearly doubled in the last 6 years and has resulted in an increase of probation staff in the State from 1,527 in 1965 to 1,956 in 1972.[5]

The States of California and Washington use a different approach in providing revenue to local jurisdictions. These States attempt to resolve a problem that is inherent when probation is a local function; namely, that financing probation is a local responsibility. However, when juveniles or adults are sent to correctional institutions, these are usually administered and financed by the State. A consequence often is the shifting of financial

5. Information supplied by the New York State Division of Probation.

responsibility from the local government to the State government by sentences of incarceration rather than probation.

California and Washington have developed probation subsidy programs in which counties are reimbursed in proportion to the number of individuals that remain in the community rather than being sent to State institutions. The subsidy program in California was developed as a result of a study that indicated that some individuals eligible for commitment to State correctional institutions could safely be retained on probation and that with good probation supervision, they could make a satisfactory adjustment. It was estimated that at least 25 percent of the new admissions to State correctional institutions could remain in the community with good probation supervision.

The California Probation Subsidy Program was instituted in 1966 by the State's youth authority. The youth authority was authorized to pay up to $4,000 to each county for every adult and juvenile offender not committed to a State correctional institution. The counties were required to demonstrate a commitment to improved probation services, including employment of additional probation workers and reduction of caseloads. In addition, each county had to demonstrate innovative approaches to probation, such as intensive care probation units for dealing with hard-core adult and juvenile offenders.

California estimates that, even with expanded probation services, the cost of probation runs little more than one-tenth of the cost of incarceration, approximately $600 per person annually for probation, compared to $5,000 annually for institutionalization. In all, the program has resulted in substantial savings to taxpayers. In the six years between 1966 and 1972, California canceled planned construction, closed existing institutions, and abandoned new institutions that had been constructed. Almost $186 million was saved in these ways, while probation subsidy expenditures came to about $60 million. Furthermore, although there has been a general decrease in commitments to State institutions throughout the United States, the decrease is sharper in those counties in California that participate in the subsidy program. The decrease in those counties almost doubles that of California counties not participating in the subsidy program.[6]

---

6. Smith, *A Quiet Revolution*, gives the background of and experience under California's probation subsidy plan.

The State of Washington has had a similar experience with the probation subsidy program begun in January, 1970. Its purpose was to reduce the number of commitments to institutions from county juvenile courts. In the 2 years the program has been in operation, there has been a marked reduction in the number of children and youth sent to State institutions. To illustrate, in 1971, the State received 55 percent fewer commitments than expected.[7]

Advantages of State Administration

Even in those instances where the State provides financial incentives to local jurisdictions, as in California, participation of counties is discretionary. Uniformity in probation can be achieved only when there is a State-administered probation system, which also has a number of other distinct advantages.

A State-administered system can more easily organize around the needs of a particular locality or region without having to consider local political impediments. It also can recommend new programs and implement them without requiring additional approval by local political bodies.

A State-administered system provides greater assurance that goals and objectives can be met and that uniform policies and procedures can be developed. Also, more efficiency in the disposition of resources is assured because all staff members are State employees and a larger agency can make more flexible use of manpower, funds, and other resources.

When it is simply not possible for a State to administer a probation system, the State, through a designated agency in the executive branch, should be responsible for developing standards for local probation systems that provide for a minimum acceptable level of functioning. State standards have a greater chance of being implemented if the State indicates a willingness to share the costs with local governments when standards are met and maintained.

In addition to setting standards for local jurisdictions, the State agency should be responsible for establishing policies, defining statewide goals, providing staff training, assisting in fiscal planning and implementation, collecting statistics and data to

7. Information supplied by the Washington State Department of Social and Health Services.

monitor the operations of local probation agencies, and enforcing change when necessary. Through these means, a state-supervised program can bring about some degree of uniformity in operations throughout the State, but not to the same degree as a State-administered program.

PROBATION ADMINISTRATION

The complexities of administering a probation system have been reflected in several studies. A poll conducted for the Joint Commission on Correctional Manpower and Training indicated that administrators felt the need for more training, especially in public administration.[8] Another study revealed support for two different types of education for administrators. One group advocated social work education, apparently representing a concern for substantive practice matters. The others advocated public administration because of a concern about managerial responsibilities.[9]

NEED FOR ADMINISTRATORS TO FORMULATE GOALS

The administrator is expected to formulate goals and basic policies that give direction and meaning to the agency. If these goals are not formulated specifically, they are made by default, for staff will create their own framework. Should policies and goals not be developed quickly, or well enough, persons outside the agency may determine policies, with or without consideration of long-range goals.

Unfortunately, clearly defined objectives for probation systems rarely are set forth. The probation administrator has contributed to variations in philosophy, policy, and practice. Often staff members of the same agency have different perceptions, with top management having one view, middle management another, and line personnel reflecting some of each.

Probation staff members bring to the organization their own backgrounds, and the beliefs they acquired before becoming employees. These in turn are modified by other staff members,

8. Joint Commission on Correctional Manpower and Training, *Corrections 1968: A Climate for Change* (Washington: JCCMT, 1968), p. 30.

9. Herman Piven and Abraham Alcabes, *The Crisis of Qualified* *Manpower for Criminal Justice: An Analytic Assessment with Guidelines for New Policy* (Washington: Government Printing Office, 1969), vol. 1.

judges, law enforcement officials, personnel of other parts of the correctional system, probationers, complainants and witnesses, lawyers, and the news media.

If an administrator has failed to define goals and policies for his organization, dysfunction within the organization must follow. Some dysfunctioning is rooted both in tradition and rapid growth.

TRAINING FOR PROBATION WORK

Since the 1920's there has been an emphasis on social work education as a prerequisite for entering probation. The preferred educational standard was a master's degree in social work. This emphasis was paralleled by the concept of professionalism. To achieve professionalism, staff members had to be provided opportunities to increase their knowledge and skills. Such a thrust created a staff expectation that they would have opportunity to use the increased knowledge and skills. However, as probation systems grow in size, agencies tend to develop the characteristics of a bureaucracy that increase constraints on staff behavior which result in frustration.

New graduates of schools of social work have been reluctant to enter probation. Newer staff members sent by probation agencies to graduate schools of social work often leave the agency as soon as they fulfill any commitment made to secure the education. Such workers are likely to express their reason for leaving as frustration over the lack of opportunity for using their knowledge and skills.

DYSFUNCTIONS IN PROBATION OPERATION

Training emphasis has been at a staff level, and this too can contribute to dysfunction. More emphasis has been placed on training probation officers than on equipping executives and middle-level managers with skills to administer effectively. Organizational change must begin with the executives and middle management if probation officers are to have an opportunity to use increased knowledge and skills acquired through training.

Another dysfunction may result from the change from one-to-one casework emphasis of the probation officer to the group emphasis needed for an administrator. Many staff members are promoted from the ranks of probation officer to supervisor and administrator. If effective organizations are to be developed, supervisors and administrators should meet and work with staff on a group basis. If the supervisors and administrators do not have the skills to do this effectively, they will revert to the pattern of one-to-one relationship.

Another form of dysfunction may stem from promotion of a probation officer to a supervisory or administrative position. Ideally a supervisor should receive training that enables him to create a supportive atmosphere for the probation officer, both inside and outside the agency. The probation officer who has been promoted but given no training for his new role has a natural tendency to see himself as doing his job well by concentrating on internal matters. Support and supervision of staff may consist of nothing more than shuffling papers, reporting statistics, and giving basic training to probation officers.

SERVICES TO PROBATIONERS

THE CURRENT SERVICE SYSTEM

Many problems have prevented development of a system for providing probationers with needed resources. For one thing, the goal of service delivery to probationers has not been delineated clearly and given the priority required. Services to probationers have not been separated from services to the court. Generally, both services are provided by the same staff members, who place more emphasis on services to the court than to probationers.

Because the goal for service delivery to probationers has not been defined clearly, service needs have not been identified on a systematic and sustained basis. Priorities based on need, resources, and constraints have not been set. Measurable objectives and ways of achieving them for various target groups have not been specified. Moreover, monitoring and evaluation of services have been almost nonexistent.

Another problem is the lack of differentiation between services that should be provided by probation and those that should be delivered by such agencies as mental health, employment, housing, education, and private welfare agencies. Because of community attitudes toward offenders, social agencies other than probation are likely to be unenthusiastic about providing services to the legally identified offender. Probation offices usually lack sufficient influence and funds to procure services from other resources and therefore try to expand their own role and services. This leads to two results, both undesirable: identical services are duplicated by probation and one or more other public service agencies, and probation suffers from stretching already tight resources.

Some probation systems have assumed responsibility for handling matters unrelated to probation such as placement of neglected children in foster homes and operation of shelter facilities, both of which are the responsibilities of the child welfare or other public agencies. Probation also has attempted to deal directly with such problems as alcoholism, drug addiction, and mental illness, which ought to be handled through community mental health and other specialized programs.

These efforts to expand probation's role have not been successful because there is not enough money to provide even the traditional basic probation services.

OVEREMPHASIS ON CASEWORK

One result of the influence of social work on probation has been an overemphasis on casework. Development of child guidance clinics in the 1920's and 1930's influenced particularly the juvenile courts and their probation staff.

The terms "diagnosis" and "treatment" began to appear in social work literature and not long after in corrections literature. Those terms come from the medical field and imply illness. A further implication is that a good probation practitioner will understand the cause and be able to remedy it, just as the medical practitioner does. Essentially, the medical approach overlooked any connection between crime and such factors as poverty, unemployment, poor housing, poor health, and lack of education.

A review of the literature of the 1930's, 1940's, and 1950's indicates that the casework method became equated with social work, and in turn, casework for probation became equated with a therapeutic relationship with a probationer. A study manual published by the National Probation and Parole Association in 1942 reflects this equation in the table of contents. The titles of three of the chapters are: "Social Casework," "Case Study and Diagnosis," and "Casework as a Means of Treatment." [10]

10. Helen D. Pigeon, *Probation and Parole in Theory and Practice* (New York: National Probation and Parole Association, 1942).

The literature discussed the development of social work skills in interviewing, creating therapeutic relationships with clients, counseling, providing insight, and modifying behavior. When practitioners began to view themselves as therapists, one consequence was the practice of having offenders come to the office rather than workers going into the homes and the communities.

Although the literature refers to probation officers working with employers, schools, families, and others in the probationer's life, the chief concern is the relationship between probation officer and probationer. Indeed, if probation staff members see casework as their model, it may well be asked how much contact and what kind of contact they should have with persons other than probationers.

Recently a much broader view of social work practice has been developed, a view that social workers in corrections have taken an active role in developing. After a 3-year study of social work curriculum sponsored by the Council on Social Work Education in the 1950's, the report of the project on "Education for Social Workers in the Correctional Field" said:

"The social task in corrections seems to call for social workers rather than for caseworkers or group workers. All social workers in corrections work with individuals, groups and communities, with less emphasis on the use of one method than is characteristic of many social work jobs." [11]

A task force organized in 1963 by the National Association of Social Workers to study the field of social work practice in corrections suggested that the offender's needs and the service system's social goals should determine methodology. The task force stated that social workers should have an array of professional skills—based on knowledge, understanding, attitudes, and values required for professional use of the skills—from which they could draw on appropriate occasions to meet the offender's needs and the goals of the probation system. [12]

When casework was applied to probation, a blurring of roles occurred between the probation officer and the probation agency. When each probation officer is assigned a certain number of cases, it is implied that he has full responsibility for all individ-

11. Elliot Studt, *Education for Social Workers in the Correctional Field* (New York: Council on Social Work Education, 1959), p. 50.

12. G. W. Carter, *Fields of Practice: Report of a Workshop* (New York: National Association of Social Workers, 1963).

uals concerned. He is expected to handle all the problems that the offenders in his caseload present and to have all the necessary knowledge and skills. The role of the agency in this arrangement is unclear.

No one person can possess all the skills needed to deal with the variety of complicated human problems presented by probationers. This situation is complicated by the diversity of qualifications required by jurisdictions throughout the country for appointment to the position of probation officer. The requirements range from high school or less to graduate degrees. Requirements for prior experience may be nonexistent or extensive.

Furthermore, few criteria exist as to what is acceptable performance. This deficiency makes it necessary for individual probation officers to set their own standards and gives them a great deal of latitude in working with probationers. Therefore it is difficult to assess the degree to which any probation officer has been successful in positively influencing a probationer.

The expectation that probation officers must know what their probationers are doing is traditional. If a probationer is arrested, the first question likely to be asked is when the probation officer last saw his client. The probation officer is expected to account for what is known, or more specifically for what is not known, about the probationer's activities. One consequence is that a probation officer quickly learns that he must protect himself. The system demands accountability when probationers get into the public view through alleged violations or new crimes. Probation staff members recognize that a high level of visibility exists, that they are answerable for their decisions, and that, if the matter comes to the attention of the court, the decisions will have to be justified.

The Caseload Standard

One impact of the casework model has been a standard ratio of probationers to staff. The figure of 50 cases per probation officer first appeared in the literature in 1917. It was the consensus of a group of probation administrators and was never validated. The recommendation later was modified to include investigations.

The caseload standard provides an excuse for officers with large caseloads to explain why they cannot supervise probationers effectively. It also is a valuable reference point at budget time. Probation agencies have been known to attempt to increase their staff and reduce the size of the caseload without making any effort to define what needs to be done and what tasks must be performed. Caseload reduction has become an end unto itself.

When caseloads alone have been reduced, results have been disappointing. In some cases, an increase in probation violations resulted, undoubtedly due to increased surveillance or overreaction of well-meaning probation officers. Some gains were made when staff members were given special training in case management, but this appears to be the exception. The comment has been made that with caseload reduction, probation agencies have been unable to teach staff what to do with the additional time available.

The San Francisco Project described in a subsequent section challenged the assumption of a caseload standard. Four levels of workloads were established: (1) ideal (50 cases); (2) intensive (25, i. e., half the ideal); (3) normal (100, twice the ideal); and (4) minimum supervision (with a ceiling of 250 cases). Persons in minimum supervision caseloads were required only to submit a monthly written report; no contacts occurred except when requested by the probationer. It was found that offenders in minimum caseloads performed as well as those under normal supervision. The minimum and ideal caseloads had almost identical violation rates. In the intensive caseloads, the violation rate did not decline, but technical violations increased.

The study indicated that the number of contacts between probationer and staff appeared to have little relationship to success or failure on probation. The conclusion was that the concept of a caseload is meaningless without some type of classification and matching of offender type, service to be offered, and staff.[13]

But the caseload standard remained unchanged until the President's Commission on Law Enforcement and Administration of Justice (the Crime Commission) recommended in 1967 a significant but sometimes overlooked change by virtue of the phrase "on the basis of average ratio of 35 offenders per officer." [14]

13. James Robison et al., *The San Francisco Project*, Research Report No. 14 (Berkeley: University of California School of Criminology, 1969).

14. President's Commission on Law Enforcement and Administration of Justice, *The Challenge of Crime in a Free Society* (Washington: Government Printing Office, 1967), p. 169.

The change was to a ratio for staffing, not a formula for a case-load.

Agencies are now considering workloads, not caseloads, to determine staff requirements. Specific tasks are identified, measured for time required to accomplish the task, and translated into numbers of staff members needed.

The Decisionmaking Framework

The framework for making decisions about probationers varies widely from agency to agency and within a single agency. Some decisions about a case, such as recommendations for probation revocation or termination, may be made only by the head of the probation agency, while other decisions about the same case may be made by any of a number of staff workers. Consequently, many probational personnel may not know who can make what decisions and under what circumstances. Part of the difficulty may come from statutes that define the responsibilities of a probation officer more explicitly than those of an agency. In addition, probation administrators often do not establish a clear decisionmaking framework.

The decisionmaking patterns vary not only for staff but for the offender placed on probation. If the system views its task as surveillance of the probationer, he has low status in any decisionmaking. The decisions are made for and about him, but not with him. If the system is oriented toward service, using the social work model, his role in decisions still is likely to be circumvented. This occurs despite the social work concept that the client has the right to be involved in what is happening to him, that is, self-determination.

This paradox exists because the probationer has an assigned status restricting his behavior. Probation conditions, essentially negative in nature although often expressed in a positive fashion, are imposed on him. The probationer may have to obtain permission to purchase a car, to move, to change a job, and this necessity restricts his choices of action. The probationer, therefore, has the task of adapting to an assigned status while seeking to perform the normal roles of a self-sufficient individual in the community: working, being a parent or a family member, paying taxes, obeying the law, meeting financial obligations, etc. Technical violations of probation conditions can result in revocation and commitment to a correctional institution.

If the client consults a noncorrectional social agency, he has the right to explain his problems and to terminate the relationship with that agency if he chooses. A probation client legally is required to appear but not legally required to ask for help. He may or may not be ready to receive help. He may be encouraged by staff to use resources of other community agencies, but the decision rests with him.

He may, however, be required to utilize some services offered by probation, such as psychiatric examination or testing. He may have some goals, but they are accepted by probation staff only if they are consistent with the conditions of probation or with the notions of the probation system, which usually means the probation officer. In short, the probationer's right to participate in decisionmaking has been limited by probation conditions and the role assigned him by the probation staff or the system.

Although probation staff members may be receptive to the social work concept of self-determination, they are aware that they occupy a position of authority. The very words, "probation officer" signify authority, indicating an assigned role of power over another individual.

Furthermore, probation staff members may not be aware of or sensitive to what it means to be a probationer. A study on the interaction between parole staff and parolees indicated that most staff were relatively unaware of the difficulties of being a parolee. Staff and parolees saw the difficulties of parolees differently. Significantly, the parolees seemed more aware than the staff of what the staff could do and consequently to whom they could turn for expert information and advice when needed.[15]

For the most part, the probation system has tended to view offenders as a homogeneous group. The assumption has been that all require the same kind of service; namely, treatment on a one-to-one basis. Confusion exists about the form of treatment to be used and what it is supposed to accomplish. Discussion with most probation staff members reveals their difficulty in explaining what they do to "treat" a probationer and why. They speak of a relationship with each probationer as an end in itself and the sole means of providing services to individuals. Proba-

15. Elliot Studt, *People in the Parole Action System: Their Tasks and Dilemmas* (Los Angeles: University of California Institute of Government and Public Affairs, 1971).

tion staff members also perceive the periodic contact they must make to account for the probationer's presence in the community as helping, treating, or rehabilitating the probationer.

Probationers are a heterogeneous group. The needs of juveniles differ from those of adults; girls and women have different needs than boys and men. There may be some common needs but one means, casework, will not meet them all. For example, casework is not a satisfactory technique for the probationer who has a drug problem. The problem of a probationer may not be interpersonal but one that should be met through specific help such as a job, employment training, or education. Reducing caseloads alone to improve supervision does not necessarily result in better probation services. Research in the past decade provides evidence that other approaches are needed.

The emphasis should be on classification of offenders and development of appropriate service programs, which usually are labeled "treatment." The impetus for this shift has been slowed by lack of research and the ideology of the caseload standard. A recent monograph from the Center for Studies of Crime and Delinquency at the National Institute of Mental Health, provides a good summary of the various models that have been or are being tested.[16] These include specialized supervision programs, guided group interaction programs, and delinquent peer group programs, as well as out-of-home placement and residential treatment. The monograph also covers specialized units in probation and parole such as the California Community Treatment Project and the Community Delinquency Control Project of the California Youth Authority.

Classification of probationers is only one approach to typology. Another is identification and classification of the probationer's needs. To date, this has not been done systematically by any probation agency; what have been identified as basic needs usually are derived from anecdotal reports concerning individual offenders.

A third approach to the typology question involves the question, "Who is to be changed?" To date the primary target for change has been the probationer. A suggestion has been made

16. Eleanor Harlow, J. Robert Weber, and Leslie T. Wilkins, *Community-Based Correctional Programs:* *Models and Practices* (Washington: Government Printing Office, 1971).

that the typological approach might be applied to families and to the community.[17]

FUTURE DIRECTIONS FOR SERVICE DELIVERY

To implement an effective system for delivering services to all probationers, it will be necessary to:

1. Develop a goal-oriented service delivery system.

2. Identify service needs of probationers systematically and periodically, and specify measurable objectives based on priorities and needs assessment.

3. Differentiate between those services that the probation system should provide and those that should be provided by other resources.

4. Organize the system to deliver services, including purchase of services for probationers, and organize the staff around workloads.

5. Move probation staff from courthouses to residential areas and develop service centers for probationers.

6. Redefine the role of probation officer from caseworker to community resource manager.

7. Provide services to misdemeanants.

Developing Goals

The probation services system should be goal-oriented, directed toward removing or reducing individual and social barriers that result in recidivism among probationers. To achieve this goal, the probation system should provide a range of services directly and obtain others from existing social institutions or resources. The goal should be to help persons move from supervised care in their own communities to independent living.

The probation system must help create a climate that will enable the probationer to move successfully through transitions from one status to another. The first is from the status of an individual charged with committing an offense to that of a probationer living in the community but not completely independent. The final transition occurs when probation is terminated and the probationer moves from supervised care to an independ-

17. Seymour Rubenfeld, *Typological Approaches and Delinquency Control: A Status Report* (Rockville, Md.: National Institute of Mental Health, Center for Study of Crime and Delinquency, 1967), pp. 21–25.

ent life. The goal should be to maintain in the community all persons who, with support, can perform there acceptably and to select for some type of confinement only those who, on the basis of evidence, cannot complete probationer status successfully, even with optimal support.

With this goal in mind, the practice of commitment to an institution for the initial period of probation (variously known as shock probation, split sentence, etc.), as the Federal and some State statutes permit, should be discontinued. This type of sentence defeats the purpose of probation, which is the earliest possible reintegration of the offender into the community. Short-term commitment subjects the probationer to the destructive effects of institutionalization, disrupts his life in the community, and stigmatizes him for having been in jail. Further, it may add to his confusion as to his status.

Identifying Needs of Probationers

To plan for services, a probation system must initiate and maintain an assessment of needs of its target group, the probationers. This assessment must be ongoing because needs change. An inventory of needs should be developed by involving probationers rather than relying solely on probation staff to identify what it believes probationers' problems to be. More specifically, needs assessment requires:

• Knowledge of the target group in terms of such factors as age, race, education, employment, family status, availability of transportation.

• Identification of what services the offender most wants and needs to remove individual and social barriers.

• Identification of services available and conditions under which they can be obtained.

• Determination of which needed and wanted services do not exist or are inadequate.

From an assessment of needs, problem areas can be highlighted and priorities determined. This process makes it possible to specify how the various needs identified are to be met; whether directly through the probation system or through other social institutions; for what number or percentage of the target group; in what period of time; and for what purpose. Specifying objectives provides a means for evaluating whether the system was able to accomplish what it set out to achieve. If an objective is not met, the basis for pinpointing possible reasons is provided.

Differentiating Internal and External Services

Direct probation services should be defined clearly and differentiated from services that should be met by other social institutions. Generally the kinds of services to be provided to probationers directly through the probation system should:

• Relate to the reasons the offender was brought into the probation system.

• Help him adjust to his status as a probationer.

• Provide information and facilitate referrals to needed community resources.

• Help create conditions permitting readjustment and reintegration into the community as an independent individual through full utilization of all available resources.

In addition, probation must account to the court for the presence and actions of the probationer.

Other needs of probationers related to employment, training, housing, health, etc. are the responsibility of other social institutions and should be provided by them. Therefore, most services needed by probationers should be located outside the system itself. These services should be available to probationers just as they are to all citizens, but some social institutions have created artificial barriers that deny ready access by persons identified as offenders.

Employment is an example. Some probation agencies have created positions of job developers and employment finders. Probation systems should not attempt to duplicate services already created by law and supposedly available to all persons. The responsibility of the system and its staff should be to enable the probationer to cut through the barriers and receive assistance from social institutions that may be all too ready to exclude him.

The probation system has a responsibility to assure that probationers receive whatever services they need. To mobilize needed resources for helping probationers, the probation system must have funds to purchase services from an individual vendor, such as a person to provide foster care for a probationer or a psychiatrist to provide treatment, or from agencies or social institutions, such as marital counseling, methadone maintenance, education, and training. The potential for purchasing services for groups has been largely untapped. For example, juvenile probationers with reading difficulties may need diagnostic testing and remedial help. If these cannot be provided through local schools, the probation agency may have to locate a resource and purchase the needed testing and remedial help.

For older probationers who are unemployed or underemployed, probation staff may interest a university or college in developing special programs. These might include courses to provide remedial education or vocational training, depending upon the identified need of a given group of probationers.

Many other kinds of services may be purchased. Regardless of the service purchased, it is essential that provision be made for monitoring and evaluation of the services to insure that they are, in fact, being provided and that they meet the specified objective.

Organizing the System to Deliver Services

To meet the needs of the increased number of individuals that will be placed on probation within the next decade, the probation service system must be organized differently than it has been. With the recognition that needs continually change, that the probation system itself will not be able to meet all the needs of the probationers, that many of the needs can be met through existing community resources, that new resources will have to be developed, and that some services will have to be purchased, the system should be organized to accomplish the following work activities:

• Needs assessment—ongoing assessment of probationers' needs and existing community resources.

• Community planning and development—establishing close working relationships with public and private social and economic groups as well as community groups to interpret needs; identifying needs for which community resources do not exist; and, in concert with appropriate groups, developing new resources.

• Purchase of services—entering into agreements and monitoring and evaluating services purchased.

• Direct services—receiving and assessing probationers; obtaining and providing information, referral, and follow-up; counseling; and supervising.

Differentiating work activities permits staff assignments to be organized around a workload rather than a caseload. Tasks directed toward achieving specific objectives should be identified and assigned to staff to be carried out in a specified time. This activity should be coordinated by a manager who makes an assessment of the staff members best able to carry out given tasks. Thus, the manager should know the capacities and capabilities of his workers and their specific areas of competence. He also should be able to help his subordinates work together as a team rather than as individuals.

A trend in modern organizational theory is to use teams of staff members with different backgrounds and responsibilities. Teams of individuals from varying disciplines and with differing skills may be assembled for a given task and project and disbanded when the project is completed. The leadership within the team may change, with a junior person serving as the team leader if there is particular need for his knowledge and skills.

In examining the various functions within the probation service delivery system it becomes apparent that there is a range of jobs requiring different kinds of knowledge and skills. Paraprofessionals and those in other "new career" occupations can provide services complementary to those of the probation officer. The potential for assigning a group of probationers to a team of probation officers, paraprofessionals, and other new careerists, headed by a team leader who does not function in the traditional social work supervisory role, is worth testing.

Location of Services

Probation services should be readily accessible to probationers. Therefore they should be based in that part of the community where offenders reside and near other community services. Staff serving probationers should be removed from courthouses and separated from staff providing services to the courts.

Services to probationers in rural areas may have to be organized on a regional rather than the traditional county basis. Service centers should be located in the more populated areas, with mobile units used for outlying districts. In such areas, where transportation is a problem, it is important that probation and other community services be in the same physical location.

Services to offenders should be provided in the evening hours and on weekends without the usual rigid adherence to the recognized work week. The problems of offenders cannot be met by conventional office hours. Arrangements should be made to have a night telephone answering service available to probationers.

Probation Officers as Community Resource Managers

The responsibility for being the sole treatment agent that has traditionally been assigned to the probation officer no longer meets the needs of the criminal justice system, the probation system, or the offender. While some probation officers still will have to carry out counseling duties, most probation officers can meet the goals of the probation services system more effectively in the role of community resource manager. This means that the probation officer will have primary responsibility for meshing a probationer's identified needs with a range of available services and for supervising the delivery of those services.

To carry out his responsibilities as a community resource manager, the probation officer must perform several functions. In helping a probationer obtain needed services, the probation officer will have to assess the situation, know available resources, contact the appropriate resource, assist the probationer to obtain the services, and follow up on the case. When the probationer encounters difficulty in obtaining a service he needs, the probation officer will have to explore the reasons for the difficulty and take appropriate steps to see that the service is delivered. The probation officer also will have to monitor and evaluate the services to which the probationer is referred.

The probation officer will have a key role in the delivery of services to probationers. The change in responsibility will enable him to have greater impact on probationers. As community resource manager, he will utilize a range of resources rather than be the sole provider of services—his role until now and one impossible to fulfill.

A THEORY OF PROBATION SUPERVISION*

As the literature of probation demonstrates, a thoroughly eclectic discipline possesses an almost infinite capacity to generate

* Carl B. Klockars, Jr. *The Journal of Criminal Law, Criminology and Police Science*, vol. 63, No. 4, 1972.

the most diverse forms of theory. Probation students' published attentions to supervision include everything from after-dinner speeches to decision models. Speeches tell the reader a good deal about the speaker and decision models tell a good deal about the officer, but neither seems to capture what probation supervision is.[1] Decision models cannot be considered inappropriate since knowledge of decision-making is certainly of legitimate scientific concern. The speeches, as well as the dozens of articles which discuss the question of what probation supervision "ought to be," can be sympathetically interpreted as teaching theories. One cannot object to the treatment of probation problems at this level either. The vast majority of improvements in probation services has resulted, not from the scientific demonstrations of efficiency, but rather through the efforts of moral men from Augustus through Charles Chute and Rufus Cook to those who wish to enter the field with "oughts" today.

Our intention is to provide a description and analysis of the standard form of probation supervision.[2] To do so four elements must be considered. The first is the working philosophy of the officer—the way he sees his job and duties. The second is the organizational context in which the officer finds himself. The third is the legal and logical definition of revocation, and the fourth is the psychological approach of the probationer. It is our observation that each of these four components responds to movement in the other. As a result, any theory of probation supervision must not only cite each of these components but also specify the nature and mechanics of their interaction.

1. Because what passes for probation supervision theory is so diverse, we shall not attempt any history of such efforts here. The best article on the subject is Lewis Diana's highly critical *What is Probation?*, 51 Crim.L.C. & P.S. 189 (1960). It has received little attention and less rebuttal. A slightly watered-down version of it appears in Probation and Parole 39–56 (R. Carter & L. Wilkins eds. 1970).

2. The theory of probation supervision presented here was developed during two years of participant observation research in a large metropolitan probation office. Nearly one hundred officers supervised more than seven thousand probationers and parolees. The theory is a revised and expanded section of a restricted circulation monograph which the author composed for the department: Make Believe Bureaucracy: A Case Study in Probation (Mimeo., 1970). All investigations were made with the full knowledge and consent of the department administration.

WORKING PHILOSOPHY OF THE
PROBATION OFFICER

The first and broadest component of the theory of probation supervision is the role which the officer sets for himself and the logic and rationale he develops to explain what he does or what he ought to do. So pervasive is this component of probation supervision, it gives particular warp and depth to all other components. Our observations yield a typology of probation officer [3] which falls roughly between the thesis, "Probation is not Casework," [4] and the antithesis, "Probation is Casework." [5]

The Law Enforcers.[6] At the probation-is-not-casework pole we find officers who stress the legal authority and enforcement aspects of their role. Of prime importance to such officers are (a.) the court order ("His only job is to help the offender comply with the order of the court."); [7] (b.) authority ("I will fully execute that authority but only that authority delegated to me by the court."); [8] (c.) decision-making power ("Once I have made a decision, I will steadfastly resist all client efforts to alter my decision by threats, tantrums, seduction, illness, etc."); [9] (d.) officer responsibility for public safety ("It is the criterion of safety for society that will determine for the parole officer whether the level of adjustment achieved is acceptable or whether he is so dangerous to society that he must be removed from its midst and returned to prison."); [10] and often (e.) police work ("What it

3. The typology we present is naturally a compromise with reality. We do not pretend that it captures all of what any officer is. Nevertheless certain characteristics of officer behavior and rationale can be separated and rendered meaningful for the ends intended here.

4. Blake, *Probation is not Casework*, 12 Fed.Probation 54 (June 1948).

5. Meeker, *Probation is Casework*, 12 Fed.Probation 51 (June 1948).

6. The terminology here is based in part upon titles and descriptions suggested for police officers in R. Taft & R. England, Criminology 321 (1964). Our categories are also similar to those suggested by Oh-

lin, Pivin & Pappenfort, *Major Dilemmas of the Social Worker in Probation and Parole*, 2 National Probation & Parole Assoc. J. 211 (1956).

7. Hardman, *The Function of the Probation Officer*, 24 Fed.Probation 4 (Sept. 1960). Hardman adds that he will "defend this definition before the parole board, the supreme court, or the angels in heaven."

8. Id. at 7.

9. Id.

10. G. Giardini, The Parole Process 265 (1959).

simmers down to is police work. We're the policemen back of the agencies.").[11]

While these characteristics are found in the officer at this pole of our typology, we must add that the philosophies and rationales which cause certain officers to gravitate to this pole are all too easily relegated to a "junior G-man" [12] model. One may find officers at this pole with examined philosophies which dictate that firmness, authority, and rule abidance are essentials of social life and ought to be enforced during the probation period. What will concern us however is that their behavior is unshakably law and rule-enforcing.

The Time Servers. For the purposes of our typology, time-serving officers are nearly the functional equivalent of the law enforcers. They comprise that category of probation officers who find no law-enforcing or casework vocation in probation. Instead, they see their jobs as having certain requirements to be fulfilled until retirement. They have little aspiration to improve their skills; they are not likely to attend seminars or training institutes, nor do they belong to professional associations. Their conduct on the job is rule-abiding and their job responsibilities are met minimally but methodically. Rules and regulations are upheld but unexamined. They don't make the rules; they just work there.

The Therapeutic Agent. At the other pole of officer role conception is the officer who considers himself a therapeutic agent. Here, the officer's role is emphasized in the administration of a form of treatment [13] artfully "introducing the probationer to a

11. Officer opinion cited in Diana, supra note 1, at 199.

12. An epithet common among officers studied by P. Takagi, Evaluation Systems and Adaptations in a Formal Organization: A Case Study of a Parole Agency 116 (unpublished Ph.D. dissertation at Stanford University, 1967). Social casework has only recently discovered the meaning of "authority" which sociology has classically held for it. As a turning point, one might suggest Fink's *Authority in the Correctional Process*, 25 Fed.

Probation 34 (Sept. 1961). See also D. Dressler, Practice and Theory of Probation and Parole 170 (1969) for a recent attempt to redefine authority in such a way as to make it palatable to those who had learned it as a synonym for "authoritarianism."

13. I have chosen to reproduce the rhetoric of the therapeutic agent to dramatize both the inseparability of form and content and the tenacious grasp on a sophmoric identity which such an acrobatic rhetoric represents. A leading so-

better way of life" [14] by the "motivation of patterns of behavior which are constructive," [15] by "giving support and guidance to those who are unable to solve their problems by themselves," [16] and by "providing an opportunity to work through his ambivalent feelings." [17] This is accomplished through the use of knowledge of the offender history "analyzed in terms of psychological, physiological, and social factors," [18] "day-by-day analyses of recorded interviews (which) develop the kind of skill needed in the evaluation of the individual considered for probation," [19] and the loan of the officer's "own ego to the client's in the perception and appraisal of reality." [20] Charles Shireman has attempted to summarize this working philosophy as follows:

1. We take conscious pains in our every contact with the offender to demonstrate our concern about him and our respect for him as a human being.

2. We seize every opportunity to help the offender come to understand the nature of the shared, problem-solving, helping process by actually experiencing it.

3. We recognize, bring into the open, and deal directly with the offender's negative attitudes toward us as the representatives of social authority.

4. We "partialize" the total life problem confronting the offender.

cial casework theorist expresses this exactly as she shares with us some insights into "process":

In short, working from a process base the social worker conceives all phenomena as unique within classes or categories, as characterized by continuous change and direction toward an end, as embodying potential for such change which itself shifts in the course of time. He uses a process, a professional social work process, to affect processes, that is, the life process of an individual, group, or community, in order that the processes affected may have the best possible chance for self-realization in relation to a purpose which has brought worker and clientele together.

R. Smalley, Theory for Social Work Practice 130 (1967).

14. Glover, *Probation: The Art of Introducing the Probationer to a Better Way of Life*, 15 Fed.Probation 8 (Sept. 1951).

15. Gronewald, *Casework in Probation*, 39 Prison J. 45 (Oct. 1959).

16. Id.

17. Id.

18. Id. at 43.

19. Id.

20. Id. at 45.

5. We help the individual perceive the degree to which his behavior has and will result in his own unhappiness.[21]

We find further that officers of the therapeutic agent type are likely to belong to professional associations, actively campaign for recognition of the professional status of probation officers, display various diplomas and certificates testifying to their skills, and speak in the argot of social casework wherever possible.

The Synthetic Officer.   The fourth and final officer type in our classification is distinguished by his recognition of both the treatment and law enforcement components of the probation officer's role.   His attempts at supervision reflect his desire to satisfy the arguments of both the therapeutic and law-enforcing agents.   Thus, he sets for himself the active task of combining the paternal, authoritarian, and judgmental with the therapeutic. In so doing, he may unknowingly solve what is alleged to be the classical dilemma of corrections.   The most common way of phrasing this dilemma is that, for therapeutic purposes, the probation officer must require the probationer to "tell all" but must also recognize that revelation of the wrong sort may result in revocation.[22]   Clearly, a central issue of probation supervision is the treatment-control dilemma and its resolution in the revocation decision.

REVOCATION AND THE LOGIC OF TREATMENT

Straightforward confrontation with the question of revocation should define a strategy of supervision, clarify it, and set its boundaries.   For the law enforcer and time server the logic is simple—revocation should be recommended whenever the rules of probation are violated.   The simplicity and directness of this answer are not available for those with a faith in probation as treatment.

Extensions of the logic of treatment demand not only that probation itself be a treating process but also that the officer be provided with therapeutic alternatives.   Such a portrait of corrections is painted when probation is treatment under supervision in society, when parole is more restricted training for social adjustment, and when prison is genuinely rehabilitative treatment

21. Shireman, *Casework in Probation and Parole: Some Considerations in Diagnosis and Treatment,* 27 Fed.Probation 51 (June 1963).

22. See Ohlin, Pivin & Pappenfort, *supra* note 6, at 211–25.

which prepares the prisoner for reentry into society. When added to this portrait of corrections, such conceptions as the halfway house suggest an even smoother curve.

This, of course, is not the case. Probation cannot operate on the assumption of the rehabilitative nature of the prison. Instead it must operate on the assumption of the destructive nature of prisons, and, if it wishes to consider itself a treatment agency, probation must do so with the simultaneous recognition of non-therapeutic alternatives. In short, revocation must be viewed as the boundary of treatment and the beginning of its compromise.

Arguments to the contrary assert that penal institutions need not be treatment facilities *in se* but may be considered so *per se*. In a variation on a behaviorist theme revocation becomes a sanction, probation and parole become rewards, and the entire correctional process emerges as an extended shaping mechanism. This argument, however, is unconvincing. Few institutions, if any, have been able to demonstrate that their inmates profited from their stay there. On the other hand, modern penology has shown that institutionalization has a high probability of damaging the inmate and returning him to society in worse condition than when he entered. Even if the institutional experience itself is harmless, the loss of employment, separation from family, and label of convict are most likely to be harmful.

Recognition of the boundaries and compromise of treatment at revocation forces those who believe in treatment to adopt a single, consistent rationale for revocation. That rationale is that the probationer is dangerous to himself or others. Considering the nature of penal institutions, no other rationale is consistent with a faith in treatment.

Such a conception of revocation bears double-edged consequences for probation. While this conception is predicated upon a faith in probation as treatment, those who hold such a faith must advocate probation even when, in treatment, it is not successful. A treatment strategy of probation with the conception of revocation we have suggested must also provide the officer with both power to guide and control the probationer during treatment and definitions of desired conduct which direct and inform him. In addition, this power can only be acquired from revocation as a threat which will usually remain unfulfilled.

Probably much probation work is conducted by threats of revocation. Our observations confirm that threats are regularly used and carried out by time servers and law enforcers. However, as a strategy for the therapeutic or synthetic officers, threats seem to dissolve quickly because with the single "clear-and-present-danger" exception they are not carried out. Nevertheless, for the majority of probationers who do not seem to break the rules of probation anyway the simple threat-of-revocation strategy probably works as well as any other.

The central problem which remains is the resolution of genuine treatment and control in an effective supervision strategy. Our observations suggest that such a resolution does exist. This resolution is removed from the boundaries of revocation. It gains its strength from the definition of the officer-probationer-department triad. It is slow to degenerate and operates on the medium of exchange.[23]

A THEORY OF PROBATION SUPERVISION

The strategy of exchange is only implicitly understood by officers who employ it. Nevertheless, it seems to be applied by all officers of the synthetic type. We know of no other form of supervision in which the synthetic officers' aspirations can be satisfied. Let us first present diagrammatically the parties involved in probation supervision:

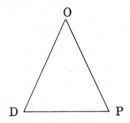

FIGURE 1: SUPERVISION TRIAD
[A8886]

wherein O represents the officer; P, the probationer; and D, the department. Let us now look sequentially at the way in which the bonds of the triad are completed.

The Initial Interview. The first meeting between the probationer and the officer serves to define the components of their relationship. It defines not only the restrictions which will be placed upon the probationer, but also suggests the medium of exchange through which exceptions may be sought. The initial interview regularly includes an explanation of the rules and regu-

---

23. The notation used in our theory is roughly appropriated from F. Heider, The Psychology of Interpersonal Relations (1958).

lations by which the probationer is expected to live. These may range from requirements such as seeking permission to marry or obtain a pilot's license, to technical violations such as using alcohol or frequenting places of probable criminal association.[24] In the department which we studied, many of these rules may be printed and distributed to the probationer. Here, the probation officer functions as an officer of the court. Our triadic diagram is now rendered as:

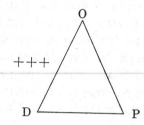

FIGURE 2: SUPERVISION TRIAD
[A8887]

indicating the officer's responsibility to the department and its regulations.

The second substantive component of the initial interview is an extension of aid, assistance, and guidance by the officer to the probationer. Statements and assurances such as "I am here to help you," "Your problems and difficulties are my responsibilities as well," and offers of referral for employment, family, medical, or psychological counselling characterize this component. While our observations reveal a wide variation in the style of such offers, all are intended to show interest and give assistance. Consequently, we may now complete the officer-probationer bond in our diagram as:

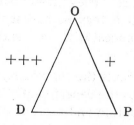

FIGURE 3: SUPERVISION TRIAD
[A8888]

24. Arluke, *A Summary of Parole Rules: Thirteen Years Later*, 15 Crime & Delinquency 267 (1969).

if the officer is able to convince the probationer of the sincerity of his interest.

At this point we have not yet completed the bond between the department and the probationer. It is the most critical bond in the triad because its completion resolves the treatment-control dilemma. As we have suggested above, the problem of the synthetic officer is that he bears two compelling but patently inconsistent roles, one or both of which are denied by other officer types. Such a problem is authentic and our initial observations and interviews in the department were bent upon articulating it. Remarkably, in our search for the classical dilemma of corrections, logically expressed in the role of the probation officer, we found no evidence of its existence. Watching, participating in, and discussing case relationships suggested to us that for probation it was a logical reality but a sociological fiction. The synthetic officer is able to dispose of it by including a managed reality of the "department" in the case relationship. In order to clarify this last statement, we report the responses of two synthetic officers to the question, "How can you tell a probationer that he should bring his problems to you and tell you honestly about the difficulties he is having when he knows that if you find out too much you can lock him up?"

Officer One: "I tell my probationers that I'm here to help them, to get them a job, and whatever else I can do. But I tell them too that I have a job to do and a family to support and that if they get too far off the track, I can't afford to put my job on the line for them. I'm going to have to violate them."

Officer Two (A Narcotics Specialist): "From the beginning I tell them what the rules are. They know, though, that more than anything else I require that they be honest with me. And they know too that if they're honest with me, (and I can tell if they're not), I won't screw them."

In each of these statements the controlling element of the officer's role is transferred to the department. In the first, the officer claims that his evaluation and position are at stake. In the second, the officer further separates himself as the mediator between departmental rules and the probationer. We may observe that "screwing the probationer" means reporting information which would be negatively judged by departmental standards. Because the department is designated as a distinct participant in the case relationship, one which bears the sanctioning and authoritative responsibility, we can now complete our triadic diagram of the initial phase of probation supervision:

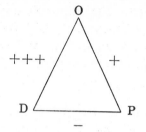

FIGURE 4: SUPERVISION TRIAD
[A8889]

THE ORGANIZATIONAL CONTEXT AND THE RULES OF PROBATION

Before we extend our theory to include the development of the relationship which our diagram signifies, it is appropriate to ask to what extent "the department" corresponds to the benevolent-but-unyielding-despot role ascribed to it. To free us, at least in part, from the real differences between departments, we can observe that no single philosophical position exists to which the field of probation is committed. Consequently, value positions are not closed and substantive evaluation is not logically possible.[25]

Since the illogic of evaluations has been of little concern to more sophisticated fields of study than probation, an examination of the rules of probation and the officer's discretion with respect to their application is more compelling. We shall consider three aspects of the rules of probation in their organizational context. First, probation rules are generally silly. If they were taken

---

25. This is in part the thrust of P. Takagi, supra note 12, whose research attempted the exploration of evaluative discrepancies suggested by Scott, *Organizational Evaluation and Authority*, 1967 Admin.Sci.Q. 93. The problem of evaluation of the probation officer's performance is elegantly assumed under Herbert Simon's observation more than a quarter of a century ago:

There is one important difference between permitting a subordinate discretion over a value premise and permitting him discretion over a factual premise. The latter can always be evaluated as correct or incorrect in an objective, empirical sense. . . . To a value premise . . . the terms correct and incorrect do not apply.

Simon, *Decision Making and Organizational Authority*, 4 Pub.Admin.Rev. 18 (1944).

seriously, very few probationers would complete their terms without violation.   Among prohibitions are liquor usage, gambling, indebtedness, and association or correspondence with "undesirables."   Among permissions necessary from the officer are marriage, change of employment, and travel out of the community.   Among requirements are curfews, treatment for venereal disease, and church attendance.[26]   Arluke's evaluation of them is worth repeating:

> Some parole conditions are moralistic, most are impractical, others impinge on human rights, and all reflect obsolete criminological conceptions.   On the whole they project a percept of a man that does not exist.[27]

Secondly, because of the nature of the rules, strict administration of them is tempered both by the officer's access to information of violations and by an attitude of reasonableness toward vigorous enforcement.   Beyond this, however, at least two authors in professional publications suggest that probation rules are to be thought of only as flexible guidelines.[28]   A final point in reference to rule violation and departmental hegemony is that the vast majority of information about a probationer's conduct can only be provided by the officer.   Thus, even if rules were practical and even if they were stipulated as inflexible and indiscriminate, the officer would still have the option of providing (albeit at his own risk) the information upon which they could be applied.   This third aspect of the character of probation rules in their organizational context is salient even under present conditions.   It is possible for an officer to "screw" his probationer.

The implication of these observations is that the "department," as the genuine bearer of the authority and control components of the officer role, is to no small extent a fiction.   The rules, their application, and their dismissal are largely a matter of the discretion of the officer, who, with very little personal risk, may conceal or permit their violation.

26. Arluke, supra note 24, at 265.

27. Id. at 269.

28. DiCerbo, *When Should Probation Be Revoked?*, 30 Fed.Probation 11 (June 1966); D. Dressler, supra note 12, at 254.

EXCHANGE STRATEGY AND THE DEVELOPMENT
OF SUPERVISION

The fictional nature of the rules of probation in their organizational setting, combined with the synthetic officer's artificial manipulation of "the department," introduce properties to the case relationship which not only increase the officer's control but also suggest patterns of case development. If we adopt a market analogy, the probationer can be considered a consumer who wishes to purchase the completion of his term. In the triadic relationship which the synthetic officer structures, the probationer is provided with two currencies. The first is compliance with the rules of his probation. In following such rules he purchases his completion by demonstrating what is thought to be satisfactory social maturity. If he can complete his term without violation, he will have little need to draw upon the second currency which is available to him.

This second currency may be called rapport. It consists of appeals for aid, assistance, or understanding combined with the confession of problems. For those probationers who are helped by probation, it is the stuff of which counselling is made. Honest counselling is possible in this case because, analogically, the department and officer are different sellers. What cannot be purchased from the department with rule compliance can be purchased from the officer with rapport.

The analogy of two sellers which the probationer perceives, however, is only an illusion. He is dealing with a near-perfect monopoly. The officer controls the definitions and resulting permissions. He is able to dramatize his own separation from his departmental superego by techniques ranging from forceful restatement ("These are the rules. I didn't make 'em; you didn't make 'em, but we both have to live with 'em.") to revelation of his own jeopardy ("My supervisor is on my neck over what I'm letting you get away with."). While maintaining the separation, he may also grant exception ("I'm going to go out on a limb for you.") or express charity ("You were right to tell me the truth. We can work on it together and keep what happened between ourselves.").

Practically, the officer who holds such a monopoly has two advantages. First, he is capable of creating "false bottoms" on the availability of pardons for violations. The criteria for satisfac-

tory conduct can be set at virtually any level. The officer's definitions are perceived as those of the department. Secondly, the
officer is able to adjust those false bottoms, while giving the impression of following departmental policy.[29]

In terms of our original diagrams, the serial development of
probation supervision, structured in the manner suggested, can
be signified as shown in Figure 5. The exchange of signs from

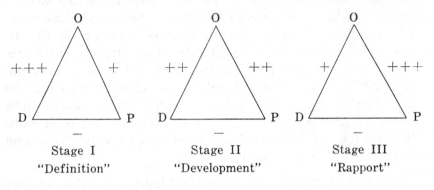

| Stage I | Stage II | Stage III |
| "Definition" | "Development" | "Rapport" |

FIGURE 5: THE DEVELOPMENT OF PROBATION SUPERVISION
[A8890]

the O–D bond to the O–P bond represent the primary process
exchange of permission for rapport as the case relationship develops. This exchange is predicated upon the recognition of some
difficulty in abiding by the defined rules. In the absence of this
difficulty, probation is essentially perfunctory and there are no
structural reasons for the supervision relationship to develop beyond Stage I. Other roles may develop based upon personal at-
traction, interests, or mutual experience, but from the reference
of an officer and a probationer they are incalculable. Consider,
for example, the officer who learns about jazz from a musician
probationer.

While the transfer of signs represents the primary process of
exchange, that is not all it represents. In addition, the officer
adds to the bargain an apparent change in his fidelity to the department. He can no longer be simply an agent. In light of the
investment which he makes for rapport with the probationer, he

29. A complication intrudes here
when the decision to revoke probation is genuinely considered. It
is that a consideration of the
judge's criteria for granting a revocation must be made by the officer. If the judges refuses to grant
revocation when requested by the
officer, the officer not only loses
face but also destroys any chance
of regaining rapport.

cannot maintain for the probationer's eyes the same strength of attachment to his officer position. He may, of course, still hold it, but, in effect, he says that the job and the rules are secondary and the man is what really matters.

Consequently, we have represented the bond between the officer and the department as minimal in the final stage. In some cases, where an apparent team of officer and probationer develops against department rules, this minimally positive bond is indeed an overstatement.

DISCUSSION

Several theoretical analyses of structurally similar positions give formal credence to the conception we have developed here. Perhaps the broadest of these is Simmel's analysis of the respective characteristics of the dyad and triad. Critical is Simmel's observation that:

> The dyad represents both the first social synthesis and unification and the first separation and antithesis. The appearance of the third party indicates transition, conciliation and abandonment of absolute contrast. . . . [30]

According to Simmel, the triad offers the advantage of non-partisanship and mediation roles. This is the intent and result of the inclusion of "the department" in the case relationship. Simmel claims further that the triad transforms the nature of conflict from its invariably personal quality in the dyad. He observes:

> A third mediating social element deprives conflicting claims of their affective qualities because it neutrally formulates and presents these claims to the two parties involved. Thus the circle that is fatal to all reconciliation is avoided: the vehemence of the one no longer provokes that of the other . . . . [31]

In the triadically-structured case relationship the officer need never come into direct personal conflict with his probationer. He can claim to be only the objective reader of departmental regulations. Furthermore, the quality of the officer's affective responses can only be interpreted as partisan to the probationer's interests.

30. G. Simmel, The Sociology of Georg Simmel 145 (K. Wolff, transl. & ed. 1964).

31. Id. at 147.

One can find similarly structured analyses of specific occupations. The most famous is the foreman. Variously called a "marginal man of industry," [32] "the man in the middle," [33] and a "master and victim of doubletalk," [34] his position is located between worker and management. He owes allegiance to both but can fully maintain the identity of neither. Effective foremanship depends upon the foreman's ability to manipulate a situation structurally similar to that of the synthetic officer. The difference between the positions is the privilege, which the officer enjoys, of defining his own criteria of conduct, while the foreman's criteria are dictated and evaluated by others.

Goffman cites baseball umpire Babe Pinelli's vision of his task as the product of the rules of the game, the player's enthusiasm and the benevolent impartiality with which they must be reconciled. Pinelli states:

> It is easy for any umpire to thumb a man out of the game. It is often a much more difficult job to keep him in the game—to understand and anticipate his claim so that a nasty rhubarb cannot develop.[35]

In contrast, however, the umpire's rules are closely supervised and his performance is both public and evaluable.

A closer parallel to the triadic case relationship and its place in a manipulatable rule structure is the drama staged regularly in many large automobile sales agencies. The plot begins with the customer's decision on a car about which to negotiate a price. The customer is then led to a room where he waits, while the salesman leaves to "find out what he can do." He invariably returns with an offer, the generosity of which he punctuates in many ways. If the customer cannot be convinced, this exit and consultation with a higher authority may be repeated. Various *leitmotifs* intervene as the climax approaches. The climax occurs when the source of authority or an available substitute appears. His performance either closes the deal or terminates the

32. Wray, *Marginal Men of Industry: The Foreman*, 46 Am.J.Sociology 298 (1949).

33. Gardner & Whyte, *The Man in the Middle: Position and Problems of the Foreman*, 1945 J. Applied Anthropology 1.

34. Roethlisberger, *The Foreman: Master and Victim of Doubletalk*, 23 Harv.Bus.Rev. 283 (1945).

35. E. Goffman, The Presentation of Self in Everyday Life 98 (1959).

negotiations. The customer never comes into direct conflict with the salesman, nor is the salesman's performance anything but accommodating.

While the similarities to the case supervision pattern we have sketched are clear in this last example, we do not wish to suggest that the intent of the case supervision drama is as crassly motivated nor as interpersonally impoverished. There is a difference, which ought not be minimized, between an artificial performance designed to increase commissions and a crescive drama based upon a genuine interest in the welfare of a client. Whether or not that drama can survive its disenchantment, remains a central problem of the social psychology of probation.

THE HUMANITY OF PROBATION OFFICERS*

The title above is not intended to imply a discussion of the foibles and human failings of probation officers, although there doubtless are many which would make interesting reading. Rather, humanity is used here to denote the best qualities of humankind: kindness, considerateness, sympathy, mercy, compassion, and understanding. In a complex society of computerized impersonality and identification by number, simple human concern is essential to a lessening of tension and turmoil. The probation officer must not grow hard and calloused in such a setting, but must maintain the "common touch" of basic human emotions.

To some this may seem to belabor the obvious and to others it may appear trite; but in an environment which creates inhumanity, it becomes necessary to remind ourselves that we—who are supposed to correct and rehabilitate—cannot allow our services to contribute to that creation through the exercise of inhumanity toward our probationers. The obvious and trite are most likely to be overlooked, especially in routine, day-to-day activity. It is this very failing on a wide scale which makes it necessary to review the need for humanity on the part of the probation officer.

* Claude T. Mangrum, *Federal Probation*, June 1972. Reprinted with permission.

Probationers Have a History of Failure

Many probationers have long histories of failure in their families, schools, jobs, marriages, and even in illegal activities. These people need successful experiences, even small and menial ones, to help them feel a part of the world. The probation officer can contribute to this success by treating the probationer with dignity and respect—not a difficult thing to do, but an action which helps him to feel that he is somebody.

We live in an environment which creates inhumanity. It has spawned poverty, violence, and crime. It has brought about rootlessness, impersonality, and noninvolvement. It has produced loneliness, restlessness, and unconcern. As a result, we have no time for people as *people*. We have lost the sense of being a vital part of something important. Consequently, we feel little commitment to others or to the welfare of our communities.

This is particularly true of most of our probationers whose environment has been such that there is little they can do to influence—to say nothing of control—the forces and factors which are vital to their dignity, well-being, or even their lives. They are frequently the victims of social injustice, social rejection, and social stigma. The insight and social skills necessary to deal with injustice, rejection, and stigma are not characteristic of our probationers. Such victimization may, indeed, convince them that they are "no good" and that they "can't make it." These feelings are quite likely, in turn, to lead to frustration, hostility, and further illegal and/or antisocial behavior.

In our dealings with them, we must not further contribute to this demeaning and dehumanizing process through actions which deny their essential dignity and worth or which further isolate them from participation in the mainstream of social activity. This is a real possibility for probation officers because of their work in an authoritative setting; and the occupancy of a position of authority often leads to arrogance; and arrogance generally results in a "put down" of others or arouses hostility in them. In either case, the probation officer loses the opportunity to be successful in his mission of "rehabilitation" because he winds up actually perpetuating the dehumanizing treatment to which the probationer has been so long subjected. The constructive use of authority is proper for probation officers; but arrogance is always destructive and has no place in a profession dedicated to serving others.

Be Genuine in Relating to Probationers

The probation officer must be real in relating to his probationers. It is easy to grow calloused toward them when all our time is taken up with trying to solve the problems of others and to enforce the regulations of the courts. But, if we become suspicious and cold, our attitude will reveal itself to the probationer. It cannot be successfully covered up by a "professional" facade—which is often disguised as being clinically objective, not getting overinvolved, or merely performing one's duty. The result is that we "professionalize" ourselves out of meaningful contact with the very people we are charged with helping.

The probation officer must be sensitive to how he appears to his probationers because they react according to how they "read" the officer, not according to the impression the officer thinks he conveys. It is difficult to long deceive people about how we really feel toward them.

A sensitive response to human needs will do away with the necessity to project an "image." Being genuine in relating to others makes its own profound impression—one on which it is probably impossible to improve. As trite as it may sound, there is nothing weak, or unmanly, or unprofessional in feelings of concern, compassion, understanding, and warmth so long as these feelings are real and are not patronizing or condescending.

Awareness of the influences of cultural differences, desire for the protection of individual rights, respect for the integrity and dignity of the probationer—all these will result in treatment of probationers as *people,* not as cases. Yet, they do not mean a disregard for the rights or welfare of the community. There is nothing necessarily incompatible between warmth and acceptance and firm enforcement of the laws of the land. We must take whatever corrective measures are necessary; but these must not permit us to demean the dignity of the individual. There must be a balance between compassion and control; between friendliness and firmness; between consideration and correction.

Effective Communication

The probation officer must talk *with* the probationer, not *to* him. This is the only way to effectively communicate. Trying to "treat" the probationer by issuing commands and directives, or giving friendly advice, or finding for him all the solutions to his problems will not be effective—either because this approach is likely to arouse hostility and resistance or because what is being said makes no impression on him.

Like everyone else, the probationer is always interpreting what he hears from the probation officer, as well as the probation officer-probationer relationship itself, in terms of its specific meaning for him.   This meaning is determined by what is traveling on what someone has called the "inner circuit."   Such things as the probationer's unique past experiences, his cultural heritage, his immediate social environment, and his pressing, current concerns all condition the meaning for him of whatever the probation officer does or says.

Consequently, the probationer does not always hear what the probation officer intends to convey.   And, to further complicate the situation, his response is based on his own interpretation of the event's meaning for him.   It is no wonder that misunderstandings arise between probation officer and probationer.   Such misunderstandings occur in everyday communication on all levels. The potential for such misunderstanding is, no doubt, much greater in the probation officer-probationer relationship with its overtones of "establishment" vs. the rebels, authority vs. resistance, we vs. they.

So often in this situation, the probation officer may come to think that the probationer's reactions are deliberate defiance, or "he just doesn't care that I'm trying to help him," or "he doesn't want to change his behavior," or "we just can't seem to communicate," or "he just won't learn."

One of the ways in which the probation officer can help overcome these interferences to clear communication between himself and the probationer is to relate to and treat him with dignity, concern, and awareness that he, too, is a man.   Of course, this will not solve all the communication problems, but it is an important step in the direction of reducing misunderstandings and of removing the barriers which frequently hinder effective treatment efforts.

Contribution to Success

There is a personal and professional "payoff" to treating people with dignity, respect, feeling; to relating to them as worthwhile and important. They will reciprocate the treatment and, thereby, contribute immeasurably to one's success as a probation officer. A fundamental treatment technique, long used by most probation officers, is a meaningful interpersonal relationship with the probationer; a relationship built on mutual trust and respect. If the probationer is not treated with concern, dignity, and respect, this most important technique cannot possibly be effective.

In the long run, this is the only way for the probation officer to behave. All else—disrespect, contempt, unconcern, facade, distrust—will fail. Only the probationer can really be successful in changing his own behavior and attitudes; and his success is the probation officer's success. We have much less control over his behavior than we like to think, especially if we get "hung up" with our position of authority.

The most effective way to turn the probationer from his illegal ways is to treat him with dignity. He is less likely to recidivate if he believes he is "somebody" and if the probation officer reinforces this feeling through considerate treatment. Does he already have a sense of his own self-worth? If so, he will react with hostility to treatment by the probation officer which denies his worth. If he does not have a positive concept of himself, try to imagine what we are doing to him when we act in such ways as to reinforce his negative self-concept. We drive him further and further away from any desire or motivation to conduct himself in a positive way.

Whatever he may have done in violating the law, he is a *man* and has the right to retain his dignity. This includes making his own decisions, within a framework of legally and socially acceptable behavior, of what he does and does not do. To strip him of all choice relative to his own conduct is to strip him of the human dignity which distinguishes man from lower orders of the animal kingdom.

There are, of course, some probationers who will take advantage of this kind of treatment—partially because it is so different from the way they usually are treated and they do not really know how to respond to such expressions of acceptance. Some will be hostile because they will consider it to be a "put on." Some will be passive because of confusion of not knowing what is the expected response. In every case, the probation officer will have to start with the probationer "where he is" and patiently demonstrate genuine respect for him as an individual. The results will be most worthwhile as he sees probationers grow as *men*. Whatever risk is involved in some probationers taking advantage is minimal compared to the awareness that one has aided another to grow and to improve his relations with the community.

Know Yourself

For the probation officer to really know his probationer, he *must* know himself. To always treat others with dignity and respect, he must respect his own integrity. To be real in his relations with others, he must know who he is, what he is doing, and why he behaves that way. This kind of self-awareness is not always easy. We all have biases, prejudices, and pet peeves— many of which were learned so early in life that we tend to regard them as part of our biological heritage. Self-discipline and control in relation to these do not come naturally. One must be aware of these feelings to be sure that they do not govern his actions. Biases can be unlearned; prejudices can be overcome; pet peeves can be tolerated. Self-discipline and rational control are necessary to guard against the problem of selective enforcement of probation conditions based on one's own biases.

One of the things with which most probationers need to deal is their feelings—about society, law, authority, themselves, and a host of other things—without being shut off by the "helping agent." Overt behavior is frequently the expression of feelings that can no longer be suppressed. The threat of punishment may have held behavior in check until the feelings were so explosive that nothing could stop the outburst. Society, in this circumstance, often deals with behavior but feeling is seldom considered. So, it is usually only a matter of time until the outburst occurs again. For the probation officer to be the "helping agent" in dealing with the probationer's feelings, he must also be aware of, and able to deal with, his own feelings regarding, among other things, authority, acceptance, his probationers, his job, and himself. If he does not "know where he is going" in this regard, he will find it extremely difficult to help the probationer know where he is going.

The probation officer who does not know himself—his strengths and weaknesses, his virtues and faults, his potentials and limitations—will never really know his probationer. Not knowing the probationer usually means insensitivity to his needs.

Insensitivity to his needs means inability to help him meet those needs. Inability to meet those needs means social failure for him. Failure for the probationer means lack of success for the probation officer. To be successful, the probation officer must know himself and must discipline himself to always treat his probationers with respect and dignity.

Conclusion

The probation officer must be aware of, concerned about, and actively engaged in changing social conditions which contribute to the dehumanizing of individuals. He must be vitally concerned with social reform and with reform of the system for administration of criminal justice. But, in his concern for changing the system, he cannot afford to neglect his probationer. There is relatively little he can do as an individual to change the overall system; but he can determine that his treatment of the probationer will not be an extension of the brutality, callousness, unconcern, and delay which so frequently characterizes the system prior to his getting the probationer for treatment.

If we can accept, with Ramsey Clark, that crime flows from acts which demean the individual, then one way to prevent a criminal and antisocial behavior is to treat probationers in a way that shows genuine respect for the dignity and worth of the individual.

Despite our traditional claims for the effectiveness of probation, treating the offender as a "second-class" citizen by denying him human dignity and worth is much worse than no probation service at all.

_____

EXPOSING THE QUASI–JUDICIAL ROLE
OF THE PROBATION OFFICER*

_____

As judges appear to be shedding more and more of their judicial functions, the role of the probation officer is undergoing sympathetic change. While there is a distinction to be made between the judicial tasks of a judge and the judge's administrative

* Eugene H. Czajkoski Federal Probation, September 1973. Reprinted with permission.

tasks, the distinction often becomes blurred in the actual operation of the court. Constitutionally, the judge may delegate his
administrative powers but he may not delegate his judicial powers. Under the circumstance where judicial powers and administrative powers are becoming increasingly confused, the probation
officer seems to find himself more and more in a quasi-judicial
position.

Unquestionably, there is a difference between administrative
decision-making and adjudication. Administrative decision-making depends on free, extensive and informal discussions with
many interests and informed individuals or groups. Adjudication
requires formalized procedures, the building of a record, and the
presentation and cross-examination of evidence. In adjudication,
the final judgment is based on the record alone. The aforemen-
tioned difference is well known and this discussion of the probation officer's quasi-judicial role does not rest on an analysis between judicial process and administrative process. Questions are
raised. It rests rather on the analysis of judicial effect. Questions are raised as to the propriety of the probation officer's
achieving judicial effect without judicial process.

The case for the quasi-judicial role of the probation officer is
made along five lines of functional analysis.

(1) Plea Bargaining and the Abdication of the Judge From Sentencing

It wasn't too long ago that plea bargaining was curtained off
in the courtroom. To insure a valid guilty plea, one which could
not later be upset on appeal, judges engaged in a litany with the
defendant wherein the question was asked, "Did anyone make
you any promises?" [1] Promises made to induce a guilty plea were,
in effect, denied in open court. Everyone involved, including the
judge, knew about the plea bargaining and the promises made
but all, especially the defendant, (lest his deal be upset) denied
the negotiated promises in open court. All seemed to have benefited from the charade except that it was unseemly for the court
to participate in subterfuge and, certainly, the recipient of justice
was often left with a quizzical notion of the basic honesty of
the court. Now that plea bargaining is openly acknowledged

1. An example of the detailed questioning pursued by a judge prior
to accepting a guilty plea can be
found in: Frank J. Remington, et
al., *Criminal Justice Administration*, New York: The Bobbs-Merrill Co., 1969, p. 567.

and has the imprimatur of the United States Supreme Court,[2] the air in the courtroom is a little clearer. Another result is that the pace of plea bargaining, with its new-found legal respectability, has been stepped up.

To even the most casual observer of the court, it is evident that the judge's role in sentencing has shrunk almost to that of a mere announcer. Not unwillingly, it seems, the judge has abdicated a major portion of his sentencing role. It is the prosecutor, the chief plea bargainer, who in reality determines sentence.

Some very large prosecution offices have gone so far as to produce handbooks to guide assistant district attorneys in fixing sentence through bargaining. Completely ignoring the generally accepted correctional philosophy that sentencing should be in accord with the individual characteristics of the offender, the guidelines used by prosecutors are usually based on the crime committed. The prosecutor's influence in sentencing is drawing us further back toward classical concepts of penology (sentencing in accordance with the crime) even while lawyers in other contexts, such as through the Model Penal Code of the American Law Institute and the Model Sentencing Act of the National Council on Crime and Delinquency, espouse sentencing in accordance with the characteristics of the individual offender. It is doubtful that prosecutors are moved by one or the other of the two philosophical stands. It is more likely that they are motivated by production goals and by bureaucratic standards of efficiency and self-interest.

By permitting plea bargaining, judges have left themselves little to do other than to certify conditions previously agreed to by defendant, prosecutor, and police. Largely relieved of their sentencing role, many judges also appear to be also giving up their role of interpreting the law for trial juries.[3] Many juries find themselves having to decide on the requirements of law as well as decide on facts to be fitted to law. The fitting is less likely to be done by judges these days.

The abdication of sentencing responsibility to the plea bargaining system leaves the probation officer in an even more peculiar position than it leaves the judge. Theoretically, the proba-

2. In Brady v. U. S., 397 U.S. 742 (1970), the Supreme Court held that plea inducements were generally compatible with the goals of the criminal justice system.

3. This phenomenon has been reported to the writer by a number of practicing trial lawyers, and it would appear to warrant some empirical investigation before a trend can be agreed upon.

tion officer is supposed to make sentencing recommendations to the judge on the basis of his professional estimate of the rehabilitation potential of the defendant. Whether or not a defendant is sentenced to probation probably depends more now on his success in plea bargaining than on his promise of reformation. How does the probation officer fit into this new scheme of extensive plea bargaining? What point is there in conducting an elaborate social investigation by way of evaluating rehabilitation potential? In answer to the first question, Professor Blumberg points out that the probation officer serves to "cool the mark" in the production-oriented and confidence game-like-system of expeditiously moving defendants through the court by means of plea bargaining.[4] The probation officer can assure the defendant of how wise it was for him to plead guilty and of how much benefit there is to be derived from the correctional efforts arising out of the sentence. In answer to the second question, social investigations of defendants (presentence reports) are becoming shorter, more factual, and less analytical.

Like the judge's role, the probation officer's role in sentencing is diminishing. If it has become the judicial role of the judge to simply certify the plea bargaining process, then the probation officer's role is quasi-judicial in that he does the same thing. It is admittedly a peculiar argument, but where the probation officer does a perfunctory presentence report and aims his recommendation toward what he already knows will be the plea bargaining sentence, then he is indeed playing out a de facto judicial role.

It has long been argued that the probation officer's role in sentencing has been a quasi-judicial one, especially where the judge more-or-less automatically imposes the sentence recommended by the probation officer. Various empirical studies have shown a very high correlation between probation officer recommendation and disposition made by the judge. Carter and Wilkins have pointed out that judges have followed probation officer recommendations in better than 95 percent of the cases.[5] Among the factors which might explain the high level of agreement between recommendations and dispositions, it was postulat-

4. Abraham Blumberg, *Criminal Justice.* Chicago: Quadrangle Books, 1967.

5. Robert M. Carter and Leslie T. Wilkins, "Some Factors in Sentencing Policy," *Journal of Criminal Law, Criminology and Police Science*, 58, No. 4 (1967), pp. 503–514.

ed that probation officers make their recommendations in anticipation of what the judge desires (second guessing the judge).
Nowadays it is more likely that the prosecutor has found a way
to communicate the plea bargaining agreement to the probation
officer and the probation officer responds with an appropriate
recommendation (or no recommendation) in his presentence report.

Insofar as it firmly determines sentence, the plea bargaining
process clearly undermines the professional role of the probation
officer. It is now probably more appropriate for the probation
officer to counsel the prosecutor on rehabilitation potential than
the judge. The prosecutor might want to use the probation officer's professional estimate in the plea bargaining. As a matter
of fact, probation officers frequently conduct "prepleading investigations" which are used by both judge and prosecutor to
decide plea matters.

(2) Intake Procedures

Intake service by probation officers in adult courts is practically unknown. At the juvenile court level, however, it is
considered good practice to have some form of intake apparatus.

When serving as a functionary in a juvenile court's intake
unit the probation officer is asked to decide which cases are appropriate for formal judicial processing. This kind of decision
is obviously a judicial one somewhat akin to those made by the
judges or magistrates at preliminary hearings. Except for supervision within an administrative hierarchy, the probation officer in intake functions quite independently in his quasi-judicial
decision-making. Despite the fact that the intake process does
not meet the ordinary requirements for adjudication, there have
been few complaints from defendants subjected to the process.
Clearly, inasmuch as intake offers the defendant an opportunity
for leniency and perhaps a chance for being saved from legal
stigmatization, there is little inclination on the part of defendants to challenge the procedure. Indeed, very many of them
consent to an informal probation supervision which is carried out
in nearly the same way as adjudicated probation. Behavior required of the defendant is almost the same in both cases and there
is a "penalty" for failure under both formal and informal
supervision. Under informal probation supervision, the penalty
becomes referral to the court for formal judicial processing, the
threat of conviction and the likelihood of incarceration.

In terms of controlling input to the court the intake probation officer is very much like the prosecutor. The pattern for both the probation officer and prosecutor usurping judicial prerogatives begins to emerge.[6]

(3) Setting the Conditions of Probation

The granting of probation always involves conditions either by specification or by implication. It is usually the court that sets conditions of probation and it has frequently been held in case law that the court may not delegate its power and responsibility to impose conditions. It has also been frequently held that the court may not delegate the setting of conditions to the probation department. It is hard to find an intrinsic legal reason why a probation department cannot be given the responsibility for imposing conditions of probation. In the legal cases which have denied probation departments such authority, there has usually been the background of statutes requiring the courts to set conditions. Where statutes do not specifically state that the court must set the conditions of probation, it appears that the setting of conditions may be left to the probation department. In any case, it is common for the judge to impose a "blanket" condition such as "heed the advice of the probation officer" which in effect gives the probation officer condition-setting power.

Oral or unrecorded conditions have been generally held to be invalid and in order for a defendant to be bound by conditions, they must be definite, clearly stated, and effectively communicated to the defendant. Unfortunately, conditions of probation are notoriously vague and poorly communicated to the defendant. Typical conditions of probation include such ambiguous requirements as: Avoid undesirable associates; stay away from disreputable places; and do not keep late hours. Such conditions are obviously very difficult for the defendant to conscientiously manage. What is "undesirable"? What is "disreputable"? Standards for adhering to such conditions are seldom adequately set down and the enforcement of those conditions, where it is done at all, is left to the personal, and frequently capricious, judgment of the probation officer. The indefinite conditions become a vehicle for maintaining the moral status quo as interpret-

6. The efforts of defense lawyers to find a role in the intake process is explained in: Margaret K. Rosenheim and Daniel L. Skoler, "The Lawyer's Role at Intake and Detention Stages of Juvenile Court Proceedings," *Crime and Delinquency*, 11, No. 2 (1965), pp. 167–174.

ed by the probation officer. According to surveys made by Arluke, conditions seem slow to change.[7] While a few jurisdictions
are turning to brief, streamlined sets of conditions, for the most
part, particularly in the juvenile courts, conditions of probation
remain moralistic, negativistic, and vague.

Apart from conditions of probation serving as a means for
controlling nonlegally proscribed behavior, in other words, behavior which is morally undesirable but not unlawful, conditions
of probation intrude upon or become substitutes for certain formal judicial processes. Many conditions of probation involve
monetary obligations. Some are the kind that any citizen may
have, e. g., support of dependents; and others arise out of criminal conviction, such as fines or restitution. Because of the existence of such monetary conditions of probation, the probationer is deprived of the usual judicial safeguards and is placed in
the administrative or quasi-judicial hands of the probation officer.

Consider, for instance, the matter of supporting dependents.
Defendants who are on probation as a result of criminal conviction are seldom brought into civil or family court on the issue of
supporting dependents. Dependents wishing support from the
probationer need only go to the probation officer to obtain satisfaction. The probation officer, using the condition of probation,
can compel support payments in amounts determined by the probation officer himself, through his own administrative investigation. Without a court hearing on the question of support payments, the order of the probation officer in enforcing the conditions of probation has significant judicial effect. Were he not
on probation for a criminal case, the defendant might easily seek
an adjudication process in the appropriate court on the question
of support. Instead he is forced to submit to the judicial effect
brought about by the probation officer enforcing a standard condition of probation. The defendant makes his case before the

7. Nat R. Arluke, "A Summary of
Parole Rules—Thirteen Years Later," *Crime and Delinquency*, 15
No. 2 (1969), pp. 267–274. Although Arluke surveyed parole
conditions (dealing with about 50
parole jurisdictions is easier than
trying to deal with literally hundreds of probation jurisdictions),
his findings are relevant to probation conditions. Probation conditions and parole conditions are
very similar and both are frequently administered in unison by a
single agency having combined
probation and parole functions.
For a specific analysis of conditions of probation and for demonstration of their similarity to conditions of parole also see: Judah
Best and Paul I. Birzan, "Conditions of Probation: An Analysis," *Georgetown Law Journal*, 51
(1963), pp. 809–836.

probation officer and not before the court which is specially set up to adjudicate the question of family support.

A similar usurpation of civil court process occurs when a restitution condition is imposed on a criminal court probationer. It is usually left to the probation officer to determine the appropriate restitution payment. Too often, victims, particularly corporate victims, seek to gain through restitution conditions that which they would have great difficulty in gaining in civil court. Civil courts are comparatively careful in restoring exactly what has been lost. Relying on adversary proceedings, they analyze and evaluate the loss in fair detail. Civil courts may hold jury trials on matters of restitution. When the criminal court probation officer is given the responsibility of settling the matter of restitution, he does not have the same resources for hearing evidence on the loss as do the civil courts. He usually accepts the victim's flat statement as to what the loss is. The probationer, since he is not arguing the matter in a genuine court setting, can do little to rebut the victim's claim. Victims frequently do far better in gaining restitution through the criminal court probation officer than through a civil court. Because he is operating on the basis of a criminal conviction having occurred, the probation officer is bound to presume in favor of the victim in terms of both the quality and quantity of the restitution claim. Since the criminal court judge rarely conducts a full-dress hearing on the question of restitution, preferring to assign resolution of the matter to the probation officer, the judicial effect of the probation officer's determination of restitution is significant indeed.

(4) Probation Violation Procedures

The traditional view of probation has been that it is a privilege rather than a right and as such the probation status does not invoke ordinary due process. While this view has experienced considerable erosion in recent years, the revocation of probation remains highly discretionary. In some jurisdictions, probation violation hearings closely approach the characteristics of a trial. Still a hearing is not a trial and the courts generally retain substantial discretion in revocation of probation proceedings.[8]

8. For a very thorough review of legal practices in probation revocation see: Ronald B. Sklar, "Law and Practice in Probation and Parole Revocation Hearings," *Journal of Criminal Law, Criminology and Police Science*, 55 (1964), pp. 175–198.

While it is the judge who actually revokes probation, it is the probation officer who initiates the revocation action and largely controls it. In a very high proportion of cases, the judge's revocation action is in accord with the probation officer's recommendation. The hegemony of the probation officer in probation violation proceedings is well known and requires little unfolding here. It plainly casts the probation officer in a quasi-judicial role.

In the case of so-called technical violations, the judicial role of the probation officer becomes amplified. Technical violations are those which are somehow covered by the conditions of probation but which are not specified in criminal statutes. Failure to report to the probation officer or failure to avoid undesirable persons might be a type of technical violation. Oftentimes probation officers proceed on the basis of technical violation when new criminal offenses are suspected but cannot be easily proved. Police and prosecutors regularly call upon the probation officer to invoke some technical violation against a probationer who they believe has committed a new crime. It is patently easier to put a defendant behind bars as a result of a probation violation hearing than it is to send him to prison as a result of a full-fledged trial. In consenting to proceed on the basis of a technical violation when the real issue is a new criminal offense, the probation officer is playing a judicial role. In effect, he is deciding that there is sufficient basis to conclude that the defendant is guilty of the new offense and thus deserves to have the technical violation placed against him. Given the vague and all-encompassing nature of conditions of probation, it is not difficult for the probation officer to muster a technical violation as needed. Many probationers are in a steady state of probation violation as a result of conditions relating to keeping "decent hours," abstaining from alcohol, and various prohibitions relating to sexual activity. These violations usually go unenforced by the probation officer until such time as he is given reason to believe that a new criminal offense has occurred. Invoking the technical violation thus becomes the result of the probation officer's making the adjudication that a crime has been committed. The probationer has a hearing on the technical violation but is denied a trial on the suspected crime which triggered the technical violation.

(5) Punishment by the Probation Officer

The legislator sets punishment, the judge imposes it, and the administrator executes it. Under our constitutional scheme, it is the judge who decides when a particular individual is to have legal punishment. While probation is a sentence, it is ideologically not a punishment. Nevertheless, implicit in probation supervision are numerous opportunities for punishment. With his awesome authority over the probationer, the probation officer may in various ways restrict his liberty. It is easily argued that restriction of liberty amounts to punishment. The probation officer, in the name of rehabilitation and under the banner of standard conditions of probation, can demand that the probationer not live in or frequent certain areas, that he not engage in certain employment, and that he refrain from a number of interpersonal associations.

Sometimes probation-officer-decided punishments are more direct than denial of freedom. In some jurisdictions, a probationer may not receive a driver's license without the specific approval of the probation officer. From place to place, various occupational licenses are subject to the approval by the probation officer. If one chooses not to regard the probation officer's withholding of license approval as punishment and therefore not in the nature of a judicial action, it is at least still possible to conceive of the probation officer's approval role in licensing as being quasi-judicial.

In sum, the probation officer's role is multi-faceted. Many of the facets are not easily recognized and may be dysfunctional to our concepts of justice and due process. It is difficult to say whether the probation officer's quasi-judicial role is increasing. It is very closely tied to the judge, but the judge seems to be giving up more and more of his own judicial role. If the probation officer ties in more with the prosecutor, then the probation officer's quasi-judicial function may paradoxically increase because of the judicial aggrandizement of the prosecutor's office through plea bargaining and other arrangements.

THE MATTER OF TRUST*

It was Friday afternoon and a party was scheduled for Baker Cottage that night. A shiny, late model car pulled to a stop in front of the administration building and two middle-aged matrons entered the foyer, bearing cookies, soda, and other goodies for the boys' party. Two boys were busy painting the ceiling of the foyer. The ladies deposited the food beside the receptionist's door and looked around briefly for someone to receive their contribution. The parole supervisor entered, and one of the women addressed him:

"These are things for the party tonight, I guess it will be all right just to leave them here?"

"Well, maybe we'd better set them inside until party time." He unlocked the receptionist's door.

It was one of those subtle interchanges that frequently escape notice. In effect the matron's query was, "Can we safely leave this food in the hall with these two kids?" And his answer was, "No. We'll be missing a few bottles of pop if we do."

But it was not sufficiently subtle to escape the boys' notice. The ladies observed the boys glance at each other; the speaker then hastily attempted to gloss over the implication in her query: "Oh, I'm sure the things will be all right here in the hall. I'm sure you can trust these boys."

Now the interaction was no longer in the realm of subtlety. Attempting to mitigate the delicate situation, she had instead brought the issue to a head-on confrontation. The boys said nothing, but I noticed a slight side-wise glance, a bit of disdain or even contempt for her quick switch. The message was unspoken but clear; it said: "Lady, you've never seen us before in your life. How the hell do you know whether you can trust us? You've already revealed your distrust by your initial question; no cover-up will get you off the hook now."

But the burden of decision—of stating a position—was now shifted to the parole man. Both boys stopped painting and waited to see how he would handle this awkward situation. Would he likewise reverse his original position in an attempt to

* Dale G. Hardman, *Crime and De-linquency*, April, 1969. Reprinted   with permission of The National Council on Crime and Delinquency.

conceal his attitude? Would he squirm and try not to remind these charitable ladies that their beneficiaries were thieves? Would he avoid a direct answer and send someone else to put away the things? He did not. He didn't bat an eye. He said, very matter-of-factly and dispassionately, with no trace of embarrassment: "Ma'am, when we're ready to trust them we'll send them home." I observed the two boys glance at each other, nod, and resume painting. This time there was no disdain, no contempt for the worker's position. It was straightforward and honest, it was consistent, there was no phoniness in it; it did not attempt to evade a most touchy subject: the matter of trust.

Center Cottage had been on unusually good behavior for several months—no runaways, no serious fights, no heavy disciplinary incidents. Mr. K, the administrator, was highly pleased and told the boys so; so pleased, in fact, that he struck an unusual bargain with them: "I'll tell you what I'm going to do: we're going to take the lock off your dormitory. As long as there are no runaways from Center Cottage that dormitory door will stand open."

This was unprecedented trust, and the boys were quite proud of this special merit. Two or three months of open-door policy passed without incident. Finally three boys, led by a diagnosed psychopath, decided to depart from our environs. One night they waited until the dorm was quiet and then broke into the adjoining linen room. The window there was covered with a heavy one-inch screen anchored with half-inch bolts. They tore some sheets into ropes and, attaching these to the screen, attempted to pull it loose. No good. They got a half dozen boys out of bed, who labored with them until they were exhausted and returned to their beds. The original group continued to struggle and sweat on through the night. Dawn found the three boys still belaboring the stubborn screen, and the change of guard caught them red-handed. They were hustled off to lock-up, where I saw them later in the morning. The interviewing lasted the balance of the morning, but no mention was made of Mr. K's bargain. Finally, at the interview's end, I said: "Now one thing is still not clear to me: how come you guys worked all night on that window when all you had to do was walk out the door?"

"Oh, no, we couldn't do that. That would be breaking our promise to Mr. K."

Has any worker in correctional practice never been confronted with decisions, large and small, concerning the matter of trust:

how far shall I trust this or that offender? What worker has never had the gratifying experience of having such trust honored and of hearing the object of that trust express his appreciation? And what worker has never had the experience of having that trust violated, with the resulting disintegration of a personal relationship? What worker has never wished for a rule of thumb to guide him at these decision points: Whom shall I trust? In what circumstances? How shall I say no? How can I reject a plea for trust without rejecting the client? How shall I approach a client who has violated my trust?

And what correctionist has never been faced with such decisions as these: "Mr. Probation Officer, can I have a minute or two alone with my mother [or wife, or girl friend, or brother] before I go back to the joint?" "Mr. Caseworker, I need to get a car for this job. Will you co-sign for me?" "Mr. Parole Supervisor, I've got my pilot's license now. Will you let me fly down to Gravelburg to see my mother [or wife, *et al.*]?" "Mr. Placement Officer, I need a driver's license on this job. Will you let me and my brother Joe use your car to take the road test?" "Mr. Work Director, can I report in to the infirmary by myself?" "Can I go up to the institutional orchard [or barn, or laundry, or cannery] by myself?" "Can I go to school off campus?" "Can I get a job downtown?" On many such decisions there will be agency policy and rules to guide us. But rules can never cover all the possible exigencies that will arise in supervising offenders. Inevitably the decision to trust or not to trust must be ours. So when shall we trust and when shall we not?

In my experience practically all workers want to trust their clients as far as is realistically possible, and conversely want their clients to trust them. And most of them believe, as I do, that it is essentially good for any person to know that he is trusted and can fulfill that trust. This is, I believe, especially true of offenders.

But no rule of thumb can guide us in our decision to trust or distrust, any more than a simple rule can predict success or failure on parole. However, a few generalizations, gleaned from the literature (very meager on this matter [1]), from research, and from the experience of correctional workers may prove helpful.

[1]. A review of twenty-four well-known texts on various therapeutic methods reveals no mention of lying as a symptom and no suggestions for handling it. A notable exception is Thomas Szasz, *The Myth of Mental Illness* (New York: Hoeber, 1961).

Trust is Therapeutic

I. *To be trusted and to fulfill that trust is basically thera-peutic.*

Discussing verbal expression in interviews, Cyril Burt says: "Treat the deceiver just as though he were trustworthy and you may shame him out of his deceit.   Grant him, therefore, the fullest credit for every particle of fact his fabrication may contain, with the dictum of the practical charlatan ever in mind." [2]

Although it is only one aspect of the matter of trust, the initial interview is a good starting point.   A client has told you something that you know or suspect is not so.   How do you handle

RANGE OF WORKER RESPONSES TO LYING

Passive Responses

Aggressive Responses

1 Supports, encourages lying
2 Accepts story at face value
3 Doesn't comment; implies acceptance
4 Withholds judgment
5 Ignores lying
6 Reflects position only
7 Makes client assess veracity
8 Reflects absurdities; implies incongruency
9 Implies rejection of story
10 Weighs evidence with client; assesses story
11 Focuses on absurdities vs. reality
12 Uses "attrition" technique
13 Frankly rejects story with explanation
14 Flatly rejects story; gives no rationale
15 Uses anxiety technique ("sweat out")
16 Interrogates
17 Cross-examines
18 Berates, accuses, scolds
19 Verbally abuses, threatens
20 Physically abuses (third degree methods)

[A9185]

2. Quoted in Pauline Young, *Social Therapy in Probation and Delin-* quency (New York: McGraw-Hill, 1952), p. 365.

this? I have observed various interviewers react to lying with a repertory of responses ranging from blows to a smiling, nodding acceptance of the fallacious statement and have ranked these responses (see the scale below) in approximate ordinal positions from passive to aggressive methods of handling. (I initially thought to call these two polarities nondirective and directive, but Rogerian [nondirective] counselors would probably object that the extreme top of this scale does not represent their position.)

I know of no author who advocates a position as extreme as No. 1 or 2 on the scale. There are a few who occasionally seem to ascribe to No. 3.

Collins and Mackay [3] believe that outright denial of reality is a defense mechanism having roots in "early loss and rejection, and [the client] controls the resulting anxiety created by his reality situation by denying it." Since they do not distinguish between deliberate lying and perceptual distortion, I assume that their article covers both. They would place themselves, I believe, at No. 4 or 5 on our scale.

I have heard the question raised: "How would Rogers [No. 6 on our sale], in a nondirective setting, handle the matter of lying?" I have not found an explicit statement on this topic by Rogers or his interpreters, but I believe they would respond that lying is much less likely to occur in a nondirective (and therefore nonauthoritarian) setting and that the worker has nothing to give or withhold if successfully "snowed." The client may deny reality to himself (perceptual distortion) and honestly report that he believes something to be fact when it is not. But the non-directive worker would not distinguish between outright lying and defensive denial to self. He would handle each the same way—by reflecting the client's underlying feeling: "You want very much for me to believe you are not the kind of person who would. . . ." Or perhaps: "From your point of view, then, you were not responsible for this act?" The non-directive worker's role is to hold the client's own feelings up to view, but not to take sides, neither condemning lying nor praising truthfulness. This, I gather, is essentially Dressler's [4] position (No. 6 on our scale): "The question was not 'Is this true?' so much as 'How does the client feel about it?'"

3. Alice H. Collins and J. R. Mackay, "Casework Treatment of Delinquents Who Use the Primary Defense of Denial," *Social Work*, January 1959, pp. 34–43.

4. D. Dressler, *Practice and Theory of Probation and Parole* (New York: Columbia University Press, 1959), p. 33.

A Wisconsin colleague of many years' experience states that his preferred method of handling lying is to use a role-reversal technique, placing the client as the hearer of the story and insisting that he assess the veracity of his own story from the standpoint of another (No. 7 on scale). This is only a short step to another common technique (no known author supporting this): "Ted, you have told me this . . . ; however, I know these . . . to be facts. Both can't possibly be true; they are mutually exclusive. Now how do you suppose your story soun ¨ ¨o me?" (No. 8 on scale.) Although phrased essentially the same as No. 8, No. 9 would end: "For these reasons I cannot accept your story."

Glasser [5] (No. 11 on scale), emphasizes, as probably the cardinal point in his reality therapy, that a client must be held accountable for his behavior, including, I gather, verbal behavior. He goes to great lengths to confront his patients with reality, and would probably act similarly in handling lying, although I have found no specific reference to this problem.

One of the most skilled interviewers I ever knew was an Austrian immigrant, a colleague of August Aichhorn for many years. He managed our reception cottage and his job was, among other things, to conduct the initial interview with each new boy. He never interviewed a boy without first reading his record. He then encouraged the boy to tell his story in his own words. Whenever the boy's story did not square with the record, he stopped the boy immediately (unlike the police interrogator who encourages the suspect to tell more and more lies that will later be used against him). But he was never punitive or unkind in doing so, just doggedly persistent: "Just a minute, please. A moment ago you said that . . . . But Mr. Zilch, your probation officer, states that. . . . I do not see how this can be if what you say is true." Usually another version of the story or another explanation was forthcoming. "But wait—I do not understand how. . . ." A second explanation follows, and a third; perhaps evasive action. "Please do not go on until I am clear on this matter. I want to understand how. . . ." "I still do not see. . . ." "I am sorry, but it is still not clear to me. . . ." With infinite patience, never raising his voice, he kept this up until by sheer attrition he wore the boy down to the

5. W. Glasser, *Reality Therapy* (New York: Harper and Row, 1965).

point where the straight story came out (No. 12 on the scale). Then, instead of berating the boy with "Why didn't you tell me the truth in the first place?" he would say: "Ach, of course! *Now* I see! How stupid of me not to understand! Please go on with your story now." I have never known a boy to attempt lying to him more than two or three times; they simply found it too much work.

Hyman, a functionalist caseworker, takes a more active part in refuting discrepancies (No. 13 on our scale) in the stories of prostitutes on probation.[6] She flatly informs the offender that she does not accept the story (she does not use the term "lying," as Glasser likely would) and states why the story does not ring true. She even suggests that probation may not work out if the client does not "level" with her, which may be considered a veiled threat not to recommend a grant of probation. My only objection to this method is that if a threat is to be used, it should be a clear-cut threat—not veiled. Rather than subtly suggesting that something dire may happen to a parolee's status, for instance, I would prefer: "Ed, I want to make clear where I stand on this matter. I regard your action as a serious violation of parole—serious enough that if it happens again I will have you picked up and recommend revocation to the parole board. Since neither of us want this, let's see what we can do to prevent recurrence." But this too is part of a larger picture. I have indicated elsewhere [7] that the hallmark of good correctional practice is clarity of expectations, defined by sociologists as role clarification. Since role theory holds that one's role affects one's behavior more than, let's say, personality traits or developmental history, then clear role definition is vital. To apply this principle to situations of trust, therefore, means that I will make certain that my client understands what I expect of him; there will be no assumptions, innuendoes, implied meanings, or veiled threats, because these violate the principle of clear role definition. I agree with Glasser [8] that "the teacher should always say, 'I want you to . . . ,' never 'we should . . . ' or 'you should . . . ,'" although my reason, a clear definition of expectations, is different from Glasser's.

---

6. Evelyn C. Hyman, "Holding the Promiscuous Girl Accountable for Her Own Behavior," *Bulwarks against Crime*, 1948 Yearbook (New York, National Probation and Parole Association), pp. 190–201.

7. Dale G. Hardman, "Authority in Casework—a Bread-and-Butter Theory," *NPPA Journal*, July 1959, pp. 249–55.

8. Glasser, op. cit. supra note 5, p. 158.

It is my belief that clear role definition defined as clarity of expectations, has been underrated as a variable of social service practice. The author of a Cleveland study hypothesized that as mental patients moved from highly controlled institutional life toward more autonomous and unstructured settings, their self-concepts would change; they would see themselves more as mentally healthy and identify more with non-patients. However, no such relationship was found; the degree of structure or autonomy of the settings had no bearing on their self-concepts. But the author accidentally discovered a factor significantly related to self-concept: role definition. Situations in which the staff consistently clarified their expectations tended to elicit the expected behavior from the patients; consequently the patients' self-concept changed in these situations, in the direction of mental health.[9] I suggest that the same dynamics will apply in correction.

I believe that Redl and Wineman's handling of lying [10] would fall in about the same area as Hyman's on our scale (No. 13 or 14). Wineman describes a youngster who refused to go to bed and led several others in a fracas in the coal bin until he cut his bare foot on a shovel. While patching up the foot, Wineman cautioned him about such exploits.

"I didn't do nothing."

"What do you mean, you didn't do anything? You were chasing around down there, weren't you, and up here too, for that matter?"

Later, in a group session, Redl handles the same boy.

"I notice that whenever you don't like something, Andy, you accuse us of always having or doing anything we want and never letting you kids do anything." [Boy merely parrots Redl's words.] "Oh, come on, Andy. Surely you have more to say than that. You're smart enough to use your own words."

"Well, it's true. We never can do what we want."

9. E. G. Shumway, *The Effects of Rehabilitation Program Structure on Mental Patients' Role Conception.* Ph.D. dissertation, Case-Western Reserve University, 1969 (unpublished at time of this writing).

10. F. Redl and D. Wineman, *The Aggressive Child* (Glencoe, Ill.: Free Press, 1957), pp. 541, 545.

"Can you really sit there after five months at Pioneer House and say that in this place the kids don't ever get a chance to do what they would like to?"

"Yeah."

"With the program we plan with you guys, and all the places you get to go, and the things we do? Let me ask you: Where can you remember any place where you lived where you had more fun?"

"Say, I lived with my grandma once and she let me do anything I wanted and gave me candy all the time, too."

"I never said we let you do whatever you wanted. I only said you do a lot of things that are fun. Do you still pretend that that isn't so?"

"Maybe not."

"Well, I wonder, then, why you keep saying that all the time?"

Aichhorn [11] (No. 15 on our scale) describes putting an offender in an anxiety-arousing situation and gradually and subtly increasing the anxiety level until the truth comes out. I believe that this can prove effective with certain naïve boys, but not with sophisticated liars who have a very high anxiety threshold.

The most aggressive, roughshod handling of lying that I have observed on a professional level (No. 17 on our scale) occurs in the group therapy sessions at Highfields, N. J.,[12] and its paratypes at Southfields, Ky., and Pinehills, Utah.[13] Here, however, it is the group, not the therapist, who picks the story to shreds, batters the liar's defenses to rubble, and leaves him in tears. That the group rejects the snow job is not accidental: the process is properly called *guided* group interaction. The group therapists, in the initial structuring of the group settings, deliberately frame the meetings so that snow jobs are taboo. If the group permits one of its members to get away with a snow job, *the group,* not the offending member, is confronted with

11. A. Aichhorn, *Wayward Youth* (New York: Viking Press, 1935), pp. 124–25.

12. See L. W. McCorkle, A. Elias, and F. L. Bixby, *The Highfields Story* (New York: Henry Holt, 1958).

13. L. T. Empey and J. Rabow, "Provo Experiment in Delinquency Rehabilitation," *American Sociological Review*, October 1961, pp. 679–95; April 1962, pp. 256–58.

this by the therapist; *the group* is required to explain why it was allowed; *the group* is forced to rehash the story and extract the truth. At times the group's approach to lying amounts to rapid-fire cross-examination by ten prosecutors at once. Sitting through an hour of this in the "red chair" can shake the strongest will.

A boy had been in group meetings for six weeks without participating. He "didn't have no problems and couldn't see no sense in makin' out like I do have." But tonight, the group decided, the red chair was his. After the group had battered his defenses mercilessly for half an hour, he finally began discussing his past, his home, his family—a pretty good job of baring his soul, I thought; kids rarely revealed so much to me in one sitting. But suddenly one of the members interjected: "Just a minute. Are you holding something back?"

"Naw, I ain't keepin' nothin'."

"Yes, he is," said another member. "He's been holdin' back for quite a while." More vehement denial, more positive assertions from the other boys—teen-agers, please note, whose perceptual acuity was much keener than mine, a professional correctionist. The intensity of the group cross-examination increased until it became almost badgering; then, finally, came the painful moment of truth. The boy suddenly covered his face and blurted: "I came home one night and found my mother in bed with a goddam Spic." He burst into tears and left the room in uncontrollable sobbing. The meeting was stone silent until his return, perhaps five or ten minutes later. When he had resumed the red seat, someone asked quietly: "Tell us honestly, now. Don't you feel better now that you've got this out?" The boy heaved a great sigh and nodded. The other continued: "Well, that's what the meetin's for—to help you with problems like this. And we can't help you if you try to bullshit us. Outside it's okay; bullshit all you want out there. But not in the meetin'."

Korn and McCorkle [14] record an individual interview in which the counselor's style is almost as roughshod as the group sessions described above (about No. 16–17 on the scale), and seemingly they hold this as the ideal approach to the "con" expert. But

14. R. R. Korn and L. W. McCorkle, *Criminology and Penology* (New   York: Henry Holt, 1959), pp. 562–67.

I can't conceive of clients coming back voluntarily for more of this, as is required in guided group interaction.

The above examples represent a rather wide spectrum of approaches to lying and various levels of worker involvement. These variations are similar to but not identical with the various degrees of direction-nondirection among workers engaged in personal counseling. I refer to this parallelism only to make a third point: several studies [15] of the effectiveness of counseling have indicated that no approach can be called the best: effectiveness is a matter of counselor skill and experience, not of technique used. With the exception of the two extremes on our scale, I believe there is no best or worst method of handling lying; another man's method will fit me no better than his shoes will. And I do not believe that interviewing liars on parole differs from interviewing those in child welfare, assistance, medical, or psychiatric settings. But the diverse aproaches cited above have one common feature; in no case did the correctionist imply that he accepted the fabrication. And this leads to the second generalization:

Snowing and Conning Harmful

II. *Knowingly to permit a client to snow or con you is never therapeutic or helpful to him.*

Occasionally I hear a correctionist indicate that he never gets snowed any more—he is now sufficiently sophisticated to recognize a snow job when presented with one. I suspect that these colleagues lie about other matters also. After nearly a quarter of a century in the business, I still get snowed occasionally—but never knowingly. I believe snowing is reinforced every time a client succeeds at it. Lippman believes conning disrupts the worker-client relationship: "The probation officer probably never will reach the stage when one of these clever delinquents will not be able to really convince him of his sincerity while he is telling a succession of lies. There are delinquents who will have no respect for the probation officer if they can outwit him." [16] Korn and McCorkle refer to the consequences as "anti-

15. See F. E. Fiedler, "A Comparison of Therapeutic Relationships in Psychoanalytic, Non-directive, and Adlerian Therapy," *Journal of Consulting Psychology,* December 1950, pp. 436–45.

16. H. S. Lippman, "The Role of the Probation Officer in the Treatment of Delinquency in Children," *Federal Probation,* June 1948, pp. 36–39.

therapeutic": "Behind this mask the delinquent, entirely un-
touched and unreached, would merely be congratulating himself
on his success in deceiving and manipulating the naïve adult
world." [17]

My own approach to lying probably falls about mid-range in
the above spectrum (about No. 10): "Sam, there are some discrepancies between your story and Mr. P.O.'s report; namely,
.   .   .   . Now so far I don't know you very well, so I don't
know yet how much I can depend on what you tell me. I hope
later I will get to know you this well. But I *do* know Mr. P.O.
Whenever I have checked on any of his reports, I have found it
to be very accurate—he is always careful to check everything he
says. So I believe you can see why I am inclined to accept his
version and not yours. Now I'll tell you what I am willing to
do: if you sincerely believe that Mr. P.O. is wrong and you are
right, we will write or talk to witnesses, write for evidence or
documents of any sort if they have not already been presented
in court—we'll even help you get a lawyer and a new hearing
if there is evidence for it. But until I see this evidence, I will go
along with Mr. P.O."

But our ground is not always as solid as that provided by the
careful and objective Mr. P.O. Not infrequently the court worker
is confronted with fantastic charges against a client, charges
made by a citizen or police or parents. But the same impartiality
should hold: we will not decide until we have all the facts. And
when we decide that our client should go to court—or be recommended for probation, or revocation, or commitment, or removal
from home—we will tell him so and tell him why.

What about other violations of trust? We let a boy leave
campus for some worthy cause and he fails to return. We give
a man a position as cashier at the PX and he embezzles. We
put a girl on the switchboard and she "smuggles" calls outside.
A boy is allowed to attend school in town to play football and he
steals the gear. A boy with a penchant for science is assigned to
count bacteria in the institution's milk samples; he steals the
microscope. How do you handle such violations of trust?

First, let us in honesty admit that we share in this violation:
we recommended him; we overestimated his readiness or his
capacity to resist temptation, or we underestimated the demoral-

17. Korn and McCorkle, op. cit. supra note 14, p. 566.

izing elements of the setting. This was our job; we blew it. This admission is in no way intended to absolve the offender of responsibility for his behavior; but if the assignment of trust is a shared decision—and it should be—then we must share in its failure, as we will gladly share in its success. We will tell the boy so and hopefully obtain from him an equally honest statement of *his* responsibility.

Next we will try to avoid a common mistake of parents whose trust has been violated. I have frequently seen them in tears sadly shaking their heads and proclaiming that they can never again trust their child as long as they live. I believe it is much more conducive to mental health and consistent with good correctional practice to say: "Jerry, it seems that we gave you a responsibility before you were ready for it. You will have to go back a step or two in our program now. You must demonstrate to us that you have sufficient maturity to handle this kind of assignment before you can have another chance like that. We are going to re-assign you to a less demanding, less tempting position—but likewise one where you have less trust. You must earn that trust before we will trust you so far again."

This approach presumes, of course, an institutional or supervisory program that has various gradations and degrees of responsibility, freedom, and trust. If I were to make a single criticism of correctional programs in general, it would be that they are graduated in steps that are too large. An example of this is found in the step from institution to parole. Not only are many subjects ill-prepared for this major step when it comes, but after release it is such a long step back that most supervisors are reluctant to recommend revocation. The parolees get away with murder and the word is passed around that the parole system is lax. Instead of returning a client to prison, I would use the halfway house in this respect, as one correctionist has suggested: [18] "Bill, this is your third violation of this type. Admittedly, no single one is serious enough to revoke your parole. But one more and the board will likely revoke you, whether I recommend it or not. Let me suggest an alternative: return to the halfway house voluntarily—long enough to get you

18. R. E. Ashpole, Department of Sociology, University of Utah. Personal communication.

away from the company you're keeping, away from the bars and babes and bookies, back to regular hours of working, eating, and sleeping. Spend maybe a month or two there, until you're back on your feet and functioning as well as you did when you were first released. I think it may save you the three years remaining on your sentence." I would approve this, with the proviso that both voluntary and involuntary return to the halfway house be permitted. If I were designing an ideal institutional program, it would have not two or three steps or stages of promotion but many—perhaps twenty or thirty, ranging from complete restriction and deprivation of privileges up to working or studying off campus and only occasional reporting. Each successive step would have slightly more freedom, trust, and responsibility than the previous one, and the step from institution to parole would be only a small one. The entire program would be growth-oriented. As fast as the subject demonstrates, by obeying clearly defined requirements, that he is ready for promotion, promotion will occur. No day will pass without his being reminded at least once of the growth-oriented nature of the program, the progress he has made, how far he must go to the next step, the advantages of additional responsibility. These daily—repeat, *daily*—reminders will be calculated for every boy and never left to chance. Violation of trust will then be interpreted as regression to a less mature position, not as lifelong rejection and eternal damnation. A third generalization concerning the matter of trust would then be:

Violation of Trust as Social Immaturity

III. *Violation of trust should be defined not as a personal affront to the worker, but as the client's social immaturity; our mutual objective is to develop his social maturity.*

So far we have evaded the troublesome question of when to trust and when to distrust. Let's say it is the second or third time we have seen the boy since he entered the institution. He asks for some privilege involving trust—perhaps to carry a message to the laundry where the girls work. "Jake, how long have you been here now—two weeks? That really isn't long enough for me to know you very well, is it? You may be a real dependable kid, or not—I don't know yet. Now when I get to know you better, if you do prove to be dependable I'll let you have an assignment like this. Until then I'll reserve these jobs for kids who have proved themselves to me." The basic ideas here are that we constantly hold forth the objective of trust as inherent in social maturation; we never flatly reject a request without explanation; and that explanation is based realistically on the degree of social maturation that our client has demonstrated.

Research has well documented that children do not mature at the same rate in all aspects of their intellectual abilities, their various organic systems, their attitudes, or their interests. To expect that a child will achieve a consistent level in all areas of social maturation is therefore unrealistic. Hartshorne and May's classic study of honesty in children [19] revealed that a child may lie but may never steal or cheat, and vice versa; they found low correlations among these measures of honesty rather than a single, distinct trait of honesty. Stating that a boy is trustworthy or untrustworthy is not nearly as helpful as knowing that he is dependable in areas A and B, only fair in C, and very questionable in D. We can utilize this knowledge in counseling: "Dave, in the ten weeks you've been with us we have never known you to lie or steal. Although you're a husky boy, you've always been good around the smaller kids, never mean or rough with them. You have a gentle hand with the livestock. You work well with or without supervision. In all these things you are ready to go home. But I find that you always have a problem when girls are around; you can't keep your hands to yourself; you make off-color remarks; you embarrass them with dirty pictures and suggestive movements. This is the main thing you must work on before we can trust you to attend school off campus, or else they'll just send you back." Boys like Dave are much more likely to take their assignment of trust seriously if they must earn it. And this introduces our fourth generalization:

Lightly Rendered—Lightly Held

IV. *Trust that is lightly rendered is apt to be lightly held.*

We initiated a system of furloughs for home visits at our institution, and the kids thought this was wonderful. For about nine months (our average tenure) no furlough was violated. By this time we had a new crop of kids who had not been present at the inception of the program. Furloughs were old hat; they

19. H. Hartshorne and A. M. May,
Studies in Deceit (New York: Macmillan, 1928).

held no special significance for the newcomers; hence a series of furlough violations began. We may enlarge on the above generalization: *any* sort of delegated responsibility will be lightly held if lightly given. One of our boys had spent most of his institutional career in the kitchen, had shown well above average responsibility, and became a fair cook. He wished to pursue this career outside. Rather than explore fry-cook jobs in local beaneries, I approached a French chef, the supervisor of food service in the finest hotel in the state. He agreed to take the boy as an apprentice (at lower starting wages than a fry-cook job would pay). "But you've got to start at the bottom if you work at the hotel," I said. "You'll have to scrub floors and wash dishes."

"That's okay."

"He won't be an easy guy to work for. I watched him awhile and he's fussy as hell. He has dozens of special cooks for meats, poultry, pastry, desserts, salads, and so on. Nothing ever goes out of that kitchen that he doesn't check personally. The dishwasher has to lay all the silverware out in a straight row on a long table covered with linen. He walks along the table picking up every knife and turning it over to inspect it. Nothing short of perfection leaves his kitchen."

"Good. That's the kind of guy I want to work for."

Now dishwashing generally is considered among the most menial of jobs, and categorically our kids despised the assignment; it was usually done as slipshod as possible. But here was a man who said by his demeanor: "I consider your assignment important—important enough to merit my most careful attention. Slipshod work is unacceptable. You are important because your job is important. When you demonstrate competence here—but not until then—we will promote you to peeling vegetables." I will render trust on the same basis. The French chef would never, for instance, assign a new man to making pastry or ice cream. Just as unrealistic is to place unlimited trust in a client who has not demonstrated trustworthiness. Neither do I believe such trust to be therapeutic or helpful to him; an "A" given to a student who has not earned it is meaningless to him. Our boys on the painting scaffold knew that the two matrons had no basis for their verbal expression of trust—the protestation was unrealistic; it *had* to be phony. The ladies' statement was intended to elicit confidence, but had the reverse effect. Thus our fifth generalization:

Trust Based on Reality

V. *Trust, like reassurance, must be rooted in reality to be helpful.*

I suggest that a client's maturation rate in the matter of trust is positively correlated to the personal integrity of his worker— his basic honesty with himself and clients. This, however, is easier to say than to achieve. We all believe we are essentially honest with our clients: we would never, for instance, tell them an outright lie, cheat them at billiards, embezzle their funds, or make passes at their wives. I am not speaking, however, of these rare opportunities which may occur once or twice during a supervisory relationship, but of the hundreds of little opportunities that occur daily in which our personal integrity is manifest. I am speaking of our numerous defense mechanisms; the evasions; the avoidance of blame, confrontation, responsibility, and decision; the subtle and not-so-subtle attempts to gloss over our mistakes and to conceal our errors and human weaknesses. All too often I find myself using such primitive defenses as: "No, Willie, I didn't forget our appointment; something came up." "I didn't really lose my temper; I was just trying to make clear. . . ." "I made this decision on purely objective bases, not on personal considerations." "No, I didn't forget to check on your request; this would just not be a good time to ask for it." "If you must get angry with somebody, place the blame where it belongs— blame the administration [or the legislature or the public]." And all too rarely do I find myself saying: "Yes, that was my mistake. . . ." "I was too hasty. . . ." "This was my fault and not the school's. . . ." "Yes, I was inconsistent. . . ." "Yes, I did neglect your best interests, Joe."

Pointing out the difficulty of maintaining a professional relationship based on unqualified truthfulness, Halleck lists seven types of lies that are built into professional relationships—"the lie of adult morality," "the lie of professional helpfulness," "the lie of confidentiality," "the lie of rewards for conformity," "the denial of limitations," the lie that says "Open up; trust me; all will go well," and the lie that says "We like you but not your behavior." [20]

20. S. L. Halleck, "The Impact of Professional Dishonesty on Behavior of Disturbed Adolescents," *Social Work*, April 1963, pp. 48–56.

Halleck could have generalized on this theme. Numerous built-in-lies are inherent in our socio-economic-political system, and we may find ourselves inadvertently attempting to support them. For example:

The *Horatio Alger Myth:* anyone can follow the footsteps of Abraham Lincoln or Booker T. Washington; our system provides equal opportunity for all.

The *Blindfolded Justice Myth:* our legal-judicial system administers justice equally to all persons, black or white, rich or poor, male or female.

The *Crime-Never-Pays Myth:* all offenders sooner or later get their just deserts.

The *Key-to-Success Myth:* the only road to success is hard work, perseverance, pluck, etc. No one ever achieves success by pull, subterfuge, petty politicking, or toadying to authority.

The *Myth of Face-Value Idealism:* a person or group proposing an ideal of service-above-self, of commitment to Hippocratic oaths, academic freedom, liberty, equality, or fraternity, will always act in accordance with that ideology.

I suspect that in no profession, field of endeavor, or human relationship is there a complete lack of duplicity, double-talk, hypocrisy, or violation of subscribed ideology. There are preachers who do not behave as they preach, teachers who do not believe what they teach, and correctionists who do not have faith in correction.[21] To tell a young client that reality is otherwise does not increase his confidence in a worker. A number of writers have commented on the role of adult deceit in the disenchantment of youth. But like all such questions concerning reality, this one distills to a matter of perception, and most offenders have perceptions of reality that strike the square world as cockeyed. A youth gets a speeding ticket on which the officer records a speed several miles faster than that on the youth's speedometer; therefore all cops are crooked. A young prostitute is visited by a man she recognizes as a minister; therefore all preachers are hypocrites. Bennie the Brown-noser gets ahead faster on the job, in the military, or in school; therefore, our client concludes, "nobody ever gets ahead by effort alone." Not only the disen-

21. A colleague has proposed a sociology course to study the inconsistency and hypocrisy inherent in major American institutions. I suspect this would make rather dull study after the first few weeks.

chanted but also the offenders use these universal tokens of hy-
procrisy as rationalizations for their non-conforming and antisocial behavior.

What, then, should be the correctionist's approach to the realities of our society? If we deny that inconsistencies and hypocrisy exist, we are perverting the facts of life; on the other hand,
if we concede the client's perception of reality, we have unwittingly supported his rationalization. Furthermore, an otherwise
constructive interview is easily turned into endless, pointless,
senseless debate about the nature of societal reality; you will, in
fact, find a few skilled subjects who can lead you off into such
polemics despite your best efforts to talk about his problems.
Can anything therapeutic ever come of an argument about what
portion of cops are crooked, what portion of ministers are hypocrites, what portion of doctors violate their Hippocratic oath?
The nearest approach to a satisfactory resolution of these discrepancies in perception runs (for me) something like this:
"Chris, I know there are crooked cops (or hypocritical ministers,
or scot-free criminals), but most of the cops I have known are
hard-working guys trying to do their jobs in the face of some
very frustrating obstacles. Perhaps you have found it otherwise.
But in any case it isn't my job to change their behavior. So let's
talk about you, since it *is* my job to change your behavior."
Someone will suggest that as a responsible citizen it *is* my job
to change crooked cops, hypocritical ministers, and wayward
physicians. As a responsible citizen, yes; but not as a parole
officer.

One of the most miserable hours I have ever spent occurred on
a Friday in a boys' cottage. Friday night was dance night—
the biggest event of the week for the boys. But several girls at
the girls' cottage had symptoms suspiciously like mumps; the
physician could not be sure. I canceled the dance and the Abbott
Cottage boys hit the ceiling. Such an outpouring of hostility I
have never encountered before or since. I could not leave the
cottage supervisor alone with them—a riot was imminent. The
tension built up for forty minutes or more. Reasoning was useless; the dire consequences of mumps in adolescent males meant
nothing to them:

"Let all us guys that's had mumps go to the dance."

"How many is that?" (All the hands went up.) "Well, I believe that settles that point." They began slamming furniture

about. They poured out venom upon the school, the teachers, the supervisors, the administration, and the physician. They finally demanded that I call that damfool doctor and set him straight. At this point I said: "Now look, the doctor didn't decide to cancel the dance; I did. He only told me about the nature of mumps and left the decision to me. It was my decision and mine alone. If you want to be mad at someone, be mad at me." From that moment their wrath subsided, and within a quarter of an hour they were laughing, playing, and planning how they might buy a television for the cottage. I think if I had evaded this bit of responsibility we might have had a riot on our hands. I cannot, in fact, recall a single instance in which forthright, scrupulous honesty with a client has had an adverse effect upon our relationship. Yet there are too many instances where my attempts to cover up my peccadilloes were discovered by the client, to the detriment of our relationship. I think clients expect us to be human. But they would like us to be honest about it. And the relationship between our own integrity and their trust is explained, in part at least, by Sykes and Matza's neutralization theory [22]: before a boy can be confirmed in delinquency he must develop a system of rationalization—e. g., "We're doing drunks a favor by rolling them; they'd just spend their dough for more booze." The same principle applies when I employ various subterfuges to conceal my human frailities—I hand them a rationalization: "Hardman has not leveled with me; therefore I am not obligated to level with him."   So our last generalization would be summed up thus:

Trust: A Two-way Street

VI. *The degree to which a client values a worker's trust is positively related to the degree of his trust in that worker.*

Only when the matter of trust has become a two-way street can it be effectively manipulated as a casework tool. I had an eighteen-year-old who was being returned to the institution; he asked to have a few moments alone with his wife. I had known him for nearly two years and figured this was a safe risk. I figured wrong; he slipped out the back door, and after giving him time for a sporting headstart his wife notified me of his de-

22. G. M. Sykes and D. Matza, "Techniques of Neutralization: A Theory of Delinquency," *Sociological Review*, December 1957, 644–48.

parture. I was angry of course, at myself, the boy, and his wife. The conversation went something like this:

"Charlene, I figure this wasn't Eddie's responsibility; you asked to see Eddie, so you were responsible to see that he went back."

"I tried to, Mr. Hardman, but he wouldn't listen."

"I think I know both of you well enough to know that you could have stopped him. At least you could have hollered when he started out the door."

Here she burst into tears. "I couldn't make him go back if he didn't want to."

"But he still has to go back, and beside that you've both broken your word to me." She nodded and continued sobbing. "Now in the time you have known me, have I ever broken my word to you or Eddie?"

She shook her head.

"Then I figure you owe me something. When you see Eddie, I want you to have him phone me." Within an hour he did so.

"What happened, Eddie? I never figured you'd pull a fast one like that on me."

"I know, Mr. Hardman, but I just couldn't go back to that place."

"But you could break the trust I put in you. How do you feel about that?"

"Awful. I'm sorry, Mr. Hardman, but. . . ."

"Have I ever broken your trust, Eddie?"

"No."

"Then do you have a right to break mine?"

The boy returned voluntarily within an hour.

Let me provide a last example of successful manipulation of trust. Three girls had run away from the institution; one had returned. The caseworker, who lived on campus, received a call about midnight from one of the runaway girls, inquiring about the one who had returned. The caseworker tried to persuade her to return voluntarily, but to no avail.

"How about just talking to me, then? Just come on out and let's talk awhile."

"I'm not comin' near that place again."

"Okay, how about letting me meet you down-town? *You* name the place."

"Naw, you'd just pick me up."

"Have I ever broken my word before?"

"No."

"Then what makes you think I will now?"

"It's your job. You're suppose to pick me up."

"That's true. Okay, let me talk to you. When we're through talking I'll give you a ten minute headstart, and then I'll start looking for you."

"That's not long enough. I want twenty minutes."

"Fifteen."

"Okay, fifteen minutes."

To his surprise both runaway girls showed up for the discussion. At the end of the period, he gave them the fifteen-minute lead as agreed, but did not find them. The next day, the girl who had phoned returned voluntarily; the other was apprehended.

Note in both of the examples above that the worker was aware of the two-way relationship of trust and that he used it purposefully as a casework technique to achieve a correctional objective. Many workers successfully use various casework techniques unconsciously; when we use them consciously we are most effective.

If consciously employed, these generalizations concerning the matter of trust will, I believe, serve to make the correctionist a more effective worker.

———

GAMES FAMILIES OF DELINQUENTS PLAY*

———

Working with delinquents and their families is like walking uphill in a mudslide. The problems abound. There are personal problems, interpersonal problems, community problems, social problems, and cultural problems. It may happen that hundreds of problems in this category are loaded on a family that is inade-

* Warren Walker, *Federal Probation*,
December, 1972. Reprinted with
permission.

quate to begin with, or an individual youth who starts with several personality deficits. When a severe dose of resistance to treatment and distrust of parental authorities is added to the goo, it becomes clear that family work with delinquents is difficult at best, and a cause for despair at worst.

The family worker addresses himself to the families in the midst of their brokenness and pain. At the very least, he communicates that he cares and that he is willing to help, even if for only a short time. He commits himself to doing the best possible job with every family he treats. He resists the temptation to work with only those families who are adequate and cooperative; and he works as hard as he can with the inadequate and unwilling clients too. At Camp Paige in the Los Angeles County Probation Department, all clients are seen with no screening. For a while, the family worker takes upon himself some of the pain experienced by his clients and he develops a deep human compassion for each of them. He discovers that the more he comes to understand his clients, the more he begins to appreciate them and their ability to survive in the midst of sometimes deplorable conditions.

Some of the families venture to expose themselves to the therapist. The dynamics of the interpersonal relations in the family rise to the surface and the therapist is free to deal with some of these dynamics while never forgetting the intricate human complexities from which the dynamics arise. Sometimes he can help the families to change destructive family patterns and occasionally he can even get the families to use family relationships as leverage with which to change delinquent behavior.

One way of understanding family dynamics is to think in terms of games the family plays. The advantage of the game category is that it provides a nontechnical language everyone can use and it relates to a common base of behavior. That is, game language suggests that we all play games, no matter whether we are in a helper or helped capacity at the moment. Further, the game category introduces a note of detachment that the therapist and clients alike abundantly need as they work on the family problems. The therapist gets himself into trouble if he takes his work too seriously. He will become deeply discouraged the first time one of his star clients is arrested if he does not maintain a kind of "hang loose" attitude toward his work.

There is a danger, however, in using the game category to describe family dynamics. The danger is that the games will be a way of putting raw human interaction with all its sensitive intricacies into neat little categories. There is even a possibility that an attitude of ridicule could develop. However, if the therapist can laugh at the games that he himself plays and laugh with, and not at, the families as they talk over games and strategies, this danger can be overcome. It is hoped then that the game category will help the therapist to maintain perspective in his work, but not be a way of maintaining distance from the clients.

The one dynamic that seems to be constant in the behavior of delinquents in and out of the family setting can be called the "burn the house down" game. The name comes from the story by Charles Lamb, "Dissertation on Roast Pig." Lamb satirically suggests that roast pig was discovered by a man who had a suckling pig which he kept in his house as a pet. One day when he left his house, he returned to find that the house had been burnt to the ground and that his little pig had been roasted. Quite by accident, he tasted the pig and made the discovery that when suckling pigs were roasted, they provided a succulent dish. Armed with this knowledge, the man went out, bought another house and another suckling pig, put the pig in the house and burned the house down. The moral of the story seems to be that, although the man was after a very good thing—the roast pig—he paid a very high price—a new house. The "burn the house down" game then refers to the dynamic of trying to get a good thing, but going about it in such a way that a terribly high price must be paid.

One incident to illustrate how this applies to the acts of delinquents is the case of a boy who stabbed himself because his mother had kicked him out of the house. The primary motivation seemed to be to get back at the mother. He wanted a good thing—her acceptance and her protestations of love—but he almost paid a rather severe price—his life—for what he wanted from his mother.

Generally speaking, what the boys and their families actually want is a rather admirable value. The problem is that they attempt to get it in a way that is destructive. The drug abuser, for example, might be simply wanting to feel good, or to break the boredom of his life, or having a daily goal such as "scoring," or he may want to impress his peers and be popular with them.

Those are certainly not demeaning or distorted values. The car thief may want the thrill of riding in a car or the prestige of being the bravest of his peers. These too are not deplorable values. What the boy wants is usually a good thing, but the way he goes about getting it is, to say the least, problematic. It is helpful to think of delinquent behavior in these terms because it gets one away from believing that delinquents are crazy and have a sense of values that is utterly different from that of nondelinquents. Thinking in terms of delinquent behavior as an inadequate approach to an adequate goal is also a helpful way of communicating understanding to the boys who have got themselves into trouble. If you can identify with wanting to be liked and wanting to have nice things, then you are likely to build a liaison between yourself and the boy who has told you about wanting such things. If you can build such a liaison, then you may be able to work together on changing the problematic behavior.

Along with this general all-inclusive game, there are some specific games which some families of delinquents play. Remember that many families are doing the best that they possibly can, and that all of them should be prized for their ability to cope with as many problems as they have to put up with, let us consider some of the games that families of delinquents play with the family workers.

Games Families Play With Family Workers

One such game is called, "I blame you for not helping me and see to it that you don't." This game might be played by a mother opening a family group meeting by stating that, since the family workers and the other parents are not Chicano, or drug addicts, or Black, or ex-convicts, they cannot understand her family's problems and, therefore, no good will come from the meeting. In one instance, I remember opening a group with a discussion of the effect that gang involvement had upon a particular boy's ability to stay out of trouble. One mother stated that boys who were in gangs would not discuss gang behavior because they were pledged to secrecy. Well, of course, the belief created the fact, and we had a rather silent meeting for a while.

Some parents appear to refuse to allow treatment to succeed where they themselves have failed. They continually remind their sons of the inadequacies of the treatment they are receiving and end up driving a wedge between the son and the treatment persons. This is rather a powerful game and the treatment person is almost helpless in the face of it. However, it does help the family worker if he is prepared for it and if he can remind himself that a game is being run on him. Sometimes he will want to confront the family with the game they are playing.

A game similar to this one is, "Your camp is messing up my son." This is often interchanged with, "The school is messing up my son," or "The boy's father is messing up my son," or any one of a number of variations. In this game the family blames some other authority or person for the difficulty in which the son has placed himself. This game blocks progress in family treatment because it keeps the family and the family workers from focusing on the behaviors and attitudes which the people involved have a good chance of changing and which are making trouble for the son and the family. It is very difficult for a son to assume responsibility for his behavior if the father blames the school authorities for all problems with which his son has been involved in school. When a father adamantly declares that a school is negligent because they forgot to immediately report his son's absence from school, it is extremely difficult for that son to grapple with the reasons for his truancy. When a mother protests her son's being deprived of a furlough from camp for fighting, it is hard for that son to improve the control of his aggressive behavior.

Another game which families play with the family workers is, "We're burning incense just because we like the smell." One time as I visited a boy while he was out on furlough with his family, I could smell incense. I asked why the incense was burning and the family members said it was because they like the smell. It later became clear that they were burning incense to hide the smell of marihuana, which they had been smoking when I knocked on the door. The family was hiding behavior which was important to the treatment process. Most delinquent boys have long histories of hiding their behavior and when the family aids secretive behavior, treatment is impeded. Being "up front" is a prerequisite for progress in treatment.

Games Parents Play With Their Sons

A game that the parents of delinquents play with their sons is, "He'll do it anyway." Some parents play this game when it is brought to their attention by the family worker that their son is doing something that is seriously problematic, for example, getting drunk in his home every day. The parents, rather than using their ability to stop the boy, might rationalize in this fashion: "Well, I certainly don't want him to drink, and it is damaging because he is becoming an alcoholic, but I let him drink at home because if I don't, he'll do it anyway."

This game is harmful because when parents play this game, they don't get around to confronting the son with their strong feelings about the son's behavior. They often seem hesitant to make bold, strong personal confrontations. This is unfortunate because the son needs to hear loudly and clearly from the parents their own feelings about his problematic acts. The parents may, in reality, be unable to prevent the delinquent behavior, but they take away even the possibility of influencing it if they play "He'll do it anyway." If they refrain from playing this game and consistently give him strong statements about his behavior, controlling it when they can and influencing it when they can, the chances are great that their son will improve his behavior.

Another game parents play is, "It's the company he keeps." Some parents seem to think that there probably is nothing wrong with what their son is doing, and certainly nothing wrong with what they themselves are doing, and that the problem is that the son has been seduced and misled by his seriously delinquent, irresponsible friends. The problem, of course, with this game is that it causes the son and the parents to avoid taking responsibility for their behavior. The son certainly may be influenced by his peers, but he, not his friends, is the one making the decisions to join in the delinquent activity. If the parents will refrain from playing this particular game, perhaps the son can come to see that there are some people who have a good influence on him, and some who have a bad influence on him. It is hoped that the son will be able to use some discrimination in the choice of his friends, and that the parents can back him up after he has made his evaluations of the effects upon him of particular friends.

Other families play the, "That kid is ruining my life" game. One boy in a family conference said, "My dad makes me uncomfortable because he is so nervous." The boy's mother immediately said, "You make him nervous." The son was being blamed for things that were not of his doing. Some parents have a way of blaming their son for every bad thing that happens to the family. They begin thinking that the son is responsible for the conflict in their own marriage, for a nervous breakdown, and for any number of things for which the parents themselves are accountable.

A variation of the "ruining my life" game is "permanent teeter-totter." This game refers to the dynamic of encouraging one child to be extremely good and the other one to be extremely bad. Some parents seem to set up such a dynamic in the family. They predict that one son will turn out an angel and the other devil, and they go about fulfilling their own prophecy. Sometimes they seem to resist the improvement of the one who is at the bottom of the teeter-totter, almost appearing to fear that if one child goes up, the other will have to come down.

A game that many parents seem to play with their sons might be called. "Here's the candy, but I hope you get pimples!" This was a statement of a mother who volunteered to bring candy to her son while he was incarcerated but secretly hoped that his face would break out from eating it. We're dealing here with a double-edged message. One mother was describing her profuse love for her son in great detail. She said, "I love that boy so. I would love him even if he were laid in his casket. I can see him lying there with his eyelids closed, his lips a pale blue, a yellow pallor stealing over his face .   .   . ." The profuse protestations of love were accompanied by a detailed fantasy of the death of the son. The mother was conveying a double message, saying in effect, "I love you," and, "I want you dead." Many families appear to play this double message game. They get into a kind of "go away closer" thing. There is, of course, a natural ambivalence in just about every parent I know, but when this ambivalence is clouded over with protestations of abundant love, it gets very confusing. It can confuse the son to the point of driving him crazy.

Along with this double-edge game, there is a double-bind game played. One set of parents bought their son a Mustang Mach II with a 392 c. inch engine capable of speeds upwards of 125 miles per hour and said, "We'll take it away from you if you ever go over 60! " This kind of situation is radically improved when the family worker can get the parents to give a straight-arrow message rather than a double-bind one to their sons. Parents can learn to deal with their negative feelings more openly. Parents are often surprised with the verbal response they get from their sons when they themselves are honest, even when the feelings with which they are honest are negative feelings.

Games Boys Play With Their Families

One game that boys often run on their mothers is, "See mommy run." This game is played by the son who gets kicked out of school, becomes embroiled in all kinds of trouble with the police, does physical harm to his body by using drugs, all at least to some degree to test his mother's love for him. That is, he wants to see if mommy will come running after him when he gets into trouble. He wants assurance that, indeed, his mother does love him and he seems to need for her to communicate it by attending him when he gets into trouble.

When a son plays this game, he almost comes to expect his mother to rescue him at the last moment. For example, one boy managed to overdose three times with the convenient faith—conscious or otherwise—that his mother would be there to rescue him before he died. A pediatrician friend of mine says that when an overdose victim is brought to the hospital, the doctors relax when they discover that the boy has a history of overdose. Doctors have learned that some boys know exactly how much dosage it will take to throw their parents into a conniption fit and still be just short of fatal. This game is sometimes broken up when the mother states she is through running and the son begins to seek love and affection in a more direct and less destructive manner.

Another game that guys sometimes play with their parents can be called, "My gang can lick my old man." The idea here is that, for many delinquents, the peers and particularly the gang have a far stronger influence than do the parents. Some boys reject the values, standards and disciplines of the parents often in the name of freedom, and unwittingly become slaves and captives to the mores and discipline of the gang. Rather than weighing the statements of the parents against the statements of their peer groups and then objectively deciding in which direction they will go, some boys go in the direction their gang indicates almost by reflex action. When a young man is thoroughly immersed in this game, it is very difficult for him to listen to an adult for his ears are shut to outer influence. Nobody, however, really wants to die or to be seriously injured, or to have his brain damaged. If it can be pointed out that an uncritical acceptance of gang ways will lead to destruction, then boys may begin to be cooperative with their parents and with the family workers.

Some boys seem to play the game, "The devil made me do it." This is a game played when something or someone else is blamed for one's own troublemaking behavior. It is a device used to avoid taking the responsibility for doing something about getting into trouble. Variations on the game are, "My friends led me astray," "I inherited my temper from my old man," "What do you expect from someone who is brain damaged?" And "I was having an acid flashback." These kinds of games prevent the youth from seeing that he did what he did because he wanted to do it, and that it is never a question of, "I can't" but always a question of, "I won't."

A game boys seem to play on their parents in the home is "shopping." This is a rather simple, obvious game. The son plays it when he is denied a request from one parent and makes the same request to another parent, making sure that one parent knows not what the other parent is doing. For example, if he wants to go out to a movie, he may ask his father if he may go and if his father says no, he may go to his mother and ask her for permission. This game tends, of course, to pit one parent against the other. Some boys are able to so skillfully manipulate one parent against the other that they can obtain permission to do almost anything they want to do. However, in so doing, they may so intensify family conflict that they may contribute to family dissension.

Obviously, this is a description of only a few games that families of delinquents play. There are many more and there are many more factors contributing to any delinquent behavior. The above represents a few of the games that families of delinquents play and it is written in the hope that people working with such families will develop a feel for some of the dynamics described and will be able to break up some of the more destructive games. One way of breaking up the games is simply to describe to the family the particular dynamic obtaining in terms of games. Most families are not threatened by having someone telling them that they are playing a particular game. Usually one member of the family wants to stop playing it. Beyond this, particular methods I find to be effective in treating the families of delinquents will be described in future writings.

Certainly working with delinquents and their families can be frustrating, but it also can be deeply rewarding. In some families there is observable movement in a few family sessions. Families come to new understandings of each other and find more effective ways of meeting their needs within the family and within the community. When a boy develops such self-direction that he can meet his real needs without getting himself into trouble and the family communicates openly and the members of the family affirm and support each other, it is a cause for celebration. When this kind of thing happens, the family worker feels more like he is walking downhill to a mudslide; he just drifts along and hopes he can stay on his feet!

THE PROFESSIONAL AND THE VOLUNTEER IN PROBATION: AN EMERGING RELATIONSHIP*

Probation began with volunteers; some believe it will end with them, with volunteer probation counselors, tutors, foster parents, office workers, and the like. However, that is taken, the early volunteers were honorably discharged as soon as we could pay people, and the pendulum swung hard toward paid professionals in the first five decades of this century. Today the pendulum swings back toward volunteers—but with a difference. Where first probation was all volunteer and later virtually all paid professional, today it is both, and both are here to stay.

Probation will never again be all volunteer. But neither will it ever again be all paid professional. Therefore, the problem of *modern* volunteerism differs crucially from the problem of early volunteerism in corrections, for it becomes an issue of *relationship* between volunteer and paid professional, a problem of defining optimum roles for each in a productive probation partnership. John Augustus, as probation's founding father, incorporated "volunteer" and "probation officer" in one body; just so, we must learn to incorporate in the body of probation, both volunteer and paid professional. As in any new marriage, we will have to work at it, and we may still have to be satisfied with something less than perfect integration; but we cannot afford to be content with as little as coexistence. Divorce is impossible. Whatever the secret hopes of some, the modern court volunteer is not going to go away.

* Ivan H. Scheier, *Federal Probation*, June, 1970. Reprinted with permission.

The Volunteer Returns to the Court

The ghost of John Augustus rose again in 1960, looking somewhat different, when Royal Oak, Michigan, began easing into the use of volunteers with misdemeanants. Juvenile courts at Lawrence, Kansas, and Eugene, Oregon, had experimented with this kind of volunteer usage, since the mid-fifties. Judge Horace B. Holmes began using volunteers at the Boulder, Colorado, Juvenile Court in 1961. But not until 1967 did the court volunteer movement really take hold. Today, some 50,000 citizens contribute several million hours of service a year, in 1,000 court probation departments, and at least one new court a day is estimated to be launching its venture into volunteerism. These figures would be approximately doubled if one included parole and detention volunteer programs, as well as probation.

Even in this infancy of the movement, there are more volunteers than paid people in probation and they may soon be contributing a larger total of service hours as well. Moreover, the explosive acceleration in current growth rate extrapolates to a near future in which one-quarter of all courts will have volunteers working in probation programs, for better or for worse, in, say, 1972.

A similar sign of the times is the recent interest in planning and implementation of court volunteer programs on a *statewide* basis. Florida and Washington are already doing so, and 20 other states have indicated to the National Information Center, serious interest at this level. This immediately raises the question whether court volunteer programs are adaptable to the variety of local court and community conditions.

Adaptability to Local Communities and Courts

There are good reasons for approaching court volunteer programs with care and caution. Not among these is saying: "It works in your town because your town is unique." In the first place, 500 communities wear out the word "unique" and, on the evidence, the volunteer penetration into probation is broad as well as deep. Thus, what was said 2 years ago is more true today:

> The court volunteer movement is already too large for the "hothouse flower" label. It is also too hardy in surviving various types of environment. One of the clearest conclusions thus far is that a volunteer probation

program is not restricted to any one unique set of court or community conditions. Volunteer programs now flourish in every size and shape of American community and court. They span rural areas, small towns, large cities and suburbia. Some volunteer courts are in communities with colleges and depend heavily on them; others do not.[1]

To be sure, very small and very large communities have been relatively slow on the uptake (the latter, probably related to the skepticism of established professionals). But the broad weight of dissemination evidence simply will not permit the "unique" shrug-off.

As for type of courts, volunteer programs tend to take root in courts with a rehabilitation rather than a purely retributive philosophy. Other than that, they are not peculiar to any particular type of court. As noted recently:

> All levels of jurisdiction are represented: municipal, county, district or superior. About half are juvenile courts with a core of professional probation officers who preceded the advent of volunteers. The remainder are misdemeanant courts which would have had no probation department at all, except for volunteers.[2]

As of today, add that a few courts are even beginning to experiment with volunteers assigned to *felons* on probation. For American service volunteerism—where too many college graduates have licked too many stamps, too long—entrusting volunteers with any kind of probationer was itself something of a pioneer venture into elevated responsibility and meaningfulness. The extension to *felon* probationers is surely on the growing edge of *serious* service volunteerism.

The Volunteer Encounter With Professionals

Increasingly we realize this difference in court setting is important. This is not so much because of the age of volunteers assigned probationers. They tend to be younger probationers in adult courts, averaging 18 to 20 years of age, which is not too

---

1. H. B. Holmes, et al., "The Volunteer Returns to the Court," *Juvenile Court Judges Journal*, Volume 18, Number 4, Winter 1968.

2. Ibid.

far from the juvenile court average. Rather, the crucial difference is that in most juvenile courts, volunteer programs have to
be grafted onto a pre-existing paid professional structure. But
misdemeanant courts, the forgotten area of probation, rarely had
probation departments of any sort prior to volunteers. Accordingly, this pre-existing staff "limitation" on the activities and
attitudes of volunteers does not usually exist in misdemeanant
courts. By the same token, volunteer programs in previously
unprofessionalized courts lack the potentialities for growth of
volunteer programs through professional leadership. Or, at any
rate, they do at first. For volunteer programs actually have
created paid leadership positions in corrections where none existed before. The evidence on this point is overwhelming and,
on the other side of the ledger, there is not one authenticated instance of a corrections professional losing his job because of volunteers.

Thus, in both juvenile court and misdemeanant systems, paid
professionals come to be involved with volunteers. But the vol-
unteer-produced type of professional is a different kind of fellow.
He is committed to volunteers by choice, and if it comes to that,
he owes his job to them. His relationship to volunteers is central and natural, if not entirely without friction, as he concen-
trates on supervising or facilitating their work. If he locks horns
with anyone, it is far more likely to be the traditional professional (whose stake is in supervising probationers, not volunteers). Let us hope this does not happen, but it could, as the
"new professional" becomes more numerous. In that sad case,
the traditional professional could have a relationship problem,
not only with the volunteer, but also with the volunteer-created
"new professional." Indeed, while our attention has been riveted
on the emerging court volunteer, we have neglected an area of
equal personnel significance: the concurrent emergence of the
volunteer-created new professional.

Visibility of this "new professional" in corrections has been
somewhat obscured because, especially in the early days of the
movement, he was called by traditional titles such as chief probation officer or director of probation services, even though that
is not what he was actually doing in the *traditional* sense. Also,
one person might perform quite successfully in both job dimensions at once. More and more, however, the new professional is
being advertised for and called what he actually is: "Volunteer

Coordinator (Corrections)," "Director of Probation Volunteer Services," "Volunteer Specialist," or even "Community Organization Specialist."

The Inspiration Issue

All the above may seem to invent fanciful problems for a profession already supplied plentifully with real ones. Let me therefore reiterate: probation volunteer programs are suddenly past the oddity stage. Present figures, and close-in projections show them upon us in ever more significant numbers, giving little quarter to leisurely reflection. In fact, they have already changed the question before the house. The question no longer is, "will it be done?"; the only question is, "will it be done well?"

It must be said that, to some, it is virtually the same question. They feel the idea is intrinsically so good it will work itself. Some mystic quality in the volunteer has only to be permitted a chance and it will succeed. That is, volunteerism is placed in the Judeo-Christian tradition rather than the more secular democratic citizen-participation tradition. Indeed, this emphasis on spiritual values frequently reaches the point where to good people who hold this view seem to be proposing that probation become an arm of Christianity (as it is actually said to be in at least one European country). In any event, the position is that you need not concern yourself overly with managerial procedures where inspiration is concerned; in fact, the idea is so good, you can scarcely "procedure yourself out of it."

To others, procedure is just about everything. Running volunteer programs is a complex, professionally demanding body of specialized *knowledge*. You *can* fail at it, and on the record, quite a few courts have. Yes, inspiration is one of the important things volunteers offer, but you'd better have a good organization behind that inspiration, if you want it to work massively in program-level interventions. Indeed, why do we feel we can show our faith in spirit only by being disorganized? Why must we suffocate goodwill in chaos, when we have applied organizational genius to just about everything else in this country? Surely, we can no longer suffer misguided sentiment to waste precious human resources. We must let hard heads help soft hearts.

Evidence of the Impact of Court Volunteers

But there is a prior question: Why invest time, intelligence, and effort in the organization of volunteers if they are not, in the first place, demonstrated to be effective agents of positive probation change? To a certain extent, the present inadequacies of probation justify trying anything that even looks hopeful, not so much because it is proved better, as that it can hardly be worse. But in the long run, we need more than desperation as justification, and we already have some evidence. Courts using volunteers consistently report reductions in institutionalization rates, as more and more, they are able to work with the offender in his home community. At the same time, striking reductions in repeat offense percentage are also claimed (although this can be a somewhat elusive statistic). Perhaps the most impressive research finding is one which has been independently confirmed in three separate courts: one juvenile, one misdemeanant-suburb, and one misdemeanant-metropolis. As recently summarized,[3] all three researches agreed in finding that a group of probationers assigned volunteers one to one showed lessening of antisocial attitudes when tested before and after probation. By contrast, groups of probationers not assigned volunteers showed actual *increase* in antisocial attitudes—a damning indictment of "empty probation."

This does not clinch the case, by any means. First of all, these positive results were produced by relatively *well-run* volunteer programs. Other programs are poorly run and, presumably, show poorer results. A second complication is the multi-dimensional impact of court volunteer programs. In addition to probationers, they have important influences on the court, the community, and the volunteers themselves.

Thus, anecdotal observation and evidential analysis in process at the National Information Center concur strongly that court volunteer programs are popular and well received in the community. Volunteers function effectively as the court's ambassadors and educators in the community. Even other social control and social service agencies in town—from whom "jealously" might conceivably be expected—tended to approve the Boulder Court's venture into volunteerism.

Impact on the volunteers themselves is less well known. There is the traditional assumption that volunteers find their work sat-

3. I. H. Scheier, "Court Volunteer Impact on Probationers: Attitudes and Personality," reprint from Volume 1, Number 18 (1969) of *The Volunteer Courts Newsletter*, published at the National Information Center on Volunteers in Courts, Hall of Justice, Division C, Boulder, Colorado 80302.

isfying—generally they do—but anecdotal observation of volunteers in action also suggests that at least some volunteers will
hang on in a poorly run program, though unhappy, just because
they think the ultimate objectives of probation so worthy. As
for statistics, Denver County Court has reported a very favorable
re-volunteer rate, well over 80 percent, but this number reflects
volunteers who have already survived the test of a year's service
during which the first 3 to 6 months appear to be the "volunteer
death" period of greatest dropout. When one is talking about
court volunteer turnover rate for a 1-year period, the figure is not
much better than 50 percent.

  Finally, the volunteer's impact on professional roles and structures in the court is a profound and complex one which we shall
touch on later in this article. But clearly, court volunteer programs are not a one-edged sword, or even a two-edged sword.
They cut many ways in the court and the community. Put otherwise, anyone who sees only black and white misses much in this
chiaroscuro world. And too many people see volunteers in this
all-or-nothing way; either anathema or panacea, with nothing
in between; either not in the ball park or the only game in town.

The Range of Court Volunteer Contributions

  Either extreme is unrealistic. Court volunteer programs are
actually a complex mix of advantage and disadvantage. Therefore, planning and evaluation must carefully balance expected
yield against necessary inconvenience, adjustment, and stress on
the court. We must be as clear as possible on the nature of this
expected yield. What precisely may a probation department expect to get out of volunteers? Generally, the answers are: (1)
amplification of services and, (2) diversification of services.

  (1) *Amplication of services.*—As for amplification, consider
the case of the probation officer who, after paperwork chores,
has an hour a month left to spend with each probationer in his
caseload. He can spend it directly (a) supervising the probationer, in which case his 1 hour input of time results in 1 hour output
of attention received by the probationer. Alternatively, he can
spend this hour directly (b) supervising a *volunteer* who then
spends much more time supervising the probationer as his "caseload of one." The 1 hour input of time by the probation officer
may thus result in 15 hours output of attention received by the
probationer ("amplied" via the volunteer).

Combinations of the two systems are possible, too, of course, where the probation officer spends part of this time supervising the volunteer and part of his time keeping some direct contact with the probationer with whom the volunteer works.

In the second system in which probation officers supervise probationers indirectly by the use of volunteers, the same probation officer input of time eventually delivers 15 hours' attention to the probationer instead of one—15 times as much time. The case is a great deal more complex than that, of course, but our calculations have indicated generally an "amplication factor" averaging between 10 and 20 for court volunteer programs. That is, for each hour of staff supervisory or facilitatory time invested (and this investment is necessary) 10 to 20 hours of volunteer service are outputted into the probation service system.

(2) *Diversification of services.*—Potentially, the probation treatment plan can now tap any skill that exists in the community, a mind-stretching prospect we have scarcely begun to absorb. Do you need a cobbler, a carpenter, a marriage counselor, cosmetologist, a psychiatrist, a guitar player, a stock market expert? They are there. The report of the Joint Commission on Correctional Manpower and Training indicates that almost 50 percent of the community would probably or certainly volunteer for juvenile corrections work if asked (see "Readings" section at the close of this article). Indeed, we know of at least 50 different types of skills that have been volunteered to courts the past few years. The breathtaking possibility for the probation officer is: Your staff *is* the community, a reservoir of skills which can be orchestrated to probation planning. Volunteers are *not* a rigid format, take it or leave it. They are a *medium with which you can work*, the bricks and stones which you select and place in order to build your own house of probation. They are not a house already built.

The facts support this variegated view of volunteers. No less than 155 distinct court volunteer job descriptions have been catalogued as actually filled by volunteers in one court or another, in 20 major categories of contribution, and several major program areas. The volunteer as a range of options, rather than a restriction, is further suggested by the types of roles volunteers can and have filled in courts (one volunteer can fill several at once, of course):

Thus, in the area of direct contact with probationers, volunteers can offer services such as: (1) support-friendship, sincere

warmth; (2) "mediation," facilitation of social-physical environment (get jobs, intercede with teacher, etc.); (3) behavior model,
good example; (4) limit-setting, social control, conscience; (5)
teacher-tutor of skills, academic, vocational or social; (6) ob-
servation-information-diagnosis-understanding [extra eyes and
ears (a) on the probationer (b) on the community, or even (c)
on court operations]; and (7) advisory or decision-making participation in formulation or modification of probation plan.

Volunteers can also do many things not primarily involving direct contact with probationers. Among these are: (8) administrative, office work, and related facilitation; (9) help recruit,
train, advise, and supervise other volunteers; (10) expert consultant to regular staff; (11) advisor to court, participation in
policy-making, formally or informally, the volunteer as a source
of ideas; (12) public relations, public education, and related impact on the community; and (13) contributions of money, materials, facilities, or help in securing them from others (e. g., fund
raisers).

As late as 1962, I remember reading an eloquent plea for citizen participation which culminated in a suggestion to this effect:
"Now, why don't you folks get together and *discuss* delinquency."
By contrast, the list above announces citizen participation at a
new pitch. And as citizens assume these new levels of responsibility, so does the court, for if citizens can do so many different
and real things, the court must take explicit responsibility for
articulating and directing the efforts of this powerful instru-
mentality.

Management of Court Volunteer Programs

The supervision of such a range of effort demands real skill
in a director of court volunteer programs. Books and big man-
uals barely scratch the surface of this subject and the introduc-
tory guidelines below are merely a shorthand for formidable complexities. They are certainly not meant to encourage the dangerous myth that "anyone can do it." Nor do they mean to impute
a tidy consensus to that special body of knowledge concerning
the purpose and conduct of court volunteer programs, which is
only now beginning to emerge from the writings of pioneers.[4]

---

4. See "Readings" section at the end
of this paper, and especially a sum-
marizing work entitled, *Using Vol-*
unteers in Court Settings: A Man-
ual for Volunteer Probation Pro-
grams.

Recruiting.—The early fear is that you will not get enough good people, but the danger is almost exactly opposite. Premature, broadcast recruiting will get you more people than you are ready to use (and they will likely resent overlong waiting). Quantity of volunteers is rarely a problem—Boulder typically has a waiting list. Talks at local groups, word-of-mouth, even "help wanted" ads, all bring their human yield.

As for volunteer quality, the ancient unconscious prejudice—what you don't pay for can't be worth much—is at last being laid to rest. Overwhelming experience and actual statistics show that today's court volunteer is well educated, successful, mature—the kind of person you would be glad to pay for if you had the money. Not incidentally, you would need quite a bit of money. Nationally, 10 to 15 percent of court volunteers are professionals contributing as professionals, without charge. Overall, in a modest-sized community such as Boulder, the purchase price of volunteer services would be $50,000 a year, at a conservative estimate. Boulder does not have that kind of money, of course, but we do have that kind of service.

Within the middle-class predominance of court volunteers (poor people usually cannot afford to volunteer) all races and religions are proportionally represented. All have a great deal more sophistication on social matters than their parents had, and anyone who thinks of them in terms of sweet, naive "Lady Bountiful," is simply whipping a dead volunteer.

There are misfits, of course, but so far as The National Information Center has been able to ascertain, the percentage is no higher among volunteers than among paid people in corrections.

Screening and selection.—The second secret nightmare of those who sleep on volunteer program planning is: "We're going to get all these kooky people and since they're volunteers we're going to have to accept them." Wrong on both counts! Begin your screening back in recruiting, by keeping your focus sharp. Recruit only where you are most likely to find the kind of people you want, e. g., church groups, colleges, labor unions, your personal friends, etc. Do not use "come one-come all" newspaper releases, especially in the early stages of the program.

After focussed recruiting, do not be afraid to screen hard. Begin by being clear in your own mind as to exactly what you want in the job and in the volunteer's qualifications. Be honest with yourself and the volunteer about it, rather than apologetic. Indeed, you will do just about everything right if you act as if you're offering the volunteer a $10,000-a-year job: application form, character references, police checks, replicated interviews, good motivation, etc. Actually, volunteers seem to appreciate it more when they are taken seriously in this way.

True, you will occasionally—not often—have to reject a nice person who is just not suitable. More often, however, they will screen themselves out if you give them a chance to do so, via honest realism in describing the job, during training, and even in trial jobs. Or there may be other less sensitive jobs to offer such a person, in the court or elsewhere in town (e. g., via a local volunteer bureau). Moreover, people come increasingly to respect your high standards. It becomes a privilege to be a volunteer at your court, and citizens understand if they do not quite make it. We know of only one case in which a rejected volunteer took his case to the Governor, won it, and did a good job. The Governor's wife is a volunteer too!

Orientation and training.—Auslander's recent M.S.W. study (see "Readings" section) confirmed that currently, what the average court is doing about training volunteers is essentially very little. Some reject it almost entirely on the grounds, plausible in themselves, that the volunteer is not supposed to be just another watered-down professional. True enough, but orientation can do other needed things.

For example, it can *familiarize* the volunteer (1) with the job and its boundaries, (2) with what probationers are like, (3) with typical problems and solutions of volunteers working with probationers, (4) with the court, the "who, what, where" of staff, procedures, laws, facilities, and (5) the same for community resources available for helping probationers.

Secondly, volunteer orientation and training has an important *morale* function. Training says to the volunteer: the court takes your work seriously. Also, the volunteer looks around and sees that he's not alone (loneliness being a real morale problem for volunteers). Nor should *staff* morale implications be overlooked. When staff have a hand in the planning and conduct of training, they have a chance and a channel for saying: This is how we would like the job done. This relieves their "loss of program control" nightmare about volunteers. Staff also can catch here, some of the enthusiasm and concern of good volunteers.

For these reasons volunteer orientation is viewed as a critical area of the court volunteer movement at this juncture, and the National Information Center will be spending the year 1970 reviewing and developing practical resources in this domain, under a grant from the Office of Juvenile Delinquency and Youth Development, U. S. Department of Health, Education, and Welfare.

Other managerial areas.—We have no space to cover entire areas of volunteer program managerial expertise, each of which would merit a chapter in any book, e. g., public relations, financing volunteer programs, volunteer incentive and support, communications and record-keeping, evaluation of individual and program performance, etc.

Changes in the Role of the Professional

Space permits mention of only one more matter—but a tremendously important one: the profound changes in professional roles produced by the introduction of volunteers into a court system. But this role change is not role *degradation*; far from it. First of all, the probation professional can do nothing but profit from enhanced interaction with the additional professionals brought in as volunteers. Secondly, leadership of the high-quality court volunteers we are getting, challenges the probation officer *professionally* as never before. Thirdly, the ability of the profession to attract and retain high quality people depends directly on improved pay scales. On the record, local volunteers have been effective allies of professionals here, in various courts around the country. All in all, the claim that volunteers deprofessionalize corrections proves on examination to be precisely contrary to fact. Volunteers will professionalize corrections as never before, and one may suspect that some old-liners who claim volunteers demand too little professionally are really afraid they will demand too much.

The really sobering role-change impact of court volunteerism is that it appears to deprive the probation officer of one of his chief satisfactions professionally: direct contact with probationers. But this is not necessarily so, or, at least, the matter is more involved than this simple statement indicates.

Let us make three assumptions about probation caseloads and from these deduce three role models for the professional of a future in which volunteers are a substantial factor in probation programming. The assumptions are: (1) Certain types of probationers can be rehabilitated primarily by what a "caseload of one" volunteer can offer, e. g., warmth, a behavior model, individualized mediation in the environment, etc.; (2) certain other cases cannot, and require the attention of a professional probation officer (or associated professional); and (3) diagnosis will increasingly develop precision in discriminating among these two types of probationer.

Given these reasonable assumptions, three professional role-types can be discerned: (1) the volunteer specialist, the "new professional" who works primarily with and through volunteers, rather than directly with probationers, (2) the traditional professional who continues to work directly with a caseload of probationers, (3) the two-way professional who derives satisfaction both from contact with volunteers and contact with probationers. Part of his caseload is carried via supervision of volunteers, while the other involves direct contact with probationers.

The professional of types two and three not only retains the satisfaction of direct work with probationers; he probably enjoys it in enhanced form. For with volunteers taking over a number of cases which do not require his attention, he now has a chance for direct work with probationers which is ideal in two senses. First, having been relieved of part of his caseload by volunteers, he can concentrate better on the fewer probationers remaining as his direct responsibility. Secondly, this reduced caseload may be composed largely of the probationers he deliberately selects to work with, as those who are most likely to benefit from his professional attention. Thus, where formerly the probation officer was something like the football coach at a school so small he had to teach flower arrangement for the girls and lacrosse for the alumni, now others take on the chores peripheral to his interest and capacity, and he can concentrate on football. This, of course, is better for the football players, and the flower arrangers too.

These new professional roles in probation are exciting and promising, yet little is being done to prepare for the dislocation and retraining the next few years will require in adjusting to them. The National Information Center's publications and institutes need to be amplified tenfold, and soon, or we shall never get the best out of our new and growing army of volunteer assistants. Instead, we will join our cousins in 30 other major areas of service volunteerism, where 60 million volunteers constitute the largest leaderless army in the world, and the most tragic, because not enough people are being trained well enough to lead them and develop their immense potential. Volunteerism has no West Points in or out of corrections, now or on the horizon, and this may be the most stupendous oversight of the century.

ROYAL OAK'S EXPERIENCE WITH PROFESSIONALS AND VOLUNTEERS IN PROBATION*

Probation officers, judges, correctional workers, and citizens, close your eyes and dream for a moment! What would you ask if your wildest dreams could come true? A probation department where hundreds of your citizens would think of and talk about "us" and "we" rather than "they" and "them"; a mayor and a city commission who, when they talk to visitors from out of state, would refer to the probation program as "we" and "us" out of a feeling of pride, even though they are not part of the staff and have nothing to do with the daily operation of the probation program—the kind of "we" and "us" a New York citizen uses when he talks about the Mets: "We sure won that game, didn't 'we'?"

Would you ask for a program so well accepted that many businessmen contribute money to it each year because they want to be involved? Or would you dream of the day you could write a letter to 40 psychiatrists asking them to volunteer their time and talent and have 35 of them respond and become part of your rehabilitative service?

With eyes closed, do you dream of the day that your professional staff would have several hours a month to spend individually with the more difficult probationers?

How about the thought of having hundreds of volunteers who will sit up all night in a hospital with a probationer in a crisis and perform hundreds of other acts of friendship?

Would you like to operate a program that furnishes as much as $250,000 a year in services on a budget of as little as $17,000 from the taxpayers and an additional $8,000 from private dona-

* Keith J. Leenhouts, *Federal Probation*, December, 1970. Reprinted with permission.

tions within the community, with only a 7 percent recidivism rate over a 10-year period? This is what happened at the Municipal Court at Royal Oak, Michigan, which had jurisdiction over persons 17 and over charged with misdemeanors.

All of these, and much more, are now being experienced by courts using volunteers. If your dreams include these thoughts, and many more, consider using volunteers.

How the Royal Oak Program Developed

How did the Royal Oak program begin?

In 1959 eight citizens sat around the table on a hot August night discussing the court's problem. All we could do was to look at the defendant for a moment or two after he pleaded guilty or was found guilty and was given a fine or a jail term. Completely without any probation program, no presentence investigation or rehabilitative service was possible. What could we do about it? The eight, all expert counselors,[1] agreed to try to change the system by accepting a caseload of five probationers each. In early 1960 the Michigan Corrections Commission appointed one of them chief probation officer and approved the plan to use volunteers. We started assigning probationers to them.

There was, of course, much that was wrong with the program. But of greater significance, there was much that was right. We began to build on the strengths and sought to overcome the weaknesses. History proved what was right was more important than what was wrong.

Volunteers Recruit Volunteers

The original eight recruited more volunteers. Soon it was possible to reduce the caseload to two or three probationers per volunteer. Eventually a one-to-one relationship was established. All of the volunteers were experts in some field of counseling. Most of them were educators, ministers, psychologists, and other professionals with at least a master's degree in counseling and guidance.

When we were about 9 months old, we had 30 volunteers and some 75 probationers. As the judge, I was spending about 20 hours weekly administering the program. This was in addition

1. A psychiatrist, a psychologist, a social worker, three clergymen, and two junior high school assistant principals. The last five had master's degrees in counseling and guidance.

to my civil, traffic, and criminal judicial duties which took some 40 hours a week. I could not do this indefinitely, for I was the only judge in a city of 90,000 which had many thousand people traveling through it each day. The fact that it is part of the metropolitan area of Detroit further complicated the situation. We needed help and we turned to the volunteer chief probation officer and the community for assistance. We asked two businessmen to each donate $25 a month to the program so we could employ the chief probation officer for 40 hours a month to supervise the program. They agreed and we had our first budget and "paid" worker. He met with all of the probationers and volunteers each month.

Many things happened after that, but a tradition was established. When a need was manifested, it was solved in one of two ways. Either volunteers were used or professionals were employed for a fraction of what their services were worth, businessmen in the community paying all or, in the later years, part of their salaries.

A few months later, a second part-time professional was added to the staff. He was also one of the original eight volunteers. Two more businessmen contributed funds. The two of them each met with half of the volunteers and probationers monthly.

Role of the Retiree

About this time I was reaching the point of exhaustion. I called a friend of many years, Harry Hassberger. Now retired from his job as an executive with a plumbing and heating company, he was working about 3 hours a day as a school street-crossing guard. He readily agreed to work 15 hours a week as a volunteer to administer the program, thus relieving the part-time professionals from burdensome details so they could spend nearly all of their time counseling and supervising the volunteers.

A few months later the school year ended and Mr. Hassberger agreed to work full time for the amount he could receive under Social Security regulations, about 50 cents an hour. Four businessmen contributed $25 each a month to "pay" for his services.

It would be difficult to underestimate his contribution. The young program took on a new dimension of pride and self-assurance. Mr. Hassberger's concern, interest, and dedication became a key part of the program. We were so proud of what he was doing, that we became more proud and confident of ourselves.

He soon earned the name, Harry "The Horse" Hassberger as he ran from room to room almost with the enthusiasm of a youngster chasing a ball.

We learned about group psychotherapy. A psychiatrist agreed to handle two groups for a year for $10 an hour. Again businessmen contributed their money. At the end of 15 months we had a good program but must more was needed.

Then, unexpectedly, the mayor called us and said, "The city commissioners are being criticized for not contributing to the program. How much do you need for next year?" We projected $4,400 and the mayor readily agreed to give it. However, we requested only $2,200. We did not want to lose our private financial contributors. Their involvement was important to us. Thus, we started the new fiscal year with a budget of $4,400, half from the city.

By 1965, the program had a budget of $17,000 from the city and about $8,000 from private contributors. The staff included seven retirees who administered the program, 12 part-time professional chief counselors who counseled the probationers and supervised the volunteers, and a part-time staff psychiatrist who coordinated the efforts of 35 volunteer psychiatrists and 15 psychologists and who also made presentence evaluations. They made one presentence evaluation every 3 months and also rendered help on a weekly basis, without cost, to well motivated probationers who needed help. Some also conducted group therapy sessions on a weekly basis for 9 months at a time.

Three of the retirees—a former labor dispute investigator, a superintendent of schools, and a recovered alcoholic—did the presentence investigations with the assistance of the volunteer psychiatrists and psychologists and the staff psychiatrist. No one committing one of the more serious misdemeanors was ever sentenced unless and until 4 to 20 hours of careful presentence work had been completed.

Those placed on probation were assigned in several different ways.

Royal Oak's Program Today

About 20 percent of all probationers are assigned to volunteers who work on a one-to-one basis with the probationer. With solid training and supervision available, both expert counselors and ordinary citizens with special aptitudes and interests are used as volunteers. These probationers also report to a member of our professional staff at least monthly in addition to their several meetings with their volunteer each month. Thus, the time and the warmth of the volunteer acting as a friend are experienced together with the skill and the warmth of the professional.

Approximately 20 percent of the probationers report to 12 part-time professional counselors. All have at least a master's degree in counseling. Some are psychologists. They have a case-load of 10 probationers each and, freed of burdensome administrative detail by the retirees, can spend all of their 15 to 20 hours a month supervising volunteers and counseling their probationers. They average about 1½ hours a month with their probationers.

About 20 percent participate in group counseling programs conducted by volunteer psychiatrists and psychologists in addition to the part-time staff psychiatrist. A few weekly sessions have also been conducted by the part-time professional counselors. These are weekly meetings.

Ten percent of the probationers attend the court's Alcoholics Anonymous program. Most of the leaders of the program are recovered alcoholics who were first assigned to the program by the court. Most of them also attend the Alcohol Information School conducted by the probation department.

Five percent attend individual and group marriage counseling sessions conducted by one of our part-time professionals who is an authority in this field.

Another 5 percent are under treatment with the volunteer psychiatrists and psychologists who agree to work with one motivated probationer at a time in addition to completing one presentence report a month.

The female probationers are referred to the head of the Women's Division which has 25 volunteers. This accounts for about 5 percent. Their program includes a charm school.

Most of the remaining 15 percent are older offenders—in their 40's, 50's, and 60's—who see the retirees only under orders to pay restitution or support. The average number on probation at Royal Oak is about 500.

Under our system it is difficult to say how many staff members are needed for a given number of volunteers. One retiree spends all of his time administering the one-to-one volunteer program. We usually have about 100 active one-to-one volunteers.

We would estimate that one professional could supervise, as distinguished from administer, this number. Perhaps one professional, responsible for both supervision and administration, for every 50 volunteers would be reasonable.

Volunteer Turnover Is Low

Except for those who move away, the turnover rate for volunteers is encouragingly low. We believe several conditions are necessary for such a fine response. The volunteer must be given serious work to do which is worthy of his abilities. If he can work on a one-to-one basis, he should not be a volunteer mailing assistant. We should be considerate of him; if he is requested to work with one probationer, we should not ask him later to work with two or three. We should be flexible within the framework and philosophy of the program so he can be innovative and imaginative. We should be sure he is appreciated, although public recognition may not be necessary. The annual "Thank You" parties in Royal Oak were poorly attended by the one-to-one volunteers, although other groups attended in larger numbers.

There are many ways volunteers can be utilized. The one-to-one relationship is only one. Volunteer medical doctors, optometrists, attorneys, dentists, and secretaries have given of their special talents to our court. The role of the psychiatrist and psychologist has already been mentioned. Dr. Ivan H. Scheier [2] of the Boulder County (Colorado) Juvenile Court and director of the National Information Center on Volunteers in Courts, one of the leaders in this field, has listed over 100 ways courts can use volunteers. (Excellent literature, a Volunteer Court Newsletter, and other services are available by contacting him at the Hall of Justice at Boulder, Colorado.)

What can the volunteer do that good, solid professional cannot do? Apart from the initial advantage where the probationer learns that the volunteer is not being paid, the answer is Nothing. To equate the one-to-one relationship, imagine a probation officer with no presentence investigation duties, no administrative details, and 22 probationers. (The average volunteer gives 5 to 10 hours a month.) Could he do a commendable job? Of course he could! Therefore, no community with 500 probationers which

---

2. See Dr. Scheier's article, "The Professional and the Volunteer in Probation: Perspectives on an Emerging Relationship," Federal Probation, June 1970.

is willing to employ about 23 probation officers and also provide adequate administration and presentence help need consider volunteers. Since this would be asking a city of about 100,000 to spend over $350,000 a year on probation, volunteers are the only answer. Rarely do these cities spend more than $25,000 a year. More often they spend nothing on court rehabilitative services.

Hard Work Is Expected

Although there is nothing particularly complex and difficult about administering a volunteer court program for experienced probation officers and judges, it is hard work. Having given some 10 to 20 hours a week for nearly 10 years in addition to my judicial duties, I say this with feeling and conviction. Thus, although dissemination of this concept is one of the main goals of our organization, Volunteers in Probation, Inc., we now try to persuade courts not to use volunteers if they will not work diligently. Most of the more than 600 courts known to be making substantial use of volunteers (there were virtually none in 1960 and only 25 or so in 1967) are doing too good a job to have courts without dedicated judges and probation officers initiate volunteer programs which are lacking in dedication and willingness to work.

When we first began to promote the volunteer program in 1965, there were three big obstacles. First, Royal Oak and its judge were said to be unique. This, of course, was not true, for Royal Oak is an average city and I am an average judge and person. Now, there are more than 600 answers, including large cities like Denver, Seattle, Houston, and Dallas, which demonstrate that it can work elsewhere.

Second, we heard many say, "prove that it works." We do not hear this much any more, probably for two reasons. It is obvious that intensive probation, which is possible only by and through the use of *volunteers and professionals*, is more effective than "paper" probation which is all that is available in the vast majority of the lower courts; research at Boulder, Denver, and Royal Oak has at least shifted the burden of proof to those who argue against intensive professional-volunteer probation programs. Research at Royal Oak compared a group of 100 probationers in our city and in a comparable city in another state. Each spent $17,000 a year on its program. The other court, for its $17,000, provided the services of one fine probation officer. He had some secretarial service and a caseload of about 250 probationers. Since the other city was one-fourth again larger than Royal Oak, one might assume that if Royal Oak had about 500 active probationers, the other court should have had more rather than less probationers. The probation officer of the second city regretfully admitted that many were not given probation because his caseload was too large already.

The one hundred probationers at Royal Oak had a recidivism rate of half that of the other court. Through psychological testing and retesting, there was evidence that attitudes were improved at Royal Oak contrary to the experience of the other court.

Each of the 1965 probationers at both courts was also considered in another recidivism study. At Royal Oak 310 defendants were placed on probation in 1965, the year of the test. In the second court, 223 were placed on probation. Over a period of 4 years and 9 months through September of 1969, 14.9 percent of the probationers in Royal Oak were convicted of additional offenses. In the other court, 49.8 percent had one or more subsequent convictions. The research also indicated that the Royal Oak probationers were convicted of 0.23 convictions per probationer during the period of study compared with a conviction rate of 2.70 per probationer in the other court. The research simply adds proof to what must be true. Many thousands of hours of intensive rehabilitative services are more effective than one overwhelmed probation officer who can only administer a telephone and letter reporting system.

Professional-Volunteer Relationship

The third obstacle is the resistance of the professional probation officer who feels threatened by volunteers. This is being overcome gradually as the professionals realize that the volunteer desperately needs the professional and is not trying to take his place. At Royal Oak we place the greatest value on the professional. A volunteer program was established rather quickly. For many years we struggled to achieve professionalism. Now that new professional positions are being created by the use of volunteers and experience has proved over a decade that no professional has ever lost a job because of a volunteer, this last obstacle is being removed. It is also interesting to note that in a few courts, through volunteer involvement, citizens are aware for the first time of the splendid job professionals are doing and the vital role they fulfill. With this new and better citizen understanding, more professionals were engaged and their pay rates were increased more rapidly than ever before. Volunteers have proved themselves valuable allies and coworkers. They work hand in glove with the professionally trained probation officer.

Some Guidelines in Using Volunteers

We strongly urge you to bear in mind that no two volunteer programs can be expected to develop in precisely the same way. To develop spirit, we believe it is essential to assess your own needs and resources and to put them together in your own way. We emphasize that no one should carbon copy the mechanics of any other program.

What are some of the factors you should consider if you decide to use volunteers? May we suggest a few, based on our experience for a decade and watching the movement grow from virtually no courts in 1960 to more than 600 known courts in 1970.

Start small.—At Royal Oak, in 1959, our adult misdemeanant court probation program began, without publicity, with eight volunteers. It probably could have begun with a hundred. Hindsight now confirms the wisdom of a small start. Virtually every successful volunteer court program has begun small. If you are starting from nothing with no pre-existing probation department, as in Royal Oak, use only expert volunteers since no staff supervision is possible at first. If there is a pre-existing professional program, the nonexpert volunteer can be used immediately.

Build spirit.—Building spirit is an essential ingredient. If you do not feel good about each other and what you are doing, forget the idea. Some years ago I had an opportunity to talk with DeWitt Wallace, founder and cochairman of *Reader's Digest*. What would Mr. Wallace talk about in the few minutes we had together? Would it be their circulation? Would it be buildings, wealth, power? No. Mr. Wallace said simply, "The story of the Digest is its spirit. We who work for the Digest like each other and have a feeling we are doing good." The same feeling must dominate a professional-volunteer probation program or it will fail. It is that important. It is that simple.

Select and screen volunteers with care.—Selecting and screening, of course, is vital in any program. If you do not select the right paid employee for the job and screen out the wrong ones, you will never be successful. The same is true of the volunteer.

You must be just as selective with a volunteer as you are with a professional. Remember that many citizens want to be volunteers and "work with" a probationer. Most programs always have a waiting list. Select only the best because this is what the probationer deserves. For many of them, it will be the first time they have had the best of anything. Recently a friend of mine said of a newly elected judge, "He has the quality most needed to be a judge. He is a warm and decent human being." The same is true of a volunteer.

We would suggest that the more general the recruitment, the more careful the screening must be. At Royal Oak, no public appeal was ever made for volunteers. No radio, newspaper, public speeches, or TV announcements were made. Recruitment was by reputation and word of mouth. Three screening devices were utilized. First, most of the volunteers were personal friends of the judge, a member of the probation staff, or another volunteer in whom we had the utmost confidence and respect. Second, acceptance of the screening process of professional organizations such as the teacher who was screened by the school board, the psychologist who was screened by the psychological association, etc. Third, an interview by a volunteer psychiatrist or psychologist when we were not satisfied by one of the first two screening devices. Many volunteers qualified under two of the three screening processes. When the recruiting is done on a broader basis, as in Denver, where public speeches and newspaper articles have been used successfully, a formal training program further screens volunteers. You can be quite sure they will be good volunteers after they have given some 8 hours or more to an intensive training program.

Counseling efforts must be constantly supervised.—Perhaps the most vital factor of all is supervision. At Royal Oak we always insist that no probationer report only to a volunteer. He also reports to a professional probation officer at least monthly. (In Royal Oak, the professional probation officers work part-time.) The professional staff should run the program, not the volunteer. At least monthly, a member of the staff should "see" the volunteer-probationer relationship through the eyes of the probationer as well as through the eyes of the volunteer by way of the volunteer's monthly written or oral reports. Thus, the staff knows where more intensive supervision is necessary and it must be supplied.

Supervision can be supplied in a variety of ways, but *it must be part of the program.* At Royal Oak it is usually quite informal and consists of one night a week when the staff is available to assist the volunteer and answer his questions. If left to himself, the volunteer feels alone and often will lose his motivation and quit. The less expert the volunteer is in counseling, the more intensive the supervision must be.

One of the encouraging facts about the current volunteer court movement is that nearly all of the courts use professionals to supervise volunteers. The exception is the small city or town where it may be volunteers or absolutely nothing for the foreseeable future. An estimate based on a recent survey conducted at Royal Oak indicates that about 90 percent of some 350 volunteer courts responding, use professionals to supervise volunteers.

Training is vital.—Training varies much with individual courts. However, in every program it must be done one way or another. At Royal Oak it is primary an inservice training program following a careful process of recruiting, selection, screening, orientation, and actual assignment of the volunteer to a probationer. In other courts a careful and substantial training course before assigning a volunteer to a probationer plays a more vital role.

Perhaps the finest training program for volunteers has been devised by Judge William H. Burnett and Professor James Jorgeson in Denver. If a more formal training program would serve you best, write to Judge Burnett at the County Court, City-County Building, Denver, Colorado. Orientation, assignment to a probationer, and careful inservice training, however, might suit you better. But if the volunteer is not a warm human being who would be a good friend for a probationer, we can't make him one with just a training program. Careful selection and training are the key.

Flexibility should be stressed.—Volunteers often put it this way. "The beauty is that, within the framework of the philosophy of the program, I can do my thing in my way." Thus, where they meet, what they do together, how much the volunteer's family is involved, what they talk about, how they help out in a crisis, when and how to give advice are left to the volunteer. Again, selection is the key. The right type of person acting as a volunteer knows what to do generally. With supervision and guidance he can be effective in problem solving.

The volunteer should be a friend.—Probation officers are professional people with skills. We do not attempt to teach these skills in a short training course. We are asking our volunteers to be friends. Even those courts which call them volunteer probation officers are using them as friends and not as probation officers. This is as it should be. As friends, they are useful and perform a role that is needed in probation. The authoritarian role is assumed by the judge and probation officers, not by the volunteer. Revocation of probation and extension of probation are for the probation officer, not the volunteer.

Learn to accept the probationer as a person.—The volunteer must learn to accept the probationer as a human being. Listening is so important in achieving this acceptance.[3] Never has this been more clearly demonstrated than in our presentence investigation department. Assisting in this area are volunteer psychiatrists, psychologists, and retirees. The late Ralph Sheppard was a retired superintendent of schools. He was a warm and understanding person. On many occasions the probationer would leave the courtroom angry and defiant. He would then spend some 2 or 3 hours with Mr. Sheppard. When the defendant came out of the room, I would hardly recognize him. So defiant, angry and hostile a few hours before, he would have just one question: "Can Mr. Sheppard be my probation officer?"

Another fine retiree is Orson Clark who formerly worked for Ford Motor Company as an administrator. Also a concerned and understanding person, he is fond of telling the story of a probationer named Eddie who came in one day, without an appointment, and asked to talk to Mr. Clark. Eddie talked and went on and on. Orson never said a word except, "Yes," "You are right," "That's right." After an hour and a half the youngster stood up, shook hands, and said, "Mr. Clark, that is the best advice anyone ever gave me." And that was the best advice anyone ever gave Eddie for two reasons: First, it came from the heart, not the lips. Second, it "said" one of the most meaningful things one person can say to another—"Eddie, you are important. I will listen to you because you are an important human being." Retirees have the time to listen.

3. A book about Royal Oak and the volunteer court movement. *Please Listen to Me*, has been published by Funk & Wagnalls. Copies are available through Volunteers in Probation, Inc., 200 Washington Square Building, Royal Oak, Michigan 48067. The cost is $2.95 plus 30 cents for mailing for paperback, and $5.95 plus 30 cents mailing costs for a cloth-covered edition.

Use of Volunteers Is Nothing New

It should also be noted that the 600 or more volunteer courts have done nothing new. Two basic concepts are involved. First, if we want to change a young offender, we must instill in him an inspirational personality. Volunteers are effective in doing this. This has been demonstrated by the Boy Scouts, Sunday School teachers, the YMCA, the Big Brothers, and many others. The greatest manifestation of this concept was some 2,000 years ago when the idea of the inspirational personality was utilized to begin the redemptive process of Christianity. "And the Word became flesh . . . ." [4] Rules, commandments, concepts, and ideas had all failed. It had to be manifested in a personality who, like ourselves, knew joy and sorrow, loneliness and companionship, triumph and tragedy, suffering and death. It could not be done any other way. We simply do not understand rules and laws. We understand blood, sweat, tears, and pain. We understand personalities. People change people. Human conduct is changed by human contact. There is no other way.

The second basic concept is also very old. People will give time and talent to causes greater than themselves. The churches of our Nation have proved this over the centuries. By and through the use of volunteers they operate programs that give $10 to $20 of services to their community for every $1 in their budget. Small church staffs direct volunteers in Sunday School teaching, finance and social action committees, fund raising, welfare services, and visitation. They support the church's cause of redemption. The same interest and support apply to the court volunteers. They give their time and effort to the court's cause of rehabilitation and change. Because of them, the courts can give services far above and beyond their budgets. On this we do not opinionate. We have experienced it.

Really, these courts have done very little that is new. The ideas they now use are very old, indeed, and have withstood the test of time.

Weakness Can Lead to Strength

A very great man once said, ". . . for when I am weak, then I am strong." [5] Referring to an affliction that was "chronic, very painful, repulsive and humiliating," St. Paul finally recog-

---

4. John 1:14.   5. II Corinthians 12:10.

nized that strength was ultimately based on humility. His weakness thus led to his great strength, humility, and reliance upon the power of God.

At Royal Oak, in 1959, our weakness was lack of money and paid professionals. Thus, in our weakness we turned to volunteers. A community responded magnificently. Out of our weakness grew our strength. If, in 1959, we had $15,000 a year to hire one professional, we would never have turned to volunteers and our strength (funds to employ one professional who would have been overwhelmed and ineffective) would have been our ultimate weakness and the cause of failure. Our weakness became our strength. Our strength would have been our weakness.

Perhaps our greatest hope for the future lies in our weakness. As a Nation, we place a high value on military defense and space programs. We will spend billions for these things. We do not place a high priority on troubled youths who appear before our juvenile and misdemeanant courts. We will not spend much on them. So, in our weakness, let us turn to our strength, the concerned citizen.

I have learned much at the 15 or more national correctional conferences I have attended. However, at the last conference I heard a professional probation officer tell an audience the same old thing: "Give us the tools and we will do the job." Perhaps he should consider the experience of those courts using professionals and volunteers *who* say, "Let us somehow do the job *together* and we will get the tools."

THE SAN FRANCISCO PROJECT: A CRITIQUE*

It has not been established that the rise in reported crime reflects basic changes in American people. It is apparent, however, that seldom in the history of our country has such a majority of law-abiding citizens been so acutely aware of crime and so concerned with its remediation. It is a concern that embraces our political system, increasing our interest in the effectiveness of crime control approaches. In view of heightened public concern,

* William P. Adams, Paul M. Chandler and M. G. Neithercutt, *Federal Probation*, December, 1971. Reprinted with permission.

research in probation and parole can no longer be regarded as a luxury; it is essential to improve program effectiveness and to increase public confidence in these processes.

Research is costly and funds for research in probation and parole have been limited. It is important, therefore, that we make our research investments wisely. In 1964 a major research effort, the *San Francisco Project* [1] was undertaken. Because the final project report revealed methodological uncertainties and equivocal results, a critique might reveal some valuable lessons for guidance in future research investments.

On June 1, 1964, the National Institute of Mental Health awarded a $275,000 grant to the School of Criminology, University of California, Berkeley for research in probation and parole. Funded for four years, the project began September 1, 1964. As then conceived, the main goals of the project were:

1. Develop discriminating criteria for the classification of federal offenders.

2. Study the effects of varied intensities and types of supervision and caseload sizes.

3. Develop a prediction table for supervision adjustment.

4. Examine decision making in presentence recommendations.

Despite its unique aspects, the San Francisco Project was more replicative than innovative. As early as 1952, for example, the California Department of Corrections commenced research with variations in caseload size and supervision.

The San Francisco Project was carried out in the U.S. probation office of the Northern District of California with headquarters in San Francisco and offices in Sacramento and Oakland. Study population problems arose during the research when the Eastern District of California was created, removing a large number of cases from the original project.

During Phase I of the research, data were gathered on almost all offenders received for presentence investigation and released for supervision from federal institutions. Data collection forms were key punched for machine tabulating. While data gathering was proceeding, extensive changes were made in caseload assign-

1. Joseph V. Lohman, G. Albert Wahl and Robert M. Carter, *The San Francisco Project*, Berkeley: University of California, April 1965.

ments. Based on the 50-unit workload concept,[2] four levels of supervision were established.

There were two *Ideal* caseloads, each containing about 40 supervision cases and two presentence investigations per month, approximating the 50-unit concept. The *Intensive* caseload represented half that standard, with two officers assigned to it, each having a supervision load of 20 and one presentence investigation per month. The *Ideal* cases were to receive supervision on the basis of at least two contacts per individual per month while the *Intensive* caseloads required contacts once weekly.

The *Normal* caseloads consisted of the usual workload in the Northern District of California which had been averaging about 100 work units per month. Since some cases were syphoned off to the other caseloads, and one *Minimum* supervision load was established (consisting of approximately 350 cases and no presentence investigations), the *Normal* caseloads were diminished in size.[3]

In Phase I of the project, clients for the various caseloads were chosen from the existing loads and from newly received probationers and parolees randomly. These random assignments to all caseloads were made from September 1964 to June 1967 with a few exceptions representing special problems.[4]

In Phase II, beginning June 1, 1967, the policy on case assignment was changed from randomness to selection based on four factors.

Probation Supervision

A variety of activities is included in "probation supervision," ranging from surveillance through group counseling to psychoanalysis. In the San Francisco Project reference is made, interchangeably, to *types*, *kinds*, and *intensities* of supervision. At no point, however, were the characteristics of differing types of su-

2. See *Manual of Correctional Standards*, New York: The American Correctional Association, 1962, p. 510. For a different standard consult *The Challenge of Crime in a Free Society*. Washington: U. S. Government Printing Office, 1967, p. 167.

3. Normal caseload sizes were quite variable. For instance, during the study one of the authors determined the range to be 70 to 130 supervision cases plus an unknown number of investigations.

4. No substantive estimate of the number and characteristics of these cases appears to be available.

pervision identified. During the period of research no extraordinary treatment programs were in progress. Types or kinds of supervision remained dependent upon the styles of individual officers. With one exception, to be discussed later, no qualitative distinction was made among the styles of individual officers. To the contrary, anonymity was ensured and an effort was limited to measurement of different intensities of supervision.

In dealing with these different intensities the number of contacts the officer had with each client was approximately [5] documented. The quality of these contacts was ignored. In keeping with the methodological components of the research, an officer maintaining *Intensive* supervision might see a person four times each month, for 10 minutes per contact. An officer providing *Ideal* supervision might see the individual twice each month, for an hour each time. The measurement used, therefore, not only failed to deal with quality but provided a poor "measure" of quantity (simple time exposure to supervision).[6]

The Selection Phase

As the shift was made from the random phase to the selection phase of the research, individuals were assigned on the basis of a four-factor profile to the four levels of supervision—*Intensive, Ideal, Normal,* and *Minimum.* Because data from the earlier phase of the project were not definitive, selection of the four factors was based upon knowledge derived from other sources.

Individual offenders were given profile numbers of 1, 2, or 3, in each of the categories *type of offense, age,* and *prior record,* and 1 or 3 on the basis of the Socialization Scale (CPI–SO) from the *California Psychological Inventory.* There were 54 possible profiles ranging from 1–1–1–1 to 3–3–3–3, the higher numbers representing those believed to have a higher recidivism probability.

In deciding which of the profile groups should be assigned to the various levels of supervision the "expert-judge" technique was

5. The word "approximately" is used here because this documentation depended on entries in records maintained by several different persons. No reliability checks, audits, etc., were used so the data depended almost exclusively on officer attention to detail.

6. Note that time exposure to an officer is an illusive index too. For instance, some officers spend half the time a client is in the office talking to someone else on the telephone.

employed. This technique is accepted in social science research, but loss of precision is inherent in its use. Generally the "expert-judge" technique employs a minimum of three "judges" making independent choices and some method to integrate their decisions. In the San Francisco Project only one such "judge" was used. One can speculate endlessly on what characteristics such a judge should have—long, successful, and recent field experience, finely tuned administrative skills, extensive familiarity with correctional research practices, etc. The point is: No one man is likely to be an adequate "judge."

To explore what losses might be experienced because of the application of the "expert-judge" technique, consider for a moment, a familiar federal offender, the postal employee embezzler. If over 40 years of age and scoring within an arbitrary range on the CPI–SO, this offender would have a profile of 1–1–1–1, the lowest recidivism probability.

Such offenders frequently fall into the "ritualist" category in Merton's classification of deviant behavior.[7] On the basis of the "expert-judge" decision, and with conformity as a singular measure, such offenders were placed on minimum supervision. True, in most instances they continued to conform and complete probation "successfully." Not known, however, is how many of these offenders returned to tight patterns of conformity with no increased realization of personal freedom. How many became mental health casualties? With existing criteria they were regarded simply as probation successes.

Minimum Supervision: Random Phase

Minimum supervision has, de facto, been the rule in probation for years, a byproduct of limited appropriations. The San Francisco Project established minimum supervision caseloads by design and much of its evaluative effort focused on this caseload.

During the random phase a representative group of clients were assigned to a single, large caseload. They were not told the nature of the supervision they were to have, but were encouraged to contact the probation office if they wished assistance. During an initial interview they received instructions regarding travel limitations and required written monthly reports. Following the initial interview no contact was initiated by the probation office

7. Robert K. Merton, "Social Struc-   *Analysis.*   New York: Harcourt,
    ture and Anomie," *Sociological*   Brace and Company, 1949, p. 775.

unless monthly reports were absent or certain events, such as an arrest, came to the attention of the probation office. In such cases contacts were assigned to a staff probation officer on the basis of availability. If assistance with a specific problem was sought, that matter was assigned to a staff officer in like manner. Many persons on minimum supervision did take the initiative in making contact.

Excluding technical violations, the violation rate for the minimum supervision caseload was reported as not significantly different from that of other caseloads. The inherent weaknesses of the violation index as a measure of probation success preclude any conclusions, however. Whether this group did or did not do any better than the others is unknown, but an inference worthy of closer attention emerges from the data.

The probability that the talents and time of probation officers might be more efficiently trained on specific needs, as opposed to making routine contacts, awaits verification or rejection through future research efforts. If, at the outset of supervision, a climate of trust and confidence is established, it seems more likely that clients will seek the assistance of a probation officer before permitting their personal adjustment to deteriorate to the point of probation or parole violation. No available evidence documents that routine contacts without goals will increase such a possibility. Clearly needed is closer attention to understanding and measuring the quality, not the quantity, of supervision.

Minimum Supervision: Select Phase

During the select phase of research a large minimum supervision caseload was formed with individuals having a low violation probability. The four-factor profile was used. This caseload was assigned to an officer who developed his own management techniques. After the select phase commenced, individuals with other than low profile scores were transferred to this caseload as a result of judgments made by officers who, until such transfers, provided them with other levels of attention.[8]

Considerable information was lost during the evaluation of the select phase of minimum supervision, due, in part, to the fact that

8. Separating these persons to control for possible contaminating effect evidently is not possible. The type of outcome distortion likely through this transfer procedure is obvious; clients transferred to minimum supervision likely would be a highly selected (for "success") group compared to the general population.

much of the collected data had not been stored properly. It appears that the loss of such documentation led, to some extent, to fantasy levels of evaluation such as reference to the "Superman" [9] qualities needed in an officer handling such a caseload.

If the violation index were valid and reliable, the reported 11.5 percent rate of violation for this group, compared to higher rates of violation for other groups, would, nevertheless, be meaningless because no control group of comparable selectivity receiving other levels of attention existed. The possibility remains that a group with a high recidivism probability might do best under minimum supervision or that persons with low recidivism probability might have even lower violation rates with closer attention.

The violation rate reported for the select group under minimum supervision becomes further suspect when it is noted, in the final report, that the officer periodically reviewed the individual cases, moving for early termination of supervision when he deemed appropriate. No criteria are provided to show under what circumstances early termination was considered appropriate. It is obvious that violation rates can be reduced to nil by terminating cases soon enough. They can also be influenced by computation techniques.[10]

In contrast to the effort made to avoid identification of individual supervision techniques in other aspects of the research project, attention was given to the approach developed by "Mr. X," the officer handling select phase minimum supervision. He attempted to establish clearly the "ground rules" for supervision. His intent was to create a "contract" detailing appropriate performance for the individual under supervision and reciprocal assistance from the probation officer. One purpose was to eliminate a sense of manipulation and shift some responsibility to the client. This could be important because it emphasizes one of the essential

9. James L. Robison, Leslie T. Wilkins, Robert M. Carter, and G. Albert Wahl, *The San Francisco Project Final Report.* Berkeley: University of California, April 1969, p. 60.

10. An example of this is apparent on page 63 of the *Final Report* (Robison, loc. cit.). There the "11½ percent" violation rate is computed by dividing number of cases permanently removed from minimum supervision as successes (124) into number of cases in which warrants were issued or where the closing was "by violation" (14). However 17 of the permanent removals were by transfer, so these were neither success nor failure cases. A transfer is not a termination. This makes the "violation rate" 13.1 percent without any change in client performance.

ingredients in a reintegration process—that of experiencing responsibility. In reviewing reports on this phase of the research one wonders, however, how consistent intent and practice were when "Mr. X" refers to knowledge not shared by the probationer/parolee as his "hole card," and says "I'll use every bloody tool I have available to get them to meet the contract."

It remains a distinct possibility, as suggested by the San Francisco Project design, that probation supervision caseloads can be organized to improve the use by well trained and highly educated probation officers of their effort and concern. In the process it might be determined that through appropriate selectivity many persons can safely be assigned to large, minimally supervised caseloads, and benefit from infrequent attention. One cannot infer, however, that meaningful selection can be made upon age, type of offense, prior record, or results from a psychological test that were not delivered to the computer for evaluation.

Violation Index as a Measure of Success

To become definitive, social research, like research in the physical sciences, requires criteria for measurement. The complex processes of probation and parole are so poorly understood that methods for evaluation often are illusive. The tendency is to focus upon the obvious, the believed level of subsequent law violations, as a measure of success.

A violation index was developed for the San Francisco Project relating the number of persons with unfavorable terminations to the number of persons with favorable terminations and during the second phase of the research, lumping all persons still active on supervision and having completed 24 months of supervision, with the favorable termination group. Therefore, completion of 24 months on supervision became equivalent to success. No information provided indicated the 24-month period has a relationship to successful community adjustment. It is an arbitrary figure, probably determined more by sample size needs than by the social phenomena.

Use of the violation index established conformity as a measure of success. Probation and parole embrace many complexities; they span human personality interacting with society. If the rate of subsequent law violations were a valid measure of these complex processes, controlled, scientific application of such an index would be essential for the development of reliable information. With the application of the outcome rate, several variables came into play without sufficient control, interfering seriously with the credibility of the findings.

During the random phase of research, with the technical violations excluded, the violation rates reported for the *Minimum* and *Ideal* caseloads were 22.2 percent and for the *Intensive* caseload, 20.0 percent. This represented no significant difference.[11] Including technical violations the violation rate for the *Intensive* group was 37.5 percent, for the *Minimum* group, 22.2 percent and *Ideal* group, 24.3 percent. Persons under supervision at the time of this evaluation had been exposed to the possibility of unfavorable terminations for significantly different periods of time. The project evaluation approach was supported with the statement, "It is believed that the first six to twelve months of supervision are generally the most critical in terms of violation rates." That appears a potentially hazardous assumption, especially since it is not tested in the project.[12]

The first 6, or the first 12 months of supervision might be the most critical in terms of violations but the use of a generalized assumption, without clearer statistical distinctions, to include in the computations persons with significantly different periods of time under supervision, and the failure to deal statistically with the violation potentials beyond a 12-month period for those persons, causes a loss of confidence in the results of those computations.

The various caseloads, during the random selections phase, were comparable initially in some respect such as *age, prior record*, and *type of offense* but significantly different in other areas, such as *family criminality, occupational skills, sex,* and *education*. The implication here is that violation rates were compared across groups dissimilar in some characteristics which may have substantial impact upon community adjustment. The existence of some of the differences has been acknowledged in report form but these differences are described as unsystematic. In fact, if one scrutinizes the six variables in which the three caseloads differ significantly, four of them indicate the intensive caseloads to

11. Robison, loc. cit., p. 6.

12. For an assessment of by-month violation rates during the first year of parole supervision in a heterogeneous parole population.

See *Uniform Parole Reports Newsletter*: Davis, California. National Council on Crime and Delinquency Research Center, April 1970, pp. 2–4.

be disadvantaged and on only one is the minimum caseload preju-
diced.

Two important factors affecting violation rates were *early terminations*, representing success, and *termination by warrant*,
representing failure. Successful termination is usually the product of agency machinery, whereas unsuccessful termination is
likely the result of specific behavior on the part of individuals
under supervision. Had the violation index been applied to groups
with comparable percentages of favorable terminations (holding
number of violators constant), the adjusted violation rates would
have been 10.5 percent for the *Minimum* group and 20.9 percent
for the *Ideal* group compared to 37.5 percent for the *Intensive*
group. Apparently, then, during the random phase the caseloads
differed significantly on outcome, albeit not in the direction that
might have been anticipated.[13] This difference devolves mainly
from the fact that the various modes of supervision differed very
significantly on number of cases terminated successfully as well
as unsuccessfully.

Termination by issuance of a warrant occurs most often from
the commission of new offenses. The second most frequent cause
is failure to meet the conditions of probation or parole. Since
probation officers differ significantly in recommendations on
judgments and the courts are influenced by officer recommendations, decisions concerning the issuance of warrants may be influenced by a variety of supervision philosophies.[14] Deliberate
effort to avoid identification of particular officer styles in the
research fostered loss of control over this potentially important
variable.

Early termination of supervision results largely from an officer's awareness and evaluation of an individual's community adjustment. Except in cases with special conditions, no criteria
have been established for early termination so such actions depend largely upon the initiative of the individual officer. Two
clients making similar adjustments might have had substantially
different chances to be terminated from supervision early, particularly if one had close attention under *Intensive* supervision,

13. The reader is cautioned to take
these analyses cautiously. The
comparisons on outcome are based
on a total of 87 cases (18 from
the minimum group, 37 from the
ideal, and 32 from the intensive).

14. See "The Decision Making Process" which follows.

and the other had little attention under *Minimum* supervision. Again, inadequate accounting of an important variable raises serious questions about the reliability of the violation index.

The final report, perhaps the most useful of the series, suggested that the high rate of technical violations for persons under *Intensive* supervision probably resulted from officer awareness of activities. Further investigation might unearth some entirely different reasons. Consider at least another possibility. Traditionally in America, imposition of authority is not assimilated easily, even by the essentially law-abiding. Understanding this, entertain the possibility that the higher number of technical violations for persons under *Intensive* supervision resulted as expressions of defiance in response to the frequent authoritative intrusions into their lives. Such a possibility applies to all violations, not technical violations alone.

Emile Durkheim, the 19th century sociologist, suggested that crime serves a social function. If this is so, perhaps by encouraging new violations our correctional processes have assured society of a criminal population. This might appear preposterous, but the efficiency with which our institutional programs have functioned in that direction remains. The "revolving door" jail treatment of skid row alcoholics intensifies rather than interrupts losses of self-respect. Such "treatment" has virtually guaranteed a supply of drunks for our city streets. Many persons are employed revolving the doors and, by offering objects for comparison, these inebriates have given many persons reason to feel better about themselves.

The Decision-Making Process

Probation officers make decisions affecting clients and communities. A goal of the San Francisco Project was to examine the practice of officers making sentencing recommendations to the court. In the Northern District of California, probation officers recommend criminal case disposition and the courts "follow" these suggestions in about nine of 10 cases.

The "decision game" described by Wilkins [15] was used with 14 United States probation officers stationed in San Francisco. Five cases in which presentence reports had been prepared were analyzed and classified under 24 subject headings. The informa-

15. Leslie T. Wilkins, *Social Deviance: Social Policy, Action and* *Research.* Englewood Clifts, N. J.: Prentice Hall, 1965, pp. 294–304.

tion was typed on 4″ by 6″ cards with a title on the lower edge, the cards being arranged in a binder for each case so that only the title showed. Each officer was asked to "conduct" the presentence investigation by selecting the information he wished to use. After each selection the officer was asked if he could make a recommendation. The researcher encouraged an early decision and recorded the selections and recommendations. After a decision was made the officer was asked to select three more cards and state whether he wanted to change his recommendation.

On the average, these probation officers selected 4.7 cards prior to decision. *Offense* and *Prior Record* were selected in every case. Six other categories, *Psychological/Psychiatric, Defendant's Statement, Defendant's Attitude, Employment History, Age,* and *Family History* being selected more than half of the time.[16] Decisions, therefore, were based on but few of the 24 factors contained in the presentence report and the additional information seldom changed recommendations. The researchers concluded that much of the information gathered in the investigation was not used in arriving at a recommendation.

The research failed to recognize that the eight categories most often chosen were likely to include information which the investigators indicated was little used. For example, the three separate categories of drug use, homosexuality, and alcoholic involvement were chosen by the officers less than 20 percent of the time, but these are items which are usually found, if present, in the psychological/psychiatric section which was chosen in the 80 percent range. The *Family History* category, chosen more than half the time, could conceivably contain almost all of the pertinent data about the offender. Nearly one-third of the 24 items were selected in the less than 10 percent range but included are such facts as race, religion, and place of birth. While these may be important for identification, or for other reasons, it is hoped and expected that they would have little or no relevance to sentencing. Thus even a casual inspection of the distribution of the information items indicates that the suggestion that a small amount of information is used in decision making is misleading.

There are other uses of the presentence report besides determination of the sentence barely acknowledged in the research

16. Joseph D. Lohman, G. Albert Wahl, and Robert M. Carter, *Decision Making and the Probation Officer.* Berkeley: University of California, June 1966, pp. 7, 10.

reports. Presentence reports may be used both as a guide for supervision and a basis for classification and treatment by institutions. For example, the Bureau of Prisons would perhaps find an evaluation of the individual's educational adjustment very significant in its attempts to develop a meaningful treatment program, although this item was rated, according to the study, at about the midpoint in decision making for sentencing. Obviously the importance of the data relates to the use to which it is to be put. While some of the data collected and recorded by the probation officer may not have significant immediate use in sentencing, he is usually in the best position to glean that information which may be of significance in the correctional process.

Two of the five cases were chosen as being clear-cut, one leading to probation, the other to confinement. In these cases there was perfect agreement among all 14 officers. The other three cases generated a wide range of opinion. In case four, for example, five officers recommended imprisonment, two probation, four split-sentence, and two county jail terms.[17] Given the evidence that there is substantial agreement among probation officers' recommendations and the actual sentence imposed, these data were interpreted as suggesting that disparity in sentencing, usually attributed to judges, may be influenced considerably by probation officers.

Because two of the cases were of the "open and shut" variety, decisions using limited categories of information were invited. To generalize about levels of information usage on the basis of five cases from a universe of thousands is indefensible; to do so when two of the five have been chosen to drive information usage down is worse. Further, officers were instructed to make decisions on as little information as possible; this constraint being the opposite of working conditions.

Minimum documentation needed here is a separate tabulation of the number of factors considered in cases really requiring a decision. Also, it is not wise to imply that because, on the average, only a few factors are used in making most decisions no data beyond those are needed.[18] Rather, one is better advised to look at the most demanding cases decision-wise and see what they require. This would mean looking at the top of the range of

17. Ibid., p. 14. The total is less   18. Ibid., p. 16.
    than 14, for one officer who recog-
    nized his own work was excluded.

factors. Here that number is 13, suggesting that the "efficiency level" may be rather high.

The statement, ". . . it appears certain that the data most significant (for decision) are the items of information most often initially collected by probation officers . . . as well as being information which serves as the basis for presentence report recommendations," [19] is unrealistic. Those items initially collected depend on what is in the case folder at assignment. The referral sheet has the name, address, offense, possible sentence, names of codefendants, custody status, sentencing judge, plea, date of plea, date of judgment, court officer's initials, and miscellaneous comments. Sometimes there is an arrest record; often there is not. These items initially collected mostly seem to have little or no bearing on judgment. Also, because the fact gathering process is fairly routinized at referral, what an officer asks for first or second may be more a matter of habit than anything else. The fact that "confinement status," though highly correlated with sentence, is seldom asked for in the decision game setting suggests pitfalls inherent in this sort of analysis.

While the authors of the San Francisco Project intimate that these findings document inefficiency in the presentence process, the data presented hardly support a dogmatic stance. The relationship between playing at decision making and actually confronting problems in the field remains a mystery. For example, "Research Report Number Seven" notes that in the decision game officers ". . . did not have to go into the field to verify information such as employment . . . ." [20] Apparent is the potential value of such verification, though, because official employment reports are notoriously misleading. That report also states ". . . participants were allowed to 'gather' information or 'conduct' the presentence investigation in any way they desired . . . ." [21] As the report unfolds, however, it becomes apparent that the only latitude in the decision game was freedom to choose cards in any preferred order.

What does one do when two pieces of information conflict? What happens when the official version of the offense and the defendant's version are not reconcilable? There are no victims in the cards to be contacted and cryptic paper entries give few

19. Ibid., pp. 18–19.   21. Ibid., p. 5.

20. Ibid., p. 5.

clues to their veracity. Who judges the "defendant's attitude"? Is he truly hostile or terribly frightened?

If the implications of this research are correct, presentence investigations could be conducted by case aides and computers at greatly reduced cost and with increased efficiency. If that be true, though, what of the vital relationships—often established between probation officer and offender during the presentence process—that are difficult to establish afterward? What if efforts to get the offender moving in a positive direction at the time when he seems susceptible to change are delayed? The "evidence" presented suggesting that probation decision making is a simple mechanical process is less than overwhelming. It fails to account for the personal "chemistry" between client and officer, the intuitive process that each officer uses to evaluate his cases, and the fitting of pieces together in understanding the offender.

Impact of Supervision

A valuable contribution to the San Francisco Project has been provided by Arthur E. Elliot, then supervisor of social work students training at the San Francisco probation office. Mr. Elliot wished to sample the effects of the project from the clients' point of view. His work on supervision impact was primarily intuitive and interpretive, but employed a systematic approach.

The aims of the study included:

1. Ascertaining the offender's view of probation or parole.

2. Determining the probation officer's concept of his role in supervision.

3. Obtaining information about supervision from persons close to offenders.

Standardized interviews were held in cases terminated successfully between September 1, 1966, and June 1, 1967. The sample contained 100 offenders, 71 of them probationers.[22]

While attitudes and experiences of successful cases may differ from those of failures, other characteristics of the sample generally paralleled the project population. It should be noted, how-

22. Joseph D. Lohman, G. Albert Wahl, Robert M. Carter, and Arthur E. Elliot, *The Impact of Supervision: Officer and Offender* *Assessment.* Berkeley: University of California, September 1967, pp. 7 & 10.

ever, that more than 40 percent of Mr. Elliot's sample had no prior record, a circumstance suggesting the group had fewer negative experiences with law enforcement than a general sample of offenders. An earlier report in the project series indicated that 26.6 percent of a sample of 500 had no prior records.[23]

There are some highly suggestive findings in Mr. Elliot's work which may be of use to the probation officer. First, there was a high degree of consensus between offender and officer regarding offender problems and available pertinent resources. This would seem a good omen for a favorable counseling relationship. The study indicated, however, that seldom was there a long-range, well-developed plan of supervision. Counseling generally focused on specific assistance requested by the client and was, of course, limited by the time and skill of the officer. In addition, much time was spent in general contact which was of questionable use to the client. Perhaps these factors explain why only 10 percent of the offenders said probation officers contributed significantly to their supervision success.

Of those who received *Intensive* treatment, not one named the probation officer as important in his adjustment. To the offenders the most important aspect of successful adjustment was assistance from family or friends, followed by having a basically noncriminal orientation. Employment and emotional growth also received priority consideration. Fear of further legal action was considered less important by the study group in preventing further criminal activity.

The results were in close agreement with the probation officer's analysis of his own work. Here is a clue, it appears, to explain why intensive supervision did not seem to reduce the rate of violation. Perhaps it is not the number of contacts but rather the *quality* of work that is vital.

Despite pessimistic evaluations of the supervision process, most offenders and their families agreed that positive changes occurred during supervision. However, 15 percent felt there were no changes while another 10 percent believed they had more problems than before. Some improvements were noted in the fields of emotional maturity, family relationships, and employment.

Despite the low regard offenders voiced for their probation officers' contributions to their success, it is interesting to note that

23. Ibid., p. 27.

60 percent of the clients rated supervision as "helpful." Some reported specific activity of the probation officer which was helpful while others saw the probation structure itself as assisting in their good adjustment.

Among those who indicated they had not benefited from supervision there was a tendency to claim competence to manage one's own affairs and to see probation as interference. There was a general feeling that the shock of apprehension and court appearances was a specific deterrent.

Of particular interest to line officers is the relationship between the offender and the probation officer. Many social caseworkers feel positive relationships in corrections are difficult or impossible to attain because of the authoritarian setting. In this study more than two-thirds of the offenders had negative ideas about the probation officers prior to contact with the agency. Officers were assumed to be harsh, punitive, critical, moralistic, and enforcement minded. Sixty-seven of the 70 offenders (96 percent) with this view, however, changed their minds after actual contact with their supervising officers. Most offenders reported forming a satisfactory relationship.

It is unfortunate that this part of the research was not extended to persons receiving minimum supervision. Views of the supervision experience from those persons compared to individuals receiving other levels of attention might provide clues to meaningful changes in the administration of probation. Offenders are capable of insights into correctional processes, and, by virtue of their experiences, can teach much with their observations and evaluations.

A Theoretical Framework Needed

Review of the San Francisco Project reveals that method and direction were sought after the research was initiated. In the final report it is suggested that the original design was too ambitious. The absence of a well-developed theoretical framework resulted in lack of orientation and loss of efficiency.

There is yet no intergrated theory of corrections.[24] Lacking such, difficulty in evaluating correctional processes, including the process of probation and parole, continues. Corrections embraces many complexities, yet in the San Francisco Project, a relatively

24. T. C. Esselstyn, "The Social System of Correctional Workers," *Crime and Delinquency*, April 1966, p. 117.

simple concept of conformity, never clearly defined, is the focal measure of supervision outcome.[25]

The San Francisco Project found early inspiration from some provocative questions posed by the late sociologist and lawyer Paul Tappan, who asked, "What part of our probation caseloads could have done as well merely on a suspended sentence without any supervision?" [26] He suggested the need for developing discriminating criteria for classifying offenders into categories: those who do not require probation, those who require differing degrees of supervision, and those who require highly professionalized services.[27]

Robert K. Merton, a contemporary sociologist noted for having attained an unusual balance between theory construction and empirical research, recalls that a 17th century columnist, John Aubrey, reported "Dr. Pell was wont to say that in the Solution of Questions, the Main Matter was the well-stating of them; which requires mother-witt and logic . . . for let the question be but well-stated, it will work almost of itself." [28] In responding to the questions posed by Professor Tappan, the San Francisco Project moved too rapidly from speculation to attempted experimentation, and failed to state well the problems to be solved. There was insufficient clarity in exploring doing "as well." No definition was given to the "requirements" which might be met through differing types and degrees of supervision. In future probation research we must endeavor to identify and state well the problems to be solved; this will require a good measure of mother wit and logic.

25. Items on which the alleged randomly assigned cases differed significantly by supervision level have been enumerated. Outcome factors on which they were significantly different include prior convictions, persons returned to federal custody as violators, time under supervision and monthly earnings under supervision. Any (or all) of these serves as an alternate outcome index. The clear tendency here, too, is for the intensive cases to fare poorly consistently.

26. Paul W. Tappan, *Crime, Justice and Correction.* New York: McGraw-Hill, 1960, p. 584.

27. Ibid.

28. Robert K. Merton, "Notes on Problem-Finding in Sociology," *Sociology Today.* New York: Basic Books Inc., 1959, p. IX.

THE PRESENTENCE INVESTIGATION REPORT*

Its Functions and Objectives

The presentence investigation report is a basic working document in judicial and correctional administration. It performs five functions: (1) to aid the court in determining the appropriate sentence, (2) to assist Bureau of Prisons institutions in their classification and treatment programs and also in their release planning, (3) to furnish the Board of Parole with information pertinent to its consideration of parole, (4) to aid the probation officer in his rehabilitative efforts during probation and parole supervision,[1] and (5) to serve as a source of pertinent information for systematic research.

The primary objective of the presentence report is to focus light on the character and personality of the defendant, to offer insight into his problems and needs, to help understand the world in which he lives, to learn about his relationships with people, and to discover those salient factors that underlie his specific offense and his conduct in general. It is not the purpose of the report to demonstrate the guilt or the innocence of the defendant.

Authorities in the judicial and correctional fields assert that a presentence investigation should be made in every case. With the aid of a presentence report the court may avoid committing a defendant to an institution who merits probation instead, or may avoid granting probation when confinement is appropriate.

Probation cannot succeed unless care is exercised in selecting those who are to receive its benefits. The presentence report is an essential aid in this selective process.

Where the defendant is committed to the custody of the Attorney General, copies of the presentence report are sent to the institution. The institution relies on the report for pertinent data relating to the kind and degree of custody required by the defendant, needed medical attention, and the needs, capacities,

---

* Division of Probation, Administrative Offices of the U. S. Courts, A Monograph. Reprinted with permission.

[1]. The Federal probation officer also supervises persons released from Federal correctional institutions and the U. S. Disciplinary Barracks.

and problems of the individual.   These data will aid the institution in making its preliminary diagnostic study and in promptly formulating a treatment and training program.   Moreover, the presentence report not only saves the time and effort of the institution in procuring essential community and family information about the defendant, but also gives this necessary information more completely and accurately than can be obtained by the institution through correspondence and questionnaires.

In considering whether to grant or deny parole, the Board of Parole finds in the presentence report helpful information not only about the offender's personal and social adjustment prior to commitment, but also about his relationships within the community to which he may return.

The Probation Officer's Part in the Investigation

The probation officer has the important task of gathering information about the defendant;   evaluating, assimilating, and interpreting the data;   and presenting them in a logically organized, readable, objective report.   Each defendant should be investigated without any preconception or prejudgment on the probation officer's part as to the outcome of the defendant's case.

The probation officer must be completely objective and impartial in conducting the investigation and in writing the presentence report.   He not only reports the tangible facts in the case, but also such subjective elements as the defendant's attitudes, feelings, and emotional reactions.   He presents them so as to give to the court an accurate, unbiased, and complete picture of the defendant and his prospects for becoming a law-abiding, responsible citizen.   Every effort must be made to check the accuracy of information which is likely to be damaging to the defendant or to have a definite bearing on the welfare of the family and the safety of the community.

Verifications should be obtained, wherever possible, in documentary form such as letters, facsimiles, and certified statements.   The Probation Division has prepared a series of forms which serve as a practical device for obtaining verified information as to prior arrests, employment, military service, education, medical history, birth, and marriage and divorce.

Wherever possible, a defendant should be seen more than once in the course of the investigation.   Seldom does a defendant reveal his true self in a single interview. Often it takes more than one interview to establish a cooperative relationship and to give the defendant confidence in the probation officer.[2]

If the investigation discloses information that is substantially different from statements given by the defendant, the probation officer should reinterview the defendant and resolve the conflicting statements. This will assist the probation officer in determining the motivation behind any erroneous statements and will help to explain the defendant's personality and character.

Generally, the probation officer should have 2 to 4 weeks to complete his investigation and write his report. If necessary, he should be given more time.

Start Where the Defendant Is

In conducting the investigation and in writing the presentence report, the probation officer should be primarily concerned with how the defendant thinks, feels, and reacts *today*. He starts with the defendant as he finds him—as of this moment—and includes in his report no more from the past than what is believed essential to help the court understand the defendant as he is *today*. This is not to say that early developmental influences have no relevance to current behavior. However, a mere recitation of experiences, relationships, and circumstances, without relating them to the present picture, offers little or no insight in understanding the defendant's present thinking, feeling, and behavior.

The Worksheet

Each probation system has some type of worksheet. In the Federal Probation System it is known as Probation Form No. 1. It is essential that all offices use the latest revision of this form.

The form is not intended to be a presentence investigation report itself but rather a guide for the probation officer in gathering basic factual information. From this information on the worksheet he selects, evaluates, and assembles the data under the major headings of the presentence report.

2. See articles on the initial interview, by Henry L. Hartman, M.D., in the September and December 1963 issues of *Federal Probation*.

Tangible Facts Not Enough

A presentence report is more than a compilation of tangible facts. Facts about family composition, employment, health, and so on, have relatively little value unless they are interpreted in relation to the defendant and how he thinks, feels, and behaves. Such facts alone do not give an account of a living person—his character and personality in action. People in the report must come to life. Instead of giving an accumulation of cold facts the report should rather present a true, vivid, living picture of the defendant.

Facts are not limited to the tangible. Attitudes, feelings, and emotional responses are facts, too. Knowledge of these more or less intangible elements is essential to really know a person and what makes him behave as he does.

How the defendant feels about those with whom he comes in daily contact, what he thinks about his family, his peers, and his coworkers—and what he believes they think about him—are essential to an understanding of his relationships with people. Also significant are his feelings about baffling problems in his life, including his offense and his reaction to opportunities, accomplishments, disappointments, and frustrations. His moral values, his beliefs and his convictions, his fears, prejudices, and hostilities explain the "whys" and "wherefores" of the more tangible elements in his life history.

Time, patience, and skill are required to uncover these more subjective factors and to develop their relevance, but they are basic in good report writing. Each of them should be interpreted in terms of the defendant's family background, culture, and environment, and in relation to the groups with whom he has associated and is closely identified. Even an untrained investigator can pull together the bare facts required in a presentence report and assemble them in an established outline and format. But the ability to select the pertinent data, to distinguish between factual data and inferences, to draw out the subjective elements, and to assess their relative importance in the personality makeup and the needs of the defendant, differentiate the trained and skilled probation officer from the untrained and inexperienced probation officer.

When Another Office Is Called On To Assist

When another Federal probation office is called on to assist in developing a presentence report, it should be made clear what specific information is desired, when the information is needed, and the probable date of sentence. No more information should be requested than is required.

The same procedure applies when requesting information from cooperating welfare agencies, institutions, and State and local probation and parole offices. The request should include sufficient data to enable the officer of the cooperating district or agency to make an intelligent inquiry.

When a request is made of another Federal probation office for a *complete* investigation report, the following minimum data should be supplied on the form 1 worksheet, if possible, or in a letter: true name; place of residence and exact address (including apartment number); birthdate; sex and race; date of arrest; status of custody; brief summary of the offense; defendant's statement; prior record; names and addresses of parents, brothers, and sisters, and other relatives close to the defendant; and places of employment. Specific directions for locating persons to be interviewed should be supplied wherever possible.

When the cooperating probation office is asked to write the report in presentence form, the office for the court in which sentence is to be pronounced (office of origin) will determine how it wishes to present the report to the court. The report from the second office may be appended to the report prepared by the office of origin or may be incorporated as a part of it. If the report from the second office is to be incorporated in the report of the office of origin, it would be desirable to indicate what information comes from the second office.

Investigations Prior to Conviction or Plea

Where a court is not continuously in session and the judge sits for only short periods in the various places of holding court a probation officer may find it difficult to complete the presentence reports within the limited time available. In these circumstances some courts request that investigations be conducted prior to conviction or plea. When such a request is made, the probation officer should ask the defendant after having advised him of his right to the advice of counsel, to sign the Probation Division's form authorizing the probation officer to institute the investigation. It is also desirable to have on file a letter from the defense attorney stating that he has no objection to the probation officer beginning the investigation prior to conviction or plea.

As provided by rule 32(c) (1) of the Federal Rules of Criminal Procedure, the presentence investigation report shall not be submitted to the court or its contents disclosed to anyone unless the defendant has pleaded guilty or has been found guilty.

Discussion of the Report With the Judge

It is the practice of most judges to call the investigating officer into chambers to discuss the various aspects of the case as reflected in the presentence report. Where certain information in the report is unfavorable to the defendant, the judge may discuss these points with the probation officer in chambers.

Confidential Nature of the Report

The presentence investigation report is a confidential document and should not be available to anyone without the permission of the court. In some instances the court delegates to the probation office the responsibility for determining what information from the report may be disclosed.

The presentence report often contains highly privileged information about the defendant and his family and also confidential data from cooperating public and private welfare agencies, law enforcement officials, employers, and others who know the defendant. This information is frequently given to the probation officer with the understanding that it is to be kept confidential.

The defendant's family, which is the best source of information about him, frequently divulges confidential information which, if disclosed, can impair the relationship between him and his family.

Welfare agencies adhere to the principle of confidentiality. When they share their case file information with the probation office they rely on the probation office to comply with the agencies' standards in the use of this information. They expect that the information will be used solely in the rehabilitation of persons under investigation and supervision by the probation officer.

Probation officers often have access to confidential information in the arrest and investigation reports of law enforcement agencies—Federal, State, and local.

An employer will be reluctant to supply information if he believes what he says will get back to the employee. There may be, for example, such on-the-job problems as drinking, quarrelsomeness, and lack of dependability.

Some defendants have had a close relationship with dangerous associates. If incriminating information about these persons is divulged, there is the risk of retaliation.

The family physician is often the source of information that is privileged as a matter of law.

A probation office will lose the respect and confidence of an informing person or agency if confidential information is disclosed. There will be a reluctance to give further information. Eventually, sources of information will dry up and the value of the report will be seriously impaired. Therefore, the probation officer must be cautious and discreet to avoid divulging confidential information.

No presentence report should be read aloud in open court.

At all times there should be a cooperative relationship between the probation office and those institutions and agencies on which the probation office calls for information and professional assistance. A mutual exchange of information may be helpful not only to the respective agencies, but also to the probation office and the court.

The presentence investigation report eventually becomes a part of the defendant's case folder. The courts generally leave to the judgment of the probation office whether cooperating agencies should be permitted to read the case record—including the presentence report—or whether the desired information should be given by individual interpretation or written summaries.

OUTLINE, CONTENTS, AND FORMAT OF THE REPORT

Identifying Information

The following identifying information is requested on Probation Form No. 2, the first page of all presentence reports (see facsimile on p. 8).

DATE. Give the date the presentence report is typed.

NAME. Enter the name of the defendant as shown on the court record. Also insert the true name, if different, and any aliases.

ADDRESS. Give the present home address.

LEGAL RESIDENCE. Give the legal residence (county and State) if different from the present home address. Otherwise insert "Same."

AGE AND DATE OF BIRTH. Give the age on last birthday and the date of birth. Use the symbol "ver." when verified by an official source.

SEX.

RACE. Race is determined by ancestry; e. g., white, Negro, American Indian, etc. It should not be confused with national origin.

CITIZENSHIP. Give name of country. Citizenship refers to the country of which the defendant is a subject or citizen.

EDUCATION. Give highest grade achieved.

MARITAL STATUS. Single, married, widow, widower, divorced, legally separated, common law.

DEPENDENTS. List those entirely dependent on the defendant for support; e. g., "Three (wife and two children)."

SOCIAL SECURITY No.

FBI No.

DOCKET No.

OFFENSE. Give a brief statement, including statutory citation; e. g., "Theft of Mail (18 U.S.C. 1708)."

PENALTY. Insert statutory penalty for the specific offense. This should be obtained from the U. S. attorney in each instance. The probation officer should not attempt to state the penalty on the basis of his knowledge.

PLEA. Nature and date.

VERDICT. Date.

CUSTODY. Give status (summons, personal or surety bond, recognizance, jail) and period in jail.

ASSISTANT U. S. ATTORNEY. Give name of the assistant U. S. attorney handing the case.

DEFENSE COUNSEL. Give name and address. When appointed by court, this should be indicated.

DETAINERS OR CHARGES PENDING. Give the name and address of the office issuing the detainer or preferring the charge. Also give the dates action was taken.

CODEFENDANTS. Enter the names of codefendants, if any, and status of their respective cases. If there are no codefendants, insert "None."

The following information, below the double rule on form 2, is inserted after the final disposition of the case:

DISPOSITION. Sentence imposed by the court.

DATE. Date of sentence.

SENTENCING JUDGE.

Presentence Report Outline

The presentence report outline adopted by the Judicial Conference Committee on the Administration of the Probation System on February 11, 1965, consists of the following marginal headings and the respective subheadings:

OFFENSE
    Official version
    Statement of codefendants
    Statement of witnesses, complainants, and victims

DEFENDANT'S VERSION OF OFFENSE

PRIOR RECORD

FAMILY HISTORY
    Defendant
    Parents and siblings

MARITAL HISTORY

HOME AND NEIGHBORHOOD

EDUCATION

RELIGION

INTERESTS AND LEISURE–TIME ACTIVITIES

HEALTH
    Physical
    Mental and emotional

EMPLOYMENT

MILITARY SERVICE

FINANCIAL CONDITION
    Assets
    Financial obligations
EVALUATIVE SUMMARY
RECOMMENDATION

In each presentence report the probation officer should follow the title and exact sequence of these headings.

The suggested contents for the marginal headings are given starting on this page. The items listed under *Essential Data* are those which should appear in *all* presentence reports. Those listed under *Optional Data* will appear in many reports, depending on their significance in the particular case. Each probation officer will determine which of the optional data are essential for the respective defendants under study and how each is to be treated.

In writing the report the probation officer need not follow the sequence of the *essential* and *optional* items. This may prove awkward, hinder readability, disrupt the trend of thought, and obstruct the logical development of the subject matter in question. He will have to shape the general content of the report according to the requirements of each case.

Offense

Official Version

    Essential Data:
        Nature and date of plea or verdict.
        Brief summary of indictment or information, including number of counts, period covered, and nature, date(s), and place(s) of offense.
        Extent of property or monetary loss.
        Extent of defendant's profit from crime.
        Aggravating and extenuating circumstances.
        Nature and status of other pending charges.
        Days held in jail.
        Reasons for inability to divert (juvenile cases).

    Optional Data:
        Date and place of arrest.
        Circumstances leading to arrest.
        Statement of arresting officers.

Attitude of defendant toward arresting officers.

Degree of cooperation.

Where detained prior to trial or sentence.

Amount of bond.

Extent to which offense follows patterns of previous offenses.

Relation of offense to organized crime or racket.

Amount of loss recovered.

Has full or partial restitution been made.

Other violations involved in addition to those charged.

Statement of Codefendants

Essential Data:

Extent of their participation in offense.

Present status of their case.

Optional Data:

Attitude toward offense.

Attitude toward defendant.

Their statement of defendant's participation in offense.

Relative culpability of defendant in relation to codefendants and coconspirators.

Statement of Witnesses, Complainants, and Victims

(Optional.)

Comment. The *official version* of the offense may be obtained from the office of the U. S. attorney. The U. S. attorney's file will give the nature of the charge, details of the offense, statements of arresting officers, statements of codefendants, complainants, witnesses, and victims, and also a summary of the arrest record.

Apprehending and prosecuting officers will give greater emphasis in their reports to the offense, the prior arrest record, and the evidence that is essential to convict a person. They are not necessarily as concerned as probation officers are with the kind of person who commits the crime, the motivations underlying the offense, and his personal and social adjustment. The probation officer is interested in the crime and its details to the extent to which they tell something about the defendant. He knows the offense represents only one facet of the defendant's behavior in general and that there is no need in telling any more about the offense than what light it sheds on the defendant. It is not necessary, for example, to give check numbers, auto serial numbers, etc.

In giving the official version of the offense, involved legal terminology should be avoided.

It is important to have the *codefendant's version* of the offense and the extent to which he may have been a leader or an aggressor. His account can be as significant in interpreting the defendant's part in the offense as the defendant's "own story." The court is generally interested in knowing the relative culpability of the defendant in relation to codefendants or coconspirators.

The report should indicate whether the codefendant has been apprehended and what disposition was made in his case.

Statements of *complainants, witnesses,* and *victims,* in some cases, can also help in understanding the defendant in relation to the offense he has committed. Their firsthand account of the offense and the defendant's attitude and conduct while carrying out the offense also can be helpful. It is important to know whether the victim is a possible contributor to the crime.

In assessing the nature of the offense and the underlying motives, the probation officer should not be carried away by the feelings, attitudes, and plight of the victim and the reactions of an indignant public. However, it must be remembered that the court before it places the defendant on probation, must be "satisfied that the ends of justice and the best interest of the public as well as the defendant will be served thereby." (18 U.S.C. 3651.)

Defendant's Version of Offense

Essential Data:
> Summary of account of offense and arrest as given by defendant if different from official version.
> Discrepancies between defendant's version and official version.
> Extent to which defendant admits guilt.
> Defendant's attitude toward offense (e. g., remorseful, rationalizes, minimizes, experiences anxiety, etc.).
> Defendant's explanation of why he became involved in the offense.

Extent to which offense was impulsive or pre-
meditated.

Environmental and situational factors contributing
to offense, including stressing situations, experiences, or relationships.

Optional Data:

Defendant's feelings from time of offense until his
arrest.

Defendant's reactions after arrest (e. g., defiant,
relieved, indifferent, etc.).

Defendant's attitude toward the probation officer
and his degree of cooperation.

Defendant's attitudes toward prior convictions and
commitments if they contribute to an understanding of the present offense.

Comment. Whatever the defendant says about the offense
and his part in it is necessary to understand him. His statements may vary from that of the law enforcement officers and
the U. S. attorney, but he is entitled, nevertheless, to make clear
his part in the offense and to give his own interpretation of the
circumstances and motivations underlying it.

Any extenuating and aggravating circumstances should be reported.

It is important to learn whether the offense was impulsive or
carefully planned. The feelings of the defendant prior to the
crime, during the commission of the crime, between the time of
the crime and arrest, and after arrest are pertinent data in many
instances. A person who had a feeling of remorse and concern
before he was arrested is likely to be different from one who is
neither remorseful nor much concerned until after he is apprehended. A person who carefully devises a plan, carries it out
calculatingly and with confidence, and is caught because of some
unanticipated circumstance or oversight, is likely to be different from one who commits a crime impulsively or who,
with some reluctance, commits a crime in which he most likely
will be caught.

The attitude of the defendant toward his offense is significant
in determining whether he should be considered for probation.
It must be kept in mind that some defendants may attempt to
rationalize or justify their crime or even place the blame on
someone else.

Prior Record

Essential Data:

> Clearance with FBI, social service exchange and police departments and sheriffs' offices in respective localities where defendant lived.
>
> Juvenile court history.
>
> List of previous convictions (date, place, offense, and disposition).
>
> List of arrests subsequent to present offense (date, place, offense, and disposition).
>
> Military arrests and courts martial (date, place, offense, and disposition) not covered in *Military Service* (see text).
>
> Institutional history (dates, report of adjustment, present release status, etc.).
>
> Previous probation and parole history (dates, adjustment, outcome).
>
> Detainers presently lodged against defendant.

Optional Data:

> Defendant's explanation why he was involved in previous offenses.
>
> Codefendants in previous offenses.

Comment. The identification record (fingerprint record) of the Federal Bureau of Investigation is the best source of information on the arrest record of a defendant. Through the office of the U.S. marshal the FBI sends a copy of the fingerprint record to the probation office. Although the FBI record has a fairly complete coverage of arrests and convictions, it is recommended that the probation office also clear with local identification bureaus, police departments, and sheriffs' offices in those cities and communities in which the defendant has resided. Particularly in smaller communities, they may have information about the defendant's reputation and his general attitude and behavior at the time of the offense.

Clearances with social service exchanges will give information regarding juvenile court contacts. Where there are no exchanges, the probation officer should check any case where it seems likely the defendant (or his parents in neglect and dependency cases) may have a juvenile court record.

Where the FBI fingerprint record does not give the disposition of a case, the probation officer should communicate with the law enforcement office which filed the print or the court in which the case was tried.

If the defendant has an institutional record, the date of commitment and release, the institutional adjustment, and the present release status should be determined by writing to the institution.

Petty offenses and misdemeanors, including arrests for drunkenness and disorderly conduct, may be summarized in a single paragraph, giving the period during which the offenses occurred, the nature of the violations, and the dispositions.

A succession of offenses resulting in acquittals, or arrests which do not result in prosecution, may reveal something significant about the defendant and may also be summarized in a single paragraph.

An extended record of traffic violations should be summarized in a single paragraph.

Where the defendant admits arrests which are not reflected in official arrest records, the report should indicate they are by his admission.

Prior convictions should be listed according to (1) *juvenile* and (2) *adult* offenses and in chronological order under each of the two headings. Serious military offenses which resulted in incarceration and also those which have a civil counterpart should be listed under adult offenses. The prior convictions should be set up as follows:

PRIOR RECORD:

Juvenile	Offense	Place	Disposition
7–2–40	Petty theft	1 yr. probation	Detroit
(Age 13)			

While in the 9th grade at junior high school the defendant and a classmate, age 15, each took a bicycle from the school's bicycle stand. They were arrested the following day and brought to the Wayne County Juvenile Court. Both were placed on probation for 1 year. According to the Juvenile Court, the defendant completed his probation satisfactorily.

Adult

4–14–55 (Age 28)	Conspiracy to steal and receive stolen property	Detroit	3 yrs. probation and $150 costs

The defendant was convicted in the Wayne County Recorder's Court of the theft of approximately 3,000 pounds of body solder from the Ford Motor Company (value $614). As a truck driver for a parts manufacturing company, the defendant made frequent trips to the Ford Motor Company. It was through his contacts there that the solder was loaded on his truck. Later, attempts were made to sell it to scrap metal dealers. He was involved with three other men, including a Detroit police sergeant who was the defendant's brother-in-law. On 10–31–55 he was placed on probation for 3 years and ordered to pay $150 costs. He was discharged from probation 10–31–58 "with improvement" (verified by Recorder's Court).

Under each offense include institutional record in a separate paragraph, giving dates of custody, escapes and returns, type of release, and expiration of sentence.

Family History

Defendant

Essential Data:

Date, place of birth, race.

Early developmental influences (physical and emotional) that may have a significant bearing on defendant's present personality and behavior.

Attitudes of the father and the mother toward the defendant in his formative years, including discipline, affection, rejection, etc.

By whom was defendant reared, if other than his parents.

Age left home; reasons for leaving; history of truancy from home.

Relationship of defendant with parents and siblings, including attitudes toward one another.

Extent of family solidarity (family cohesiveness).
Relatives with whom defendant is especially close.

Optional Data:
Naturalization status (country of birth and place
and date of entry into United States).
Order of birth among siblings.

Parents and Siblings

Essential Data:
(All information optional.)
Optional Data:
Parents (name, age, address, citizenship, natural-
ization status, education, marital status, health,
religion, economic status, general reputation).
If deceased, also give age at death and cause.
Siblings (same as parents, above).
History of emotional disorders, diseases, and crim-
inal behavior in the family.
Attitude of parents and siblings toward defendant's
offense.

Comment. No more of the family background should be included in the report than is necessary to understand the defendant and to help him in his personal and social adjustment. As
has already been emphasized, the probation officer should start
where the defendant is *now*.

Defendant. Attitudes and relationships between the defendant and his parental family are especially significant if the defendant lives or has regular contact with them. In some instances where there is little or no contact, it may be helpful to
determine what relationships exist and what effect it has on
the defendant.

Are there interfering relatives?

Include here the defendant's role in the parental family as he
sees it, particularly if he is single. Does he feel he is part of
the family, that he is wanted, appreciated, understood? Does
he feel left out, discriminated against, rejected?

What does he say that is favorable about his parental family? What is unfavorable? What family problems and relationships disturb him and with which ones is he unable to cope?
What the defendant thinks about his parental home, family

background, and family relations will help the probation officer to understand why he thinks, responds, and behaves as he does.

Parents and siblings. The probation officer should resist the tendency to give in the report too much extraneous information about parents and siblings. Such information as dates and places of birth, residence, health, education, religion, employment, and earnings may, in some instances, have little or no relevance.

What is the cultural background of the family? What family influences are apparent? What stabilizing factors are there in the parental family? To what community agencies is the family known?

As a general rule detailed information about the family is more pertinent in understanding juvenile and youth offenders than it is in the case of the older offender.

Data about each member of the parental family may be presented in the following format, giving the name, age and address in each instance:

> Father. Donald Jones, died in 1958 from a heart attack at age 52. For 17 years prior to his death he worked as a cook at various restaurants.

> Mother. Violet (nee Thomas) Conrad, 54, lives at 1928 Chestnut Street, Detroit, with her second husband, Noel Conrad, a factory worker. She is employed as a cook at a bar and restaurant.

> Brother. William Jones, 35, 423 Elm Street, Ann Arbor, Michigan, is married, has two children, and is employed in his own business as a house painter. He has not been seen by the defendant in 5 years. They are distant in their relationship.

> Sister. Mary Louise Jones, 32, 5127 Foster Avenue, Detroit, single, is a saleslady with the Hudson Department Store. The defendant has always maintained close ties with his sister. She visits the defendant's family every other week.

Marital History

Essential Data:
> Present marriage, including common law (date, place, name and age of spouse at time of marriage).

Attitude of defendant toward spouse and children and theirs toward him.

Home atmosphere.

Previous marriage(s) (date, place, name of previous spouse, and outcome; if divorced, give reasons).

Children, including those from previous marriage(s) (name, age, school, custody, support).

Optional Data:

Significant elements in spouse's background. History of courtship and reason for marriage. Problems in the marriage (religion, sex, economics, etc.).

Attitude of spouse (and older children) toward offense.

Attitude of defendant and spouse toward divorce, separation, remarriage.

Contacts with domestic relations court.

Juvenile court record of children.

Social agencies interested in family.

Divorce data (including grounds, court, date of final decree, special conditions, and to whom granted).

Comment. A disorganized family life can contribute in large measure to unbecoming conduct. The wife can be a contributing factor to the defendant's difficulties with the law. It is just as important to know about the wife's personality and character, and her problems and needs and social adjustment, as it is to have that knowledge about the defendant.

The wife can be a valuable source of information about the family and the marriage relationship. It is not sufficient to have only the defendant's account of the marriage. The wife's statements can be significant, too. She should be interviewed by the probation officer regarding many of the defendant's problems and needs. No presentence report is complete without interviewing her. But it should be kept in mind that the wife can also be a biased informant. She can be against her husband or be protective of him.

Sometimes neighbors and relatives can throw considerable light on the marriage relationship.

The attitudes between husband and wife and their relationship with one another and the children, may have a significant bearing on the emotional responses of the defendant and his behavior in general. It is important to know how both husband and wife assess their marriage and their family life and what their children mean to each of them. It is helpful to know what family problems each finds especially difficult to cope with. The probation officer should know in what ways they are not compatible and what problems each creates in the home. He should know to what extent the marriage has not been successful and what history of discord there may have been in previous marriages.

What stabilizing influence can the wife and children have? To what extent can the wife help resolve his problems and needs and in what ways can he help her? She may need help, too.

It should be known with what welfare agencies the family has had contact.

Home and Neighborhood

Essential Data:

> Description of home (owned or rented, type, size, occupants, adequacy, and general living conditions).
>
> Type of neighborhood, including any desirable or undesirable influences in the community.
>
> Attitude of defendant and family toward home and neighborhood.

Optional Data:

> Date moved to present residence and number of different residences in past 10 years.
>
> How long has defendant lived in present type of neighborhood.
>
> What race, nationality, and culture predominate.
>
> Prior home and neighborhood experiences which have had a substantial influence on the defendant's behavior.

Comment. In commenting on the home the probation officer is interested not only in the type of construction, costs, size, conveniences, and furnishings. He is also interested in what they reflect about the cultural background and the social and economic status of the family. What do they mean to the family in terms of attitudes, feelings, and relationships, and in what ways do they affect the behavior of the family members?

What the defendant and his wife are willing to put up with in the home and neighborhood tells something about them. How do they feel about the home? Are they dissatisfied with what they have? Does the wife feel her husband should have provided a better home? Is he disturbed by the way she keeps their home? Do the conditions of the home suggest any breakdown in the personality of the defendant or his wife?

Are the husband and wife trying to maintain a home above their earning capacity? Is the home a financial burden?

Meaningless "label" terms should be avoided in describing the home. Moreover, the probation officer should not judge the home by his own standards or by the way his wife keeps their home. Rather, it should be judged by what is expected in the general neighborhood. And it should be remembered that a nicely furnished and well-maintained home does not necessarily mean that family life is well organized.

In describing the neighborhood it is not only important to know about neighborhood influences—good and bad—but also to know how the defendant and his family feel about the area and what effect living in the area may have on their feelings, status, and behavior.

Education

Essential Data:
>Highest grade achieved.
>Age left school and reason for leaving.
>Results of psychological tests (IQ, aptitude, achievement, etc.), specify test and date.

Optional Data:
>Last school attended (dates, name, address).
>Previous schools attended covering 5-year period (dates, name, address).
>School adjustment as evidenced by conduct, scholastic standing, truancy, leadership, reliability, courtesy, likes and dislikes, special abilities and disabilities, grades repeated, and relationships with pupils and teachers.

Business and trade training (type, school, dates).
Defendant's attitude toward further education and train-
  ing.
Ability to read and write English.

Comment. The school is a valuable source of information about
the defendant, particularly in juvenile and youth offender cases.
Through its teachers, attendance officers, guidance counselors,
social workers, and school nurses it has accumulated pertinent
information about the family and family relationships.

Only so much of the school record as will help understand the
defendant as he responds and behaves *today* should be included
in the report. Any significant patterns of behavior which persist
from school days should be reported.

Reactions to schools, teachers, and classmates are important
in juvenile and youth offender cases.

Religion

Essential Data:
  Religious affiliation and frequency of church attendance.

Optional Data:
  Church membership (name, address, pastor).
  Member of what church organizations.
  What has religious experience meant to defendant in the
    past and at present.
  What are defendant's moral values.
  What is the pastor's impression of the defendant.

Comment. Centuries of human experience have given testimony to the dynamic qualities of religion. Depending on the defendant's past church experiences, a renewal of interest in church
affiliation or religious expression may be a significant factor in
helping him overcome some of his difficulties. If church participation had meaning for him at one time, it may be important to
know at what point and for what reason he lost interest in church
activities. His clergyman may be in a position to tell how his
church experience in the past may be utilized in his reclamation.
He can also be of assistance in pointing out the defendant's
strengths and weaknesses.

Of what importance is his church participation and religious
experience? Where there is no history of church affiliation it
would be helpful to know what guides the defendant follows for

his moral and spiritual values. It may be important to know where there are conflicts in family relationships because of differences in faith of family members.

Interests and Leisure-Time Activities

Essential Data:

> Defendant's interests and leisure-time activities (including sports, hobbies, creative work, organizations, reading).
>
> What are his talents and accomplishments.

Optional Data:

> Who are his associates; what is their reputation.
> Extent to which he engages in activities alone.
> Extent to which he includes his family.
> Extent to which his leisure-time pursuits reflect maturity.

Comment. How a person spends his leisure time may offer leads to problems the defendant might have in his social adjustment. The character and extent of his recreational pursuits and his special interests help the probation officer to understand the defendant's sense of values, social needs, outlook on life, and his goals. Frequently they tell something about the character of his family life and how they hold the family together or pull them apart.

Does the defendant have a well-balanced array of interests and recreational activities? Do physical or emotional handicaps limit him in his social relationships? With what groups does he identify? Is he a leader or a follower? What are his hobbies? What are his active sports interests? In what creative work is he engaged? To what organizations does he belong? Which of them may be a source of help in his social adjustment?

Health

Physical

Essential Data:

> Identifying information (height, weight, complexion, eyes, hair, scars, tattoos, posture, physical proportions, tone of voice, manner of speech).
>
> Defendant's general physical condition and health problems based on defendant's estimate of his health, medical reports, probation officer's observations.

Use of narcotics, barbiturates, marihuana.

Social implications of defendant's physical health (home, community, employment, associations).

Optional Data:

History of serious diseases, including venereal disease, tuberculosis, diabetes (nature, date, effects).

History of major surgery and serious injuries (nature, date, effects).

Hospital treatment (hospital, dates, nature, outcome).

Last medical examination (date, place, pertinent findings).

Current medical treatment (prescribed medicine and dosage).

Use of alcohol.

Allergies (especially penicillin).

Mental and Emotional

Essential Data:

Probation officer's assessment of defendant's operating level of intelligence as demonstrated in social and occupational functions.

Personality characteristics as given by family members and as observed by probation officer.

Attitude of defendant about himself and how he feels others feel about him (parents, siblings, spouse, children, associates).

Social adjustment in general.

Social implications of mental and emotional health (home, community, employment, associations).

Optional Data:

IQ (support with test scores).

Findings of psychological and psychiatric examinations (tests, date, by whom given).

Emotional instability as evidenced by fears, hostilities, obsessions, compulsions, depressions, peculiar ideas, dislikes, sex deviation (include any history of psychiatric treatment).

Defendant's awareness of emotional problems and what he has done about them.

Comment. The probation officer is concerned with the social implications of the defendant's physical, mental, and emotional health as they relate to his family life, his relationships with people, and his ability to earn a living. It is not unusual for a defendant to say he has "good" health. But on further inquiry, health problems and concerns about health come into focus. It is important to know how the defendant actually feels about his health in general and to report what health conditions need special attention.

Where authorization is required to release medical information, a copy of a form authorizing release of confidential information should accompany the request.

Physical. Physical ills can lead to aberrations in behavior. Physical disabilities and deformities may be related to the offense and the defendant's behavior in general.

No more than is necessary to understand the defendant's present health condition should be included in the report. A listing of injuries, diseases, and surgery serves no purpose unless they have a bearing on the defendant's present health or are connected in some way with the offense. Ordinary childhood diseases or surgery without serious after effects would be classed as extraneous information. The test of what to include in the report should be: Is the disease, injury, or surgery likely to be related in any way to the defendant's present health and behavior?

Mental and Emotional. The statement of the defendant's mental health should be supported wherever possible by psychiatric and psychological reports. A mere diagnostic label serves little or no purpose. The diagnosis should be expressed in understandable terms in relation to the specific problems and needs of the defendant.

Whether or not an IQ is available, the probation officer should assess the defendant's operational level of intelligence as demonstrated in social and occupational functions.

As pointed out on page 3, "Tangible Facts Not Enough," it is important to know something about the attitudes, feelings, and emotions of the defendant and also his relationships with people. How does he feel about himself? In what ways does his image of himself differ from how others see him?

A description of the defendant's personality may be presented in this portion of the presentence report. In describing his personality and traits of character such descriptive labels as high strung, timid, sullen, boastful, impulsive, suspicious, remorseful, etc., may be used. But each should be supported by examples to help clearly portray the trait or quality.

Employment

Essential Data:

> Employment history for past 10 years (dates, nature of work, earnings reasons for leaving).
>
> Employer's evaluation of defendant (immediate supervisor, where possible), including attendance, capabilities, reliability, adjustment, honesty, reputation, personality, attitude toward work, and relationships with coworkers and supervisors.
>
> Occupational skills, interests, and ambitions.

Optional Data:

> If unemployable, explain.
>
> Means of subsistence during unemployment, including relief and unemployment compensation.

Comment. A job is different things to different people. It is a means of livelihood; to some it is pleasant and to others it is not so pleasant. Others regard it as a necessary evil—a frustrating experience. It can be status-giving. It can provide a feeling of belonging and fellowship with friendly people. Particularly in creative work, or employment requiring special skills, it gives a sense of achievement and a partnership in a worthwhile enterprise. One-third of an adult's life is spent on his job. Hence, a defendant's employment adjustment and his attitude toward his job can be significant factors in his personal and social adjustment.

Wherever possible, the employment history should be verified by each employer. What the employer (particularly the immediate supervisor) says about the defendant's job adjustment is significant. It may differ considerably from the statement of the defendant.

It is not necessary, in most cases, to report on the employment history beyond a 10-year period.

It is important to know in what ways the defendant's personality, physical condition, and appearance may have contributed to his spotty employment record and his inability to get and to hold a job. If he is unemployable, the nature of his limitations or handicaps might be mentioned again. (*Note:* His disabilities and handicaps will have already been covered under *Health.*)

The employment record should be set up in the following format, giving at the start of each paragraph the dates of employment, name of the employer, nature of work, and the salary or wage. This should be followed by the reason for leaving the job, an evaluation of the defendant's job adjustment, and an estimate of the skills achieved.

EMPLOYMENT:

September 1950 to April 1955 (4 years 7 months). The defendant was employed at the Fitzsimmons Manufacturing Company, 3775 E. Outer Drive, Detroit, as a semi-truck driver at $2 per hour (verified). Employment was terminated when he was arrested 4–10–55 for involvement in theft of material from the Ford Motor Company (see PRIOR RECORD).

May 1955 to February 1963 (7 years, 7 months). Employed at the Acme Manufacturing Company, 1400 E. Nine Mile Road, Ferndale, Michigan, as a stock handler and crib attendant at $2.94 per hour (verified). The firm's records show that employment was terminated because of the defendant's arrest in the present case, that he had violated a shop rule by leaving the premises during the lunch period, and had failed to punch out or notify his foreman. When he returned to work 2 days later he was notified of his dismissal.

April 1963 to February 1964 (10 months). Employed as a toolmaker's helper at the Broaching Specialities, Inc., 1500 E. Eleven Mile Road, Madison Heights, Michigan, at $2 per hour. According to the company he was a satisfactory employee and left voluntarily to accept a better-paying job.

February 1964 to present (9 months). Employed at the Vulcan Engineering Company, 222 Conner Street, Detroit, as a bench hand helper at $2.49 per hour. His supervisor describes him as a dependable employee and believes he has the potential for advancing to a higher-skilled and better-paying job. His employer knows about his present offense.

The defendant's wife is employed as a saleslady at the Hudson Department Store where the defendant's sister is also employed. Her earnings are $52 a week.

Military Service

Essential Data:

> Branch of service, serial number, and dates of each period of military service.
>
> Highest grade or rank achieved and grade or rank at separation.
>
> Type and date of discharge(s).
>
> Attitude toward military experience.

Optional Data:

> Inducted or enlisted.
>
> Special training received.
>
> Foreign service, combat experience, decorations and citations.
>
> Disciplinary action not covered in *Prior Record* (see text).
>
> Veteran's claim number.
>
> Selective Service status (local board, classification, registration number).

Comment. The military service record of *former* military personnel should be obtained in each instance from the Military Personnel Records Center. Requests for information on *active* personnel should be sent directly to the defendant's commanding officer.

The medical history supplied by the Military Personnel Records Center should be reported under the marginal heading, *Health.* Only minor military offenses should be included here. As already pointed out, serious military offenses which resulted in incarceration and also those which have a civil counterpart should be listed under *Prior Record.*

Financial Condition

Assets

Essential Data:

> Statement of financial assets.
>
> General standard of living.

Optional Data:
> Net worth statement.
> Property (type, location, value, equity).
> Insurance (type, amount, company).
> Checking and savings account (bank, amount).
> Stocks and bonds (type, value).
> Personal property (car, furniture, appliances).
> Income from pensions, rentals, boarders.
> Family income.
> Available resources through relatives and friends.

Financial Obligations

Essential Data:
> Statement of financial obligations.

Optional Data:
> Current obligations, including balance due and monthly payment (home mortgage, rent, utilities, medical, personal property, home repairs, charge accounts, loans, fines, restitution).
> Money management and existing financial delinquencies.
> Credit rating.

Comment. How a defendant handles his finances sometimes tells a lot about him—the things he buys, the number of items he purchases on time, regularity of payments, the extent to which purchases have been picked up for nonpayment. Knowledge of the defendant's debts and financial obligations helps the probation officer to understand the defendant. To what extent are there money-management problems and current delinquencies in the payment of financial obligations? The defendant's credit rating may offer helpful leads to his financial status.

Evaluative Summary

Essential Data:
> Highlights of body of the report.
> Analysis of factors contributing to present offense and prior convictions, (motivations and circumstances).
> Defendant's attitude toward offense.
> Evaluation of the defendant's personality problems and needs, and potential for growth.

Optional Data:
    Reputation in the community.

Comment. Writing the evaluative summary is perhaps the most difficult and painstaking task in the entire presentence report. It has a significant bearing on the future course of the defendant's life. It is here that the probation officer calls into play his analytical ability, his diagnostic skills, and his understanding of human behavior. It is here that he brings into focus the kind of person before the court, the basic factors that brought him into trouble, and what special helps the defendant needs to resolve his difficulties.

The opening paragraph of the evaluative summary should give a concise restatement of the pertinent highlights in the body of the report. There should follow in separate paragraphs those factors which contributed in some measure to the defendant's difficulty and also an evaluation of his personality. (*Note:* A fuller description of his personality should appear under *Health —Mental and Emotional.*)

Recommendation

Essential Data:
    Recommendation.
    Basis for recommendation.
Optional Data:
    Suggested plan, including role of parents spouse,
        pastor, further education, future employment.
    Sentencing alternatives.

Comment. Some judges ask for the probation officer's recommendation regarding probation or commitment. Where recommendations are requested, they should be a part of the presentence report. If the judge does not wish to have the recommendations included as a part of the report, they may be given on a separate sheet which may be detached if the presentence report is later sent to an institution.

If it is recommended that the defendant be placed on probation, the proposed plans for residence, employment, education, and medical and psychiatric treatment, if pertinent, should be given. The part to be played in the social adjustment of the defendant by the parental and immediate family, the pastor, close friends, and others in the community should also be shown. If commitment is recommended, the probation officer should indicate what special problems and needs should receive the attention of the institutional staff.

Where the judge asks for sentencing alternatives, they may be included in this part of the report.

SOME GENERAL SUGGESTIONS

Writing the Report

The presentence report should be dictated at the earliest possible time following the investigation. Notes "grow cold" if they are not dictated relatively soon. Moreover, the longer the delay, the greater is the chance of overlooking significant observations.

Prior to dictating, the worksheet information and other interview notes, together with reports and correspondence regarding the case, should be well organized. This is especially true in dictating directly to the stenographer. Attempting to organize notes during dictation results in a waste of time.

The probation officer who dictated the presentence report should sign the report—not the chief probation officer. It is not necessary to have the names of both the chief probation officer and the investigating officer on the report.

Objectivity and Accuracy

Objectivity is one of the essential attributes of a probation officer. Impartiality in his report writing will depend to a large extent on the degree of objectivity he has achieved. The trained and skilled probation officer will not read into situations what is not there. He recognizes his own prejudices and blindspots and makes allowances and adjustments for each of them. He is careful not to assess the defendant's behavior and actions on the basis of his own standards of conduct and moral values. He does not allow himself to overidentify with the defendant. He guards against the psychological mechanisms of rationalization and projection. He rids himself of any preconceived notions about the defendant, for he knows that premature or snap judgments can be not only embarrassing to the defendant, the probation office, and the court, but damaging as well. He is never guilty of "slanting" a report.

Facts contribute to objectivity, but it is possible to misrepresent or distort facts. In evaluating or reporting the statements, impressions, and observations of collateral contacts, the reliability of the informant should be made clear in the report. Where there is an element of uncertainty about the informant's statement, this should be made known.

Inferences, impressions, and opinions are important at times and may have a place in the presentence report. But a clear distinction should be made between what is factual and what is inference. Facts are more likely to be presented accurately than inferences, impressions, and interpretations. It is better to say "Mr. Brown impresses one as honest and sincere" than to say "Mr. Brown *is* honest and sincere."

Indicating Sources of Information

Sources of information should be shown in the report, not at the close of the report. In reading about the defendant's employment record, for example, the reader should know whether the statement is given by the defendant himself, his wife, the employer, or some other source. When reporting that the defendant gets along well with his wife it is essential to know whether it is based on his statement only, the wife's, or the statement of each of them.

Ways in which the source may be reported are the following: "According to the defendant's wife . . ."; "The report from Central High School indicates that . . ."; "The defendant insisted that . . ."; "The report of the psychiatrist disclosed . . ."; "The defendant's pastor states . . ."

Unverified statements should be clearly shown as "unverified," "rumor," or "unconfirmed report." Immeasurable harm and irreparable injury may result from unverified information presented as fact.

Only in most unusual circumstances should a presentence report be based solely on the defendant's statement. When this is done, it should be made clear in the report, preferably at the beginning.

Selectivity in Writing the Report

The presentence report should not be cluttered with extraneous information which has little or no relation to the personality, character, and behavior of the defendant. Information about the defendant's birth and his early development, for example, may be irrelevant in the case of an adult who appears to have normal intelligence and seems to behave in a relatively normal way. Detailed information about family members with whom an adult defendant has had no contact in many years may be of little significance. A comprehensive school report will be more pertinent in understanding a juvenile or youth offender than a person in his forties and fifties.

A verbatim account of the indictment would seem to have no place in the report. A brief summary should suffice since the judge has before him the indictment or information from the official file of the court. A lengthy recital of every detail in the offense serves no purpose unless it tells something about the defendant, his personality, and his conduct in general.

An extended history of employment instability, family discord, similar types of offenses, inability to tolerate tedium, and the need to be on the go, do, of course, throw light on the defendant.

The average length of the presentence report should generally be six to eight pages of single-space typing on 8- by 10½-inch sheets. This does not include the face sheet (form No. 2), the evaluative summary, and any recapitulation the probation officer may carry at the close of the report.

Brevity

Needless repetition and wordiness should be avoided. Redundancy often occurs when the probation officer has no opportunity to edit a preliminary draft of the report before it is typed in final form. Too many persons tend to waste words.

All data in the report should be concise and to the point, but brevity should not be sought at the expense of completeness. Discriminating selection of relevant material is one means of shortening the report.

Negative statements of no significance should be omitted. The following "irrelevant negatives" contribute nothing to an understanding of the defendant. "This juvenile has had no military experience"; "The defendant had no brothers or sisters"; "There is no history of hospitalization for emotional disorders."

Complete, short sentences and paragraphs confined to a single topic or thought are an aid to clarity and help to sustain the interest of the reader. In general, sentences should be brief. Paragraphs should be held to about 15 typed lines.

Style and Format in Writing the Report

Good report writing adheres to the rules of rhetoric. A good style need not be elaborate. A simple, direct, lucid style is most effective. Time and effort should not be wasted to achieve a dramatic effect. However, the report should be written so that the defendant comes alive. It should present him as a living person. Enlargement of descriptive vocabulary enhances the ability of the probation officer to describe for the court the kind of a person it has before it.

"Subject" should not be used in referring to the defendant; it is much too impersonal. The defendant is a human being to be helped. Some refer to him as "the defendant" and others prefer to call him "Mr. Brown" or by his first name if he is a juvenile or youth offender. An adult should never be referred to by his first name. The usual alternatives of "mother," "father," "sister," "wife" may be used as called for.

The repetitious use of "he said" should be avoided. Some more descriptive variations are: mentioned, asserted, replied, recalled, admitted, suggested, promised, emphasized, disclosed, revealed, divulged. Variations which describe the mood or manner in which the defendant made his statements are especially helpful, for example: objected, confided, argued, mumbled, interrupted, volunteered, contested, denounced, confessed, warned.

The probation officer should avoid the use of "I" in his reports. He should refer to himself as little as possible. Third person makes for readability.

The general format for setting up the presentence report is that shown in the facsimile in the appendix, starting on page 29.

Use of "Label" Terms

The use of generalized terms and unsupported adjectives should be avoided. These so-called "label" or "blanket" terms fail to define sharply the differences between persons, situations, and circumstances. Terms such as "disorderly home," "shocking conduct," "lacking in judgment," "poor disciplinarian," "undependable person," "makes a good living," "heavy drinker" have varied interpretations and meanings to different people. The judge, the probation officer, the defendant, the employer do not give the same evaluation to these vague terms.

"Highly emotional" gives little insight into the personality makeup of the defendant. A "bad" heart does not tell whether the defendant is bedridden or ambulatory, or to what extent he is handicapped or unable to work. Stating that the defendant can do "light work" has little significance because persons interpret "light work" differently. Medical diagnostic terms will have more meaning if the social and physical implications of the disease are spelled out.

If used at all, blanket terms should be supported by meaningful, descriptive information. For example, "irresponsible husband" may be followed by statements such as "fails to bring home the pay check"; "deserted the family 3 days last month"; "overlooks paying rent and utilities."

Clichès and stereotyped terms and phrases have no place in report writing.

Technical Words and Phrases

Technical words and phrases, in general, should be used only if they have wide usage and a common meaning. Such terms as sociopath, schizophrenic, moron, paranoid, sex psychopath, neurotic, psychotic, character disorder—which often are used indiscriminately by the public and the press, and sometimes probation officers, too—have a distinctive professional meaning to psychiatrists and psychologists. They should be restricted to these specialists in behavior. The probation officer should not attempt to apply them on his own.

Where psychiatric, medical, or psychological terminology is used in the presentence report, it may be accompanied by an explanation of the diagnostic statements.

Verbatim Reporting

Verbatim reporting may be helpful at times in portraying the feelings, attitudes, and responses of a person. But the direct quotation should be used only if it gives a better picture of the defendant or the situation and circumstances than would a paraphrased statement. Where quotation marks are used, the quoted portion should contain the *exact* words of the person quoted— not an interpolation. Moreover, the language should *not* be taken out of context. Meanings can be distorted or altered if any statement preceding or following, or any part of the quoted portion, is omitted.

Verbatim reporting is helpful for the unbiased picture it presents of the defendant's thinking processes, attitudes, and feelings, and the precise way in which he expressed himself. On the other hand, verbatim reporting is unreliable unless full notes are taken in the presence of the defendant. Recording direct quotations following the interview cannot be reliable. Without shorthand devices, the probation officer will have difficulty in recording word-for-word statements.

Handwritten statements by the defendant on certain aspects of the presentence investigation fall in the category of verbatim reporting and should be carried in quotes.

THE IMPACT ON JUDICIAL DISPOSITIONS*

The probation officer as a member of the court staff has two major functions to fulfill. The first is to conduct an investigation of an offender which culminates in a presentence or probation report. This report is frequently accompanied by a recommendation to the court as to the selection of an appropriate sentence. The second function is to provide supervision for offenders placed on probation or some other form of conditional liberty. Despite the recent focus of correctional interest and attention, and a considerable volume of literature, the terms and conditions of these functions remain relatively vague. It is proposed to examine here a segment of one of these, namely the presentence report recommendation and its relationship to the court disposition. Our purpose is not so much to provide data, but to make explicit some questions about presentence report recommendations and their relation to court dispositions.

. . . The following discussion relates mainly to the federal probation system, and we are indebted to the Administrative Office of the United States Courts for furnishing pertinent data. Information has also been drawn from the San Francisco Project, a study of the federal probation system, supported by the National Institute of Mental Health.[1] It should be noted that these data cover different populations over different periods of time, and are not to be seen as interesting in themselves, but as throwing light on the presentence report recommendation and court disposition.

* Reprinted from Robert M. Carter and Leslie T. Wilkins, "Some Factors in Sentencing Policy," *Journal of Criminal Law, Criminology* and *Police Science* 584 (1967): 503–514.

1. See Lohman, Wahl & Carter, *A Non-Technical Description of the*

Recommendations and Dispositions

The Relationship

The presentence report is a document basic to the functioning of both judicial and correctional administrations. The contents of the report, including the recommendation, assist the court in making a judgment consistent with its dual responsibilities to society and the defendant. Within the federal system the report aids the institutions within the Bureau of Prisons in determining classification and treatment programs and also in planning for subsequent release. The report provides information to the Board of Parole, furnishing information believed to be pertinent to its deliberations. Furthermore, the report contributes to the probation officer's rehabilitative efforts while an offender is under his supervision.[2]

In February, 1965, with the publication of a 39 page monograph entitled *The Presentence Investigation Report,* a standard outline and format were adopted for the preparation of presentence reports in the federal courts.[3] The final paragraph headings of the report are "Evaluative Summary" and "Recommendation." The importance of these paragraphs is recognized by the American Correctional Association which includes among its standards for the preparation of presentence reports a "recommendation for or against probation, or for other disposition according to court policy." [4]

The fact that there is a substantial number of sentencing alternatives available to federal judges also means that an equal number of possible recommendations may be considered by the probation officer. The selection ranges, of course, from probation with or without a fine or restitution, and/or a jail sentence, and imprisonment under various statutes which determine parole eligibility, to other dispositions which include commitment for observation and study and continuances for community observation.

Because of this variety of available disposals, the relationship between a recommendation and a disposition may be more simply

San Francisco Project, The San Francisco Project series (April 1965).

2. The federal probation officer supervises persons released on parole or mandatory release from federal correctional institutions or the

United States Disciplinary Barracks.

3. *The Presentence Investigation Report* (Adm.Off.U.S.Cts.) (1965).

4. *Manual of Correctional Standards* (Am.Corr.Assn.) 521 (2d ed. 1959).

considered from one of two directions. The first method would
be to contrast recommendations for probation made by probation officers with actual court dispositions resulting in probation.
The second would be from an opposite direction, viewing recommendations against probation (or for imprisonment) with
actual court dispositions for probation.

Data developed during the San Francisco Project contrast
recommendations and dispositions for 500 consecutive cases
processed through the United States District Court in the
Northern District of California between September 1964 and
August 1965.[5] These data indicate that:

.   .   .   there is a close relationship between the recommendation of probation and the actual granting of probation. Probation
was recommended in 227 cases and was granted in 212 of those
cases. If the 7 cases of "observation and study" are not included, probation was granted, when recommended, in 212 of the
220 cases or in 96 percent of the cases. In only 2 of the 227
cases was there a substantial difference between the probation
officer's recommendation and the court's disposition of the cases.
In these instances, prison sentences were ordered where probation had been recommended.[6]

These data closely parallel the California data. The percentages of probation officer recommendations for probation
followed by California Superior Courts, for the years cited, are
shown in Table 35-1.

Table 35-1

*Percentage of Probation Officer Recommendations
for Probation Followed by California Superior Courts*

1959	95.6%
1960	96.4%
1961	96.0%
1962	96.5%
1963	97.2%
1964	97.3%
1965	96.7%

Source: State of California, Department of Justice. *Delinquency
and Probation in California*, 1964, p. 168; and *Crime and Delinquency in California*, 1965, pp. 98–99.
[A8885]

5. Carter, *It Is Respectfully Recom-*   6. Ibid. 41.
   mended   .   .   ., 30 Fed.Prob. 2
   (1966).

Data on the federal system, arranged by the ten judicial circuits, indicate the relationship, shown in Table 35–2, between

Table 35–2

*Percentage of Probation Officer
Recommendations for Probation
Followed by Ten Judicial Circuits, Fiscal Year 1964*

First Circuit	99.4%
Second Circuit	96.0%
Third Circuit	93.2%
Fourth Circuit	93.3%
Fifth Circuit	95.2%
Sixth Circuit	93.9%
Seventh Circuit	89.9%
Eighth Circuit	95.0%
Ninth Circuit	93.5%
Tenth Circuit	97.8%
Overall	94.1%

Source: Data furnished by the Administrative Office of the United States Courts.

[A8884]

probation officer recommendations for probation and such dispositions in court for Fiscal Year 1964.

The patterns in these first two tables exhibit almost total agreement between a probation officer's recommendation for probation and an actual disposition of probation. However, this trend appears less stable when viewed from the opposite perspective—the relationship between recommendations against probation (or for imprisonment) and court dispositions of probation. California data reveal, in Table 35–3, the percentages

Table 35–3

*Percentage of Probation Officer Recommendations
Against Probation Not Followed by California
Superior Courts*

1959	13.5%
1960	12.8%
1961	14.8%
1962	17.4%
1963	21.6%
1964	21.1%
1965	19.9%

Source: State of California, Department of Justice. *Delinquency and Probation in California,* 1964, p. 168; and *Crime and Delinquency in California,* 1965, pp. 98–99.

[A8891]

of "against probation" recommendations and probation dispositions in court.

It is noteworthy that California authorities indicate the "superior court judges are more lenient than probation officers as
to who should be granted probation." [7] This pattern has already
been observed by one of the authors,[8] and by others,[9] in respect
to the federal probation officer. Further confirmation of this
pattern is found throughout the federal system as indicated by
a review, in Table 35–4, of "against probation" recommendations

Table 35–4

*Percentage of Probation Officer
Recommendations Against Probation Not
Followed by Ten Judicial Circuits, Fiscal Year 1964*

First Circuit	7.3%
Second Circuit	9.5%
Third Circuit	27.4%
Fourth Circuit	31.8%
Fifth Circuit	11.5%
Sixth Circuit	19.3%
Seventh Circuit	15.9%
Eighth Circuit	16.5%
Ninth Circuit	23.3%
Tenth Circuit	9.2%
Overall	19.7%

Source: Data furnished by the Administrative Office of the United
States Courts.
[A8892]

and probation dispositions according to the ten judicial circuits
for Fiscal Year 1964.

As already indicated, the probation officer has a wide latitude
in his choice of a recommendation. Table 35–5 presents data
on the specific recommendations of probation officers in the
Northern District of California between September 1964 and
February 1967, and shows the wide variety of possible recommendations.

Table 35–6 presents overall data on the relationship between
recommendations and dispositions of 1,232 cases processed

7. *Delinquency and Probation in
California, 1964* (Calif.Dept. of
Justice) 166 (1964).

8. Carter, supra note 11.

9. Lohman, Wahl & Carter, *San
Francisco Project* series (Report
#2) 8 (Berkeley: June 1965).

through the District Court in Northern California. The reader will note that of 601 cases recommended for probation, 15 were ordered imprisoned; of 334 cases recommended for imprisonment, 31 were placed on probation.

These data seem to support certain generalizations about the nature of the relationship between probation officer recommendations and court dispositions. We have seen that there is a very strong relationship between recommendations *for probation* and court dispositions of probation, an average agreement of about 95 percent. It has also been observed that the strength of the relationship diminishes slightly when recommendations *against*

Table 35–5

Probation Officers' Recommendations as to Sentence
Northern District of California
September 1964 to February 1967

Recommendation	Total	Percent of Total
All Cases	1,232	100.0
No Recommendation	67	5.4
Mandatory Sentence (Under Certain Narcotic Law Violations)	45	3.6
Probation	601	48.9
Regular	(284)	(23.1)
With Fine and/or Restitution	(197)	(16.0)
Split Sentence (Imprisonment up to Six Months Followed by Probation)	(49)	(4.0)
Under Youth Corrections Act	(71)	(5.8)
Fine only	38	3.1
Jail only	35	2.8
Imprisonment	334	27.1
Parole Eligibility After 1/3 Sentence	(234)	(19.0)
Parole Eligibility at Any Time	(64)	(5.2)
Under Youth Corrections Act	(36)	(2.9)
Observation and Study	51	4.2
Adult	(39)	(3.2)
Youth	(12)	(1.0)
Continuance for 90 Days Observation	16	1.3
Deferred Prosecution	3	.2
Commitment Under Federal Juvenile Delinquency Act	2	.2
Other Recommendations	40	3.3

Source: Unpublished *San Francisco Project* data.   [A9414]

TABLE 35–6

Probation Officers' Recommendation and Subsequent Court Dispositions
Northern District of California
September 1964 to February 1967

Recommendation	Total	Disposition								
		Mandatory	Probation	Fine only	Jail only	Imprisonment	Observation and Study	Continuances	Deferred Prosecution	Other
All Cases	1,232	45	671	30	27	337	73	18	2	29
No Recommendation	67	–	44	2	2	14	1	–	–	4
Mandatory	45	45	–	–	–	–	–	–	–	–
Probation	601	–	551	5	3	15	17	2	–	8
Fine only	38	–	14	22	–	1	–	–	–	1
Jail only	35	–	5	1	19	8	2	–	–	–
Imprisonment	334	–	31	–	2	281	13	5	–	2
Observation and Study	51	–	3	–	–	9	38	1	–	–
Continuances	16	–	6	–	–	–	–	10	–	–
Deferred Prosecution	3	–	–	–	–	–	–	–	2	1
Federal Juvenile Delinquency Act	2	–	1	–	–	–	–	–	–	1
Other	40	–	16	–	1	9	2	–	–	12

Source: Unpublished *San Francisco Project* data.   [A9413]

probation (or for imprisonment) are contrasted with court dispositions of probation. Thus, it may be concluded that where disagreements exist between recommendations and dispositions, they occur when the officer recommends imprisonment. In a sense, if this relationship measures "punitiveness" then it may be concluded that the probation officer is more punitive than the judge.

Outcome of Supervision According to the Recommendation

Very limited data are available on the outcome of the supervision, i. e., the violation rate, according to recommendations of probation officers. The 1964 cohort study of Davis [10] examined the violation status of 11,638 adult defendants granted probation in California Superior Courts between 1956 and 1958. Davis showed that 27.1 percent of the defendants recommended for and placed on probation were "revoked," while 36.7 percent of the defendants placed on probation against the recommendation of the probation officer were revoked. Davis concluded that the "difference in revocation rates was very significant and indicates that the two groups were not alike in their tendency to recidivism."

It is questionable that this single explanation for the 10 percent differential in revocation rates occurs simply because of differ-

10. Davis, *A Study of Adult Probation Violation Rates by Means of* the *Cohort Approach*, 55 J.Crim. L., C. & P.S. 70 (1964).

ences in the two groups.   There are two other possible explanations for this.   One explanation may be that subtle differences
exist in the supervision provided by a probation officer who may
feel "resentful" in having an individual placed on probation
against his recommendation.   The second possibility is that the
defendant's attitude toward a probation officer who recommended that he be imprisoned instead of placed on probation
may affect the outcome of supervision.   While there are no measures of these two negative factors, it is possible that they account for a large portion of the observed differential.   There are
other interesting studies which support the hypothesis of self-
fulfilling prophecies.

Another way of viewing Davis' data is to emphasize that 63.3
percent of those who received an unfavorable probation recommendation but were placed on probation completed their probation without revocation.   Thus, to deny probation to all those
with negative recommendations from probation officers would
suggest that approximately two out of every three defendants
with such recommendations would be denied the opportunity
to complete probation successfully.   Davis inquired as to the
number of defendants who, denied probation on unfavorable
recommendations, would have succeeded on probation if given
the opportunity.   There are, at this time, no data to answer
this question.[11]

Other data are available from the Administrative Office of
the United States Courts which indicate that despite considerable
variation in the use of probation, the overall violation rates, or
the rates broken down by "major," "minor," or "technical" are
almost identical.   Table 35–7 of the Administrative Office report
is reproduced here to show probation violation rates for 1965, according to the actual percentage of persons placed on probation
by the 88 U.S. District Courts, arranged by quartiles.

The data in Table 35–7 reveal that approximately 19 percent
of those placed under probation supervision violate the terms
of this conditional liberty, regardless of the percentage of the
offender population on probation.

11. Wilkins, *A Small Comparative
Study of the Results of Probation*,
8 *British J. Crimino.* 201 (1958).

TABLE 35–7

(Table A 18 of the Administrative Office of the U. S. Courts
Covering 88 United States District Courts)
Comparison of the Use of Probation in District Courts,
by Type of Violation, Fiscal Year 1965
(Excludes Violators of Immigration Laws, Wagering Tax Laws and
Violators of Federal Regulatory Acts)

Item	88 District Courts	Quartile Groups of District Courts			
		First 22 District Courts	Second 22 District Courts	Third 22 District Courts	Fourth 22 District Courts
Average Actual Percent Placed on Probation	49.0	65.9	53.8	47.2	36.9
Total Removed	11,259	2,263	2,759	3,678	2,559
No Violations	9,157	1,843	2,267	2,973	2,074
Violated Probation	2,102	420	492	705	485
Technical Violation	344	78	85	106	75
Minor Violation	577	111	120	216	130
Major Violation	1,181	231	287	383	280
Percent Violated Probation	18.7	18.5	17.8	19.2	18.9
Technical Violation	3.1	3.4	3.1	2.9	2.9
Minor Violation	5.1	4.9	4.3	5.9	5.1
Major Violation	10.5	10.2	10.4	10.4	10.9

Source: Administrative Office of the United States Courts, *Persons Under the Supervision of the Federal Probation System* (Washington, D.C., 1965), p. 33.

[A9417]

Factors Affecting the Agreement between Recommendations and Dispositions

Reverting to the possible explanations for the high degree of agreement between probation officer recommendations and court dispositions, it is possible that four factors, operating independently, but more probably simultaneously, account for this relationship:

1) The court, having such high regard for the professional qualities and competence of its probation staff, "follows" the probation recommendation—a recommendation made by the person (probation officer) who best knows the defendant by reason of the presentence investigation;

2) There are many offenders who are "obviously" probation or prison cases;

3) Probation officers write their reports and make recommendations anticipating the recommendation the court desires to receive. (In this situation, the probation officer is quite accurately "second-guessing" the court disposition);

4) Probation officers in making their recommendations place great emphasis on the same factors as does the court in selecting a sentencing alternative.

Data from the San Francisco Project confirm the fact that probation officers and judges apply approximately equal significance to similar factors.[12]   Examination of 500 probation officer recommendations according to the major categories of recommendations for probation and recommendations for imprisonment (or against probation) produced data on the legal and demographic characteristics of the offender population which had an important effect upon the recommendation selected. In general terms, the proportion of recommendations for probation increased with the number of years of education, average monthly income, higher occupational levels, residence, marital and employment stability, participation in church activities, and a good military record. Recommendations for imprisonment (or against probation) increased proportionately when offenders exhibited such characteristics as homosexuality, alcoholic involvement, the use of weapons or violence in the commission of the offense, the existence of family criminality, and drug usage. Age (in the range examined) did not significantly distinguish between the two recommendations, and racial and religious affiliation differences were absent. The female, however, was more likely to be recommended for probation than the male offender.

Certain offense categories (e. g., embezzlement, theft from interstate shipments or theft of government property, and false statement) usually produced recommendations for probation, while other offense categories (e. g., bank robbery, the interstate transportation of stolen motor vehicles [Dyer Act], and National Defense law violation) usually resulted in recommendations for imprisonment. Offenders who entered a plea of guilty retained their own attorneys, or who were released to the community on

12. See Lohman, Wahl & Carter, *San Francisco Project* series (Re-   ports 4 and 5) (Berkeley: December 1965, February 1966).

bail, bond, or personal recognizance while the presentence investigation was being conducted, had significantly greater chances of being recommended for probation. It is recognized, of course, that a recommendation for or against probation is generally based upon some combination of characteristics—some obvious, others subtle—rather than upon any single characteristic or piece of information.

It is apparent that not all factors are of equal significance in determining the probation officer's recommendation. Accordingly, statistical computations produced a general ranking of the significance or importance of various factors.[13]

A further examination of the 500 cases was made, reviewing the selection of the sentencing alternative by the court. Again, statistical computations were completed and a second rank order of the signficant or important factors was produced.

These two sets of data—one relating to the recommendation, the other to the disposition—are summarized in Table 35-8. The rankings were based on probability and contingency coefficient values. A correlation was computed and a significant value of .90 was obtained. These data indicate that there is considerable agreement between probation officers and judges as to the significance of certain factors and characteristics for decisions relating to probation or imprisonment recommendations and dispositions.

Another possible explanation of the close agreement between recommendations and dispositions is certainly that some cases are clearly probation or imprisonment cases. However, there are no "hard" data to identify which cases are "clearly" probation or prison cases. An actual but extreme example of an "imprisonment case" is the bank robber who, armed with an automatic pistol and with an accomplice waiting in a stolen automobile, robbed a bank of $35,000, pistol-whipped a teller, and in the flight from the scene, engaged in a gun battle with pursuing police. It is doubtful that probation officers or judges would be inclined to see probation as a suitable disposition for such a case, regardless of any other factors involved. An example of the "probation case" is the young married offender, who, unemployed prior to the Christmas season, made a false statement to the Post Office for employment, concealing a prior misdemeanor arrest. In general terms, this type of offender would normally be seen as a suitable candidate for probation.

13. Id.

Table 35–8

Rank of Demographic Factors Utilized by
Probation Officers for Recommendations and
District Court Judges for Sentencing
Alternatives, According to Probability
and Contingency Coefficient Values
500 Federal Offenders
Northern District of California
September 1964 to August 1965

Demographic Factors	Probation Officers' Ranking	District Court Judge's Ranking
Prior Record	1	3
Confinement Status	2	2
Number of Arrests	3	4
Offense	4	1
Longest Employment	5	5
Occupation	6	8
Number of Months Employed	7	6
Income	8	10
Longest Residence	9	7
Military History	10	9
Number of Residence Changes	11	17
Distance to Offense	12	14
Number of Aliases	13	24
Marital Status	14	11
Legal Representation	15	13
Weapons and Violence	16	15
Family Criminality	17	21
Plea	18	18
Education	19	12
Church Attendance	20	16
Narcotics Usage	21	23
Sex	22	19
Alcoholic Involvement	23	25
Crime Partners	24	20
Homosexuality	25	26
Race	26	28
Age	27	22
Religion	28	27

Source: Joseph D. Lohman, Albert Wahl and Robert M. Carter. *San Francisco Project* series, Report 5 (Berkeley: February 1966), p. 68.

Spearman's p = .90 [A9415]

From observation and conversations with judges and probation officers during the past years, it appears that judges do indeed have a high regard for their probation staff and value their professional judgment as to the disposition of a case. It is suspected that this is especially true in the federal system in which probation officers are appointed by the court and serve at its pleasure. This esteem for probation officers and their services by the court may also contribute to the high agreement between recommendations and dispositions, even though there are no statistical data to support this.

The fourth potential explanation for the close agreement between recommendations and dispositions—probation officers anticipating the recommendation the court desires—is now to be discussed.

Variation Among Probation Officers and Probation Offices

Disparities in sentencing have been of considerable interest in recent years and attempts to reduce these frequently observed differentials have normally been focused on judges. For example, sentencing institutes for judges have been developed at the federal and state level, as well as training programs for newly appointed or elected judges. That attention should be directed toward judges—for they impose the sentences—is certainly normal and, on the surface, a logical approach to resolving disparities. However, this pattern ignores one of the facts of community life—in this case the judicial community and its social system—that many persons play a part in the functioning of the community. Included in the judicial community are probation officers, prosecutors, defense attorneys, perhaps to a lesser extent the law enforcement agencies, and other judges on the same bench.

It seems to have been generally assumed that the judges are solely responsible for the disparities and that the remainder of the judicial community plays only a minor role which remains constant, neither supporting nor contributing to the disparities. Although we do not have complete data upon which a judicial "community-effect" can be shown to be a basis for disparities, there are data available which demonstrate the supporting role of at least one member, namely the probation officer.

If we assume that probation officers are "constant" and that judges are "variable," we would expect to find significant differences in the relationship between officer recommendations and

court dispositions as we move toward extremes in the use of probation or imprisonment. We would not, in the federal system,
for example, expect to find the more than 94 percent agreement
between recommendations and dispositions spread uniformly
throughout the system, for some courts use probation frequently,
others infrequently. In Fiscal Year 1965, individual federal
courts had a range of probation usage in excess of 50 percent,
with one court using probation for 23.8 percent of its cases, another for 75.7 percent of its cases. The percentage of defendants
on probation in Fiscal Year 1965 by the ten judicial circuits is
shown in Table 35–9.

Table 35–9

Percentage Use of Probation in Ten Federal Judicial Circuits	
First Circuit	53.0%
Second Circuit	45.2%
Third Circuit	63.8%
Fourth Circuit	60.8%
Fifth Circuit	44.8%
Sixth Circuit	44.3%
Seventh Circuit	44.4%
Eighth Circuit	49.9%
Ninth Circuit	49.0%
Tenth Circuit	43.7%
Overall	49.0%

Source: Administrative Office of the United States Courts. *Persons
Under the Supervision of the Federal Probation System, Fiscal Year
1965*, pp. 103–105.

[A9401]

Thus, on a circuit-wide basis, there is a high of 63.8 percent
in the usage of probation ranging to a low of 43.7 percent, an
overall spread of 20 percent, and as noted above, the variation is
even more marked among individual courts. Six of the eighty-
eight district courts used probation in excess of 70 percent for
their defendants; twelve courts used probation for less than 40
percent of their defendants.

Despite the variation among courts, individually or circuit
wide, the relationship between probation officer recommendations and court dispositions is generally quite constant, whether
there is high, moderate, or low usage of probation. This may
be seen more precisely in Table 35–10 which provides data for
Fiscal Year 1964 on sixteen selected federal courts: the five with
the highest usage of probation, the five with the lowest use of

probation, and the six courts which were within one percent of the national average for use of probation.

It will be seen, for example, that in District *A* probation was recommended for approximately three of each four defendants (147–55); in District *H*, the recommendations are about equal (152–149), while in District *N*, probation is recommended for about one defendant in three (148–310). However, the "agreement" rate between probation recommendations and dispositions in District *A* is 97.3 percent, in District *H*, 95.4 percent, and in District *N*, 93.7 percent.

These data indicate clearly that the recommendation-disposition relationship does not vary greatly from court to court, and that disparities in sentencing are supported, at least in terms of recommendations, by the probation officer member of the judicial "influence group." To be sure, there may be differences in the Districts which justify high or low use of probation, but thus far these have not been demonstrated. These data raise some interesting and important questions regarding the utility of sentencing institutes for judges, by themselves, as the solution to disparities, and suggest that probation officers, and perhaps prosecuting and defense attorneys, be included in such institutes.

The data in Table 35–10 have indicated that there is considerable variation in officer recommendations for or against proba-

TABLE 35–10

Use of Probation and Recommendations for and against Probation by Selected United States District Courts Fiscal Year 1964

	Percentage Use of Probation	Recommended for Probation			Recommended against Probation			Recommendations Given by Probation Officers: Percent of Total Cases
		Number of Defendants	Number Granted Probation	Percentage Granted Probation	Number of Defendants	Number Granted Probation	Percentage Granted Probation	
A	78.3	147	143	97.3	55	20	36.4	73.2
B	71.4	144	137	95.1	90	31	34.4	88.0
C	70.7	27	26	96.3	7	0	–	82.9
D	70.4	20	19	95.0	11	2	18.2	43.7
E	70.2	125	125	100.0	28	1	3.6	77.3
F	50.8	106	100	94.3	112	17	15.2	89.3
G	50.0	16	16	100.0	17	1	5.9	82.5
H	50.0	152	145	95.4	149	19	12.8	80.9
I	50.0	14	13	92.9	9	0	–	60.5
J	49.7	12	12	100.0	36	6	16.7	15.4
K	49.6	29	28	96.6	36	0	–	47.4
L	36.8	28	28	100.0	19	0	–	13.6
M	36.5	61	61	100.0	117	14	12.0	73.0
N	35.6	158	148	93.7	310	21	6.8	87.8
O	28.5	92	82	89.1	74	25	33.8	35.1
P	26.3	44	38	86.4	174	24	13.8	90.8
Total for All District Courts	50.2	6,868	6,463	94.1	7,691	1,518	19.7	63.1

Source: Data furnished by the Administrative Office of the United States Courts.   [A9412]

tion in different Districts, but that rate of agreement between recommendations and dispositions is relatively constant between Districts. Accordingly, we would expect to find a common frame of mind, or "influence group set," among officers in a single District which leads to the agreement in that District, regardless of the frequency of probation or imprisonment dispositions. Thus, where probation is used frequently, we would expect the officers in that court to be sympathetic to such usage and we would anticipate that little variation would exist among officers. If this is the case, we would not expect to find much significant variation among probation officers in a single District. We would not expect to find large differences among colleagues appointed by the same court, operating in a similar fashion as regards court and office policies and directives, appointed under uniform standards, paid identical salaries, and theoretically sharing similar views of the correctional process.

Let us return to our data on the 1,232 recommendations made by the probation officers in the Northern District of California as shown in Table 35-5. By restricting ourselves to a probation-imprisonment dichotomy, we observe that probation was recommended 64.3 percent of the time (601 of 935 cases) and that imprisonment was recommended 35.7 percent (334 of 935 cases). The recommendations of 19 probation officers in Northern California for probation or imprisonment are presented in Table 35-11. (Officers who made less than 15 recommendations are excluded.)

The percentage of recommendations for probation is almost 50 percent—from a low of 40.0 to a high of 88.9 percent. Three officers recommended probation for less than 50 percent of their cases; three officers between 50 and 60 percent, six between 60 and 70 percent, five between 70 and 80 percent, and two in excess of 80 percent.

While this individual variation may be attributed, in part, to the geographic basis for assignment of cases or to other administrative reasons it is statistically significant and suggests that probation officers, even in the same District, do not view the correctional process from identical perspectives.

What accounts for this variation among officers? In part, administrative and geographic consideratons may be an explanation. There may be differences in probation-suitability among persons from metropolitan areas, (e. g., San Francisco-Oakland)

Table 35–11

Individual Probation Officer Recommendations
for Probation and Imprisonment
Northern District of California
September 1964 to February 1967

Probation Officer	Number of Recommendations	Number of Probation Recommendations	Number of Prison Recommendations	Percentage of Probation Recommendations
1	55	40	15	72.7
2	39	25	14	64.1
3	46	21	25	45.7
4	57	35	22	61.4
5	16	14	2	87.5
6	20	13	7	65.0
7	55	22	33	40.0
8	38	22	16	57.9
9	22	17	5	77.3
10	58	46	12	79.3
11	59	32	27	54.2
12	57	35	22	61.4
13	54	42	12	77.8
14	36	17	19	47.2
15	56	34	22	60.7
16	46	31	15	67.4
17	60	43	17	71.7
18	18	16	2	88.9
19	42	24	18	57.1

Source: Unpublished *San Francisco Project* data.   [A8991]

and less developed or rural areas such as the northern coast or central valleys of California. But it is equally possible that these variations are due to personal characteristics, including academic training, age, and vocational background. Some general but not conclusive observations can be made based on the probation officers in northern California. For example, probation officers with graduate training or graduate degrees in social work or social welfare recommended probation for 56.3 percent of their cases; officers with graduate work or graduate degrees in criminology in 69.6 percent of their cases, and officers with graduate work or graduate degrees in sociology in 67.7 percent of their cases. Officers with the longest service recommended probation for 54.0 percent of their cases, while the "newer" officers recommended probation for 68.4 percent. Three hypotheses are suggested by these and other data:

1) Some of the variation in probation officer recommendations is a product of the individual background of the officer and includes vocational experience and academic training.

2) The differences of variations tend to diminish with the period of employment; that is, officers with different backgrounds are far more dissimilar upon entering the probation service than after exposure to the agency.

3) With an increase in the period of service (i. e., more experience) there is a decrease in recommendations for probation. This may represent a more "realistic" or less "optimistic" view of the benefits of probation treatment for a greater number of offenders than was the view held by the officer earlier in his professional career.

"Second-Guessing" or "Following"

There is, in our search for variation, the possibility that the probation officer attempts to second-guess the court by making recommendations which are anticipated to be those desired by the court. If this were the case, one measure of this factor would be that different judges receive different rates or percentages of probation or imprisonment recommendations. Thus, properly "second-guessing" a punitive judge would require a larger proportion of imprisonment recommendations; second-guessing a "lenient" judge would require more probation recommendations. Returning to the data on the 1,232 cases in the Northern District of California, and again restricting ourselves to a probation-imprisonment dichotomy, we find some, but not significant variation in the percentage of probation recommendations to individual judges. These data are in Table 35–12. Since none of these judges has a reputation of being punitive or lenient, we can only surmise that in this District there is little if any second-guessing.

A review of Table 35–12 will also indicate that individual judges are equally receptive to recommendations for probation; the relationship between recommendations for probation and such dispositions being 97.2 percent overall and constant between judges.

It appears that judges "follow" probation officer recommendations; there is no other ready explanation of the individual officer variation in probation recommendations and the high over-

TABLE 35–12

Recommendations for and against Probation According to
United States District Court Judges
Northern District of California
September 1964 to February 1967

Judge	Number of Cases Disposed of in Court	Number of Recommendations for Probation	Number of Recommendations against Probation	Percentage of Cases Recommended for Probation	Number of Cases Granted Probation	Number of Cases Denied Probation	Percentage Agreement Between Probation Recommendations and Dispositions
Total	831	527	304	63.4	512	278	97.2
1	64	40	24	62.5	38	23	95.0
2	58	30	28	51.7	29	23	96.7
3	160	103	57	64.4	99	53	96.1
4	156	114	42	73.1	111	38	97.4
5	88	57	31	64.8	57	30	100.0
6	100	58	42	58.0	56	36	96.6
7	60	39	21	65.0	38	18	97.4
8	73	46	27	63.0	44	26	95.7
9	72	40	32	55.6	40	31	100.0

Source: Unpublished *San Francisco Project* data.   [A9416]

all relationship between recommendations and dispositions. This also tends to confirm the observation that probation officers contribute to the problems of disparities in sentencing. From these data, all four previously suggested explanations of the close agreement between recommendation and disposition (probation officers and judges giving approximately equal weight to similar factors, the "following" of recommendations by the court, the presence of "obvious" probation or imprisonment cases, and some "second-guessing") appear appropriate.

Summary

In this chapter, some of the dangers of continued reliance on tradition and the development of a body of correctional folklore have been pointed out. It has been determined that the relationship between recommendations for and dispositions of probation is high and that the relationship diminishes when viewed from the recommendations against and the subsequent grant of probation perspective. Limited data on the outcome of supervision by recommendation and by percentage use of probation are provided. We have inquired into the reasons for the close agreement between recommendation and disposition and suggest that four factors, in varying degrees, account for it. We have observed that the overall relationship between recommendation and disposition does not vary from District Court to District Court, but rather remains relatively constant, regardless of the percentage use of probation. We suggest that disparities in sentencing are supported by the probation officer and it appears that these differences, in part, are a reflection of the officer's individual academic training and experience. Length of service brings about a trend toward conformity with colleagues and the development of a more conservative perspective toward the use of probation.

There are other segments of the presentence report process to which questions should be addressed. These include operational and administrative considerations, the decision-making processes of probation officers, and an examination of the nature and impact of the social system of correctional agencies. Within the operational considerations would be inquiries as to the role of subprofessionals in presentence investigations, the rearrangement of the standard presentence format to provide a developmental sketch instead of the current segmented report, a determination as to the appropriateness of "confidential" presentence reports, the collection of presentence data in a fashion which allows computer analysis, and the separation of the investigation and supervision functions. Although some examination has been made of the decision-making process,[14] we need additional information about the sequence of data collection, the relative importance of certain kinds of data, and the eventual use of the data for decision-making within the correctional system. We find almost a complete void in knowledge on the social systems of correctional agencies, although available data indicate that the system itself has a profound influence on job behavior, beliefs, values, and the definition and achievement of correctional goals. Indeed, we know more about the social systems of the offenders with whom we deal than about the systems of the agencies which provide correctional services.

There are vast gaps in our knowledge about the entire correctional process, but these gaps may be closed by imaginative, innovative, and creative research and operational designs and programs. This requires a willingness to subject our current traditional, correctional models to scrutiny and a willingness to set aside those features, cherished though they may be, which are inefficient and ineffective.

14. Id.

DISCLOSURE OF THE PRESENTENCE INVESTIGATION REPORT*

FOR THE PAST 20 years there has been considerable debate over the issue of disclosure of the presentence investigation report to the defendant and his attorney. A majority of the judiciary and their probation staffs have argued strongly against disclosure or even partial disclosure of the report.

The issue of disclosure has been the subject of recommendations from the Advisory Committee on the Federal Rules of Criminal Procedure in 1944, 1962, 1964, 1966, and 1970.

The present Rule 32(c)(2) authorizes the court to release presentence information.

> The court before imposing sentence may disclose to the defendant or his counsel all or part of the material contained in the report of the presentence investigation and afford an opportunity to the defendant or his counsel to comment thereon. Any material disclosed to the defendant or his counsel shall also be disclosed to the attorney for the government.[1]

The preliminary draft of proposed amendments (January 1970) to the Federal Rules of Criminal Procedure for United States District Courts enlarges the rule of disclosure. (Rule 32.2(c)(1).)

> Before imposing sentence, the court shall permit the defendant and his counsel, if he is so represented, to read the report of the presentence investigation unless in the opinion of the court the report contains information which if disclosed would be harmful to the defendant or other persons, and the court shall afford the defendant or his counsel an opportunity to comment thereon.

The proposed amendments also provide a safeguard for handling such information the court believes may be harmful to the defendant or others. (Rule 32.2(c)(2).)

---

* William G. Zastrow, *Federal Probation*, December, 1971. Reprinted with permission.

1. Rule 32(c)(2), Federal Rules of Criminal Procedure.

If the court is of the view that there is information
in the presentence report, disclosure of which would
be harmful to the defendant or other persons, the court
in lieu of making the report or part thereof available
shall state orally or in writing a summary of the background information contained therein to be relied on in
determining sentence, and shall give the defendant or
his counsel an opportunity to comment thereon. The
statement may be made to the parties in camera.

The report of studies and recommendations made by the Bureau of Prisons and the Youth Corrections Division of the U. S.
Board of Parole pursuant to 18 U.S.C. 4208(b), 5010(e), or 5034
would be considered a presentence investigation within the meaning of the rule.

In recent years three organizations have recommended that
the presentence report be disclosed to the defense—the American
Bar Association in its *Standards Relating to Sentencing Alternatives and Procedures,* the American Law Institute in its *Model
Penal Code,* and the National Council on Crime and Delinquency
in its *Model Sentencing Act.*

From my contacts with federal and state probation officers,
it is obvious that the practice of disclosing the presentence report varies greatly from district to district and from state to
state. In some federal districts the presentence is completely
confidential. In other districts, one of the judges may reveal the
presentence report while his fellow judges in the same district
maintain that it is a confidential document.

In some districts a copy of the statement of the offense, the
defendant's version of the offense, and the prior record are
routinely made available to the defendant and his attorney.
Some courts direct that the full presentence be reviewed by the
defendant and his attorney.

Some judges will argue that due to their extensive law training
and years on the bench presiding at trials, they are able to carefully evaluate information in the presentence report and separate
fact from hearsay. Unless the report is carefully written and
hearsay is so labeled, it may be difficult to perform the necessary winnowing.

Arguments Against Disclosure

A number of arguments have been advanced against the release of the presentence report to the defendant and his attorney. Some of them are the following:

1.   Confidential sources will "dry up." This would deprive the court of information both useful and necessary in the sentencing process.

2.   The sentencing process would be delayed, sentence hearings would be protracted, the probation officer would be required to testify at such hearings and reveal his sources of information.

3.   Revealing information to the defendant would damage the working relationship between the defendant and the probation officer and might, in certain instances, hurt him emotionally.

4.   Informants might be subject to retribution at the hands of the defendant or the disclosed information might prove embarrassing to both the defendant and the informant.

5.   Disclosure would result in fewer probation grants.

Arguments for Disclosure

Proponents for disclosure base their arguments on fairness to the defendant.

> Although due process probably does not require disclosure of the presentence report (Williams vs. Oklahoma, 358 U.S. 576), if the fact basis of the report is incorrect, re-sentencing may be required by the Fifth Amendment (Townsend vs. Burke, 334 U.S. 736 and Baker vs. U. S., 388 Fed. 2nd 931). If disclosure is not permitted, such inaccuracies are uncovered only if a judge has articulated his reasons for imposing a particular sentence.[2]

Following are some of the arguments for disclosure:

1.   Proponents for revealing the presentence report maintain that disclosure helps the defendant better understand the reason for the court's disposition of his case and may well be the first step in his rehabilitation.

2. *Georgetown Law Journal*, Vol. 58, No. 3, February 1970.

Killinger & Cromwell—Corr. in Comm. CrJS—24

2. At the trial level, the defendant and his attorney have available to them the evidence which will be presented and consequently an overview of the entire trial process. But nondisclosure of the presentence report excludes the defendant from the sentencing process.

3. The defendant is given an opportunity to refute damaging information which may be based solely on hearsay. Or he may clarify statements that are inaccurate or are exaggerated. On this point Justice Williams O. Douglas has made a succinct statement in support of disclosure of the presentence report.

> The imposition of sentence is of critical importance to a man convicted of crime. Trial judges need presentence reports so they may have at their disposal the fullest possible information. . . . But while the formal rules of evidence do not apply to restrict the factors which the sentencing judge may consider, fairness would, in my opinion, require that the defendant be advised of the facts—perhaps very damaging to him— on which the judge intends to rely. The presentence report may be inaccurate, a flaw which may be of constitutional dimension. . . . It may exaggerate the gravity of the defendant's prior offenses. The investigator may have made an incomplete investigation. . . . There may be countervailing factors not disclosed by the probation report. In many areas we can rely on the sound exercise of discretion by the trial judge; but how can a judge know whether or not the presentence report calls for a reply by the defendant? Its faults may not appear on the face of the document. . . . Whatever should be the rule for the federal courts, it ought not to be one which permits a judge to impose sentence on the basis of which the defendant may be unaware and to which he has not been afforded an opportunity to reply.[3]

Practice of Disclosure in the Eastern District of Wisconsin

In the Eastern District of Wisconsin the presentence report has been routinely available to the defense counsel for approximately 5 years. Needless to say, when we commenced disclosure

---

3. Opinion of Mr. Justice Douglas, 39 F.R.D. 276, 278 (1966), dissenting from promulgation of changes in F.R.Crim.P. 32(c)(2).

of the presentence report on direction of the court, we approached our task of report writing with some misgivings. We consequently developed some "mechanics" which we believed would be helpful in the preparation of our reports. These "mechanics" have led to a more thorough, accurate, and objective report.

In our district, immediately after the defendant has entered a plea of guilty or has been found guilty, he is directed to contact our office, accompanied by his attorney. In the presence of his attorney, the defendant is informed of the purpose of the presentence investigation, the areas covered by the report, and the material which we believe is essential. He is also told that the presentence report will be available to his attorney for review and comment.

In the course of the investigation attorneys have volunteered to secure medical and psychiatric data or other documented information which they believe will be helpful in the preparation of our report. The defendant, in the presence of his attorney, is asked to sign releases for confidential information such as school records, medical history, and employment.

Family members interviewed are informed that information they present to us will be available to the defense attorney.

Where we obtain information which is contrary to that furnished by the defendant, he is re-interviewed. If the defendant maintains that his initial statement is correct, both versions are placed in the presentence report.

Arrest records are reviewed with him to determine whether he attests to their accuracy. If any arrest is challenged, the arresting agency is contacted to determine whether there is an error. Arrests which did not result in a conviction are eliminated from the presentence report.

When the report is completed, the defense attorney is invited to our office at his convenience to read the report, take such notes as he desires, and to discuss the report with the probation officer who conducted the investigation or, if he is not present, with the chief probation officer. He is also invited to challenge such portions of the report he believes may be inaccurate. In 5 years, only three minor challenges have resulted which the court quickly resolved at the time of sentence.

It is the opinion of the staff that through disclosure of the presentence report, we have received considerably more help from the defense attorney in the presentence investigation and that the defendant has a better understanding of the disposition ultimately arrived at by the court.

After reviewing the presentence report, the defense attorney often is aware of certain facets of his client's life about which he had no previous knowledge. In some instances the attorney has assisted his client in setting up a probation plan and at the time of sentencing has made a recommendation to the court based on this plan.

Where the defense attorney is aware that there is a probability of commitment, he often reviews with the probation officer the type of dispositions available to the court and in his statement of mitigation often has proposed a disposition which he believes best meets the needs of his client.

In the Eastern District of Wisconsin the court has asked for a specific recommendation in each case. We have eliminated from the presentence report our recommendation to the court. The reason for this is obvious. Should we recommend a commitment and the court disagrees and places the defendant on probation, our relationship with the client at best would be off to a poor start.

The argument that revealing the presentence investigation would probably lead to less probation grants has not been proved. During calendar year 1970, dispositions in our district resulted in approximately 70 percent probation grants compared to 30 percent commitments.

In Conclusion

Release of the presentence report to the defense attorney has not resulted in the problems we at first anticipated.

Sources of information have not dried up.

In many instances we have observed a more helpful and cooperative attitude on the part of the defendant and his counsel.

There is less "sparring" between the client and officer at the outset of probation. The probationer is aware that we have knowledge of many of the facets of his life—his problems, his strengths, his weaknesses, his potential.

The probation officer becomes a better and more objective investigator, carefully screening fact from hearsay.

Presentence summaries are less judgmental and more analytical.

The presentence investigation is a basic working document in the judicial and correctional process. Fairness to the defendant should require its release to the defendant and his defense attorney.

> Fundamental fairness to the defendant requires that the substance of all derogatory information which adversely affects his interests and which has not otherwise been disclosed in open court should be called to the attention of the defendant, his attorney, and others who are acting on his behalf.—American Bar Association *Standards Relating to Sentencing Alternatives and Procedures.*

PRESENTENCE INVESTIGATION REPORT DISCLOSURE IN ALBERTA*

At a time when society is closely scrutinizing the functioning of our judicial system, and when people are coming to the realization that probation is a valuable tool in the correctional cycle, it is apparent that the question of whether to divulge the information of the presentence investigation report to the defendant or to limit this disclosure needs to be further evaluated. As noted by Zastrow, considerable discussion has resulted over this question, and over the noted disparity of courts in utilizing the power of disclosure in different parts of the United States.[1] It might therefore be worthwhile to look at probation in Alberta and how the presentence investigation report is handled by our courts.

In 1968–1969 the sections of the Criminal Code of Canada dealing with probation were amended. The Code now requires that any information concerning the subject and made available to the courts in the presentence investigation report also be made available to the defense and crown counsels. Disclosure of in-

---

* Norm Larkins, *Federal Probation,* December, 1972. Reprinted with permission.

1. William G. Zastrow, "Disclosure of the Presentence Investigation Report," Federal Probation, December 1971, pp. 20–22.

formation has led probation officers to develop techniques whereby the information obtained by them and presented in the report is more objective and accurate (with less reliance on hearsay information), which requires a thorough analysis of events surrounding the criminal charges. A somewhat standardized procedure has been adopted in carrying out such an investigation.

In Alberta, immediately after the defendant has entered a plea of guilty or has been found guilty by trial, the presiding judge may, upon his own initiative or as a result of a submission from the defense counsel, request that a presentence report be prepared. At the time of such a request, the court worker of the Adult Probation Branch immediately contacts the individual and requests that he arrange an interview with our office at his earliest convenience. Information is obtained so that the probation officer can contact the offender should he fail to report directly to the office.

At the time of the initial interview the purpose of the presentence investigation report is explained, along with the information it will cover and the material which we believe is essential, such as family history and employment background. Before the interview is conducted, it is explained that a copy of the report will be made available to the offender or his legal counsel prior to sentencing. It is the duty of the offender to bring to the judge's attention any mistakes or omissions which he feels would be important in influencing the sentencing. After this has been explained the major interview is then conducted.

The interview proper proceeds with the purpose of obtaining a social history of the individual. Information as to the offender's education, employment history, and family situation is obtained, as well as a recapitulation of the offense through the offender's eyes.

Following this, it is the responsibility of the probation officer to go into the community to obtain information about the offender, and to corroborate the information obtained in the interview. As much information on the individual is obtained from as many sources as is feasible without jeopardizing the offender in any way. Should the offender request that certain persons not be contacted, his wishes are usually met unless it is felt that elimination of this information would seriously distort the report.

It should be noted that the probation officer is to remain objective in his searching out of information. As an officer of the court he is neither to defend the defendant, nor is he to prosecute him. It is the duty of the probation officer to be impartial. The purpose of the report is not to prove the innocence or guilt of the defendant, but to present information about him so that the courts have a better basis on which to pass a just sentence. From this information it is hoped some insight into the cause of the difficulty can be determined.

When all the information has been accumulated and compiled, it is the duty of the probation officer to evaluate the information and to make a recommendation to the court. The Report is then given to the court worker who, on the day of sentencing, ensures that the offender is given a copy of the report and made aware that any mistakes or omissions are to be brought out before sentencing. If the offender has counsel, the report is made available to him rather than the offender. At the discretion of the judge, the probation officer may be required to defend or substantiate any or all information he has presented in the report, or may be requested to elaborate on some aspect or circumstance mentioned in the report. However, this is the exception rather than the rule. Thus, it is usually only in Supreme Court that the probation officer is required to be in attendance at the time of sentencing.

Arguments Against Disclosure Evaluated

Zastrow has listed five common arguments which have been used against the release of the presentence report to the defendant and his lawyer. Analysis of these as they apply to the situation in Edmonton, Alberta, might give some indication as to their validity.

(1) "Confidential sources will 'dry up.' This would deprive the court of information both useful and necessary in the sentencing process."

Unfortunately this may be true if the probation officer does not maintain an attitude of cooperative assistance with those with whom he deals. Good public relations prevents the buildup of any barriers to communication. Rather it can lead to closer cooperation between the probation officer and the source. Schools are beginning to recognize the value of a probation officer's being assigned to each separate high school both as an aid to school counselors and also as a crime prevention program. As a result the schools as a confidential source of information have not "dried up" but rather have become even more free with information despite the legislative changes of 1968–1969 which effected the disclosure of the presentence investigation report.

(2) "The sentencing process would be delayed, sentence hearings would be protracted, the probation officer would be required to testify at such hearings and reveal his sources of information."

The first two points should not be considerations, since the desire to pass a just sentence should outweigh the need for speed. In most instances, however, the presentence report disclosure does not delay sentencing, since all concerned read the written report prior to the court session. Occasionally sentencing may be protracted because of errors or omissions in the report. It should also be noted that the probation officer seldom testifies at such hearings. Rather he prepares a written report which reveals the sources of his information and presents this at court. Occasionally further information may be requested but this is the exception rather than the rule, and the probation officer is not required to attend court unless it is the Supreme Court. Revealing of the sources of the information maintains credibility and objectivity on the part of the probation officer.

(3) "Revealing information to the defendant would damage the working relationship between the defendant and the probation officer and might, in certain instances, hurt him emotionally."

Contrary to expectations, revealing the information to the offender may develop a certain trust of the offender for the probation officer. He is able to evaluate how well the probation officer has investigated the offense and the offender. When it is apparent that the probation officer has some insight into the problems of the offender, the offender frequently is more willing to accept further counseling. Although his behavior may indicate immaturity, it would appear that the offender is usually a reasonable and mature individual in assessing his situation and frequently is more critical of himself and would make harsher recommendations than the probation officer. As a result, the majority are satisfied with the information presented in the presentence investigation report, and thus the report acts as the basis on which to base probation supervision and counseling.

Occasionally offenders become upset because of more severe sentences than they anticipated. Naturally the blame is placed on the presentence report, since it probably contained negative information. However it seems that it is the exception rather than the rule that this attitude remains for any considerable length of time, although there are no statistics available to substantiate this point.

(4) "Informants might be subject to retribution, at the hands of the defendant or the disclosed information might prove embarrassing to both the defendant and the informant."

If one remembers that the purpose of the presentence report is not to defend or acquit but rather to be objective, then one should realize that both the good and the bad will be referenced, and hopefully the offender will recognize the objectivity of the report. When information is factual, whether positive or negative, the offender usually is much more accepting of it. Thus, the threat of retribution is extremely remote, and probably would be found only with the most hardened criminal, an individual who is less likely to obtain a presentence investigation report and not likely to receive probation. Retribution as a fact does not exist at this point in time.

That information would be embarrassing to the defendant and the informant is difficult to understand. Should the information be embarrassing to the informant, it is doubtful that he would bring it to the probation officer's attention. That the information would be embarrassing to the defendant should be of little consideration if the information is important in the dispensing of justice.

(5) "Disclosure would result in fewer probation grants."

This definitely is not the case in Edmonton, Alberta. Since the passage of the amendment requiring disclosure the number of persons on probation has increased between 1969 and 1971 by 218 percent while the crime rate has increased by approximately 5 percent. With disclosure, the probationer must be more objective and thus the report is more valuable as a tool in reaching a just sentence. This is recognized not only by the probation service, but also by the courts requesting such reports.

Further to this, it should be noted that the increase in requests for such reports has been dramatic while the change in percentage of commitments where probation was not granted after a presentence report has been approximately 13 percent.

Arguments for Disclosure Evaluated

Since it would appear that arguments against disclosure are tenuous, it might be worthwhile to also evaluate the arguments for disclosure as noted by Zastrow.

(1) "Proponents for revealing the Pre-Sentence Report maintain that disclosure helps the defendant better understand the reasons for the Court's disposition of his case and may well be the first step in his rehabilitation."

It is generally accepted that understanding of the cause is the necessary first step in any treatment. If through the presentence report the subject is made aware of the reasons for his behavior then we have the basis for changing this behavior. As mentioned before, the objectivity of the probation officer will lead the defendant to greater acceptance and trust and respect in the probation officer, all of which are essential for the establishment and growth of an effective counseling environment.

Further to this, in a presentence report the offender can frequently see that someone really understands him, and really accepts him for what he is. This can be the most remarkable effect for it immediately establishes a strong link between the offender and the probation officer.

(2) "At the trial level, the defendant and his attorney have available to them the evidence which will be presented and consequently an overview of the entire trial process. But nondisclosure of the presentence report excludes the defendant from the sentencing process."

This argument is little more than a superficial glossing over of the entire process. Why this argument would support disclosure is difficult to elaborate upon since it is a statement of fact rather than effect. I would suggest that nondisclosure does not exclude the defendant from the sentencing process, but I would suggest that the defendant will have greater reason to believe he has received an opportunity to challenge any discrepancies which may exist and thus see the reasons for the sentence imposed.

(3) "The defendant is given an opportunity to refute damaging information which may be based solely on hearsay. Or he may clarify statements that are inaccurate or are exaggerated."

This is perhaps the most obvious argument for disclosure. We presume that a person is innocent until proven guilty. If we find a person guilty by trial then pass sentence upon the offender after utilizing presentence investigation report information which the offender has not seen and thus cannot defend himself against, we then are going against this basic premise of our legal system. Where there is no disclosure the information contained in the report may be distorted or inaccurate such that justice may not prevail. The basic ideas which evolve from the point are apparent.

A less apparent aspect of this is that the individual is placed in a position to defend himself, and before there can be a defense there must be an evaluation. If the offender is unable to defend himself then he must realize the report is an objective evaluation of himself, and self-realization is the beginning of the rehabilitative process.

A Further Point of Contention

Zastrow states that they have eliminated the specific recommendation as to sentencing from their presentence reports for a reason that is obvious to them. He states, "Should we recommend a commitment and the court disagrees and places the defendant on probation, our relationship with the client at best would be off to a poor start." I doubt this would be the case in the majority of instances in which this occurred.

The occurrence of such disparity between the recommendation and adjudication in Edmonton would appear small, although no statistics are available to support this position. The judges appear to follow the presentence report recommendations with consistency, although recommendations are general and adjudications are specific. At all times the judge gives close consideration to the information and recommendation which are included in the report. Occasionally, however, the judge does not follow the recommendation, and during his adjudication will point out his reasons for his sentencing.

In cases where one has recommended incarceration and probation has been granted, one might anticipate a certain barrier to effective counseling, but this generally is not the case. The offender usually is able to evaluate the report more objectively than one might anticipate, and frequently is able, not only to foster the probation relationship, but also to shed further light on his own problems and perhaps reflect on ways and means of rehabilitating himself.

In the exceptional instance the offender is greatly relieved to have been placed on probation and is willing to cooperate in any way possible with the probation officer.

In Conclusion

The release of the presentence report to the Crown and to the defendant has not resulted in the problem which one might have anticipated. Rather, it has led the probation service to develop skills which more objectively analyze the offense and the offender. With greater objectivity has come greater reliance by the courts on the reports, with a resultant increase in reports requested and the number of persons granted probation. The analytical rather than judgmental aspect of the reports makes them not only of greater value to the courts, but also more acceptable to the offender, for in them he may see that perhaps someone understands or at least attempts to understand his problems. This latter frequently results in a closer relationship between the offender and the probation officer. Further, disclosure is a requirement for fairness to the defendant. Thus, the presentence investigation report is an integral part of the correctional system and should be made available to the defendant or his counsel.

> What, then, is the best procedure to follow in making presentence disclosure to individuals and institutions other than the court? While a good case can be made for maintaining strict confidentiality, there is no doubt that the trend toward liberalization of disclosure will continue. The defense counsel should have a general idea of the contents of the presentence report. This information can probably be best given in conference with the probation officer prior to sentencing. However, in order that community sources of information will not be jeopardized, the attorney should *not* have access to the names of individuals interviewed by the probation officer. In effect, the defense attorney should probably have access to all of the objective material contained in the report.—JOHN R. MANSON

STANDARDS WITH COMMENTARY: DISCLOSURE OF THE PRE–SENTENCE REPORT

THE AMERICAN BAR ASSOCIATION*

4.3 Presentence report: disclosure; general principles.

The presentence report should not be a public record. It should be available only to the following persons or agencies under the conditions stated:

> (i) The report should be available to the sentencing court for the purpose of assisting it in determining the sentence. The report should also be available to all judges who are to participate in a sentencing council discussion of the defendant (section 7.1);

> (ii) The report should be available to persons or agencies having a legitimate professional interest in the information likely to be contained therein. Examples of such persons or agencies would be a physician or psychiatrist appointed to assist the court in sentencing, an examining facility, a correctional institution, or a probation or parole department;

> (iii) The report should be available to reviewing courts where relevant to an issue on which an appeal has been taken;

> (iv) The report should be available to the parties under the conditions stated in section 4.4.

Commentary

a. Confidentiality

In several states, the presentence report is in effect a public record. In California, for example, the full report "must be made available to the Court and the prosecuting and defense attorneys at least two days prior to the time fixed by the court for the hearing and determination of such report and must be filed with

* *Sentencing Alternatives & Procedures*, Approved Draft, 1968. Reprinted with permission of the American Bar Association.

the clerk of the court as a record in the case at the time of said hearing." Cal.Penal Code § 1203 (1966 Supp.). And in Virginia,

> the probation officer shall present his report in open court in the presence of the accused who shall be advised of the contents of the same and be given the right to cross-examine the investigating officer as to any matter contained therein and to present any additional facts bearing upon the matter which he may desire to present. The report of the investigating officer shall be filed as a part of the record in the case.

Va.Code Ann. § 53–278.1 (1967).

On the other hand, in most states the report is confidential, at best available only on a limited basis. For example, the provision in Ohio is that the report "shall be confidential and need not be furnished to the defendant or his counsel or the prosecuting attorney unless the court, in its discretion, so orders." Ohio Rev.Code Ann. § 2951.03 (1965 Supp.). Compare N.C.Gen.Stat. § 15–207 (1965); N.J.Crim.Prac.Rules, Superior and County Courts, Rule 3:7–10(b) (1967); Fed.R.Crim.P. 32(c) (2).

This section begins with the assertion that the presentence report should not be a public record. No affirmative purpose is seen for making the document public, whereas there are discernible detriments. The defendant, for example, is not served by a public disclosure of the intimate—and possibly irrelevant or unverified—details of his background. Those who are concerned that sources of information might be affected by disclosure might also be heard to object. But whereas competing considerations may overcome such an argument in other contexts, no such reasons are observable here.

The conclusion is thus expressed that the report should not be spread upon the record, and that it should only be available as circumstances warrant. What those circumstances are likely to be is developed in subsections (i) through (iv).

b. Sentencing court

The basic purpose of the report is to assist the court in the sentencing decision, and it must of course be available to that end. By the same token, the report should not be used by the court for other purposes, particularly on such questions as guilt in the case before it or in other cases against the same defendant. It is also provided in subsection (i) that the report should be available to the sentencing council described in section 7.1, infra.

c. Professional agencies

It is quite common for presentence report statutes to provide that in the event of the defendant's commitment the report should be transmitted to the corrections authorities. See, e. g., Ala.Code tit. 42, § 21 (1959); Cal.Penal Code § 1203 (1966 Supp.); Conn.Gen.Stat.Ann. § 54–109 (1960); Ind.Stats.Ann. § 9–2252 (1966 Supp.); Mich.Stat.Ann. § 28.1144 (1954); Minn. Stat.Ann. § 609.115(5) (1964); Mont.Rev.Code Ann. § 94–7831 (1967 Supp.); N.J.Crim.Prac.Rules, Superior and County Courts, Rule 3:7–10(b) (1967); N.M.Stat.Ann. § 41–17–23 (1964); N.Y. Code Crim.Proc. § 931(1) (1966 Supp.); Ohio Rev.Code Ann. § 2951.03 (1965 Supp.). See also NCCD, Standard Probation and Parole Act § 11 (1964); Model Sentencing Act § 4, Appendix C, infra; Model Penal Code § 7.07(7), Appendix B, infra. Although the statutes are normally silent on the point, it is also common for the report to be available to the officer who is to supervise the defendant's probation, whether or not the officer has himself prepared the report. The reasons for such provisions are sound: both the corrections authorities and the probation officer can better perform their tasks with the information contained in a good presentence report.

There are likewise good reasons for making the report available to other persons and agencies with a legitimate professional interest in the information it is likely to contain. A diagnostic facility, such as is contemplated by section 4.6, infra, will be provided with a good start on its inquiry if it can begin with a carefully prepared presentence report. There would likewise seem no reason why a private treatment institution should not have access to the report if its interest is legitimate. See generally Sharp, *The Confidential Nature of Presentence Reports,* 5 Catholic U.L.Rev. 127, 129 (1955).

d. Reviewing courts

Disclosure of the report to appellate courts follows from the Advisory Committee's position on appellate review of sentences. See ABA Standards, Appellate Review of Sentences (Tent.Draft, April 1967). However, even if sentences are not to be reviewed, disclosure of the report to reviewing courts would be necessary in order to permit review of matters relating to sentencing procedure, such as the duty to obtain a complete and accurate report. Cf. State v. Laird, 85 N.J.Super. 170, 204 A.2d 220 (1964).

e. Parties

The question of disclosure of the presentence report to parties presents issues which are difficult of resolution and highly controversial. Because of the complexity of the problem, it is dealt with in the separate section which follows.

4.4 Presentence report: disclosure; parties.

(a) Fundamental fairness to the defendant requires that the substance of all derogatory information which adversely affects his interests and which has not otherwise been disclosed in open court should be called to the attention of the defendant, his attorney, and others who are acting on his behalf.

(b) This principle should be implemented by requiring that the sentencing court permit the defendant's attorney, or the defendant himself if he has no attorney, to inspect the report. The prosecution should also be shown the report if it is shown to the defense. In extraordinary cases, the court should be permitted to except from disclosure parts of the report which are not relevant to a proper sentence, diagnostic opinion which might seriously disrupt a program of rehabilitation, or sources of information which has been obtained on a promise of confidentiality. In all cases where parts of the report are not disclosed under such authority, the court should be required to state for the record the reasons for its action and to inform the defendant and his attorney that information has not been disclosed. The action of the court in excepting information from disclosure should be subject to appellate review.

(c) The resolution of any controversy as to the accuracy of the presentence report should be governed by the principles stated in sections 4.5(b), 5.3(d), 5.3(f), and 5.4(a).

Commentary

a. Background

The question of disclosure of the presentence report to parties has produced much heated debate in the literature. See, e. g., Lorensen, *The Disclosure to Defense of Presentence Reports in West Virginia,* 69 W.Va.L.Rev. 159 (1967); Guzman, *Defendant's Access to Presentence Reports in Federal Criminal Courts,* 52 Iowa L.Rev. 161 (1966); Roche, *The Position for Confidentiality of the Presentence Investigation Report,* 29 Albany L.Rev. 206 (1965); Higgins, *In Response to Roche,* 29 Albany L.Rev. 225 (1965); Higgins, *Confidentiality of Presentence Reports,* 28 Albany L.Rev. 12 (1964); Parsons, *The Presentence Investigative Report Must be Preserved as a Confidential Document,* Fed. Prob., March 1964, p. 3; Thomsen, *Confidentiality of the Presentence Report: A Middle Position,* Fed.Prob., March 1964, p. 8; *Symposium on Discovery in Federal Criminal Cases,* 33 F.R.D. 47, 122–28 (1963); Sharp, *The Confidential Nature of Presentence Reports,* 5 Catholic U.L.Rev. 127 (1955); Rubin, *What Privacy for Presentence Reports,* Fed.Prob., Dec. 1952, p. 8; Note, *Right of Criminal Offenders to Challenge Reports Used in Determining Sentence,* 49 Colum.L.Rev. 567 (1949); Hincks, *In Opposition to Rule 34(c)(2), Proposed Federal Rules of Criminal Procedure,* Fed.Prob., Oct.-Dec. 1944, p. 3.   Other articles are collected in Committee on Rules of Practice and Procedure, Second Preliminary Draft of Proposed Amendments to Rules of Criminal Procedure for the United States District Courts, p. 41 (March 1964) (Advisory Committee's note).   See also Proposed Amendments to Rules of Criminal Procedure for the United States District Courts, 39 F.R.D. 168, 193–94 (1966).

There is also a division among statutes on the point, although none has been found which flatly forbids disclosure to the defendant.   Most maintain a position of silence which is usually interpreted as placing disclosure within the discretion of the sentencing court.   This, for example, was the position of the Federal Rules of Criminal Procedure prior to the 1966 revision.*   There are a few statutes, however, which specifically require disclosure, or which in terms leave the issue to the court.   In addition to the statutes cited in comment *a* to section 4.3, supra, see Minn.

---

* The results of a survey conducted to determine how federal district judges exercised this discretion are set forth in Higgins, *Confidentiality of Presentence Reports,* 28 Albany L.Rev. 12, 39–44 (1964).

Stat.Ann. § 609.115(4)(1964): "Any report made pursuant to subdivision 1 of this section shall be open to inspection by the prosecuting attorney and the defendant's attorney prior to sentence. . . ."

Finally, it should be noted that there have been numerous proposals which have attempted to draw an intermediate line between complete disclosure and complete secrecy. The President's Crime Commission recommended, for example, that "in the absence of compelling reasons for nondisclosure of special information, the defendant and his counsel should be permitted to examine the entire presentence report." President's Comm'n, The Challenge of Crime 145. See also President's Comm'n, The Courts 20. Other proposals have often proceeded from the view that what the defendant needs is not the whole report, but merely the facts on which it is based. Sources of information, together with opinions of the probation officer, properly can remain a privileged communication between officer and judge. See, e. g., Higgins, *Confidentiality of Presentence Reports,* 28 Albany L.Rev. 12 (1964). The Model Penal Code, on the other hand, has varied slightly from this conclusion by suggesting that the Court should advise the defendant or his attorney "of the factual contents and conclusions" of any presentence or psychiatric reports. Again, "the sources of information need not . . . be disclosed." Model Penal Code § 7.07(5), Appendix B, infra. Still a fourth view was expressed by an amendment once proposed to the Federal Rules of Criminal Procedure. By this view, the disclosure requirements would be different depending on whether the defendant was represented by counsel: if he is represented, "the court before imposing sentence shall permit counsel for the defendant to read the report of the presentence investigation (from which the sources of confidential information may be excluded)"; if the defendant is unrepresented, "the court shall communicate, or have communicated, to the defendant the essential facts in the report of the presentence investigation (from which communication the sources of confidential information may be excluded)." Committee on Rules of Practice and Procedure, Second Preliminary Draft of Proposed Amendments to Rules of Criminal Procedure for the United States District Courts, p. 39 (March 1964). A previously suggested revision was to the effect that the court be required to disclose "a summary" of the material contained in the report. See Higgins, *Confidentiality of Presentence Reports,* 28 Albany L.Rev. 12, 13 (1964).

b. Considerations

There have been three basic arguments made against disclosure of the presentence report to the defendant. First, it is suggested that disclosure would dry up sources of information. "To get information, especially of an intimate sort, the social investigator must be able to give firm assurances of confidentiality; if people generally learn that supplying information will get them into court or plunge them into a neighborhood feud, they will no longer share their knowledge and impressions . . . ." Paulsen, *Kent v. United States: The Constitutional Context of Juvenile Cases,* 1966 Sup.Ct.Rev. 167, 180. Compare United States v. Fischer, 381 F.2d 509 (2d Cir. 1967). In addition, the files of social agencies, open only on a confidential basis, would have to be closed to probation officers if the information were required to be disclosed to the defendant. In other cases, the lives of informants may be endangered if their identity were disclosed.

The second reason commonly advanced for not disclosing the presentence report is that disclosure would interminably delay the proceedings: "To require the court to permit examination and controversy over each part of a probation report would, in large part, defeat the very purpose of the report by extending the process to the point at which it is no longer a practical tool for the court's guidance in the exercise of its discretion." People v. Peace, 18 N.Y.2d 230, 237, 219 N.E.2d 419, 423 (1966), cert. denied 385 U.S. 1032 (1967). The fear is thus that the defendant will challenge everything in the report, and thereby transform the sentencing process into a much more lengthy affair than it has to be. In turn, it is predicted, this could lead to dispensing with the report altogether in order to avoid the delay.

Thirdly, there is the argument that disclosure of parts of some presentence reports would be affirmatively harmful to the rehabilitative efforts of the defendant: a psychiatrist hardly reveals his complete diagnosis to his patient at the beginning of their relationship. Similarly, and particularly if the defendant is to be supervised on probation by the same officer who compiled the report, it can impede the defendant's progress from the beginning if complete disclosure is made.

Finally, each of these arguments is buttressed by the contention that it is not unfair to the defendant to proceed against him in this manner. "After conviction a case ceases to be an action at law and becomes a social problem." Hincks, *In Opposition to*

Rule 34(c)(2), Proposed Federal Rules of Criminal Procedure, Fed.Prob., Oct.-Dec. 1944, p. 7. Viewed in this light, there is not the scrupulous need for trial-type hearings with full disclosure and confrontation that properly governs the determination of guilt. The probation officers can be as trusted as can the defense attorney to ensure the accuracy of the report; and ensuring accuracy is the only interest which the defendant would protect if he were afforded full disclosure.

The major difficulty with the arguments in favor of the secrecy of the report is that each is aimed at a specific evil which may indeed be a legitimate cause for concern, but yet is generally asserted as supporting non-disclosure in all cases irrespective of the existence of even a remote possibility in the particular case of the actual occurrence of the feared result. There cannot possibly, for example, be a valid reason for withholding from the defense attorney a statement in the presentence report describing the defendant's prior criminal record. Yet such statements are withheld daily because the disclosure of a diagnosis might be harmful or because sources of information might dry up.

The position of the Advisory Committee thus begins with a sense of relevance, coupled with the principle that at the very least fairness to the defendant should dictate disclosure in the absence of countervailing reasons which are in fact applicable to his case. Consider, for example, State v. Pohlabel, 61 N.J.Super. 242, 160 A.2d 647 (App.Div.1960). The defendant had been employed to paint the interior of an apartment and while there had stolen the owner's checkbook. He wrote seven checks, totaling $1467. Seven indictments were returned, to each of which he pleaded *non vult*. He was sentenced to seven consecutive three-to-five year terms, thus resulting in a term of twenty-one to thirty-five years. Eight years after the conviction, the defendant for the first time was able to examine the presentence report. In it he discovered the statement of the probation officer that he was a "master of deception" and had a "contemptuous attitude toward law enforcement agencies." The report indicated that the defendant had "spent the greater part of his life in penal institutions" and that he had numerous prior convictions, including one life sentence for escape from a California prison. The fact, however, was that he had had only one prior conviction, and that for stealing an automobile seven years before at the age of eighteen. He had served only four years for that offense. The disclosure of these discrepancies moved the prosecutor to join in a motion for re-sentencing, which was finally granted some nine years after the original conviction and sentence. Had the discrepancies been pointed out at the time of sentencing, the defendant well might have been given concurrent terms, and might thus have been free for at least four years by the time he finally was able to discover the errors. For other examples of similar difficulties, see United States v. Myers, 374 F.2d 707 (3d Cir. 1967); State v. Killian, 91 Ariz. 140, 370 P.2d 287 (1962); *Symposium on Discovery in Federal Criminal Cases*, 33 F.R.D. 47, 124–25 (1963). See also Newman, Conviction: The Determination of Guilt or Innocence Without Trial 222–23 (1966), quoted on p. 275, infra.

Because such incidents can and do occur, and for other reasons to be developed below, the Advisory Committee is persuaded that fairness to the defendant requires disclosure of all information in the report which is adverse on the sentencing issue and which has not previously been disclosed by prior proceedings in open court. The Committee thus unanimously supports the statement in subsection (a) which would place upon the sentencing court the duty to apprise the defendant, his attorney and others acting on his behalf of the existence in the report of all such information. For reasons which are set forth in a separate statement in Appendix A, infra, one member of the Committee would stop at this point. The remainder of the Committee, however, believes that the simplest and fairest method of implementing this principle is to permit the parties to inspect the report. The details of this recommendation are set forth in subsection (b).

The view which is reflected in subsection (b) is based upon both an assessment of the values which are served by non-disclosure and a balance of these values against basic fairness to the defendant. Specifically, the argument that sources of information will dry up if the defendant's attorney is permitted to examine the report falters on two grounds.

The first is based on the experience of those members of the Committee who have lived under a system in which disclosure is routine, and is supplemented by the Committee's examination of sample reports produced under such a system. The conclusion is that there is little factual basis for the fear that information will become unavailable if the report is disclosed. The quality and value of a presentence report will turn to an infinitely greater extent on the skill of the probation service and the availability of adequate supporting facilities than it will on whether its contents remain a secret. This view is further supported by the experience of the Legal Aid Agency in the District of Columbia. In order to meet the informational needs of defense counsel who were denied access to the presentence report, the Agency instituted a program to supply the attorney with a separately prepared report for the defense. It was reported to the Advisory Committee that only rarely was difficulty encountered by reason of the fact that such reports were expressly prepared for the defendant. For a description of the project, see Keys, *Extra-Legal Help for Defendants,* Legal Aid Brief Case, Oct. 1965, p. 15.

The second reason is more fundamental. One of the basic values underlying the manner in which the guilt phase of a criminal case proceeds is that the defendant is entitled to know the details of the charge against him and is entitled to an opportunity to respond. It is believed that this value is subverted by a system which does not require disclosure of the information contained in the presentence report.

Perhaps an example can best make the point. Assume two statutes, one defining the offense of robbery and providing a ten-year maximum term and the other defining the offense of armed robbery and providing a twenty-year maximum. It would be unthinkable in this country to permit the defendant to be convicted of robbery under the first statute and yet sentenced to twenty years under the second because of a report submitted to the court by a probation officer which disclosed for the first time the fact that the defendant was armed. Defense of this result on the ground that the sources of such information would dry up if the defendant were told about it would be dismissed out of hand.

But contrast a jurisdiction which takes a different approach. Assume here that the legislature has defined only one offense of robbery and has remitted to the sentencing court the job of grading the offender within the range of a twenty year maximum term. In this context we seem quite prepared to admit the propriety of the same twenty year term on the same ground, namely that the defendant was armed. Yet this time we make no requirement that the defendant be informed that the judge may act on this basis.

Is there a relevant difference between the two cases? Why is it that when the legislature grades the severity of different circumstances under which the same basic offense can occur we require notice of the facts that distinguish the different levels of punishment which are available, and yet when the courts are given unlimited discretion to engage in the same grading process no notice is necessary? Is there not an argument that the defendant in the latter case is *more* in need of notice as a practical matter than he is in the former?

Consider a further refinement of the example cited above. Assume that the legislature has defined an offense of robbery with a maximum term of five years, and further has authorized an additional or supplemental term of ten more years if the defendant exhibited tendencies of sexual dangerousness or if he had committed the offense twice before. Again, it is perfectly clear that our system as now structured, and for good reason, would require that the defendant be notified of the grounds on which such a supplemental term could be based prior to its imposition. See Specht v. Patterson, 386 U.S. 605 (1967); Oyler v. Boles, 368 U.S. 448 (1962). Yet our system would seem also to permit imposition of the identical fifteen year term for the identical offense for the identical reasons without notice of the grounds if the decision were left to a judge, unguided by legislative criteria.

The irony is clear. The Committee majority believes that the need to protect sources of information should be given no more weight on the disclosure issue at the sentencing stage than it would be at the guilt stage or at a hearing on recidivist or sex offender proceedings. It can see no relevant distinction. Long since exploded is the theory that a defendant who has been convicted of crime no longer has any rights, or that any sentence less than the maximum is the result of an act of grace. See, e. g., Kadish, *Legal Norm and Discretion in the Police and Sentencing Processes*, 75 Harv.L.Rev. 904, 919–25 (1962). In terms of impact on the defendant, it would not seem to be maintainable that he is hurt more by the deprivation of notice on the guilt issue than he would be on the sentencing issue. Coupled with the belief that the system can function in just as informed a manner with disclosure as without it, this conclusion leads the majority to the view that with respect to the occurrence of historical events the presentence report should not be a sacrosanct document. As the Supreme Court recently observed in a different, but still strikingly similar context, "perhaps the point of it is that while non-disclosure may contribute to the comfort of the staff, disclosure does not cause heaven to fall." Kent v. United States, 383 U.S. 541, 564 n. 32 (1966).

Nor can the majority of the Advisory Committee accept the argument that non-disclosure should follow because the proceedings will be delayed by disclosure. In the first place, such an argument is a difficult one to make in the face of a conclusion that basic fairness requires disclosure; it completely avoids the fundamental relevance of justice to the defendant as a factor in determining procedural requirements. In the second place, the majority believes that this too is a straw man which both is not likely to find support in the facts of many cases and which in most can be avoided by the presentence conference proposed by section 4.5, infra.

Most importantly, however, it is the conviction of the majority that a properly conducted sentencing proceeding could, and perhaps should, be *more* protracted rather than less because of non-disclosure of the report. As expressed in support of section 5.3(f) (iii), infra, one of the functions of the defense attorney is to assure that the sentence is based on adequate and accurate information.* The only way he can meet this duty if not allowed access to the report is by painstaking investigation, followed by the detailed presentation of evidence which may already be contained

---

* Compare the Supreme Court's conclusion in *Kent* that: "We do not agree with the Court of Appeals' statement, attempting to justify denial of access to these records, that counsel's role is limited to presenting 'to the court anything on behalf of the child which might help the court in arriving at a decision; it is not to denigrate the staff's submissions and recommendations.' On the contrary, if the staff's submissions include materials which are susceptible to challenge or impeachment, it is precisely the role of counsel to 'denigrate' such matter. There is no irrebuttable presumption of accuracy attached to staff reports. If a decision on waiver is 'critically important' it is equally of 'critical importance' that the material submitted to the judge—which is protected by the statute only against 'indiscriminate' inspection —be subjected, within reasonable limits having regard to the theory of the Juvenile Court Act, to examination, criticism and refutation. While the Juvenile Court judge may, of course, receive *ex parte* analyses and recommendations from his staff, he may not, for purposes of a decision on waiver, receive and rely upon secret information, whether emanating from its staff or otherwise. The Juvenile Court is governed in this respect by the established principles which control courts and quasi-judicial agencies of the Government." Kent v. United States, 383 U.S. 541, 563 (1966). See also the statement by Mr. Justice Douglas dissenting from the recent changes in the Federal Rules, 39 F.R.D. 276, 278 (1966).

in the report. An attorney who is to assure himself that an item of information—which may have been furnished to the probation officer by the defendant in the first place—will be before the sentencing court must delay the proceedings to determine whether it has already come to the attention of the judge.

Finally, the majority cannot accept the proposition that historical facts should be withheld because the disclosure of a diagnosis might harm the defendant's chances for rehabilitation. The majority would be quite prepared to accept the legitimacy of the thesis underlying this argument, as expressed in subsection (b), but at the same time cannot accept it as a reason for denying disclosure of information not relevant to the point.

The reaction of the majority is not unlike that expressed by the Supreme Court in the *Kent* case, which involved the disclosure of social records of a juvenile to his attorney to permit preparation for a hearing on whether the juvenile should be waived to a criminal court for the trial of several serious felonies. The Court noted that "with respect to access to the social records of the child, we deem it obvious that since these are to be considered by the Juvenile Court in making its decision to waive, they must be made available to the child's counsel." Kent v. United States, 383 U.S. 541, 562 (1966). Indeed, the language of the *Kent* opinion strongly supports the conclusion that disclosure was necessary in order to provide the effective assistance of counsel to which the child was entitled at the waiver hearing. No less is a defendant at sentencing entitled to the assistance of counsel, and no less should that assistance be provided in a context where it can be effective. Sentencing on the basis of undisclosed factual information is inconsistent with this objective. Compare Note, *Due Process and Legislative Standards in Sentencing,* 101 U.Pa. L.Rev. 257, 263–71 (1952); Model Sentencing Act § 4, comment, p. 15 (1963). See also Paulsen, *Kent v. United States: The Constitutional Context of Juvenile Cases*, 1966 Sup.Ct.Rev. 167, 178–83.

Finally, it should be noted that there may be constitutional grounds on which disclosure of the presentence report should be required. Already noted is the possibility of an argument proceeding from the need for the effective assistance of counsel. Cases such as Townsend v. Burke, 334 U.S. 736 (1948), and United States v. Myers, 374 F.2d 707 (3d Cir. 1967), strongly support the position that the purpose of counsel at the sentencing proceeding is to assure the accuracy of information to be used in framing the sentence, a function which he cannot perform without access to the presentence report. The constitutional requirement of notice prior to the taking of adverse action—heretofore operative in civil contexts as well as criminal—may also operate in this context. But whatever the result of the constitutional cases of the future, two points must be made. First, the Supreme Court has never explicitly held that disclosure is not required. Neither Williams v. New York, 337 U.S. 241 (1949), nor Specht v. Patterson, 386 U.S. 605 (1967), deals specifically with this issue. The second point is that the disclosure decision is not in any event a decision which should exclusively be controlled by constitutional considerations. The Committee majority is persuaded as a matter of policy that disclosure of the report ought to be required because such a practice will increase the fairness of the system, because it will increase the appearance of fairness, and because it will assure a greater degree of accuracy in the sentencing determination.

c. Subsection (b)

It remains to deal with several of the specifics of subsection (b). It is appropriate in the ordinary case that it be the attorney rather than the defendant who is to examine the report because of the need for an expert evaluation of its strengths and weaknesses and because it will be the attorney who is to prepare the presentations to be made at the sentencing proceeding. Of course if the defendant is to represent himself at the sentencing proceeding, then it is he who must have access to the report. The court in such a case should advise him of his rights in this respect.

In addition, subsection (b) provides that there should be full disclosure to the prosecuting attorney. On this point, the majority follows the suggestion of the revision of Federal Rule 32(c) (2). Compare Minn.Stat.Ann. § 609.115(4) (1964), quoted in comment a, supra. The major reason for such a provision is that the prosecutor too should be concerned with the accuracy of the facts on which the sentence is based, and that his interests will thus be served by being able to compare the report against information at his disposal. See § 5.3(d)(i), infra. He also needs to be in a position to challenge or concede any inaccuracies asserted by the defendant.

Subsection (b) also provides that in extraordinary cases the court may withhold three types of information for stated reasons. There would be no purpose advanced if the defendant were shown scurrilous information which was clearly irrelevant to the sentencing decision. Of course such information should not be in the report in the first place, and in most instances will not be. But if it is there, the principle which generally supports disclosure need not be pushed to extremes if there is a chance that the information may do some positive harm. There are likewise good reasons for withholding from the defendant personally information of a diagnostic nature which may do positive harm to any effective program of rehabilitation. Similarly the sources of information actually obtained in exchange for assurances of confidentiality could in some cases be properly withheld. To the extent that disclosure of the information is tantamount to disclosure of its source, on the other hand, the balance would seem clearly in favor of the defendant's need to know.

The difficulty with exceptions such as these is that they may be abused, and result as a practical matter in little improvement in the disclosure patterns which presently exist. In an attempt to confront this danger directly, the majority would require that the court explicitly state for the record the reasons for the non-disclosure of any item of information, and that it inform the defendant that a deletion has occurred so that he may have the matter, along with all of the other issues in the case, reviewed on appeal. By endorsing a general policy in favor of disclosure, by making non-disclosure of specific items a burdensome task to be justified as an exception, and by providing for review to determine whether non-disclosure was justified, the majority believes that the danger will be minimized, but that an outlet will be available to accommodate justifiable fears in particular cases. In a very few cases, this position will result in disclosure of information which the advocates of secrecy would prefer not to disclose. Such is the price of a system which derives value from the fairness with which it operates.

4.5   Presentence report: time of disclosure; presentence conference.

(a) The information made available to the parties under section 4.4 should be disclosed sufficiently prior to the imposition of sentence as to afford a reasonable opportunity for verification.

(b) In cases where the presentence report has been open to inspection, each party should be required prior to the sentencing proceeding to notify the opposing party and the court of any part of the report which he intends to controvert by the production of evidence. It may then be advisable for the court and the parties to discuss the possibility of avoiding the reception of evidence by a stipulation as to the disputed part of the report. A record of the resolution of any issue at such a conference should be preserved for inclusion in the record of the sentencing proceeding (section 5.7[a][iii]).

Commentary

a. Timing

Since a major purpose of access to the information in the presentence report is to assure its accuracy, it follows that disclosure of the report itself or the information it contains should occur at a time sufficiently prior to sentencing to afford a reasonable opportunity for verification. Under a provision such as section 4.4 (a), which contemplates informal disclosure by the court at the sentencing proceeding of most of the information in the report, this requirement could be met by permitting a delay in the imposition of sentence in the rare case where the defendant took issue on a matter which the court considered important to a proper sentence. In most cases the proceeding could continue without delay, either because the defendant admitted the truth of the information disclosed to him or because his challenge was of such a minor sort as not to have any particular bearing on the sentence to be imposed. In other cases correction could occur in open court by stipulation of the parties.

On the other hand, if the parties are to be permitted to inspect the report under a provision such as section 4.4(b), disclosure should occur prior to the sentencing proceeding by a sufficient time so as to permit independent verification and, if necessary, preparation for the elaboration of parts which are deemed inadequate.

ADDITIONAL VIEWS OF JUDGE STANLEY WITH RESPECT TO THE COMPULSORY DISCLOSURE OF PRESENTENCE REPORTS

Because the issue is so fundamental, and the evidence against non-disclosure is so overwhelming, I feel compelled to register my views with respect to the portion of this report which favors compulsory disclosure of presentence reports.

The problem has recently received the attention of the Judicial Conference of the United States and the United States Supreme Court.   After a study extending over a period of some three years, the Judicial Conference and the Supreme Court, acting upon the recommendations of the Advisory and Standing Committees on Rules of Practice and Procedure, approved Rule 32(c) (2) of the Federal Rules of Criminal Procedure, which makes disclosure of presentence reports discretionary.   During the course of its study, the Advisory Committee obtained the views of circuit judges, district judges and federal probation officers.   The survey disclosed the following:

Circuit Judges	— 40 opposed compulsory disclosure,
	7 were in favor of compulsory disclosure,
	4 expressed no opinion;
District Judges	—250 opposed compulsory disclosure,
	18 were in favor of compulsory disclosure,
	2 expressed no opinion;
Federal Probation Officers	—340 opposed compulsory disclosure,
	20 were in favor of compulsory disclosure,
	8 expressed no opinion.

It has been repeatedly held that there is no denial of due process of law for a court to consider the report of a presentence investigation without disclosing its contents to the defendant, or giving him an opportunity to rebut it.   Williams v. Oklahoma, 358 U.S. 576 (1959); Williams v. New York, 337 U.S. 241 (1949).

A majority of the Committee not only recommends compulsory disclosure to counsel for the prosecution and defense, but also recommends that provision be made for any part of the report to be controverted by the production of evidence.   In the recent case of Specht v. Patterson,* decided April 11, 1967, the United States Supreme Court reaffirmed its decision in Williams v. New York, supra, which recognizes that probation workers "have not been trained to prosecute, but to aid offenders"; that most of the information "relied upon by judges to guide them in the intelligent imposition of sentences would be unavailable if information were restricted to that given in open court by witnesses subject to cross-examination"; and that the type and extent of information gathered by probation officers "make totally impractical if not impossible open court testimony with cross-examination," since such a procedure could "endlessly delay criminal administration in a retrial of collateral issues."

For other convincing arguments opposing compulsory disclosure, see Judicial Conference Committee on Administration of the Probation System, Judicial Opinion on Proposed Change in Rule 32(c) of the Federal Rules of Criminal Procedure—A Survey (1964); Keve, The Probation Officer Investigates 6–15 (1960); Parsons, *The Presentence Investigation Report Must be Preserved as a Confidential Document*, Fed. Prob., March 1964, p. 3; Barnett and Gronewold, *Confidentiality of the Presentence Report*, Fed. Prob., March 1962, p. 26; Wilson, *A New Arena is Emerging to Test the Confidentiality of Presentence Reports*, Fed. Prob., Dec. 1961, p. 6; *Federal Judge's Views on Probation Practices*, Fed. Prob., March 1960, p. 10; Sharp, *The Confidential Nature of Presentence Reports*, 5 Catholic U.L.Rev. 127 (1955).

Perhaps the overriding issue involved is that most of the valuable information contained in presentence reports would no longer be available if disclosure should be made mandatory. Certainly, former employers and members of a defendant's family would hesitate to give information if the report is to be read by the defendant or his counsel, and such persons are subject to being brought into court to establish the accuracy of the information given. Further, experience teaches that a disclosure of information given by members of the defendant's family would often result in a complete breakdown of family relationships. It is no answer to the problem to say that sources of confidential information can be withheld, because anyone experienced in the field knows that more often than not the information itself discloses the source.

* 386 U.S. 605 (1967).

It is the considered judgment of most experts in the field that compulsory disclosure would result in a presentence report containing nothing more than information related by the defendant himself, and that obtained from public records and documents. In my judgment, this would work to the detriment of defendants, since it would require judges to sentence on the basis of guesswork and inadequate information. It has always been my practice, and the practice of most judges with whom the matter has been discussed, to voluntarily disclose derogatory information, not testified to by witnesses, that affects the length of the sentence. Such practice should be encouraged, but is a matter that should be left to the enlightened judgment and sound discretion of the trial judge.

Since the evidence against compulsory disclosure is so overwhelming, and the Supreme Court has repeatedly held that no constitutional issue is involved, I simply see no basis for embarking upon a course that "would undermine modern penological procedural policies that have been cautiously adopted throughout the nation after careful consideration and experimentation." Williams v. New York, supra.

EDWIN M. STANLEY
*Member of Advisory
Committee on
Sentencing and
Review*

STANDARDS RELATING TO PROBATION*

PART I. GENERAL PRINCIPLES

1.1   Nature of sentence to probation.

(a) The legislature should authorize the sentencing court in every case to impose a sentence of probation. Exceptions to this principle are not favored and, if made, should be limited to the most serious offenses.

(b) In this report the term "probation" means a sentence not involving confinement which imposes condi-

* The American Bar Association, Project on Standards for Criminal Justice, Approved Draft, 1970. Reprinted with permission of the American Bar Association.

tions and retains authority in the sentencing court to modify the conditions of the sentence or to resentence the offender if he violates the conditions. Such a sentence should not involve or require suspension of the imposition or the execution of any other sentence.

(c) Upon a sentence to probation, the court should not be required to attach a condition of supervision by the probation department if in its judgment supervision is not appropriate for the particular case.

(d) The court should specify at the time of sentencing the length of any term during which the defendant is to be supervised and during which the court will retain power to revoke the sentence for the violation of specified conditions. Neither supervision nor the power to revoke should be permitted to extend beyond a legislatively fixed time, which should in no event exceed two years for a misdemeanor or five years for a felony.

(e) A sentence to probation should be treated as a final judgment for purposes of appeal and similar procedural purposes.

(f) Upon revocation of probation the court should have available the same sentencing alternatives that were available at the time of initial sentencing. The could should not foreclose any of these alternatives before revocation.

1.2 Desirability of probation.

Probation is a desirable disposition in appropriate cases because:

(i) it maximizes the liberty of the individual while at the same time vindicating the authority of the law and effectively protecting the public from further violations of law;

(ii) it affirmatively promotes the rehabilitation of the offender by continuing normal community contacts;

(iii) it avoids the negative and frequently stultifying effects of confinement which often severely and unnecessarily complicate the reintegration of the offender into the community;

(iv) it greatly reduces the financial costs to the public treasury of an effective correctional system;

(v) it minimizes the impact of the conviction upon innocent dependents of the offender.

1.3 Criteria for granting probation.

(a) The probation decision should not turn upon generalizations about types of offenses or the existence of a prior criminal record, but should be rooted in the facts and circumstances of each case. The court should consider the nature and circumstances of the crime, the history and character of the offender, and available institutional and community resources. Probation should be the sentence unless the sentencing court finds that:

(i) confinement is necessary to protect the public from further criminal activity by the offender; or

(ii) the offender is in need of correctional treatment which can most effectively be provided if he is confined; or

(iii) it would unduly depreciate the seriousness of the offense if a sentence of probation were imposed.

(b) Whether the defendant pleads guilty, pleads not guilty or intends to appeal is not relevant to the issue of whether probation is an appropriate sentence.

PART II. THE PRESENTENCE REPORT

2.1 Availability and use.

(a) All courts trying criminal cases should be supplied with the resources and supporting staff to permit a presentence investigation and a written report of its results in every case.

(b) The court should explicitly be authorized by statute to call for such an investigation and report in every case. The statute should also provide that such an investigation and report should be made in every case where incarceration for one year or more is a possible disposition, where the defendant is less than [21] years old, or where the defendant is a first offender, unless the court specifically orders to the contrary in a particular case.

2.2 Purpose of report.

The primary purpose of the presentence report is to provide the sentencing court with succinct and precise information upon which to base a rational sentencing decision. Potential use of the report by other agencies in the correctional process should be recognized as a factor in determining the content and length of the report, but should be subordinated to its primary purpose. Where the presentence investigation discloses information useful to other correctional agencies, methods should be developed to assure that this data is made available for their use.

2.3 Content, scope and length of report.

Presentence reports should be flexible in format, reflecting differences in the background of different offenders and making the best use of available resources and probation department capabilities. Each probation department should develop gradations of reports between:

(i) a short-form report for primary use in screening offenders in order to assist in a determination of when additional and more complete information is desirable. Short-form reports could also be useful in courts which do not have adequate probation services;

(ii) a full report, which normally should contain the following items:

(A) a complete description of the offense and the circumstances surrounding it, not limited to aspects developed for the record as part of the determination of guilt;

(B) a full description of any prior criminal record of the offender;

(C) a description of the educational background of the offender;

(D) a description of the employment background of the offender, including any military record and including his present employment status and capabilities;

(E) the social history of the offender, including family relationships, marital status, interests and activities, residence history, and religious affiliations;

(F) the offender's medical history and, if desirable, a psychological or psychiatric report;

(G) information about environments to which the offender might return or to which he could be sent should probation be granted;

(H) supplementary reports from clinics, institutions and other social agencies with which the offender has been involved;

(I) information about special resources which might be available to assist the offender, such as treatment centers, residential facilities, vocational training services, special educational facilities, rehabilitative programs of various institutions to which the offender might be committed, special programs in the probation department, and other similar programs which are particularly relevant to the offender's situation;

(J) a summary of the most significant aspects of the report, including specific recommendations as to the sentence if the sentencing court has so requested.

A special effort should be made in the preparation of presentence reports not to burden the court with irrelevant and unconnected details.

2.4   When prepared.

(a) Except as authorized in subsection (b), the presentence investigation should not be initiated until there has been an adjudication of guilt.

(b) It is appropriate to commence the presentence investigation prior to an adjudication of guilt only if:

(i) the defendant, with the advice of counsel if he so desires, has consented to such action; and

(ii) adequate precautions are taken to assure that nothing disclosed by the presentence investigation comes to the attention of the prosecution, the court, or the jury prior to an adjudication of guilt. The court should be authorized, however, to examine the report prior to the entry of a plea on request of the defense and prosecution.

2.5 Availability of report; challenge of its contents.

Standards dealing with the disclosure of the presentence report and the resolution of controversy as to its accuracy are developed in the separate report of this Advisory Committee on Sentencing Alternatives and Procedures.

PART III. CONDITIONS OF PROBATION

3.1 Imposition and implementation of conditions.

(a) All conditions of probation should be prescribed by the sentencing court and presented to the probationer in writing. Their purpose and scope and the possible consequence of any violations should be explained to him by the sentencing court or at an early conference with a probation officer.

(b) Probation officers must have authority to implement judicially prescribed conditions; but the conditions should be sufficiently precise so that probation officers do not in fact establish them.

(c) The probationer should have the right to apply to the sentencing court for a clarification or change of conditions.

3.2 Nature and determination of conditions.

(a) It should be a condition of every sentence to probation that the probationer lead a law-abiding life during the period of his probation. No other conditions should be required by statute; but the sentencing court should be authorized to prescribe additional conditions to fit the circumstances of each case. Development of standard conditions as a guide to sentencing courts is appropriate so long as such conditions are not routinely imposed.

(b) Conditions imposed by the court should be designed to assist the probationer in leading a law-abiding life. They should be reasonably related to his rehabilitation and not unduly restrictive of his liberty or incompatible with his freedom of religion. They should not be so vague or ambiguous as to give no real guidance.

(c) Conditions may appropriately deal with matters such as the following:

(i) cooperating with a program of supervision;

(ii) meeting family responsibilities;

(iii) maintaining steady employment or engaging or refraining from engaging in a specific employment or occupation;

(iv) pursuing prescribed educational or vocational training;

(v) undergoing available medical or psychiatric treatment;

(vi) maintaining residence in a prescribed area or in a special facility established for or available to persons on probation;

(vii) refraining from consorting with certain types of people or frequenting certain types of places;

(viii) making restitution of the fruits of the crime or reparation for loss or damage caused thereby.

(d) Conditions requiring payment of fines, restitution, reparation, or family support should not go beyond the probationer's ability to pay.

(e) The performance bond now authorized in some jurisdictions should not be employed as a condition of probation.

(f) Probationers should not be required to pay the costs of probation.

3.3 Modification and termination of conditions.

Conditions should be subject to modification or termination by the court. All changes in conditions should be presented to the probationer in the manner prescribed in

section 3.1 of this Report.   Where the proposed modifications would result in a form of confinement as a condition of continued probation, the probationer should be
afforded the procedural rights set forth in Part V of this
Report.

PART IV.   TERMINATION

4.1   Satisfactory completion of probation term.

It should be provided that probation automatically
terminates upon the successful completion of the term
set by the court at the time of sentencing. It is nevertheless desirable that the fact of termination be recorded
in an order of the court, a copy of which should be furnished to the probationer.

4.2   Early termination.

The sentencing court should have the authority to
terminate probation at any time. Such authority should
be exercised prior to the term fixed in the original
sentence if it appears that the offender has made a good
adjustment and that further supervision or enforced
compliance with other conditions is no longer necessary.

4.3   Criminal record.

Every jurisdiction should have a method by which the
collateral effects of a criminal record can be avoided or
mitigated following the successful completion of a term
on probation and during its service.

PART V.   REVOCATION OF PROBATION AND
OTHER SANCTIONS

5.1   Grounds for and alternatives to probation revocation.

(a) Violation of a condition is both a necessary and a
sufficient ground for the revocation of probation. Revocation followed by imprisonment should not be the disposition, however, unless the court finds on the basis
of the original offense and the intervening conduct of
the offender that:

(i) confinement is necessary to protect the public from further criminal activity by the offender;
or

(ii) the offender is in need of correctional treatment which can most effectively be provided if he is confined; or

(iii) it would unduly depreciate the seriousness of the violation if probation were not revoked.

(b) It would be appropriate for standards to be formulated as a guide to probation departments and courts in processing the violation of conditions. In any event, the following intermediate steps should be considered in every case as possible alternatives to revocation:

(i) a review of the conditions, followed by changes where necessary or desirable;

(ii) a formal or informal conference with the probationer to reemphasize the necessity of compliance with the conditions;

(iii) a formal or informal warning that further violations could result in revocation.

5.2   Arrest of probationers.

(a) Formal arrests of probationers for the alleged violation of conditions of their probation should be preceded by the issuance of an arrest warrant based upon probable cause that a violation has occurred. Arrests without a warrant should be permitted only when the violation involves the commission of another crime and when the normal standards for arrests without a warrant have otherwise been met.

(b) Probation officers should not be authorized to arrest probationers.

5.3   Proceedings following commission of another crime.

A revocation proceeding based solely upon commission of another crime ordinarily should not be initiated prior to the disposition of that charge. However, upon a showing of probable cause that another crime has been committed by the probationer, the probation court should have discretionary authority to detain the probationer without bail pending a determination of the new criminal charge.

5.4 Nature of revocation proceedings.

(a) The court should not revoke probation without an open court proceeding attended by the following incidents:

(i) a prior written notice of the alleged violation;

(ii) representation by retained or appointed counsel; and

(iii) where the violation is contested, establishment of the violation by the government by a preponderance of the evidence.

Sentence should be imposed following a revocation according to the same procedures as are applicable to original sentencing proceedings.

(b) The government is entitled to be represented by counsel in a contested revocation proceeding.

(c) As in the case of all other proceedings in open court, a record of the revocation proceeding should be made and preserved in such a manner that it can be transcribed as needed.

(d) An order revoking probation should be appealable after the offender has been resentenced.

PART VI. PROBATION DEPARTMENT ADMINIS-
TRATION, SERVICES AND PERSONNEL

6.1 Legislative responsibility; administrative structure.

(a) Legislative bodies should appropriate sufficient funds so that all trial courts administering criminal justice will have adequate probation services and personnel in order to implement properly the standards developed in this Report.

(b) It is appropriate for probation services to be administered at either the state or local level, but in no event should control be vested in an agency having prosecutorial functions.

6.2 Establishing minimum standards.

Minimum standards for probation services should be formulated and enforced by an appropriate state agency and should be applicable to all probation departments within the state. In addition to the standards recommended in this report, the following general principles are important in developing minimum standards:

(i) Supervision of probationers.

There should be a sufficiently low average caseload to provide adequate supervision for probationers and to encourage the development of variable caseloads for different types of offenders and assignment techniques which will maximize the benefit of offered supervision. In appropriate cases, supervision should be supplemented by group counseling and therapy programs. Where feasible, branch probation offices should be located in the community in which probationers live so as to meet more effectively the demands of supervision. To complement supervision, helping services should be obtained from community facilities in appropriate cases and, where necessary, probation personnel should actively intervene with such facilities on behalf of their probationers;

(ii) Research and statistics.

Accurate and uniform records and statistics should be available as a foundation for research into sentencing criteria and probation department programs. Continuous research and evaluation, involving a cooperative effort among operations and research personnel, should be an integral part of probation departments;

(iii) Working conditions.

To help achieve the standards recommended in this Report, probation personnel should have adequate office space, clerical assistance and conference facilities.

6.3 Collateral services.

In appropriate cases, probation departments should be prepared to provide additional services which may be foreign to the traditional conceptions of providing presentence reports and supervising convicted offenders. Examples of such additional services include the preparation of reports to assist courts in making pretrial release decisions and assistance to prosecutors in diverting selected charged individuals to appropriate noncriminal alternatives.

6.4   Appointment of probation personnel.

(a) Responsibility for appointing chief probation officers in local probation departments should reside solely in the chief judge of the court or an appropriate judicial body. Consideration should be given to the creation of an agency or committee to advise in recruiting and screening chief probation officers. Such a committee should consist of representatives of government, the judiciary, the bar, and the community.

(b) Chief probation officers should make all appointments of probation personnel in accordance with a merit system. After a probationary period, tenure should be granted and removal permitted only after a hearing conducted by a civil service commission or other career service organization.

6.5   Qualifications for probation officers; other personnel.

(a) The educational and occupational requirements for probation officers should be possession of a bachelor's degree supplemented by:

(i) a year of graduate study in social work, corrections, counseling, law, criminology, psychology, sociology, or related fields; or

(ii) a year of full-time casework, counseling, community or group work experience in a recognized social, community, correctional or juvenile agency dealing with offenders or disadvantaged persons, or its equivalent as determined by the hiring agency.

(b) A significant number of probation officers in a department should have graduate degrees in one of the subjects enumerated in this section.

(c) While the core of any probation department should be professionally educated and trained personnel, it is desirable that the staff include individuals who may lack such professional qualifications but have backgrounds similar to those of the probationers themselves.

In addition, in appropriate cases citizen volunteers should be used to assist probation officers.

6.6   Education and training.

(a) Fellowships for graduate study should be made available to probation officers and college graduates interested in probation.   In addition, probation officer trainee programs combining work and education should be established for high school graduates and college students.

(b) In-service education and training programs should be jointly planned and developed by appropriate state agencies, universities, and local probation departments.   In state and larger local probation departments, implementation of these programs should be made a full-time responsibility.

6.7   Salaries of probation personnel.

(a) Entry salaries should be competitive with entry salaries offered in related fields such as welfare, education, and community action programs.

(b) Salaries should be structured so that promotion to an administrative or supervisory job is not the only means of obtaining a higher salary.   Merit pay increases should be available for outstanding job performance, advanced academic achievement, or completion of special in-service training.

Chapter 4

PAROLE

THE ORIGINS OF PAROLE*

A number of false beliefs exist regarding parole and its administration and at least two of these misconceptions which are current, have so little basis in fact that it is difficult to understand their widespread acceptance. There is, for example, the popular conception that parole developed from the Australian system of Ticket of Leave. The other equally fallacious belief is that rules and regulations of parole now in operation are those originated by members of boards of parole or administrators of parole.

Parole is the conditional release of an individual from a penal or correctional institution, after he has served part of the sentence imposed upon him. Parole did not develop from any specific source or experiment, but is an outgrowth of a number of independent measures, including the conditional pardon, apprenticeship by indenture, the transportation of criminals to America and Australia, the English and Irish experiences with the system of Ticket of Leave, and the work of American prison reformers during the Nineteenth Century.

Conditional Pardons and Transportation To America

The transportation of criminals to the American Colonies began early in the Seventeenth Century. The precedent for this removal of criminals from England can be found in a law passed in 1597 providing for the banishment "beyond the seas of rogues" who appeared to be dangerous. As early as 1617, the Privy Council passed an order granting reprieves and stays of execution to persons convicted of robbery, who were strong enough to be employed in service beyond the seas.

* Reprinted in part by permission of the New York State Division of Parole. From *Manual for Parole Officers*, 1953, p. 1–19 Footnotes omitted.

400

The transportation of criminals to America was backed and supported by the London, Virginia and Massachusetts companies, and similar organizations. At the time the plan was proposed, acute economic conditions prevailed in England. Unemployment was widespread. Taxes, particularly for the relief of the poor, were high and the English labor market was overcrowded. In spite of the existing situation, there were groups in England who opposed colonization, although the insistent demands for labor in the American Colonies could not be met. It was in an effort to avoid antagonizing these groups, and at the same time to satisfy the need for labor in the Colonies, that the Government devised the plan to transport convicted felons to America. The plan was presented to the King and he approved the proposal to grant reprieves and stays of execution to the convicted felons who were physically able to be employed in service.

The procedure developed to select individuals to be recommended to the King was somewhat similar to the present day methods followed by prison officials in recommending to the governor or parole boards in various states, the names of prisoners whose minimum terms are to be decreased by compensation or commutation allowance for good conduct and work willingly performed.

In England lists of names were compiled by court officials and signed by the judge or frequently by the mayor and recorder. The lists were then presented to the Secretary of State. In cases wherein a death sentence had been imposed, a stay of execution was automatically granted until the King had reviewed the recommendation made by the judge. The pardons granted by the King were written in Latin and accompanied by a docket in English, giving the name of the prisoner, his crime and, in some instances, a statement was added giving the reason why clemency had been granted.

In the beginning no specific conditions were imposed upon those receiving these pardons. However, a number of those pardoned had evaded transportation or had returned to England prior to the expiration of their term, it was found necessary to impose certain restrictions upon the individuals to whom these pardons were granted. It was about 1655 that the form of pardon was amended to include specific conditions and providing for the nullification of the pardon if the recipient failed to abide by the conditions imposed.

Transportation To America

During the early days of transportation, the Government paid to each contractor a fee of approximately five pounds for each prisoner transported. However, under the provisions of a law enacted in 1717, this procedure was discontinued and the contractor or shipmaster was given "property in the service" of the prisoner until the expiration of the full term. Once a prisoner was delivered to the contractor or shipmaster, the Government took no further interest in his welfare or behavior unless he violated the conditions of the pardon by returning to England prior to the expiration of his sentence.

Upon arrival of the pardoned felons in the Colonies, their services were sold to the highest bidder and the shipmaster then transferred the "property in service" agreement to the new master. The felon thereupon was no longer referred to as a criminal but became an indentured servant.

The system of indenture dates back to the Statute of Artifices enacted in 1562, and originally it had no relation to persons convicted of crime. Blackstone defined apprentices as "another species of servants who were usually bound out for a term of years by deed indenture." The contract of indenture was written on a large sheet of paper, the halves separated by a wavy or jagged line called an indent. The master and the apprentice or his guardian signed the form thereby agreeing to conform with the conditions specified. Van Doren in his biography of Benjamin Franklin quotes the conditions imposed upon Franklin in 1718, when at the age of twelve, he became indentured to his brother:

> ".   .   .   During which term the said apprentice his master faithfully shall or will serve, his secrets keep, his lawful demands everywhere gladly do. He shall do no damage to his said master nor see it done to others, but to his power shall let or forthwith give notice to his said master of the same. The goods of his said master he shall not waste, nor the same without license of him to give or lend. Hurt to his said master he shall not do, cause or procure to be done. He shall neither buy nor sell without his master's license. Taverns, inns or alehouses he shall not haunt. At cards or dice tables or any other unlawful game he shall not play. Matrimony he shall not contract nor from the services of his master

day or night absent himself but in all things as an honest faithful apprentice shall and will demean and behave himself toward said master all during said term."

This indenture bears a similarity to the procedure now followed by parole boards in this country. Like the indentured servant, a prisoner conditionally released on parole agrees in writing to accept certain conditions included on the release form which is signed by the members of the parole board and the prisoner. Even some of the conditions imposed today on conditionally released prisoners are similar to those included on the indenture agreement.

Transportation was, of course, terminated by the Revolutionary War, but for some time before this, the Colonists had vigorously protested against the importation of criminals. A tax was levied on each poor, disabled individual or felon received in the Colonies but even the imposition of the tax did not end the practice.

Bentham in reviewing criminal laws, comments that transportation had all the defects punishment can have and none of the qualities it might have; that under the transportation system, bondage was added to banishment but the convict who was able to offer the shipmaster a sum larger than that offered by an American Colonist could procure his liberty at the first port of call en route to America.

Transportation To Australia

The termination of the Revolutionary War ended transportation to America but England did not repeal her transportation law. Judges continued to impose sentences of transportation and the places of detention for prisoners awaiting transportation became overcrowded. Some attempt was made to relieve the situation by granting pardons freely but when a serious outbreak of crime occurred, the public demanded that the transportation law be enforced.

The Pitt Government had no interest in the rehabilitation of criminals. However, faced with a crime wave and the unsanitary conditions and overcrowding in the criminal detention quarters, the Government recognized the need for some immediate action. Australia had been discovered by Captain Cook in 1770 and the Government deliberated whether to use this land as a refuge for the thousands of American Royalists who had returned to England and were starving, or to establish Australia as a new colony for the reception of transported felons.

In 1787, the King announced that Australia was to be used for convict settlement and in May, 1787 the first fleet sailed, arriving at Botany Bay on January 18, 1788.

A different procedure was followed by the Government in dealing with prisoners transported to Australia than had previously been followed in transporting prisoners to America. All the expense incurred was met by the Government and the criminals transported did not become indentured servants but remained prisoners under the control of the Government which assumed responsibility for their behavior and welfare.

More conservative writers like Ives admit that the system of transportation had some value. He stated he believed transportation was to some extent "the wisest method of dealing with major criminals." O'Brien asserts: "It afforded an army of more than one hundred thousand persons a fresh start with real possibilities of rehabilitation."

No unbiased account of the history of transportation to Australia has been published. Authors who have dealt with this subject have dilated upon the primitive conditions which prevailed and the horrors which existed at Norfolk Island, Port Arthur, and the other penal settlements. The murders resulting from the sadistic treatment accorded to prisoners have been stressed and there are even accounts of prisoners who escaped and later practiced cannibalism.

The first governor of the penal settlement was given "property in service" for all felons under his supervision. He inaugurated the plan of assigning prisoners to the free settlers and when this transfer became effective, the settler or new custodian took over the "property in service" agreement.

From the days of Henry VIII, power to pardon felons could not be delegated to any individual without statutory authority. In 1790 a special enabling act gave to the governors of the penal settlements, power to remit sentences of transported prisoners. The first governor of Australia received instructions from the Government regarding the emancipation and discharge from servitude of prisoners whose conduct and work records indicated they were worthy to receive a grant of land. At first, these prisoners received an absolute pardon but later a new form of conditional pardon was instituted which became known as "Ticket-of-Leave." This Ticket-of-Leave was merely a declaration signed by the governor or his secretary, dispensing a convict from attendance at government work and enabling him, on condition of supporting himself, to seek employment within a specified district. No provision was made for his supervision by the government, the Ticket merely stating:

> "It is His Excellency, the Governor's pleasure to dispense with the government work of......tried at...... convicted of......and to permit......to employ...... (off government stores) in any lawful occupation with the district of......for his own advantage during good behavior or until His Excellency's further pleasure shall be made known."

This type of permit also took its origin from the Statute Artifices which provided that a servant, having lawfully terminated his employment, must be given a testimonial by his master. This testimonial gave the servant license to depart from the master and liberty to work elsewhere. No employer could legally accept anyone for service unless this testimonial or certificate of availability was produced.

Until 1811, Tickets-of-Leave were freely granted to prisoners for good conduct, meritorious service, or for the purpose of marriage. In 1811 a policy was adopted requiring that prisoners serve specific periods of time before being eligible to receive Tickets-of-Leave. This procedure, however, was not strictly adhered to until 1821, when a regular scale was formulated. Those who had a sentence of seven years could obtain a Ticket-of-Leave after serving four years; those with sentences of fourteen years, after serving six years, and those with life sentences, after serving eight years.

Great stress has been placed upon the experience of Alexander Maconochie, who was assigned as Governor of Norfolk Island in 1840. He devised new methods of treating prisoners but his experiments were limited to the prisoners confined in Norfolk and the success he achieved can hardly be attributed to the entire Australian system.

Maconochie said that in Van Dieman's Island he had "witnessed the dreadful state of depravity" to which the men in the public gangs had sunk, and the idea occurred to him that these conditions arose from the state of slavery to which the prisoners had been reduced. He originated the experiment of granting marks as a form of wages by which the state of slavery might be obviated and whereby the act of punishment would not be eliminated. He brought his proposed plan to the attention of the House of Commons in 1837, three years prior to his appointment as Governor of Norfolk.

He proposed that the duration of the sentence be measured by labor and good conduct within a minimum of time; that the labor thus required be represented by marks proportional to the original sentence, the prisoner to earn these marks in penal servitude before discharge. Marks were to be credited day by day to the convict, according to the amount of work accomplished. Maconochie, however, remained at Norfolk Island for a period of only four years and while his ideas were progressive and his experiments successful, his term of office was so limited that his achievements did not have any revolutionary effect on the system of transportation.

With the increase of free settlers, Australian Colonists began to protest the Government's use of the land for what they termed "a dumping ground for criminals." Although there were other reasons, the contributing factor in the decision of the Government to terminate transportation to Australia, was the threat of the Colonists to revolt.

Prior to the decision to terminate transportation, some effort had been made to alleviate some of the caustic criticism of the system by careful selection of the prisoners to be transported to Australia. The proposal was made that prisoners would first have to undergo a period of training and discipline in penal servitude in England, before transportation was effected. It was planned that this training period would cover a period of eighteen months. However, the experiment of selection was a failure, but it did mark the beginning of the utilization of trained and experienced individuals who were made responsible for the selection of the prisoners who had profited by the training program.

Three prison commissioners were appointed to accomplish the selection. The membership of this group may have established the precedent followed by American prison reformers in creating boards of parole consisting of three members.

The final termination of transportation to Australia did not occur until 1867, although opposition to the plan had been expressed as early as 1812.

England's Experience With Ticket-of-Leave

In America, as early as 1817, provisions had been made for the reduction of sentences by allowances for satisfactory work and conduct. The English Penal Servitude Act of 1853, governing prisoners convicted in England and Ireland, substituted imprisonment for transportation. By this Act, prisoners who received sentences of fourteen years or less were committed to prison, but the judge was granted permissive power to order the transportation or imprisonment of individuals who had received terms of more than fourteen years. This law also specified the length of time prisoners were required to serve before becoming eligible for conditional release on Ticket-of-Leave.

Those who had sentences exceeding seven years but not more than ten years, became eligible for Ticket-of-Leave after they had served four years and not more than six years. Prisoners who had sentences of more than ten years but less than fifteen, were required to serve at least six but not more than eight years, and those with sentences of fifteen years or more were required to serve not less than six nor more than ten years. America did not develop the use of the indeterminate sentence until nearly a quarter of a century after the enactment of the English Act of 1853.

The Act of 1853 related to conditional release and gave legal status to the system of Ticket-of-Leave. It provided:

> "It shall be lawful for Her Majesty by an order in writing under the hand and seal of one of Her Majesty's principal secretaries of State, to grant to any convict now under sentence of transportation, or who may hereafter be sentenced to transportation, or to any punishment substituted for transportation, by this Act, a license to be at large in the United Kingdom and the Channel Islands, or in such part thereof respectively as in such license shall be expressed, during such portions of his or her term of transportation or imprisonment, and upon such conditions in all respects as to Her Majesty shall deem fit; and that it shall be lawful for Her Majesty to revoke or alter such license by a like order at Her Majesty's pleasure.

> "So long as such license shall continue in force and unrevoked, such convict shall not be liable to be im-

prisoned or transported by reason of his or her sentence, but shall be allowed to go and remain at large according to the terms of such license.

"Provided always, that if it shall please Her Majesty to revoke any such license as aforesaid, it shall be lawful for one of Her Majesty's principal secretaries of State, by warrant under his hand and seal, to signify to anyone of the Police Magistrates of the Metropolis that such license has been revoked, and to require such Magistrate to issue his warrant under his hand and seal for the apprehension of the convict to whom such license was granted, and such Magistrate shall issue his warrant accordingly and such warrant shall and may be executed by the constable to whom the same shall be delivered, for that purpose in any part of the United Kingdom or in the Isles of Jersey, Guernsey, Alderney or Sark, and shall have the same force and effect in all the said places as if the same had been originally issued or subsequently endorsed by a Justice of the Peace or Magistrate or other lawful authority having jurisdiction in the place where the same shall be executed, and such convict, when apprehended under such warrant, shall be brought, as soon as he conveniently may be, before the Magistrate by whom the said warrant shall have been issued or some other Magistrate of the same Court, and such Magistrate shall thereupon make out his warrant under his hand and seal, for the recommitment of such convict to the prison or place of confinement from which he was released by virtue of the said license, and such convict shall be so recommitted accordingly, and shall thereupon be remitted to his or her original sentence, and shall undergo the residue thereof as if no such license had been granted."

The following conditions were endorsed on the license of every convict liberated on a Ticket-of-Leave in England:

"1.   The power of revoking or altering the license of a convict will most certainly be exercised in the case of misconduct.

2.   If, therefore, he wishes to retain the privilege, which by his good behavior under penal discipline

he has obtained, he must prove by his subsequent conduct that he is really worthy of Her Majesty's clemency.

3.　To produce a forfeiture of the license, it is by no means necessary that the holder should be convicted of any new offense. If he associates with notoriously bad characters, leads an idle or dissolute life, or has no visible means of obtaining an honest livelihood etc., it will be assumed that he is about to relapse into crime, and he will be at once apprehended and recommitted to prison under his original sentence."

The British public accepted that in compliance with the provisions of the law, the programs followed in the prisons would be reformative and that prisoners selected for release on Ticket-of-Leave represented definite proof of having profited by the training and, therefore, their conditional release would not be incompatible with the welfare of society.

Long before the termination of transportation, it had been recognized that the experiment followed in Australia of releasing prisoners on Ticket-of-Leave without further supervision, was a serious mistake. However, this knowledge did not prevent a repetition of the procedure. The public had assumed that the Home Office planned to enforce the conditions imposed upon prisoners on Ticket-of-Leave during the first two years after the enactment of the Servitude Act of 1853. The outbreak of serious crimes which occurred within the next three years was attributed to the lack of supervision accorded the released prisoners. A campaign of criticism was carried on and Ticket-of-Leave men were blamed for most of the crimes committed. The public became convinced that the Ticket-of-Leave system was not only a menace to public safety but was an absolute failure.

The public was vociferous in its demands for action to correct the misuse of Tickets-of-Leave. A select committee was appointed to hold hearings and at one of the meetings a representative of the Home Office testified that no efforts had been made to develop any plan for the supervision of Ticket-of-Leave men after release. The Home Office had merely accepted that Ticket-of-Leave men were prisoners who had completed their sentences. The head of the London Police admitted that he had also misinterpreted the Provisions of the Act of 1853 and had, in fact, issued orders to the police that they were not to interfere with Ticket-of-Leave men.

Representatives of other law enforcing agencies asserted that it was not possible to identify Ticket-of-Leave men because no report on the convicts was furnished them by the officials granting the Ticket and they learned that Ticket-of-Leave men had destroyed their licenses to be at large as a means of avoiding apprehension and identification. The only result of these hearings was the adoption of a Resolution by the Select Committee:

1. That the system of license to be at large, or Ticket-of-Leave, has been in operation too short a time to enable the committee to form a clear and decided opinion either as to the effect which it had already produced or to its probable ultimate workings.

2. That the system appears to be founded upon a principle, wise and just in itself, viz., that of enabling a convict to obtain by continued good conduct, while undergoing punishment, the remission of a portion of his sentence upon the expressed condition, however, that in case of subsequent misconduct, he should serve the residue of the original term specified in the original sentence.

3. That to render this system of Ticket-of-Leave, adopted both for the reformation of offenders and the interest of the public, the conditions endorsed on the Ticket-of-Leave ought to be enforced more strongly than appears to have been hitherto the case.

4. That every convict on his release was a Ticket-of-Leave ought to be reported to the Police of the town or district to which he is sent.

A series of prison riots occurred in the English prisons in 1862. Coupled with another serious crime wave, this again focussed attention on the administration of prisons and the Ticket-of-Leave system. The public again demanded that effective measures be taken to change the administration of prisons and correct the weaknesses of the Ticket-of-Leave system. Although the intent of the Act of 1853 had been to make prisons reformative in character, this objective had not been achieved. No real labor was performed in the prisons, discipline was lax, and the prison officials, apprehensive of the dangerous convicts, freely granted credit for good conduct to make prisoners eligible for release at the earliest possible date.

The House of Commons was petitioned to bring the situation to the attention of the Queen, who appointed a Royal Commission. At the public hearings held by the Commission, it was discovered that during the seven years which had elapsed since 1856, when the Select Committee had adopted its resolution, no system had been put into operation to supervise prisoners after their release. The fact that no understanding or cooperative agreement existed between the Home Office and the law enforcing agencies was also brought out. The head of the London Police openly admitted that until a few minutes prior to his appearance before the Royal Commission he had never seen a Ticket-of-Leave and had no knowledge of the conditions endorsed thereon.

Individuals who favored supervision by the police and those who opposed it, appeared before the Commission. Ticket-of-Leave men testified that they objected to reporting to the police because the latter were considered their "special enemies who dogged them and informed their employers of their criminal status." These criminals stated that they would be forced to steal or starve if supervised by the police, as no employer would hire them if aware of thier criminal record. The police testified that if a Ticket-of-Leave man were required to report to the police in each community he visited, the need for watching would cease. They urged that the system of irregular supervision be abolished and that some uniform procedure with prescribed rules and regulations be established.

The Royal Commission in its report stressed the unreformative programs in operation in the prisons which rendered the prisoners unprepared for freedom. They also expressed the opinion that a large proportion of the prisoners released on Ticket-of-Leave had given no reliable proof of their reformation prior to release. The Commission strongly urged that England adopt the system followed in the prisons of Ireland.

As a result of the report of the Royal Commission, the services of the police were used for supervision and later a number of Prisoner's Aid Societies, supported partly by the Government, were established. These agencies followed the methods of supervising prisoners which had proven effective in Ireland.

The Irish System of Ticket-of-Leave

Sir William Crofton became head of the Irish prison system in 1854, one year after the enactment of the Servitude Act. He accepted the idea that the intent of the law was to make penal institutions something more than places of safe keeping, and that the programs in the prisons should be designed toward reformation and Tickets-of-Leave granted only to prisoners who gave visible evidence of definite achievement and change of attitude.

The Irish convict system under Crofton's administration, became famous for its three stages of penal servitude, particularly the second stage where classification was governed by marks obtained for good conduct and achievement in education and industry. So-called "indeterminate prisons" were also utilized, where conditions were made as nearly normal as possible and no more restraint was exercised over the inmates than was necessary to maintain order.

The administrators of the Irish System maintained that its success was due to the cooperation extended by the convict toward his own amendment and his conviction sooner or later that the system, however penal in its character, was designed for his benefit and that stringent regulations imposed for his supervision after release rendered a vocation of crime unprofitable and hazardous to follow. The form of Ticket-of-Leave issued in Ireland was slightly different than the one used in England. Known as Form E, it reads:

> "Number of Convict's Book .... Order of License to be a convict made under Statute 27 and 28 Victoria, Chapter 47, Dublin Castle .... day of .... 18.... Her Majesty is graciously pleased to grant to .... of .... who was convicted of burglary first degree, at .... the .... thereupon sentenced to be kept in penal servitude for the term of .... and is now confined in the .... Convict Prison, Her Royal license to be at large from the day of his liberation under this order, during the remaining portion of said time of penal servitude, unless the said .... shall before the expiration of the said time be convicted of some indictable offense within the United Kingdom,

in which case such license will be immediately forfeited by law, or unless it shall please Her Majesty sooner, to revoke or alter such license. This license is given subject to the conditions endorsed upon the same. Upon the breach of any of which it will be liable to be revoked whether such breach is followed by conviction or not, and Her Majesty hereby orders that the said .... be set at liberty within thirty days from the date of this order."

The Ticket-of-Leave was signed by the Chief Secretary of the Lord Lieutenant of Ireland, and imposed the following conditions:

"1.　The holder shall preserve this license and produce it when called upon to do so by a magistrate or police officer.

2.　He shall abstain from any violation of the law.

3.　He shall not habitually associate with notoriously bad characters, such as reported thieves and prostitutes.

4.　He shall not lead an idle and dissolute life, without means of obtaining an honest livelihood."

"If the license is forfeited or revoked in consequence of a conviction of any felony, he will be liable to undergo a term of penal servitude equal to that portion of his term of .... years, which remains unexpired when his license was granted, viz., the term of .... years .... months."

Each Ticket-of-Leave man was further instructed as follows:

"Each convict coming to reside in Dublin City or in the County of Dublin will, within three days after his arrival, report himself at the Police Office, Exchange Court, Dublin, where he will receive instructions as to his further reporting himself.

"Each convict, residing in the provinces, will report himself to the constabulary station of his locality within three days after his arrival and subsequently on the first of each month.

"A convict must not change his locality without notifying the change to his constabulary in order that his
registration may be changed to the locality to which he
is about to proceed.

"Any infringement of these rules by the convict will
cause to be assumed that he is leading an idle, irregular
life and thereby entail a revocation of his license."

A description of the convicted man granted a Ticket-of-Leave
was fully outlined on the back of the form.

Ticket-of-Leave men residing in rural districts were supervised entirely by the police, but those residing in Dublin were
supervised by a civilian employee who had the title of Inspector
of Released Prisoners. He worked cooperatively with the police but it was his responsibility to secure employment for the
Ticket-of-Leave men. He required them to report at stated
intervals and visited their homes every two weeks and also
verified their employment. The problem of hounding by the
police, which had been stressed at the hearings before the Select
Committee and the Royal Commission in London, did not arise
in Ireland. It was accepted that conditionally released prisoners
would inform their employers of their criminal record and if
they failed to do so, the head of the police was responsible for
this action. Many of the problems being discussed by present
day parole executives were confronted by the administrators
of the Irish System and they adopted their policies to meet the
needs. Contrary to the experience in England, the Irish System
of Ticket-of-Leave had the confidence and support of both the
public and the convicted criminal.

Prisoners Aid Societies

In England and Ireland after 1864, Prisoners Aid Societies
were established, the Government contributing a share of funds
equal to the sum raised by the Society for its work. These Societies employed agents who devoted their full time to the supervision of released prisoners, and whose duties were outlined
as follows:

1. To visit the local prisoners weekly or oftener, if
    ordered by the Honorable Secretary and to take his
    instruction as to dealing with the cases selected for
    aid.

2. To visit local employers of labor taking every opportunity of seeing and becoming personally acquainted with foreman and other officials explaining to them the objectives of the Society and endeavoring to secure their cooperation.

3. To see the prisoner at the jail and accompany him to the railway station when needed, and to provide board and lodging for him for a limited time.

4. To visit constantly all persons under the care of the Society so long as they were unemployed and after employment is found.

5. To enter daily in a journal all parties seen and places visited and to submit the journal to the Committee at the monthly meeting.

6. To expend, under the direction of the Honorable Secretary, the money of all Ticket-of-Leave men under his supervision and to lose no opportunity of procuring suitable employment for them.

Developments in the United States

By 1865, the Crofton System had been widely publicized in America and prison reformers who were critical of the conditions existing in our prisons, suggested the adoption of new methods based on the Crofton plan. Although there were some critics of the Irish System, little attention was given to their opposition and American reformers continuously enunciated the need for new types of prison programs to provide for the grading of criminals, according to the degree of their reformation, and the use of the mark system as a check on their progress and restraint against disorder.

Propagandists for the Crofton System, however, did not believe in the adoption of the Ticket-of-Leave and specifically stated that "no Ticket-of-Leave system will ever be made acceptable and proper in the United States." Their attitude was apparently based on the conception that it would be un-American to place any individual under police supervision and they did not believe that any form of supervision would be effective. A letter written by Crofton in 1874, in reply to an inquiry sent him by the Secretary of the New York Prison Association, may have been responsible for a change in their viewpoint. In his communication, Crofton stressed that the police of Ireland were permitted to delegate competent individuals in the community to act as custodians for Ticket-of-Leave men. He suggested that America follow the practice of having prisoners about to be released name a "next friend" to whom they would be willing to make their reports, a person "likely to befriend them" and then to arrange with competent persons for supervision of a friendly character to the well-doer, but at the same time of a nature which will restrain the evil disposed by compelling them to observe the conditions upon which they have been liberated.

At the time the propaganda was being carried on for the adoption of the Crofton plan, the Elmira Reformatory in New York State was being constructed. Because of the widespread interest in prison programs, it would logically be assumed that before the new institution was opened, a suitable plan or organization would have been developed and necessary legislation enacted, or at least suggested by the Board of Managers of the State Government.

Elmira Reformatory was formally opened in July 1876, and had been operating for almost a year before its first Superintendent, Z. E. Brockway drafted a measure establishing a definite policy.

Prior to his appointment to Elmira Reformatory, Mr. Brockway had been head of the House of Correction in Detroit and while there, had drafted an indeterminate sentence law. His proposed measure outlined the following special features for the Elmira System:

1. An indeterminate or indefinite sentence, the length of time served to be dependent upon the behavior and capacity of the prisoner, within statutory limitation.

2. The status and privileges accorded to the prisoner, as in the Crofton plan, were to be determined by his behavior and progress.

3. Education was to be compulsory.

4. Provision was made for the release on parole of carefully selected prisoners.

Although no novel idea was included in the organization and administrative plan for Elmira, in its operation the system combined principles, the validity of which had been recognized separately.

The acceptance of the indeterminate sentence is so general today that it is difficult to comprehend why it should have become a serious controversial issue. The movement to substitute the indeterminate or reformative sentence for the fixed or definite term, began in England early in the Nineteenth Century.

As early as 1839 George Combs, a Scotch philosopher, visited America to lecture and it was he who suggested the idea of a sentencing board, the indeterminate sentence, parole, and what later became the basis for the system under which modern boards of parole function. In one of his lectures he said:

"If the principles which I advocate shall ever be adopted, the sentence of the criminal judge, on conviction of a crime, would simply be one of finding the individual has committed a certain offense and is not fit to live in society, and therefore granting warrant for his transmission to a penitentiary to be there confined, instructed, and employed until liberated in due course of law.

"The process of liberation would then become one of the greatest importance. There should be official inspectors of penitentiaries invested with some of the powers of a court, sitting at regular intervals and proceeding according to fixed rules. They should be authorized to receive applications for liberation at all their sessions and to grant the prayer of them on being satisfied that such a thorough change had been effected in the mental condition of the prisoner that he might safely be permitted to resume his place in society.

"Until this conviction was produced upon examination of his disposition, of his attainment, in knowledge of his acquired skills or some useful employment, of his habits of industry, and, in short, of his general qualifications to provide for his own support, to restrain his criminal propensities from committing abuses and to act the part of a useful citizen, he should be retained as an inmate of a penitentiary."

The vital principle of the indeterminate sentence was that no prisoner would be paroled until he was fit for freedom. Those who campaigned for the adoption of the indeterminate sentence recognized that in itself it had no mystic power but that its real strength was in the reformatory agencies—labor, education, and religion. It was also recognized that the indeterminate sentence placed in the hands of competent prison officials a tool which could be effectively used.

The main opposition to the enactment of indeterminate sentence laws came from the judges who were unwilling to relinquish their traditional privilege of fixing the time prisoners must serve. Despite their opposition, however, the law was enacted and provisions were also made for the parole of prisoners. At the beginning of the Twentieth Century, twenty-six states had adopted these measures.

The Elmira Reformatory and the Inception of Parole

Parole originated at the Elmira Reformatory and hence the procedures as they were initiated, may have some historical interest. Before being considered for parole, each inmate was required to maintain a good record of conduct for a period of twelve months. He was expected to have gained the confidence of the superintendent and the managers and before being released, he was required to present suitable plans for permanent employment. When his release had been approved, he was given a new suit of clothing and sufficient funds to reach his destination and to pay his immediate expenses. The superintendent then interviewed him on the day of his release and instructed him to proceed to his employment and remain there, if practicable, for at least six months. He was required to report to a guardian on his arrival and write directly to the superintendent notifying him that he had done so.

One of the conditions of his parole was that he must report on the first of every month to his guardian and report his situation and conduct. The guardian's report and certification by the parolee's employer as to his wages, were transmitted to the superintendent of Elmira. A record was kept of all paroled men who were required to report for a minimum period of six months. It was the belief that a longer period under supervision would be discouraging to the average paroled man.

According to the philosophy of the Reformatory officials it was considered preferable to have the paroled prisoner return to the place from which he was committed or the place of his usual habitation, on the basis that "recuperation from a damaged reputation and recovery of public confidence are easiest in the community where the misconduct occurred." The employer and the parole supervisor were "always made fully acquainted with all the facts, this for the sake of honesty, safety, and for the salutary mutuality of the confidential relations involved." Paroled prisoners were not permitted to conceal or deny their history. Monthly reports certified by the employer and supervisor were required. The officals considered the chief of the local police—"not the average policeman in the great cities, nor indeed a religious or philanthropical organization or private individual" the most satisfactory individual to supervise paroled prisoners.

American prison reformers were aware of the conditions under which prisoners conditionally released from institutions in England and Ireland were granted their liberation. Although for the most part, the same restrictions were enforced, certain new procedures were developed in the supervision of released prisoners in this country.

One of the first institutions for juvenile delinquents was established in New York State in 1820. An Indenturing Committee of three members was appointed and they adopted the policy of requiring written reports from the sponsors and the children who were released from the institution.

Early in the history of prisons in the United States, public interest and one of the major considerations of the penologists was centered in the problems presented by discharged prisoners. Prisoners Aid Societies were established early in the Nineteenth Century to give needed relief to prisoners discharged from the institutions and to aid them in securing employment. Each prisoner who was given assistance by the Society was required to submit written reports to the Society covering his progress, behavior, earnings, and savings. This policy of requiring written reports from prisoners was later adopted by the officials at the Elmira Reformatory.

With the great stress placed upon reformation, and the knowledge of England's experience with Ticket-of-Leave men, it should have been obvious that if the new system was to be given a fair trial, prison programs would have to be revolutionized. Ignoring this important factor in the treatment of criminals, state after state proceeded to enact indeterminate sentence and parole laws and the abuse of them became widespread.

No thought was given to the training of prisoners toward their future adjustment in the community and both prison administrators and inmates soon accepted the idea that reformed or unreformed, allowance of time for good behavior was automatic and release at the earliest possible date was a right, rather than a privilege. After release, supervision was either non-existent or totally inadequate if it was required. The result was a duplication of the English experience.

Every charge that had been made against the operation of the early English system of Ticket-of-Leave was leveled against the administration of parole in the United States.

It has been only within the past two decades that drastic action has been taken by a number of states to render prison reform and parole effective parts of the state system of correctional care. It is now recognized that parole can be an effective method of community protection and at the same time offer constructive aid to released prisoners. To achieve these objectives, however, the system must be adequately financed, non-political in operation, and supported by public trust and confidence.

PAROLE*

Almost every offender who enters a correctional institution is eventually released. The only relevant questions are: When? Under what conditions?

Most offenders released from a correctional institution re-enter the community on parole. In 1970, the latest year for which complete data are available, almost 83,000 felons left prison; 72 percent of them were released by parole. Nineteen percent were released by discharge and 9 percent by other forms of conditional release.[1] Parole is the predominant mode of release for prison

---

* The National Advisory Commission on Criminal Justice Standards and Goals, *Report on Corrections*, 1973.

1. *National Prisoner Statistics: Prisoners in State and Federal Institutions for Adult Felons, 1970* (Washington: Federal Bureau of Prisons, 1970), p. 43.

inmates today, and it is likely to become even more so. This trend can be highlighted by comparing the figures for 1970 stated above with those from 1966, when 88,000 felons left prison; 61 percent were released by parole, 34 percent by discharge, and 5 percent by other forms of conditional release.[2]

A 1965 study by the President's Commission on Law Enforcement and Administration of Justice (the Crime Commission) showed that slightly more than 112,000 offenders were then under parole supervision. By 1975, the Commission estimated, this number would be more than 142,000.[3]

These figures include only those offenders sentenced to State prisons. They do not include youth committed to juvenile institutions, virtually all of whom are released under some form of supervision at the rate of about 60,000 a year.

None of these figures include persons sentenced to jail, workhouses, and local institutions. More than one million persons were released from such facilities in 1965, according to the Crime Commission. It is in these facilities that some of the most significant gaps in parole services exist.

The National Survey of Corrections made for the Crime Commission found that almost all misdemeanants were released from local institutions and jails without parole. Of a sample of 212 local jails, the survey found, 62 percent had no parole programs at all. In the 81 jails that offered parole, only 8 percent of the inmates actually were released through this procedure.[4] There is little reason to believe the situation has changed radically since 1965, although efforts have been made in several jurisdictions to extend parole services to jail populations. The need for parole services is acute at the misdemeanant level.

Parole has been attacked as leniency, but its proponents argue that it is both humanitarian and designed to protect the public. They advance these arguments on two grounds. First, virtually everyone convicted and sent to a correctional institution will return to the community. He can be turned loose by discharge

2. *National Prisoner Statistics: Prisoners in State and Federal Institutions for Adult Felons, 1966* (Washington: Federal Bureau of Prisons, 1968), p. 43.

3. President's Commission on Law Enforcement and Administration

on Justice, *Task Force Report: Corrections* (Washington: Government Printing Office, 1967), pp. 6–8. Publication referred to hereinafter by title.

4. *Task Force Report: Corrections*, p. 61.

with no continuing responsibility on his part or the State's, or he can be released under supervision at what appears to be an optimal time and be assisted in reintegration into the community. From this perspective, parole is simply a form of graduated return to the community, a sensible release procedure.

A second major argument is that the sentencing judge cannot anticipate what new information may be available to a parole board or what circumstances might arise to indicate the optimum release date. Unlike the judge, a paroling agency has the advantage of being able to observe the offender's behavior. Furthermore, decisions on release made at the time of sentencing may be more angry than rational. Greater objectivity in appraising the offender may be achieved by a parole board when the passions that may have been aroused by an individual's offense have cooled.

Available evidence supports the view that parole does not lead necessarily to a lessening of the amount of time inmates actually serve in prison. In fact, one major criticism of present parole laws is that their administration tends to result in more severe penalties in a criminal justice system that already imposes extensive State control.

Inmates released on parole in the United States in 1964, the last time national data of this kind were available, actually served slightly *more* time than those released through unconditional discharge (Table 12.1). The table does not show the additional time served by offenders returned to prison as parole violators, a hazard to which those discharged unconditionally are not subject. In the major proportion of parole revocation cases, violation of parole rules rather than new felony offenses cause the offender's return to prison to serve more of his sentence. Thus arguments

Table 12.1. Number and Types of Releases in 1964 and Median Time Served

Type of release	Number	Median time served
Discharge	22,883	20.1 months
Parole	42,538	21.1 months

Source: *National Prisoner Statistics, State Prisoners: Admissions and Releases, 1964* (Washington: Federal Bureau of Prisons, 1967.)

[A9403]

are made that the sentencing structures supporting extensive
parole use should be severely modified because of their capacity
to inflict additional and unwarranted "punishment."

DEFINITION IN HISTORY

The classific definition of parole was provided in the Attorney
General's Survey of Release Procedures in 1939 as "release of an
offender from a penal or correctional institution, after he has
served a portion of his sentence, under the continued custody of
the state and under conditions that permit his reincarceration in
the event of misbehavior." [5]   Though some jurisdictions impose
limitations on parole use, offenders generally can be released on
parole and repeatedly returned to confinement for parole violation until the term of their original commitment has expired.

Yet to many, parole is still seen as "leniency" for offenders.
Others contend that, in well-operated systems, different types
of offenders should serve differing periods of time, and the more
dangerous and violence-prone should serve more time.   This is
seen as a proper use of sentencing and parole flexibility.   To actually understand parole and to make it a more effective instru-
ment of public policy requires sophisticated knowledge of all its
processes, procedures, and objectives.   Understanding is obscured
by the use of such value-laden terms as leniency, harshness, punishment, or coddling.   All of them oversimplify what is a complex administrative, legal, and political issue.

Parole resembles probation in a number of respects.   In both,
information about an offender is gathered and presented to a
decisionmaking authority with power to release him to community supervision under specific conditions.   If he violates those conditions, the offender may be placed in, or returned to, a correctional institution.   Parole, however, differs from probation in a
significant way.   Parole implies that the offender has been incarcerated in a correctional institution before he is released, while
probation usually is granted by a judge in lieu of any kind of
confinement.

Recent development of informal institutions (halfway houses,
etc.) used by both courts and parole boards make the distinction
between probation and parole increasingly difficult to sustain.

5. *Attorney General's Survey of Re-*   Government Printing Office, 1939),
   lease   Procedures   (Washington: vol. IV, p. 4.

To add further confusion, some jurisdictions use the term "bench parole" to refer to a form of minimally supervised probation.

Parole and probation also differ significantly in terms of who makes the decision. Parole is almost always an administrative decision; the granting of probation, a court function.

The power to determine when an offender may be released from an institution, to fix the conditions of his supervision, and to order parole revocation almost always passes from the court to an agency within the executive branch. In the case of adults this agency is usually a parole board; in the case of juveniles, an institutional official. As a condition of probation, a sentencing judge may require an offender to spend some time in an institution before he is released under community supervision, as in the "split sentence" in Federal jurisdictions. In this situation, authority to fix conditions and powers of revocation and discharge continue with the court after the offender is released from confinement. Therefore, the case almost always is classified as probation.

Parole also needs to be distinguished from one other kind of release. In a number of jurisdictions—New York, Wisconsin, the Federal system—adult offenders are automatically released under supervision when they have served a portion of their sentence and have earned a specified amount of time off for good behavior. Legislation specifies the calculation of "good time," and the parole authority exercises no discretion in the matter. The procedure is called "mandatory" or "conditional" release and is used to provide supervision for those offenders who have been denied parole, are ineligible for it, or have previously refused it. Although released automatically, such offenders may be returned to serve the remainder of their terms if they violate any of the release conditions. The advantage of mandatory release is that supervision is provided for those not paroled. Its main disadvantages are that time under supervision usually is short, and inmates are released simply because they have earned time off for good behavior, with little regard for their readiness to return to the community.

The beginning of parole in the United States generally is identified with the Elmira Reformatory in New York, which opened in 1876. In the Elmira system, sentences were indeterminate, dependent on "marks" earned by good behavior. Release was for a six-month parole term, during which the parolee had to report regularly to a volunteer guardian or sponsor.

Elmira drew wide attention by its new approach to imprisonment, which was markedly different from the tradition of incarceration for a term fixed at the time of sentence. The designation of certain institutions for youthful felons as "reformatories," and the accompanying practice of permitting indeterminate sentences and parole, spread rapidly through the United States in the last quarter of the 19th century and the beginning of the 20th. This sentencing system, including its provisions for parole, soon was extended to prisoners of all ages. By 1922, parole laws had been passed by 45 States, and in 1945 Mississippi became the last State to develop parole legislation.

This does not imply, however, that either parole laws or practices have developed uniformly. States still vary widely in the proportion of inmates released under parole supervision. In 1968, for example, the National Prisoner Statistics of the Federal Bureau of Prisons showed that among offenders released in the States of Washington, New Hampshire, and California, more than 95 percent were released under parole supervision. During the same period, less than 10 percent of inmates released in Oklahoma were released on parole. In Nebraska the comparable figure was 20 percent. Nationwide, releases to parole supervision were approximately 60 percent of all releases.

The history of parole for juvenile offenders is different from that for adults. For juveniles, parole usually is traced to the houses of refuse for children in the latter part of the 19th century. From these settings, children were released to work for several years in private homes. Total control of the child was vested in the family to whom he was released. It was the family's responsibility to determine when he had earned his freedom.

The child protection programs developed later assumed many of these activities. Although in recent years juvenile programs have become more correctional, they have continued to be involved closely with child welfare activities.[6] In many States, juvenile aftercare services are the responsibility of the welfare department or a similar agency containing a broad range of serv-

6. See Anthony Platt, "The Rise of the Child-Saving Movement: A Study in Social Policy and Correctional Reform," *Annals of the* *American Academy of Political and Social Sciences*, 381:21 (January 1969).

ices. In these settings, delinquency is seen as merely a symptom of a young person's need for State services. Labels such as "delinquent," "dependent," or "neglected" are de-emphasized. The general thrust is to treat these children within the context of child welfare.

Juvenile parole authorities usually are more than willing to distinguish their services from those for adults. Juvenile officials typically use the term "aftercare" as a synonym for parole, but in many ways the difference is more than semantic. The problems presented by the young releasee are different from those of the adult offender. School attendance and vocational training programs are much more likely to be a central feature of programs for juveniles, while employment is the major concern for adult offenders.[7] The two concerns might be cursorily equated. But no one may be legally required to work, while school attendance is compulsory for juveniles. In fact, chronic truancy is a juvenile "crime."

Juvenile and adult parole services usually are not organized similarly. The National Survey of Corrections showed that in 1965 parole boards decided on the release of juveniles in only two States, although such boards released adults almost everywhere in the country.

SENTENCING STRUCTURES

Any parole system and set of standards designed to improve its functioning can be understood and evaluated only in terms of the structure in which it exists. All parole systems, no matter how autonomous, are part of a larger process—not only of corrections generally, but also of a complex sentencing structure involving trial courts and legislative mandates. The structure and functions of parole systems and their relative importance in the jurisdiction's total criminal justice picture all depend largely on the sources of sentencing authority and limits on sentencing alternatives and lengths.[8] In most jurisdictions, for most offense categories, the sentences that can be imposed and the proportion of sentences actually served are determined by a balance of decision-making powers among legislatures, trial courts, and pa-

7. See William Arnold, *Juveniles on Parole* (Random House, 1970).

8. See Chapter 5 of this report. See also Daniel Glaser, Fred Cohen, and Vincent O'Leary, *The Sentencing and Parole Process* (Washington: U. S. Department of Health, Education, and Welfare, 1966).

role authorities. As noted in Chapter 5, there is no sentencing structure common to all jurisdictions. The relative importance and power of parole determinations vary markedly from one jurisdiction to another and within jurisdictions from one offense category to another.

VARIATIONS IN STRUCTURE

Throughout the history of American criminal justice, there have been various models of "ideal" sentencing structures proposed in different jurisdictions. Some have been tried, all have been debated, most have been modified. But there is still no uniform sentencing structure. The Model Penal Code of the American Law Institute, the Model Sentencing Act proposed by the National Council on Crime and Delinquency, suggestions of the Crime Commission, and the American Bar Association's Minimum Standards for Sentencing are recent attempts to propose sentencing structures suitable for all offenders in all jurisdictions. Because there have been no common standards for sentencing structures and processes, establishing standards for parole functions is extremely complex.

It might be possible to reach agreement on matters such as structure and composition of parole boards, appropriate workloads, staff training and development, and proper procedures for granting and revoking. But it must be remembered that the meaning and importance of the paroling function vary from one postconviction system to another. For example, in jurisdictions where legislatures set long maximum terms that trial judges cannot modify where good-time laws are stringent, or where pardon is almost unheard of, parole becomes not only an important method of release but virtually the *only* method. Furthermore, where sentences are long, it may mean that parolees must be supervised for decades.

The situation is different in systems that have relatively short legislative limits on sentences, with judges empowered to fix upper terms less than statutory maxima, and with liberal good-time allowances or frequent use of pardon. In such cases parole determinations may play a relatively minor part in overall release processes. In short-sentence jurisdictions, parolees terminate supervision fairly quickly. In jurisdictions in which minimum sentences are not required by either legislation or court determination, parole authorities have wide discretion to release inmates at any time.

Variations also exist among jurisdictions in regard to institutionalized juvenile delinquents, but they are not nearly as disparate as in the case of adults. The extent of control by the State over juvenile offenders generally is fixed by age rather than by offense. In most jurisdictions juvenile commitments do not have fixed minimum terms, so that release authorities have wide discretion.

But laws relating to juveniles are by no means uniform in all jurisdictions. For example, the National Survey of Corrections reported that in five States juveniles can be paroled from State training schools only with the committing judge's approval. In three States, the time a juvenile must serve before release is fixed in advance by the court. In effect, these are minimum sentences.

The sentencing system finally adopted is crucial to the parole function because it fixes the amount and the character of discretion a parole system can exercise. Seeking to eliminate the abuses that lurk in discretion, some persons would eliminte any form of discretionary release after sentencing by the trial judge.[9] However, most authorities hold that discretion is inevitable; the task is to limit and control it. From this view, many more problems arise when the entire releasing decision is placed in the hands of the trial judge or made dependent on a system of totally fixed sentences set by the legislature than if the decision is shared with a parole authority.[10]

On the other hand, most parole officials do not want the amount of power implicitly delegated by completely indeterminate sentencing. They feel that the awesome task of determining sentence limits should be left to judicial and legislative branches.

9. See *Struggle for Justice: A Report on Crime and Punishment in America*, Prepared for the American Friends Service Committee (Hill and Wang, 1971), ch. 8.

10. See American Bar Association Project on Minimum Standards for Criminal Justice, *Sentencing Alternatives and Procedures* (Institute for Judicial Administration, 1967), Sec. 3, pp. 129–199.

Sentencing Consistent With Parole Objectives

The sentencing system that seems most consistent with parole objectives has the following characteristics:

1.   Sentence limits set by legislation, with the sentencing judge having discretion to fix the maximum sentence, up to legislative limits.

2.   No minimum sentences, either by mandate or by judicial sentencing authority.

3.   Comparatively short sentences for most offenses, with a legislative maximum not to exceed five years for most offenders.

4.   Mandatory release with supervision for offenders ineligible for parole, so that they are not held in an institution until their absolute discharge date.

5.   All parole conditions set by the paroling authority, but with opportunity for a sentencing judge to suggest special conditions.

6.   Legislative prohibition of offenders' accumulating consecutive sentences if it interfers with minimum parole eligibility.

7.   Legislative provisions for alternatives to reimprisonment upon parole revocation.

8.   No offenses for which parole is denied by legislation.

In general, the intent of such a system is to give to the legislature and sentencing judges the authority to set outer limits of sentence but not to restrict parole authorities by setting minimum terms.   At the same time, the sentencing structure provides supervised release for those offenders whom parole authorities cannot conscientiously release under regular parole criteria.   The sentencing structure may provide for extended terms for dangerous offenders, though parole eligibility requirements should remain roughly the same in these cases.

A system of this kind would give parole authorities discretion over the release of offenders whom trial courts decided need incarceration.   Yet it would be a limited discretion.   Parolees would not be under supervision for excessive time periods nor, if parole were denied, would they be incarcerated for unnecessarily long terms.

PURPOSES OF PAROLE

The objectives of parole systems vary widely. Without clearly stated and understood objectives, the administrator cannot make the most basic decisions regarding effective resource allocation. Even a casual attempt to clarify the purposes of parole will reveal that objectives frequently are in conflict. One of the parole administrator's chief tasks is to minimize this conflict.

A Basic Purpose: Reduction of Recidivism

Few things about parole evoke consensus, but there is some agreement that one objective and measure of success is reduction of recidivism. Even this consensus quickly becomes less firm when two specific functions are examined: (1) provision of supervision and control to reduce the likelihood of criminal acts while the offender is serving his sentence in the community (the "surveillance" function), and (2) provision of assistance and services to the parolee, so that noncriminal behavior becomes possible (the "helping" function).[11]

To the extent that these concerns can be integrated, conflicts are minimized, but in the day-to-day activity of parole administration they frequently clash. Decisions constantly must be made between the relative risk of a law violation at the present time and the probable long-term gain if a parolee is allowed freedom and opportunity to develop a legally approved life style. Resources are needed to clarify the choices and risks involved. Key requirements for this kind of assistance are development of clear definitions of recidivism and creation of information systems that make data available about the probabilities of various types of parole outcome associated with alternative decisions. (These requirements are discussed in some detail in Chapter 15.)

Varied Concerns of Parole Boards

Reducing the risk of further criminality is not the sole concern. In fact, it actually may be secondary in some instances. A wider variety of concerns was expressed in a questionnaire completed by nearly half the parole board members in the United States in 1965, who were asked to indicate what they considered the five most important factors to be weighed in deciding on pa-

11. American Correctional Association, *Manual of Correctional Stand-* *ards* (Washington: ACA, 1966), p. 114.

role. Table 12.2 shows the items selected by at least 20 percent of those responding as being among the five most important considerations. The first three items selected as being the most important were related to the risk of violation. However, the next four related to three other concerns: equitable punishment, impact on the system, and reactions of persons outside the correctional organization.

Table 12.2. Items Considered by Parole Board Members to be Most Important in Parole Decisions

Item	Percent Including Item as One of Five Most Important
1. My estimate of the chances that the prisoner would or would not commit a serious crime if paroled.	92.8
2. My judgment that the prisoner would benefit from further experience in the institution program or, at any rate, would become a better risk if confined longer.	87.1
3. My judgment that the prisoner would become a worse risk if confined longer.	71.9
4. My judgment that the prisoner had already been punished enough to "pay" for his crime.	43.2
5. The probability that the prisoner would be a misdemeanant and a burden to his parole supervisors, even if he did not commit any serious offenses on parole.	35.3
6. My feelings about how my decision in this case would affect the feelings or welfare of the prisoner's relatives or dependents.	33.8
7. What I thought the reaction of the judge might be if the prisoner were granted parole.	20.9

Source: National Parole Institutes, *Selection for Parole* (New York: National Council on Crime and Delinquency, 1966).

[A9419]

A number of other studies have noted the same phenomenon.[12] Most parole board members consider risk a paramount concern,

12. See Robert Dawson, *Sentencing: The Decision as to Type, Length,*   *and Conditions of Sentence* (Little, Brown, 1969).

but other factors assume such importance in certain cases that
risk becomes secondary. A well-known inmate convicted and
sentenced for violation of a public trust may be denied parole
repeatedly because of strong public feelings, even though he
might be an excellent risk. In another type of case, an offender
convicted of a relatively minor crime may be paroled even though
a poor risk, because in the opinion of the board he has simply
served enough time for the offense committed. To some analysts
these other-than-risk considerations are viewed simply as con-
tingencies that arise from time to time; to others they involve
objectives central to parole decisionmaking. In either case, considerations other than risk assessment figure prominently in
parole decisionmaking and must be accounted for in any discussion of objectives. To judge from questionnaires returned by
parole board members and from studies in the field, there seem
to be at least three core sets of concern other than reducing recidivism,[13] which significantly and regularly impinge upon most
parole decisionmakers.

FAIRNESS AND PROPRIETY

Parole programs are part of larger systems of criminal justice.
They are governed by concepts of propriety and modes of conduct
arising from American culture and law. Especially in recent
years, parole systems have been expected to conform with practices that enhance the ideals of fairness and reflect hallmarks of
American justice such as procedural regularity, precedent, and
proof.

Most recently these issues have been reflected in increased
sensitivity to inmates' or revokees' rights to counsel, the right of
a hearing on parole grant and revocation, and disclosure of information used in decisionmaking. Reflecting this emphasis,
some parole board members may even refuse to consider at a
parole violation hearing evidence that might have been secured
by questionable search procedure. Comparable issues also arise
in establishing conditions for parole supervision, which are expected to meet the tests of relevance, reasonableness, and fairness.

13. Keith Hawkins, "Parole Selec-   unpublished doctoral dissertation,
tion: The American Experience,"   Cambridge University, 1971.

Appropriate Sanctions and Public Expectations

Though it seldom is stated openly, parole boards often are concerned with supporting a system of appropriate and equitable sanctions. This concern is reflected in several ways, depending upon a jurisdiction's sentencing system. One of the most common is through decisions seeking to equalize penalties for offenders who have similar backgrounds and have committed the same offense but who have received different sentences.

Alternatively, decisions to grant or deny parole, particularly in well-known cases, often may hinge on the question, "Has this person served enough time for the act he committed?" Considerable differences in these matters exist from one system to another, as well as among individuals in the same system. Such concerns usually are less apparent in, and perhaps less relevant to, juvenile agencies. However, in many parole systems, maintaining an appropriate system of sanctions directly or indirectly underlies most decisionmaking. How significant these considerations are depends on the kind of sentencing framework in which the parole system is operating.

In addition to issues of equity, parole decisionmakers sometimes respond to actual or anticipated public attitudes. Such concerns for public acceptance of parole generally, and case decisions specifically, govern the kinds of risks that are acceptable and the actions considered feasible by parole decisionmakers. This public reaction issue is particularly acute in cases affecting society's core beliefs. Criteria having little to do with the question of risk may be used by parole officials in dealing with certain cases, particularly those involving crimes seen as "heinous." The concern is more for meeting general social norms and responding according to public expectations.

Maintenance of the Justice System

A third set of concerns that influences parole decisionmaking relates to support of other criminal justice operations. Parole boards play a crucial role as a kind of system regulator, influencing other parts of the justice system, from police to prisons. For example, in some systems where a parole board has extensive control over the amount of time a large proportion of inmates will serve, institutional populations can change dramatically depending on board policy. Not only do parole board decisions influence institutional size, but they also reinforce behavior that can have profound effects on the kinds of programs sustained. Inmates are more likely to participate in a program the parole board explicitly values than in one to which the board pays no attention.

Institutional staff members have an obvious stake in the programs in which inmates are involved. Hence they too are affected by parole decisions. Various parole officials are sensitive to the correctional impact of their decisions and some take this factor into account in their decisions.[14] In some instances, boards will be reminded forcefully of their effect on inmates and institutions. For example, it is not uncommon during times of high prison tension (as after riots), when parole policy is under attack by inmates and sympathizers, for boards to become more "liberal." In such instances, the degree of risk acceptable for parole, conditioned by pressures within the institutions, shifts perceptibly. Parole boards directly affect parole supervision staff by the kind of offenders they release and revoke, and by the policies surrounding these actions.

System maintenance and other basic concerns cited clearly influence parole decisionmaking. However, questions of risk, fairness, public expectation, and system maintenance are not the only considerations affecting parole authorities. Of great importance as well are the beliefs they hold concerning the sources of criminality, strategies for changing offenders, and the nature of the relationship between the correctional system and the offender.

ORGANIZATION OF PAROLING AUTHORITIES

Most persons concerned with parole decisionmaking for juveniles are full-time institutional personnel. Only a few juvenile jurisdictions have noninstitutional personnel determining parole releases.

Different circumstances prevail in the adult area. For example, adult boards tend to carry many more direct State-level administrative responsibilities than do releasing authorities for ju-

14. Keith Hawkins, "Some Consequences of a Parole System for Prison Management," in D. F. West, ed., *The Future of Parole* (London: Gerald Duckworth, 1972).

veniles. Table 12.3 shows that in 1965, 14 adult parole boards supervised probation services for the courts of the State. Few parole decisionmaking groups for juvenile offenders had a similar responsibility. The table also shows the historical link in many States between parole and the clemency or pardon authority of the governor. Many boards carried out advisory functions for the governor in executive clemency matters and in one State, Alabama, the board granting paroles also had the power to pardon.

Although there is considerable variety in the organizational settings in which parole decisionmakers work, at least two dominant organizational strains can be identified—the institutional model, which largely predominates in the juvenile field, and the independent model, the most common in the adult field. Considerable controversy has arisen around these two models.[15]

THE INSTITUTIONAL MODEL

In general, the institutional model perceives parole as being bound closely to institutional programs. It places the release decision with the correctional facility's staff. Parole is simply

Table 12.3 Responsibilities of Adult Paroling Agencies Other Than Parole, 1965

Additional Responsibility	Number of Boards
Holds clemency hearings	28
Commutes sentences	24
Appoints parole supervision staff	24
Administers parole service	20
Paroles from local institutions	19
Grants or withholds "good time"	17
Supervises probation service	14
Grants pardons, restorations, and remissions	1
Fixes maximum sentence after 6 months	1
May discharge prior to sentence expiration	1
Sets standards for "good time"	1
Acts as advisory board on pardons	1
None	5

Source: National Council on Crime and Delinquency, *Correction in the United States* (New York: NCCD, 1967), p. 215.

[A9402]

15. *Task Force Report: Corrections*, pp. 65–66.

one more of a series of decisions affecting the offender. The persons most familiar with the cases make the releasing decision; and this makes it possible to develop a rational and consistent set of decisions that affect the inmate. The Crime Commission reported that 34 of 50 States used this form of organization in the juvenile field.

The major arguments raised against the institutional model is that too often institutional considerations, rather than individual or community needs, influence the decisions. Overcrowding in the institution, desire to be rid of a problem case or to enforce relatively petty rules, or other concerns of institution management easily become the basis of decisionmaking. Institutional decisionmaking also lends itself to such informal procedures and lack of visibility as to raise questions about its capacity for fairness or, what may be as important, the appearance of fairness.

THE INDEPENDENT AUTHORITY

In the adult field, a good deal of reform was associated with removing parole decisionmaking from institutional control to an independent authority. Undoubtedly much of the basis for this reform came from the view that paroling authorities were being swayed too easily by institutional considerations or were not being objective enough.[16] The change was so complete that today no adult parole releasing authority is controlled directly by the operating staff of a penal institution.

Whatever its merits in fostering objectivity, the independent parole board also has been criticized on several counts. First, the claim is made that such boards tend to be insensitive to institutional programs and fail to give them the support they require. Second, independent boards are accused of basing their decisions on inappropriate considerations, such as the feelings of a local police chief. Third, their remoteness from the institutional program gives independent boards little appreciation of the dynamics in a given case; their work tends to be cursory, with the result that too often persons who should be paroled are not, and those who should not be paroled are released. Fourth, the argument is made that independent systems tend to place on pa-

16. *Attorney General's Survey of Release Procedures* (1939), vol. IV, p. 49.

role boards persons who have little training or experience in corrections.

Lack of knowledge about corrections, combined with the distance of the parole board from institutional programs, builds unnecessary conflicts into the system. The rapid growth of partway release programs and halfway houses has increased the probability of those conflicts. In short, critics of the independent model assert that important decisions are being made concerning the correctional system, its programs, and the offenders in it by persons far removed from the system who have little appreciation of its true nature.

THE CONSOLIDATION MODEL

While these arguments and their rebuttals continue, an alternate system has gained considerable support in recent years, tending to cut the ground away from both major models. This system is linked with a general move toward consolidation of all types of correctional services into distinctive departments of corrections that subsume both institution and field programs. The consolidation model, emerging from the drive toward centralized administration, typically results in parole decisions being made by a central decisionmaking authority organizationally situated in an overall department of corrections but possessing independent powers. The director of corrections may serve on such a releasing authority, or he may designate a staff member to do so. In the youth field, the centralized board may have policy responsibilities for institutions as well as parole decisionmaking.

Proponents of the consolidation model argue that there is increased concern for the whole correctional system in departments where parole releasing authority is part of a centralized system. They claim that sensitivity to institutional programs seems more pronounced in consolidated systems than in completely autonomous ones. They also contend that removal of parole decisionmaking from the immediate control of specific correctional institutions tends to give greater weight to a broader set of considerations, a number of which are outside direct institutional concerns.

Although variations in organizational or administrative arrangements may be required to meet special circumstances, certain general organizational requirements seem clear. Among the most essential requisites is that the organizational structure of parole authorities should foster close coordination between parole decisionmakers and the increasingly complex set of programs throughout the correctional network. Yet sufficient autonomy should be preserved to permit parole boards to act as a check on the system.

The trend in this country clearly is in the direction of consolidation. More than 60 percent of the State parole boards responsible for release of adult offenders now function in common administrative structures with other agencies for offenders.[17] This trend enhances integration of correctional operations. If parole boards are to function as useful and sophisticated decisionmaking units that balance a wide set of concerns, they also must achieve and maintain some degree of autonomy from the systems with which they interface. This issue involves appointment and tenure methods, as well as the tasks and functions for which parole authorities take responsibility.

ARTICULATION OF CRITERIA FOR DECISIONS

Articulation of criteria for making decisions and development of basic policies is one of the chief tasks that parole decisionmakers need to undertake. While discretion is a necessary feature of parole board operations, the central issue is how to contain and control it appropriately. Few parole boards have articulated their decision criteria in much detail or in writing, even though research has shown that criteria exist. Parole board members tend to display, with slight variations, a consistent response to case situations of which they may be only marginally aware.[18]

Articulating the basis of decision systems is crucial to improving parole decisions, because criteria must be specified before they can be validated. For example, 75 percent of 150 board members queried in 1965 by the National Probation and Parole Institute asserted that rapists generally were poor parole risks. Research data have shown such an assumption to be wrong.

17. National Probation and Parole Institutes, *The Organization of Parole Systems for Felony Offenders in the United States.* 2d ed. Hackensack, N. J.: National Council on Crime and Delinquency, 1972). Unless otherwise stated, factual data on State parole systems given in this chapter are from this publication.

18. Don Gottfredson and Kelly Ballard, "Differences in Parole Decisions Associated with Decision Makers," *Journal of Research in Crime and Delinquency,* 3 (1966), 112.

Articulation of criteria is crucial to staff and inmates alike. The notion of an inmate's participation in a program of change depends on an open information system. His sense of just treatment is inextricably bound with it. As one parole board member put it:

> It is an essential element of justice that the role and processes for measuring parole readiness be made known to the inmate. This knowledge can greatly facilitate the earnest inmate toward his own rehabilitation. It is just as important for an inmate to know the rules and basis of the judgment upon which he will be granted or denied parole as it was important for him to know the basis of the charge against him and the evidence upon which he was convicted. One can imagine nothing more cruel, inhuman, and frustrating than serving a prison term without knowledge of what will be measured and the rules determining whether one is ready for release.
> . . . Justice can never be a product of unreasoned judgment.[19]

And without valid information on the basis of parole decisions, correctional staffs hardly can be expected to deal realistically with offenders or to shape meaningful programs with them.

In most parole systems, board members are so heavily committed to case-by-case decisions that these additional tasks, and those to be suggested subsequently, will require a substantial alteration in work style. Smaller States will need to shift from part-time to full-time parole boards. Other States will require additional personnel at the parole decisionmaking level.

NEED FOR APPEAL PROCEDURES

Besides the pressure for clearly articulated policies, there also is a rapidly developing demand for mechanisms by which correctional, and specifically parole, decisions can be appealed. The upsurge of cases being considered by the courts documents this need.[20] The courts can and will test at least certain aspects of parole decisions. Yet if parole authorities are to develop correc-

19. Everette M. Porter, "Criteria for Parole Selection" in *Proceedings of the American Correctional Association* (New York: ACA, 1958) p. 227.

20. For examples of this growth in interest by the courts, see Comment, "The Parole System," *Pennsylvania Law Review*, 120 (1971), 282.

tional policy consistent with correctional needs and judicial standards, they need to establish self-regulation systems, including internal appeal procedures.[21]

Where the volume of cases warrants it, a parole board should
concentrate its major attention on policy development and appeals. The bulk of case-by-case decisionmaking should be done
by hearing examiners responsible to the board and familiar with
its policies and knowledgeable as to correctional programs.

Hearing examiners should have statutory power to grant, deny,
or revoke parole, subject to parole board rules and policies. In
cases of offenders serving long sentences, those involved in cases
of high public interest, or others designated by the parole board,
two or more parole members personally should conduct the hearings and make decisions. Hearing examiners operating in teams
of two should handle the large part of day-to-day interviewing
and decisionmaking for the board. Inmates and parolees should
be entitled to appeal decisions to the parole board, which could
hear cases in panels or en banc. As action is taken on these cases
and the system of appeals refined, the board should further ar-
ticulate its policies against which unwarranted uses of discretion could be checked.

Instead of spending his time routinely traveling from institution to institution hearing every type of case, the board member
should be deciding appeals and hearing cases of special concern.
He should be developing written policies and using monitoring
systems by which decision outcomes could be observed and strategies for improvement developed. The use of the board for all
types of appeals from correctional decisions (loss of good time,
denial of privileges) also should be considered.

In smaller systems, many of these activities would have to be
carried out by the same persons. However, procedures can and
should be developed to assure attention to each separate function
—policy development, hearings, and appeals. Only a few of these
crucial activities now are carried out by the average parole
board. They are critically needed, and the kind of system described here would greatly facilitate their attainment. Parts of
such a system have been used successfully by the California and
Federal parole boards and other governmental agencies.

21. Edward Kimball and Donald   and Response," *Crime and Delin-*
      Newman, "Judicial Intervention in   *quency,* 14 (1968), 1.
      Correctional Decisions: Threat

An advisory group, broadly representative of the community and specifically including ex-offenders, should be established to assist the parole board by reviewing policies and helping shape and implement improvement strategies developed. This kind of link to the public is critically needed if sensible policies are to be developed and support for their adoption achieved.

PAROLE AUTHORITY PERSONNEL

The most recent data available on members of juvenile parole releasing authorities indicate that by far the largest number are full-time staff of juvenile correctional institutions.[22] In several States, such as California and Minnesota, youth commissions parole juveniles. In others, such as Wisconsin and Illinois, the same board is responsible for release of both juveniles and adults.[23] The issues of appointment, qualifications, and training raise precisely the same questions for juvenile release authority members as they do for board members responsible for adult release.

In 41 States, adult parole board members are appointed by the governor. In seven jurisdictions, they are appointed in whole or in part by the department of corrections.

A similar problem exists with any part-time member of a paroling authority. In 18 States, parole board members responsible for the parole of adult males are part-time employees. In six others only the chairman is a full-time employee. Part-time board members tend to be located in the smallest States, but there are exceptions. Tennessee and South Carolina, for example, with part-time boards, have larger populations than several other smaller States that have full-time boards. If parole services were extended to local jails and one board was made responsible for jails, training schools for delinquents, and adult prisons, a full-time board would be needed in virtually every State.

For larger States, the relevant question is, What is the optimum size of the parole decisionmaking authority? Almost half of parole boards for adult offenders consist of three members; 18 jurisdictions have five members; six have seven members; and one parole board, New York's, consists of 12 members. Some

22. National Council on Crime and Delinquncy, *Correction in the United States* (New York: NCCD, 1967), p. 104.

23. *Correction in the United States*, p. 86.

parole authorities argue that boards could grow indefinitely. But with a shift in emphasis toward policy articulation and appeals, it would seem prudent to hold the size to a manageable level. Few, if any, State boards should exceed five members. As the workload expands beyond the capacity of these members, hearing examiners should be appointed. The largest States might need 20 hearing examiners or more.

QUALIFICATIONS OF BOARD MEMBERS

Two dilemmas that are common to most appointive public offices are also seen in deciding on the best method of selecting parole board members: first, how to secure appointees with expertise and willingness to challenge the system when necessary rather than merely preserving it; second, how to select parole board members who will be responsive to public concern, as expressed through elected officials, without making politics rather than competence the basis for appointment.

Parole decisionmakers too frequently have shown the negative possibilities of both dilemmas. In many instances they have become so coopted by a correctional system that there is no independent check against abuses of public or offender interests. Too many times appointments have been governed by patronage considerations, a dangerous criterion when human freedom is at stake and the most difficult moral, legal, and scientific issues are involved.

If parole authorities are to have the competence required for their tasks, specific statutory qualifications for board members must be developed. In 24 States there are no statutory requirements for parole members responsible for the release of adult offenders. In one State generalized references to character are made. In another 21 only the broadest references to experience or training are enunciated.

According to the findings of the first National Parole Conference in 1939, board members "should be selected on the basis of their integrity and competence to deal with human and social problems, without reference to political affiliations." [24] More recently the standards proposed by the American Correctional Association required that parole board members should "command respect and public confidence," be "appointed without reference

---

24. *Proceedings, National Parole Conference, 1939* (Leavenworth, Kan.: Federal Prison Industries, Inc., 1970), p. 113.

to creed, color or political affiliation," possess "academic training which has qualified the board member for professional practice in a field such as criminology, education, psychiatry, psychology, law, social work and sociology," and "have intimate knowledge of common situations and problems confronting offenders." [25]

No single professional group or discipline can be recommended as ideal for all parole board members. A variety of goals are to be served by parole board members, and a variety of skills are required. Knowledge of at least three basic fields should be represented on a parole board: the law, the behavioral sciences, and corrections. Furthermore, as a board assumes responsibility for policy articulation, monitoring and review, the tasks involved require persons who are able to use a wide range of decisionmaking tools, such as statistical materials, reports from professional personnel, and a variety of other technical information. In general, persons with sophisticated training and experience are required. In this context, the standards suggested by the American Correctional Association should be statutorily required for each jurisdiction.

Hearing examiners require less specialized education and training. More critical in these roles are persons with educational and experiential qualifications that allow them to understand programs, to relate to people, and to make sound and reasonable decisions. These roles should offer particular opportunities for ex-offenders and for those persons most sensitive to the implications of offenders' lifestyles.

MAKING THE APPOINTMENT

A critical question concerns who should make the actual appointment to the parole board. Two basic choices are the governor or the head of the department of corrections. Appointment by the governor provides the board increased autonomy and greater responsiveness to public influence. But it increases the likelihood of lack of coordination with the corrections agency, oversensitivity to public reactions, and appointment of unqualified personnel. Selection by the director of corrections, who is himself selected on the basis of professional qualifications, is

25. American Correctional Association, *Manual of Correctional Standards*, p. 119.

more likely to secure appointment of knowledgeable persons, protection from political influence, and some shielding from an undue concern for public criticism. The major disadvantage is the possible appointment of a "rubber stamp" decisionmaking body.

Some type of device must be employed if competent board personnel are to be selected. Each State should require by law that nominees for parole board positions first be screened by a committee broadly representative of the community. Representatives of groups such as the State bar and mental health associations should be included, as well as representatives of various ethnic and socioeconomic groups. The law should require that appointments be made only from the approved list of nominees.

TERMS OF OFFICE, SALARY

A number of other suggestions to improve parole board appointments have been made and should be adopted. One of these is to provide parole board members with substantial terms of office, as long as 12 years, during which they cannot be removed except for good cause.[26]

A matter of particular importance in attracting well-qualified persons to parole positions is the compensation. According to the most recent data available, the median salary for full-time parole board members is $19,000 a year. This is not a salary which in 1972 can attract the type of personnel needed for parole decisionmaking posts. The salary for such positions should be equivalent to that of a judge of a court of general jurisdiction.

TRAINING FOR BOARD MEMBERS

Improvement in the performance of parole members depends heavily on the availability of a training program. The National Probation and Parole Institutes have undertaken to provide biennial training sessions for new members. But much more needs to be done in this area. Ongoing training is needed by both new and experienced board members.

An effective ongoing program should inform board members of recent legal decisions and advances in technology and acquaint them with current correctional practices and trends. Because of the relatively small number of parole board members in each State, such a program would have to be national in scope. An

26. Phillip E. Johnson, *Federal Parole Procedures* (Washington: Administrative Conference of the United States, 1972).

exchange program of parole board members and hearing officers also should receive support. Recent experiments carried out by the National Probation and Parole Institutes, in which parole board members had the opportunity to visit other States, proved to be valuable experience for participants.

THE PAROLE GRANT HEARING

The parole hearing is a critical moment for inmates. At this point they are legally "eligible" for release, their case is studied, they are interviewed, and the decision is made. In all States except Texas, Georgia, and Hawaii, adult felony offenders are present at hearings at the time of parole consideration. Four States screen files and grant interviews only to eligible inmates who seem to merit parole consideration. All other States hear every offender at least once, even those unlikely to be released. Many parole authorities see an inmate several times during the course of his sentence. In fact, a number of States provide for at least annual review of each case, no matter how remote release may be.

Formal hearing procedures are much less common with juveniles. More often, primary emphasis is placed on written reports or staff conferences at which the youth may or may not be present.

Procedures followed at parole hearings for adult offenders are extremely diverse. In some States, each parole applicant is heard by the full parole board. In others, especially those with many correctional institutions, boards are split into smaller working panels, each of which conducts hearings. In several jurisdictions, a single parole board member may conduct a hearing unless the case is regarded as unusually important, when a larger subcommittee or the entire board conducts the hearing. In the Federal system and in California, the parole boards appoint "hearing officers" to assist in some hearings. The number of cases considered in a single day by boards or panels for adult offenders ranges from 15 to 60.

INFORMATION BASE

Information available to the parole board at the time of a hearing typically is prepared by institutional staff. It is usually based on reports on the offender's adjustment to prison life. Some parole boards request special investigations of release plans for all inmates, while others prefer to wait until they make a tentative decision that parole is indicated. A few States have reports prepared by professional clinical personnel. Since these professionals are scarce, most reports prepared for parole boards are written by caseworkers who actually have relatively little opportunity to observe inmates.

Glaser has suggested use of revised reporting systems, wherein staff members who have the most contact with inmates would be involved most directly in providing data for the board's decisions.[27] With the increasing stress on reintegration, most parole board members need a great deal more information about community services available to released offenders, as well as on feasible programs that might be undertaken. This lack is not solely an information gap; unfortunately, the basic problem is that community resources are meager.

RIGHT TO A HEARING

In most jurisdictions the offender has no statutory rights in the parole consideration process, except in some instances the right to a personal appearance before the parole board. Yet at these hearings, the traditional stance has been that the inmate and his record must make an affirmative case for parole. The Model Penal Code represents a turn-around in the traditional assumption that the burden of proof (however evaluated) rests on the inmate. It proposes that an inmate is to be released on parole when he is first eligible unless one of the following four conditions exists:

1.   There is a substantial indication that he will not conform to conditions of parole.

2.   His release at that time would depreciate the seriousness of the crime or promote disrespect for the law.

3.   His release would have substantially adverse effects on institutional discipline.

4.   His continued correctional treatment, medical care, or vocational or other training in the institution will substantially enhance his capacity to lead a law-abiding life when released at a later date.[28]

Recently the National Commission on Reform of Federal Criminal Laws substantially endorsed the presumption and the four considerations of the Model Penal Code. It offered in addition

27. Daniel Glaser, *The Effectiveness of a Prison and Parole System* (Bobbs-Merrill, 1964), ch. 9.

28. American Law Institute, *Model Penal Code*, (Philadelphia: ALI, 1962).

the proviso that, once an inmate has served the longer of five years or two-thirds of his sentence, he should be paroled unless the board is "of the opinion that his release should be deferred because there is a high likelihood that he would engage in further criminal conduct." [29]

PROCEDURAL GUIDELINES

In the past few years there has been a noticeable increase in complexity of procedural requirements for parole hearings. Of those jurisdictions holding personal interviews, for example, 21 now permit the "assistance" of attorneys in behalf of the inmate. Seventeen allow the inmate to be represented at the hearing by persons other than counsel whom he feels will help him present his case for granting parole. A verbatim record of proceedings is made in 11 jurisdictions.

Development of guidelines for desirable parole hearings should attend to several concerns simultaneously. First, such hearings should provide parole authorities with as much relevant and reliable information about each case as possible. Second, the hearing process itself should carry the hallmark of fairness. Not only should it be a fair determination in substance, but to the extent possible it also should be perceived by the inmate as fair. Third, as far as practicable the hearing should enhance the prospects for an inmate's successful completion of his parole.

To these ends the hearing can make a number of contributions. The manner in which the inmate is interviewed and notified of decisions affecting him can support or undermine respect for the system of justice. Any opportunity for the offender's active participation in decisions can greatly affect his commitment to the plans made. In the final analysis, *his* commitment is the crucial factor in whether or not these plans will be carried out.

In keeping with the reintegration emphasis, a modern corrections system should embrace a wide variety of alternative programs, not only for institutions, but also for release or partway release. Except in rare cases it will probably be too cumbersome for a parole board to approve specific actions in detail. With community corrections, halfway houses, prerelease centers, split sentences, and similar developments, the line between parole and prison already is becoming blurred. It therefore appears neces-

29. National Commission on Reform   *Report* (Washington: Government
    of Federal Criminal Laws, *Final*   Printing Office, 1971), p. 300.

sary that the parole board increasingly test the appropriateness of programs and match individuals with them by criteria fixed in advance, rather than try to make clinical decisions on an individual's readiness for release.

THE AUTOMATIC FIRST HEARING

A number of practical steps for parole hearings flow from these changes in overall correctional processing. Every inmate should routinely be seen by a parole authority during the first year of incarceration. This review should be automatic and no application by the inmate should be required. Such a hearing might result in consideration of early parole. More often, it would be devoted to a review of the particular objectives and programs developed by the inmate and staff. Any program involving release for long periods should involve the parole board hearing staff.

The important element of this first, automatic hearing is that the board approves program objectives and program categories for offenders rather than attempting to make detailed clinical judgments about each case. The objective of the hearing, however, should not be to coerce the inmate to subject himself to specific institutional treatment programs. The traditional ineffectiveness of such programs does not make participation a good basis for a parole decision.

A particularly critical determination during this initial interview is scheduling another interview or hearing, if one is necessary before the inmate's release. It should be increasingly common to approve an inmate's program, including a full-time parole release date, as far as a year in advance without requiring another hearing or further interviews by the parole board. If the objectives of the program are met, administration of the parole board's plan would be left to the offender and institutional and field staffs. Should substantial variations occur or important new information develop, the board could be notified and a new hearing scheduled. On the other hand, not all release dates can be predetermined at an initial interview. Additional hearings may be required either because of the length of the inmate's sentence or by the circumstances of a particular case. In such instances, a new hearing date would be fixed after the initial interview. In no case should more than a year transpire between hearings.

Under this plan, the parole board would function more to monitor the decisions of others than to make detailed judgments in individual cases. The plan should also reduce the number of individual release hearings conducted by board representatives. This is particularly important since there is a practical limit on the number that can be conducted in a day. An effective hearing requires close attention of board representatives, institutional staff, offenders, and other persons involved in tailoring programs and releases to individual cases. It also requires careful recording of plans and decisions. With a system of this kind, no more than 20 cases should be heard in a day.

PROMPT DECISION AND NOTIFICATION

If this system is to work, it requires involvement of at least two representatives of the parole authority who are empowered to grant parole in all but the most exceptional cases. A current problem in a number of parole jurisdictions is that only a single representative of the parole authority actually hears offenders' cases. He is not able to take final action on any case until he returns to a central point where other board officials can join him in making a decision. Hence there is often inordinate delay, while the inmate and others involved must simply mark time. Not only does such delayed decisionmaking lower morale, but also available parole resources may deteriorate and no longer be open to the inmate when the parole finally is granted. The job that was waiting is lost; the chance to participate in vocational education programs is gone.

Delay in making parole decisions should be eliminated. The key lies in sufficient decisionmaking power being allocated at the point of hearing. In almost all cases two examiners can perform the necessary hearing functions if they can agree.

Allied to prompt decisionmaking is the manner in which an inmate is notified of determinations affecting him. About half of the State jurisdictions now inform inmates of the decision and the reasons for it as soon as it is made, at the hearing itself. This practice is relatively new. Formerly, the almost universal practice was to send word of release or deferral to the inmate through a board representative or an institutional official. Such officials have no way of clarifying the meaning of the decision or its implications to the inmate. This task can and should be done only by parole decisionmakers, not by others trying to represent them. Parole authorities should explain the reasons for their decisions directly to the inmate and answer any questions he has.

WRITTEN DECISIONS

Also critical in this respect is the necessity for parole decision-makers to spell out in writing the reasons for their decision and to specify the behavioral objectives they have in mind. Currently only about 12 parole boards dealing with adult offenders document the reasons for their decisions. It should be a universal practice. It is important for future hearing representatives to have available the reasoning of prior hearing officials.

Likewise, it is important for institutional officials to have the written parole opinion to assist them in shaping future programs for offenders denied parole. It also is important for board self-evaluation; research should be able to measure the relationship between reasons for actions and subsequent events and decisions. Board documents provide a basis for checking the reasons for decisions against the criteria used. This is particularly crucial in a two-tiered system of decision and review in which appeals can be made.

DUE PROCESS REQUIREMENTS

Provisions for sharing the bases of decisions with offenders, making a written record of proceedings, requiring written reasons for decisions, and allowing a two-tiered appeal process not only are good administrative practice but also are consistent with legal requirements of procedural due process. They may come to be viewed as legally necessary. So far, however, courts have been restrained in requiring elaborate procedural safeguards during parole consideration. For example, the Federal Second Circuit Court of Appeals in the recent case of Menechino v. Oswald, 430 F.2d 403 (2d Cir. 1970), in referring to the parole board's function said:

> It must make the broad determination of whether rehabilitation of the prisoner and the interest of society generally would best be served by permitting him to serve his sentence beyond the confines of the prison walls rather than by being continued in physical confinement. In making that determination, the Board is not restricted by rules of evidence or procedures developed for the purpose of determining legal or factual issues.

However, the Supreme Court, in a recent case involving parole revocation hearings, laid down strict procedural requirements to safeguard due process. (See subsequent section on revocation.)

It may well be that such requirements will be deemed necessary for the grant hearing as well.

Trends in court decisions are difficult to predict. Certainly in the last few years appellate courts have ordered changes in parole proceedings, particularly those surrounding revocation. There is sound basis in correctional terms alone for elements in the parole hearing that embrace some characteristics of administrative hearings occurring at other points in the criminal justice process. The value of information disclosure, for example, does not rest simply upon legal precedent. Parole boards have as much stake in the accuracy of records as other criminal justice officials. Evidence indicates that decisions are much more likely to be documented carefully and fully when information is disclosed and when those whose interests are at stake have a chance to examine and test it. Rather than resulting in an adversary battle, disclosure more often than not provides information not contained in the report. This is an important addition for decisionmakers.

Information sharing underlies much of the emphasis in modern corrections that is moving toward an open, reality-testing base. From this perspective, it is expected that offenders will be given available evidence and facts. In the average parole file little material is so sensitive that it cannot be reviewed with the inmate. Of course, if there is a need to treat with caution professional material such as certain types of psychiatric reports, it can be held back.

The suggested procedures of the American Bar Association for disclosure of presentence investigation material seem eminently suitable for the parole hearing stage. Materials could be withdrawn when deemed necessary, with a notation made of this fact in the file. In case of appeal, the full parole board would be notified as to what material had been withheld from the inmate and could take this into consideration.

REPRESENTATION

The issue of inmate representation by lawyers or other spokesmen causes difficulty for many parole board members because it seems to create an unnecessarily adversarial system out of essentially a "clinical" decision process. However, several arguments for representation can be advanced. The offender's representative has the freedom to pursue information, develop resources, and raise questions that are difficult for an inmate in a helpless position. To the extent that the information base can be enlarged by representatives and issues sharpened and tested more directly, there is likely to be improvement in the whole process of parole board decision-making. Equally important, however, is the impression of fairness given to the inmate who is represented. Indeed in many cases it is more than simply a feeling of fairness. It is clear that, in too many situations, the lack of ability to communicate well, to participate fully in the hearing, and to have a sense of full and careful consideration, is extremely detrimental.

Representation also can contribute to opening the correctional system, particularly the parole process, to public scrutiny. It is important that more people become personally involved in the correctional process, since the reintegration movement rests on the involvement of community resources and representatives. Involvement of persons from the outside also provides opportunity for remedy of any abuses in parole processes.

Ultimately the credibility of a parole system will rest on its openness to public scrutiny. For these reasons, a system of providing, or at least allowing, representation for the offender at parole hearings should be sponsored by parole officials. Because of the diversity in parole eligibility and program administration among parole systems, the precise interviews with inmates at which representation is appropriate or feasible will vary. But the principle of allowing representation when crucial decisions regarding the offender's freedom are made should guide the board in fixing policies. Lawyers are only one possible kind of representative; citizen volunteers also could serve as offender representatives.

The idea of representation at hearings may be annoying to parole officials. Implementation may increase costs. On balance, these inconveniences seem a small price for the prospective gains. Assuming representation, the board should be able to prevent

abuses in the conduct of hearings. It is crucial for parole boards to develop appropriate policies for information disclosure, forms and methods of representation, and procedural rules to be followed at the hearings.

MODEL FOR THE PAROLE GRANT HEARING

The hearing examiner model can be easily adapted to parole systems from administrative law. Hearing examiners play a

central role in an administrative agency's treatment of controversy. Matters are scheduled before the examiner who conducts
a full hearing and then prepares a report which contains findings
of fact, conclusions of law, and recommended order. This report, the transcript, and the evidence introduced constitute the
exclusive basis for decision. The hearing examiner makes the
initial decision which, unless appealed to the full Board or Commission, becomes the decision of the agency.

A party dissatisfied with the recommendations or findings of
the hearing examiner can appeal his decision to the full agency
board which, being charged with the responsibility for decision,
may overturn the findings of the examiner. The full board does
not hear the matter de novo, but on briefs and arguments. The
final order of the board can then be appealed to court by a dissatisfied party. Court review would determine whether there is

FIGURE 12.1.　HEARING EXAMINER MODEL

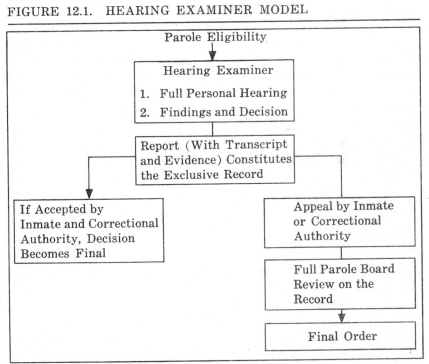

[A8990]

substantial evidence on the record as a whole to support the agency decision, or whether it is erroneous as a matter of law.

Adaptation of the administrative law model for use of hearing
examiners in parole grant hearings is represented in Figure 12.1.

When a parole grant hearing is scheduled, a hearing examiner should conduct a full personal hearing with the inmate, his representative, and appropriate institutional staff members. Contents of any written reports supplied to the hearing examiner should be openly disclosed and become a part of the record, except that the parole board may establish guidelines under which certain sensitive information could be withheld from the inmate with notation of this fact included in the record.

A verbatim transcript of the proceedings should be made. The hearing examiner should make his decision on the basis of criteria and policies established by the parole board and specify his findings in writing. He should personally inform the inmate of his decision and provide him a copy of the full report. The hearing examiner's report, with the transcript and evidence, should constitute the exclusive record.

If the decision of the hearing examiner is not appealed by the inmate or the correctional authority within five days after the hearing, the decision of the hearing examiner should be final. If the decision is not accepted by the inmate or the correctional authority, appeal should be made to the parole board. The full parole board should review the case on the record to see if there is substantial evidence to support the finding or if it is erroneous as a matter of law. The order of the parole board should be final.

REVOCATION HEARINGS

Until the late 1960's, procedures in many jurisdictions for the return of parole violators to prison were so informal that the term "hearing" would be a misnomer. In many instances revocation involved no more than the parole board's pro forma approval of the request of the parole officer or his field staff supervisor. In many jurisdictions the revocation decision represented almost unfettered discretion of parole authorities. In addition to minimal procedural formality, the grounds for revocation also were non-specific, involving such assessments as "generally poor attitude" or allegations of "failure to cooperate," rather than specific breaches of conditions or commission of new offenses.

This was particularly true in revocation of the aftercare of juveniles, where the decision to revoke was viewed primarily as a casework determination. Ostensibly, it did not involve a breach of conditions but was simply an action for the youth's welfare.

This general stance of casual and quick return of both adults and juveniles rested primarily on the "privilege" or "grace" doctrine of the parole grant. To many parole officials, revocation did not warrant much concern with due process, procedural regularity, or matters of proof, hearing, and review.

In 1964 a study of parole board revocations showed that there was no hearing at all in at least seven States. In those States providing a hearing, the alleged violator frequently was returned to prison directly from the field on allegation of the field agent or on a warrant issued by the board. An actual hearing or review of this return by the parole board did not take place until weeks, sometimes months, after the parolee had been returned to the institution.[30] In most cases, then, revocation was a fait accompli by the time the board's representative next visited the institution to review the revocation order and officially declare the parolee a violator.

In a small minority of cases, board members canceled the warrant or field complaint and permitted the prisoner again to resume parole. However, since the parolee had been moved to the institution, employment and family relationships already were disturbed. In effect a canceled revocation order meant that the parolee once again had to be transported to his local community and begin the readjustment process all over again. Counsel rarely was permitted to represent the alleged violator at such hearings. Any witnesses to the alleged violation almost always were seen outside the hearing at the parole board offices, rarely subject to confrontation or cross-examination by the parolee. While at the time of the survey some States allowed parolees to have "assistance" of lawyers, no jurisdiction assigned counsel to indigent parolees.

INTERVENTION BY APPELLATE COURTS

Since the 1960's there has been considerable appellate court intervention in the parole process generally and in revocation procedures specifically. This new vigor is consistent with a general distinction in administrative law between granting a privilege (as in parole) and taking it away once it has been given (as in revocation). Courts generally have held that initial granting

30. Ronald Sklar, "Law and Practice in Probation and Parole Revocation Hearings," *Journal of Criminal Law and Criminology*, 55 (1964), 75.

or denial of a privilege can be done much more casually and with fewer procedural safeguards than taking away a privilege once granted.

Development of court-imposed requirements for procedural due process in parole revocation has been somewhat erratic. One of the important leading cases in the Federal jurisdiction was Hyser v. Reed, decided in the D.C. Circuit in 1963 (318 F.2d 225, 235). The decision in this case generally supported the common position that revocation was strictly a discretionary withdrawal of a privilege not requiring adversarial hearings at which inmates are represented by counsel and so forth. This part of the decision was consistent with both the law and the general sentiment of most parole authorities at the time. What *Hyser* did do, however, was to deal with the venue question of where the revocation hearing should take place.

The court supported the U. S. Parole Board practice of conducting a fact-finding hearing on the site of the alleged offense or violation of condition, with review at the institution only if the first hearing determined the offender should be returned. This decision was sensible, particularly in those cases involving a mistake or failure to find any infraction. If in fact the parolee did not commit the alleged infraction he could continue his parole uninterrupted.

Subsequent to the *Hyser* decision, however, courts in some Federal and State jurisdictions reversed the first part of the decision; namely, the lack of any right, constitutional or otherwise, for due process to be applied at revocation proceedings. Most courts that departed from *Hyser* in this regard did so on the basis of the Supreme Court decision in a case involving "deferred sentencing" or probation revocation. In Mempa v. Rhay, 389 U.S. 128 (1967), the Supreme Court held in 1967 that a State probationer had a right to a hearing and to counsel upon allegation of violations of probation. A number of courts interpreted the principle of *Mempa* to apply to parole as well.

The extension of *Mempa* procedural requirements to parole revocation was fairly common in both State jurisdictions and in various Federal circuits. In almost all cases, conformity with *Mempa* requirements meant a reversal of former legal positions and a major change in administrative practices. For example, the New York Court of Appeals, resting its decision on the *Mempa* case, reversed its former position and required the New York

Parole Board to permit inmates to be represented by counsel at
revocation hearings, People ex rel. v. Warden Greenhaven, 318
N.Y.S.2d 449 (1971). The rationale most often used as a basis for
the requirement of procedural due process at parole revocation
was expressed in another Federal Circuit Court case, Murray v.
Page, 429 F.2d 1359 (10th Cir. 1970):

> Therefore, while a prisoner does not have a constitution-
> al right to parole, once paroled he cannot be deprived of
> his freedom by means inconsistent with due process.
> The minimal right of the parolee to be informed of the
> charges and the nature of the evidence against him and
> to appear to be heard at the revocation hearing is invio-
> late. Statutory deprivation of this right is manifestly
> inconsistent with due process and is unconstitutional;
> nor can such right be lost by the subjective determina-
> tion of the executive that the case for revocation is
> "clear."

By and large parole officials have resisted attempts by courts,
or others, to introduce procedural due process requirements
into parole revocation and at other stages of parole. Resistance has rested not simply on encroachment of authority but
also on the possible negative effects of stringent procedural requirements on parole generally and on administrative costs.
Some parole officials argue that elaborate revocation hearings
would create demands on the parole board's time grossly incom-
mensurate with personnel and budget. Other opponents of procedural elaborateness have argued its negative effects on the purpose and use of revocation.

Resistance to increased procedural requirements in revocation
apparently is diminishing, whether by persuasion or court order.
As of 1972, 37 jurisdictions allow counsel for adult inmates at
the time of parole revocation. Nineteen permit disclosure of the
record to the offender or his lawyer. Thirty-two States provide
for the right to hear witnesses. In some places due process procedures have been extended even to the operation of juvenile
aftercare revocation. For example, in Illinois a juvenile parolee
is notified in writing of the alleged parole violation and of the
fact that he has a right to a hearing.

The State of Washington has developed perhaps the most elaborate system for handling adult parolees accused of violation. It
affords them the following rights and procedures: the right to a

hearing before parole board members in the community where the violation allegedly occurred; the right to cross-examine witnesses; the right to subpena witnesses; the right to assistance of counsel, including lawyers provided at State expense for indigent parolees; and the right to access to all pertinent records.

SUPREME COURT DECISION

The Supreme Court on June 29, 1972 dealt with several crucial issues relating to parole revocation in the case of Morrissey v. Brewer, 408 U.S. 471 (1972). Two parolees appealed an appellate court's decision on the ground that their paroles were revoked without a hearing and that they were thereby deprived of due process. The appellate court, in affirming the district court's denial of relief, had reasoned that parole is only "a correctional device authorizing service of sentence outside a penitentiary" and concluded that a parolee, who is thus still "in custody," is not entitled to a full adversary hearing, as would be mandated in a criminal proceeding.

In reversing the Court of Appeals decision, the Supreme Court held that:

> . . . the liberty of a parolee, although indeterminate, includes many of the core values of unqualified liberty and its termination inflicts a "grievous loss" on the parolee and often on others. It is hardly useful any longer to try to deal with this problem in terms of whether the parolee's liberty is a "right" or a "privilege." By whatever name the liberty is valuable and must be seen as within the protection of the Fourteenth Amendment. Its termination calls for some orderly process, however informal.

In considering the question of the nature of the process that is due, the Court delineated two important stages in the typical process of parole revocation: the arrest of the parolee and preliminary hearing; and the revocation hearing.

While the Court stated it had no intention of creating an inflexible structure for parole revocation procedures, making a distinction between a preliminary and a revocation hearing was an important decision, since many of the jurisdictions that do grant hearings grant only one. The Court also laid out a number of important points or steps for each of the above two stages which will undoubtedly apply to future parole actions.

In regard to the arrest of the parolee and a preliminary hearing, the Court indicated that due process would seem to require some minimal prompt inquiry at or reasonably near the place of the alleged parole violation or arrest. Such an inquiry, which the Court likened to a preliminary hearing, must be conducted to determine whether there is probable cause or reasonable grounds to believe that the arrested parolee has committed acts that would constitute a violation of parole conditions. It specified that the hearing should be conducted by someone not directly involved in the case.

In interpreting the rights of the parolee in this process, the Court held that the parolee should be given notice of when and why the hearing will take place, and the nature of the alleged violation(s). At the hearing, the parolee may appear and speak in his own behalf. He may bring letters, documents, or individuals who can give relevant information to the hearing officer. On request of the parolee, persons who have given adverse information on which parole revocation is to be based are made available for questioning in his presence unless the hearing officer determines that the informant would be subjected to risk of harm if his identity were disclosed.

The Court also specified that the hearing officer should have the duty of making a summary or digest of what transpires at the hearing and of the substance of evidence-introduced. On the basis of the information before him, the officer should determine whether there is probable cause to hold the parolee for the final decision of the parole board on revocation.

The Court said there must also be an opportunity for a hearing, if it is desired by the parolee, prior to the final decision on revocation by the parole authority. This hearing must be the basis for more than determining probable cause; it must lead to a final evaluation of any contested relevant facts as determined to warrant revocation. The parolee must have an opportunity to be heard and to show, if he can, that he did not violate the conditions, or, if he did, that circumstances in mitigation suggest the violation does not warrant revocation. The revocation hearing must be tendered within a reasonable time after the parolee is taken into custody.

The minimum requirements of due process for such a revocation hearing, as set by the Court, include (a) written notice of the claimed violations of parole; (b) disclosure to the parolee of evidence against him; (c) opportunity to be heard in person and to present witnesses and documentary evidence; (d) the right to confront and cross-examine adverse witnesses (unless the hearing officer specifically finds good cause for not allowing confrontation); (e) a "neutral and detached" hearing body such as a traditional parole board, members of which need not be judicial officers or lawyers; and (f) a written statement by the factfinders as to the evidence relied on and reasons for revoking parole.

ISSUES STILL UNRESOLVED

The Court left several questions unresolved. The extent to which evidence obtained by a parole officer in an unauthorized search can be used at a revocation hearing was not considered. Nor did it reach or decide the question whether the parolee is entitled to the assistance of retained counsel or to appointed counsel if the parolee is indigent.

While the Court did address certain features of the parole revocation process prior to a formal revocation hearing, it did not specify requirements for the process by which offenders are taken and held in custody. Present law and practice in many jurisdictions empower individual parole officers to cause the arrest of parolees for an alleged violation and to hold them in custody for extensive periods.

It is a power that needs careful control because it is easy to abuse, especially in those cases in which the arrest does not lead to a hearing, in which there is no review, and in which the parolee simply is held for a while in jail and then released back to parole status. This is a practice called "jail therapy" by which the parole officer "punishes" the parolee briefly (if he is a drunk, for example, he may be held in "protective custody" over New Year's Eve), then releases him back to community status. While this short-term confinement may not be undesirable in all cases, the lack of administrative control over its use is.

The use of all arrest and hold powers should be carefully narrowed. Parole field agents should be able to arrest and hold only when a warrant has been secured from a representative of the parole board on sufficient evidence. The warrant or similar document requiring parole commissioner approval of administrative arrest should be universally used. At present, only about half the State jurisdictions require such a warrant; in the remainder the parole agent can pick up an alleged violator on his own initiative and have him detained by signing a "hold" order. Initial two-step review of administrative arrest should be established, with appropriate provisions for emergency situations but with no application to law enforcement officer arrests for new offenses.

It must be remembered that taking no action and returning the parolee to the institution are not the only two courses open. The work of the California community treatment programs shows that the availability of alternative measures—short-term confinement or special restrictions—can be extremely useful in dealing with parolees instead of causing them a long-term return to an institution. Likewise, the Model Penal Code suggests that jurisdictions develop alternatives to the no action vs. full revocation dilemma. Such alternative modes need to be developed and formalized and used much more extensively.

ORGANIZATION OF FIELD SERVICES

TRANSFER OF ADULT PAROLE TO CORRECTIONAL DEPARTMENTS

One of the clearest trends in parole organization in the last few years is consolidation of formerly autonomous agencies or functionally related units into expanding departments of corrections. Some of these departments have been made part of still larger units of State government, such as human resources agencies, which embrace a wide range of programs and services. One clear indication of this trend is the number of States that have shifted administrative responsibility for parole officers from independent parole departments to centralized correctional agencies.

Most recently the States of Oregon, New York, and Georgia have made such transfers. A number of smaller States still have parole supervision staffs responsible to an independent parole board. Practically every large State now has adult parole field staff reporting to the same administrative authority as the personnel of the State penal institutions. Today, the majority of parole officers at the State level work for unified departments of correction.

The emergence of strong and autonomous correctional agencies represents an important step toward removal of a major block to needed correctional reform—fragmented and poorly coordinated programs and services. It is important that such consolidations continue, particularly among the services available for misdemeanants, where the more serious program gaps now exist. How quickly and effectively consolidation will take place depends largely on development of coordinated corrections units in large urbanized regions or absorption of these facilities and services into State programs.

JUVENILE PAROLE ORGANIZATION

The problems in parole services for juvenile delinquents had some of the same characteristics. The National Survey of Corrections found tremendous shortcomings in juvenile aftercare programs. In some States young persons released from training schools were supervised by institutional staff. In others they were made the responsibility of local child welfare workers, who simply included these youngsters in their caseloads of dependent or neglected children. In some States no organized program of juvenile parole supervision existed. Whether distinct juvenile correctional agencies should exist or whether such services should be carried out as a regular part of welfare services has been a matter of controversy for years.[31]

The events of the last years have virtually ended that argument. Distinct divisions and departments of juvenile correctional services are emerging. There is less agreement about whether such departments should be combined with agencies serving adult offenders. Yet it is widely agreed that separate program units should be maintained, even if adult and juvenile programs are combined in a single agency. Statewide juvenile correctional services embracing both institutions and field aftercare represent an established trend that should be supported.

Consolidation is not simply a matter of administrative efficiency; it facilitates important parole objectives as well. From the reintegration perspective, the task of parole staff is to intervene between the offender and his world and, if needed, to work with him to find satisfying and legal modes of behavior.

31. See, for example, State of New York, Governor's Special Committee on Criminal Offenders, *Preliminary Report* (1968), pp. 61-66.

Confinement is minimized and made to serve as much as possible the goal of dealing with problems in the community. Pre-release activities and community-based correctional facilities, through which offenders can participate increasingly in community life, are central. To be effective, both of these programs require extensive involvement of field staff. It is no longer sufficient to wait for the "transfer" of a case from an institution to a parole staff. The system now must work in such a way that heavy expenditures of field staff energy in the community and with the offender are made for many months prior to his "release" on parole. This requires a close interrelationship between institution and field staffs.

LINKING INSTITUTIONAL AND FIELD STAFFS

The lack of continuity and consistency of services between institutional and field services has been a severe problem to many jurisdictions. It often is further complicated by what could be described as rural vs. urban perspective. Institutions generally are located miles from population centers. The manpower they tend to recruit is drawn largely from small town and rural areas. The result is that institutional staff may have little understanding of city and especially ghetto life. In contrast, most field workers live in or near the large population centers in which most offenders reside, and more field workers than institutional workers are from minority groups. This cultural difference contributes to feelings of mistrust, hostility, and incredulity that handicap communication between institutional and field staffs.

A number of steps are needed to overcome this communication breakdown. An ongoing series of joint training sessions involving field workers and institutional counselors can be helpful in achieving mutual understanding. Promotions from institutional services to field services and vice versa also can have some effect in building communication channels.

Most important is that institution and field staff be under common administrative direction. It is not enough that they be simply linked administratively at the top; linking must be at the program level as well. This can be done in several ways. One is to provide that both institutional and field services be regionalized and placed under common administrators in each area. Obviously, in States where there are only one or two institutions, problems are compounded for the whole community-based thrust.

But even here some program consolidations are possible by devices such as placing all institutional programming responsibilities under full control of the head of parole field services for the last months of the inmate's confinement.

The stress on linking institutional and community supervision also has implications for systems that combine probation and parole services in a common administrative unit. Although this combination is infrequent among juvenile services, in 38 States the same State agency carries responsibility for the supervision of adult parolees and probationers. Having these services in a single agency has great economic advantages and provides an even quality of service to all areas of a State. There also are significant advantages in being able to influence staff toward more consistent programs for offenders. Tying staff to locally based institutional resources can work well for both probationers and parolees. However, in urban areas where case volume is sufficient, specialized staff who work with specific institutions are needed. Such tasks demand considerable time and require field staff to become intimately familiar with institutional personnel and participate actively in their programs.

CASELOAD VS. TEAM ASSIGNMENTS

The caseload—the assignment of individual offenders to individual officers—is the almost universal device for organizing the work of parole officers. This concept is being modified importantly in a number of offices through development of team supervision. A group of parole officers, sometimes augmented with volunteers and paraprofessionals, takes collective responsibility for a parolee group as large as their combined former caseloads. The group's resources are used differentially, depending upon individual case needs. Decisions are group decisions and generally involve parolees, including the parolee affected by the decision. Tasks are assigned by group assessment of workers' skills and parolees' objectives and perceptions.

Under the reintegration model, for example, various groups or organizations such as employers, schools, or welfare agencies may become someone's "caseload" and the major targets of his activities. Community representatives are dealt with directly, are directly involved, and help to shape programs. The parole office, instead of being located in a State office building, shifts to the community. The staff becomes expert in knowing both the formal and informal power structure of the community in which it operates and works closely with police, schools, employers, and probation officers. Such functions have a significant impact on the kind of manpower and training required for field staff. For example, there is a heavy involvement of volunteers as tutors and job finders that requires a staff able to use and work with such personnel.

The emphasis in a traditional parole agency is directed toward the proper administration of the specific caseload assigned to each individual officer. It is an administrative style familiar to most large bureaucracies. Front-line workers have responsibility for specific and clearly defined tasks and are checked by their supervisors to see that those tasks are carried out. The supervisors are under the command of middle managers who in turn report to someone above them.

Although the rhetoric of the organization is couched in such phrases as "helping the offender" and "developing a positive relationship," organizational controls tend to be attached to activities designed largely to foster the surveillance work of the agency or protect it from outside criticism. Parole officer performance most often is judged by the number of contacts that have been made with parolees, often with little regard for the quality of events that transpired during these contacts. Complete and prompt reports showing compliance with agency policies, such as written travel permits for parolees, are valued highly and require a major investment of parole officer time.

The result of this kind of administration is a rigid chain of command that is regimented, standardized, and predictable and that allocates power to persons on the basis of their position in the hierarchy. The parolee, being the lowest, is the least powerful.

FLEXIBILITY IN ORGANIZATIONAL STRUCTURE

A correctional policy that assumes parolees are capable of making a major contribution toward setting their own objectives and sees the parole agency's main task as helping the parolee realistically test and attain those objectives also must place a premium on developing an organizational structure that promotes flexibility. This means that managers must learn how to administer a decentralized organization that must adhere to broad policies and yet allow for a high degree of individual autonomy.

The dilemmas that arise when a manager tries this style of administration are many. Their resolution requires a sophisticated knowledge of administration and organizational techniques. One of the highest priorities for effective development of community-based services lies in providing managers with precisely this kind of skill.

Nelson and Lovell summarize the issues well:

> The correctional field must develop more collaborative, less hierarchical administrative regimes in order to implement its reintegration programs. The hierarchical format was developed to achieve the goal of production and orderly task performance. When individual change is the prime purpose of the organization, this format is inappropriate for people cannot be *ordered* to change strongly patterned attitudes and behavior. Nor is change apt to come about through the ritual performance of a series of tasks. . . . Power must be shared rather than hoarded. Communication must be open rather than restricted. Thus the managers of reintegration programs will need the skills of cooperation, communication, and collaboration.[32]

Resistance to reintegration-style programs can be widespread. Take for example a job function that has been interpreted traditionally as one of surveillance, head-counting, and maintenance of order. Management says the job is best accomplished by a new set of techniques—including relaxed, open and free communication, and decisionmaking involving parolees. Staff members should perceive themselves less as policemen than as counselors. It is highly likely in such a case that some staff will resist the changes.

Persons who see themselves as professionals also can be major obstacles to change. The trend toward a reintegration model and away from a rehabilitation model has been frustrating to several traditional professional groups who perceive their "expertise" as being challenged or, at worst, rejected. Meetings are held to or-

32. Elmer K. Nelson and Catherine H. Lovell, *Developing Correctional Administrators* (Washington: Joint Commission on Correctional Manpower and Training, 1969), p. 14.

ganize opposition to "nonprofessional practices" and to changes
that are "untested" and that have strayed from the "tried and
true." It is not surprising that administrators sometimes capitu-
late. But "let's not rock the boat" or "let's wait till next year"
are the cliches of timid leadership that lead to stagnant bureaucracies. It takes great skill and perseverance to change an agency. There is no substitute for intelligence, skill, and above all,
courage.

COMMUNITY SERVICES FOR PAROLEES

A significant number of parolees can do very well without much
official supervision, according to repeatedly validated research.[33]
Many offenders can be handled in relatively large caseloads simply by maintaining minimum contact with them and attending
to their needs as they arise. Most of these parolees probably
should be released from any form of supervision at all. Outright
discharge from the institution would be an appropriate disposition and should be used much more frequently than it is. Failing that, minimum supervision can and should be employed for
a significant group.

For those parolees requiring more intensive help, the emphasis
in recent years, and one worthy of support, has been toward effecting as many needed services as possible through community
resources available to the general population. To the extent that
offenders can gain access to these opportunities on the same basis
as other citizens, the additional blocks that arise when parolees
attempt to move into the mainstream of community life are reduced.

Moreover, more resources usually are available to programs
designed to deal with a broad public spectrum. For example, vocational training programs operated by correctional agencies cannot begin to offer the range of services offered by government
agencies to economically deprive groups in general. Skills developed in programs for these groups are usually much more
marketable. Job placement is also more likely to be operating
effectively.

Finally, using such services allows flexibility and speed in
adapting to needs. It avoids creation of additional specialized

---

33. See Joseph D. Lohman, Albert Wahl, and Robert Carter, *The San Francisco Project: The Minimum* *Supervision Caseload*, Research Report No. 8 (Berkeley: Univer- sity of California, 1966).

bureaucracies on State payrolls that respond more readily to their own survival needs than to changing needs of offenders. Provision of funds to parole agencies to purchase resources in the community represents an important new approach to the problems of securing needed services.

From this perspective, a major task of parole officers is to make certain that opportunities in community services and programs actually exist for parolees and to prepare and support parolees as they undertake these programs. Offenders often are locked out of services for which they apparently qualify according to the criteria established by the agency, not because of any official policy barring them but because of covert resistance to dealing with persons thought to be troublesome. Mental health agencies deny assistance to offenders on grounds that such persons cannot benefit from their programs. Public employment offices often are reluctant to refer to an employer a person viewed as unreliable. Public housing resources may be restricted because of biases against persons with records.

Considering these reactions and the discrimination that too often exists against minority group members, who constitute a significant portion of the offender population in many areas of the country, the need for a parole staff that is willing and able to play the role of broker or resource manager for parolees is clear. This need involves more than skills at persuasion or aggressive argument. It also requires a knowledge of the sources of power in a community and the ability to enlist those sources in changing agency behavior.[34]

Undoubtedly, the trend toward creating new ways of delivering services to meet human needs—mental health, family counseling, physical rehabilitation, employment, and financial assistance—will modify the parole officer's tasks in several important respects. Human service centers designed to deliver a wide range of programs will develop.[35] Part of the task of parole staff will be to support such efforts and play an appropriate role in a coordinated human-services delivery system. Increasingly, the pa-

34. John M. Martin and Gerald M. Shattuck, "Community Intervention and the Correctional Mandate," consultant paper prepared for the President's Commission on Law Enforcement and Administration of Justice, 1966.

35. U. S. Department of Health, Education, and Welfare, Community Service Administration, *Toward a Comprehensive Service Delivery System through Building the Community Service Center* (1970).

role officer's unique responsibility will be to make certain that offenders obtain the benefit of available resources, to counsel parolees about the conditions of their parole, and to help them meet those conditions.

FINANCIAL ASSISTANCE

Perhaps the most common problem immediately confronting offenders released from adult correctional institutions is the need for money for the most basic needs—shelter, food, and transportation. Most States provide new releasees with transportation, some clothes, and modest gate money totaling perhaps $50. Inmates fortunate enough to have been assigned to programs in which money can be earned in prison frequently are much better off financially than those who were not. Those who have participated in work-release programs usually will have saved a portion of their salary for the time of their release.

Data that show parole failure rates clearly related to the amount of money an offender has during the first months of release can be explained in a number of ways.[36] Nevertheless, it is a consistent finding and, in the day-by-day existence of parolees, lack of funds is a critical problem.

A number of solutions to this problem have been tried over the years, the most common being a loan fund arrangement. Although there are several difficulties in administering such a fund, it is a practical necessity in every parole system until arrangements for sufficient "gate money" or other subvention can be provided.

The most practical and direct way to meet the problem is to provide offenders with opportunities to earn funds while they are incarcerated. For those who are unemployed, funds should be provided, much in the manner of unemployment compensation, when they are first released until they are gainfully employed. The State of Washington recently has adopted precisely such legislation. It should be adopted in every jurisdiction.

EMPLOYMENT

Closely related to the problem of finances is that of getting and holding a decent job. While it is difficult to demonstrate ex-

36. Glaser, *The Effectiveness of a Prison and Parole System*, pp. 333–348.

perimentally a precise relationship between unemployment and recidivism, the gross picture does show a fairly consistent link between unemployment and crime.[37]   Hence every parole system should maintain its own measures of unemployment rates among its populations.

For the offender already on the street, the most critical skill required of a parole officer is directing him to a wide variety of services available in the community.   A prime resource is the State employment service.   Almost everywhere such services have commitments at the policy level to extend special assistance in the placement of parolees.

However, the test of these programs is found in the day-by-day working relationships between local employment personnel and parole officers.   How well they cooperate is colored by the attitudes of local employment department staff but more importantly by the skill of the parole staff in maintaining relationships.   A wide variety of other programs exist; for example, those sponsored by the Office of Economic Opportunity, the Office of Vocational Rehabilitation, and the large number sponsored by the Department of Labor.   The key issue in using these programs is good communication at the local operational level.

The most acute employment problems are those associated with persons about to be released on parole.   It is a time of great strain on the parolee.   The difficulty of finding employment often is an additional source of anxiety because the most common reason why offenders are held beyond the date fixed for their release is that they have no job to go to.

Many States have developed systems of "reasonable assurance," under which a definite job is not required before an inmate is released, provided some means can be found to sustain him until one can be found.   This generally is a far better practice than holding him until a job is promised.   Parolees find it much easier to get a job if they can personally interview employers.   Research consistently has shown offenders do as well, if not better, if they can find their own job.[38]

Partial release programs in the community go a long way toward eliminating many of these problems.   While the offender

37. Glaser, *The Effectiveness of a Prison and Parole System*, ch. 14.

38. John M. Stanton, "Is It Safe to Parole Inmates Without a Job?" *Crime and Delinquency*, 12 (1966), 149.

still is confined, he has the chance to make contacts in the community, be interviewed by employers, work directly with a parole officer, or actually begin an employment program through work release. In terms of a broad correctional strategy aimed at coping with employment problems, prerelease programs are of pivotal importance.

Another activity that has grown in recent years, under sponsorship of both private and public sources, is job training programs in institutions that are connected to specific job possibilities on the outside. The Office of Vocational Rehabilitation has programs in a number of institutions. The Department of Labor has made numerous efforts in this area. Such programs need to be supported because of the large-scale resources and expertise they represent and the network of relationships they possess in the free community.

RESIDENTIAL FACILITIES

Another major need of many newly released offenders is a place to live. For some, the small, community-based residential facility is extremely useful in a time of crisis.

Young persons particularly need to have a place to go when events begin to overwhelm them. Such centers also can be useful for dealing with offenders who may have violated their parole and require some control for a short period, but for whom return to an institution is unnecessary.

To the extent that such facilities can be obtained on a contract basis, the flexibility and, most probably, the program quality increase. For young offenders especially, bed space in small group facilities can be secured through many private sources. This is less true for adults, and development of State operated centers may be required.

DIFFERENTIAL HANDLING

Making all programs work requires a wide variety of resources, differential programming for offenders, and a staff representing a diversity of backgrounds and skills. Some offenders may be better handled by specialized teams. Drug users of certain types may be dealt with by staff who have considerable familiarity with the drug culture and close connections with various community drug treatment programs. Other offenders may require intensive supervision by officers skilled at maintaining close controls and surveillance over their charges. While the latter may be assigned to a specialized caseload, assignments to specialized treatment caseloads in general should involve a great deal of self-selection by the offender. Arbitrary assignments to "treatment" groups easily can result in the offender's subversion of program objectives. An ongoing program of assessment and evaluation by staff and parolees is needed to make certain that offenders are receiving the kind of program most appropriate for them.

MEASURES OF CONTROL

There is an increasing tendency to minimize use of coercive measures and find ways by which offenders' goals and aspirations can be made congruent, if not identical, with agency goals. These trends can be seen in the shifting emphasis of parole rules, the clearest manifestation of the coercive power of parole.

Until the 1950's parole rules heavily emphasized conformity to community values and lifestyles with little or no relationship to the reason why a person originally committed a crime. One State's rules, only recently amended, give the flavor of such conditions. They provided in part that:

> The person paroled shall in all respects conduct himself honestly, avoid evil associations, obey the law, and abstain from gambling and the use of intoxicating liquors. He shall not visit pool halls, or places of bad repute, and shall avoid the company and association of vicious people and shall at least once each Sunday attend some religious service or institution of moral training.

In the 1950's many rules of this type were replaced by more specific conditions such as requiring the parolee to obtain permission to purchase a car. Until the late 1960's almost every State had a long list of parole conditions.[39] As "tools of the parole officer," these conditions gave reason to expect that violations would occur often although official action would not be taken unless the parole officer felt the case warranted it. Problems of differential enforcement were bound to occur, and did. A great deal of ambiguity developed for both parolees and parole officers as to which rules really were to be enforced and which ignored. Studies have demonstrated that officers tend to de-

---

39. Nat Arluke, "A Summary of Parole Rules," *Journal of the Nation-* *al Probation and Parole Association*, 218 (January 1956), 2–9.

velop their own norms of behavior that should result in return to prison. These norms among parole officers became very powerful forces in shaping revocation policies.[40]

The recent trend has been toward reducing rules and making them more relevant to the facts in a specific parole case. Part of this move undoubtedly has been stimulated by the interest of the courts in parole conditions. Conditions have been struck down by the courts as unreasonable, impossible of performance, or unfair. Additional principles constantly are being developed, as when a Federal court recently restrained the State of California from prohibiting a parolee from making public speeches. Hyland v. Procunier, 311 F.Supp. 749, 750 (N.D.Calif.1970).

Several States have reduced the number of parole conditions considerably. In 1969, 45 jurisdictions prohibited contact with undesirable associates; today 35 do so. Ten States removed the requirement of permission to marry or file for divorce. Oregon, as a specific example, has removed nine discernible general conditions, including the requirement of permission to change residence or employment, to operate a motor vehicle, or to marry; the proscription of liquor or narcotics and contacts with undesirables; and dictates that the parolee maintain employment, support his dependents, and incur no debts. Idaho has removed seven such rules from its agreement of release.

Perhaps the most substantial change in procedure occurred in the State of Washington, where the standard parole conditions imposed on all inmates were reduced to four. They required the parolee to (1) obey all laws, (2) secure the permission of a parole office before leaving the State, (3) report to the officer, and (4) obey any written instructions issued by him. The State parole board imposes additional conditions in individual cases as seems appropriate. Conditions also may be added during the course of parole on the parole officer's application.

The advantage of this system is that both the parolee and parole officer know which conditions are to be enforced, although obviously violations of the remaining rules are judged individually and may not result in a return to prison. The other advantage is that much unnecessary anxiety is avoided over rules that rarely,

40. James Robinson and Paul Takagi, "The Parole Violator as an Organization Reject" in Robert Carter and Leslie Wilkins, eds., *Probation and Parole: Selected Readings* (Wiley, 1970).

if ever, would result in a return to prison. More such candor should be encouraged in parole supervision practice.

The removal of unnecessary rules also helps to shape the activity of the parole officer more positively. When unclear or unnecessary rules exist, the effect is twofold: a great deal of busy work by a parole officer; and a corruption of his relationship with the parolee. The trust of the reintegration approach is toward an open problem solving relationship between the parole officer and the parolee in which the parolee's objectives are clarified and tested against the limits under which both he and the parole officer must live. The fewer the limits required by the parole system, the greater the opportunity of locating alternative behavior styles that are satisfying and meet the tests of legality. This is not to say that rules should not be enforced, but that there should be as much honesty in the enforcement process as possible.

Some parolees do require fairly intensive and directive supervision. In such cases, parole officers with the skill and aptitude for this kind of case should be assigned. Some intensive supervision caseloads (12 to 20 parolees) can be differentiated as caseloads for surveillance rather than for counseling and support. The parolee may not be in a position to see the relevance of any services offered, but he can respond positively to the knowledge that his daily whereabouts and activities are under careful scrutiny. In the eyes of the parolee, the efficacy of intensive surveillance caseloads resides in the credibility of the counselor and those he recruits to assist.

The need for high surveillance and intensive supervision for some offenders raises directly the question of the extent to which parole officers should assume police functions, such as arresting parolees, and the associated question as to whether they should be armed. A 1963 survey of parole authority members in the United States revealed that only 27 percent believed that parole officers should be asked to arrest parole violators. Only 13 percent believed that parole officers should be allowed to carry weapons.[41] In general, most parole officers accept the proposition that arrests by parole officers may be necessary on occasion but strong liaison with police departments should be depended on in the majority of instances when arrests are needed.

41. National Parole Institutes, *Description of Backgrounds and Some Attitudes of Parole Authority* Members of the United States (New York: National Council on Crime and Delinquency, 1963).

Guns are antithetical to the character of a parole officer's job. Much concern among some parole officers as to the need to be armed arises from their anxiety in working in areas of cities in which they feel alienated and estranged. This anxiety can be allayed by assigning to such districts persons who live in them. The RODEO project in Los Angeles, where probation officers are assigned two community assistants drawn from the neighborhood, is an excellent example. Because of their intimate knowledge of the community, such workers are able to keep well informed of the activities of their charges without the necessity of using tactics normally associated with police agencies.

MANPOWER

Problems of manpower for corrections as a whole are discussed in Chapter 14 of this report. Here the discussion will be limited to special manpower problems of parole systems.

RECRUITMENT AND PERSONNEL PRACTICES

Nothing indicates more starkly the relatively low priority that parole programs have received in governmental services than parole officers' salaries. The National Survey of Corrections indicated that in 1965 the median starting parole officer salary in the United States was approximately $6,000 a year. Although the studies of the Joint Commission on Correctional Manpower and Training three years later showed this salary base had risen, most of the gain could be accounted for by a national upswing in salary levels. It did not represent a substantial gain compared to other positions in government and industry.

The essence of an effective parole service lies in the caliber of person it recruits. Until salaries are made attractive enough to recruit and hold competent personnel, parole programs will be sorely handicapped. Almost half of the State agencies responsible for parole services surveyed by the Joint Commission reported serious difficulties in recruiting new officers.[42]

Though merit system procedures have significantly dampened political patronage influences in staff selection and promotion, they have brought a series of built-in restrictions. These must be overcome if a reintegration style for parole agencies is to be effected. The great difficulties attached to removing incom-

42. Joint Commission on Correction-   *Time to Act.* Washington: (JCCMT,
    al Manpower and Training, *A*   1969), p. 13.

petent employees and the lack of opportunities for lateral entry are two examples. The most acute problems are those surrounding the criteria for staff selection and promotion. The issue bears most specifically on the employment and advancement of minority group members. For example, in 1969, while blacks made up 12 percent of the general population, only 8 percent of correctional employees were black, and they held only 3 percent of all top and middle level administrative positions.[43]

Some reforms are beginning, but merit systems are traditionally suspicious of new job titles and slow to establish them. When a new program is initiated, existing job titles frequently do not fit. The red tape and delays encountered in hiring staff often seriously damage programs. A sense of the frustration felt by administrators who are trying to modernize their programs is captured in the statement of one State parole system head, who asserts that merit systems can be and frequently are the single largest obstacle to program development in community-based corrections.

MANPOWER REQUIREMENTS

The problems of trying to determine staffing needed to carry out an effective parole supervision program is complicated tremendously by lack of agreement on objectives and knowledge of how to reach them. Within any correctional policy, a number of alternative styles are needed, ranging from no treatment at all to a variety of specific and carefully controlled programs. Perhaps the most discouraging experiments in parole supervision were those that sought to test the thesis that reducing caseloads to provide more intensive services would reduce recidivism.

The project that broke most completely from this notion was the Community Treatment Project of the California Youth Authority. The program involved classification of offenders by an elaborate measure of interpersonal maturity or "I-level" and use of treatment techniques specifically designed for each "I-level" type. Treatments ranged from firm, controlling programs for manipulative youths to supportive and relatively permissive approaches for those assigned to a category that included neurotic and anxious youngsters. With certain exclusions, offenders were assigned randomly to 10-man caseloads in the community, each of which was designed to carry out treatments consistent

43. *A Time to Act*, p. 14.

with a particular classification, or to a term in a training school followed by regular parole supervision.[44]

The results of the project were impressive. After 24 months, those assigned to special caseloads had a violation level of 39 percent. Those assigned to a regular program had a 61 percent failure rate. Of interest also was the variation in success rates among "I-level" types. Some researchers argue that some of the research results should be attributed to differences in official reaction to the behavior of those in special caseloads as opposed to those in regular ones,[45] rather than improvements in the offenders. Yet results in the context of other research efforts described by Stuart Adams make the argument for a differential treatment approach fairly strong.[46]

The Work Unit Parole program in effect in the California Department of Corrections since 1964 divides parolees into several classifications (based in part on their prior record and actuarial expectancy of parole success). It requires certain activities from the parole officer for each classification of parolee and thereby is able to control the work demands placed on an individual officer.

In this system, the ratio of officers to parolees is approximately 1 to 35.[47] Two facts about the program should be noted.

1. The ratio of 1 to 35 does not express a caseload. Officers are assigned to a variety of tasks that are quantifiable. These task related workloads are the basis for staff allocation.

2. The workload ratios for a specific agency would depend on the kinds of offenders they have to supervise and the administrative requirements of that agency.

The important point is that the concept of a caseload as a measure of workload is outmoded, especially in an era stressing a variety of skills and team supervision. The task is to spell out the goals to be accomplished and the activities associated with

44. Marguerite Q. Warren, "The Case for Differential Treatment of Delinquents," *Annals of the American Academy of Political and Social Science*, 381 (1969), 46.

45. Paul Lerman, "Evaluating the Outcomes of Institutions for Delinquents," *Social Work*, 13 (1968), 3.

46. Stuart Adams, "Some Findings from Correctional Caseload Research," *Federal Probation*, 31 (1967), 148.

47. California Department of Corrections, *Work Unit Program, 1971* (Sacramento, 1971).

their attainment, and to assign staff on that basis. Research information must continuously inform the judgment by which these allocations are made.

EDUCATION AND TRAINING NEEDS

Both the Corrections Task Force in 1967 and the Joint Commission in 1969 agreed that a baccalaureate degree should be the basic education requirement for a parole officer, and persons with graduate study might be used for specialized functions. Both also stressed the need to create opportunities for greater use of persons with less than college-level study. Many tasks carried out by a parole officer can be executed just as easily by persons with much less training, and many skills needed in a parole agency are possessed by those with limited education. As observed earlier, persons drawn from the areas to be served are good examples of staff with needed specialized skills. Ex-offenders also are an example of a manpower resource needed in parole agencies. A growing number of agencies have found such persons to be an immensely useful addition to their staffs.[48]

Ways of recruiting, training, and supervising these relatively untapped sources of manpower for parole and other elements of corrections are discussed in Chapter 14.

STATISTICAL ASSISTANCE

Proper organization, selection, and training of personnel are necessary for improved parole services, but in themselves they are insufficient. The crucial task of making the "right" decision remains for whoever must make it, whatever his position in the organization. Although the typical parole board member deals with a variety of concerns in decisionmaking, his basic objective is to lessen as much as possible the risk that an offender will commit another crime. This criterion remains paramount, but it is so variably interpreted and measured that severe handicaps impede its attainment.

To begin with, the measures of recidivism currently used in individual jurisdictions vary so much that useful comparisons across systems, and indeed within systems, are virtually impossible. In one jurisdiction, only those parolees who return to

48. Vincent O'Leary, "Some Directions for Citizen Involvement in Corrections," *Annals of the American Academy of Political and Social Science*, 381 (1969), 99.

prison are counted as failures, no matter what may have transpired among those parolees not returned. In another, everyone who has been charged with a violation as measured by the number of parole board warrants issued is treated as a failure.

The length of time under parole supervision confounds other comparisons. Thus recidivism variously includes the rest of the parolee's life, the span of the parole period only, or the time immediately following discharge.

The computational methods used in developing success or failure ratios also can do more to confuse than to assist understanding. In one State, recidivism is measured by the proportion of offenders returned to prison compared with the number released in the same period. In another, a much lower rate is shown for exactly the same number of failures because it is arrived at by computing the number of persons returned to prison in a given period compared with the total number of persons supervised during the same period. Until uniform measures are developed, vitally needed comparisons are not possible. Nor will meaningful participation in policy decisions be possible for agencies and persons outside the parole system.

UNIFORM PAROLE REPORTS SYSTEM

A major effort to help solve the problem of uniform measures of recidivism was development of the National Uniform Parole Reports System, a cooperative effort sponsored by the National Parole Institutes. This program enlisted the voluntary cooperation of all State and Federal parole authorities having responsibility for felony offenders in developing some common terms to describe parolees—their age, sex and prior record—and some common definitions to describe parole performance. Parole agencies for the last several years have been sending this information routinely to the Uniform Parole Report Center, where it is compiled. The results are fed back to the contributing States. Comparisons across the States thus are beginning to be possible. This effort represents a long step in developing a common language among parole systems.

Although this national system has made great strides, many additional steps need to be taken to develop its capacity fully. The Uniform Parole Report System needs to tie into a larger network that includes data from correctional institutions, so that information collected on the offender can be linked to parole outcome and crucially needed comparative data on discharged offenders can be obtained.

Important also is the need to tie in, on a national basis, to crime record data systems so that followup studies extending beyond parole periods can be carried out. The Uniform Parole Report System should have access to national criminal history information so that the experiences of parolees who have been classified according to a set of reliable factors can be checked. Attempts to use the usual criminal identification record alone to describe the results of parolee performance inevitably suffer from such gross inadequacies as to be almost completely useless. The careful definitions built into the Uniform Parole Report System should be combined with access to criminal data. This would enable tracing of subsequent parolee histories and could be a powerful tool for policy development and research.

A comparable system for releases from juvenile institutions also is needed. Information on misdemeanants released on parole is almost nonexistent. Development of statewide statistical services in corrections is the key for such misdemeanant recordkeeping.

USES AND LIMITATIONS OF STATISTICS IN PAROLE

Thus far the stress on statistical development has been on its utility as a national reporting system. But equally needed is a basic statistical system in each parole jurisdiction to help it address a variety of concerns in sufficient detail for practical day-to-day decisionmaking. There are a number of ways such data can be used.

Since the 1920's a number of researchers have concerned themselves with developing statistical techniques for increasing the precision of recidivism probability forecasting, as noted in Chapter 15. Although the methods may vary in detail, the basic aim of the studies has been to identify factors that can be shown to be related statistically to parole outcome and, by combining them, to ascertain recidivism probability for certain parolee classes. These statements usually have been labeled "parole predictions."

Typically, the probability statements produced by statistical techniques are more accurate in estimating the likely outcome of parole than are traditional case methods. There has been relatively little use of these devices in the parole field, although some experimentation has been carried on in several jurisdictions.

A major source of resistance to the use of prediction methods is found in the nature of the parole decision itself.[49]　Parole board members argue, for example, that simply knowing the narrow probability of success or failures is not nearly as helpful as knowing what type of risk would be involved.　For example, they are more likely to tolerate higher risks if an offender is likely to commit a forgery than if he is prone to commit a crime against a person.　Most prediction systems depend largely on prior events, such as criminal age and criminal record.　This does not help a parole board that must deal with the offender as he is today within the realities of the decisions and time constraints available to them.

Technology is capable of dealing with a number of the additional concerns of parole authorities and probably will continue to make statistical information increasingly valuable.　Currently a major research project is under way with the U.S. Parole Board seeking ways in which statistical material can assist the parole board member in his decisionmaking.　Significant help lies in this direction, and each jurisdiction should be made fully aware of the possibility of using statistical information in parole decisionmaking.

With computer technology and the possibility it offers of instant feedback, the usefulness of this kind of system should increase.　It seems doubtful, however, that statistical methods in the foreseeable future can substitute entirely for the judgments of parole board members and examiners.　The impact and the variety of elements other than the estimation of risks are profound.　The intricacies that arise in the individual case make total dependence on any statistical system highly risky at best.

Statistical predictions can be helpful in giving guidelines to parole board members as to general categories into which particular inmates fit, how other inmates similarly situated were treated earlier, and what the trends are in broad decisions.　This information is important for parole decisionmakers.　But most experts are convinced that the optimum system is one in which both statistical and individual case methods are used in making decisions about individuals.

49.　Norma S. Hayner, "Why Do Parole Board Members Lag in the Use of Prediction Scores?"　Pacific Sociological Review, (Fall 1958), 73.

Daniel Glaser sums up the issue as follows:

> I know of no instance where an established academic
> criminologist, judge or correctional administrator has
> advocated the replacement of case studies and subjective
> evaluation by statistical tables for sentencing, parole or
> other major decisions on the fate of an offender. The
> many reasons for insisting upon case data may be group-
> ed into two categories. First of all, these officials must
> make moral decisions for the state as a whole in deter-
> mining what risks would justify withholding from or
> granting freedom to a man. . . . Secondly, there
> always is some information on a case too special to be
> readily taken into account by any conceivable table in
> estimating what risks are involved in a specific official
> action. Thirdly, there are many types of predictions be-
> sides the overall prospect of violations which judges and
> parole board members must consider. These include
> the type of violation, and the consequences of certain
> types of violations for community treatment of other
> parolees.[50]

THE RISK OF FAILURE DURING THE EARLY PAROLE PERIOD: A METHODOLOGICAL NOTE*

Correctional administrators have long placed a heavy emphasis on the critical importance of the first few months on
parole. They have used the claim that the risk of failure is at
its highest during the first few months following release to justify halfway houses, preparole programs and intensive supervision by parole agents during the early parole period. The following statement is representative of that point of view:

> It had been known for a long time that the highest per-
> centage of postprison failures occurs within 6 months

50. *The Effectiveness of a Prison and Parole System*, p. 304.

* John E. Berecochea, Alfred N. Himelson, Donald E. Miller, *The Journal of Criminal Law, Criminology and Police Science*, Vol. 63, No. 1, 1972. Reprinted with permission.

after release, with the greater number taking place during the first 60 days. But it was not until the early forties that penal and correctional institutions realized that something must be done to help inmates bridge the gap between the prison community and life in free society. . . .[1]

Statistical evidence purporting to support this claim has been gathered and reported from many jurisdictions. Lunden in discussing his data on recidivism among boys and girls released from training schools in Iowa stated:

The data reveals that the first three months con-stitutes the crucial period for parole violation. If the juvenile does break parole the boy or girl is most apt to do so within the first three months after the date of parole from the institution.[2]

Another study, using statistical data on federal parole vio-lators during the 1949 fiscal year, reported that 30 percent of the violations occurred within less than three months after re-lease, 57 percent within six months and 82 percent within a year.[3] The prestigious President's Commission on Law En-forcement and the Administration of Justice reported, using information from the State of Washington prison system, that ". . . violations on parole tend to occur relatively soon after release from an institution, nearly half of them within the first 6 months after offenders are released, and over 60 percent within the first year."[4] Numerous other studies using the same method could be given.

This paper will focus on the method of assessing failure rates which was used in these studies and compare the question it answers and the results it achieves with the questions answered and the results realized by two alternative methods.

The method used in each of the studies cited above answers the question: "Of all those who violated their parole during a given period, how long had they been on parole at the time of

1. Baker, *Preparing Prisoners for Their Return to the Community,* 30 Fed.Probation 43 (1966).

2. Lunden, Statistics on Delinquents and Delinquency 267 (1964).

3. Killinger, *The Federal Govern-ment's Parole System,* 14 Fed.Pro-bation 61 (1950).

4. President's Commission on Law Enforcement and Administration of Justice, The Challenge of Crime in a Free Society 68 (1967).

their failure?" While this is a legitimate question, is it the proper question to be asked? Should not the question be: "What are the chances of failure on parole during the early period of parole compared to later periods?" This is not the question answered by the studies cited above. In each they considered only those persons who failed. The question of risk, however, must be answered in terms of the entire population who risk parole failure. This includes those who do not fail as well as those who fail. Thus, these studies do not provide risk rates and cannot be used to answer the question of risk.

The proper statistical method for answering the question of risk during a specified period of time following release to parole is simple. In question form it is: "Of all those at risk during the specified period of time following release to parole, what proportion violate their parole during that period?"

SOME FICTIONAL EXAMPLES

In order to demonstrate empirically that different methods of computing failure rates yield different results, a fictional parole system was created. Five hundred men were released to parole per month in this fictional system. In the first statistical experiment, the failures were computed at a constant rate of 2.0 percent per month based on the survivors, i. e., 2.0 percent of the 500 releases each month failed during the first month following release giving 10 failures, 2.0 percent of the surviving 490 releases failed during the second month giving 9.8 failures, 2.0 percent of the 480.2 survivors failed during the third month giving 9.6 failures, and so forth [5] for thirty-six months at which time the rate was arbitrarily reduced to zero.[6] This method might be referred to as the *survivor cohort base follow-up method.*

In order to produce the type of data which has been cited in the prior literature, this procedure was carried out for four years (48 monthly release cohorts) and all those who failed parole during a given system year were tabulated to produce a distri-

---

5. This method of computing period-specific failure rates has also been used in Mannheim & Wilkins, Prediction Methods in Relation to Borstal Training 127 (1955).

6. The rate was reduced to zero in order to simplify the computations. This is only a slight departure from "reality" in as much as the rate of failure, no matter how it is computed, falls to a very low level after three years on parole.

bution of time on parole among the failures. These frequencies were then converted to proportions of the total number of failures during the given system year. This method might be referred to as the *ex post facto failure base method.*

In order to produce yet another set of rates based on another method, the number of failures per month produced by the fixed rate of 2.0 percent per month among the survivors was expressed as a proportion of the total number of men released to parole in each release-month cohort which was 500. This method might be referred to as the *total release cohort base follow-up method.*

The rates resulting from these three methods of computing failure rates are shown in Table 1.

TABLE 1

COMPARISON OF THREE METHODS OF COMPUTING "FAILURE RATES"
IN A FICTIONAL PAROLE SYSTEM HAVING A CONSTANT
MONTHLY FAILURE RATE

Months to Failure	Survivor Cohort Base Follow-up Method *		Ex Post Facto Failure Base Method **		Total Release Cohort Base Follow-up Method *	
	No. of Failures	Failure Rate	No. of Failures	Failure Rate	No. of Failures	Failure Rate
1–3	29.4	5.9	352.8	11.4	29.4	5.9
4–6	27.6	5.9	331.2	10.7	27.6	5.5
7–9	26.1	5.9	313.2	10.1	26.1	5.2
10–12	24.5	5.9	294.0	9.5	24.5	4.9
13–15	23.0	5.9	276.0	8.9	23.0	4.6
16–18	21.7	5.9	260.4	8.4	21.7	4.3
19–21	20.5	5.9	246.0	7.9	20.5	4.1
22–24	19.2	5.9	230.4	7.4	19.2	3.8
25–27	18.1	5.9	217.2	7.0	18.1	3.6
28–30	17.1	5.9	205.2	6.6	17.1	3.4
31–33	16.0	5.9	192.0	6.2	16.0	3.2
34–36	15.0	5.9	180.0	5.8	15.0	3.0

* Number of failures and failure rates based on one month of releases in the fictional system; increasing the number of months of releases would have no effect on the analysis. In the survivor cohort method, the Failure Rate is a quarterly rate based on a monthly survivor rate of 2.0 percent.

**Number of failures based on all returns during a system year after the system stabilized.

[A9425]

From Table 1 it can be seen that a constant failure rate (of 2.0 percent per month) using the *survivor cohort base follow-up method* produces "failure rates" in the other two methods which seem to show that the rate of failure decreases over time. Thus what is in actuality a constant rate of failure over time would, using the traditional method, give the appearance of a higher risk during the early parole period.

In order to demonstrate the obverse situation, namely that increasing rates of failure over time might not be detected using the traditional failure base method, Table 2 was constructed

TABLE 2

COMPARISON OF THREE METHODS OF COMPUTING "FAILURE RATES" IN A FICTIONAL PAROLE SYSTEM HAVING A CONSTANT NUMBER OF FAILURES PER MONTH

Months to Failure	Survivor Cohort Base Follow-up Method *		Failure Base Method **		Total Release Cohort Base Follow-up Method *	
	No. of Failures	Failure Rate	No. of Failures	Failure Rate	No. of Failures	Failure Rate
1–3	21.516	4.30	258.192	8.33	21.516	4.30
4–6	21.516	4.50	258.192	8.33	21.516	4.30
7–9	21.516	4.71	258.192	8.33	21.516	4.30
10–12	21.516	4.94	258.192	8.33	21.516	4.30
13–15	21.516	5.20	258.192	8.33	21.516	4.30
16–18	21.516	5.48	258.192	8.33	21.516	4.30
19–21	21.516	5.80	258.192	8.33	21.516	4.30
22–24	21.516	6.16	258.192	8.33	21.516	4.30
25–27	21.516	6.56	258.192	8.33	21.516	4.30
28–30	21.516	7.02	258.192	8.33	21.516	4.30
31–33	21.516	7.55	258.192	8.33	21.516	4.30
34–36	21.516	8.17	258.192	8.33	21.516	4.30

* Number of failures and failure rates based on one month of releases in the fictional system; increasing the number of months of releases would have no effect on the analysis. In the survivor cohort method, the failure rate is based upon a constant number of failures expressed to the base of the number of people at risk at the beginning of the quarter.

** Number of failures based on all returns during a system year after the system stabilized.   [A89751]

using a constant number of failures (7.172) per month for each month following release to parole (up to four years). This statistical experiment produces an increasing failure rate over time in the survivor base method but a flat rate in the other two methods. Again the results of the different methods are different.

Tables 1 and 2 demonstrate that different questions are being asked by the three methods in as much as they yield different answers. Thus, the choice of the proper method depends upon a precise statement of the question to be answered. Some of the questions which might be answered using these methods are:

1. At what period of time following release to parole is the risk of failure at its highest or lowest point? The proper method for answering this question is the survivor method.

2. At what point in time following release to parole does the risk of failure stabilize, if at all? Again the survivor method is the appropriate one.

3. At what point in time following release to parole can the most failures or the highest proportion of failures be expected? The proper technique here is the total cohort base follow up method.

4. Among those who fail parole during a given period of time such as a calendar year, how many can be expected to have been on parole for any specified length of time? The failure base method should be used to answer this question.

5. Do different kinds of parolees survive parole for different lengths of time? The total cohort base method is the method of choice here.

6. Is the risk of failure over time different for different kinds of parolees? For instance, is the risk level fairly stable over time for those convicted of homicide as compared to those convicted of narcotics crimes? The survivor cohort method is appropriate here.

Before leaving the discussion of the several methods, some further comments should be made on the failure base method. This method has several characteristics which would seem to limit its usefulness. First, as we have seen, it does not provide a measure of risk. Second, it tells us nothing about those who do not fail. Third, the findings are very dependent upon changes in releasing practices. For instance, if the failure rate using the total release cohort base method was constant over time and if this constant rate was the same for successive release cohorts and if the number of releases per month increased steadily over successive cohorts, then the failure rate using the failure base method would yield a relatively high proportion of failures who had been on parole for a relatively short period of time. Thus the failure base method does not lead to the same results as the total release cohort base method. The rates produced by this method are influenced by changes in the number of people being paroled while the other two methods are not.

AN ACTUAL EXAMPLE USING NARCOTIC ADDICTS

The purpose of this part of the paper is to apply the procedures discussed in the fictional examples to an actual parole system. Two sets of data will be used to make this demonstration. Both sets of data are from the Civil Addict Program operated by the California Department of Corrections. It is essentially a correctional program for civilly committed narcotic addicts and has been described elsewhere.[7] While any narcotic addict may commit himself to the program, most of the addicts in the program were committed to it following a felony or misdemeanor conviction, usually for drug use or sales. The program consists of an institutional phase followed by release to the community under supervision, i. e., parole, called outpatient status. Those who violate their conditions of release may be returned to the institution; the majority of those who are returned violated their conditions of release by the use of narcotics.

During the year 1966, 1,270 men were returned to the institution from the community. Table 3 gives a distribution of time spent in the community by these failures. It can be seen that most of these returnees (violators) had been in the community for only a short period of time. But, as argued above, this failure base method does not answer the question of risk as it does not include those who did not violate the conditions of their release and were not returned.

In order to answer the question of risk we must use the survivor cohort base method, i. e., we must know the total number at risk and the number of those at risk who violated their release status in each successive time period. To obtain this information, all men released to outpatient status for the first time

---

7. Kramer, Bass & Berecochea, *Civil Commitment for Addicts: The* *California Program,* 125 Am.J.Psychiatry 128–36 (1968).

from June 1962 through June 1964 were used as the study sample, or population.[8] Each releasee was studied for a period of three years. For each period following release the number of men who violated their conditions of release during that period was expressed as a percentage of the total number of those at risk at the beginning of the period. Those at risk were defined as all those in the community and under the supervision of the Department who were outpatients at the beginning of that period. All those who had their outpatient status suspended during prior periods were removed from the at risk population. For example, during their first three months on outpatient status, 227 of the 919 men at risk were returned or suspended giving a violation rate of 24.7 percent. During the second period

TABLE 3

TIME FROM LAST RELEASE TO OUTPATIENT STATUS TO RETURN
TO THE INSTITUTION FOR MALES RETURNED AS VIOLATORS
IN 1966: CALIFORNIA CIVIL ADDICT PROGRAM

Months in Outpatient Status	Number Returned	Percent Returned	Cumulative Percent Returned
1–3	205	16.1	16.1
4–6	384	30.2	46.3
7–9	244	19.2	65.5
10–12	119	9.4	74.9
13–15	93	7.3	82.2
16–18	66	5.2	87.4
19–21	57	4.5	91.9
22–24	32	2.5	94.4
25–27	27	2.1	96.5
28–30	13	1.0	97.5
31–33	10	0.8	98.3
34–36	10	0.8	99.1
37 or more	10	0.8	99.9
Totals	1270	99.9	

[A8976]

8. This data is taken from that used in Bass, *Narcotic Addict Outpatient Program*, Research Rep.No. 36, Calif.Dept.Corrections (1969). The data used in this report excludes fifteen people who died while on outpatient status or who were discharged from outpatient status as a result of technical errors in their commitment process. It also excludes one case which was lost in the process of analysis.

(months four through six) 187 of the 692 men at risk were returned or suspended giving a violation rate of 27.0 percent. The same procedure was followed for each of the 12 follow-up periods and the results of this analysis are presented in Table 4.

TABLE 4

PROBABILITY OF FAILURE DURING GIVEN TIME PERIODS USING THE TOTAL COHORT METHOD AND THE SURVIVOR COHORT METHOD FOR 919 SUBJECTS RELEASED TO OUTPATIENT STATUS IN THE CALIFORNIA CIVIL ADDICT COMMITMENT PROGRAM—JUNE 1962–JUNE 1964.

Months on Outpatient Status	Number Failures During Period	Failures as a Pct. of Number Released	Number Available Beginning of Period	Probability of Failure During Period
1–3	227	24.7	919	.247
4–6	187	20.3	692	.270
7–9	114	12.4	505	.226
10–12	79	8.6	391	.202
13–15	47	5.1	312	.151
16–18	23	2.5	265	.087
19–21	17	1.8	242	.070
22–24	20	2.2	225	.089
25–27	16	1.7	205	.078
28–30	11	1.2	189	.058
31–33	14	1.5	178	.079
34–36	5	0.5	164	.031

[A9420]

The answer to the question as to the relative risk of parole violation over time for civilly committed narcotic addicts is that the rate of suspension (here taken as a measure of the risk of parole failure) is higher during the earlier periods following release and does decline over time until the risk levels off at about the fifteenth month. However, the rate of failure using the survivor method (exhibited in Table 4) is not nearly so high in the early months as it would appear if it were estimated using either the traditional failure base method (exhibited in Table 3) or the total cohort base method (also exhibited in Table 4).

It should be noted that this study is based on narcotic addicts who, at least according to correctional and medical experts, would be expected to return to the use of narcotics as soon as they are released to the community. Thus if the theory did not hold for addicts it is unlikely that it would hold for other offender types. In this light this study casts some doubts upon the validity of the theory that the risk of parole violation is highest during the first few months following release. For the risk of failure during the first few months on outpatient status is not nearly so high in comparison to the second half of the first year as the theory would predict. In fact the largest change in the risk of failure occurs during the first half of the second year so that the risk is relatively high during the entire first year.

SUMMARY AND DISCUSSION

This study, utilizing several different methods of assessing the risk of failure during the early parole period, raises some question about the adequacy of a method based only on failures—which seems to be the most prevalent model today. Using an artificial data base, a comparison of the failure base method with two other methods based on cohorts followed over time revealed that each method yields sometimes radically different results. An analysis of some real data drawn from the California Civil Addict Program also revealed that the failure base method tends to exaggerate the risk factor in the first few months on parole as compared to a cohort method using survivors as its base.

In view of this evidence, both logical and empirical, it would seem necessary to re-evaluate the notion that the first few months on parole represent a "crucial" period in the career of the average parolee. Further research would seem to be needed to establish the validity of this early risk period for various classes of offenders. Further inquiry is also needed into the question of *how* these rates are generated. It may be for example that part of the phenomenon results from organizational behavior; the parole system may act in such a way that early deviance is more likely to be noted and more likely to be reacted to in a negative fashion than is deviance in later periods.

RELEASE FROM PRISON: TRANSITION AND RE–ASSIMILATION*

It has long been known that the greatest rate of post-release failures occur within the first sixty days.[1] Only within the past few years, however, have correctional authorities realized that something must be done to enable inmates to bridge the gap between prison and freedom. The most comprehensive treatment program within the institution may meet with complete failure if it does not provide for this transition. Too often the newly realized individual is simply placed on the street upon release with little or no preparation for the role of free-world citizen.

Ideally the preparation of the offender for his return to the free world should begin the moment he enters the correctional process. The transition from prison to community life, if it is to be a smooth re-assimilation, must be preceded by treatment programs which are unique to the particular inmate and dedicated to the singular purpose of providing that individual with the necessary strengths to succeed on the outside.

One of the reasons for the lack of release preparation in the past has been the lack of understanding of the psychological and social mechanisms at work in the mind of the released inmate. The public conception that release from prison is an end—a goal—is often inaccurate.

Robert Lindner has suggested that the moment of release is a time of apprehension and self-examination, of discomfort and questioning, of self-doubt, inadequacy, inferiority, and fear of the future and the unknown.[2] More true to life than the layman's consensus is the following account of an inmate of his release from prison in Texas:

> It was the day I had been waiting for eight years. I felt self-conscious in my new suit and stiff new shoes. As I walked through the front door of the institution,

* Paul F. Cromwell, Jr. prepared especially for this volume.

1. Baker, "Preparing Prisoners for Their Return to the Community," 30 *Federal Probations*, 43, (1966).

2. Linder, Robert, *Stone Walls and Men* (Odyssey Press, New York), 1946, p. 470.

past the highly polished brass bars and down the front steps to freedom I realized just how scared I was. I had heard from others what to expect but I knew things would be different with me. It was five blocks to the bus station and as I walked them I began to feel stares from passers-by and I knew that they knew I was a convict. It was a feeling and whether they really knew or not, I knew, and thought they knew.

The bus trip to Houston wasn't bad except that I felt, again, terribly self-conscious. When a woman sat down beside me I forced myself not to look at her. She smiled at me once but I turned my head, afraid that my status would show on my face.

At the bus terminal in Houston I felt lost. Everything had changed in eight years. The town was larger, busier and the telephone book was twice its previous size. I looked for the names of several friends in it but they were not there, and then I realized; all my friends were in prison, not here.

I went into the restaurant of a large department store and sat down. I wasn't hungry, but was searching for a friendly face, a kind word or just a smile. The waitress, expressionless and tired looking, dropped a menu in front of me. I ordered coffee and a piece of pie, half ate it, and left. No smile, no kind word; just efficiency.

I walked away; unconsciously drifting back to the old neighborhood. Within a few hours I was again among friends. Within a few days I had made connections and taken my first heroin in eight years.

I'm back again. Looking forward to release. I wonder if it will be the same next time. I know it will be, but I'm still anticipating the next time.

As in this case, the releasee too often appears outside the gates with no family, no friends. He has lost contact with free society. This loss is engendered by the lock-step routine of prison life. The institutionalizing process of prison robs him of initiative; makes him dependent. He leaves the institution and enters the free world in much the same condition as a new born infant leaves the security of the womb and enters the world, kicking and screaming in protest. The releasee, unlike the new-born, often finds a rejecting or apathetic world. He is scared, dependent; psychologically naked, and often in attempting to pick up the threads of a past life returns to the environment he once found most comfortable; his former criminal subculture.

Anthropologist Ruth Benedict has discussed continuities and discontinuities in cultural conditioning.[3] The term "continuities" refers to training which gradually prepares an individual to move from one role to another with a minimum of strain, thus helping to prevent maladjustment in the new role. The transition from childhood to an adult role is an example of this process.

Discontinuity occurs when the training in one role develops patterns which are dysfunctional in a subsequent role. The released inmate faces a discontinuity of conditioning. With seemingly purposeful training we condition the inmate to become institutionalized. He awakens at a certain hour, goes to meals on signal, reports to work assignments when told, showers in the evening at a predetermined time, takes part in highly structured recreational and educational programs and retires, again at a specific time. He may learn a vocational trade and become highly skilled or improve his academic background yet in all this he is rigidly scheduled, tightly controlled and given almost no initiative nor opportunity to make choices or decisions.

The roles of inmate and free-world citizen are strongly differentiated. A "Good" inmate is highly tractable and assumes little responsibility in decision making; a successful free-world citizen assumes responsibility, makes the proper decisions and choices and determines his own schedules and activities. An individual in one role must revise his behavior from almost all points of view when he assumes the second role.

Dr. Benedict Alper recently told a group of correctional administrators of a man who had spent nineteen years in a correctional institution:

> He told an audience to whom I introduced him that one of the hardest things for him to learn to do when he got out was to open a door. If he came to the door of an office or a private home, or a lavatory, or a station, or wherever it might be that he found himself

3. Benedict, Ruth, "Continuities and Discontinuities in Cultural Conditioning," *Psychiatry*, Vol. I (1938), pp. 161–167.

facing a door, his first reaction was to stand there and wait for somebody to open it. For nineteen years he had never turned a knob or lifted a latch, he had to wait on the pleasure and the keys of somebody else to do that. And so he said to his audience, "What is for you in private life the easiest thing to do—to open a door and walk through—is for a person who has been conditioned to confinement the hardest thing to re-learn." It took him several weeks before he got over that conditioned feeling of having to stand stockstill when he came to a door to wait for somebody else to open it. I know of no more forceful illustration of the "theoretical" reason for alternatives to present dealing with convicted offenders.

Reconditioning to the free world must become as important a task to correctional personnel as is conditioning the newly arrived inmate to prison life.

The necessity of abrupt revision of behavior brings about a form of cultural shock to the released inmate. Thus, our thesis: *The prison often does not adequately furnish support to the individual as he progresses from role to role.* Even the most well-developed treatment program, if totally contained within the institution, will lack one ingredient essential to an inmate's success after release. The missing factor is contact with the community and family.

The discontinuity between prison house and free world can be and must be relieved by a planned program of transition.

Community Treatment Centers

Several states and federal institutions have introduced innovative programs to aid the releasee in making the transition with a minimum of role strain and cultural shock. One such program is the Community Treatment Center concept developed by the United States Bureau of Prisons.

The Community Treatment Centers provide a program of graduated release, which permits the resident to solve his social and his economical problems piecemeal and reduces prospects of finding himself in desperate circumstances soon after release. Graduated release reduces the tension and anxiety and most importantly the shock of an abrupt release. It also creates a continuity of roles consistent with a maximum adjustment upon

final release. The dichotomy between imprisonment and freedom loses some of its distinction, thus causes the released inmate
to move from role to role with greater ease.

Graduated Responsibility

An essential element of graduated release is a concomitant
program of graduated responsibility. As the inmate is continuously conditioned toward responsible social participation, the
standards of conduct expected of him should be adapted to his
capacity. It is of special interest that society demands almost
perfection of behavior from the newly released offender, the person least apt to be capable of such a high standard. From the
"normal" citizen we easily forgive minor and temporary devi-
ances from the norm. Petty transgressions such as overindul-
gence in alcohol, tardiness in paying debts, family arguments,
and occasional absenteeism on the job are regarded little concern, yet any of these on the part of the released offender are
considered as "proof" that the offender has not been properly
rehabilitated. Expectation of immediate adaptation to the
normative structure are not consistent with the concept of graduated release. Therefore, minor deviations should be viewed as
natural and should be expected and even programmed within the
structure of the post-release period. The goal should be growth,
not total and immediate normative adherence. The responsibility for growth is with the releasee, the responsibility of requiring growth with the supervising agency.

The Blackburn House Experience

One such program was developed at Blackburn House, a private non-profit Half-Way House in San Antonio, Texas. Blackburn House is a contract facility offering services to U. S. Bureau
of Prison's inmates who are to soon be released to the San Antonio vicinity.

Counselors provide center residents with a supervised environment, help them find jobs and give them needed guidance and
support. Family problems and special difficulties, such as drug
addiction and alcoholism get special attention. Group sessions
and individual counseling are mandatory.

The staff recognized that the success of the post-release period
depends heavily upon the resident's ability to adjust to new social and cultural conditions which will be encountered upon final

release. The treatment program therefore is oriented toward providing these strengths and insights which will facilitate the adjustments.

Phases of Adjustment

Blackburn House counselors have delineated four phases through which residents tend to pass during their 90–120 day stay in the center.

Observer Phase

Upon release from the institution and entry into the Center, the average resident maintains himself as a somewhat detached spectator. This period of detachment is analogous to the situation a child is confronted with on his first days in a new school. The surroundings and people are new and somewhat mystifying. After a few days the expectations and rules of the place become familiar, strange faces gain names and a more comfortable feeling develops.

The staff is especially sensitive to the feelings of the resident during the Observer Phase for this is the time during which the foundation must be laid for the remainder of his stay and during which his specific treatment needs should be identified, and a treatment modality designed specifically for his needs.

Involvement Phase

Upon successful resolution of the Observer Phase the resident usually enters a period of involvement. His first steps into the free world culture are experienced. Job hunting and home visits on weekends and evenings may bring about the first serious, adjustment problems. Attempts at family reintegration often create severe anxieties. The resident often realized that many of his preconceptions about release were false. The liabilities and stigma of his conviction and incarceration make themselves readily apparent when searching for employment and housing.

Staff members must be aware of the potential problems inherent in the Involvement Phase and work toward maximum supportive counseling at this time. The emphasis of both group and individual counseling is toward guidance and support in resolving these anxieties and frustrations.

Coming to Terms

If resolution of the Involvement Phase is successful the inmate enters a stage of adjustment which enables him to function with minimal problems and anxieties. He spends less time in the Center and the thrust of this period is toward maximum community involvement.

Pre-Release

At a point two to three weeks previous to final release, problems often reappear which have been latent during the Coming to Terms Phase. Final release is looked forward to with both anticipation and apprehension. Counselors again must watch for indications of anxiety. Problems may again erupt which were seemingly resolved weeks before. Even in its openness, the Center has institutionalizing qualities and the fear of leaving is often present. The institutionalizing quality is illustrated by the number of ex-residents who seek housing in the immediate vicinity of the Center and who almost daily return to visit staff members. Not only anxieties, but behavior problems often manifest themselves and the Pre-Release Phase may be a period of frustration for both resident and staff.

Maximum awareness of the potential hazards at each stage of adjustment allows the staff to anticipate and prepare the resident to resolve those problems. Re-assimilation into the free world community is thus facilitated and role conflict reduced.

The Community Treatment Center concept is, of course, only one of several options available to corrections to ease the transition from prison to the community. Work release, study release, furloughs, and increased use of parole all aid in the reduction of "release shock" and subsequent recidivism.

The Prison of the Future

Daniel Glaser has predicted that the prison of the future will maintain extensive links with community organizations. "Churches, social and fraternal organizations, service clubs, hobby groups, professional or trade associations, as well as societies and persons aiding each other in the control of vices (e. g., Alcoholics Anonymous), will participate in the prison more actively than heretofore." [4]

4. Glaser, Daniel, "The Prison of   *City*, (Harper & Row Publishers, the Future," from *Crime In the*   1970), p. 262.

Such cooperation should go far toward the goal of providing for each releasee the ability to move from the role of prisoner, with its attendant handicaps, to the role of the useful, productive citizen.

Summary

The released inmate, contrary to popular myth, greets his freedom with fear and trepidation. Anxiety-ridden, he may drift back into old and familiar patterns of delinquent activities and to the comfort of past criminal acquaintances.

Due to the critical nature of the post-release period the onus is upon correctional authorities to provide comprehensive preparation for the inmates release into the community. Traditional programs such as institutional pre-release do not provide for gradual transition from total confinement to total freedom. This abrupt role change by the inmate creates a form of cultural shock which manifests itself in high recidivism rates. This phenomenon has been termed "discontinuity of conditioning." The role behavior required of a free world citizen is strongly differentiated from that of the inmate culture. The inmates conditioning within the institution prepares him to play a submissive role with little opportunity for individual initiative. Free world success requires a degree of autonomy, initiative, and assumption of responsibility.

A successful pre-release program must provide a gradual transition from one role to another and should be accomplished outside the institution. A graduated release program can most efficiently provide this necessary element of the total rehabilitative process. Essential elements of graduated release are: (1) an in-community setting, (2) close supervision, (3) allowance for expected deviations from the norm, (4) releasee growth in responsibility and capabilities, and (5) a gradual programmed transition from total confinement to absolute release. Only in this manner may the released inmate experience continuity of roles consistent with a successful adjustment to free world expectations.

SUPERVISION OF PAROLE AND PROBATION CASES*

During the past fifteen years, over five as a Parole Officer and over ten as an Area Supervisor, the writer has become increasingly concerned about the lack of supervision of parole and probation cases. It is the purpose of this paper to focus attention on the importance of supervision. Supervision on all parole and probation cases, which involves investment on the part of the Parole or Probation Officer, is of paramount importance. There are no ready answers and no infallible solutions, but we must continue to forge forward. We must become more involved with the client, and we must continue to seek the answers and solutions to the problems confronting the parolee and probationer.

The moment of decision with regard to the future of parole may be upon us. Historically, parole and probation, in various forms, goes back several hundred years. More study, research, money and energy have been devoted to the problem of the paroled and probated prisoner during the past quarter-century than in all previous recorded history. More has been published on the subject in recent years than ever before. Although the surface has only been slightly dented, there is now available a considerable amount of literature devoted to the field.

It is suggested that in our concern about the multitude of problems that confront the Officer and his client, we have become enmeshed in a tangle of theories, a mass of words, and a bog of philosophy, that has literally obliterated our primary objective. We attend schools, read everything that is available, accumulate great amounts of knowledge, acquire any number of degrees. We spend hundreds of hours together discussing what to do and how to do it. We figuratively sprain our arms with our back-patting over the marvelous work we are accomplishing. Are we? How much have we put into the actual supervision of our cases? Have we not, at times, completely overlooked the fact that supervision is the reason for our being? Have we not become so theory and philosophy oriented that we are prone to overlook the client-counselor relationship?

* Terry A. Cromwell, a paper prepared especially for this volume.

There appears to be almost as many definitions of supervision as there are Parole and Probation Officers. There is one inescapable conclusion—there must be a workable relationship between the counseled and the counselor. A relationship of mutual respect and regard is ideal, but too rarely attained. However, it must be remembered that we are not working in ideal situations or with ordinary people. They have a myriad of problems—they have committed crimes—they have been convicted—their sentences probated or they have served varying amounts of time in penal institutions. Parolees come to us from controlled environments where virtually every move is dictated, where the population is manipulated and manipulative. They come from an atmosphere of suspicion, distrust, and even fear. The probationer comes from the trial and, in some cases, from jail. Then, in a matter of minutes or hours, we have them as our responsibility to function in a free society with us as their mentor and guide. Where do we go from here?

Supervision and Supervision Contacts

They must be supervised! A new relationship must be created. The questions are immediate to both parties of this relationship and, in most instances, too numerous to enumerate. It all begins with the initial interview. In almost every case, it is a rather traumatic experience for the parolee. In some instances, the same is true of the Officer. It is a beginning! We will not attempt to delve into the dynamics of this interview—there are many informative sources from which we may obtain the knowledge that is applicable to this interview.

In an alarming number of cases, the supervision of a client consists solely of an office interview once or twice a month and the completion each month of the monthly report. The information obtained is only that which the client wants to divulge and, in many instances, completely erroneous. Verification is absent. The chronological record on many cases is loaded with summaries of office visits, telephone calls, and letters. There is no reference to home and field visits. Yet the formal reports will contain detailed descriptions of the home and the employment environments with pertinent comments on existing relationships. Obviously, this information has been "fed to the Officer" and has been rather thoroughly digested. The value and importance of the office interview cannot and must not be minimized. It is so often here that the involvement and subsequent relationship really solidifies.

To depend solely, however, on this phase of the total supervision experience as a means of effecting change in an individual is sheer folly. Supervision must encompass all environments. Home visits on a regular basis with the parolee, plus collateral contacts in the same environment with the family, are an absolute necessity. The same is true with visits in the employment setting (where possible) and with the employer. Some types of employment preclude this type of visit. In the larger percentage of cases, however, visits with the employer and with the client on the job are not only possible but are extremely important to the total supervision program.

A Parole Officer recently expressed it this way: "It's amazing how the pieces all fit together to form an accurate picture of the parolee's adjustment". Leave out one segment and the picture is most often distorted. This same officer also expressed concern about the frequency of home and field visits. "More times than not," he said, "if I miss seeing a case at home or on the job during any given month, a problem will develop that *might* have been circumvented had I made my usual visit". One thing is certain—this officer is involved with his cases and he is concerned. The reality of each individual's problems is of significant importance to him.

No one can legitimately argue with the thesis that some cases need more supervision than others. First of all, we are working with people and no two of them are alike. Secondly, we are working with people who have had, and do have, problems with attitudes and behavior beyond that point which is considered acceptable. Their value systems in many cases are in variance with those expected by the society in which they live. However, to say there are cases who need no supervision at all, except for the monthly office visit, is to virtually abrogate one's responsibilities as a counselor. Assuming that there was such a case, we still have a responsibility to the public and, under the law, an obligation to render some form of supervision. The important point here is that if this supervision is totally office oriented, can we truthfully state that we are supervising? Supervision in all environments must be considered essential.

Supervision contacts are defined and labeled in many ways. In truth, there are more types of supervision than have yet been defined. We speak of supervision as treatment, as supportive, surveillance, preventive, authority oriented, and the list goes on and on. We speak of ourselves as Officers, Agents, agents of change, caseworkers, etc. We would hopefully say that we are there to help the offender help himself, to motivate him in the so-called right direction, and by doing these things, protect society. While the offender is serving his sentence and until such time as he discharges from his sentence, is legally released from super-vision, pardoned, or dies, we have a responsibility and an obliga-tion to society and to the offender that we cannot ignore.

Supervise? Why?

Many arguments have come forth against frequent contacts with clients at home, in the field, or even in the office. The propo-sitions are as many and varied as the colors of a rainbow. Ex-amples—"leave them alone and let them work out their own problems"; "the client resents your intrusion"; "he does not need supervision as long as he reports regularly, works regularly, and gets into no trouble with the law; why supervise?" "I can do more supervision in the office and by telephone than I can anywhere else;" "there isn't enough time to devote to each case;" "I do not supervise outside the office and I have very few revoca-tions;" "if they get into trouble, I'll hear about it;" "I am chained to my desk by administrative work and do not have time to work outside the office;" "I have too many cases". "How can I super-vise a hundred or more people?" It is saddening to review and meditate on the extensive list of reasons why supervisory contacts are not desirable or not possible.

Let us now attempt to analyze the reasons listed above. How can we leave them alone and let them work out their own prob-lems? They have failed in this all or part of their lives—this is one of the reasons they are where they are. Certainly, in some instances, the client resents our intrusion. The truth is, he re-sents the authority we represent—in fact, he has rebelled against authority and this has accounted, at least in part, for his behavior. It is our job to become involved with him, as unpleasant as it may be in the beginning for each of us, and help him solve the problem.

So he doesn't need supervision because he reports every month, tells us he is working every day, staying out of debt, and has not had any problems? Is it a fact that these people never tell a lie or never misrepresent the truth? What about the nagging wife, the problems with the employer, the regular visits to the neigh-borhood tavern, the sick children, and so on? There are so many things about him that we will never know if *he* is our only source of information.

Exactly what kind of supervision can we do in the office and by telephone? Assuming that this constitutes our total supervision, the only possible answer is, practically none. The client often presents one picture in the office, another one at home, and even a slightly different one at work. Oftentimes a few minutes in the livingroom of his home, with his wife present, is more revealing than an hour's groping session in the office. The telephone is an impersonal and inanimate object—it involves distance and distance destroys intimacy.

It is felt that we should thank a kind providence that we do not have enough time for each case. Certainly the client is often grateful. Long and extended (sometimes distended) interviews more often than not are more harmful than beneficial. Many offenders have relatively short attention spans, and once it is exhausted, further conversation is not fruitful.

It is quite possible that the Officer who does not extend his services beyond the office would not have many revocations. In the first place, the only information he has about his client is what the client wants him to have plus that which he has obtained through the use of a telephone or through police sources. We all know that a client may violate many of the rules over an extended period of time and not violate the law. Clients who are guilty of violations have been known to complete their sentences and discharge. However, it is a matter of record that their names are frequently noted at a later date on police, court, and institutional records. Is it possible that this type of case is a successful one?

Even the most skeptical of persons must admit that the client *might* have never returned to the institution had the counselor *worked* at establishing a helpful relationship with him prior to discharge. Undoubtedly, there are revocations which could have been avoided if the supervising officer, through frequent and meaningful contacts with the subject, at home, on the job, and in the office, plus the appropriate collateral contacts, had worked at creating a workable relationship with his client. If the officer had supervised his cases elsewhere other than the office, he would have possibly learned that some of his cases who seemed to be adjusting so well, were in fact, on the verge of serious problems with the law, as well as with the parole or probation authority.

As the result of case contacts, he would be able to take immediate action. Some cases would, of course, be recommended for revocation. In other cases, revocation could be avoided—corrective action could be initiated. In most instances, when he receives word from the police that the client is in trouble, it will most certainly be the first indication of a problem. What happened to preventive supervision?

There are not any known instances of an Officer being "chained" to his desk by anything or anyone other than his own lack of initiative, organization, and planning. Lack of experience and training could also account, in part, for the condition. The truth is—supervision comes first, and the Officer who supervises nearly always has time for the more tedious and time-consuming administration. With training and study, he will always find the time he needs for office matters. There are many officers who now make frequent supervisory contacts who would, without hesitation, say that the fact that they do work at supervision makes their administrative work easier. They are so well acquainted with their cases that routine or violation reports do not entail extensive preparation. Their chronological records not only reflect numerous contacts, but are documented in a brief, concise, and summarized style that makes report writing much less of a chore.

The most frequently voiced reason for lack of supervision is— "I have too many cases. How can I supervise a hundred or more people?" There is some validity to this statement. Some, but not much. A caseload of from 30–40 cases is very near to ideal and this size load can be supervised. A caseload of a hundred or more is not at all desirable, but it can be supervised. The first ingredient is composed of desire and work! The second is a combination of planning and organization. Finally, one must look for the ways and means to do, *not* the reasons why it can't be accomplished. Large caseloads can be classified in terms of case needs and requirements. Some cases need more supervision than others, some can adjust quite favorably with normal supervision, and there is a small group who will do well with a minimum of supervisory contacts. Therefore, it is safe to say that even the largest caseloads could be so organized that at least most of those cases in particular need of assistance would find it forthcoming.

The Officer who has no desire to supervise and who may, at the same time, have an allergy to work, has possibly already lost the battle. It is assumed that almost all Officers have the desire to help. If they do not possess this quality, they should look elsewhere for a livelihood. Unfortunately, there are those who possess some degree of desire, but little energy. It is so easy to stay in the office, adopt an air of omnipotence, let the cases come in and fill them with good, solid fatherly advice. The same attitude can be, and is applied to dependence on the telephone. It is suggested that the office desk and telephone are, in many cases, the greatest barriers to effective supervision that are known to the field of corrections.

The relationship between the Officer and the client could be called the key to supervision. As has been mentioned, it may not be warm (hot, yes). It may not be one of mutual regard and respect. It may be directive on the part of the Officer with the parolee in a resistive role. In spite of all obstacles and problems, if the client is motivated toward a more acceptable attitude and behavior pattern, then the relationship has been successful. When the Officer is a warm person who is willing to become involved, to invest something of himself and his knowledge in his cases, the success rate rises. A danger arises here. Over-identification and over-involvement must, at almost all costs, be avoided. Our role is *not* one of complete sympathy, toleration of excuses, encouragement of dependence, or as a sponge to soak up the sad stories that come our way. We are here to recognize a problem, define it, and then ask, "what are you going to do about it?" We are here to help the parolee help himself. We are not so much interested in the "whys" as we are the "whats".

We are at the crossroads. We know why we are here—the question is, what are we going to do about it? Quite obviously, we must "gird our loins" and get to the task at hand. We must supervise and we know that it must be total supervision and must apply, to a marked degree, to *all* cases. It may be called supportive, preventive, surveillance, authoritative, or it may well bear a variety of labels. All of the knowledge, theory, and philosophy in the universe will not be of any value at all if there is no application.

Examples—Lack of Supervision

There are many case histories that are available which graphically illustrate the need for supervision and also are good examples of what can and does happen when there is none.

Client X had been under supervision for a number of years. He had never been arrested on any charge, had reported regularly, but he was not a young man and was in relatively poor health. He had not, in recent years, worked with any degree of regularity. He was not old enough to qualify for Old Age Assistance and had no income other than that which he received from performing menial labor at a variety of jobs. A neighbor looked in on him occasionally and assisted him with his daily needs. His attitude toward supervision was good and he was considered in such a favorable light by his Officer that supervision had been reduced to an absolute minimum. Result—the parolee was arrested for stealing. What? Food! Why? He was hungry and had no funds with which to purchase anything. There were several sources available from which assistance could have been obtained. The Officer was not aware of the client's condition because he had not been in the man's home in months.

Another client had been under supervision for a period in excess of seven (7) months. He was seen and interviewed at home on two (2) occasions during this period. During the four (4) month period just prior to the murder that he committed (while under supervision), only one (1) contact was made and this was a field collateral contact with the Volunteer Parole Officer. Even office contacts were missing. The parolee was tried and convicted of the murder. At the time of the offense, he had seen his Officer just three (3) times—once in the office and the two (2) occasions at home. During the investigation of the murder charge, it was learned that within a period of two weeks of the date he committed murder, he had been involved in a fight in which he was so vicious that a witness stated "he acted like an animal". The Officer had no knowledge of the incident.

A client was permitted to mail his reports to the Parole Officer. He had been on parole for several years. It had long ago been decided that he needed no supervision. A period of about six (6) months went by without a supervisory contact. Then, when an attempt was made to see him, it was discovered that he had absconded from supervision and a parent had been submitting his reports.

Smith had been on Parole for approximately fourteen (14) months. He had worked every day, reported in person every month, and had not been arrested or apparently involved in any illegal activities. He had paid off a number of old debts and receipts were turned over to the supervising Officer. A study of his reports and his file indicated that his adjustment was excellent. Two mistakes were made. The parolee's past history was all but ignored and home visits with him and his family were, for the major portion of the parole period, minimal. In fact, he was seen at home on just four occasions. There were four home collateral contacts made on the same dates. Overnight he was in serious trouble. He was arrested for a series of felony thefts, was able to post bond, and then absconded from supervision before his Parole Officer could contact him. A subsequent investigation revealed that he was traveling rather extensively out of his county of residence and, during these travels, was engaged in illegal activities. Regular and frequent home visits might well have uncovered early indications of his activities and possibly would have enabled the Parole Officer to initiate action to bring the case under control. At the very least, a number of the crimes he committed might have been avoided through early detection and subsequent reincarceration.

During an audit of a caseload, the Supervisor questioned the scarcity of supervision contacts on a case. There had been no home or field contacts over a period of several months. Yet, among other things, the client had been reporting that he was working at a business establishment within a few blocks of the parole office. The employer, according to the client, knew of his criminal history. At the insistence of the Supervisor, the Officer contacted the employer by telephone immediately, only to learn that the client had terminated his employment several months prior to the call. Immediate and intensive supervision brought the case back under control and the client successfully completed his sentence.

Every one of the Officers whose cases have just been described are good Officers. It must be remembered, though, that they are much like the rest of us. They make mistakes. Happily, in each instance, the Officer profited. It is extremely doubtful that any of them will repeat the same mistake. Unfortunately, many of us have to learn so many things the hard way. These officers are concerned, they are working hard at their jobs, and they are involved with their clients.

Initiating Supervision—Approach and Conversation

Almost any Parole or Probation Officer who has been in the field for even a few months has been bombarded with lectures, literature, and advice. He has learned a prescribed method (or methods) of conducting every conceivable type of interview. He has been exposed to the attitudes, customs, and traditions of the various ethnic groups and cultures. The do's and don'ts have been carefully explained to him. The policies and procedures of the agency have been at least partially digested and he has acquired a token knowledge of criminal law and court procedures.

Then comes the day of reckoning. He has a caseload. Sooner or later (usually sooner) it suddenly occurs to him that he is now confronted with a multitude of problems. What does he talk about when he visits the client's home? Job? What do you say to a client in the office? Naturally, there are cases with plenty of problems and these clients are "easy" to talk to—more often than not it is "listen to". Of course, there is always the old standby— THE RULES. Are you working regularly? Are you staying home at night? How many of your old criminal friends have been by to see you? What about drinking?

A casual conversation involving such mundane things as the weather, latest news, athletics, or his hobbies (our clients usually have some type of hobby other than crime) will probably elicit as much information as is needed regarding not only his habits but his attitude. With perhaps a majority of cases, it is unlikely that the rules need to be mentioned in most of the interviews. There are exceptions to everything. A few clients need to be reminded more than others of the responsibilities and obligations of parole or probation. Most of these cases, though, can be handled without a didactic approach. Even the most distant and suspicious client will, in time, relate more comfortably in a relaxed atmosphere. The Officer needs to show interest in the individual. This interest should not only embrace the client, but his family, friends, employer, and even his pets. A moments attention to a child or a pet has been known to open a lot of doors. When they are opened, it is sometimes surprising what comes out!

Summation

Parole and Probation cases can be supervised. Supervisory contacts outside of the office can be made even with large caseloads and all the inherent problems. The knowledge and skills that go into it are not easily acquired. One must know from the very beginning that there are no experts. There is no manual that answers all of the questions. No procedures have yet been evolved that solve all of the multitude of problems that confront the correctional worker. If there is an answer, it must involve education, experience, more education, more experience and, above all things, desire and work. A recognizable degree of proficiency in all areas is a must factor. New skills must be added, developed, and put to use. The word "can't" needs to be buried and forgotten. Supervisory contacts with the client must be frequent, be as meaningful as possible, and must encompass all those environments within which society expects (and, yes, even demands) a nominal conformity. You may not be supervising your cases now, but you can start today.

THE FUNCTION OF COERCIVE CASEWORK IN CORRECTIONS*

One hears a great deal today about social permissiveness, individual freedom, right of free speech, and allowing everyone to "do his thing." These ideas have been made the topics of books, magazine articles, newspaper editorials, protest demonstrations, and political speeches; everyone seems to be getting into the act. On the one hand our courts are badgered for legal approval of more liberal expressions of individual freedom and on the other hand they are ridiculed for their lenient rulings which protect the criminal and tie the hands of law enforcement. There are alternating cries of anguish over the breakdown of law and order and of indignation over the development of a police state.

The writers, speakers, and demonstrators cite the rising crime rates, campus disorders, police brutality, the generation gap, youthful disrespect for authority, authoritative disregard for the individual, and a host of other themes to support their respective theses. They all imply, and often state, that it is a matter of unrealistic leniency or unconstitutional restriction—depending on which side the complainant finds himself—which is at the root of all our problems.

These are not tides of controversy which swirl outside the field of corrections. Indeed, some of our new recruits, especially those

* Claude T. Mangrum, *Federal Probation*, March, 1971. Reprinted with permission.

young people just out of college, may be particularly susceptible to being caught up in these controversies. They have been trained in times of less social restraint, exposed to the philosophy that every man should be free to "do his own thing," and, perhaps, influenced by the spirit of disrespect for law, order, and authority which infects our society today. Yet, they are coming into a field specifically assigned the responsibility of protecting society through the exercise of restraints, the enforcement of law and order, and the use of authority. It is little wonder that some of the young enforcers of society's regulations may have conflicts of identification between society and the violators of society's laws.

In this setting, it seems important—indeed, imperative—to draw the attention of the newcomer and the veteran to these conflicts and to explore some ideas which may help to orient us to a resolution of them.

What Is Coercive Casework?

At the heart of the philosophy of correctional work is the two-fold concept of social control and social treatment. They are not mutually exclusive or separate entities, but intertwined—the one impinging on the other, modifying and shaping, being modified and shaped in turn. Ideally, of course, we attain the goal of control through the means of treatment. However, this statement taken alone is easily misconstrued; therefore, it needs some explanation and analysis.

There is, in the minds of many practitioners of the "helping professions," an irreconcilable conflict between the use of casework techniques and the use of authority. This apparent dichotomy has been the topic of many debates and journal articles and need not be belabored here. The conflict remains unresolved and will probably continue so for a long time to come. We do not expect to resolve it here; only to try to approach it from a slightly different perspective.

The definitions of social casework are almost as numerous as are the numbers of persons defining it. However, they all generally are focused on the processes by which the individual is helped to more effectively function within his social environment. The emphasis is on the individual in the recognition that no matter how similar one's situation may appear to be to that of another, each problem, and each attempt and method to resolve it, has its own unique meaning to each individual. The method which works for one person may not work with another. One of the basic and most important tasks of the caseworker is to fit his treatment methods and techniques to the unique needs of his client.

To coerce is to restrain or constrain by force, especially by the use of legal authority. "Restrain" carries the idea of holding in check, controlling, curbing. "Constrain" gives the idea of forcing into, compelling, obliging to action.

By coercive casework, then, we mean the use of restraining and constraining legal authority in the processes of helping the offender to function in his social environment without resorting to illegal or antisocial behavior.

This is, ideally, the underlying philosophy of establishing and enforcing specific conditions of probation and parole because those conditions are to be used for guidance of the client's behavior. He is placed under restraints when instructed not to associate with certain kinds of people, not to leave the jurisdiction without permission, or not to possess a weapon. He is constrained when instructed to report regularly to the probation or parole officer, to maintain gainful employment, or to make restitution to the victim of his offense.

Perhaps a graphic example of this approach is the condition of probation which requires the probationer to participate in a program of psychotherapy. Despite some objections that such an order violates the basic need for client motivation for such therapy to be effective, most of us know of specific instances where the proper motivation has developed *after* the therapy program has begun.

There are many who hold that the foundation of effective casework is the belief that motivation to improve or to resolve problems must come from within, that casework is not effective unless it is desired and voluntarily requested by the client. Somehow, the client must engage himself in grappling with his own problems if they are to be resolved. They believe that every man has the right of choice and it is wrong to impose on him official values or solutions to problems from without.

We do not deny the innate dignity of man, nor his right to freedom to make choices. We do not deny the validity of the above-noted ideas, nor of the basic responsibility of the individual to deal with his own problems with his own resources; but, neither can we deny the necessity of the orderly functioning of society, nor of all citizens to behave so as not to disturb that orderly functioning. Neither can we deny the importance of client and worker alike recognizing that the exercise of the right of choice carries with it the necessity of accepting the consequences of that choice.

It is essential to recognize that underlying our highly developed society are orderly behavior and relationships, without which society could not exist. When individuals act so as to disrupt this order, some action must be taken to restore it. In the case of the criminal offender (and many others, for that matter) this action may be through coercion—for his own and society's welfare.

The Function of Coercive Casework

While it is true that effective casework is not something done *to* or *for* the client, but *with* him, it is also true that sometimes it is a matter of some action which "gets his attention" or "holds him still" long enough for him to recognize that there *is* motivation from within; he may only need to make way for it to begin to function. Or, it may be necessary, through restraint and constraint, to structure action until the validity of it can be understood and accepted for itself as a way of life.

In this initial stage of the correctional treatment process, one need not necessarily be complicated in the design of his casework methods and techniques. He may need only to set, and enforce, some behavioral limits—to inform his client, "You can go this far, but no further"; to say, "No! You cannot do that."

If it is true that "nothing succeeds like success," it is also true that nothing fails like failure. In direct proportion to his lack of success, the individual is likely to feel ineffectual, then powerless, then useless, then helpless. At this point he also ceases to care; and that is when he is the most disruptive and dangerous.

The offender, often habitually unsuccessful in his attempts to adjust to the pressures and demands of society, needs to have successful experiences—even if they are at first coerced. A definite "shall and shall not" approach is often necessary until the client reaches the point where he can be comfortable with the restraints and constraints imposed on his conduct; until the motivation for lawful and acceptable behavior comes from within himself, from the knowledge of the benefit to be derived from avoiding the kind of disruptive behavior which subjects him to penalty and social rejection.

The aim of providing success experiences is to persuade the offender of the validity of society's ideals and to have him internalize them as his own. He must come to view his behavior in the light of its impingement on others and learn to regulate it accordingly. To reach this goal requires not only casework treatment but behavior control as well.

There is a common misconception that delinquent and criminal groups have "their own set of values," so will not accept and live by the values of the larger community. However, making the values of society meaningful and relevant to these groups can provide the motivation for them to modify their own value systems and to incorporate society's values into their own codes of conduct.

This will entail the application of realistic values that are relevant to present conditions, not merely harping on traditional concepts based on outmoded social codes. To sharp and inquiring youth, it will also require pertinent explanations of the "why" of these values.

It is imperative, in this regard, for society to propagate its value of the necessity to behave in accordance with law. Various subgroups, including the criminal and delinquent subcultures, actively propagate their value codes. It is no less acceptable for society to vigorously engage in such activity—despite current criticisms of such practice. The correctional worker needs occasionally to remind himself—and others, including his clients—that society also has rights and needs.

A Positive Approach

We readily recognize the necessity of forcible restraint of those who represent a violent threat to society; and, for the protection of others, we put these persons behind bars. This is a negative action. There is a positive side to this same coin, however, especially in regard to those offenders who are not placed or continued behind bars, but are allowed to remain in the community on probation or parole.

This positive action—what we have termed coercive casework —is that restraint and constraint on the individual's behavior designed to help persuade him of both the short- and long-run validity of accepting society's values and regulating his conduct accordingly. The goal, of course, is to have him internalize these values, making coercion unnecessary. It is the same kind of discipline we enforce with our children as we try to instill within them acceptable standards of conduct. These standards are at first enforced through various restraints and constraints. As the child matures and restraint becomes self-discipline, the enforced standards become clear through understanding and habitual through regular observance.

It is behavior, illegal and antisocial, which brings the individual into the correctional system. It is both behavior and the attitudes leading to it which we must help to change. While the, techniques for accomplishing this goal may be varied and require individual application according to need and circumstances as well as an explanation of "why," the underlying philosophy is as simple as "thou shalt not" and "thou shalt." This is not a new concept, certainly; but it is a basic and necessary one both in terms of individual benefit and the ongoing and orderly functioning of society.

CALIFORNIA'S PAROLE RULES*

Psychologically, the first sixty to ninety days of parole are the most difficult. The former prisoner has been incarcerated from one year to perhaps twenty or thirty years in a regimented institution, where many everyday decisions were made for him. Although many of the more progressive parole systems have programs that aid the parolee in the transition from incarceration to freedom, to assume that these programs fully prepare him for return to civilian life would be unrealistic. Consequently, he returns to free society somewhat frightened, bewildered, and perhaps embittered.

Before release, a work or home program is arranged for the parolee, enabling him to look forward to a constructive life during his rehabilitation. Often, however, subconsciously he has built up this home life or employment out of proportion to reality. He is disillusioned when he finally realizes life is not

* William D. Milligan, *Crime and Delinquency*, April, 1969. Reprinted with permission of the National Council on Crime and Delinquency.

what he had remembered or envisioned during his years of confinement.

Most parolees are emotionally immature and, in many respects, must be treated accordingly. Thus, certain restrictions, defining the limits to which he may go without endangering his freedom, must be imposed.

Before his release, the inmate signs a document describing the conditions of his parole. Copies are then distributed to the parolee at the time of his release, to the district or out-of-state office having supervision, and to the central file office in Sacramento.

California's Department of Corrections makes every effort to insure that the individual rights of the parolee will not be violated. Accordingly, much legal research was undertaken before the conditions were drafted, and they are revised if any section appears inequitable or unrealistic.

California Penal Code Sections 3052 and 3053 provide statutory authority for the establishment and enforcement of the conditions of parole. If any of the conditions is violated to the extent that reincarcerating the parolee for part or all of the remainder of his term is deemed necessary by the Adult Authority, this may be done,[1] but cause must be shown in the order suspending or revoking the parole.[2]

The following description of California's parole conditions includes an explanation of their purposes and various meanings.

Release

> 1. *Release*: Upon release from the institution you are to go directly to the program approved by the Parole and Community Services Division and shall report to the Parole Agent or other person designated by the Parole and Community Services Division.

The purposes of this clause are to guarantee that the parolee reaches his destination and, further, to determine whether any assistance can be rendered upon his arrival. For example, the parole agent may wish to introduce him to his new employer if they have not already met or perhaps he can drive the released prisoner home. Often, having a person with him who is aware of his past and present problems as well as those that will con-

---

1. Cal.Penal Code § 3056.   2. Id., § 3063.

front him in the near future will lessen much of the parolee's anxiety. Therefore, compliance with this condition is for the parolee's benefit, not punishment.

Residence

2. *Residence*: Only with approval of your Parole Agent may you change your residence or leave the county of your residence.

Violation of this provision, as with most of the other restrictions, will not of itself be sufficient to return the parolee to prison; however, a continual changing of address may result in such action. Past experience has shown that the parolee who constantly changes his residence is trying to evade his parole agent, usually because he is involved in some sort of illegal behavior.

Approval for change of residence is seldom, if ever, denied. The main reason for the regulation is to keep the officer informed of the whereabouts of the parolee. This is necessary for the protection of society, particularly if a recent crime has been committed of the type or nature for which the parolee had been convicted.

Permission to leave a county is seldom refused if the reason is legitimate, as for a vacation or a visit, even if it means leaving the state. Geographic limits are set for prisoners released on parole, but they are not meant to be unduly restrictive.

Employment

3. *Work*: It is necessary for you to maintain gainful employment. Any change of employment must be reported to, and approved by, your Parole Agent.

After several years of incarceration a man becomes overly dependent on others because he has few decisions to make. He is told when to eat, work, sleep, and bathe. A signal begins his day and ends it. A long period of such routine seems to sap him of initiative and ambition. Most prisoners have never held a job for more than a few months at a time; consequently, upon release the average parolee is ill equipped to hold a job for an extended period. If this regulation were applied strictly the vast majority of parolees would soon be back behind prison walls for violation of parole. The rule is used, however, as a lever or forced incentive for the parolee to maintain steady employment.

It is doubtful that inability to hold a steady job would be enough to warrant a return to prison. Coupled with some other violation, however, it may constitute a valid reason for revocation of parole.

As indicated above, the parolee's transition from prison to free society is characterized by immature emotions: he reacts quickly to a situation without considering the consequences. Therefore a work requirement is imposed on the parolee for much the same reasons justifying the residence requirements. For instance, the parolee might become irritated with his employer and, instead of looking at the situation maturely, might rashly quit his job. He would thus be without financial backing to sustain him and his family until another position is found. The restriction compels him to think *twice* before quitting and, instead, discuss the matter with his employer.

If employment is not maintained, the parolee may look for "easy" money and resort to robbery or burglary. If employed, he is less apt to succumb to the impulse of returning to a criminal life. Also, the working parolee has a chance to achieve a sense of accomplishment and personal pride. He can prove to himself that he is part of society and can function accordingly.

One last rationale for this restraint concerns the narcotics addict and the sex offender. To place a dog near food or a child near candy and tell him not to touch it would be foolish. To allow an addict to work in an area where drugs are available or to permit a sex offender to be employed around young children would be tempting him beyond reason. He may fool himself into believing that he will not revert to his former way of life, but in the interest of society and the parolee, to take such a chance would obviously be unwise.

Reports

4. *Reports*: You are to submit a written monthly report of your activities on forms supplied by the Parole and Community Services Division unless directed otherwise by your Parole Agent. This report is due at the Parole Office not later than the fifth day of the following month, and shall be true, correct, and complete in all respects.

Generally these reports are submitted monthly. However, if progress and stability are shown, plus steady residence (e. g., the parolee has bought a home), fewer reports may be required. Some parolees, in fact, have been instructed that no reports are necessary unless residence or employment has changed. As with most of the conditions, an occasional infraction will not necessarily mean reimprisonment. Parolees are not less susceptible to forgetfulness than others, and to revoke their parole for a minor mishap would be grossly unfair and unjust.

Alcohol

5. *Alcoholic Beverages*: The unwise use of alcoholic beverages and liquors causes more failures on parole than all other reasons combined.

*A. You shall not use alcoholic beverages or liquors to excess.

B. You shall not use *any* alcoholic beverages or liquors.

(* Strike out either A or B, leaving whichever clause is applicable.)

Condition A is invoked for practically all parolees. The only exceptions are those cases in which the authorities feel that complete abstinence is necessary for successful parole. The justification for this regulation is the direct relationship between alcoholism and recidivism.

The California Penal Code [3] and the Adult Authority [4] are explicit in their regulation of the use of alcohol by sex offenders, and the court has upheld the rule. Sex offenders have little control over their sexual desires; it takes very little to precipitate their aggressive behavior.

Narcotics

6. *Narcotics and Dangerous and Hypnotic Drugs:* You may not possess, use, or traffic in any narcotic drugs, as defined by Division 10 of the Health and Safety Code, or dangerous or hypnotic drugs as defined by Section 4211 of the Business and Professions Code, in violation of the law. If you have ever been convicted of possession, sale, or use of narcotic drugs, or have ever

3. Id., § 3053.5.   4. Cal.Adult Authority Res. 159.

used narcotic drugs, and are paroled to a section of California where an Anti-Narcotic Program is, or becomes available, you hereby agree to conform to the instructions of your Parole Agent regarding your participation therein.

Possession, use, or trafficking in certain drugs is a crime whether or not a person is on parole. Hence, this imposition is no more onerous to the parolee than to the ordinary citizen. The purpose of this condition is to serve as a reminder to the parolee that any infraction will invoke immediate jailing until an investigation has been completed, with revocation of parole the probable result. This restriction appears to have a deterring effect upon the parolee. The necessity for it is clearly indicated, as addicts are difficult to control. Constant supervision over them is essential for rehabilitation.

Weapons

7. *Weapons*: You shall not own, possess, use, sell, nor have under your control any deadly weapons or firearms.

The California Penal Code [5] specifies that no felon may own or possess any pistol, revolver, or other firearm capable of being concealed upon the person and that this rule does not apply to antique pistols or revolvers incapable of use as such or to a gun barrel more than twelve inches in length.[6] "It is the purpose of the statute to make it unlawful for ex-convicts to carry a gun that will shoot and not merely objects that look like usable guns." [7]

How does the constitutional right to bear arms affect a parolee? The California courts have taken the position that regulation of firearms is a proper exercise of the police power of the state and does not violate state constitutional provisions or the Second Amendment of the U. S. Constitution.[8]

The Adult Authority is empowered to place reasonable restrictions upon the parolee.[9] Therefore, to impose a greater

5. Cal.Penal Code § 12021.

6. Id., § 12001.

7. People v. DeFalco, 176 Cal.App. 2d 590 (1960).

8. People v. Garcia, 97 Cal.App.2d 733 (1950).

9. Cal.Penal Code §§ 3052, 3053.

restraint upon him than that described in the Penal Code would not necessarily violate the state constitution. For example, the Adult Authority prohibits the possession of rifles and shotguns, although it allows some exceptions to this rule. If a parolee lives or works on a farm or a ranch and is having trouble with rodents or other animals destroying crops or small farm animals such as chickens, permission may be granted by his parole agent, with the approval of the district supervisor, to purchase and maintain a rifle or shotgun. Occasionally, permission may also be granted to an avid hunter whose previous crime or crimes did not involve firearms or other means of violence. However, under no condition may a parolee carry an operative pistol or revolver.

Problems could result when a parolee's parent has a firearm on the premises. If the parolee is potentially violent a special condition could be imposed whereby he is not to maintain a residence where firearms are present. However, the parent usually is willing to cooperate by disposing of the weapon.

Another difficult situation arises with firearms "incapable of use as such." [10] Although the Penal Code does not include this type of weapon in the firearm category, the gun still *appears* to be capable of being fired despite the absence of a firing pin. Many robberies have been committed successfully by persons carrying nonfunctioning weapons. Therefore, the Department of Corrections ordinarily will not permit the parolee to possess even nonoperative firearms. Since hardware stores and pawnshops deal in firearms, the parolee would, in most instances, be precluded from employment in these places.

Associates

8. *Associates*: You must avoid association with former inmates of penal institutions unless specifically approved by your Parole Agent; and you must avoid association with individuals of bad reputation.

This condition is based on the assumption that association with past criminals does not provide an environment conducive to rehabilitation. An infraction of this rule, when other conditions have been violated, may be enough to cause a revocation of parole.

10. Id., § 12001.

Special permission may be granted in certain situations for two or more parolees to get together (e. g., in riding to and from work or at group counseling sessions) but the permissible circumstances would be clearly defined.

Motor Vehicles

9. *Motor Vehicles*: Before operating any motor vehicle you must secure the written permission of your Parole Agent, and you must possess a valid operator's license.

This limitation applies to any motor vehicle, including motorcycles and airplanes. Permission is seldom denied, as long as the parolee has a valid operator's license and can afford the proper insurance. The chief aim of this clause is to enable the parole agent to maintain a copy of the description and license plate number of the car or cars the parolee will be driving. This precautionary measure often has been useful to the police during criminal investigations.

Cooperation and Attitude

10. *Cooperation and Attitude*: At all times your Parole Agent and your good behavior and attitude must justify the opportunity granted you by this parole.

Taken at face value, this appears to be a catchall, making it easier to re-incarcerate a parolee for some vague and nebulous infraction. However, experience has shown that this condition is rarely enforced. When used, it is usually in conjunction with other, more severe parole violations that would be sufficient justification by themselves for parole revocation.

Would parole be revoked for violation of this condition alone? It is doubtful that this would be sufficient grounds under the existing policies and procedures. Accordingly, this constraint is not as disadvantageous to the parolee as it may first appear.

Laws and Conduct

11. *Laws and Conduct*: You are to obey all municipal, county, state, and federal laws, ordinances, and orders; and you are to conduct yourself as a good citizen.

Like many of the other conditions, this restriction is imposed upon all citizens regardless of their status. Violation of this clause by commission of a felony will invariably result in return to prison. Conviction of a misdemeanor, however, does not necessarily require re-incarceration, depending, of course, on the facts of the particular case.

Civil Rights

12. *Civil Rights*: Your Civil Rights have been suspended by law. You may not marry, engage in business, nor sign certain contracts unless your Parole Agent recommends, and the Adult Authority approves, restoring such Civil Rights to you. There are some Civil Rights affecting your everyday life which the Adult Authority has restored to you, *but* you may not exercise those without first getting written approval from your Parole Agent. You should talk to your Parole Agent about your Civil Rights to be sure you do not violate this condition of your parole. The following Civil Rights *only* are hereby restored to you at this time.

A. You may make such purchases of clothing, food, transportation, household furnishings, tools, and rent such habitation as are necessary to maintain yourself and keep your employment. You shall not make any purchases relative to the above on credit except with the written approval of your Parole Agent.

B. You are hereby restored all rights under Workmen's Compensation Laws, Unemployment Insurance Laws, Social Security Laws, etc. [Reference is here made to Adult Authority Resolution No. 199.]

The power vested in the Adult Authority to alter or amend a parolee's civil rights originates from the California Penal Code.[11] The Adult Authority's Resolution No. 199 restored many civil rights that may be exercised by the parolee with permission of the parole agent. Further, all parolees may purchase necessities on credit in an amount not exceeding $1,000, provided permission is first granted by the Parole and Community Services Division. Any other rights not mentioned re-

11. Id., § 3054.

quire authorization by the Adult Authority after a parolee, via his parole agent, has explained the reason for his request.

Contracts

What if a parolee enters into a contract not authorized by the Adult Authority? Is it void *ab initio* under section 1556 of the California Civil Code, or are there mitigating circumstances that would make it voidable or valid under the estoppel doctrine? Recent court decisions [12] have established that when a parolee attempts, for example, to buy an automobile and the salesman is informed of his status as a parolee and his incapacity to contract, the parolee would not be estopped from later asserting that he had no capacity to contract. He could do so because, as a convicted felon, he normally has no legal right to make a contract. However, if the salesman was not told of the parolee's status and was thus not aware that the parolee had no capacity to make a contract, then the parolee would be estopped from asserting his inability to contract. He would not be able to use his loss of civil rights as an excuse to have the contract set aside. The California Appellate Court stated: "While such penal provisions work a hardship . . . on the person convicted of crime, a person dealing with a parolee in the ordinary course of business, without notice or knowledge of his status, should not be brought within the orbit of such hardship." [13] A further provision states that the canceling of civil rights because of a parolee's return to prison shall not affect any contractual obligations he had made during the time his civil rights were restored when he was on parole.[14]

Civil Suits

What if a parolee is civilly sued or wishes to sue? A prisoner or parolee is still liable to suit and "this liability necessarily carries with it the right to defend." [15] This right is qualified by the rule that the prisoner is not entitled to be personally present at any part of the proceedings.[16] Although this restric-

12. Rosman v. Cuevas, 176 Cal.App. 2d 867 (1959); Jones v. Allen, 185 Cal.App.2d 279 (1960).

13. Jones v. Allen, supra note 12.

14. Cal.Adult Authority Res. 199, revised and reissued Oct. 15, 1957.

15. People v. Lawrence, 140 Cal.App. 2d 133 (1956).

16. Cal.Civil Code of Procedure § 1997.

tion applies to prison inmates, there is no law that applies the same rationale to a parolee who is present in the jurisdiction where the action may be brought.

The Adult Authority does not favor restoration of civil rights to permit inmates to file civil action suits. However, the Authority will consider allowing an agent with a special power of appointment to represent inmates in civil suits. The same restriction would not be placed on a parolee, however, because he is not within the confines of prison and he has more freedom of movement. This particularly holds true when his purpose for bringing the suit seems valid. However, his civil rights must still be restored and permission granted.

Marriage

A marriage contracted by adults legally free to do so is valid. However, such a marriage contracted by a parolee in California before restoration of his civil rights is void *ab initio*, regardless of the spouse's knowledge of the facts. What about the marriage of a parolee who broke his parole by leaving the state to get married? The California attorney-general has held that a marriage contracted in another state is valid if the law of such state so provides, whether the parolee is there by consent of the Adult Authority or as an escapee.[17] If the parolee is already married, the second purported marriage in another state, if valid there, would constitute bigamy.

Voting and Holding Public Office

During the period of parole a parolee may not vote, hold public office, or serve as a juror. This is made clear not only by case law [18] and the Penal Code [19] but also by the California Constitution [20] and the Government Code.[21] Upon discharge from parole all civil rights are restored except the right to act as trustee, to vote, and to hold public office.[22] However, if a pardon is later granted, the right to vote and probably the other rights are restored.[23]

17. 18 Op.Cal.Atty.Gen. 275 (1951).

18. Stephens v. Toomey, 51 Cal.2d 864 (1959).

19. Cal.Penal Code § 2600.

20. Cal.Const. Art. II, § 1.

21. Cal.Gov.Code § 1021.

22. 2 Op.Cal.Atty.Gen. 98, 101 (1943).

23. Cal.Penal Code § 4853.

In General

The suspension of civil rights during parole is as valid as that imposed during incarceration. The numerous reasons for this rule are much beyond the scope of this paper. Two examples must suffice. If a parolee wishes to marry, permission generally is granted without hesitation, assuming he has not had excessive trouble with women in the past. If this type of trouble has occurred it is better to exercise the power of refusal than to allow the parolee to marry.

As a parole agent, I supervised a parolee who, though having dull-normal intelligence, still had the intellectual capacity to contract. He bought a faulty car but failed to inform the salesman of his parolee status and inability to contract. However, the estoppel doctrine was invoked by the salesman under the *Jones v. Allen* rationale, discussed above.[24] That is, he could not set aside the contract. This parolee was not able to discern when he was being "hooked" and, easily persuaded by a suave salesman, was stuck with a car for which he could not pay.

Thus, the suspension of civil rights is not meant as a form of harassment to make it more difficult for a man to complete his parole. To the contrary, it is meant to help him and to protect society at the same time.

Cash Assistance

13. *Cash Assistance*: In time of actual need, as determined by your Parole Agent, you may be loaned cash assistance for living expenses or employment; or you may be loaned such assistance in the form of meal and hotel tickets. You hereby agree to repay this assistance; this agreement and obligation remains even though you should be returned to prison as a parole violator. Your refusal to repay, when able, may be considered an indication of unsatisfactory adjustment.

This condition is illustrative of the steps taken by the Department of Corrections to assist the parolee. Cash assistance generally is used by a parolee who has only seasonal employment. As with any debt or obligation, it is incumbent upon the debtor to repay the loan when finances permit, but no interest

24. Jones v. Allen, supra note 12.

is charged regardless of the time needed for payment. Repayment is required because only a limited budget is available for this assistance.

Special Conditions

14. *Special Conditions*: _____

This space is left blank and filled in when the Adult Authority feels the need to impose a special condition in light of the parolee's personality or past criminal background.

Some of these conditions are required by law, such as the registration of sex offenders, narcotics addicts or peddlers, and arsonists. If the restrictions are not imposed by law, they can be removed only by Adult Authority action.

Conclusion

The California conditions of parole are not harsh or intended to be unduly restrictive. They are designed mainly to protect society and to serve as guidelines for the parolee as he begins his life anew. Good conduct may loosen some of the restrictions. On the other hand, if he begins to regress, he will obviously have to be supervised more stringently. If a parolee cannot live successfully under these restrictions, to confer total freedom upon him immediately after release from prison will not bring about any greater conformity to society's standards.

SOCIETY PERPETUATES THE STIGMA OF A CONVICTION*

According to the generalized theory of punishment, once a person has "paid his debt to society," he is free of stigma. Schwartz and Skolnick, however, have shown that stigma may linger on.[1] In "Two Studies of Legal Stigma" prospective employers in the resort hotel business refused to hire a hypothetical employee who had contact with the criminal justice system. Once contact had

* John P. Reed, Dale Nance, *Federal Probation*, June, 1972. Reprinted with permission.

1. Richard D. Schwartz and Jerome H. Skolnick, "Two Studies of Legal Stigma," *Social Problems*, 10 (Fall 1962), pp. 133–142.

occurred the individual was contaminated even though official agents of control had completed their work with the offender.

The view is generally accepted. Deviant status may transcend "time, place, organizational setting, and indeed, sometimes even truth or falsity." [2]   In similar research, others have noted the severe negative effects of imprisonment on employment opportunities, bonding, and licensing.[3]   A record of conviction produces a loss of status which has lasting consequences.

> For purposes of effective social control, this   .   .   .
> may heighten the deterrent effect of conviction   .   .   .
> Any such contribution to social control, however, must
> be balanced against the barriers imposed upon rehabili-
> tation of the convict.   If the ex-prisoner finds difficulty
> in securing menial kinds of legitimate work, further
> crime may become an increasingly attractive alterna-
> tive.[4]

Contrary to the above view, we maintain that a durable or permanent loss of status has additional dimensions.   It is not the offender's "ex-criminal" status *alone* which creates a kind of *reflected status* (mirroring some past disability), but also the perpetuation of stigma by the justice system itself and a supportive morality in some segments of the body social.

Under a variety of guises the status of criminal is legally maintained.   A number of examples will illustrate what we mean. Probation and parole are rehabilitatively thought of as more desirable for the convicted offender than the completion of a sentence in prison.   Yet both visibly display the offender in the community under a disability—his conditions of probation or parole. In some jurisdictions, he must register as a criminal, supposedly for the protection of the community.   The unintended effects of registration are to broadcast his conviction and preserve his

---

2. Earl Rubington and Martin S. Weinberg (eds.), *Deviance: The Interactionist Perspective.* New York: The Macmillan Company, 1968, p. 168.

3. William J. Byron, S. J., "Needed: A Special Employment Clearinghouse for Ex-Offenders," Federal Probation, 34 (September 1970),
pp. 53–57; B. F. McSally, "Finding Jobs for Released Offenders," Federal Probation, 24 (June 1960), pp. 12–17; Sol Rubin, *Crime and Juvenile Delinquency* (New York: Oceana, 1958), pp. 151–56.

4. Schwartz and Skolnick, op. cit., p. 136.

criminal stigma. In most states, his police and court records are public documents available for the asking.

Stigma, however, may also be patently prescribed. As an automatic accompaniment of either conviction for felony or imprisonment, the criminal may be deprived of some or most of his civil rights (called "civil disability" and sometimes "civil death"). The deprivation of civil rights is not presently thought of as a primary sanction but rather as supplemental restrictions upon the offender.[5] What the modern version of "civil death" [6] accomplishes is not too far off from its common law antecedents. The convicted offender returns to the community *sans* a full status and *sans* his respectability. The law keeps his life in bondage for his past misdeeds. True, there is no corruption of the blood or forfeiture of property to the state; nevertheless, the restoration of his lost or suspended rights is neither automatic or certain in most places.

In a number of jurisdictions, "civil death" is imposed only upon the life-term prisoner. This has been taken to mean that he loses most of his civil rights. He cannot, for example, sue but he may be sued. His power to contract is limited. In a few states his property descends as though he were dead; in others, he may will his possessions. In a majority he may convey title and inherit property. In a small minority his marriage is automatically dissolved and his spouse may remarry without securing a divorce.[7]

According to other statutes, an offender sentenced to a term less than life merely has his civil rights suspended. Such legislation either removes or restricts the right to contract, to sue, to transfer property, to vote, to hold public office or position of trust, to perform jury duty, to testify in legal proceedings or to retain marriage rights.[8] Rights may be suspended whether the sentence is imposed or suspended as in probationary outcomes.

5. Paul W. Tappan, *Crime, Justice and Correction.* New York: Mc-Graw-Hill Book Co., 1960, pp. 427–430.

6. "Disabilities Attending Conviction," American Jurisprudence 2d (Rochester: The Lawyers Co-Operative Publishing Co., 1965), Vol. 21, pp. 566–574.

7. Neil P. Cohen and Dean Hill Rivkin, "Civil Disabilities: The Forgotten Punishment," Federal Probation, 35 (June 1971), pp. 19–25; Edwin H. Sutherland and Donald R. Cressey, *Criminology*, 8th ed. (New York: J. B. Lippincott Co., 1970), p. 309.

8. *American Jurisprudence* 2d, op. cit., pp. 572–574; Harry E. Barnes and Negley K. Teeters, *New Horizons in Criminology*, 3rd ed. (Englewood Cliffs: Prentice-Hall, Inc., 1959), pp. 544–546.

In a majority of the states, lost rights may be partially or completely restored by pardon, but in a number of these the rights must be expressly mentioned in the pardon. For others certain privileges of citizenship are lost forever. In a considerable number of states the convicted offender loses the right to practice his profession, to hold public office, to serve on a jury, and to take certain kinds of state examinations.[9]

There are many anomalies in the law. In growing like a patch quilt, the law creates asymmetrical areas which require special attention if public policy is to be realized. "Civil death" is one of those areas out of our historical past that needs illumination. No general theory of punishment is likely to be operative where normative conflict is so obvious. The deck is stacked before the rehabilitation game really begins.

The argument may be made, of course, that the practice of depriving criminals of their civil rights is unknown to the public. If unknown, it cannot be said to be related to continued stigma in personal relations. We would then have to accept the Schwartz and Skolnick finding that the "criminal" label (particularly "ex-con") *alone* carries enduring stigma. We think otherwise. Either the public has some knowledge of, and continues to support deprivation of, rights or else it subscribes to a morality that demands continued status degradation. Both are likely explanations for the perpetuation of criminal stigma.

Nature of the Study

To test our hypothesis a questionnaire was administered to 204 farmers, Kentucky public school teachers, and maintenance men at a medium-sized southern university. Farmers were obtained from the northern and southern parts of the state; male and female public school teachers and maintenance men from classes and on-campus activities during the spring and summer of 1971. The questionnaire included a cover sheet and a series of questions on the loss and restoration of civil rights. Specifically, we sought to determine if members of our sample were aware (1) that prisoners lose some of their civil rights; (2) what rights, if any, prisoners should have in prison; and (3) what rights, if any, the "ex-prisoner" should have after his release from prison.

9. "Attorneys at Law: Conviction of Commission of Crime," *American Jurisprudence* 2d, op. cit., Vol. 7, pp. 77–82. See also for "Elections," "Physicians and Surgeons," and "Public Officers."

We asked these questions of three occupational groupings (including female teachers) we thought might produce a "continuum effect" in their responses and provide us with additional insights into the public's image of the criminal.

Results of the Study

Analysis of our data reveals that the public has some knowledge of the loss and restoration of civil rights. The amount and kind of that knowledge varies by social grouping or category. In our sample, teachers were the most informed and maintenance men the least informed. Seventy-one percent of the teachers, 45 percent of the farmers, and 37 percent of the maintenance men said they were aware that criminals lost some of their rights when they went to prison and did not regain all of them when they were released. Most respondents were uncertain about which rights these were or about the meaning of the concept "civil death." Teachers who taught social science and the humanities were the best informed of all occupational categories on the deprivation of civil rights. Both the order of the three categories and the percent of positive replies, however, are probably a function of the educational level of this particular sample. Most teachers had some graduate work and 39 percent of the farmers said they had either attended college or gotten a college degree. We wonder how many probation and parole officers know which civil rights are lost, suspended, and restored in their respective states.

On the question of prisoner rights, teachers again were a conspicuous category. They would not only permit the prisoner to retain more of his civil rights than maintenance men and farmers but would also provide more amenities for the incarcerated. Comparatively, teachers favored "overnight stays with wives or a girl friend (including conjugal visits)," "occasionally clothing of choice," and "personalized rooms" in the prison. Among civil rights they were for letting the prisoner "vote in elections" and "receive dividends from stock" he owned.

Maintenance men and farmers took more traditional stances, although less punitive than expected.[10] Both would allow a few amenities and rights in prison. Of the three occupational group-

10. For concordance and discordance between primary legal sanctions and social attitudes, see Don C. Gibbons, "Crime and Punishment: A Study in Social Attitudes," *Social Forces*, 47 (June 1969), pp. 391–397.

TABLE 1.—*Responses as to what rights persons should retain while confined in prison*

Right	Percent favoring retention of right		
	Teachers	Maintenance men	Farmers
Maintain control of business	13.9	2.6	8.0
Save and invest his money	68.7	55.3	48.0
Vote in elections	24.3	5.3	10.0
Sue for damages	23.5	13.2	12.0
Have privacy of room where he may add items of choice	67.0	44.7	34.0
Receive unlimited mail	69.6	65.8	58.0
Receive dividends from stock	50.0	23.7	40.0
Buy and sell property, etc.	20.0	5.3	10.0
Get married	27.0	18.4	20.0
Overnight stay or conjugal visit with wife or girl friend in special prison facilities	55.7	42.1	28.0
Inherit property	58.3	47.4	60.0
Occasionally wear clothes of his own choice	69.6	57.9	38.0
Have no rights outside prison while he is inside prison	23.5	23.7	44.0

[A9404]

ings, farmers were the most conservative with 44 percent calling for "no rights outside the prison while the criminal is inside." Something of a continuum effect was thus evident. Lining the three groups up according to the manifest liberalism-conservatism of their answers, teachers would be at the liberal end of the continuum, maintenance men in the middle, and farmers at the conservative end. We presume there would be other occupational groupings more liberal or conservative than those involved here.

When respondents were querried about "ex-prisoner" rights similar results were produced. Teachers were the most favorably oriented towards the exercise of a wide spectrum of rights on release from prison. They would allow the "ex-con" to resume his profession, vote in elections, serve on juries, live where he chooses, and hold public office and positions of trust (45 percent versus only 18 percent of the farmers). Overall, teachers seemed to be more in line with the general theory of punishment, "that once you have served your time, you're a free man. You have paid your debt to society, and now you can start anew." Maintenance men and farmers did not go quite that far. They still held out for occupational and public service disabilities for the ex-prisoner.

TABLE 2.—*Responses as to what rights*
ex-prisoners should have on release

| | Percent favoring resumption of right | | |
Right	Teachers	Maintenance men	Farmers
Resume his profession	76.5	68.4	56.0
Vote in elections	88.7	71.1	70.0
Attend college	94.8	86.8	90.0
Live in area or town he chooses	94.8	81.6	82.0
Get a job	99.1	100.0	92.0
Get married	97.0	89.5	96.0
Conduct business	92.0	78.9	80.0
Hold public office or positions of trust	45.6	34.2	18.0
Inherit property	88.7	84.2	86.0
Serve on juries	57.0	39.5	34.0
Have children	93.0	84.0	81.6

[A9418]

To get at female attitudes on prisoner civil rights, we included 65 female teachers in our sample. The speculation was that they would be less harsh than males on criminals both inside and outside the prison. For after all, women are socialized somewhat differently in our society, develop somewhat distinctive personalities which are said to harbor the humanizing elements in the species.

The data bear this out in part. When females were eliminated from our sample our percentage and chi-square values for several items fluctuated noticeably. First, inside the prison there was a decline in the number and kinds of rights and amenities our male occupational categories would allow. Males turned out to be strong on property rights; our departed females, on voting, overnight stays (including the conjugal visit) with wife or girl friend, clothes, and a personalized room. Teachers, however, remained the most liberal of the three occupational groupings.

On "ex-prisoner" rights, the effects of controlling for sex was mainly occupational. After eliminating female teachers, chi-square values on occupational items (better called "bread" items) increased. Male teachers, particularly, were heavily in favor of the "ex-con" resuming his profession, holding public office and positions of trust, inheriting property, and serving on juries. The loss of chi-square values was limited to "voting in elections" and "living where he chooses." Amenity items were not involved —since that issue was associated with imprisonment.

Finally, we differentiated our population on rights inside and outside of prison. Other than occupation and sex, age, education, and locality proved to be the more volatile of the variables we used. The young, the urbanite, and the more educated would allow more amenities and rights than rurals, the old, and the less educated. The young (under 30) especially were the most liberal of all categories on room, intimacies, and voting. Other variables such as marital status, church preference, and church attendance indicated trends but produced little in the way of significant values.

Summary and Conclusions

The public has some knowledge of "civil disability." That knowledge, however, is not particularized. Few know the meaning of the term "civil death" yet many are aware that the convicted criminal loses some of his civil rights. In three occupational groups we examined, teachers proved to be the most knowledgeable and maintenance men the least.

On questions about rights in prison and outside, the order was somewhat reversed. Teachers were the most liberal with maintenance men and farmers following in that order. Teachers would allow voting by prisoners, personalized rooms, overnight visits (conjugal or otherwise) by a wife or girl friend, occasionally clothing of choice, and minor "bread and butter activities" (dividends, investments, and buying and selling property). Maintenance men and farmers were more punitively oriented. Not only were many against simple amenities in prison but farmers, particularly, were against any rights outside the prison while the criminal was in prison. After release from prison, teachers were more for a return to a conventional status. On resuming one's profession, public office, and jury service maintenance men and farmers opted in large numbers for continued criminal disability.

When we eliminated female teachers from our sample some of our percentage and chi-square values changed pronouncedly. Within prison, the female effect was noticeable mainly in reduced values for voting and amenity items. It may be, as some have suggested, that the female is a humanizing factor in social relations. Outside prison, the absence of amenity items produced somewhat different results. "Bread" and occupational values increased, indicating the male (teacher) preoccupation with making a living.

With further differentiation of our population, age, education, and locality provided additional chi-square values. The younger and more educated respondents were far more liberal on rights than the old and less educated. A few values were also produced by locality (urban-rural) but church preference, marital status, and church attendance were not as volatile.

All of which suggests that some stigma is perpetuated by the legal system itself. As long as there is some awareness in the public of the deprivation of civil rights (and registration laws, etc.) the "ex-prisoner" travels under a disability that is self-defeating. The law preserves his prison stripes despite the myth of "having paid one's debt to society." In a computerized state, that is comparable to a permanent reminder that one cannot play conventional games because he does not have the credentials. There may be little left for the "ex-con" but illegitimate activities to satisfy normal needs. His rehabilitation is not convertible into public acceptance and legitimate pursuits.

This is a form of value conflict. Protective concerns reflected in the law are running counter to rehabilitative philosophy and the general theory of punishment. If nothing else were involved in the perpetuation of stigma, the problem would be solely one of legislative reform. The law could be brought into harmony with rehabilitative ideals.

We think there is something more here. Our study suggests that stigma is also a function of morality. Youth, the educated, urbanites, and teachers turn out to be more liberal than maintenance men, farmers, ruralites, the old, and the less educated. One grouping seemingly supports and extends the rehabilitative ideal; the other, is more supportive of current legal definitions of criminal disabilities—the older punitive ideal. Both the high value items and the demographic characteristics of our conservative category imply a morality difference. Trends on church preference and church attendance items indicate a possible source. Fundamentalists and evangelical sects, Protestants, and frequent church attenders were the most traditionally oriented of all our religious categories. By comparison, Catholics and infrequent (or never) attenders were the most liberal.

These are the sources for the perpetuation of stigma. There is nothing mysterious about the status of the convicted offender. Morality of the legal system preserve the stigma of conviction and sentence. Is this a modern version of "civil death"? We get similar results although we euphemistically label them something else.

AN EMPLOYER'S VIEWS ABOUT
HIRING EX–CONVICTS*

This section contains a verbatim account of a meeting at the United States Penitentiary at McNeil Island, Washington, of a prerelease group of fifty together with the owner of a drug firm who had been invited to discuss the attitude of employers toward hiring persons who had served time. The questions and concerns of the men and the replies of the employer are characteristic of those that come up for discussion at prerelease meetings. (Editor's note).

Employer.—"Fellows, let's get something straight to start with; I came here to talk to you, not to preach. I'm not much of a speaker, so if you'll all relax I think we'll get along.

"A few weeks ago I was asked to talk to you on how an employer feels about hiring a man that has served time and while you may not believe some of the things I say—they might not represent what a lot of other people would say or believe—I want you to know, here and now, that what I say, I believe.

"I don't particularly feel I am experienced enough in the ways of the world to give advice unasked, but you want to know how an employer feels and I'm going to do my best to tell you how one employer feels.

"First, perhaps I should make my position clear. It is that of the operator of a small drug firm. I know all the people who

* Reprinted by permission of *Federal Probation*. An Employer's Views About Hiring a Man Who Has Served Time, *Federal Probation*, Vol. 17, No. 4, Dec. 1965, pp. 43–46.

work for me and know how much I depend upon them. If they were to quit I'd be out of business because I couldn't do all the work myself. Between me and my employees there is a relationship that grounds on mutual respect and understanding and this is also true of most of the employers I have met while I've been in the drug business. Regardless of what you may have heard of the hardheartedness and money-grubbing of businessmen, it just isn't so. No, I'm not trying to tell you the average businessman isn't there to make every dollar he can, but the longer you are in your own business, the more you find out that your biggest business asset is satisfied employees. The most important asset is not the store, not the merchandise, not the money I have in the bank, but my personnel. And how I learned it during the last five or six years when merchandise was hard to get, and good employees even harder!

"During those years when a person came in and wanted a job you looked up and asked the personnel man: 'Can they walk?' If he nodded his head you hired the person immediately. It's a bit different now. Our employees get a thorough checking before we let them come to work. We're in a position to pick and choose, and naturally we take only the best. Why? Because a good employee makes the most money for you and to keep a good employee you go to quite some lengths. At present we are encouraging our employees to buy a share in the company and make it easy for them to do it with small monthly deductions. And we do this because we want them to feel more than that they are just coming to work. We want them to feel they own part of every article they sell, and the better service they give the more goods they sell and the more money we'll all make.

"As I said before, we have passed the state where we had to take anyone. We can now pick and choose, and the basis of our selection is that we pick the person we feel is best fitted for the job. When we get that person the job is done better and we make more money. And how do you get the best person? You hire the best available and then develop him. And if he can't be developed, can't be improved, you fire him!

"When I was asked to talk to you my first reaction was to say, 'No.' I wondered what I could say that would matter. And then I was handed a list of questions you asked. I'll read it to you now, or perhaps I'd better just take the questions the writers proposed and answer them one by one. Now whether you like it or not, believe it or not, I'm going to answer these questions as I see the answer."

"Should I Tell My Employer of My Record?"

Employer.—"Put yourself in my place or any employer's place. What do you want? You want a man who can do the job and you want to know about the man that is going to work for you. You give him an application to fill out. It asks: 'Name and address; and then, previous employment: begin with the last employer first, fill out length of time you worked for employer, work you did, salary and reason for leaving.' If I filled out one for you and I'd worked last in 1944, what is the first question you'd ask me? You're damn right you would! 'Where have you been the last several years?' and I'd have to tell or you wouldn't give me the job.

"Put this in your mind and keep it there. If your employer fires you because you have a record, you didn't have a job in the first place!

"There is only one answer to the question. Certainly you should tell him. And if you don't tell him then every checkup, every bit of criticism, every heavy look you're going to feel is directed right at you, and you'd really get that if you worked for me. But how the devil are you going to do your job right if you're worried every hour of the day that you are going to lose your job? By not telling you're being unfair to yourself. You just cannot go to an employer with dirty hands and expect his hands to be clean.

"Don't think just going in and telling an employer, 'I've got a record,' is going to get you a job. You've got to have the qualifications the employer is looking for. If you haven't the qualifications, you're not going to get the job and that isn't being discriminated against.

"And you're not always going to get the job you want even if you have the qualifications. Sure you're going to have to walk up and down the street and take just whatever you can get, and while you're doing it don't think you're the only one that ever did the same thing. Shortly after the first World War, in 1919 that was, I walked up and down the streets of Vancouver, B.C., looking for a job. There I was, a college graduate, and couldn't get a job of any kind. Sure, I thought I was being discriminated against. Everybody in all the stores was busy and I couldn't even get anywhere near the kind of job I wanted. Yes, I found a job, at $18 per week. Nice salary for a college graduate, but it was a job I could do and that's why I was hired. And that's the only way anyone gets a job. Because the employer is convinced you can do that job and do it better than someone else. I say this in answer to the second question, which asks:

"Will the Employer Because of My Record Refuse to Start Me in a Position for Which I Qualify?"

Employer.—"Look, fellows, the average employer is damn glad to get a competent employee and he's going to try to keep this employee as well satisfied as he can, within reason. So if you're a topnotch salesman you're not going to make the employer any money sweeping the floor. If you want to work for me, you are not going to start in my job, but if you're good I'm sure going to do everything I can to keep you."

"Will My Employer Tell the Office Manager and Staff of My Record?"

Employer.—"You're here for a reason. You got out for a reason. And if you're made of the right stuff, you belong out and you stay out. And it's the way you conduct yourself that will give people your measure. I know that this sounds a bit like 'blarney,' but I don't think people pay much attention to what's happened in the past. So don't worry about what the other person thinks. Most people don't give your record a thought, and feeling they think about you is a condition largely created in your mind. Your boss isn't going around to tell the staff whom he hires, or why. After all, that is his job, to hire people. If he hires you, you're going to be with the company until he gets ready to fire you. Don't worry about that record."

"What Are My Chances of Advancement if My Record Is Known?"

Employer.—"If you want one man's idea—and it may not be worth anything and I may be the only guy in the world that feels that way—you would be advanced as rapidly as it was possible if you worked for me. Actually I'd have more faith and trust and confidence in you simply because you told me about your record. I am naïve enough to believe you are a little smarter than the average fellow because of your experience and that you wouldn't let me down. If you did let me down, I'd just say you weren't half as smart as I thought you were. But if you made good don't you see what a smart man you'd make out of me? People feel good when their judgment is substantiated. I could say: 'I gave him a place of trust and look at him now.' And everytime I pushed you up another notch my chest would swell out a little. Why shouldn't I advance you? You bet your boots I would, just as long as you warranted it."

"Did He Hire Me Out of Pity?"

Employer.—"If you had a job someone gave you out of pity you wouldn't be working for me. Maybe some philanthropic organization might hire you that way, but if I hired you, it would be because you could do the work and make some money for me."

"Will I Be Under Constant Supervision?"

Employer.—"Yes! That's how you get the most out of people. You keep prodding them. All of my people are under constant supervision. As an employer that's all I have to do and if I didn't do it the people who work for me would feel neglected and hurt. And incidentally, anytime you're working for anyone, make sure they see you. That's the way you get ahead, by someone noticing what you are doing. If you think I'm going to open your hand every time you take it out of the till—no. But I'll be around to know whether you're making money for me or not."

"If Something Went Wrong Would I Be Automatically Blamed?"

Employer.—"Get away from the persecution complex. The guys who ask these questions sound like they're scared to death something's going to happen to them. But there is no reason in the world to feel that way if you do your job, regardless of what goes wrong. It makes me think the guy feels that he is prone to accident. You know, one man can walk down the street through broken glass barefoot and nothing happens. And this guy comes along in high-top boots and gets cut. If something goes wrong, someone was negligent. Whoever was negligent is going to hear from me.

"How could I run a business under conditions other than that? You're not going to be blamed unless I'm damned sure you were to blame. You'd probably get more leeway than would an ordinary employee because I'd hesitate to accuse you wrongfully. Forget those thoughts. Come to work ready to look the world in the eyes. You're as good as any man on the job or you wouldn't have been hired. No employer has money to waste on worthless employees.

"When people hire people they try to get as much information as they can possibly get about them. The employer wants to find out everything he can. What they like; what they don't like; where they go to church; and where they spend their spare time. That's what application blanks are for. And this is why they are studied. The personnel manager doesn't just take your blank and toss it in a drawer. He studies it, and after he's talked to you he has almost as much to fill out as you did. Some of the important factors the personnel manager must consider are: appearance, dress and grooming, knowledge of the job, grasp of job principles, and familiarity of job.

"In my business when I hire a man I want him to look neat. He has to meet the public and scores of people look at him during the day and judge our store by him. We figure, too, if a man looks neat it also indicates character and habits. And knowledge of the job. Sure, some guy shows up and says: 'I have worked in a drug store all my life.' So I ask him, 'If a customer came in and asked for something for a cold what would you recommend?'"

Answer from members of group: "Castor oil!"

Employer.—"You're fired, even before you're hired! In the first place castor oil isn't worth a damn for a cold, but more than that, we don't make a nickel on it. What kind of an employee are you. You've got to recommend something that will help the customer and at the same time make money for the store. You see, we're in a position to pick and choose. We look for a man with business acumen, with essential knowledge, and with qualities we can develop,

"This pamphlet I'm now reading from is developed to aid men in evaluating new employees or would-be employees. It's developed through the research of thousands of people who looked for jobs and a lot of employers use it.

"We employers look for self-assurance. Now that doesn't mean cockiness and playfulness. We look for men who look like they can take care of themselves and not be easily upset. We may even needle a would-be employee to get his reaction. I might even make some remark about your record just to see what you would do. I take a jab at you. I try to get you sore, just to see the reaction.

"Cooperation—ability and willingness to work with others. Now a lot of us think we're cooperative, but we aren't. I have seen a whole organization torn to pieces because some guy came in that wouldn't cooperate. He felt that someone wasn't doing quite all he should, so he didn't either. Result: pretty soon no one was doing his work.

"Command of language and handling of ideas are other factors. Naturally in my business, which is primarily selling, command of language is most important. So if you want to be a salesman you have to know how to use your language.

"Health, stamina, physical drive, and record of previous employment are also important. I'm going to read you part of a letter that came to the institution. It's from the Blank Company. 'We are glad to aid Mr. Inmate in his rehabilitation. We notice he has operated a jumbo-drilling machine and as part of our project is 4000 feet of tunnel drilling, he can join our tunnel crew.' "

"And there you have it. This man had something to offer. Something the Blank Company could use. He had experience with the drilling machine. Blank Company didn't care about the record, they wanted a man to operate a drilling machine. Experience! I have a dozen applications on my desk right now, all of them from people I would like to hire, except they don't have the right experience.

"And here's another letter the institution received. It's from a union in San Francisco and states: 'We cannot aid you in finding this man a job. At the present time several hundred of our own members are out of work.'

"So you see sometimes even when you have experience, you can't locate a job. So how much tougher it's going to be for the fellow without experience.

"Now fellows, I have given you the facts as I see them. I'm just one employer but what I've said, I believe. And I believe, too, that if there's a job open where you make your application, and you have the skill to fill that job, no one's going to give that record of yours much thought as long as you do a good job. If I've done you fellows some good I'm glad and I want you also to know it's done me some good to talk to you."

COLLEGE AS A PAROLE PLAN*

In one evening we attended two parties, one the celebration of the end of parole, and the other the first birthday party a 40-year-old man ever had.   Each, in itself, was exceedingly meaningful; to us, these events symbolized the potential of a program of parole based upon college attendance.

Four years earlier, the concept of college as a parole plan had grown out of getting acquainted with the staff and leaders among the inmates at the California Correctional Institution at Tehachapi, California.   Superintendent G. P. Lloyd, with his typical forward vision, had made possible the on-site participation of Professor Murphy's class of social welfare students from San Diego State College.   These students and the inmates shared in group discussions.   It became obvious that the goals and aspirations of students and inmates were more alike than different. That is, with one major exception: The students could look forward to the kind of life work which would be emotionally and intellectually satisfying and financially rewarding.   The inmates could look forward to parole and probable employment, the satisfactions and rewards of which would be markedly less because they would be destined to the kinds of jobs available to "uneducated" men with prison records.

Some of these men had been imprisoned as a result of acting out their frustration over inability to make productive use of their high intellectual capacity.   They could look forward to more of the same frustration and anger.   Those in touch with prisons know this is a prime factor in the high recidivism rate of capable men.

After the students' 1966 session at Tehachapi, Professor Murphy's dream took substance.   Through the cooperation of the State Board of Parole, the San Diego State College Administration, and the staff at the Tehachapi institution, with the full encouragement of Mr. Lloyd, the first man was paroled with the understanding that he would attend college.   From the start this was no easy route for Ken: His release came 2 weeks too late for him to enroll in the fall semester, and he had to face the prob-

* Melvin L. Murphy and Maribeth Murphy, *Federal Probation*, March, 1971.   Reprinted with permission.

lems of earning his living until the next semester. At age 26, Ken started college as a freshman in February 1967. His parole period ended in November 1969. He is now in his junior year and has maintained approximately a 2.5 grade point average, and has been productively employed and active as a leader in social causes.

Ken, and the 21 who followed him, have proved that this could be a tremendous forward step in the rehabilitation program of the correctional institutions.

Social Implications

In a period of international awareness of the problems of deprived peoples, and especially in the United States where it has been possible to develop opportunities for these groups, there has been consideration of the potential intellectual capabilities of these peoples. Educational programs have been developed from the elementary grades through college for the culturally deprived, gifted students. Society must also concern itself with another deprived minority, the parolees and prison inmates whose educational opportunities were prematurely curtailed.

There is a high recidivism rate among parolees in spite of the facts that: (1) The parolee has served the length sentence deemed necessary after careful study by the parole board and is ready for the next step; (2) the intent of parole is continuation of the rehabilitation program; and (3) the parole agent is in a supervisory role with the goal of providing the supportive service necessary for the parolee to make a successful readjustment to society.

It would appear that in some way either the rehabilitation program or the parole criteria are not filling the need and might be modified.

If an assumption is made that the parole board's criteria for the inmate's readiness for parole, based upon his record of progress in the institution, is an accurate assessment, then it would seem that the parole situation is not providing the needed factors for rehabilitation.

The current parole plan assigns a parole agent to help with job placement and counseling, if indicated, give assistance in finding adequate housing, and in some cases to provide a minimal financial loan. The high recidivism rate seems to indicate that for some parolees this plan is not adequate.

If one assumes that rehabilitation for parolees should include (a) developing the potential of the individual and (b) providing training for living in a new situation, then educational intervention becomes an essential consideration.

Many of these individuals are academically capable, but unqualified for college by previous poor grades, lack of finances, or cultural and social inertia in their early lives. Prison educational services both permit and encourage this group to achieve a high school education. With only a few exceptions, as first instituted at San Quentin where a limited number of college courses have been made available in the institution, and through correspondence courses, there has been no opportunity for an inmate to educate himself beyond the high school level. It has been nearly impossible for an ex-convict, even released, to gain a college education, without which his productive life is limited to manual or, at best, technical employment.

This can be changed. Paul Cossette, district administrator of the Parole and Community Services Division, San Diego, concluded in a September 1969 paper describing the educational program: "We have a start. College as a Parole Plan can be a meaningful statewide resource to help people reconstruct their lives into worthwhile productive experiences."

S. A. Whiteside, regional parole administrator, sent the article with this memorandum to Dr. H. J. Hastings, supervisor of education for the California Department of Corrections:

> Since 1967, by reason of a three-way cooperative effort—San Diego State College, California Correctional Institution at Tehachapi, and Parole and Community Service Division, San Diego—we have instituted a program known as College as a Parole Plan.
>
> Our experience to date would indicate this may prove to be an excellent program for a select group of students. Mr. Cossette has indicated step-by-step as to how this can be initiated . . . .

On October 14, 1969, Dr. Hastings sent a memorandum to all superintendents of education in California's Department of Corrections:

> I concur with Mr. Whiteside that this may prove to be an excellent program for a select group of inmates and feel that San Diego State College, the California Cor-

rectional Institution at Tehachapi, and the Parole and Community Services Division, San Diego, are to be commended for the development of this forward-looking program.

Thus, the dream became actuality and was given official sanction.

The College Plan

The first step for an inmate interested in the college program upon parole, if he has completed high school, is to discuss his interest with one of the institution's educational counselors. If the plan seems feasible and in accordance with the inmate's ability, and if the counselor believes the individual is sincere, according to Mr. Cossette's outline, the counselor will

> . . . direct the inmate to communicate directly with Professor Melvin Murphy, School of Social Work, San Diego State College, either by letter or by personal contact . . . . If, after contacting the inmate, Professor Murphy believes the inmate is qualified and capable of entering college, he will advise the inmate to direct a letter . . . to the Educational Opportunities Program, San Diego State College . . . .

The responsibility for deciding whether a person is "qualified and capable" is hardly a comfortable one. How does one assess intangibles: motivation, emotional stamina, resourcefulness, ability to maintain the necessary better-than-average conduct? There is no proved method; each must be screened as an individual human being, on the basis of personal interviews and letters of recommendation, in terms of his own unique strengths and weaknesses.

There are tests to assess ability: the American College Test (ACT), the College Aptitude Test (CQT), and the Writing Competency Test. Then comes the "admissions ordeal" which every student must go through, followed by the wait for notice of admission from the college—and the wait for the granting of parole.

With admission to college, the parolee receives an identification card. From this time on, he follows the established student program. In addition, he must inform the Community Services and Parole Division of the State Department of Corrections of his date of release, the fact that his parole plan includes college, when he will arrive in San Diego, and by what means. He must report to his parole agent within 24 hours.

Each parolee must arrange for his own arrival in San Diego. If he arrives in advance of the semester's start, he must house and support himself until he can be on campus. If he arrives within appropriate time, he can go directly into campus dormitory housing. If married, or if he has a family locally, he can live with his family.

Financial Arrangements

Since no parolee to date has been financially self-sufficient, and it is not likely that any will be, living expenses have been a major problem. In the first place, the imprisonment itself has removed the man from financial responsibility. In actuality, few prison inmates have a history of financial responsibility, and this becomes an area of difficulty from the beginning for most.

Arrangements have been made for most parolees to work on campus under the work-study program of the Educational Opportunities Program. The money earned is disbursed through the Financial Aids Office. The parolee must assume responsibility for making arrangements for his own allocation, and is expected to set up an account at any of the banks within walking distance of the campus. Usually he is "walked through" this process by a parolee who has preceded him on campus, and who also helps him through the registration procedure, including the payment of fees and registration for a minimum of 12 units.

Each month the parolee-student must be responsible for submitting his work-study time card, and for reporting to get his pay check. At the end of each semester he must reapply for financial aid and work out a budget for the coming semester.

The Parolee's Student Responsibilities

Parolees melt into the educational institution program with less difficulty than they adapt to unregulated living patterns. They are students, friendly and participating with other students, and must attend their classes and meet the course requirements. Some have difficulty with certain classes and must seek tutoring. All must learn the study habits so necessary for successful achievement.

The first semester is a period of contrast—the joy of freedom and the adventures of rediscovering the "world outside" with recreation and companionship and social life, contrasted with the frustration of coping with unfamiliar academic jargon, remembering the content of daily lectures, and overcoming test panic at exam time.

The financial stress of the first semester exceeds the parolee-student's expectations: movies, concerts, dates, and social activities are all freely available—and a strain on his meager budget. Transportation becomes a problem; most try to find "wheels" of their own: a bike, motorcycle, or old car. Even the commodities in the local supermarket, or the articles available in the overstocked drug stores, or the stereos and tape decks, provide a temptation which a newly released parolee finds almost irresistible. All of these interests, and many more, keep crowding into the study time.

The first semester is an ordeal; yet of the total group who have chosen and been selected for this plan of parole, all but one have "made it"—and that one, despite his high intelligence, was not as motivated toward college as were we who selected him. He dropped out before the end of the first week of classes, but has had three-and-a-half successful years "on the outside."

The parolees' orientation group is a means of keeping contact with each other, a place for sharing problems and concerns, and hopefully for finding solutions. In addition to the parolee-students, Professor and Mrs. Murphy and Dr. Gwen Onstead of the San Diego State College Counseling Department have served as regular facilitator-participants. When special problems arise, such as summer employment or legal questions, resource people are invited to discuss the situation.

At the end of the school year a major problem for discussion, in addition to employment and summer classes, is the problem of housing after the dormitories close in June.

Administrative Assistants

During the 1969–70 school year an innovation under the work-study program provided for the employment of two administrative assistants to Professor Murphy. These two parolee-students serve a liaison function, handling correspondence with inmate applicants, seeing that all necessary forms are received, meeting parolees upon arrival in town, arranging for the first meal and for housing, "walking" the newcomer through registration, Financial Aids, banking procedures, and seeing that he gets to the first parolee orientation meeting. In addition, they act in a supportive role during the early adjustment period, seeing that problems are communicated to the proper person—program administrator, parole agent, counseling office, the professor, social worker, etc.

Current Status of the Program

After 3½ academic years, 41 people have participated in the San Diego State College program. Two students have completed their period of parole and are now free citizens continuing their education. No paroles have been completely violated, although two men have returned for brief (45-day) periods following temporary difficulty.

Twenty-three are pursuing studies at San Diego State College; of the other 18, all but two completed at least one full year of college, and all are "making it" as citizens in the community.

Among the employment responsibilities held by parolee-students are:

• Research assistant in a federally funded educational grant;

• Community organization agent for the Educational Opportunities Program;

• Recruiter of trainees for Philco-Ford Job Development Department;

• Associate Director of New Careers;

• Assistant Manager for five men's clothing stores.

If we measure the efficacy of the program in terms of the recidivism rate—the California State Department of Corrections sets the percent of returnees at 80 percent in the first year—we would consider the program a success.

If we consider the cost of maintaining a man in prison for a year ($3,200) compared to maintaining a man in college on this minimal financial basis ($2,600), we would consider the program a success.

If we consider the feasibility of college as a parole plan for those who are intellectually capable and motivated toward college, we would consider these 41 men to have at least substantiated the feasibility. We cannot, however, overlook a possible "halo" effect related to the newness of the venture.

We believe that a major consideration of the program's effectiveness must also be the level of productivity attained in society over a period of years by parolees who attend college compared to those who do not. This must be dealt with at a future date.

Meanwhile, last week, we . . .

. . . sang "Happy Birthday" to a tall, handsome black man and danced till dawn at his first real birthday party.

. . . went to a swimming party and buffet supper in celebration of the end of a family man's parole.

. . . heard a man say in despair, "Let me stay with you for 3 days—I'm afraid I'll louse up if I'm alone."

. . . rejoiced because one of "our fellows" who had to go back for a brief time would be out in time for the fall semester.

STANDARDS WITH COMMENTARY: PAROLE*

ORGANIZATION OF PAROLING AUTHORITIES

Each State that has not already done so should, by 1975, establish parole decisionmaking bodies for adult and juvenile offenders that are independent of correctional institutions. These boards may be administratively part of an overall statewide correctional services agency, but they should be autonomous in their decisionmaking authority and separate from field services. The board responsible for the parole of adult offenders should have jurisdiction over both felons and misdemeanants.

1. The boards should be specifically responsible for articulating and fixing policy, for acting on appeals by correctional authorities or inmates on decisions made by hearing examiners, and for issuing and signing warrants to arrest and hold alleged parole violators.

2. The boards of larger States should have a staff of full-time hearing examiners appointed under civil service regulations.

* National Advisory Commission on
Criminal Justice Standards and
Goals, *Report on Corrections*, 1973.

3.   The boards of smaller States may assume responsibility for all functions; but should establish clearly defined procedures for policy development, hearings, and appeals.

4.   Hearing examiners should be empowered to hear and make initial decisions in parole grant and revocation cases under the specific policies of the parole board. The report of the hearing examiner containing a transcript of the hearing and the evidence should constitute the exclusive record. The decision of the hearing examiner should be final unless appealed to the parole board within 5 days by the correctional authority or the offender. In the case of an appeal, the parole board should review the case on the basis of whether there is substantial evidence in the report to support the finding or whether the finding was erroneous as a matter of law.

5.   Both board members and hearing examiners should have close understanding of correctional institutions and be fully aware of the nature of their programs and the activities of offenders.

6.   The parole board should develop a citizen committee, broadly representative of the community and including ex-offenders, to advise the board on the development of policies.

Commentary

Parole authorities are criticized both for being too closely tied to the institution (as with juveniles) and too remote from the realities of correctional programs (as with adults). Most persons concerned with parole decisionmaking for juveniles are full-time institutional staff. In the adult field, most parole boards are completely independent from the institutions whose residents they serve. In fact, no adult parole releasing authority is controlled directly by the operating staff of a penal institution.

Parole boards that are tied to, or part of, institutional staff are criticized mainly on the grounds that too often institutional considerations, rather than individual or community needs, influence the decisions. Institutional decisionmaking also lends itself to such informal procedures and lack of visibility as to raise questions about its capacity for fairness.

On the other hand, independent parole boards are criticized on the grounds that they tend to be insensitive to institutional programs; to base their decisions on political considerations; to be too remote to fully understand the dynamics of a given case;

and/or that they and their staff have little training in or knowledge about corrections.

An organizational arrangement lying between these two extremes is now gaining prominence. In the new model, the parole authority is organizationally situated in a unified department of corrections but possesses independent powers. This arrangement is desirable in that paroling authorities need to be aware of and involved with all aspects of correctional programs. Yet they should be so situated organizationally as to maintain sufficient independence and capacity to reflect a broader range of decisionmaking concerns than efficient correctional management.

The absence of written criteria by which decisions are made constitutes a major failing in virtually every parole jurisdiction. Some agencies issue statements purporting to be criteria, but they usually are so general as to be meaningless. The sound use of discretion and ultimate accountability for its exercise rest largely in making visible the criteria used in forming judgments. Parole boards must free themselves from total concern with case-by-case decisionmaking and attend to articulation of the actual policies that govern the decisionmaking process.

In addition to the pressure for clearly articulated policies, there is also demand for mechanisms by which parole decisions can be appealed. It is important for parole systems to develop self-regulation systems, including internal appeal procedures. Where the volume of cases warrants it, a parole board should concentrate its attention on policy development and appeals.

Case-by-case decisionmaking should be done by hearing examiners responsible to the board who are familiar with its policies and knowledgeable about correctional programs. Hearing examiners should have statutory power to grant, deny, or revoke parole subject to parole board rules and policies. Appeals by the correctional authority or inmates on the decisions of hearing examiners should be decided by the parole board on the basis of the written report of the hearing examiner. The grounds for review would be whether or not there is substantial evidence in the report to support the finding or whether the decision was erroneous as a matter of law.

In smaller states, many of these activities would have to be carried out by the same persons, since the size of the system would not justify hearing examiners in addition to a parole board. However, procedures can and should be developed to assure at-

tention to each separate function—policy development, hearings, appeals, and decisionmaking.

An important component of the parole decisionmaking function which currently exists in few, if any, parole jurisdictions is the involvement of community representatives. Policy development offers a particularly suitable opportunity for such citizen participation. It is likely to improve the quality of policies and almost certainly will improve the probability of their implementation.

PAROLE AUTHORITY PERSONNEL

Each State should specify by statute by 1975 the qualifications and conditions of appointment of parole board members.

1. Parole boards for adult and juvenile offenders should consist of full-time members.

2. Members should possess academic training in fields such as criminology, education, psychology, psychiatry, law, social work, or sociology.

3. Members should have a high degree of skill in comprehending legal issues and statistical information and an ability to develop and promulgate policy.

4. Members should be appointed by the governor for six-year terms from a panel of nominees selected by an advisory group broadly representative of the community. Besides being representative of relevant professional organizations, the advisory group should include all important ethnic and socio-economic groups.

5. Parole boards in the small States should consist of no less than three full-time members. In most States, they should not exceed five members.

6. Parole board members should be compensated at a rate equal to that of a judge of a court of general jurisdiction.

7. Hearing examiners should have backgrounds similar to that of members but need not be as specialized. Their education and experiential qualifications should allow them to understand programs, to relate to people, and to make sound and reasonable decisions.

8. Parole board members should participate in continuing training on a national basis. The exchange of parole board members and hearing examiners between States for training purposes should be supported and encouraged.

Commentary

In a number of States, parole authority positions are held by part-time personnel. With expanded responsibilities for such boards, effective membership will require a full-time commitment of time and energy. Thus part-time parole authorities should be replaced in virtually every jurisdiction. In larger States, the use of hearing examiners reduces the necessity of expanding parole boards to unwieldy proportions and makes emphasis on policy development more feasible.

The chief obstacle to creating effective parole authorities is the appointment of unqualified persons to parole boards, a practice which can have disastrous effects. More often than not, such appointments are made by political criteria. Use of nonpartisan citizen nominating panels is vitally needed in the appointment process.

There is no one profession or set of experiences known to qualify an individual automatically for the role of parole board member. The variety of goals of parole boards requires a variety of skills. At the least, knowledge of the fields of law, the behavioral sciences, and corrections should be represented. It is also desirable for persons selected to be able to utilize statistical materials, reports from professional personnel, and a variety of other technical information.

Besides improving the appointment process, it is important that qualifications for parole authority membership be spelled out by law. Terms of appointment should be long and sufficient salaries provided.

Training opportunities specifically designed for parole decisionmakers also are vitally needed. Training programs should be designed to keep board members informed on recent legal decisions and advances in technology, as well as acquainting them with current correctional practices and trends.

THE PAROLE GRANT HEARING

Each parole jurisdiction immediately should develop policies for parole release hearings that include opportunities for personal and adequate participation by the inmates concerned; procedural guidelines to insure proper, fair, and thorough consideration of every case; prompt decisions and personal notification of decisions to inmates; and provision for accurate records of deliberations and conclusions.

A proper parole grant process should have the following characteristics:

1. Hearings should be scheduled with inmates within one year after they are received in an institution. Inmates should appear personally at hearings.

2. At these hearings, decisions should be directed toward the quality and pertinence of program objectives agreed upon by the inmate and the institution staff.

3. Board representatives should monitor and approve programs that can have the effect of releasing the inmate without further board hearings.

4. Each jurisdiction should have a statutory requirement, patterned after the Model Penal Code, under which offenders must be released on parole when first eligible unless certain specific conditions exist.

5. When a release date is not agreed upon, a further hearing date within one year should be set.

6. A parole board member or hearing examiner should hold no more than 20 hearings in any full day.

7. One examiner or member should conduct hearings. His findings should be final unless appealed to the full parole board by the correctional authority or the inmate within 5 days.

8. Inmates should be notified of any decision directly and personally by the board member or representative before he leaves the institution.

9. The person hearing the case should specify in detail and in writing the reasons for his decision, whether to grant parole or to deny or defer it.

10. Parole procedures should permit disclosure of information on which the hearing examiner bases his decisions. Sensitive

information may be withheld, but in such cases nondisclosure should be noted in the record so that subsequent reviewers will know what information was not available to the offender.

11. Parole procedures should permit representation of offenders under appropriate conditions, if required. Such representation should conform generally to Standard 2.2 on Access to Legal Services.

Commentary

Although every standard-setting body attests to the crucial part the parole hearing plays in an effective correctional system, substantial shortcomings exist in this procedure. In some jurisdictions large numbers of inmates do not get an opportunity to appear before parole authority representatives. In others, so many offenders are moved through parole hearings in a single day that the process becomes meaningless. Even in jurisdictions where regular interviews are conducted with all inmates and the number interviewed is reasonable, grave deficiencies exist.

Perhaps the most pervasive shortcomings are the undue emphasis in parole hearings on past events and the extreme vagueness about the necessary steps to achieve parole. Badly needed are clearly defined objectives for the inmate, attainment of which will result in his parole. This need is highlighted by the difficulties being experienced by parole and correctional officials when parole decisions must be made on offenders already under part-time release programs. Increasingly, parole authorities must be oriented to the future, spelling out what is required for parole in a given case. They also will need to emphasize to institutional authorities the type and quality of programs to be undertaken by inmates under the direction of correctional personnel.

In the past, most jurisdictions have operated on the premise that the offender has no statutory rights in the parole consideration process, except in some instances the right to appear before the board. Yet the traditional stance has also been that the inmate and his record must make an affirmative case for parole. The Model Penal Code reflects a growing dissatisfaction with this position. It proposes that an inmate be released on parole when he is first eligible unless certain specific obstacles exist.

The notion that the preference should be for releasing an inmate on parole when he is first eligible may require some modification if minimum sentences are eliminated, but the correctional authority, rather than the inmate, should bear the burden of proof (however evaluated from jurisdiction to jurisdiction) that an inmate is not ready for release.

Consistent with this is the concept that all inmates should have a parole hearing within one year after they are received in an institution. Such a hearing might result in consideration of immediate parole. More often it would involve review of the particular objectives developed by the inmate and staff. The board's representative would approve the inmate's category and program objectives, especially those involving combinations of institutional activities and periods of temporary release.

A particularly critical determination during this initial interview is scheduling another interview or hearing, if one is necessary, before the inmate's release. It should be increasingly common to approve an inmate's program, including a parole release date, as far as a year in advance without requiring another hearing or further interviews by the parole board. If the plan for the inmate that is agreed to by the board's representative at the initial hearing were carried out to the institutional staff's satisfaction, parole would be automatic. Only if substantial variations occurred or new information developed would another hearing be required. In any event, no more than one year should pass between hearings.

The nature of these hearings, involving close attention to tailoring programs and releases to individual cases, would require careful recording of plans and decisions. With a functional system of this kind, a maximum of 20 cases a day should be heard.

As to the hearing itself, in few jurisdictions are parole authorities required to write the detailed reasons for their decisions. Future decisionmakers are left with little information, and effective review is impeded. The failure to record reasons for action also means loss of a critical information source for policy formation.

Closely allied to the failure to record reasons for parole decisions is the manner in which the offenders are notified. In many jurisdictions inmates learn of the decision through a cryptic written communication or verbally through a correctional staff member who tries to interpret the reasons for a parole action without really knowing them, instead of obtaining such information directly from the parole authority representative who conducted the hearing.

The key to rectifying this situation lies in allocating sufficient decisionmaking power to the hearing examiners. They should be able to make the final decision, based on board policy, and notify inmates personally of the results before the examiners leave the institution. In addition, the examiners should specify the reasons for their decision in writing both for the record and for the inmate to retain a copy.

In few States can inmates review, even selectively, the information on which decisions affecting them are based. In few States are offenders given an opportunity to be represented by others at a parole hearing. Effectiveness and fairness argue for the existence of both of these provisions in every jurisdiction.

The issue of inmate representation by lawyers or other spokesmen has been highly controversial. If the offender can have a representative who is free to pursue information, develop resources, and raise questions, decisions are more likely to be made on fair and reasonable grounds. The inmate will be more likely to feel that he has been treated fairly and that there is definitely someone who is "on his side." Furthermore, such representation would do much to increase the credibility of the parole system in the public's view.

————

REVOCATION HEARINGS

Each parole jurisdiction immediately should develop and implement a system of revocation procedures to permit the prompt confinement of parolees exhibiting behavior that poses a serious threat to others. At the same time, it should provide careful controls, methods of fact finding, and possible alternatives to keep as many offenders as possible in the community. Return to the institution should be used as a last resort, even when a factual basis for revocation can be demonstrated.

1. Warrants to arrest and hold alleged parole violators should be issued and signed by parole board members. Tight control should be developed over the process of issuing such warrants. They should never be issued unless there is sufficient evidence of probable serious violation. In some instances, there may be a need to detain alleged parole violators. In general, however, detention is not required and is to be discouraged. Any parolee who is detained should be granted a prompt preliminary hearing.

Administrative arrest and detention should never be used simply to permit investigation of possible violations.   •

2.   Parolees alleged to have committed a new crime but without other violations of conditions sufficient to require parole revocation should be eligible for bail or other release pending the outcome of the new charges, as determined by the court.

3.   A preliminary hearing conducted by an individual not previously directly involved in the case should be held promptly on all alleged parole violations, including convictions of new crimes, in or near the community in which the violation occurred unless waived by the parolee after due notification of his rights. The purpose should be to determine whether there is probable cause or reasonable grounds to believe that the arrested parolee has committed acts that would constitute a violation of parole conditions and a determination of the value question of whether the case should be carried further, even if probable cause exists. The parolee should be given notice that the hearing will take place and of what parole violations have been alleged. He should have the right to present evidence, to confront and cross-examine witnesses, and to be represented by counsel.

The person who conducts the hearing should make a summary of what transpired at the hearing and the information he used to determine whether probable cause existed to hold the parolee for the final decision of the parole board on revocation. If the evidence is insufficient to support a further hearing, or if it is otherwise determined that revocation would not be desirable, the offender should be released to the community immediately.

4.   At parole revocation hearings, the parolee should have written notice of the alleged infractions of his rules or conditions; access to official records regarding his case; the right to be represented by counsel, including the right to appointed counsel if he is indigent; the opportunity to be heard in person; the right to subpoena witnesses in his own behalf; and the right to cross-examine witnesses or otherwise to challenge allegations or evidence held by the State. Hearing examiners should be empowered to hear and decide parole revocation cases under policies established by the parole board. Parole should not be revoked unless there is substantial evidence of a violation of one of the conditions of parole. The hearing examiner should provide a written statement of findings, the reasons for the decision, and the evidence relied upon.

5.   Each jurisdiction should develop alternatives to parole revocation, such as warnings, short time local confinement, special conditions of future parole, variations in intensity of supervision or surveillance, fines, and referral to other community resources.   Such alternative measures should be utilized as often as is practicable.

6.   If return to a correctional institution is warranted, the offender should be scheduled for subsequent appearances for parole considerations when appropriate.   There should be no automatic prohibition against reparole of a parole violator.

Commentary

A great deal of attention, stemming largely from court interventions, has been focused recently on processes by which an offender, once paroled, is returned to confinement.   For years, substantial debate has centered around the issue of whether parole was a privilege or a right, proponents of the former arguing that parole was something to which an individual had no statutory right and thus it could be summarily revoked.   Recently, however, there has been a growing consensus that the recommitment of a parolee represents a substantial denial of freedom and words like "privilege," "grace," or "contract" cannot blur the loss of liberty so clearly at stake.   This has perhaps been best articulated by the Supreme Court, in its finding in Morrissey v. Brewer, 408 U.S. 471 (1972):

> We see, therefore, that the liberty of a parolee, although indeterminate, includes many of the core values of unqualified liberty and its termination inflicts a "grievous loss" on the parolee and often on others.   It is hardly useful any longer to try to deal with this problem in terms of whether the parolee's liberty is a "right" or a "privilege."   By whatever name the liberty is valuable and must be seen as within the protection of the Fourteenth Amendment.   Its termination calls for some orderly process, however informal.

The issues of parole revocation typically are drawn around four areas: how a parolee is taken and held in custody, when and where he is heard, what procedures are employed at revocation hearings, and what the nature of the dispositions employed is.

In a large number of jurisdictions, parole officers have wide discretion in causing the arrest of the parolee and holding him in custody. In some jurisdictions a parole warrant is issued automatically whenever a parolee is charged with a new offense, and the existence of this warrant almost always prevents bail. The unfairness of such an automatic procedure is obvious.

The place of the hearing has become a critical issue. Under former practice the parolee was heard after his return to the institution from which he was paroled. The hazards of this procedure to a fair hearing and to the parolee's sense of its being fair have inclined some parole authorities to grant hearings near the site of the alleged violation. Now the Supreme Court requires that a preliminary hearing to determine probable cause be held at or near the site of the alleged violation.

The rights to representation, to disclosure of information, to witnesses, and to cross-examination increasingly are being given to alleged parole violators in a continuing reversal of the procedures existing before the late 1960's. This increased emphasis on the components of a fair hearing usually has been the result of court edict and is being continually strengthened.

The growing emphasis of community supervision is encouraging a much wider use of measures such as short-term confinement or additional restrictions and warnings instead of return to close confinement. Such innovations should be encouraged. The possibility of reparole for offenders returned to confinement also is a desirable program direction.

ORGANIZATION OF FIELD SERVICES

Each State should provide by 1978 for the consolidation of institutional and parole field services in departments or divisions of correctional services. Such consolidations should occur as closely as possible to operational levels.

1. Juvenile and adult correctional services may be part of the same parent agency but should be maintained as autonomous program units within it.

2. Regional administration should be established so that institutional and field services are jointly managed and coordinated at the program level.

3. Joint training programs for institutional and field staffs should be undertaken, and transfers of personnel between the two programs should be encouraged.

4. Parole services should be delivered, wherever practical, under a team system in which a variety of persons including parolees, parole managers, and community representatives participate.

5. Teams should be located, whenever practical, in the neighborhoods where parolees reside. Specific team members should be assigned to specific community groups and institutions designated by the team as specially significant.

6. Organizational and administrative practices should be altered to provide greatly increased autonomy and decisionmaking power to the parole teams.

Commentary

Lack of coordination among correctional programs and functions has for years been a grave impediment to development of effective correctional programs. The separation of field parole services from the rest of corrections has been no exception. The growing complexity and interdependence of correctional programs require more than ever that parole field staff be integrated more closely with institutional staff.

As the philosophy of reintegration gains prominence, many correctional staff relationships will change. Parole staff will be concerned with prerelease activities and halfway house programs. It will no longer be the practice to wait for the "transfer" of a case from an institution to a parole staff. Rather, the lines of responsibility between institution and parole staff will become increasingly blurred. They will either perform similar roles or cooperate closely. While organizational change will not automatically create such a close interrelationship, it certainly will facilitate the goal of functional integration.

A crucial first step to this goal is to place both of these units under one administrative head. In a number of States, some parole field staffs report to independent parole boards. These staffs should be transferred to the department of corrections to enhance correctional program integration and to free parole boards for their prime task of parole policy formation and decisionmaking.

The move to consolidate parole services should also involve increasing emphasis on providing services for misdemeanants, a function currently characterized by large gaps in services. Likewise, to assure continuity of services for juveniles, juvenile programs should be encompassed in statewide correctional agencies.

This is not to say that separate divisions focusing on juvenile institutional and field services should not be maintained, but they should be organizationally tied to such services for adults so that consolidated planning may occur. For both juveniles and adults, regional administration will provide for a coordinated flow of services regardless of an offender's legal status at any given time.

However, more than a common administration is needed to coordinate field and institution staffs. Ideological differences between the two divisions, augmented too often by empirical, educational, and cultural differences, are a hazard. Badly needed are mechanisms that foster a focus on program objectives rather than on organizational function. These include training programs, common administrative controls at lower levels, and personnel policies that encourage transfers across functional areas.

The organization of field services also requires fundamental restructuring in the way its services are delivered. Organizational patterns based on the notion of a single parole officer responsible for a specific caseload of parolees should give way to those facilitating team methods. With a team approach a group of parole personnel including volunteers and paraprofessionals works with a group of parolees, with tasks being assigned on the basis of the team's assessment of services needed and staff most able to provide for them. In many cases, parole staff's efforts will be focused on various community groups or organizations rather than directly on a parolee. The variety of needs presented by parolees and the objective of involving the community more directly in programs require such methods.

Moving from the traditional caseload orientation to a team approach will not be easy. Formerly, the tasks and responsibilities assigned to individual parole officers were fairly easy to manage and supervise. Often the performance of parole officers was evaluated on the number of contacts made with each parolee assigned to each officer. Complete and prompt reports, often emphasizing compliance with rules and policies, were also valued highly. Under a team approach, however, parole managers must learn to administer a decentralized organization that must both adhere to broad policies and allow for a high degree of individual autonomy. Communication must be open, and power must be shared. There will be no set formula for how a "case" should be handled, and strong administrative leadership will be crucial.

COMMUNITY SERVICES FOR PAROLEES

Each State should begin immediately to develop a diverse range of programs to meet the needs of parolees. These services should be drawn to the greatest extent possible from community programs available to all citizens, with parole staff providing linkage between services and the parolees needing or desiring them.

1. Stringent review procedures should be adopted, so that parolees not requiring supervision are released from supervision immediately and those requiring minimal attention are placed in minimum supervision caseloads.

2. Parole officers should be selected and trained to fulfill the role of community resource manager.

3. Parole staff should participate fully in developing coordinated delivery systems of human services.

4. Funds should be made available for parolees without interest charge. Parole staff should have authority to waive repayment to fit the individual case.

5. State funds should be available to offenders, so that some mechanism similar to unemployment benefits may be available to inmates at the time of their release, in order to tide them over until they find a job.

6. All States should use, as much as possible, a requirement that offenders have a visible means of support, rather than a promise of a specific job, before authorizing their release on parole.

7. Parole and State employment staffs should develop effective communication systems at the local level. Joint meetings and training sessions should be undertaken.

8. Each parole agency should have one or more persons attached to the central office to act as liaison with major program agencies, such as the Office of Economic Opportunity, Office of Vocational Rehabilitation, and Department of Labor.

9. Institutional vocational training tied directly to specific subsequent job placements should be supported.

10. Parole boards should encourage institutions to maintain effective quality control over programs.

11. Small community-based group homes should be available to parole staff for prerelease programs, for crises, and as a sub-

stitute to recommitment to an institution in appropriately reviewed cases of parole violation.

12. Funds should be made available to parole staffs to purchase needed community resources for parolees.

13. Special caseloads should be established for offenders with specific types of problems, such as drug abuse.

Commentary

Attempts to improve parole outcome by providing all parolees with closer supervision have proved to be quite fruitless. A number of parolees require little supervision, others none at all. For those requiring supervision, the most recent emphasis has been directed toward finding and using existing community resources. A number of advantages accrue: better and more relevant services usually can be obtained; less stigma is attached to services offered by noncorrectional agencies; and more flexibility is provided when services are not entrenched in the organizational structure of a correctional agency.

To obtain these resources parole staffs must gear their attention to other community service agencies and develop greater competence in acting as resource managers as well as counselors. A parole staff has a specific task: to assist parolees in availing themselves of community resources and to counsel them regarding their parole obligation. Parole staff also must take responsibility for finding needed resources for parolees in the community.

Of course, the time when parole staff can function as brokers or resource managers will be a while in coming. In the near future, parole officers will have to continue to deal directly with many of the very real problems parolees face. Chief among these is making sure that persons recently released have adequate financial support. There are a number of ways in which this need can be met. Where offenders have been involved in work-release programs, no major problems should be encountered. For other offenders, however, or for those who have large families or wish to continue education or training, other arrangements may be needed.

All States should consider establishing a form of unemployment compensation for released offenders until they are gainfully employed. The State of Washington has adopted such legislation. Where this is not instituted loan funds for parolees should be established. Neither of these two alternatives is really an adequate solution. All persons confined in correctional institutions should be given opportunities to earn funds while they are incarcerated. Adequate "gate money" should be provided for those who have been involved in programs with no financial rewards. The high correlation between parole failure and the amount of money an offender has during the first months of release makes it clear that these investments would be sound ones.

Apart from the immediate need for money, however, most re- leasees will be interested in securing employment. This is not to say that all parolees should be required to obtain employment. Parole conditions should allow parolees to maintain themselves by any of the legal means of support available to citizens in gen- eral. But for those having difficulty finding employment, parole staff should develop working relationships with agencies and organizations in the community whose purpose is to help citizens find jobs and should make arrangements for parolees to continue in educational or training pursuits.

An additional resource with which parole personnel should be concerned is the small, community-based residential facility. Be- sides serving as the last stage of release for many offenders, such facilities can serve as a place to go during times of crisis for the parolee, whether to engage in activities offered or to live tempo- rarily. These facilities can also be utilized for offenders who have violated their parole and require a brief period of control short of return to an institution. Finally, they can serve as a meeting place for community residents, offenders, and ex-offenders. They make an ideal place to hold group meetings such as team planning sessions or a drug treatment group.

Before acting to secure such needed services in the community, it must be remembered that responsibility of parole personnel be- gins before an offender formally leaves an institution. They should work with institutional staff to assure that institutional programs are operating to meet the needs of the inmates. If an offender leaves an institution with all his needs yet to be met, the parole officer's task is an almost impossible one. In addition, while community involvement efforts are under way, the parole system may have to purchase services needed by parolees rather than trying to provide all of them directly. Funds for this pur- pose should be made available. Finally, to make sure that services are being provided which meet, as nearly as possible, the needs of the offenders released, parole staff must know what those needs are. They may find that needs vary over time and that many of the releasees at any given time have similar problems. Special teams should then be assigned to concentrate on providing services to groups of parolees with like needs.

MEASURES OF CONTROL

Each State should take immediate action to reduce parole rules to an absolute minimum, retaining only those critical in the individual case, and to provide for effective means of enforcing the conditions established.

1. After considering suggestions from correctional staff and preferences of the individual, parole boards should establish in each case the specific parole conditions appropriate for the individual offender.

2. Parole staff should be able to request the board to amend rules to fit the needs of each case and should be empowered to require the parolee to obey any such rule when put in writing, pending the final action of the parole board.

3. Special caseloads for intensive supervision should be established and staffed by personnel of suitable skill and temperament. Careful review procedures should be established to determine which offenders should be assigned or removed from such caseloads.

4. Parole officers should develop close liaison with police agencies, so that any formal arrests necessary can be made by police. Parole officers, therefore, would not need to be armed.

Commentary

The chief expression of the coercive power of parole agencies, and consequently a potential source of great abuse, is found in the conditions governing the conduct of parolees and the measures taken to enforce those rules. Some of the major criticisms against parole rules are that they often are so vague as to invite serious problems of interpretation by both the parolee and the parole officer, and that they frequently embrace such a wide portion of the parolee's potential and actual behavior as to become unnecessarily restrictive of his freedom and do little to prevent crime.

Any conditions set for parole continuance should be as specific as possible and reasonably related to the facts of the specific parole case. In formulating conditions, the offender's wishes and interests should be taken into account. Maximum consideration should also be attached to guarding the individual's constitutional and legal rights, remembering that offenders retain all rights that citizens in general have, except those necessarily limited for the purpose of confinement or control.

It is of utmost importance that the parolee know the conditions of his parole and the reasons for them. If the number of conditions is limited to those deemed absolutely necessary, the parolee will understand that these conditions are meant to be enforced, a situation which is uncommon at the present time. The removal of unnecessary rules also helps the parole officer in his relationship with the parolee. If both parties know and understand the reasons for rules in the case in question, it is less likely that the parole officer will have to either ignore rules he sees as frivolous or jeopardize his relationship with the parolee by reporting them. Furthermore, the more open the parole system, the more possibilities exist for working out postrelease arrangements that are conducive to leading a law-abiding life. Again, this means that the system will have to be ready to tolerate more diversity. Citizens in general find many satisfying lifestyles that meet the tests of legality. Parolees should have the same opportunities.

Closely related to formulation of fair and effective parole rules is the issue of their enforcement. In a number of parole systems, too many parole officers still see their major role as that of policeman-enforcer. Although close supervision may be indicated in individual cases, it should be done on a highly selective basis. Close coordination with police agencies should obviate the necessity of arming parole officers or requiring them to arrest parole violators. To the extent that a parole agency can reduce emphasis on surveillance and control and stress its concern for assisting the parolee, it probably will be more successful in crime reduction.

MANPOWER FOR PAROLE

By 1975, each State should develop a comprehensive manpower and training program which would make it possible to recruit persons with a wide variety of skills, including significant numbers of minority group members and volunteers, and use them effectively in parole programs.

Among the elements of State manpower and training programs for corrections that are prescribed in Chapter 14, the following apply with special force to parole.

1.   A functional workload system linking specific tasks to different categories of parolees should be instituted by each State and should form the basis of allocating manpower resources.

2.   The bachelor's degree should constitute the requisite educational level for the beginning parole officer.

3.   Provisions should be made for the employment of parole personnel having less than a college degree to work with parole officers on a team basis, carrying out the tasks appropriate to their individual skills.

4.   Career ladders that offer opportunities for advancement of persons with less than college degrees should be provided.

5.   Recruitment efforts should be designed to produce a staff roughly proportional in ethnic background to the offender population being served.

6.   Ex-offenders should receive high priority consideration for employment in parole agencies.

7.   Use of volunteers should be extended substantially.

8.   Training programs designed to deal with the organizational issues and the kinds of personnel required by the program should be established in each parole agency.

Commentary

Typically, manpower allocation in parole agencies has been based on a ratio of a fixed number of parolees to one parole officer.   Little experimental evidence is available on the optimal allocation of manpower, and any ratio would probably be quite specific to an individual agency depending on the character of the parolees supervised, geographic factors, and the administrative tasks the officer must carry out.   It is essential that parole agencies develop workload data, especially in an era of team supervision, so that manpower can be reasonably related to activities to be done.   Present workloads are too burdensome and immediate steps are needed in a number of States to augment parole staffs with additional manpower.

Parole manpower should consist of persons with a variety of skills and aptitudes. While a bachelor's degree generally is agreed to be the appropriate entering requirement for the parole officer position, it is also widely agreed that persons with less than a college education can be employed quite effectively to handle a number of tasks for which they may be uniquely qualified. However, career ladders that permit opportunities for advancement for such personnel must be established.

Minority groups in the community should be the targets for special efforts in recruiting for parole personnel. Not only are they familiar with the life styles of many parolees but also they know both formal and informal resources of the community.

Major manpower resources also are to be found in the use of volunteers and ex-offenders from the community. New and innovative training programs in organizational development are needed to integrate successfully the variety of skills involved in a modern parole agency and to deal with the tensions and conflicts which will inevitably arise from mixing such a variety of personnel in team supervision efforts.

Appendix

DATA ON CORRECTIONAL ORGANIZATION

NATIONAL ADVISORY COMMISSION ON CRIMINAL JUSTICE STANDARDS & GOALS

The reports of the National Institute of Law Enforcement and Criminal Justice cited in Chapter 13 carry this caveat:

Readers should be cautious in interpretations of these counts, keeping in mind that this survey did not include agencies of those municipal governments with a 1960 population of less than 1000. The figures in this report reflect the *October 1971* update of the directory, particularly in the courts sector and the juvenile corrections sector, and consequently may differ from figures presented in the summary Report (Statistics Division Report SD–D–1). Moreover in deciding whether an agency belonged in the directory or not, the general rule was to be inclusive rather than exclusive.

While numbers will help describe the scope and diversity of the system, the size and range of activity of criminal justice agencies within a State may not always be reflected by simple counts of agencies. Organizational complexity varies considerably from one governmental unit to another, even within a single State. Of the categories enumerated in the directory, the counts of local adult correctional facilities are the most reliable due to the refinement of this sector through the National Jail Census conducted in the Spring of 1970.

Correctional Institutions

General Definition—An individual facility, such as a prison, jail, farm, or annex, which is either separately administered or administratively dependent upon a parent institution and located in a separate geographical area. Hospitals for the criminally insane and halfway houses for narcotic addicts and alcoholics were not count-

571

ed in this sector but in the "all other criminal justice agencies" sector.

Juvenile Correctional Facilities—Included are those facilities which detain juveniles only, for 48 hours or more. This includes detention centers, reception and diagnostic centers, some halfway houses and other probation or work-release type facilities; that is, institutions detaining juveniles for court disposition as well as those holding juveniles for rehabilitation after court disposition. At the local level of government an agency was considered to be a juvenile agency if the administrator considered it as such. At the State level, facilities were assigned juvenile status if they were administered by the State juvenile corrections agency.

Adult Correctional Facilities—Included are those institutions which detain adults only or a combination of prisoner populations. Drunk tanks, lock-ups and other facilities which detain persons for less than 48 hours are excluded.

Probation and Parole Agencies

Included are probation and parole departments, commissions, boards or agencies operated by the State or local government, including those administratively dependent on the courts. The assignment of a probation officer to a particular level of government was an involved process related to both the type of area served and administrative responsibility. As a rule a probation department serving more than one borough was assigned to the State level of government. Probation services provided on a contractual basis were not included.

The following display of the organization of responsibility for administering corrections services in the several States is from a report of the Advisory Committee on Intergovernmental Relations. (See source note at end of table.)

Table

PARENT AGENCY RESPONSIBILITY FOR ADMINISTERING CORRECTIONAL SERVICES, BY STATE 1

January 1971

State	Juvenile Detention	Juvenile Probation	Juvenile Institutions	Juvenile Aftercare	Misdemeanant Probation	Adult Probation	Local Adult Institutions and Jails	Adult Institutions	Parole
Alabama	Local	Local	3 Separate & Independent Boards	Dept. of Pensions & Security & Local	Board of Pardons & Paroles	Board of Pardons & Paroles	Local	Board of Corrections	Board of Pardons & Paroles
Alaska	Dept. of Health & Welfare	Dept. of Health & Welfare	Dept. of Health & Welfare	Dept. of Health & Welfare	Dept. of Health & Welfare	Dept. of Health & Welfare	Dept. of Health & Welfare	Dept. of Health & Welfare	Dept. of Health & Welfare
Arizona	Local	Local	Dept. of Corrections	Dept. of Corrections	None	Local	Local	Dept. of Corrections	Dept. of Corrections
Arkansas	Local	Dept. of Welfare & Local	Juvenile Training School Dept.	Juvenile Training School Dept.	None	Local	Local	Dept. of Corrections	Board of Pardons & Parole
California	Local	Local	Dept. of Youth Authority	Dept. of Youth Authority	Local	Local	Local	Dept. of Corrections	Dept. of Corrections
Colorado	Local	Local & District	Dept. of Institutions	Dept. of Institutions	Local	Local	Local	Dept. of Institutions	Dept. of Institutions
Connecticut	Juvenile Court Districts	Juvenile Court Districts	Dept. of Youth Services	Dept. of Youth Services	Dept. of Adult Probation	Dept. of Adult Probation	Dept. of Corrections	Dept. of Corrections	Dept. of Corrections
Delaware	Dept. of Health & Soc. Servs.	Local	Dept. of Health & Soc. Servs.	Dept. of Health & Soc. Servs.	Dept. of Health & Soc. Servs.	Dept. of Health & Soc. Servs. & Local	Dept. of Health & Soc. Servs.	Dept. of Health & Soc. Servs.	Dept. of Health & Soc. Servs.

[A9406]

Table (Continued)

PARENT AGENCY RESPONSIBILITY FOR ADMINISTERING CORRECTIONAL SERVICES, BY STATE 1

January 1971

State	Juvenile Detention	Juvenile Probation	Juvenile Institutions	Juvenile Aftercare	Misdemeanant Probation	Adult Probation	Local Adult Institutions and Jails	Adult Institutions	Parole
Florida	Local	Local	Dept. of Health & Rehabilitative Services	Dept. of Health & Rehabilitative Services	Local & Probation & Parole Commission	Local & Probation & Parole Commission	Local	Dept. of Health & Rehabilitative Services	Probation & Parole Commission
Georgia	Division of Children & Youth & Loc.	Division of Children & Youth & Loc.	Division of Children & Youth	Division of Children & Youth	Dept. of Probation & Local	Dept. of Probation & Local	Local	Dept. of Corrections	Board of Pardons & Parole
Hawaii	Local	Local	Dept. of Social Service	Dept. of Social Service	Local	Local	Local	Dept. of Social Service	Board of Parole & Pardons
Idaho	State Board of Health & Local	State Board of Health & Local	State Board of Health	State Board of Health	None	Board of Correction	Local	Board of Correction	Commission for Pardons & Parole
Illinois	Local	Local	Dept. of Corrections	Dept. of Corrections	Local	Local	Local	Dept. of Corrections	Dept. of Corrections
Indiana	Local	Dept. of Welfare & Local	Dept. of Corrections	Dept. of Corrections	Local	Local	Local	Dept. of Corrections	Dept. of Corrections
Iowa	Local	Local	Dept. of Social Services	Dept. of Social Services	None	Dept. of Social Services	Local	Dept. of Social Services	Dept. of Social Services
Kansas	Local	Local	Dept. of Social Welfare	Dept. of Social Welfare	Local	Loc. & Board of Probation & Parole	Local	Director of Penal Institutions	Board of Probation & Parole

[A9405]

Table (Continued)

PARENT AGENCY RESPONSIBILITY FOR ADMINISTERING CORRECTIONAL SERVICES, BY STATE 1

January 1971

State	Juvenile Detention	Juvenile Probation	Juvenile Institutions	Juvenile Aftercare	Misde-meanant Probation	Adult Probation	Local Adult Institutions and Jails	Adult Institutions	Parole
Kentucky	Local	Dept. of Child Welfare & Loc.	Dept. of Child Welfare	Dept. of Child Welfare	Dept. of Corrections	Dept. of Corrections	Local	Dept. of Corrections	Dept. of Corrections
Louisiana	Local	Dept. of Public Welfare & Local	Dept. of Corrections	Dept. of Public Welfare & Local	None	Dept. of Corrections	Local	Dept. of Corrections	Dept. of Corrections
Maine	Local	Dept. of Mental Health & Corrections & Loc.	Dept. of Mental Health & Corrections	Dept. of Mental Health & Corrections	Dept. of Mental Health & Corrections	Dept. of Mental Health & Corrections	Local	Dept. of Mental Health & Corrections	Dept. of Mental Health & Corrections
Maryland	Dept. of Juvenile Services	Dept. of Juvenile Services	Dept. of Juvenile Services	Dept. of Juvenile Services	Dept. of Parole & Probation & Local	Dept. of Parole & Probation & Local	Local	Dept. of Correctional Services	Dept. of Parole & Probation
Massachusetts	Youth Service Board	Local	Youth Service Board	Dept. of Youth Services	Local	Local	Local	Dept. of Correction	Parole Board
Michigan	Local	Local	Dept. of Social Services	Dept. of Social Services	Dept. of Corrections & Local	Dept. of Corrections & Local	Local	Dept. of Corrections	Dept. of Corrections
Minnesota	Local	Dept. of Corrections & Local	Dept. of Corrections	Dept. of Corrections	Dept. of Corrections & Local	Dept. of Corrections & Local	Local	Dept. of Corrections	Dept. of Corrections
Mississippi	Local	Local	Board of Trustees	State DPW and Local	None	Board of Probation & Parole	Local	Dept. of Correction	Board of Probation & Parole

[A9408]

Table (Continued)

PARENT AGENCY RESPONSIBILITY FOR ADMINISTERING CORRECTIONAL SERVICES, BY STATE [1]

January 1971

State	Juvenile Detention	Juvenile Probation	Juvenile Institutions	Juvenile Aftercare	Misdemeanant Probation	Adult Probation	Local Adult Institutions and Jails	Adult Institutions	Parole
Missouri	Local	Local	Board of Training Schools	Board of Training Schools		Board of Probation & Parole	Local	Dept. of Correction	Board of Probation & Parole
Montana	Local	Local	Dept. of Institutions	Dept. of Institutions	Local	Board of Pardons	Local	Dept. of Institutions	Board of Pardons
Nebraska	Local	District Courts & Local	Dept. of Public Institutions	Dept. of Public Institutions	District Courts & Local	District Courts	Local	Dept. of Public Institutions	Board of Parole
Nevada	Local	Local	Dept. of Health & Welfare	Dept. of Health & Welfare	Dept. of Parole & Probation	Dept. of Parole & Probation	Local	Board Prison Commissioners	Dept. of Parole & Probation
New Hampshire	Board of Parole	Dept. of Probation & Local	Board of Parole	State Industrial School	Dept. of Probation & Local	Dept. of Probation & Local	Local	Board of Parole	Board of Parole
New Jersey	Local	Local	Dept. of Institutions & Agencies	Dept. of Institutions & Agencies	Local	Local	Local	Dept. of Institutions & Agencies	Dept. of Institutions & Agencies
New Mexico	Local	Local	Dept. of Corrections	Local	Dept. of Corrections	Dept. of Corrections	Local	Dept. of Corrections	Parole Board
New York	Local	Local	Dept. of Social Services	Dept. of Social Services	Division of Probation & Local	Division of Probation & Local	Local	Dept. of Correctional Services	Dept. of Correctional Services
North Carolina	Local	District & Local	Board of Juvenile Correction	Local	Probation Commission	Probation Commission	Dept. of Corrections	Dept. of Corrections	Board of Parole

[A9407]

Table (Continued)

PARENT AGENCY RESPONSIBILITY FOR ADMINISTERING CORRECTIONAL SERVICES, BY STATE [1]

January 1971

State	Juvenile Detention	Juvenile Probation	Juvenile Institutions	Juvenile Aftercare	Misdemeanant Probation	Adult Probation	Local Adult Institutions and Jails	Adult Institutions	Parole
North Dakota	Local	DPW & Local	Dept. of Institutions	Public Welfare Board	None	Board of Pardons	Local	Dept. of Institutions	Board of Pardons
Ohio	Local	Local	Youth Commission	Youth Commission	Local	Local	Local	Dept. Mental Hygiene & Correction	Dept. Mental Hygiene & Correction
Oklahoma	Local	Loc. & Dept. of Welfare & Institutions	Dept. of Welfare & Institutions	Dept. of Welfare & Institutions	None	Local & Dept. of Corrections	Local	Dept. of Corrections	Pardon & Parole Board
Oregon	Local	Corrections Division & Local	Corrections Division	Corrections Division	Corrections Division	Corrections Division	Local	Corrections Division	Parole Board
Pennsylvania	Local	Local	Board of Training Schools	Board of Training Schools & Local	Board of Probations & Parole & Local	Board of Probations & Parole & Local	Dept. of Justice & Local	Dept. of Justice	Board of Probations & Parole
Rhode Island	Dept. of Social Welfare	Dept. of Social Welfare	Dept. of Social Welfare	Dept. of Social Welfare	Dept. of Social Welfare	Dept. of Social Welfare	Dept. of Social Welfare	Dept. of Social Welfare	Dept. of Social Welfare
South Carolina	Local	Local	Dept. of Juvenile Corrections	Dept. of Juvenile Corrections	Probation, Parole & Pardon Board	Probation, Parole & Pardon Board	Local	Dept. of Corrections	Probation, Parole & Pardon Board
South Dakota	Local	Local	Board of Charities & Corrections	Board of Pardons & Parole	None	Board of Pardons & Parole	Local	Board of Charities & Corrections	Board of Pardons & Parole

[A9410]

Table (Continued)

PARENT AGENCY RESPONSIBILITY FOR ADMINISTERING CORRECTIONAL SERVICES, BY STATE 1

January 1971

State	Juvenile Detention	Juvenile Probation	Juvenile Institutions	Juvenile Aftercare	Misdemeanant Probation	Adult Probation	Local Adult Institutions and Jails	Adult Institutions	Parole
Tennessee	Local	Dept. of Corrections & Local	Dept. of Corrections	Dept. of Corrections	Local	Dept. of Corrections	Local	Dept. of Corrections	Dept. of Corrections
Texas	Local	Local	Youth Council	Youth Council	Local	Local	Local	Dept. of Corrections	Board of Pardons & Paroles
Utah	Local	Juvenile Court Districts	Dept. of Social Services	Juvenile Court Districts	Division of Corrections	Division of Corrections	Local	Division of Corrections	Division of Corrections
Vermont	Dept. of Corrections	Dept. of Corrections	Dept. of Corrections	Dept. of Corrections	Dept. of Corrections	Dept. of Corrections	Dept. of Corrections	Dept. of Corrections	Dept. of Corrections
Virginia	Local	Dept. of Welfare & Institutions & Local	Dept. of Welfare & Institutions	Dept. of Welfare & Institutions & Local	Dept. of Welfare & Institutions	Dept. of Welfare & Institutions	Local	Dept. of Welfare & Institutions	Dept. of Welfare & Institutions
Washington	Local	Local	Dept. of Social & Health Services	Dept. of Social & Health Services	Local	Dept. of Social & Health Services	Local	Dept. of Institutions	Board of Prison Terms & Paroles
West Virginia	Local	Dept. of Welfare & Local	Commissioner of Public Institutions	Commissioner of Public Institutions	Local & Div. of Probation & Parole	Local & Div. of Probation & Parole	Local	Commissioner of Public Institutions	Div. of Probation & Parole
Wisconsin	Local	Dept. of Health & Soc. Services & Local	Dept. of Health & Social Services	Dept. of Health & Social Services	Dept. of Health & Soc. Services & Local	Dept. of Health & Social Services & Local	Local	Dept. of Health & Social Services	Dept. of Health & Social Services

[A9409]